Cultivating Successful Software Development

Science Applications International Corporation

Science Applications International Corporation, SAIC, is the largest employee-owned research and engineering company in the United States. Based in San Diego and international in scope, SAIC offers a broad range of expertise in technology development and analysis, systems development and integration, technical support services, and high technology hardware and software products. SAIC scientists and engineers work to solve complex technical problems of significance to federal, commercial, and international customers in a variety of market areas, including: Energy, Environment, Government, Health Care, Technology, Information Technology, Internet, and Transportation.

Founded by a small group of scientists in 1969, SAIC has had a continuous record of growth in its financial performance and technical scope. SAIC attributes its success to a decentralized, flexible working environment that promotes and rewards technical excellence, individual initiative, and entrepreneurship. The company's ability to attract and retain the best qualified people, coupled with an environment that fosters team building, has led to 27 years of sustained growth—with over 35,000 employees, more than 400 locations worldwide, and annual revenues exceeding $3 billion.

Bob Beyster, SAIC's founder, Chairman, and Chief Executive Officer, credits the success of the company to its employee ownership culture. The hallmark of SAIC through the years has been the principle that "those who contribute to the company should own it, and the ownership should reflect an individual's contribution and performance as much as feasible."

From the start, SAIC was established for professional people who sought to perform superior scientific and technical work, who wanted a stake and a voice in the company's development and direction, and who expected fair rewards for doing excellent work. SAIC's successful track record demonstrates that employee ownership creates the incentives and the environment for excellence and growth.

SAIC has a corporate commitment to software process improvement. The focus of this commitment is to build software systems that do what customers want them to do and to deliver these systems on time and within budget—consistently.

Cultivating Successful Software Development

A Practitioner's View

Scott E. Donaldson and Stanley G. Siegel

To join a Prentice Hall PTR Internet mailing list, point to:
http://www.prenhall.com/register

Prentice Hall PTR
Upper Saddle River, New Jersey 07458
http://www.prenhall.com

Library of Congress Cataloging-in-Publication Data

Donaldson, Scott E.
   Cultivating successful software development: a
practitioner's view / Scott E. Donaldson & Stanley G. Siegel.
     p. cm.
   Includes index.
   ISBN 0–13–754268-2
   1. Computer software—Development.   I. Siegel, Stanley G.   II. Title.
QA76.76.D47D65 1997
005.1'2—dc20   96-36598
                                                  CIP

Acquisitions editor: Paul Becker
Cover designer: Wanda Espana
Cover design director: Jerry Votta
Manufacturing manager: Alexis R. Heydt
Marketing manager: Dan Rush
Compositor/Production services: Pine Tree Composition, Inc.

Selected clip art images in this book are
copyrighted, New Vision Technologies Inc. 1994
and are used by permission.

© 1997 by Prentice Hall PTR
Prentice-Hall, Inc.
A Simon & Schuster Company
Upper Saddle River, New Jersey 07458

The publisher offers discounts on this book when ordered in
bulk quantities. For more information contact:

> Corporate Sales Department
> Prentice Hall PTR
> One Lake Street
> Upper Saddle River, New Jersey 07458
>
> Phone: 800-382-3419
> Fax: 201-236-7141
> email: corpsales@prenhall.com

Printed in the United States of America
10 9 8 7 6 5 4 3 2 1

ISBN: 0-13-754268-2

Prentice-Hall International (UK) Limited, *London*
Prentice-Hall of Australia Pty. Limited, *Sydney*
Prentice-Hall Canada Inc., *Toronto*
Prentice-Hall Hispanoamericana, S.A., *Mexico*
Prentice-Hall of India Private Limited, *New Delhi*
Prentice-Hall of Japan, Inc., *Tokyo*
Simon & Schuster Asia Pte. Ltd., *Singapore*
Editora Prentice-Hall do Brasil, Ltda., *Rio de Janeiro*

To the memory of Roy G. Donaldson and Edythe Siegel

Also to:

Jessica
Melanie
Stephanie
Laura

Bena
Gary
Deborah
Rachel

Contents

List of Figures

chapter 2—Project Planning Process

chapter 3—Software Systems Development Process

chapter 4—Change Control Process

chapter 5—Product and Process Reviews

chapter 6—Measurement

chapter 7—Cultural Change

chapter 8—Process Improvement Planning

List of Tables

Preface

Software process is this book's focus. Processes examined include (1) project planning (2) software systems development, and (3) change control. We show you how to achieve effective communication between software customers and software developers. We show you how to measure software processes and the products they yield. We show you how to use measurements to improve processes and products. We show you how to implement processes by examining organizational cultural change factors. We show you how to plan process improvement so that you can bring about organizational cultural change.

This book features the following:

- Approximately 240 figures to help you quickly assimilate ideas and their relationships
- A list of key ideas (called "nuggets") at the outset of each chapter (except the first) to help you work your way through the chapter and organize what you want to take from the chapter
- Process diagrams that you can easily adapt to your environment
- Annotated outlines to help you overcome the blank-page syndrome in commiting your processes to writing.

We wrote this book because the software industry is struggling to find ways to achieve *consistent* success. In particular, we wrote this book to help software systems developers achieve consistency in turning out systems that do what they are supposed to do—on time and within budget. And we wrote this book to help software systems buyers and users get systems that do what they are supposed to do—on time and within budget.

This book is for software practitioners. People are still the most important part of the equation for successful software development projects. As competition continues to increase and budgets continue to shrink, practitioners need to continue improving their skill sets. This book contains practical guidance for building good software systems *consistently*. Simply stated, our definition of a "good" software system is one that does what it is supposed to do and is delivered on time and within budget. *Successful* software systems development in this book means "consistently building good software systems."

You are a software practitioner if you perform one or more of the following activities:

- Develop computer code, software-related products such as specification documents, databases, user's manuals, and test documents.
- Directly manage people who do the preceding.
- Manage the preceding managers.
- Buy/use products from the preceding.

A practitioner can be new to the software game or can be a veteran. The newcomer will want to study and apply what is said; the veteran will want to adapt what is said.

There is no one way to build software systems. If there were, software systems development would have been reduced to an assembly-line process long ago. However, we believe there are fundamental engineering and process principles whose application can increase the likelihood that software systems development projects will be successful. This book highlights and illustrates these principles so that you can apply them to *your* way of contracting for and/or building software systems.

This book stresses achieving *consistent* software development results. It helps the practitioner build a mature software systems development process so that consistently good systems are a natural outcome. As we explain, achieving maturity is more than a matter of defining engineering practices. Raising the maturity of your software systems development process is also an exercise in bringing about organizational cultural change. For example, if you are using the Software Engineering Institute's various capability maturity models to foster software development consistency in your organization, this book will help you institutionalize your processes. Similarly, if you are trying to gain, or maintain, ISO 9001 certification, this book can help you. Whatever your approach, this book can help you consistently achieve effective software systems development.

Figure P–1 captures the book's essence—cultivating successful software systems development. This book helps you acquire a green thumb for this cultivation exercise. If your organization has been in the software business for some time, we offer you guidance for nurturing what you have to achieve consistent success. If your organization is just getting started in the software business, we provide you with the tools and materials to grow your organization into one that consistently achieves software success. If you are a software customer, we provide you with the means to nourish the client/developer environment so that it breeds software success. Just as growing crops is subject to many perils (such as bad weather, insects, and uncertain seed quality), so too is software systems development (e.g., unanticipated change, requirements creep, and miscommunication). Our objective is to help you anticipate these perils so that you consistently produce the software equivalent of good crops.

The book has the following eight chapters.

1. *Motivation*, whose purpose is to convince you that the rest of the book is worth reading.

2. *Project Planning Process*, whose purpose is to provide you with practical guidance for effectively planning software systems development work.

3. *Software Systems Development Process*, whose purpose is to (1) define principles for putting together a software systems development process that breeds success and (2) illustrate these principles by defining a top-level process that you can use to formulate a process for your environment.

4. *Change Control Process*, whose purpose is to define change control board (CCB) mechanics and provide you with practical guidance for setting up a CCB for your software systems development process.

5. *Product and Process Reviews*, whose purpose is to describe basic processes associated with the various reviews called out in Chapter 3 as a means for reducing software systems development risk.

6. *Measurement*, whose purpose is to provide you with practical guidance for measuring the "goodness" of products and the "goodness" of the software systems development process that produced the products; the focus is on how to use measurement to achieve *consistent* product and process "goodness."

FIGURE P–1   How can you cultivate successful software development? This book gives you practical guidance for answering this question.

7. *Cultural Change*, whose purpose is to address human issues bearing on bringing about organizational cultural change during implementation of your systems engineering environment (SEE).

8. *Process Improvement Planning*, whose purpose is to provide practical guidance on how to write an SEE implementation plan to establish the framework for doing the things discussed in the preceding chapters.

Table P-1 highlights what you will learn from each chapter. To help you extract each chapter's messages and subsequently apply its concepts, we condense each chapter's key points (except Chapter 1) into what we label "nuggets." In general, the material is organized to help you extract what you need. The book's approximately 240 figures aim at highlighting essential points. In these figures, we communicate ideas through icons to facilitate information retrieval and assimilation.

We also include worked-out examples containing sufficient detail so that you can adapt the concepts illustrated to your organization. For instance, in Chapter 6, we address measurement. We focus

TABLE P-1	Summary of Chapters.	
Chapter	*Title and Purpose*	*What You Will Learn*
1	**Motivation**—convinces you that the rest of the book is worth reading.	■ A working vocabulary for the rest of the book (e.g., software, software process, software process capability, software process maturity, product and process "goodness," software process improvement, culture).
		■ Software process improvement is first and foremost a cultural change exercise.
		■ Requisite software systems development disciplines—management, development, product assurance.
		■ A key element of achieving software systems development success is effective communication between the software systems development enterprise (the entity we call the "seller") and the customer (the entity that we call the "buyer/user"). Customer/seller faulty communication underlies a majority of software systems development problems.
		■ Obstacles to improving software systems development cultures.
		■ Cultivating successful software systems development extends far beyond (1) management edicts, (2) assembling a team of experienced and good people, and (3) a five-minute conversation with a customer and a three-week coding frenzy.
		■ The focal point of software process improvement is a mechanism for effecting good seller/customer communication—the change control board (CCB).
		■ Alternative approaches to software process improvement.
		■ What "prescriptive application" of an organization's documented software systems development process means and why prescriptive application holds the key to institutionalizing the process.
		■ A *systems engineering environment* (SEE) provides a means for effecting successful software systems development—whether systems are developed sequentially or in parallel.
2	**Project Planning Process**—provides you with practical guidance for effectively planning software systems development work.	■ Life cycle role in project planning.
		■ Planning is an ongoing negotiation between the buyer/user and the seller.
		■ How to account for the interaction among the three sets of disciplines that come into play in software systems development— management, development, and product assurance— throughout the project life cycle.
		■ How to plan for change.
		■ Ideal, real, and realistic project planning.
		■ How to design a simple risk assessment approach for project planning use.
		■ How to incorporate risk reduction explicitly into your project plan budget.
		■ How to develop an ADPE element defining your organization's project planning process.
3	**Software Systems Development Process**—(1) defines principles for putting together a software systems development process that breeds success and (2) illustrates these principles by defining a top-level process that you can use as a starting point to formulate a process for your environment.	■ Guidance for buyers and users regarding contractual agreements that can arise in the software systems development game.
		■ Guidance for the buyer/user for writing a "good" statement of work (SOW).
		■ How the seller can constitute a project team and define associated responsibilities to carry out project plan work.
		■ How the buyer/user can effectively interact with the seller project team.
		■ How the seller can define a software systems development process that (1) explicitly includes the customer throughout the process and (2) can incorporate any product development life cycle.
		■ How to plug the seller organization and the customer organization(s) into the software systems development process so that both sides know how business is to be transacted.
		■ More about "prescriptive application" of the product development process.
		■ How to address process issues relevant to those environments in which numerous software systems development projects are unfolding more or less in parallel.
		■ The relationship between life cycle stages and your software systems development process.

TABLE P–1 *Continued*		
Chapter	*Title and Purpose*	*What You Will Learn*
3	**Software Systems Development Process** (*continued*)	■ How to design a form that helps you track a product as it wends its way through your software systems development process.
		■ The responsibilities of the user/buyer and seller after the seller has delivered the product to the buyer/user.
		■ How to develop an ADPE element defining your organization's software systems development process.
		■ Why this element is a good place to begin setting up your ADPE.
4	**Change Control Process—** defines change control board (CCB) mechanics and provides you with practical guidance for setting up a CCB for your software systems development process.	■ How to manage unplanned, as well as, planned change.
		■ Change control mechanics of the software systems development process.
		■ How to establish seller and customer accountability through the CCB.
		■ The three scenarios that govern all of change control:
		1. Do we want something new or different?
		2. Is something wrong?
		3. Should we baseline the product?
		■ CCB mechanics (e.g., what to record at CCB meetings, CCB role in traversing a project life cycle, who should be the CCB chairperson, what should be the CCB voting mechanism).
		■ What are information requirements for CCB minutes.
		■ When are CCB hierarchies appropriate and how to set them up.
		■ How to design change control forms that make sense for your organization.
		■ How to develop an ADPE element defining the workings of CCBs in your software systems development process.
5	**Product and Process Reviews—** describes the basic processes associated with the various reviews called out in Chapter 3 as a means for reducing software systems development risk.	■ Principles pertaining to the purpose of reviews.
		■ How to resolve key issues regarding the review process involving peers.
		■ The mechanics of document reviews and acceptance testing conducted by an independent product assurance organization.
		■ How to make software requirements testable so that the software systems development process can be brought to a successful conclusion.
		■ The key role that acceptance testing plays in harmonizing seller and customer understanding of what the delivered software system and supporting databases are to contain.
		■ Senior management's visibility needs.
		■ How technical editing can be incorporated into your software systems development process to help prevent compromising good engineering work.
		■ Technical editing suggestions that you can use as a starting point for an organizational technical editing guide.
		■ How to develop ADPE elements addressing (1) independent product assurance, (2) peer reviews, and (3) the acceptance testing cycle.
6	**Measurement—** provides you with practical guidance for measuring the "goodness" of products and the "goodness" of the software systems development process that produced the products; the focus is on how to use measurement to achieve *consistent* product and process "goodness."	■ Knowing when it makes sense for you to try to improve your software systems development process.
		■ How to avoid "measurement-for-the-sake-of measurement" activities.
		■ How to establish benchmarks to give meaning to product and process measurements.
		■ How to measure customer satisfaction.
		■ How to quantify the concept of product integrity as a means for assessing software product "goodness."
		■ How to extend the quantified product integrity concept to the software systems development process domain to assess process "goodness."
		■ How to measure the integrity of the process described in Chapter 3.

TABLE P–1 *Continued*

Chapter	Title and Purpose	What You Will Learn
6	**Measurement** (*continued*)	■ Ideas for developing your own product and process metrics in addition to the product and process integrity metrics.
		■ How to set up product and process measurement scales that make sense for your environment.
		■ How to use the product integrity metric to track product evolution through the software systems development process to head off product development problems.
		■ How to set up process measurement scales for alternative improvement approaches such as those developed by the Software Engineering Institute.
		■ How to integrate measurement with your process.
		■ How to develop an ADPE element to incorporate the product and process metrics and apply them to measure and improve your software products and processes.
7	**Cultural Change**—addresses human issues bearing on bringing about organizational cultural change during implementation of your systems engineering environment (SEE).	■ How to anticipate and manage the cultural changes that go hand-in-hand with any program designed to improve the software systems development process through the establishment of an SEE.
		■ The role in bringing about cultural change of the organization responsible for writing the ADPE elements and seeing to it that they are implemented and continually improved.
		■ How to deal with the challenges to ADPE implementation arising from the seller project-level individuals who will have to adapt to the policies, guidelines, procedures, and standards that govern their work.
		■ How to deal with the challenges to ADPE implementation arising from those buyer/user individuals who give technical direction to seller project managers for accomplishing project work.
		■ The impact on buyer/user senior management that ADPE implementation brings about.
		■ The key role seller senior management plays in effecting software systems development cultural change through ADPE implementation.
		■ How business pressures affect seller senior management support for ADPE implementation and how to accommodate these pressures.
		■ More about "prescriptive application" of the product development process as it applies to empowerment and bringing about cultural change.
		■ The customer's role in ADPE implementation.
		■ The role of training in effecting cultural change.
		■ How to sell ADPE implementation as a career growth opportunity.
		■ The organizational factors bearing upon how long it takes to bring about cultural change.
		■ Why an ADPE element defining the ADPE element development and improvement process is intimately tied to organizational cultural change.
		■ How to develop an ADPE element defining the ADPE element development and improvement process.
8	**Process Improvement Planning**—provides practical guidance on how to write an SEE implementation plan to establish the framework for doing the things discussed in the preceding chapters.	■ Timeline considerations for SEE implementation tasks and their phasing.
		■ How ADPE elements should be phased in.
		■ ADPE elements that should be included in your SEE.
		■ How the ADPE should be constituted—(1) from a small number of elements (i.e., approximately ten), each consisting of tens of pages or more, or (2) from a large number of elements (i.e., tens or more), each consisting of a couple of pages, or (3) some combination of (1) and (2).
		■ How frequently an ADPE element should be updated.
		■ The amount of detail to include in individual ADPE elements.
		■ How to define a plan for an application development technology environment (ADTE) for your organization.

TABLE P–1	*Continued*	
Chapter	*Title and Purpose*	*What You Will Learn*
8	**Process Improvement Planning** (*continued*)	■ How to package ADPE elements and related items.
		■ How to handle ADPE implementation if your organization is small—here, *small organization* means "an organization having only a few projects, each involving only a small number of people (say, up to ten) so that all involved parties frequently come in contact with one another."
		■ How to set up an austere SEE implementation approach.
		■ How to leverage mentoring and coaching to facilitate implementation of ADPE practices.
		■ Strategies that can be adopted to meet the cultural change challenges posed by SEE implementation.
		■ How to deal with the business reality of the almighty dollar in bringing about ADPE implementation.
		■ How to account for the reality that people within an organization span a broad spectrum of willingness to adapt to the engineering environment.
		■ Who should develop the SEE in your organization.
		■ How to frame an SEE implementation policy.
		■ How to plan ADPE implementation improvement at the project level.
		■ How process and product measurement can be integrated with your organizational process.
		■ How an SEE implementation plan should be structured.

on two metrics that we call "product integrity index" and "process integrity index." We give general formulas for these indexes. We show you how to set up value scales for these indexes in terms that make sense to your organization. Through detailed, worked-out examples, we show you how to calculate these indexes. Finally, we explain what these numbers mean.

At the end of the book, we include an annotated bibliography. Most of the bibliographic entries have been selected because of their practitioner bent. This bibliography is intended to (1) point you to alternative treatments of topics that we discuss, (2) help you gain greater insight into topics that we address, and (3) help you pursue topics that we only touch upon that may be of greater interest to you.

The book's central concept for housing an organization's development processes is the *systems engineering environment* (SEE). The SEE consists of the following two complementary components:

- An application development process environment (ADPE) and

- An application development technology environment (ADTE).

The ADPE is that set of policies, guidelines, procedures, and standards defining an organization's way of doing business. These entities we call "ADPE elements." The ADTE is that set of technologies (e.g., personal computers, networks, CASE tools) used to develop the organization's software products and software-related products. The book focuses on the ADPE because its elements define the software systems development process. We show you how to capture successful software development concepts in a handful of these elements. We also give you practical guidance for taking the words in these elements and infusing them into your organization. This infusion is perhaps the most challenging aspect of maturing your organization's software systems development capability—because change is mostly emotional, not cognitive.

We stress that this book is not tied to the use of any particular software systems development technology. You will find this book helpful whether you are using object-oriented technology, automated tools, prototyping, or some combination of these and other technologies.

Please join us now by turning to Chapter 1.

Acknowledgments

What no wife of a writer can ever understand is that a writer is working when he's staring out the window.

—Burton Rascoe (1892–1957), American writer, editor.

We thank William Bryan for giving us carte blanche to use material that he previously published with one of us. He unhesitatingly granted this permission at the outset of this project.

To Gary Donaldson, we are grateful for his insight into the social and cultural factors governing organizational change. We especially appreciate his help with Chapter 7.

We thank the reviewers of early drafts of some chapters. Their comments helped us adjust the book's tone and orientation.

We wrote this book while employed full time with Science Applications International Corporation. We are grateful to many of our colleagues and coworkers for helping us orgainze our thoughts and enrich our experience. To our colleague Janet Vasak go our special thanks for her support from the time the book was just an idea. We are grateful to Larry Peck for his support. We thank Andy Meranda for his help reviewing the page proofs. To Louise Pearson go our thanks for her help with obtaining permissions.

To Paul Becker of Prentice Hall, we wish to express our appreciation for his encouragement and support (both material and emotional) throughout this entire project. His patience with us is appreciated.

To Pine Tree Composition go our thanks for patience, understanding, and suggestions during the production stages of this project. The book's 240+ figures proved to be a considerable production challenge—even with software tools. The Pine Tree staff went above and beyond in dealing with this and other challenges that arose during production.

Any book project cannot be accomplished without some impact on home life. To our families, we express our gratitude for their patience while we took a lot of time away from them on evenings and weekends to write this book. Because this time can never be reclaimed, we are grateful for their understanding. Special thanks go to Bena Siegel. This trip down the book-project path was her third. Despite what she knew lay ahead, she graciously consented.

chapter 1

Motivation

1.1 INTRODUCTION

This book presents an experienced-based approach for improving an organization's software systems development process. It is written for development, product assurance, and management practitioners in the business of creating software systems or related products for commercial or public-sector customers.

The software industry recognizes that the way in which software systems and products are developed needs to be changed. The following remarks echo this need:

"Stop providing short-term fixes for long-term problems."

"Reduce the number of overlapping systems."

"Reduce our organization's dependency on individuals to create and maintain software."

"Replace our aging legacy systems with modern, maintainable, standardized systems."

"Develop new systems with lower life cycle costs."

As illustrated in Figure 1–1, this book presents ideas for making a planned transition to well-defined software systems development practices. This growing recognition of a need for change demands that organizations think in strategic terms and simultaneously deal with the day-to-day reality of getting the job done. For many organizations, software is produced by some amorphous process. Actually, software often emerges from the individual heroics of the people doing the work. To transition to well-

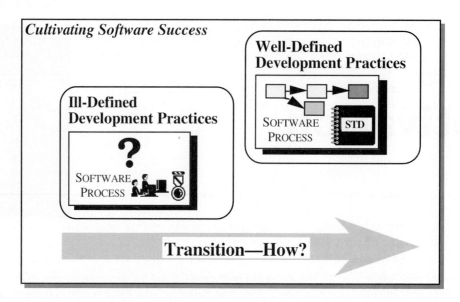

FIGURE 1–1   This book offers ideas on how to transition to well-defined software systems development practices.

defined development practices, an organization needs to institutionalize a documented process that can then be prescriptively applied to individual software systems development projects. By *prescriptively applied,* we mean "application of the documented process consistent with available time and resources." Even with time and resources, the critical element of cultivating software success is an organization's commitment to make the transition. Commitment involves people. Top-down support and bottom-up action need to be visible, consistent, and rewarded; else the critics are heard and the transition is delayed.

Part of the institutionalized process may involve automated development tools, such as computer-aided software engineering (CASE) tools. We believe the need for change cannot be solved simply with more automated development tools. Tools can help, but without a "new way of doing business" the need for change remains unanswered.

1.2 SOFTWARE SYSTEMS DEVELOPMENT CONCEPTS

To understand more specifically how to transition to a "new way of doing business," we need to establish a working vocabulary of concepts. We do not intend to present all software or software-related concepts, but we do want to introduce or review some fundamental concepts. This section presents the following concepts:

- Software.

- Software-related products.

- Software process, capability, performance, and maturity.

- Systems engineering environment (SEE).

- Culture.

Software   What do we mean when we use the term "software"? Classically, software has been looked upon as computer code (or programs) that, once installed on computer hardware, makes the hardware do its intended job. We find this viewpoint too restrictive in presenting our ideas on software process improvement. To unify many existing software systems development management concepts that are scattered around under different names, we prefer to think of software in more panoramic terms.

Specifically, in this book, *software* is formally defined as "information that has the following three distinguishing characteristics:

- Structured with logical and physical properties.

- Created and maintained in various forms and representations during the software systems development life cycle.

- Tailored for machine processing in its fully developed state".

As shown in Figure 1–2,[1] we use a sponge to represent software. A sponge is used throughout the book to portray software's susceptibility to change.

Software systems development typically proceeds from broadly defined statements of customer needs, to a specification of how these needs are to be designed into the system, to the construction of the physical entity that is the system. In engineering parlance, this evolutionary process is often described in terms of a life cycle. Such customer need statements are frequently expressed in terms of *what* the customer wants done. Besides being derived from a customer need statement (commonly called a "requirements specification"), computer code is also based upon a specification of *how* (commonly called a "design") the customer need statements are to be implemented. Consequently, computer code operating in the customer's environment can be viewed as the fully developed state of the information embodied in design and requirements specifications tailored for machine processing. In

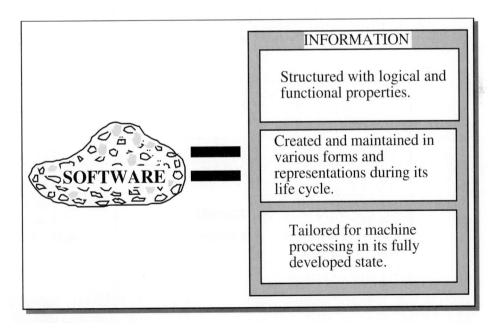

FIGURE 1–2 Our concept of software consists of three characteristics that distinguish software from other types of information.

---

[1]E. H. Bersoff, V. D. Henderson, and S. G. Siegel, *Software Configuration Management: An Investment in Product Integrity* (Englewood Cliffs, NJ: Prentice-Hall, 1980), p. 10. The discussion of the software concept in this chapter is adapted from W. L. Bryan and S. G. Siegel, *Software Product Assurance: Techniques for Reducing Software Risk* (Englewood Cliffs, NJ: PTR Prentice-Hall, 1988), pp. 36 ff.

other words, these specifications and computer code—with its many possible representations, such as source and object code on various media (e.g., disks, tapes, microprocessor chips, paper)—can be viewed as different forms and representations of a set of information with logical and functional properties (i.e., information specifying a sequence of functions to be accomplished).

Consequently, our conceptual definition of software includes not only computer code but also all associated documentation that represents an immature form of the code. For example, both the software requirements specification documentation and the software design specification documentation are considered software. Suppose we had defined software to be simply "computer code." Then, strictly speaking, software systems development process improvement would be restricted to consideration of computer code development. Such development activities would involve only overseeing the activities of coding, testing, recoding, retesting, . . . until the code is determined to be ready for customer delivery.

As illustrated in Figure 1–3, software is also the specification documentation that leads to computer code. To understand the concepts presented in this book, you need to be constantly aware of our definition of software. If you consider software only as computer code, you will often be confused in the pages that follow. Examples of software include the following:

- **Requirements specification.** This document specifies what functions a system is to do. In general, some functions will be performed by hardware, people, and computer code. Thus, a requirements specification usually consists of information, only some of which is software.

- **Design specification.** This document specifies how a requirements specification is to be implemented. In contrast to the customer-oriented language of a requirements specification, the language of a design specification is couched in computer terminology.

- **Computer source code and computer object code.** Source code is the first step in a two-step process by which software physically interacts with computer hardware. Source code is (or at least should be) produced from a design specification and is written in one of the many source code languages. These languages are based on logic constructs and syntax rules that bridge the gap between the way people think in

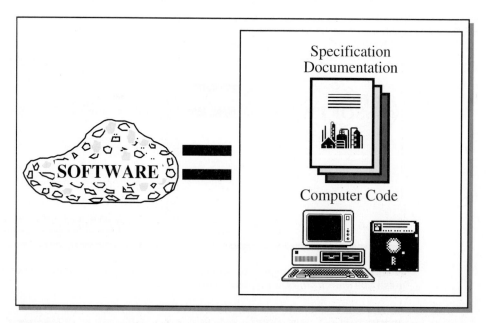

FIGURE 1–3 Our definition of software encompasses both specification documentation and computer code. Computer languages and database languages are merging. Consequently, our notion of computer code includes these blended languages.

solving problems and the way computer hardware functions in solving problems. To effect communication with this hardware, these languages must be processed by other software called compilers and assemblers, which produce object code. This latter code directly communicates with the hosting computer hardware in the binary language of zeros and ones that the hardware can understand.

With the advent of computer-aided software engineering (CASE) tools, source code can be automatically generated from CASE design documentation. From this perspective, source code can be viewed as if it were object code. In the future, CASE technology may replace the coding activity, just as compilers and assemblers replaced machine-level coding.

■ **Computer code executing on hardware.** This concept is perhaps the most difficult to visualize. It is the information embodied in object code that streams through the logic circuits of computer hardware, making the hardware do its intended job.

Computer languages and database languages are merging. In the past, computer code acted upon data. However, the distinction between these two complementary technologies is blurring. Consequently, sometimes, we think of database management systems and their associated databases as software.

Software-related Products   Besides considering the preceding examples of software, it is often convenient to discuss and associate other software-related products with our concept of software. As shown in Figure 1–4, these software-related products are not a form of software but rather serve to provide additional insight into the software. Such software-related products include the following:

■ **User's manuals.** This documentation explains to a user how to use the system containing software.

■ **Test documentation.** This documentation describes the strategy and specific test steps for exercising the system containing software to determine that the software is making the system do what it is supposed to do.

■ **System concept documentation.** This documentation describes in broad terms what a system that is to contain software is intended to do.

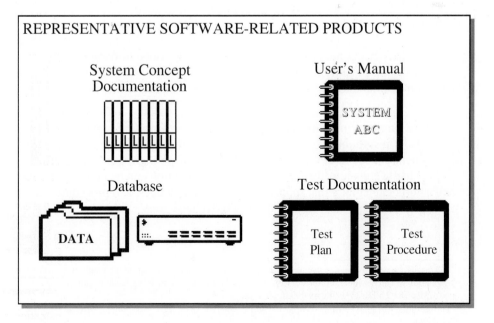

FIGURE 1–4   Software-related products augment and complement our definition of software.

Given this definition of software (and software-related products), we address the concept of "software process" and related concepts.[2] According to Webster's Dictionary, a *process* is "a series of actions or operations (leading to) an end."[3] The Institute of Electrical and Electronics Engineers (IEEE) defines a process as "a sequence of steps performed for a given purpose; for example, the software development process."[4]

Software Process A software process can be defined as a set of activities, methods, practices, and transformations that people use to develop and maintain software and associated products (e.g., project plans, design documents, code, test cases, and user manuals). As an organization matures, the software process becomes better defined and more consistently implemented through the organization.

Software Process Capability The range of expected results that can be achieved by following a software process can be thought of as an organization's software process capability. This capability provides one means of predicting the most likely outcomes to be expected from the next software project that the organization undertakes.

Software Process Performance The actual results achieved by following a software process can be referred to as software process performance. This performance focuses on the results achieved, while software process capability focuses on results expected. Based on the attributes of a specific project and the context within which it is conducted, the actual performance of the project may not reflect the full process capability of the organization; i.e., the capability of the project is constrained by its environment. For instance, radical changes in the application or technology undertaken may place a project's staff on a learning curve that causes their project's capability, as well as performance, to fall short of the organization's full process capability.

Software Process Maturity The extent to which a specific process is explicitly defined, managed, measured, controlled, and effective can be thought of as an organization's software process maturity. Maturity implies a potential for growth in capability. Also, maturity indicates both the richness of an organization's software process and the consistency with which it is applied in projects throughout an organization. This maturity is usually supported through documentation and training, and the process is continually being monitored and improved by its users. Software process maturity implies that the productivity and quality resulting from an organization's software process are known and can be improved over time through consistent gains in the discipline achieved by using its software process.

Systems Engineering Environment (SEE) As a software organization gains in software process maturity, it institutionalizes its software process through a systems engineering environment. As we subsequently discuss, this environment consists of policies, guidelines, procedures, and standards, as well as hardware and software tools. Institutionalization entails building and refining an infrastructure and a corporate culture that support the methods, practices, and procedures of the business so that they endure after those who originally defined them have gone.

---

[2]The discussion of software process and related concepts here is adapted from M. C. Paulk, B. Curtis, M. B. Chrissis, and C. V. Weber, "Capability Maturity Model for Software, Version 1.1," Software Engineering Institute and Carnegie Mellon University Technical Report CMU/SEI-93-TR-24 (February 1993), pp. 3 ff.

[3]This definition is adapted from *Webster's Ninth Collegiate Dictionary* (Springfield, MA: Merriam-Webster Inc., 1984). The words "leading to" were substituted for "conducing to."

[4]IEEE Std 610.12-1990, "IEEE Standard Glossary of Software Engineering Terminology," The Institute of Electrical and Electronics Engineers, Inc. (1990), p. 57.

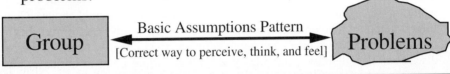

Culture is

- a pattern of basic assumptions
- invented, discovered, or developed by a given group
- as the group learns to cope with its problems of external adaptation and internal integration
- that has worked well enough to be considered valid and, therefore,
- is taught to new members as the
- correct way to perceive, think, and feel in relation to those problems.

Group ⟷ Basic Assumptions Pattern [Correct way to perceive, think, and feel] ⟷ Problems

FIGURE 1–5   A definition of "culture."

Culture   Software process improvement is an ongoing exercise of elevating software process maturity. Bringing about software process improvement requires bringing about cultural change within an organization. Thus, to describe software process improvement techniques, an understanding of the elusive term *culture* is needed. Figure 1–5 defines culture; this definition is taken from the field of psychology.[5] Throughout this book, we expand upon the notions embodied in this definition of culture to explain software process improvement techniques.

1.3 PRODUCT "GOODNESS" AND PROCESS "GOODNESS"

What is a "good" software product? What is a "good" software systems development process? "Goodness" is a multidimensional concept that depends on your point of view. What is important to one person may not be important to another person. We take the position that good people produce good products and that good processes produce good products. Evidence abounds that "good" software(-related) products can be produced without a defined software development process. Evidence also abounds that, turning out such products *consistently* more often than not depends on having a defined software systems development process.

A developer of software(-related) products wants to stay in business. It is axiomatic that "staying in business" is strongly tied to customer satisfaction, which can be expressed in many ways. First and foremost, a product should do what the customer wants it to do. In addition, when a customer pays a developer to develop software products, the customer wants these products to be delivered according to some established schedule and for some established amount of money. In this book, we choose to fold considerations such as these into our concept of "product goodness." More specifically, "product

[5]E. H. Schein, "Organizational Culture," *American Psychologist*, vol. 45, no. 2 (February 1990), p. 111.

goodness" includes an attribute related to the content of the product itself (i.e., it does what it is supposed to do) as well as attributes related to the development of that product (e.g., being developed on time and within budget).

For us, then, "product goodness" is a multidimensional concept. The label we put on this concept is *integrity*. One dictionary definition of *integrity* is "completeness."[6] For us, completeness is tied to multiple perspectives and attributes. Often people think of goodness from one perspective, (e.g., manager or developer) or in terms of an attribute (e.g., budget, schedule, or requirements). Our integrity concept allows for blending multiple perspectives and attributes. For example, a manager may think of product goodness as the product being delivered on time and/or within budget. A developer may think of product goodness as the product doing what the customer wants. We think of product goodness as product integrity that folds in all of the perspectives and attributes. We say that the product has integrity if the product is delivered on time, within budget, and doing what the customer wants. We believe that it is not "good" enough to develop a product to do what the customer wants, if the product is ten weeks late and costs three times its original estimate. Product integrity is tied to certain attributes that characterize its content and the way it was developed.

We recognize that the attributes we may choose to fold into our notion of "product integrity" would not necessarily be the same as the attributes that you would choose. Consequently, this book allows you to mold the product integrity concept to the needs of your organization. To help you do this molding, we introduce here one way to define product integrity based on the considerations previously discussed. This definition provides you with a starting point to define product integrity that makes sense for your organization. Therefore, one definition of a software product with integrity[7] is one that

- Fulfills customer needs.
- Can be easily and completely traced through its life cycle.
- Meets specified performance criteria.
- Meets cost expectations.
- Meets delivery expectations.

In Chapter 6, we show you how to quantify product integrity. The approach there is to illustrate this quantification in specific terms. We do that by using the preceding definition of product integrity. However, the quantitative treatment given in Chapter 6 is general so that you will be able to apply it to your definition of product integrity.

Several observations of the five integrity attributes are worth making.

Fulfills Customer Needs   A product that has the integrity attribute of fulfilling customer needs is one that satisfies stated customer requirements. The point is that software systems development is a challenge to the inventive nature of both the customer and the developer. They get ideas and try to flesh them out during subsequent development stages. At any particular point in this development process, they generally do not have all the answers regarding how well the software system will satisfy customer needs. Thus, to a certain extent, software systems development is a process of trial and error in which each error makes the customer and the developer a little smarter regarding how they should proceed (if they are willing to learn from their mistakes). But this trial-and-error process is simply another

---

[6]It should be noted that the dictionary gives a spectrum of definitions for *integrity*. For example, one dictionary defines the word *integrity* as follows: 1. an unimpaired condition: SOUNDNESS; 2. firm adherence to a code of especially moral or artistic value: INCORRUPTIBILITY; and 3. the quality or state of being complete or undivided: COMPLETENESS. *Webster's Ninth Collegiate Dictionary* (Springfield, MA: Merriam-Webster, Inc., 1984).

[7]The discussion of the product integrity concept is adapted from Bryan and Siegel, *Software Product Assurance*, pp. 73 ff.

way of saying that change is indigenous to software systems development. The developer develops, and then the customer and the developer analyze the results of this development. In response to the analytic results, they change their minds. The developer develops some more, and the cycle continues until they achieve what they want—or they run out of time or money. From the perspective of software development management, achieving closure between the customer and the developer includes other important considerations that should be constantly kept in mind. These considerations are embodied in the other product integrity attributes.

Can Be Easily and Completely Traced Through Its Life Cycle   A product whose evolution lacks the integrity attribute of traceability lies at the heart of the classical software maintenance problem. If the software life cycle is difficult or impossible to trace, either the software must be forever frozen, or its subsequent evolution becomes a high-risk venture with a small likelihood of a good return on the development investment.

Meets Specified Performance Criteria   A product that has the integrity attribute of meeting specified performance criteria can be viewed as a special case of the first attribute—fulfilling the customer's needs. What are performance criteria? Generally, performance criteria address such issues as the following:

- How many? For example, a customer may have a requirement for the software to process ten thousand incoming messages.

- How often? For example, a customer may have a requirement for the software to suffer no more that two failures during a month.

- How long? For example, a customer may have a requirement for the software to operate eighteen hours a day.

On some software systems development projects, significance is attached to the difference between a functional requirement (what the software is to do) and a performance criterion (how well the software is to perform). For example, a developer may be paid a certain amount for producing software that meets all functional requirements, and be paid a bonus for producing software whose operation exceeds specified performance criteria. On other software projects, there may be no reason to distinguish between "customer needs" and "performance criteria," in which case our first (i.e., fulfills customer needs) and third (i.e., meets specified performance criteria) product integrity attributes merge into a single attribute.

Meets Cost and Delivery Expectations   A product that has the integrity attributes of meeting cost and delivery expectations focuses attention on the effectiveness of the software systems development process that yields the software products. Accordingly, these integrity attributes reflect management's effectiveness in getting the job done. Part of the software manager's job is to plan the software development cycle, direct others to produce software products, and control activities during plan execution. This job, in part, is one of managing project budget and schedule. A product that has the integrity attributes of meeting cost and delivery expectations can also be viewed as a special case of fulfilling customer needs. Generally, a customer stipulates (1) what is to be done (and how well), (2) how much he or she is willing to pay, and (3) how long he or she is willing to wait for the software.

Now, just as we define product integrity in terms of attributes such as the ones previously discussed, we can similarly define a concept called "process integrity" to characterize "process goodness." What are the analogues to product attributes? In simple terms, a process is made up of components, which in turn are made up of activities. An example of a process component would be "project planning"; examples of activities associated with this process component would be the following:

- The software developer reviews a customer statement of need, communicates with the customer, and assembles a project planning team.

- The software developer formulates resource estimates based on the customer statement of need.

- The software developer business manager calculates dollar estimates from the resource estimates.

So, as we show in Chapter 6, we can define process integrity in terms of process components and associated activities. As we explain there, measuring product integrity and process integrity enables you to measure the "goodness" of the products and the "goodness" of the software systems development process used to develop the products.

1.4 REQUISITE SOFTWARE SYSTEMS DEVELOPMENT DISCIPLINES

Proper understanding of process begins with a top-level understanding of the roles of those who should be involved with a software project if it is to turn out products with integrity. For this purpose, consider Figure 1–6.[8] This figure depicts three groups of related disciplines—development, product assurance, and management. Attaining and maintaining software product integrity on a software project requires judicious application of these three groups of disciplines. We believe that achieving product integrity is accomplished with the interplay of all three discipline groups.

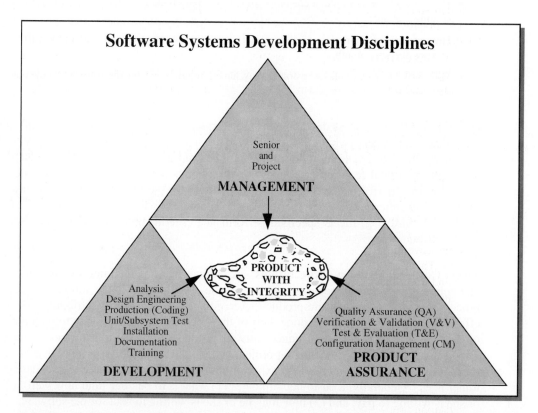

FIGURE 1–6   The requisite software systems development disciplines for attaining and maintaining software product integrity are development, product assurance, and management.

---

[8]Adapted from W.L. Bryan, C. Chadbourne, and S.G. Siegel, Tutorial: Software Configuration Management (Los Alamitos, CA: IEEE Computer Society Press, 1980), p. 452.

Development Disciplines   Development disciplines are typified by the following activities: analysis, design engineering, production (coding), unit/subsystem testing, installation, documentation, and training. The developers need to be disciplined technically and managerially to cope with a software project at all stages of development—from requirements definition through operational use. Part of this coping means knowing what technical and dollar resources are needed to get the job done, when these resources are needed, and then applying them vigorously in the right mix at the right time. These resource allocation tasks are typically the responsibility of management within the development group. The developers need to ensure not only that adequate documentation is produced but also that it is produced systematically.

What do we mean by "systematically"? Software in the form of documentation produced out of sequence—for example, computer code developed before a design specification—can disrupt traceability back to customer needs and thus detract from the product's integrity. Systematically produced software, particularly in the form of documentation, serves to maintain visibility of the evolving software product for management and the customer. We believe such visibility increases the likelihood of a good return on the development investment.

A frequent problem during software systems development is the development group's reluctance to have someone review its work. The development group needs to accept and support review activities as constructive, allied, and indispensable to the success of the project. It is counterproductive for the developers not to have their work reviewed. For example, if computer code is reviewed and it is discovered that several of the key customer requirements have not been incorporated, then management can start working on the issue before it becomes a problem. Management's job of making resource allocation decisions is more difficult if managers cannot judge where the developers are in the development process. Developers should take advantage of the review resources to increase the likelihood of successfully meeting the customer's requirements. The development organization must be ever cognizant of the customer and of the need for accurately and completely communicating project progress—and problems—to management and to the customer.

Product Assurance Disciplines   The product assurance group's disciplines provide management with a set of checks and balances with respect to the state of the software. These checks and balances offer a measure of *assurance* that *product* integrity is attained and maintained. The product assurance group includes four disciplines—quality assurance (QA), verification and validation (V&V), test and evaluation (T&E), and configuration management (CM). As illustrated in Figure 1–7, the product assurance disciplines of QA, V&V, and T&E can be represented as a set of comparison activities where "what is expected" is compared to "what is observed." The fourth discipline is the formal control (CM) of software changes. Product assurance acts as a checking and balancing mechanism on the software systems development activities, and it provides management with insight into the development process. This mechanism helps to stabilize the software systems development process by giving it visibility and traceability.

In a constructive, nonconfrontational, nonjudgmental way, product assurance plays the role of the devil's advocate. There is a natural inclination to view anyone who reviews someone else's work as an adversary (the "bad guy"), but when performed properly, product assurance supports and contributes to the software systems development process. By *performed properly* we mean, for example, "benevolent (but probing) questioning of a software product's contents." The object of the questioning should always be determination of the extent to which the product conforms to customer requirements, thereby helping to achieve convergence between the customer and the developer. By establishing agreed-upon procedures for constructive interchange among the management, development, and product assurance groups, product assurance can institutionalize a set of checks and balances serving both management and the developers throughout the software life cycle.

Typically, the development disciplines and the product assurance disciplines perceive project progress from different viewpoints. Developers tend to look for solutions that "work" but often do not worry how the solutions "will not work." Product assurance tends to look at developer solutions from

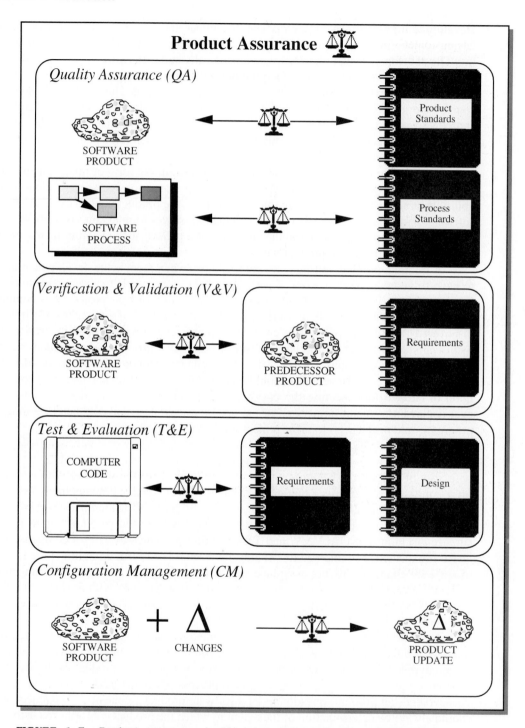

FIGURE 1–7 Product assurance is the integrated application of the three comparison processes of QA, V&V, T&E, and the CM process that formally controls changes.

the view of how the solutions "work" and "will not work." This second look both helps to ensure that the customer's needs are being satisfied and increases the likelihood of a good return on the development investment.

The product assurance disciplines provide management with insight as to the state of the software. For example, it is Friday afternoon and the product assurance group has just completed performing the agreed-upon acceptance test procedures for software code that is due for installation at the customer's site on Monday morning. Assume that the product assurance tester(s) recorded five instances (i.e., test incident reports) when "what was expected" to happen was different from "what was observed." The test incident reports (TIRs) are not judgmental but simply record the differences. Subsequently, the TIRs are provided to management. Management can focus its attention and resources on those areas that must be redone for Monday's release. Also, management may make a decision that directs the developers to work on the two most important TIRs. Product assurance is directed to rerun the acceptance tests and make sure new secondary and tertiary errors do not develop as a result of the new or changed computer code. Assuming all goes well and no new errors are introduced, on Monday morning the software code is released to the user community with accompanying release notes. These release notes inform the users that (1) there are known problems that exist and (2) resolutions to these problems are being sought. Through the use of agreed-upon testing procedures, management was able to make an informed, intelligent decision as to where to allocate project resources to meet the Monday morning deadline. At the same time, management was able to (1) effectively communicate to the user community the state of the software and (2) manage user community expectations of what the state was.

Product assurance also needs to confirm that product development is disciplined by providing the procedures for creating and controlling baselines and baseline updates—configuration management (CM).[9] To confirm that product development is disciplined, product assurance needs to apply a balanced blend of product assurance activities commensurate with project complexity and importance. How is this balanced blend realized? Management, developers, and product assurance mutually agree on what makes sense to do consistent with project schedules and resource constraints. That is, product assurance is prescriptively applied.

It is particularly important to note that product assurance does not normally address the "goodness" of a product through subjective judgments. Product assurance primarily addresses the degree to which a product satisfies customer requirements. Requirements satisfaction is determined through objective comparisons. A software product is "good," by our definition, if it embodies all customer requirements and does not embody anything the customer did not ask for.[10]

Management   The disciplines in the management group provide direction to development and product assurance activities to effect synergism among these activities. This group consists of the disciplines of senior management and project management. Senior management provides direction generally at the level above a particular project organization and promulgates corporate guidelines and policies. Typically, this direction concentrates on sorting things out with respect to two or more projects that may be competing for corporate resources. In this book, when we refer to *senior management,* we mean (unless otherwise indicated) "the person or organization to which the project manager reports."

Senior management has a key role to play at the outset of a project. It must see to it that a project is given stature within the corporate structure commensurate with the project's importance as perceived by senior management, its complexity, and its projected cost. Lacking this stature, the project may be pushed to the bottom of the corporate stack and thereby be stifled in the competition for lim-

---

[9]A *baseline* is an approved snapshot of the system at a given point in its evolution. As the word literally implies, *baseline* is a line that establishes a formal base for defining subsequent change. Without a baseline (i.e., reference point), the notion of change is meaningless. While a baseline is being established, it may be revised one or more times. These drafts are *not* baseline updates. As used in this book, *baseline update* refers to each "approved reissue" of a baseline after the baseline is first established.

[10]Remember, in Chapter 6, we show you how to quantify product "goodness" in terms that make sense for your organization.

ited corporate resources and thus lose visibility within the overall corporate context. Senior management must also ensure that a qualified project manager is assigned to lead the project. In addition, senior management must delineate the project manager's responsibilities, particularly with respect to the product assurance disciplines. It must give the project manager sufficient authority to marshal adequate corporate resources to support product development. Senior and project management must establish a well-defined accountability chain so that "who is supposed to do what for whom" is clearly understood at project outset and throughout product development.

Project management provides direction to the development and product assurance groups at the level of day-to-day activity associated with product development. Project management must also adequately distribute project resources between development and product assurance organizational entities. The practice in the software industry has too often been to dump resources into the development disciplines in an attempt to meet fast-approaching product delivery dates. The all-too-typical mad scramble to meet delivery dates often comes about because management did not ensure a front-end investment, particularly in the product assurance disciplines.

The principle of "pay now versus pay much more later" is an issue that both senior and project management must face squarely at the outset of a project. Many managers probably do not find it difficult to accept the need for front-end endeavors and concomitant expenditures in order to increase the probability of project success. What is generally difficult for managers to appreciate is the extent to which they must act to effect a disciplined approach to product development and to effect a balanced application of available resources to the development and product assurance disciplines. The project manager, in particular, must see himself or herself as a catalyst to be added continually to project activity to stimulate interaction between the development and product assurance disciplines and to make things happen effectively. This book offers some techniques (but no formulas!) for performing this catalysis.

1.5 GENERIC FOUR-STAGE SOFTWARE SYSTEMS DEVELOPMENT LIFE CYCLE

Lacking physical characteristics, software is inherently difficult to see. This inherent lack of visibility must be addressed to keep software systems development focused. One fundamental way of raising the visibility of the software systems development process is to divide the process into pieces or stages. The idea of dividing a software project into smaller, more manageable pieces gives rise to the notion of attributing a life cycle to software development (and maintenance).

The stages in a life cycle are analogous to courses in a meal. Just as a meal is divided into courses so that it can be consumed without causing indigestion, so a software project is divided into courses that individually are easier to manage than the uncut whole. There is no unique way to divide software systems development into stages. What is important is that the development is divided into some set of stages to facilitate development of the software and the management of the project. The principle is to divide the development effort into *some* set of stages.

The life cycle concept became part of the computer sciences literature in the 1960s. Since that time, a variety of life cycle concepts have appeared in the engineering literature. In this book, our life cycle concept focuses on the interactions of the requisite disciplines of development, product assurance, and management. Figure 1–8 illustrates our software development life cycle model that has four generic development stages and a review area.

The stages symbolize the activities of the development disciplines and the customer's use of the developed software system. The review area symbolizes (1) the activities of the product assurance disciplines associated with reviews, (2) the outputs from the development disciplines, and (3) the activities of the management disciplines associated with deciding what to do next based on the reviews and other factors. The review area also includes other activities of the development discipline coupled to management decision making.

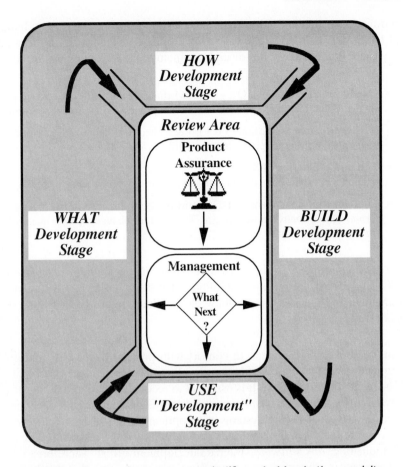

FIGURE 1–8 Our four-stage generic life cycle blends the requisite software systems development disciplines of development, product assurance, and management.

Each software systems development effort requires a unique set of the development, product assurance, and management disciplines. These required disciplines will interact throughout the development effort—i.e., throughout the life cycle.

Development   Reduced to the simplest terms, there are four development stages of software maturation:

- What—Specification of **WHAT** the software is to do.
- How—Specification of **HOW** the software is to do the **WHAT**.
- Build—Development or **BUILD** of the computer code that implements the **HOW**.
- Use—Operational deployment or **USE** of the computer code to perform the **WHAT**.

Although developers may not **USE** the software, they will probably need to provide software maintenance. The arrows leading into the **Review Area** represent the development disciplines submitting their work from each stage to independent Product Assurance for review.

Product Assurance   Product assurance serves as a checking (nonjudgmental examination of results) and balancing (alternative viewpoint of progress) mechanism on the product development activities performed. Product assurance disciplines include the following four processes:

- **Quality assurance (QA).** QA checks whether the software or software processes conform to established standards and identifies software or software processes that do not conform to standards.

- **Verification and validation (V&V).** V&V checks for any oversights or deviations from customer requirements and predecessor products and identifies them.

- **Test and evaluation (T&E).** T&E, which exercises the coded form of software, checks for shortfalls from requirements and design documents and identifies them. T&E is a special case of V&V.

- **Configuration management (CM).** CM balances the need to make changes with a visible, traceable, and formal way to control those changes. The need for change arises primarily from the application of the other three product assurance processes.

There is no uniformity in the software engineering community regarding the definitions of QA, V&V, T&E, and CM. The preceding definitions have proven to be a useful way of describing the control mechanism and the classes of review checks that need to be instituted on software systems development efforts.

Management   Management, in concert with product developers and product assurers, uses product assurance results to gain insight into product development work to make intelligent, informed decisions about what to do next. It is essential to recognize that, unlike the stages in human development, a software life cycle stage is *not* something that is passed through once, never to be revisited. From the point of view of software systems development, any life cycle stage may be revisited a number of times before the software is retired. This notion of stage revisits is a key element of planning for, and accomplishing, *any* software systems development effort. Therefore, a management decision may be made to revisit a previous or current life cycle stage to modify work already accomplished or to proceed to a subsequent life cycle stage. Thus, the life cycle is traversed by a series of one or more revisits to a life cycle stage.

For a particular software systems development effort, each generic stage unfolds into one or more stages defining the particular work to be accomplished in terms that the customer and developer mutually understand. This unfolding, or *instantiation*, gives visibility to that particular effort, thereby helping the customer and developer mutually progress in their understanding of the remaining work that needs to be accomplished. Note that the life cycle concept implies a sequence of stages, but multiple stages may be ongoing in parallel. For example, some members of the development effort may be working in the *HOW* stage on a draft design specification, while other members are working on a refinement of the requirements from the *WHAT* stage. Thus, software systems development proceeds iteratively through a life cycle via synergistic interplay among the following: (1) product developers, (2) product assurers, and (3) management.

1.6 USER, BUYER, AND SELLER ORGANIZATIONS INVOLVED IN SOFTWARE SYSTEMS DEVELOPMENT

As we explained, the development, product assurance, and management groups must interact on any software project if software products with integrity are to result. However, to appreciate more fully the implications of this concept in terms of an actual project environment, we need to say something about the three archetypical parties that interact on most software projects. As Figure 1–9 shows, these parties are the following:

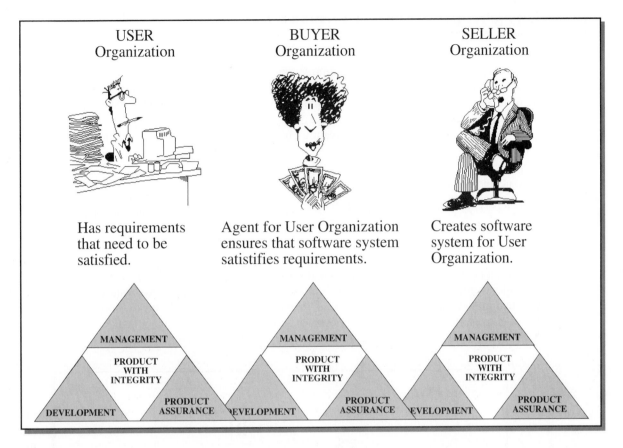

FIGURE 1–9 The three archetypical organizations that interact on most software projects may or may not have the requisite software systems development disciplines for attaining and maintaining software product integrity.

- **The user of the software system.** This party generally is the one with the requirements that the software is being developed to satisfy.

- **The buyer of the software system.** This party generally is the agent for the user and thus can be thought of as a surrogate user. The buyer typically interacts with the seller in seeing to it that the software system is being developed in accordance with user requirements. Sometimes the buyer and the user are the same. The buyer and the user are the "customer" to whom we have been referring in preceding discussions. In subsequent discussions, we generally use the terms *customer* and *buyer/user* interchangeably.

- **The seller of the software system.** This party is hired by the buyer to create the software system for the user.

If the user, buyer, and seller organizations have corresponding development, product assurance, and management personnel, the likelihood of achieving a software product with integrity is increased. For example, the seller should have a project manager and of course developers who produce a product as requested by the customer. The seller should have a product assurance group that reviews the products before they are shown to the customer. Correspondingly, the buyer/user should have a project manager who should interface with the seller project manager. Also, the buyer/user should have a staff skilled in the development disciplines to support the buyer/user project manager. Finally, the buyer/user should have a staff skilled in the product assurance disciplines to review the products received from the seller.

1.7 OBSTACLES TO IMPROVING SOFTWARE SYSTEMS DEVELOPMENT CULTURES

This book approaches software process improvement as a cultural change exercise that modifies one or more of the factors making up the previously introduced definition of culture. This section presents some of the impediments to effecting cultural change. This presentation lays the groundwork for the technical issues that this book addresses.

As depicted in Figure 1–10, cultivating software development cultural change involves more than the following elements:

- Management edicts.
- Team of experienced and good people.
- Casual conversations with the customer.

Management Edicts As discussed earlier, software systems development is an activity that requires many disciplines. It is rare that one individual possesses all the required skills to effect successful system development. In addition, it is basic human nature that creative people want to contribute to the culture that they work and live in. Therefore, management edicts may result in short-term gains. These gains are often nullified by mounting resistance and resentment that management is not willing to listen to the people who actually have to do the work. On the other hand, the antithesis of management

FIGURE 1–10 Cultivating successful software systems development extends far beyond (1) management edicts, (2) assembling a team of experienced and good people, and (3) a five-minute conversation with a customer and a three-week coding frenzy.

edicts—pure democracy—is also not the answer; a democratic approach to systems development can often result in not ever completing what needs to be done. Someone has to be in charge. Thus, effecting software systems development cultural change involves a careful blending of both extremes—dictatorship and democracy.

Let us illustrate the preceding remarks—first regarding dictatorship and then regarding democracy. Many project managers view independent product assurance as an impediment to getting the job done. Managers of project managers simply cannot edict that project managers will do product assurance. Experience has shown that project managers will perform product assurance in a perfunctory fashion or will state that the development staff will take care of product assurance. It is thus senior management's job to sell project management on the idea that independent product assurance contributes to a product's integrity. Project managers believe that their senior management does not understand what really needs to be done to get a product out the door and satisfy the customer. From their perspective, senior management is too far removed from the day-to-day realities. Rather than through edict, senior management needs to work with project managers to show in budget and schedule terms that independent product assurance *is* necessary to get a product out the door and satisfy the customer. An objective of this book is to provide senior management with insight into how to work with their project managers to effect cultural change in the product assurance realm.

Regarding pure democracy, turning the running of the project ship over to the entire development team is a recipe for shipwreck. Somebody has to be in charge to ensure that the project stays on course. Thus, another objective of this book is to provide project management (on both the developer and customer sides) with guidance on how to run a project like a participatory democracy—that is, having someone in charge, and at the same time, having this leader listening to the development team members. For this purpose, we detail a concept that we call a *change control board* (CCB) where participatory democracy works. Project work stays focused, and the participants definitely contribute.

Team of Experienced and Good People   Good people—that is, people with the applicable software systems development skills highlighted earlier—need to be blended on a software systems development effort to achieve success. The trend in the software industry is toward teaming—because, in part, systems are increasing in complexity. Thus, in general, no one corporation has the full complement of skills available to tackle the problem. (We also recognize that there are political reasons for teaming.) Even if a corporation is stable, personnel turnover and technology advancements demand continual examination of the corporate culture. Thus, assembling a team of good people requires a careful blending of the associated cultural diversity.

Compounding the challenge is the fact that each company itself consists of various software systems development cultures. For example, cultural clashes can arise in the independent product assurance area. For some companies, this independent product assurance is not a part of the culture. Senior management on both the development and customer side often recognize that independent product assurance is one way of avoiding repetition of past problems. Yet, at the working level, project managers on both the development and customer side, as well as the development team members, are often reluctant to adapt to the "new" idea of independent product assurance. Their past "successes" (without independent product assurance) makes acceptance of this form of cultural change difficult. We hope to provide management, developers, and product assurers with insight on how to blend corporate and customer cultures to achieve software systems development success.

Casual Conversations with the Customer   Software systems development is a challenge to the inventive nature of both the customer and the developer. They get ideas and try to flesh them out during subsequent development stages. Software systems development is a partnership that requires continual participation by both the customer and the developer. The notion that a customer states requirements and the developers go away and produce a working system with little or no subsequent interaction with the customer does not work. Both participants need continual visibility into the development process and products. No matter how well each participant thinks he or she understands the requirements at project outset, the reality is that both participants progress in their understanding of what needs to be done as the project proceeds.

Sellers are in the business of solving problems and providing solutions. In the commercial world, this approach translates into sellers making money. In the noncommercial or government environment, this approach translates into career advancement. There is a tendency in both environments for the developers to sign up for doing the job before the job's scope of effort is well bounded. Consequently, the customer's expectations are set that the job is well understood and that the necessary resources are in hand to complete the job. In the zeal to make money or to advance a career, an effort to manage the customer's expectations of what is really needed often falls by the wayside. Managing customer expectations is a culture change problem. Another of our objectives is to provide guidance on managing customer expectations.

To illustrate the preceding remarks, a commonly occurring software systems development problem is that of producing "user friendly systems." Figure 1–11 illustrates, in the extreme, how customer/developer misunderstandings regarding what "user friendly" means can lead to customer dissatisfaction.

Software process improvement is a cultural change that takes time. It is an exercise that is accomplished in concert with existing work. Senior management cannot afford to put today's work on hold while a new development environment is established. However, progress is needed in effecting the change to stay in business and advance careers. William Bridges, in his work on effecting cultural change, stresses the following in this regard:

> When a business or industry is going through a profound transformation—and there is hardly one that is not doing so today—competition blinds people to the real challenge, which is *capitalizing on that change*. Competing for market share in today's markets is like fighting for deck chairs on the *Titanic*.[11]

FIGURE 1–11 Customer/developer misunderstandings arising during software systems development—such as the meaning of "user-friendly system"—can adversely affect customer expectations.

---

[11]William Bridges, *Managing Transitions: Making the Most of Change* (Reading, MA: Addison-Wesley Publishing Company), 1991 (Sixth printing, April 1993), p. 82.

FIGURE 1–12 "My schedule simply doesn't permit me or my coworkers to document before we code. Anyway, the documentation is too difficult to keep up to date because the code keeps changing."

In other words, many people do not capitalize on the change because of the realities of staying in business and advancing individual careers. This constant change produces a wide spectrum of obstacles. Figure 1–12 illustrates a frequently encountered problem in the software industry—"I don't have time to document my computer code."

Too frequently, developers focus only on computer code, which is just one component of software. Part of software systems development cultural change is institutionalizing the software definition that encompasses both documentation and computer code. Once this definition is institutionalized, project planning can account for the resources needed for the documentation. Given the appropriate resources to develop documentation and computer code, the likelihood of successful software systems development efforts increases.

Many people in the software industry believe that, with the advent of computer-aided software engineering (CASE) technology, the documentation problem is a memory from a bygone era. While CASE technology produces some of the required documentation form of software, the technology generally does not produce documentation that senior management readily understands. The technologists understand the matrices and engineering diagrams that this technology turns out. Unfortunately, many of the people making the decisions regarding project resource allocation simply cannot relate to these CASE outputs. Sensitized to this potential problem, project management can set aside the appropriate resources and plan for the adaptation of CASE outputs to meet the needs of senior management and others.

Some people are receptive to change—others are not. In the latter category are those people who have achieved success in the past doing development their way. As shown in Figure 1–13, these people can be quite stubborn and disruptive to effecting software process improvement. Often they have not bought into the organization's mission regarding software process improvement. The Not-Invented-Here (NIH) syndrome manifests itself in different flavors depending upon where the individual is in the organization's hierarchy. If a senior manager suffers from the NIH syndrome, the impact on an organization can be significant. The senior manager exerts influence over immediate subordinates and others. The result is a counterculture that can splinter the organization, causing it to work at cross pur-

FIGURE 1–13 An impediment to software process improvement—the Not-Invented-Here (NIH) syndrome.

poses. If a project manager suffers from the NIH syndrome, the organizational impact can be more easily contained through senior management. (Assume that the senior management does not suffer from the NIH syndrome.) One of the objectives of this book is to provide guidance on how to achieve organizational buy-in from people who are resistant to change. However, it should be recognized that not all people will accept change. There will always be outliers.

Other cultural change challenges that we address in this book are as highlighted by the following quotations:

> "Now is not the time to sit with the customer and my software development staff to mutually agree upon what needs to be done next. Besides, my customer is paying me to figure out what he really needs. All I need to do is demonstrate the system to him after we are finished coding—and then he will know what he really wants."

> "Our Software Engineering Process Group is tying my hands with this silly procedure that defines the way we are suppose to do business with the customer. Even my customer thinks the procedure is too bureaucratic. Besides, before I came to this place to work, I already knew how to work with customers who wanted me to produce working computer systems."

> "Why do I need an independent product assurance group looking over my shoulder? My engineering staff is experienced and knows how to turn out good products. They are better able to write and execute acceptance test procedures than any outsiders could."

> "I don't see why I have to keep a written record of my interactions with the customer. I trust her, and she trusts me. Besides, the only written record that counts is the customer's letter of acceptance of the products that I and my staff deliver."

> "Another project is running into schedule and cost problems. The customer just called and said that our development team is not building what the customer needs."

> "I'm the government customer. Why can't I go around the contractor management and tell the developers how to do their job?"

"I don't understand. I've worked with this company before, and this current effort just doesn't match up with what they've done in the past."

"I don't care what our software development plan says. The customer wants the system tomorrow. If we can't deliver, he'll take his business elsewhere."

"I told you what I wanted you to do, and I assumed that you understood what I meant. But what you just delivered is not what I asked for!"

"How can you tell me that what you just delivered is what I asked for? This is *not* what I asked for, and I am not going to accept it!"

People are not afraid of change. They are afraid of what they will lose if change occurs. One of our objectives is to provide insight into how to overcome such fears.

1.8 ALTERNATIVE APPROACHES TO SOFTWARE PROCESS IMPROVEMENT

How do we overcome the obstacles to effecting cultural change to realize software process improvement? There is no simple answer. Many people in the software industry have been working this problem. Early system development efforts were concerned with keeping the hardware up and running. As the hardware stabilized and became less expensive, the emphasis in systems development shifted to software engineering considerations. To illustrate this point, consider the following remarks about software that appear in *War and Anti-war: Survival at the Dawn of the 21st Century*:

> Software is changing military balances in the world. Today weapons systems are mounted on or delivered by what the jargon calls "platforms." A platform can be a missile, a plane, a ship, or even a truck. And what the military is learning is that cheap, low-tech platforms operated by poor, small nations can now deliver high-tech smart firepower—if the weapons themselves are equipped with smart software. Stupid bombs can often have their I.Q. raised by the addition of retrofitted components dependent on software for their manufacture or operation.
>
> . . . Today the "machine tool" that counts most is the software used to manufacture software that manufactures software that manufactures software. For much of the processing of data into practical information and knowledge is dependent on it. The sophistication, flexibility, and security of the military software base is crucial.
>
> Policies that guide the development and use of information technology in general, and software in particular, are a crucial component of knowledge strategy.[12]*

These remarks are not restricted to the military domain. They apply equally well to any enterprise that relies on systems that contain software.

The demand for more intelligent information technology systems is increasing as enterprises attempt to implement effective knowledge strategies. What is needed are systems that process data and produce information that enables the enterprise decision makers to make informed decisions. Such systems are intertwined with many organizational facets of the enterprise, and the life of a system generally exceeds the tenures of individuals within the enterprise. One consequence of this continuing trend is that systems are increasing in their complexity, and thus software systems development is resource intensive. Concomitant with the resource and system complexity issues is the recognition by enterprises that they need to reduce their dependence on transient system developers. The decision makers are searching for more effective software systems development strategies. There are no simple solutions. Figure 1–14 illustrates three possible approaches for effecting software process improvement

---

[12]A. Toffler and H. Toffler, *War and Anti-War: Survival at the Dawn of the 21st Century* (New York: Little Brown and Company, 1993), p. 144.

*SOURCE: Reprinted by permission of Curtis Brown, Ltd. Copyright © 1993 by Alvin and Heidi Toffler. Published by Little, Brown and Company, 1993.

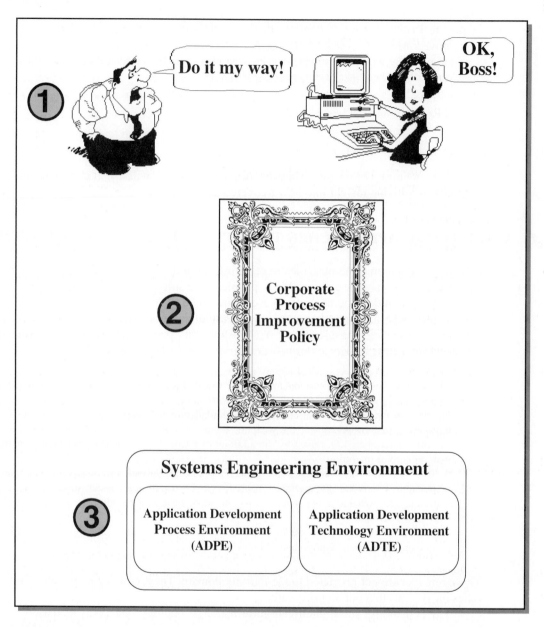

FIGURE 1–14 Alternative approaches to software process improvement—(1) management edict, (2) organizational policy, and (3) systems engineering environment (SEE). This book focuses on the SEE approach.

within an enterprise—management edits, corporate process improvement policy, and systems engineering environment.

Management Edicts As an enterprise grows, so does its complexity. An individual's capability to maintain pace with the expansion correspondingly diminishes. Replicated across an enterprise, the management edict approach often leads to the competing fiefdoms or subcultures. Over the long term, the result undermines organizational effectiveness. More organizational resources are poured into internecine struggles rather than being directed toward furthering the goals of the enterprise.

Corporate Process Improvement Policy   As an enterprise recognizes its expanding requirements for effective knowledge strategies, it often formalizes its vision for software process improvement with corporate policy. Such policy heightens the corporate awareness of the need to change the way software systems are developed. Often this approach does not reach down to the day-to-day working level of activities. Changing how the "work in progress" needs to be accomplished is disruptive and can lead to unhappy customers. While well-intentioned, this first step in software process improvement often falls short of influencing how systems are actually developed.

Systems Engineering Environment (SEE)   This software process improvement approach extends down to the day-to-day development activities. As discussed in this book, the SEE (1) accounts for the increasing complexity issues associated with enterprise growth, (2) accommodates the problems of transient developers, and (3) serves to overcome development subcultures within an enterprise. The SEE consists of two complementary components:

■ **Application Development Process Environment (ADPE)**—the set of those policies, guidelines, procedures, and standards defining the *processes* for developing deliverable products (i.e., documents or computer code or databases). A policy is high-level statement of principle or course of action governing software activity. A guideline stipulates a sequence of broadly stated steps for producing a software product or accomplishing a software process. A procedure is a detailed prescription for the sequence of steps to accomplish some software-related activity. A standard stipulates format and content conventions for software products or stipulates activity conventions for software processes. The ADPE is a framework for bringing about consistent product development.

■ **Application Development Technology Environment (ADTE)**—the *technology* as embodied in hardware and software development tools, and associated procedures for their use, required to develop products. These tools include, but are not limited to, CASE tools, programming language compilers, LAN application development tools, PC application development tools, database management systems, configuration management tools, and project management tools.

This book shows how to develop and implement application development process environment (ADPE) elements (i.e., policies, guidelines, procedures, and standards) to support the practical development of software products. This environment helps to increase the likelihood of developing usable products on time and within schedule by infusing engineering discipline into the process. Through this discipline infusion, the development process is transformed from an ill-defined process (i.e., lacking repeatability) to a well-defined process (i.e., one that is visible and traceable). We believe that visibility and traceability enable both customer and product developer management to communicate effectively with one another. They can make intelligent, informed decisions regarding how product development should proceed. This communication helps to remove ambiguities and misunderstandings. We believe practitioners are better positioned to (1) provide the customer with usable products, (2) repeat their successes and avoid their mistakes, and (3) reduce reliance on individuals for these repeatable successes.

We recognize that some in the software industry have observed that software engineering is not a discipline. Peter J. Denning, former President of the Association for Computing Machinery (ACM), made the following observation:

> Software engineering is not a discipline. Its practitioners cannot systematically make and fulfill promises to deliver software systems judged by their customers as usable and dependable, on time and fairly priced. The illusion that software engineers possess a discipline has produced the major breakdown called the software crisis.[13]

Denning's statements have much merit. However, we believe that software systems development can be disciplined. This book is about the practical application of software engineering principles. We de-

---

[13]P. Denning, "Designing a Discipline of Software Design," *Proceedings of the 7th SEI CSEE Conference*, San Antonio, Texas, January 1994 (Berlin, Germany: Springer-Verlag, 1994), Abstract of Keynote Address.

scribe techniques for injecting discipline into the software systems development process. Since this book is intended for practitioners, our emphasis is on practical means for disciplining the process. By *practical,* we mean "application of techniques consistent with available time and resources." We label this type of application "prescriptive application." Software systems development is not a cookie-cutter exercise. Management skill in applying available techniques is a key ingredient to achieving software systems development success. This book offers guidance for prescriptively applying these techniques.

But this book is more than an exposition on the engineering techniques to select for building usable software products. It is one thing to come up with ADPE elements. It is another thing to have these elements adopted and practiced within an organization. Thus, this book delves into the cultural change considerations needed to bring about ADPE adoption by the people making up an engineering organization. We address organizational culture questions such as the following:

- How do you involve the individuals in an organization in the definition of ADPE elements to achieve their buy-in to the changes that ADPE implementation implies?

- How does a seller involve the customer in the ADPE development and implementation?

- How does a seller extend the cultural change activity associated with ADPE implementation beyond the seller's environment into the customer's environment?

- How can seller senior management support be orchestrated to facilitate ADPE implementation?

- How frequently should promulgated ADPE elements be updated to tune their effectiveness without disrupting the overall state of the development environment associated with changing the elements?

- How do you promulgate ADPE elements? How many? How often? What sequence?

- Given that there are always organizational outliers, what are reasonable goals to set for how much of an organization ADPE implementation should encompass?

- How do you sell engineering activities such as product assurance when seller organizational players and/or customers question the value added of these activities?

- How do you encourage change within an organization while at the same time avoiding organizational fragmentation into competing subcultures?

- How should sellers deal with customers who are not prepared to buy into one or more key ADPE elements of the seller's process?

- How should customers negotiate with sellers on what makes sense to do on a development effort?

As many of these questions suggest, transitioning to a software systems development process that is repeatable, risk-contained, and businesslike involves blending (1) cultural, (2) organizational, and (3) engineering considerations. As illustrated in Figure 1–15, our approach to achieving this blending is through the development and implementation of a systems engineering environment (SEE).

A feature of this book is the attention given to communications issues. More than anything else, the software industry has unequivocally demonstrated that customer/seller faulty communication underlies a majority of software systems development problems. This book addresses techniques for improving customer/seller communication. In particular, this book elaborates on how to improve communications by bringing the requisite disciplines (i.e., product assurance, development, and management) together in a businesslike forum. This forum provides a management mechanism where issues are discussed, actions are assigned, and decisions are made. Such mechanisms are easy to set up, and they are extremely powerful.

Another feature of this book is our emphasis on the prescriptive application of the techniques described. When it comes to applying almost any software engineering technique, there are no fixed rules. After introducing techniques, we present specific suggestions for adapting these techniques to different organizational setups. Clearly, what makes sense to do processwise on a five-person project

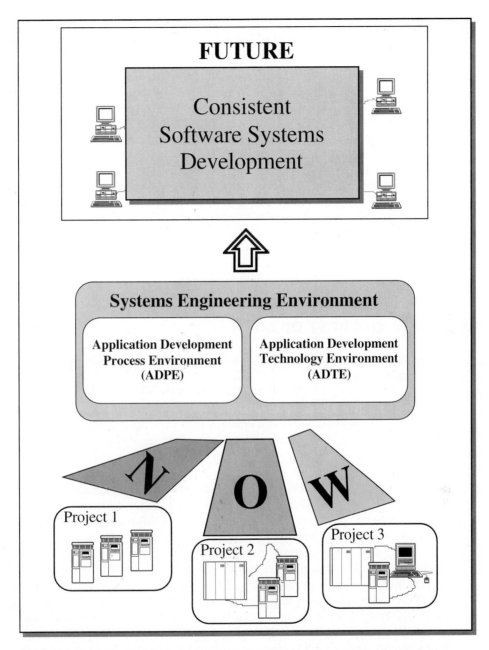

FIGURE 1–15 A systems engineering environment (SEE) provides a means for effecting consistent software systems development—whether systems are developed sequentially or in parallel. For parallel systems development, the SEE also provides a means for coordinating these development activities, thereby potentially leveraging resources and adding value to individual projects.

within an organization in all likelihood will not make sense to do on a twenty-five-person project (and vice versa) without some adaptation. What makes sense for an aging system scheduled for retirement does not necessarily make sense for a new development effort. We address these adaptation considerations, which we put under the umbrella of the previously described notion of "prescriptive application."

Another feature of this book is our approach to transitioning from ill-defined to well-defined software development practices (i.e., improving process maturity). Practice within the industry tends to focus on so-called maturity levels. Improving software process maturity is correspondingly articulated in terms of achieving Process Maturity Level 1, 2, 3. . . . This book focuses on what are termed by some in the software industry as *key process areas* that make up a given maturity level. We describe software process improvement in terms of ADPE elements that address these key process areas. From our perspective, software process maturity improvement is an exercise in ADPE element implementation. *Implementation* means "the promulgation of ADPE elements, and the prescriptive application of these elements by an organization." And, as we stated previously, this prescriptive application is tantamount to a cultural change within the organization.

Finally, another feature of this book is the scope of our cultural change perspective. The trend in industry is for corporations to team to win business. Thus, when such wins occur, the cultural change associated with setting up an ADPE extends beyond the confines of a single corporation. More and more, winning sellers are a united nations in microcosm. Customers of course are not interested in dealing with an engineering polyglot. The challenge to a winning seller is to blend this corporate diversity so that a customer sees a unified engineering organization. This book addresses the sticky issues associated with blending diverse corporate cultures.

1.9 PREVIEW OF THE REST OF BOOK

Figure 1–16 is an overview of the entire book. In the following paragraphs, we give a summary of each of the remaining chapters.

Chapter 2—Project Planning Process   The purpose of this chapter is threefold. First, it explains that there are key process elements within any life cycle. Specifically, we show how the life cycle concept brings to the fore the key process elements of (1) product assurance, (2) management review, (3) iteration within the seller organization during product development, and (4) iteration between the seller and buyer/user during product development. This section shows how this need for iteration naturally arises from the interplay among the user, buyer, and seller as each refines his or her understanding of what needs to be done as a project's life cycle unfolds. We stress that, at any given point, a project may be in more than one life cycle stage. A consequence of this reality for the practitioner is that this paralleling of activity needs to be accounted for in project planning and project tracking.

Second, the chapter explains how the life cycle concept is a key element of the software project planning process. We use life cycle examples to demonstrate this concept. We discuss project risk assessment and the way to integrate this activity into project planning. We introduce a matrix whose columns are life cycle stages and whose rows are the disciplines of management, development, and product assurance. Each entry in the matrix is one or more tasks associated with a life cycle stage and one of these disciplines. These tasks are the entities that define the technical approach in a project plan. Three cases are illustrated: (1) classical system development (including so-called "maintenance"), (2) prototyping, and (3) information engineering.

Third, this chapter includes guidance on how to develop a project planning process for your organization. We pull together the concepts discussed in the chapter and detail the project planning process activities, major communication paths, and individual roles and responsibilities. We then present an annotated outline for a project planning ADPE element.

Chapter 3—Software Systems Development Process   This chapter starts with a discussion of software process and software development organizations. We present an example software systems development process. Also, we discuss each of the process's major elements: customer, seller process engineering group, customer/seller development team, change control board, seller senior management, and major communication paths. We stress that an organization's software systems development

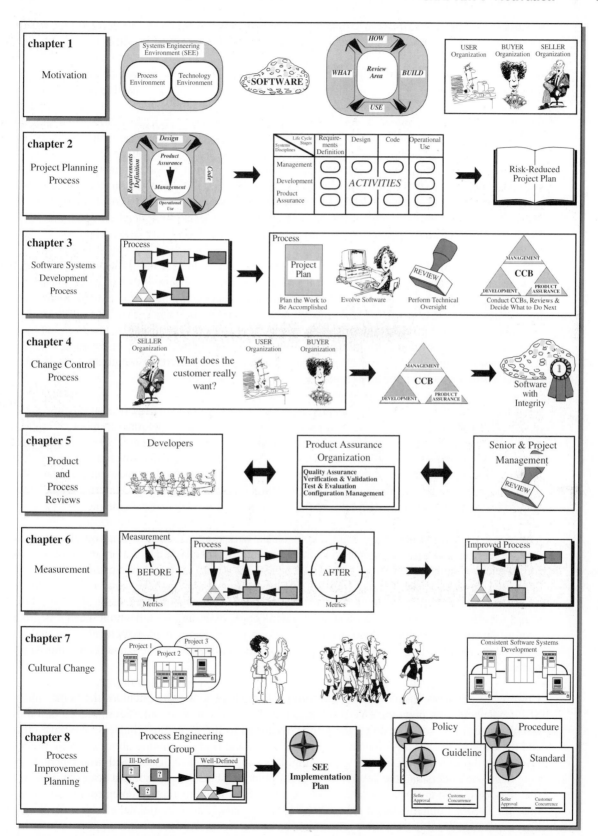

FIGURE 1–16 This figure provides an overview of this book.

process should be "prescriptively" applied to each project because no two projects are the same. In addition, we present an annotated outline for a development process ADPE element.

Chapter 4—Change Control Process   This chapter is devoted to answering the question, "What does the customer really want?" In this chapter, we show how the CCB is used to address the communications problems that plague *any* software project. We introduce the notions of planned change and unplanned change and show how they are a natural fallout of any march around the life cycle. We discuss how the classical configuration management CCB concept needs to be generalized to consider both programmatic as well as product changes, so that the seller and user/buyer are not surprised as the project life cycle unfolds. We talk about the inevitability of change and the need to plan for change. We talk about the processing of software changes and illustrate this processing for a design specification, a requirements document, and for an incident report. Next we address who sits on the board, what decisions it makes, and how it operates. Also, we describe the paperwork needed to support CCB operation. We close the chapter by presenting an annotated outline for a CCB ADPE element.

Chapter 5—Product and Process Reviews   This chapter addresses the subject of software product reviews and software systems development process reviews. The purpose of product and process reviews is to give decision makers and other software systems development project participants visibility into the project state of affairs. These reviews serve to lessen guesswork on what to do next. We present a set of software product and project process review concepts organized by management, development, and product assurance disciplines. We illustrate the review concepts with examples drawn from the real world. This chapter presents annotated outlines for a peer review guideline, an independent product assurance policy, and an acceptance testing cycle procedure.

Chapter 6—Measurement   This chapter addresses the subject of metrics. Measurement for the sake of measurement is a waste of time and resources. This chapter presents measurement techniques that enable you to measure software products (i.e., product integrity measurement) and software systems development processes (i.e., process integrity measurement) in everyday terms familiar—and therefore meaningful—to your organization. We explain and illustrate general measurement formulas. We also apply these techniques to the Software Engineering Institute's Capability Maturity Model for Software. This chapter concludes with an annotated outline for a measurement guideline.

Chapter 7—Cultural Change   This chapter deals with human issues bearing on effecting cultural change. The chapter presents views from the following perspectives: (1) the organization responsible for developing and promulgating process elements, (2) seller project participants and project managers, (3) buyer/user project management, (4) buyer/user senior management, and (5) seller senior management. Here we talk about what to expect when trying to implement an SEE. We talk time scales for effecting change. We look at how to win people over, and we talk about when it is prudent to give up on some individuals. Also, we discuss the key role senior management plays in making cultural change happen. This chapter includes an annotated outline for defining and improving ADPE elements.

Chapter 8—Process Improvement Planning   This chapter, which concludes the book, talks about SEE implementation planning. We provide guidance on how to write an SEE implementation plan to establish the framework for doing the things discussed in the preceding chapters. We have chosen to end the book by discussing what should normally be done first in bringing about software process improvement through an SEE—namely planning. It is simply easier to discuss SEE implementation planning once you understand the key issues to address in the plan. We present and discuss nineteen issues that may be important for an organization regarding SEE implementation. We provide annotated outlines for an SEE implementation plan, a configuration management guideline, a project tracking guideline, a software development life cycle definition guideline, and a document templates standard.

Project Planning Process

chapter

2

It's a bad plan that can't be changed.

—Publilius Syrus, *Moral Sayings* (First century B.C.E.).

2.1 INTRODUCTION

This chapter provides you with guidance for effectively planning software systems development work. We refer to the document containing planning information as the "project plan." In some systems development communities, the plan is called a "software development plan." The project plan is a gauge used, in part, to think through what needs to be done, to estimate how much the effort may cost, and to determine whether software systems development work is unfolding as it was envisioned.

Just as the software systems development process is iterative, so too is the planning process. No matter how well a project has been planned, there will always be changes. We stress that the project plan should be a living document. Although many may agree with this point, they experience repeated difficulties in managing the anticipated, but unknown, change. The message here is that project planning involves (1) planning the work to be accomplished before the work begins and (2) planning how to manage the changes to this work as the work is being accomplished. Thus, project planning, like software systems development, is an exercise in change management.

The emphasis in this chapter is on the project planning *process*. We present the activities involved with putting together a project plan, as well as the project plan's contents. Also, we give you an outline for a project plan to help you overcome the blank-page syndrome. The key to running any good business—software development or otherwise—is effective business processes. In the software world, one element crucial to software systems development success is the project planning process.

■ **31** ■

We need to stress one more point at the outset regarding project planning. While much of what we have to say is from the seller perspective, we also address the customer perspective. The project plan is indeed a seller document. However, the project plan is not developed in a vacuum. It is usually developed in response to a customer's or surrogate customer's (e.g., marketing organization or venture capitalist) statement of need. In this book, we refer to such a statement of need as a "statement of work," or SOW for short. This terminology carries with it the appropriate connotation of expressing the customer's statement of what that customer believes the seller needs to do for the customer. One key SOW issue that we address is that of SOW risk assessment.

With no pun intended, the plan for this chapter is the following:

- In **Section 2.2—Project Planning Nuggets**, we present the nuggets that you can expect to extract from this chapter.

- In **Section 2.3—Life Cycle Role in Project Planning**, we bring together the Chapter 1 concepts of the generic life cycle, project disciplines, and project players to show you how they bear upon the planning process.

- In **Section 2.4—Ideal, Real, and Realistic Project Planning**, we discuss the planning process in terms of three instantiations of the generic life cycle.

- In **Section 2.5—Risk Assessment and Project Planning**, we discuss project risk assessment and how to integrate this activity into project planning.

- In **Section 2.6—Project Planning Process**, we present you with guidance for developing an Application Development Process Element (ADPE) that defines the project planning process for your organization's Systems Engineering Environment (SEE).

- In **Section 2.7—Project Plan Contents**, we discuss project plan content. This discussion pulls together the project planning process concepts introduced in the preceding sections to give you ideas on how to generate a project plan.

- In **Section 2.8—Project Planning Summary**, we summarize the chapter's key points by presenting an annotated outline of an ADPE procedure as a starting point for defining your organization's project plan development process.

2.2 PROJECT PLANNING NUGGETS

Figure 2–1 lists the nuggets that you can extract from this chapter. We begin each chapter with such a list to facilitate your task of mining the chapter's contents to meet your specific needs. To introduce you to this chapter, we briefly explain these nuggets. Their full intent will become apparent as you go through this chapter.

1. **Planning requires a software systems development life cycle to provide a framework for considering the specific tasks to be accomplished.** Here, we expand upon the generic life cycle concept introduced in Chapter 1. From this generic life cycle, we "derive" examples of project-specific life cycles. This chapter offers you ideas for how such project-specific life cycles naturally bring to the fore the tasks that need to be incorporated in the project plan to accomplish the work defined in the customer's SOW.

2. **Planning needs to account for the interaction among management, development, and product assurance disciplines throughout the project life cycle.** How do you transform through project planning the software systems development process into a business proposition in which both the customer and seller are accountable for their decisions? This chapter offers you ideas for incorporating a businesslike forum into your software systems development project. This forum—which we call a change control board (CCB)—is a key element of dealing with the inevitable change that arises during any software systems development effort. Our CCB concept is a generalization of the classical configuration management concept of configuration control board.

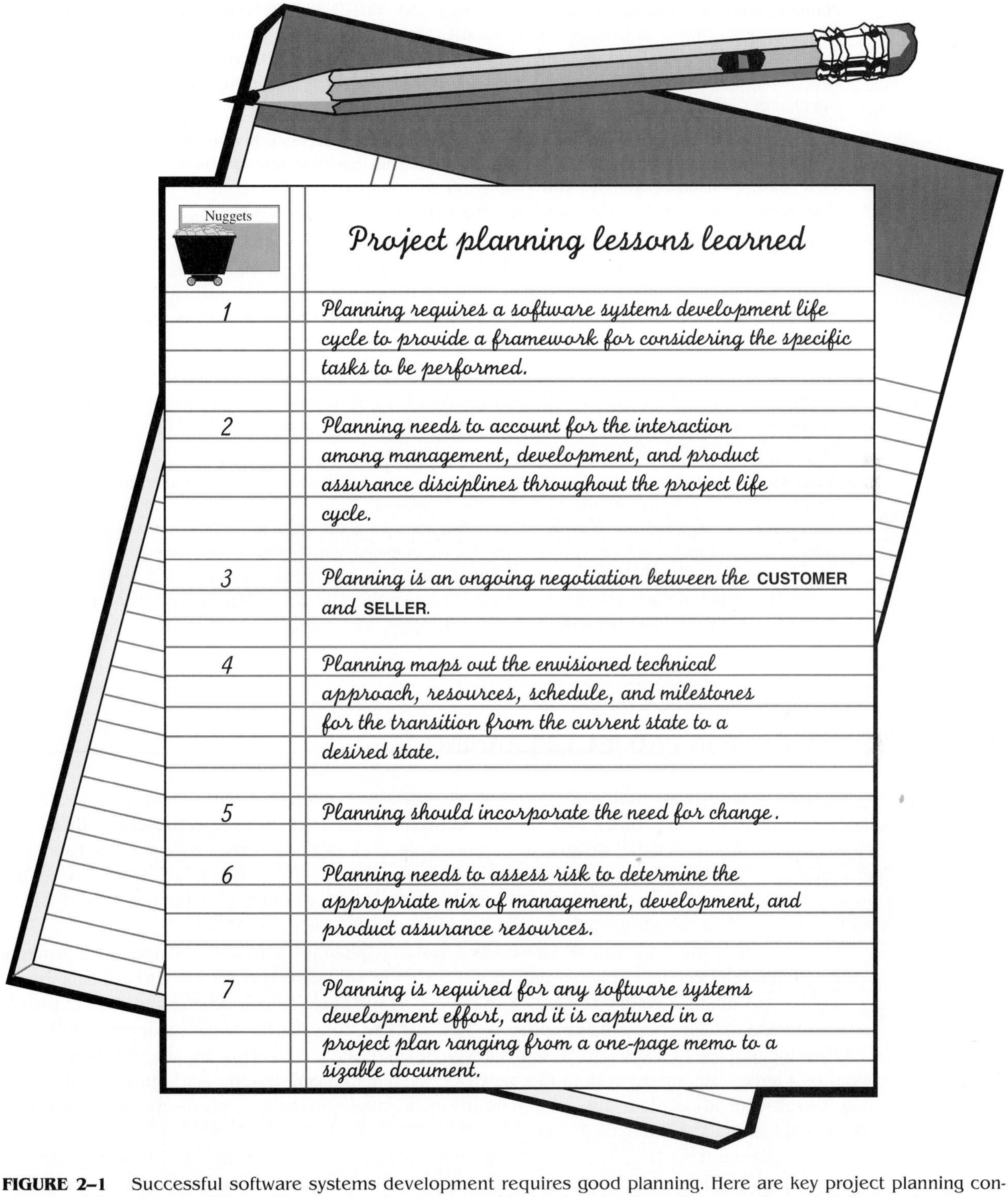

Project planning lessons learned

Nuggets	
1	Planning requires a software systems development life cycle to provide a framework for considering the specific tasks to be performed.
2	Planning needs to account for the interaction among management, development, and product assurance disciplines throughout the project life cycle.
3	Planning is an ongoing negotiation between the CUSTOMER and SELLER.
4	Planning maps out the envisioned technical approach, resources, schedule, and milestones for the transition from the current state to a desired state.
5	Planning should incorporate the need for change.
6	Planning needs to assess risk to determine the appropriate mix of management, development, and product assurance resources.
7	Planning is required for any software systems development effort, and it is captured in a project plan ranging from a one-page memo to a sizable document.

FIGURE 2–1 Successful software systems development requires good planning. Here are key project planning concepts explained in this chapter. These nuggets are your guide to planning for software systems development success.

3. **Planning is an ongoing negotiation between the CUSTOMER and the SELLER.** Underlying this negotiation process is the art of gaining closure between the customer and seller regarding SOW content before the project begins, and regarding anticipated, but unknown, changes during project plan accomplishment. This chapter offers to both the user/buyer and the seller ideas for accomplishing this negotiation in a win-win manner.

4. **Planning maps out the envisioned technical approach, resources, schedule, and milestones for the transition from the current state to a desired state.** This transition sets the overall boundary conditions for the project planning activity. This chapter offers you ideas for relating the project life cycle, project tasks, resource and schedule constraints, and risk to planning for this transition.

5. **Planning should incorporate the need for change.** It is evident from Syrus's quote at the start of the chapter that this nugget is not a new idea. However, too many people view the project planning process as an exercise in fantasy. If you paradoxically do not plan for change, your project will likely waste a lot of time and money in thrashing instead of progressing. This chapter offers you ideas for making "plan for change" integral to your project planning process.

6. **Planning needs to assess risk to determine the appropriate mix of management, development, and product assurance.** There is a strong correlation between project risk and the way resources should be allocated during project planning to these three sets of disciplines to mitigate risks. This chapter offers you ideas for doing this risk assessment and resource allocation.

7. **Planning is required for any software systems development effort, and it is captured in a project plan ranging from a one-page memo to a sizable document.** The world of software systems development spans orders of magnitude of complexity. Just as it does not make sense to use a pile driver to crack a nut, so too it does not make sense to shoehorn the project planning activity into a "one size fits all" framework. Many contractual vehicles exist for establishing a formal working relationship between a seller and a customer. The nature of these vehicles has some impact on the software systems development process. We touch upon these different vehicles.

2.3 LIFE CYCLE ROLE IN PROJECT PLANNING

In what sense does software have a *life* cycle? At the beginning of a project, the software is in a state of infancy—its features are outlines and sketchy definitions. Later in the project, these outlines and sketches are filled in with detail on structure, processing, and data; the software acquires a distinctive "personality." Ultimately (barring sickness, such as faulty design), the software achieves its fully developed state when it becomes operational and ages gracefully through a metamorphosis resulting from the incorporation of enhancements, new capabilities, and fixes to latent defects.

The concept of life cycle can be viewed as a tool to explain the activities involved with bringing software from a relatively amorphous state in someone's or some enterprise's head to a finished state in which the operating software code does useful work. A life cycle helps management acquire insight into the software systems development process. For example, consider the situation depicted in Figure 2–2. Often the purpose of a software systems development project is to bring about a transition from a manual or a legacy automated system to a new/improved automated system. As Figure 2–2 indicates and as we subsequently explain, a development life cycle integrates the systems disciplines of development, product assurance, and management.

The numbered tasks (i.e., 1, 2, 3, 4, 5, 6) represent one software systems development path that integrates development, product assurance, and management disciplines. The development disciplines are represented by the four generic development stages of WHAT (task 1), HOW (task 2), BUILD (task 4), and USE (task 5). Each stage yields one or more software or software-related products. In the earlier stages of the software life cycle, requirements specifications are typically produced. These

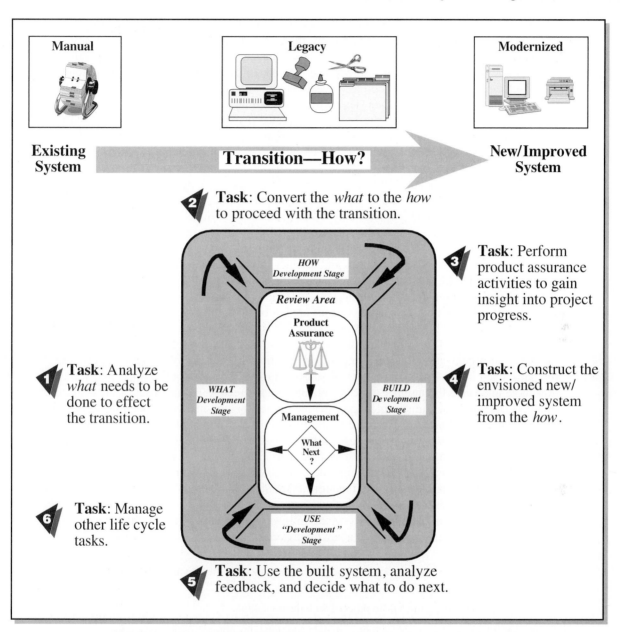

FIGURE 2–2 Software systems development projects transition manual or automated legacy systems to new/improved systems. A development life cycle brings to the fore the disciplines and tasks needed to (1) effect a successful transition and (2) respond to postdeployment needs.

specifications express the WHAT that is to be done. In subsequent stages, design specifications (HOW) and computer code and databases (BUILD) are typically produced.

Throughout this book, we rely on the life cycle concept to explain and amplify software systems development process concepts. It is therefore important for you to realize at the outset that a life cycle "stage" is *not* something that is passed through once, never to be revisited. As we mentioned in Chapter 1, from the viewpoint of software systems development, any life cycle stage may be revisited a number of times before the software system falls into disuse (i.e., dies). We prefer to think of a revisit to a life cycle stage as the enhancing, correcting, and/or adapting of what was done during the previous visit to that stage. Revisits are nothing more than "maintenance" in the dictionary sense of the word (namely, "the act of keeping in existence or continuance; the act of keeping in a specified state"[1]) In this book, we therefore adopt the attitude that "maintenance" is an integral part of the activities associated with *any* life cycle stage. Therefore, we do not distinguish between software systems development and software systems maintenance. The required disciplines and processes are the same.

As shown in Figure 2–2, the product assurance disciplines are represented in the review area, along with the management disciplines. Product assurance activities (task 3) provide developers with alternative views of the product under development (e.g., requirements specification), and management with insight to where the developers are in the development process. Product assurance seeks to compare life cycle products with one another to determine the extent to which they logically follow from one another and the extent to which they conform to the customer's stated needs. This comparison helps to build a thread that explicitly traces product to products from predecessor stages (or products from the same stage—such as an earlier draft of a specification document)—which, in turn, raises the visibility of the software systems development process. The management activities (task 6) include oversight of the development activities and product assurance support activities. Management uses the visibility provided by product assurance to make decisions on what to do next. For example, after management reviews product assurance test results, the management may decide to revisit the WHAT stage if it is believed that the customer needs are not being met by the software code.

The number of life cycle stages utilized on a particular project is a function of how much visibility is desired (and affordable). This number may also be a function of organizational policies. For example, your organization may have a policy stipulating that for planning purposes, all projects should be partitioned into a specified number of stages. Furthermore, once a project is under way, it may be desirable to change the number of stages planned and agreed to at the outset of the project. Examples that might change the number of stages include the following: changes to the project budget, changes to the customer's desire to have more visibility into the development process, or changes to customer delivery dates. The idea of partitioning a software systems development effort into stages is useful for avoiding management indigestion. Just as a number of factors govern how someone chooses to slice up the elements of a meal before consuming it, so too there may be a number of factors governing how a life cycle should be partitioned. The fundamental point is that there is no single "preferred" partition of the life cycle that should be applied to all projects.

The project team members perform the following generic software systems development tasks to transition from an existing system to a new/improved one:

- Analyze *what* needs to be done to effect the transition from the existing system to the new/improved system.
- Convert the *what* to the *how* to proceed with the transition.
- Perform product assurance activities to gain additional insight into project progress.
- Construct the envisioned new/improved system from the *how*.
- Use the built system, analyze feedback, and decide what to do next.

We illustrate this fundamental point of transition with two examples: (1) off-the-shelf software and (2) software maintenance. These examples provide insight into what we mean by software systems development. This insight is needed to clarify the scope of the project planning process as we deal with it in this book.

---

[1]*Random House College Dictionary* (New York: Random House, 1982).

Example 1—Off-the-Shelf Software

Our first example deals with an enterprise or organization that decides to rid itself of typewriters and bring in personal computers with word processing software. Here, the office is effecting a transition from a manual system to an automated system. At this point, some of you are saying, "This is not software systems development! It is just a simple equipment purchasing exercise."

First, consider how the word processing vendor developed the word processing software. One typical scenario is that the vendor's marketing organization assesses the marketplace to determine WHAT the user community wants in a word processing package. This marketing organization is a surrogate customer (i.e., surrogate buyer/user) for the vendor's product development organization. The development organization, presumably working with the marketing organization, transforms the vendor's WHAT into a HOW. Here, such things as the nature of the user interface (e.g., pull-down menus) takes shape. Then, the product development organization BUILDs to the HOW and WHAT to produce the word processing product. Before releasing the product for sale, the vendor may test market the product (typically called "beta testing") to work out problems and refine features. Subsequently, the vendor releases the product for sale where it is USEd by buyers/users.

Now, consider things from the perspective of an actual customer purchasing the equipment and word processing software. The purchase of this material presumably did not take place in a vacuum. Someone in the customer's organization compiled a list of capabilities (i.e., requirements) that the equipment and word processing software needed to satisfy. Among other things, then, somebody presumably needs to determine whether the installed system satisfies the requirements. In addition, once the office personnel start using the installed equipment, new requirements may emerge—which may or may not be satisfied by more off-the-shelf software applications.

In terms of our generic life cycle, then, we can say that the WHAT stage corresponds to compiling the list of capabilities. What about the other stages in the generic life cycle? How do they come into the picture? Typically, many personal computer software packages have to be installed before they can be used. Installation typically involves the selection of various combinations of options. Deciding which options to select depends on the buyer's WHATs. These WHATs may include a need for such capabilities as (1) grammar checking, (2) synonym finding, and (3) foreign language spell checking. Thus, by comparing the WHATs to the available options, the buyer selects the options needed to meet these requirements (e.g., grammar checker, thesaurus, foreign language dictionaries). This selection activity can be viewed as the HOW stage of off-the-shelf systems development.

It should be noted that there may also be other factors governing this option selection—such as hardware constraints (e.g., available memory, available hard disk space). Once this selection is accomplished, the buyer enters the INSTALL command and BUILDs the word processing system to USE the word processor thus developed that satisfies the requirements. Since it is generally a good idea to check that the INSTALL proceeded properly, the installed system should be turned over to product assurance to determine whether all the required capabilities have been properly installed. Then, the word processing system can be turned over to the enterprise/office users for training and for operational USE.

From the preceding discussion, it would seem that, in general, there is more to using off-the-shelf software than opening the shrink wrap and popping the diskettes into the hardware. Planning for activities such as those just discussed can make the development of off-the-shelf systems relatively free from pain.

One final comment is in order about this off-the-shelf systems development example. Many off-the-shelf purchases frequently evolve toward the use of software customized to the particular needs of the purchaser (by means other than selecting vendor-supplied options)—either by modifying vendor-supplied software or producing new software. If for no other reason, planning for such inevitable migrations saves additional time and money. Furthermore, planning for such migrations at the time of original purchase pays even greater dividends. Among other things, the plan needs to address what happens if the vendor-supplied software does not do what was asked for in the SOW.

Example 2—Software Maintenance (i.e., Life Cycle Stage Revisits)

Our second example deals with an enterprise or organization that currently has an automated system and wants to upgrade this system to incorporate new features and fix latent defects. In the software engineering literature, this scenario is frequently termed "software maintenance." In this book, we choose to include this type of project in the domain of software systems development. In other words, we believe that software maintenance requires the same activities and disciplines as new software development.

For software maintenance, the WHAT stage is the (1) specification of the requirements for new features, (2) restatement of the unsatisfied requirements (i.e., bugs), and (3) possible modification (i.e., enhancements) of existing requirements. The HOW stage is the specification of the design of the new features, the corrections to the design to correct the bugs, and the augmentation of the design to incorporate enhancements.[2] The BUILD stage corresponds to the development of code from the requirements and design specifications.

Thus, in this book, software systems development spans the gamut from the purchase of off-the-shelf software to classical maintenance. So, in terms of Figure 2–2, we see that software systems development—whether it involves the (1) development of computer code where none previously existed, (2) purchase of off-the-shelf-code, or (3) maintenance of existing code—involves the tasks shown in Figure 2–2. Every project plan, then, needs to incorporate these tasks to some degree. As we subsequently explain, the particular character of these tasks is a function of how the generic life cycle is instantiated.

To summarize the preceding discussion, the key project planning principal is the following:

> The tasks in a project plan is the seller's "how-to-do-it" response to a customer's (i.e., user/buyer) statement of need (e.g., SOW). These tasks are simply a statement of how (1) the products emerging from each life cycle stage are to be developed, (2) this product development activity is to be managed, (3) the products are to be checked for compliance with customer needs (i.e., product assurance), and (4) project accomplishment is to be checked for compliance with the project plan (i.e., process assurance).

Figure 2–3 lays out the preceding project planning principle in "tabular" form. The figure illustrates that the tasks to be performed by management, development, and product assurance can take place in one or more life cycle stages. In addition, the figure also shows that the change control board (CCB) provides a forum for review of task accomplishment during the project. The project plan is a description of the tasks that the seller team, working with the customer, are to (iteratively) perform through the life cycle that transitions the customer from the existing system to the new/upgraded system. During the project, no matter how well a project is initially planned, the details of what actually happens differ from what was planned. The change control board (CCB) provides a forum to discuss what needs to be done to respond to the changes that occur. As decisions are made with respect to what needs to be done next, the project plan is updated to reflect the refined understanding of what needs to be done to ensure a successful project. Updating the project plan as the project unfolds is critical to project success. The updated plan offers the seller the means for ensuring that the development is proceeding profitably.

Another aspect about the life cycle concept needs to be stressed. A life cycle stage is a conceptual way of visualizing a related set of software systems *development* activities. On an actual software project, these activities are, in general, not restricted to a particular time interval (even though in project planning that are typically assigned to a particular time from, e.g., the first two months of the project). Revisits make it clear that WHAT activities, for example, may be performed during various time

---

[2]For legacy systems with little or no documentation, it may be necessary for the developers to spend time examining the existing computer code to understand how the code works before they specify a design for the new features. However, design options may be limited because of the existing design.

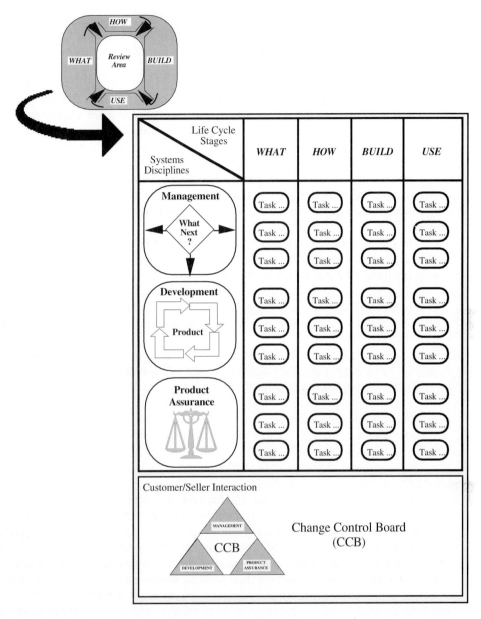

FIGURE 2–3   The generic software systems development life cycle provides a starting point for identifying management, development, and product assurance tasks to be accomplished on your project.

intervals through out a project. Thus, on a real software project, WHAT, HOW, BUILD, and USE activities will be interspersed with one another.

Furthermore, at any given point within a project, some members of the project team may be doing, for example, HOW work, while other members may be doing WHAT work. Consequently, a project may be in more than one life cycle stage at the same time. Even though we represent the life cycle concept as a sequence of stages, this sequencing of related project activities does not, in general, occur on an actual software systems development project.

A software life cycle is in reality a series of recycles through part or all of a sequence of stages that begins with a statement of customer need and ends with customer acceptance of software code and supporting databases operating in the customer's environment in accordance with this need. Any software systems development process must explicitly incorporate this series of recycles. Otherwise, it does not account for the customer/seller mutual refinement of understanding that is integral to any software systems development effort.

The following question naturally arises: *What if I can't define a specific life cycle for my project?* Suppose, for example, that the customer tells the seller to code first and ask questions later (a frequent occurrence in the real world). Alternatively, consider the case when a seller does not define a life cycle for a project and tells the customer that the seller's developers are going to code first and ask questions later. We assert that even in such circumstances, you can use the generic life cycle to help identify the tasks to be accomplished. In fact, if defining a life cycle proves to be a stumbling block, you can use the generic life cycle model during project planning to work with a customer to help define a life cycle appropriate to the work at hand. That is, the generic life cycle can be used as a tool for defining a project-specific life cycle—and, in the process of defining this life cycle, the tasks to be performed will emerge.

The role of the life cycle as portrayed in Figure 2–3 can be viewed as a task definition checklist. For example, by looking at the intersection of Management with the WHAT life cycle stage, the following planning guidance naturally emerges:

> Part of managing the project must include oversight of the development of a requirements specification (or, in the case of a "maintenance" project, the oversight of the development of a modification to an existing requirements specification).

Similarly, by looking at the intersection of Product Assurance with the WHAT life cycle stage, the following planning guidance naturally emerges:

> Product assurance must include review of a requirements specification (update), including drafts of this specification.

The following question also naturally arises: *What if the customer does not care how the product is developed?*

We refer to this situation as one in which the customer lacks "visibility" into the seller's development process. How does the seller know when the customer's needs are satisfied by the developed software system? How does the seller know how much it will cost to develop the required product? One way for the seller to approach this situation is to try to get the customer to agree that no matter what the seller delivers, the product is acceptable and payment is made. If the customer considers the risks associated with such an approach, a possible solution may arise such that the seller gets the buyer to accept intermediate products and partial payments are made. Other factors (e.g., possible customer job loss, untested technologies, large sums of money, loss of life) may also influence the customer's thinking. As the customer's risks increase, the customer's involvement often increases. To mitigate the risks, the customer may even hire consultants to provide additional insight (i.e., visibility) into the project. The project plan provides both the customer and seller a tool that gives them visibility into project progress or lack of progress.

Figure 2–4 provides you with the next level of detail regarding the perspectives of the customer (i.e., user/buyer) and the seller. As shown in the figure, both the customer and the seller can have management, development, and product assurance personnel. Each group of disciplines has its own perspective with respect to what is required in a project plan that covers the spectrum of development activities, yet remains flexible enough to respond to the anticipated, but unknown, changes.

One of the exceptions to this balance between customer and seller organizations is in product assurance. The customer organization may not have product assurance personnel. If the customer starts to question the value added of product assurance activities, the seller should listen carefully. The customer may not truly understand what it is that product assurance does to reduce the risk of not accom-

CUSTOMER (User/Buyer) Organization:
Has requirements that need to be satisfied.

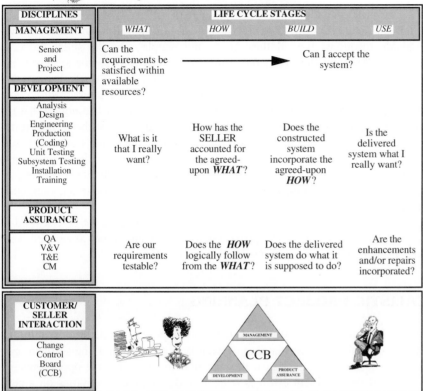

DISCIPLINES	LIFE CYCLE STAGES			
MANAGEMENT	*WHAT*	*HOW*	*BUILD*	*USE*
Senior and Project	Can the requirements be satisfied within available resources?	→	Can I accept the system?	
DEVELOPMENT				
Analysis Design Engineering Production (Coding) Unit Testing Subsystem Testing Installation Training	What is it that I really want?	How has the SELLER accounted for the agreed-upon *WHAT*?	Does the constructed system incorporate the agreed-upon *HOW*?	Is the delivered system what I really want?
PRODUCT ASSURANCE				
QA V&V T&E CM	Are our requirements testable?	Does the *HOW* logically follow from the *WHAT*?	Does the delivered system do what it is supposed to do?	Are the enhancements and/or repairs incorporated?

CUSTOMER/ SELLER INTERACTION	
Change Control Board (CCB)	CCB (MANAGEMENT, DEVELOPMENT, PRODUCT ASSURANCE)

SELLER Organization:
Creates software system for User Organization.

DISCIPLINES	LIFE CYCLE STAGES			
MANAGEMENT	*WHAT*	*HOW*	*BUILD*	*USE*
Senior and Project	Can the requirements be satisfied within available resources?	→	Is the system ready to be delivered?	
DEVELOPMENT				
Analysis Design Engineering Production (Coding) Unit Testing Subsystem Testing Installation Training	What is it that the CUSTOMER really wants?	How do we account for the agreed-upon *WHAT*?	How do we construct the agreed-upon *HOW*?	How do we enhance and/or repair the built system?
PRODUCT ASSURANCE				
QA V&V T&E CM	Are the CUSTOMER requirements testable?	Does the *HOW* logically follow from the *WHAT*?	Does the built system do what it is suppose to do?	Are the enhancements and/or repairs incorporated?

FIGURE 2–4 Consistent project planning records management, development, and product assurance responses to what needs to be done. These responses are tasks that the different disciplines are to accomplish. These tasks make up the heart of the project plan. In addition, no matter how well planning is done, unknown, but expected, changes will arise. The change control board (CCB) is a forum for systematically accounting for such changes. The project plan needs to incorporate CCB activities to account for responding to these deviations.

plishing the project. Conversely, the seller organization may not have product assurance personnel. If the seller does not present product assurance activities as part of the project plan, the customer should question whether or not the seller's organization is mature enough in its systems development processes to ensure success.

The customer's senior- and project-level management evaluate the seller's "proposal to do work" or "actual performance of agreed-upon work" in terms of whether or not the seller can satisfy the requirements within the available resources (i.e., dollars, time, and people). As the seller proceeds through the software systems development life cycle, the customer decides whether the system is acceptable. From the customer's and seller's perspectives, the fundamental question is the following: Are the requirements embodied in the software system? Both the customer and seller interact throughout the visits and revisits to the life cycle stages to answer this fundamental question. The notion that the customer hands over a set of requirements and then comes back towards the end of the project to review what has been done is a prescription for failure. From the beginning, the seller's product assurance organization should be asking whether or not the requirements are testable. If the requirements are testable, then it can be demonstrated to the customer that the fundamental question is being partially answered as the project proceeds. As indicated in Figure 2–4, this customer/seller interaction takes place, in part, at change control board meetings.

In Chapter 1, we introduced a generic four-stage life cycle. In the next section, we give several illustrations of how to transform this generic life cycle into a specific set of stages and associated tasks that can then be used to plan a specific software systems development effort.

2.4 IDEAL, REAL, AND REALISTIC PROJECT PLANNING

The planning process is essential to successful software systems development. As illustrated in Figure 2–5, planning begins with the fundamental understanding of what is to be built, how the software system is to be built, actually building the system, and how the system is to be used in the operational environment. Critical to a successful development effort is reviewing development activities on a periodic and event-driven basis to ensure that (1) customer requirements are being incorporated correctly and (2) information is available for making intelligent decisions on what to do next.

Figure 2–5 shows that the generic life cycle can be tailored to a life cycle that makes sense for your particular situation. By utilizing seller and customer experiences, a specific set of affordable life cycle stages and systems disciplines activities can be defined. Specific management, development, and product assurance tasks, milestones, schedules, and resources can be defined for each life cycle stage. Integral to the interaction between the customer and seller is the CCB. The CCB is a business forum in which the customer and seller interact to ensure that what the customer wants is built. Many, if not most, software systems development projects suffer from poor communications—customer to seller, seller to customer, developer to user, product assurance staff to managers, etc. The CCB helps to reduce the communication risks. We cannot overemphasize the importance of the CCB. Plan on establishing a CCB as soon as possible.

At this point, we describe, in a simplified way, the software development activities associated with illustrative life cycles. In particular, we illustrate the following three potential life cycles:

- **Traditional systems engineering.** A six-stage life cycle that uses systems engineering to produce detailed specification documentation and computer code.
- **Prototyping.** A three-cycle life cycle that uses prototyping to refine requirements that are not well understood.
- **Information engineering.** A six-stage life cycle that uses information engineering to develop a logical design that is then used to generate the physical implementation using a computer-aided software engineering (CASE) tool.

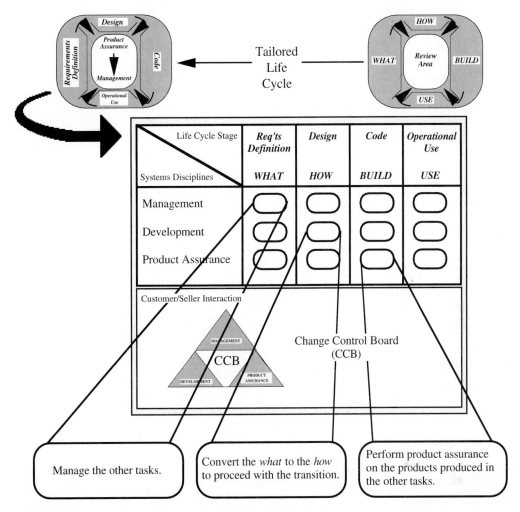

FIGURE 2–5 Using your experience to tailor the generic life cycle, you define the specific management, development, and product assurance tasks to be accomplished, and associated estimated resources, milestones, and schedule.

These three examples provide additional insight into the planning of software systems development projects. The purpose here is merely to introduce these "tailored" life cycles for your consideration when you define your own specific management, development, and product assurance tasks. These life cycles are presented from the seller's perspective because the seller is responsible for developing the product. In some instances, the SOW may specify that a customer's life cycle is to be used. The seller's project plan should take into account a learning curve for implementing what may be an unfamiliar software systems development life cycle.

Traditional Systems Engineering Life Cycle Example

The first of our three life cycle examples is Figure 2–6. This figure depicts the generic four-stage life cycle as the following six-stage systems engineering life cycle:

- Requirements definition.
- Preliminary design.

SELLER
Organization

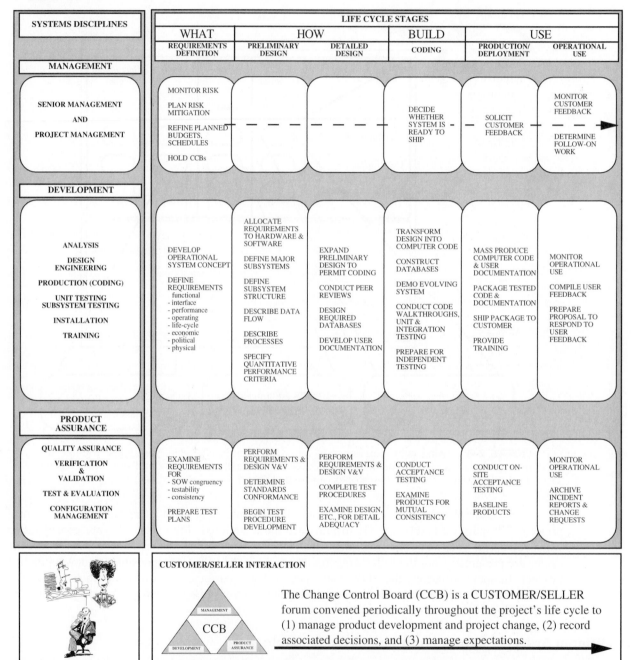

FIGURE 2–6 This six-stage life cycle gives added visibility to the design activity by dividing the HOW into two separate stages—PRELIMINARY DESIGN and DETAILED DESIGN. Such added visibility is desirable when the HOW is assessed to be particularly risky. Each round-edged rectangle shows example activities to be addressed in the project plan for each life cycle stage. The plan should account for multiple iterations of the activities shown in correspondence with the risk assessed for these activities.

- Detailed design.

- Coding.

- Production/Deployment.

- Operational use.

Each of the six stages is described below.

Requirements Definition Stage   Activity in this stage focuses on what the software is to do. In many cases, it is probably more appropriate at this stage to refer to what the system is to do—that is, the functions to be performed by the integrated operation of hardware, software, and people. At this stage of the software life cycle, it may not be evident what each of these three generic system components is to do. The boundaries separating these components from one another may be amorphous. However, these boundaries will be better understood as the actual project work unfolds. Over the life cycle of the system, the elements of this subset may change as decisions are made regarding what the hardware is to do and what the people are to do (and hence what the software is to do).

The management tasks include monitoring the assessed risk and planning risk-mitigation strategies as needed. Management refines planned budgets and schedules. It is important to establish the change control board (CCB) early on in the life cycle. As the project progresses, both the customer and seller refine their understanding of what needs to be done. These project dynamics result in the need to refine planned activities. To specify and agree to refinements, the customer and seller use the CCB meetings as a forum for recording the agreed upon refinements. Assessing risk, planning risk-mitigation strategies, detailing budgets, holding CCBs, etc., continue throughout the life cycle stages (as indicated by the dashed arrow in the figure). Once the software system is built, management decides whether the system is ready to ship to the customer. Input into this decision comes from the visibility that the product assurance acceptance testing activities provide. Acceptance testing helps management answer the following question: Does the built system do what it is supposed to do? Once the system is shipped to the customer, seller management solicits customer feedback to ensure, in part, proper system operation. During operational use, management monitors customer feedback and determines if there is follow-on work.

The development tasks include developing an operational system concept. Depending upon the overall size of the project, the concept may consist of a one-page graphic, a detailed written report, or something in between. The description of each software function embodied in the operational system concept may simply be a one-sentence definition or one or more paragraphs amplifying particular aspects of the function (e.g., its scope, qualitative performance, characteristics, and/or subfunctions). For example, a requirements specification for a system to count the number of rain days during a month may contain a statement such as the following:

"The software shall maintain monthly counts of the number of days during the month when rain fell."

As the project unfolds, the Requirements Definition Stage may be revisited and the requirements specification may be further detailed as follows:

"If rain totaling at least 0.02 inch fell during the 24-hour period, the number of rain days shall be incremented by one."

Various standards exist for writing software requirements specifications. The Institute of Electrical and Electronics Engineers (IEEE) produces one such standard.[3] This standard, first issued in 1984 and re-

---

[3]"IEEE Recommended Practice for Software Requirements Specifications." IEEE Standard 830-1993 (New York: Institute of Electrical and Electronics Engineers, Inc., April 8, 1994).

published with revisions in 1994, defines eight characteristics of a good requirements specification. These characteristics include "unambiguous," "complete," and "traceable." This standard provides guidance on how to write an unambiguous and complete software requirements specification.

The product assurance tasks include examining the requirements for SOW congruency, correctness, ambiguity, completeness, consistency, stability, verifiability, modifiability, and traceability. The seller's product assurance personnel may begin preliminary testing work by delineating a test strategy. The product assurance tasks include asking the following fundamental question: Are the requirements testable? If the requirements are not testable, it is hard, if not impossible, to demonstrate to the customer that the software system fulfills the customer's needs.

Preliminary Design Stage   Activity in this stage focuses on making the transition from *what* the software is to do to *how* the software is to accomplish the *what*.

The management tasks continue from the requirements definition stage. CCB meetings are held as often as necessary to ensure the customer and seller agree on how the requirements are designed into the envisioned computer code. The frequency of CCB meetings may increase just before and just after agreed-upon milestones. The increased meeting frequency helps to keep the management informed on the project's progress so that they can respond to any potential problems immediately. We have found that when there is more communication, the customer's expectations are met more often, and the seller's insight into what its project team can actually accomplish is well understood. Consequently, the customer gets what is wanted, and the seller does a better job of estimating what needs to be done to ensure successful completion.

The development tasks include allocating the functions defined in the Requirements Definition Stage to software and hardware (if this allocation was not performed in the Requirements Definition Stage). The outline of what eventually will become computer code is specified. Major subsystems are defined, and the top-level structure within each of these subsystems is broken out. Data-flows into and out of the system are described together with the processing within each subsystem that transforms inflows to outflows. Quantitative performance criteria (e.g., how fast, how accurate, how frequent) are specified.[4]

The product assurance tasks include verifying and validating the requirements and preliminary design, determining whether the requirements and preliminary design conform to established project standards, and developing test procedures in accordance with the test strategy.

Detailed Design Stage   Activity in this stage focuses on expanding the design outline from the preceding stage.

The management tasks are essentially the same as during the preliminary design stage. Management needs to monitor closely the schedules and to get together with the customer as soon as it is apparent that there is a schedule slip. Simply stated, good management is no surprises.

The development tasks include prescribing the software structure in sufficient detail to permit coding. Consider the following simple example. Assume that the preliminary design specification contains the following statement:

"Sum the hourly rainfall amounts [for day *x*]. If the sum is greater than 0.02 inch, increment the value of RAINDAYS in file PRECIPCOUNT."

---

[4]Such quantitative performance criteria may sometimes be specified in the Requirements Definition Stage. For example, a customer may want a message processing system that, because of known message volumes, must be capable of processing a specified number of messages per hour. Frequently, however, quantitative performance criteria derive from qualitative statements of customer requirements. These quantitative criteria thus represent *how* to accomplish *what* the customer asked for—and thus represent design. For example, a customer may have a qualitative requirement for display of realistic animation of human motion. From this (qualitative) requirement for realistic (as opposed to, say, freeze-frame or jerky) animation may be derived a (quantitative) software design performance criterion of a specified number of display images that the software must produce each second on a video device.

Assume that the preliminary design specification is expanded during this stage and the following additional detail (i.e., bolded text) is added:

> "Sum the hourly rainfall amounts [for day x]. If the sum is greater than 0.02 inch, **add 1** to the value of RAINDAYS in file PRECIPCOUNT."

Ideally, the level of detail in the Detailed Design Stage should be such that the activity in the Coding Stage is little more than a simple transcription into some computer language of the words in the design documentation. The detailed design for software is like an engineering drawing of a hardware component showing all the parts, their dimensions, their interconnections, and the material from which they are to be constructed. Also during the Detailed Design Stage, the databases needed for system operation are designed. In addition, user documentation (i.e., manuals prescribing the commands and other procedures for operating the software) is developed.

The product assurance tasks include verifying and validating the requirements with the detailed design, and examining the design for detail adequacy. Product assurance also prepares plans and procedures for testing the software code in subsequent stages. Completing the test plans and procedures is a time-consuming exercise. In addition, many times the development work does not finish as planned, and the product assurance schedules are affected. Project planning activities should account for such potential schedule slippages.

Coding Stage   Activity in this stage focuses on turning the detailed design into language that computer hardware can understand.

The management tasks include deciding whether the computer code is ready to ship to the customer. This management decision is tied, in part, to the CCB meetings that take place, and the testing that the developers and product assurance personnel conduct. Assume that early in the life cycle the customer and seller management establish the CCB as one forum for obtaining agreement. As the project life cycle unfolds, the customer and seller management routinely meet to discuss and agree upon what needs to be done. The product assurance personnel work with the developers both to ensure that the requirements are testable and that the design specifications logically follow from the testable requirements. Test plans and detailed testing procedures are developed and presented to the customer. The test procedures lay out the button-pushing steps to be performed. The procedures simply compare what is specified to be seen (as detailed in the requirements and design specifications) with what is actually observed (as detailed in the actual computer code) by the testers. If what is specified matches what is observed, then the seller management can make an informed decision to ship the product to the customer. This simple example illustrates an approach for determining "acceptance criteria" that can be presented to a potential customer. Using this approach, both seller and customer management can make an informed decision to ship and accept the product.

The development tasks include coding activities that ultimately yield a product for end use by the user in the user's own environment. CASE technology has blended the design and coding stages; moreover, it helps the developers lay out the logical design and also provides an automated capability to generate the physical computer code. In addition, CASE technology has shifted some of the burden of computer code generation from the developers to software tools. Regardless of how the computer code is generated, the code must be tested at multiple levels as it is being put together and on completion of this integration. This testing helps to assure that the computer code embodies the detailed design and the user's needs.

The product assurance tasks include acceptance testing, as well as examining the software or software-related products for mutual consistency. Customer-approved acceptance test plans and procedures, in part, can help make acceptance of a product a moot point. From the seller's perspective, acceptance testing is a value added discipline. From the customer's perspective, acceptance testing helps to reduce the risk of not getting what is needed.

Production/Deployment Stage   Activity in this stage focuses on (1) producing the software code after satisfactory completion of all testing in the Coding Stage, (2) packaging the tested software code (with user documentation), and (3) shipping it to the customer for operational use.[5]

The management tasks include monitoring the delivery of the product to the customer and solicitating customer feedback on the project activities. Such feedback is used to improve the overall software systems development process.

The development tasks include tailoring the product, if the product is intended for a range of customers with specialized needs, from the Coding Stage to these needs. In conjunction with this tailoring, testing similar to that performed in the Coding Stage is conducted to provide a degree of assurance that the tailored product conforms to customer needs.

The product assurance tasks include performing on-site installation and acceptance testing, as well as ensuring that the product(s) are baselined in accordance with organizational standards.

Operational Use Stage   Activity in this stage focuses on use of the software by the customer in her or his environment.

The management tasks include monitoring customer feedback on the performance of the product and determining potential follow-on work.

The development tasks include monitoring the operational use of the product, compiling and analyzing customer feedback (particularly user feedback), and preparing development proposals to respond to the user feedback. A by-product during this stage is customer detection of latent software defects and customer definition of enhancements or new capabilities that precipitate revisits to one or more of the preceding stages.

The product assurance tasks include testing bug fixes and archiving problems that were not solved (test incident reports) and change requests that were not incorporated into the product.

Prototyping Life Cycle Example

Figure 2–7 depicts the following three-cycle prototyping life cycle:[6]

- *Definition Cycle.* The objective of this cycle is to define the overall system concept and the set of requirements that the prototype is to satisfy. The user's perspective of the system via the user's interface is specified. In addition to defining the human computer interface, all other interfaces to the system's surrounding environment are established and validated. The emphasis is on defining all data flowing in and out of the system, and the format and manner of data transmission. The primary evaluators for this cycle are from the end user community. The end users' objectives are focused on evaluating the needs and effectiveness of the human computer interface. The operational concept is validated in terms of ease of use, ease of learning, timeliness and appropriateness of outputs, and complementation of the users' abilities. The primary output of the Definition Cycle is the skeleton version of the prototype.

- *Application Cycle.* The object of this cycle is to evaluate the design of the system. This refinement cycle is characterized by extensive knowledge acquisition efforts with the domain experts. The design is evaluated in terms of both the chosen knowledge representation and the accompanying problem solving methods. The primary evaluators for this cycle are the experts. The primary objective is to verify and validate the knowledge and problem solving methods as an accurate representation and model of cognitive skills brought to bear in solving the stated problem. The main portions of the system architecture and design are considered complete. The primary output of the Application Cycle is the essential version of the prototype.

---

[5]For some organizations, "producing" the software code may mean "mass-producing" the software code. Such organizations may produce hundreds, thousands, or millions of copies of the software code for distribution to their customer community.

[6]This discussion is an adaptation of D.A. Fern and S.E. Donaldson, "Tri-Cycle: A Prototype Methodology for Advanced Software Development," *Twenty-Second Annual Hawaii International Conference on System Sciences (HICSS-22),* IEEE Catalog No. 89TH0243-6, Volume II, Software Track (Los Alamitos, CA: IEEE Computer Society Press, 1989), pp. 377–386. The conference, held in Hawaii on January 5–6, 1989, was sponsored by the University of Hawaii in cooperation with the Association for Computing Machinery, the IEEE Computer Society, and the Pacific Research Institute for Information Systems and Management.

SELLER
Organization

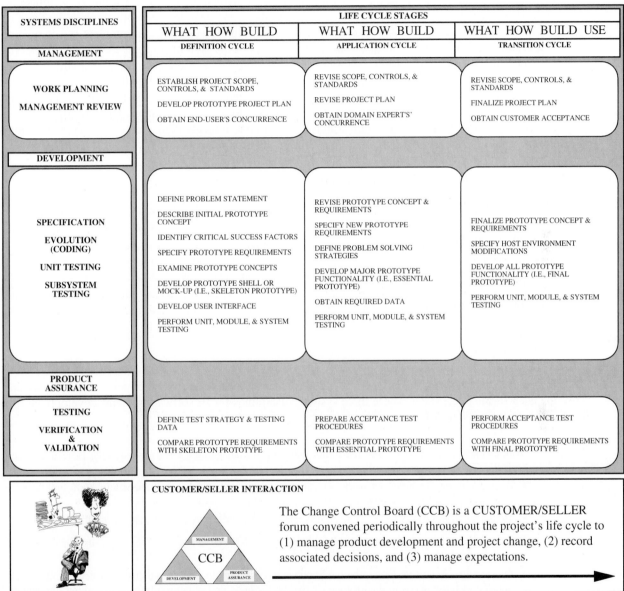

SYSTEMS DISCIPLINES	LIFE CYCLE STAGES		
	WHAT HOW BUILD	WHAT HOW BUILD	WHAT HOW BUILD USE
	DEFINITION CYCLE	APPLICATION CYCLE	TRANSITION CYCLE
MANAGEMENT			
WORK PLANNING **MANAGEMENT REVIEW**	ESTABLISH PROJECT SCOPE, CONTROLS, & STANDARDS DEVELOP PROTOTYPE PROJECT PLAN OBTAIN END-USER'S CONCURRENCE	REVISE SCOPE, CONTROLS, & STANDARDS REVISE PROJECT PLAN OBTAIN DOMAIN EXPERT'S' CONCURRENCE	REVISE SCOPE, CONTROLS, & STANDARDS FINALIZE PROJECT PLAN OBTAIN CUSTOMER ACCEPTANCE
DEVELOPMENT			
SPECIFICATION **EVOLUTION** **(CODING)** **UNIT TESTING** **SUBSYSTEM** **TESTING**	DEFINE PROBLEM STATEMENT DESCRIBE INITIAL PROTOTYPE CONCEPT IDENTIFY CRITICAL SUCCESS FACTORS SPECIFY PROTOTYPE REQUIREMENTS EXAMINE PROTOTYPE CONCEPTS DEVELOP PROTOTYPE SHELL OR MOCK-UP (I.E., SKELETON PROTOTYPE) DEVELOP USER INTERFACE PERFORM UNIT, MODULE, & SYSTEM TESTING	REVISE PROTOTYPE CONCEPT & REQUIREMENTS SPECIFY NEW PROTOTYPE REQUIREMENTS DEFINE PROBLEM SOLVING STRATEGIES DEVELOP MAJOR PROTOTYPE FUNCTIONALITY (I.E., ESSENTIAL PROTOTYPE) OBTAIN REQUIRED DATA PERFORM UNIT, MODULE, & SYSTEM TESTING	FINALIZE PROTOTYPE CONCEPT & REQUIREMENTS SPECIFY HOST ENVIRONMENT MODIFICATIONS DEVELOP ALL PROTOTYPE FUNCTIONALITY (I.E., FINAL PROTOTYPE) PERFORM UNIT, MODULE, & SYSTEM TESTING
PRODUCT **ASSURANCE**			
TESTING **VERIFICATION** **&** **VALIDATION**	DEFINE TEST STRATEGY & TESTING DATA COMPARE PROTOTYPE REQUIREMENTS WITH SKELETON PROTOTYPE	PREPARE ACCEPTANCE TEST PROCEDURES COMPARE PROTOTYPE REQUIREMENTS WITH ESSENTIAL PROTOTYPE	PERFORM ACCEPTANCE TEST PROCEDURES COMPARE PROTOTYPE REQUIREMENTS WITH FINAL PROTOTYPE

CUSTOMER/SELLER INTERACTION

MANAGEMENT

CCB

DEVELOPMENT PRODUCT ASSURANCE

The Change Control Board (CCB) is a CUSTOMER/SELLER forum convened periodically throughout the project's life cycle to (1) manage product development and project change, (2) record associated decisions, and (3) manage expectations.

FIGURE 2–7 This prototyping life cycle gives added visibility to the (1) evolving customer requirements, (2) most difficult requirements to be implemented, and (3) transition from the development environment to the operational environment.

■ *Transition Cycle.* The objective of this cycle is to achieve customer acceptance of the system as a deliverable product. This acceptance entails a detailed evaluation of the system design as a whole. Additional functionality not deemed essential, and consequently deferred until this cycle, are resolved. For example, issues such as the integration and handling of exceptional cases are resolved and implemented during this cycle of system evolution. Additional rounds of knowledge acquisition may be necessary to include the deferred functionality. The increased depth of the software must be consistent with design decisions made earlier in the process. Thus, some components of these so-called "nonessential" software modules, are addressed in this cycle. The primary output of the Transition Cycle is the final version of the prototype.

This model of software development is a blend of evolutionary prototyping and classical software management techniques that progresses through three refinement cycles (i.e., Definition, Application, and Transition). The entire process, which can consists of one or more iterations through the three refinement cycles, culminates with a clear and concise problem statement, a complete set of requirements and associated specifications, a succinct statement of the system concept, and an operational (albeit, possibly incomplete) prototyped system. This prototyping model attempts to instill increased discipline into the prototype development process. This model also brings together four diverse groups of people: (1) system developers, (2) domain experts, (3) end users, and (4) customers. Each group has different interests, concerns, and motivations for the development of a system. The prototyped system provides a common language through which they can communicate their views and serves as a tangible means to analyze and evaluate system requirements and concepts.

Information Engineering Life Cycle Example

Figure 2–8 depicts the following six-stage information engineering (IE) life cycle:

- Information Strategy Planning.
- Business Area Analysis.
- Business Systems Design.
- Technical Design.
- Construction.
- Retirement.

In general, management, development, and product assurance systems disciplines come into play during each IE life cycle stage. These three systems disciplines for IE software systems development projects are described as follows:

- **Management** tasks involve both the senior and project management ensuring that what is needed is built correctly. These tasks are the following:
  - *Work Planning.* Refining the work plan, including the scope of the work, schedule, staff, and other resources required for the life cycle stage.
  - *Management Review.* Verifying the completeness and consistency of each stage's results.
- **Development** tasks add increased detail and specificity as work in a given stage proceeds. These tasks are the following:
  - *Information Gathering.* Obtaining the knowledge necessary to understand customer needs and the relationship of those needs to the customer's overall business and obtaining information about the data and activities associated with the business.
  - *Data Analysis.* Developing and refining information about the data—beginning with defining high-level activities in the Information Strategy Planning and Business Area Analysis Stages and continuing through construction of physical database models during the Technical Design Stage.
  - *Activity Analysis.* Developing and refining information about business activities, from identifying business functions to generating and maintaining source code.
  - *Interaction Analysis.* Assessing the effect of the business activities and data on each other.
- **Product Assurance** tasks provide the development project with a system of checks and balances. These checks and balances are realized through the integrated application of the following four processes:

SELLER
Organization

SYSTEMS DISCIPLINES	LIFE CYCLE STAGES					
	WHAT HOW BUILD		WHAT HOW BUILD		WHAT HOW BUILD USE	
	INFORMATION STRATEGY PLANNING	BUSINESS AREA ANALYSIS	BUSINESS SYSTEMS DESIGN	TECHNICAL DESIGN	CONSTRUCTION	RETIREMENT
MANAGEMENT						
WORK PLANNING	SCOPE STANDARDS PROJECT PLAN	SCOPE STANDARDS ANALYSIS PLAN	SCOPE STANDARDS IMPLEMENTATION PLANNING DESIGN PLAN	SCOPE STANDARDS DEVELOPMENT PLAN	TRAINING NEEDS & SCHEDULE	RETIREMENT PLAN
MANAGEMENT REVIEW	INFO NEEDS PROJECT PLAN ARCHITECTURES	CONSISTENCY CHECKS BUSINESS MODEL REVIEW	CONSISTENCY CHECKS DESIGN MODEL REVIEW TEST PLAN REVIEW	CONSISTENCY CHECKS UNIT TESTS MODULE TESTS SYSTEM TESTS	CONSISTENCY CHECKS ACCEPTANCE TEST RESULTS REVIEW	RETIREMENT PLAN REVIEW
DEVELOPMENT						
INFORMATION GATHERING	ORGANIZATION CRITICAL SUCCESS FACTORS INFO NEEDS	BUSINESS SYSTEMS KNOWLEDGE	USER SCREENS ON-LINE HELP TARGET ENVIR.	USER & ADMIN MANUALS	CUTOVER SCHEDULES	RETIRE SCHEDULE SYSTEM COMPONENT DISPOSITION
DATA ANALYSIS	SUBJECT AREAS	ENTITY TYPES RELATIONSHIPS ATTRIBUTES	RECORDS LINK RECORDS FIELDS	PHYSICAL DATA BASE MODEL	DATA TRANSFER TABLES VIEWS	AFFECTED DATA
ACTIVITY ANALYSIS	FUNCTIONS FUNCTION DEPENDENCIES	PROCESSES PROCESS DEPENDENCIES	PROCEDURES DIALOG FLOW	LOAD MODULE DEFINITIONS	CUTOVER	AFFECTED PROCEDURES HARDWARE DISPOSITION
INTERACTION ANALYSIS	INFOR ARCH. BUSINESS SYSTEM ARCH. TECHNICAL ARCH.	PROCESS LOGIC ENTITY LIFE CYCLE PROCESS ACTION DIAGRAMS	PROCEDURE ACTION DIAGRAMS	SOURCE CODE	APPLICATION PROGRAMS	AFFECTED APPLICATIONS USER NOTIFICATION
PRODUCT ASSURANCE						
QUALITY ASSURANCE	ISP <->STANDARD PROJECT PLAN <-> CHECK LIST	ERD <->STANDARD ANALYSIS PLAN <-> CHECK LIST	USER SCREENS <-> STANDARD DESIGN PLAN <-> CHECK LIST	PHYSICAL DATABASE <-> STANDARD DEVELOP PLAN <-> CHECK LIST	APPLICATION PGMS, TABLES, VIEWS <-> STANDARDS IMPLEMENT PLAN <-> STANDARD	AFFECTED DATA <-> STANDARD RETIRE PLAN <-> CHECK LIST
VERIFICATION & VALIDATION	ISP <-> ISP	ERD <-> SUBJECT AREAS	PROCEDURES <-> PROCESSES PROC ACTION DIAGRAMS <-> PROCESS ACTION DIAGRAMS	PHYSICAL DATABASE <-> RECORDS, LINK RECORDS, FIELDS LOAD MODULES <-> DIALOG FLOW, PROCs, ...	TABLE VIEWS <-> PHYSICAL DATABASE, APPLICATION PROGRAMS <-> SOURCE CODE	AFFECTED DATA & PROGRAMS <-> IMPLEMENTATION PLAN
TEST & EVALUATION	ISP TEST STRATEGY SECTION	ISP TEST STRATEGY SECTION	TEST PROC FOR USER SCREENS, DATA TRANSFER,...	PERFORM TEST PROCEDURES IN DEVELOPMENT ENVIRONMENT	PERFORM TEST PROCEDURES IN OPERATIONAL ENVIRONMENT	REPERFORM TEST PROCEDURES BECAUSE OF AFFECTED DATA & PROGRAMS
CONFIGURATION MANAGEMENT	BASELINE PROJECT PLAN ...	BASELINE PROJECT PLAN ...	BASELINE DESIGN PLAN, RECORDS ... UPDATE PLANS ...	BASELINE DEVELOPMENT PLAN, DATABASES ... UPDATE PLANS ...	BASELINE IMPLEMENTATION PLAN,TABLES,PGMS ...UPDATE PLANS ...	BASELINE RETIREMENT PLAN, CATALOG& ARCHIVE PRODUCTS

CUSTOMER/SELLER INTERACTION

The Change Control Board (CCB) is a CUSTOMER/SELLER forum convened periodically throughout the project's life cycle to (1) manage product development and project change, (2) record associated decisions, and (3) manage expectations.

FIGURE 2–8 This information engineering life cycle gives added visibility to enterprisewide (1) information needed to support development of business systems, (2) data, (3) activities needed to process the data, and (4) activity/data interaction.

- *Quality Assurance—Checks* whether the software conforms to established standards and exposes parts that don't conform. If under "standards" are included things like software development plans, the QA process *checks* whether the product development process itself conforms to what the software development staff said it was going to do. Thus, with these definitions, product quality and process quality mean, respectively, conformance with product standards and conformance with process standards.

- *Verification and Validation. Checks* for any oversights or deviations from customer requirements and predecessor products and exposes them.

- *Test and Evaluation.* Exercises software code and data, *checks* for shortfalls from requirements and design documents and then exposes them. T&E is thus a special case of V&V.

- *Configuration Management. Balances* the need to make changes with a visible, traceable, and formal way to control those changes. The need for change arises primarily from the application of the other three product assurance processes.

As shown in Figure 2–8, the individual tasks to be performed in a given life cycle stage for a given systems discipline are shown as a rounded box. The following is an interpretation of these boxes:

- For the **Management Review** task during the Information Strategy Planning Stage (i.e., first row, first column, of IE life cycle work stages), the *information needs* of the organization, the *project plan*, and the supporting *architectures* are defined by project staff, then reviewed and approved by both customer and seller management.

- For the **Information Gathering** task during the Information Strategy Planning Stage (i.e., third row, first column, of IE life cycle work stages), the project team performs this task using project work groups and facilitated workshop sessions, such as joint requirements planning (JRP) and joint application design (JAD) sessions. Programmatic experts and customer representatives supply information about the customer's mission, organization, critical success factors, and information needs in order to plan the project work group sessions. Seller project team members and customer representatives jointly develop the agenda, invite the attendee list, and conduct the workshops with middle-level customer organization managers. Information is collected about the organization, information architecture, and technical architecture. Quality assurance tables are constructed, capturing key quality characteristics for organization data and activities. After the information has been analyzed, workshops are conducted with the customer's top-level managers and staff. Following each workshop, minutes are prepared and the information that has been gathered is analyzed.

- For the **Data Analysis** task during the Business Area Analysis Stage (i.e., fourth row, second column, of IE life cycle work stages), the data are analyzed for the customer's business area. The subject areas identified in the Information Strategy Planning Stage are expanded in detail and evolve into the definitions for *entity types*, *relationships*, and *attributes*, which are captured in an entity relationship diagram (ERD). Partitioning, attribute classification, and value derivation lead to an entity hierarchical diagram (EHD). Together, these two types of diagrams form the logical data model that is a picture of the data required and their relationships for the defined business area.

- For **Activity Analysis** during the Business Area Analysis Stage (i.e, fifth row, second column, of IE life cycle work stages), the functions and their dependencies defined in the Information Strategy Planning Stage are further decomposed into *processes* (and corresponding *process dependencies*). The hierarchical relationships of the activities performed by the business are determined, as well as, the description of what each process does and what entity types each process affects. A dependency analysis is performed to relate the lowest level processes to each other to validate that all the activities have been identified. The result of this activity analysis is a set of dependency diagrams and an activity hierarchy diagram.

- For **Interaction Analysis** during the Business Area Analysis Stage (i.e., sixth row, second column, of IE life cycle work stages), the processes are related to the entity types, attributes, and relationships. Changes to each entity type by various processes—from their creation to termination—are analyzed and documented in an entity life cycle or entity state transition diagram (also referred to as life cycle analysis). This step validates the data and processes by verifying that the entire life cycle of the particular entity type is addressed. As part of the interaction analysis, the process logic for the lowest level processes is defined and represented as process action diagrams. These process definitions are part of the building blocks for the Business Systems Design Stage.

■ For the **Quality Assurance** task during any IE life cycle stage, process and product quality are checked, respectively, by (1) checking a product against a standard for that product and (2) checking a process against a plan defining how the process is to be carried out. For example, to check for process quality in the Business Area Analysis Stage, a checklist is derived from the analysis plan and is used as the basis for determining whether the engineering process defined in the plan is followed. An example of a product QA check in the Business Area Analysis Stage would be comparing an Entity Relationship Diagram (ERD) against a standard defining how ERDs are to be constructed.

■ For the **Verification and Validation** task during any IE life cycle stage, a product is checked against predecessor products. For example, this activity checks that an ERD, defined in the Business Area Analysis Stage, is carrying through the intent of the subject areas, defined in the Information Strategy Planning Stage.

■ For the **Test and Evaluation** task during early IE life cycle stages, test planning documentation indicating *what* testing is to be performed is prepared; during later IE stages, test procedure documentation indicating *how* the testing is to be performed is prepared. For example, in the Business Area Analysis Stage, a test plan is developed that specifies what tests are to be performed to exercise user screens, on-line help, . . . that were defined during the Information Strategy Planning Stage.

■ For the **Configuration Management** task during any IE life cycle stage, plans and products are baselined and updated in a controlled manner. For example, the analysis plan that is initially created in the Business Area Analysis Stage is baselined; the initial version of the project plan (baselined during the Information Strategy Planning Stage) is updated.

Project planning for traditional systems engineering, prototyping, or information engineering systems development tasks not only entails a fundamental understanding of life cycles but also requires insight into the hazards that typically arise in the real world of software systems development. The following discussion describes alternative project planning views of the work to be accomplished.

Project Planning Views

Figure 2–9 depicts these three views of project work accomplishment:

■ **Ideal view of work accomplishment.** The ideal view puts the seller project team (i.e., management, development, and product assurance staff) on a straight-line development path from the first task to be accomplished to the envisioned software system to be developed. The tasks are laid out in a sequential and somewhat overlapping sequence from beginning to end. The project team starts with the first task and drives towards the next task, then the next task, etc. The ideal view of work accomplishment can result in ideal project plans that understate what is needed to get the job done.

■ **Real view of work accomplishment.** It is difficult, if not impossible, to plan every step along the way. No matter how well a plan is put together, there is always a difference between planned and actual. The real view of work accomplishment puts the seller project team on a straight-line development path, but the team realizes that there are real-life hazards in the way of a successful development effort. One frequent hazard is personnel turnover. People change jobs, move, get married, and retire. Another hazard is the lack of project documentation, such as requirements specifications, domain knowledge, mission statements, and so on. Then, of course, there are those unanticipated requirements that the customer did not anticipate at project start. The seller project team is faced with deciding what to do next to navigate around these hazards. The real view of work accomplishment poses a planning challenge to account for these hazards.

■ **Realistic planning view of work accomplishment.** The realistic planning view puts the seller project team on a straight-line development path, but the team realizes that the real-life hazards can be dealt with and/or avoided. The team deals with these real-life hazards by planning a CCB mechanism into their project plan. The CCB provides the team with a decision forum to review progress, analyze hazards, and discuss alterna-

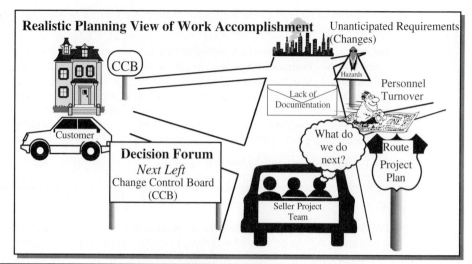

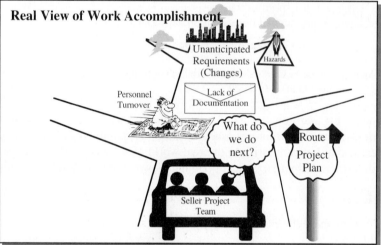

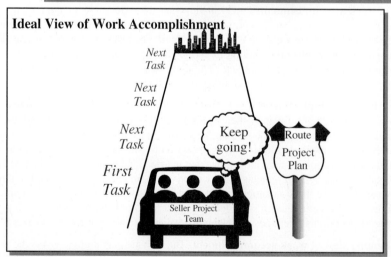

FIGURE 2–9 Although the shortest distance between two points is a straight line, project planning needs to account for the hazards that typically arise in the real world of software systems development. Successful software systems development involves planning for the hazards and establishing a means—the CCB—for preventing the hazards from jeopardizing project completion.

tive solutions. At this forum representatives from both the seller and the customer meet to discuss and decide what to do next to respond to and/or avoid real or potential hazards. If personnel turnover is a potential problem, a CCB decision might be to cross-train personnel. If there is a lack of documentation (e.g., requirements specification) for a legacy system, a CCB decision might be to substitute an existing user's manual for the requirements specification and then to develop a specification. If unanticipated requirements need to be addressed, then the CCB can decide what to do next. We are not suggesting that every decision needs to take place at a CCB. However, when decisions could affect project deliverables, schedule, resources, or project plan accomplishment, then we recommend a meeting between the customer and seller. Good management is no surprises. A subsequent CCB meeting can record the fact that a customer/seller meeting did take place, decisions were made, and action items assigned. People's memories fade quickly, and writing things down helps to avoid potential misunderstandings. The point here is that a project plan needs to account for CCB-like meetings to handle the changes and/or hazards that are a part of any software systems development effort.

Successful software systems development projects involve (1) assessing the risk of accomplishing the customer's statement of work, allocating appropriate resources to mitigate the identified risks, monitoring the risks throughout the project, and deciding how to deal with the risks. The next section describes an approach for risk assessment and risk-derived resource allocation while developing and maintaining a project plan.

2.5 RISK ASSESSMENT AND PROJECT PLANNING

Developing a project plan includes the determination that a project is high risk, medium risk, or low risk. As shown in Figure 2–10, risk criteria are applied to a customer's SOW to help determine the risk associated with the project. The assessed risk is represented by a propeller-driven airplane. Hopefully, a good job is done assessing the risk, and the seller's project team can see it coming. Appropriate management, development, and product assurance resources can be allocated for risk reduction. We define *risk reduction* to mean "reducing the likelihood that software systems development products will (1) not be delivered on time, (2) not be delivered within budget, and (3) not do what the seller and customer mutually agreed that the products are supposed to do."

Our approach for allocating appropriate management, development, and product assurance resources is repeatable. This approach includes the following:

■ A set of risk assessment criteria derived from both your organization's and industry-wide experience correlating project characteristics with project outcome.[7]

■ Iteration among the parties involved with applying these criteria to achieve consensus.

Figure 2–11 shows an example set of risk criteria used for risk assessment and corresponding risk-derived resource allocation percentages. Your organization will have its own set of risk criteria. It is important to establish a database of risk criteria for your software systems development projects. You should involve both the project team staff and your business and finance staff in establishing your organization's risk criteria. Risk comes in many forms.

Resource estimating is not an exact science, but if the risk assessment criteria provided in Figure 2–11 are applied to a given SOW by different groups within your organization, the outcomes of this risk assessment would be predominantly one of the three risk categories, i.e., high, medium, and low. High-risk projects demand more risk reduction; therefore, product assurance is allocated 20 percent of the resources, management is allocated 15 percent for oversight, and development is allocated 65 percent. Medium-risk projects require less risk reduction, and low-risk projects require even less.

---

[7]One way to define a set of risk criteria is to review your organization's projects and compile a list of lessons learned.

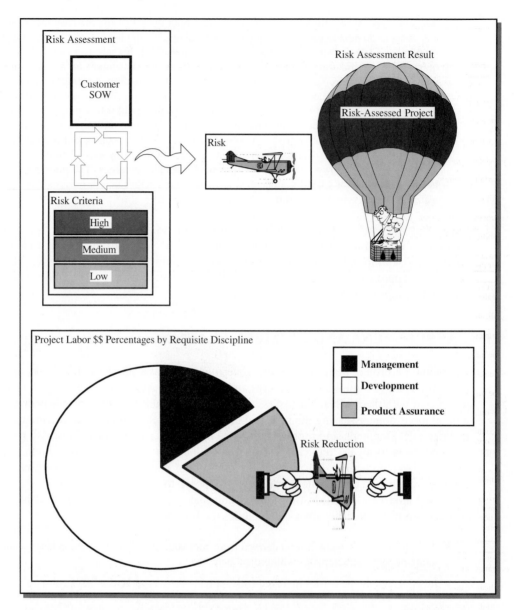

FIGURE 2–10 Project planning involves assessing the risk of accomplishing the customer's statement of work. Product assurance serves to mitigate the project risk and should therefore be commensurate with the assessed risk.

The rationale underlying the percentages in the pie charts is the following:[8]

■ The medium-risk pie chart is assumed to be the "average software systems development project." Industry experience shows that allocating approximately 10 percent of the total project labor to product assurance is a good risk reduction strategy for a broad range of projects. This experience is the basis for the medium-

---

[8]See, for example, the following references for insights into product assurance budget percentages:

1. K. Shere, *Software Engineering and Management* (Englewood Cliffs, NJ: Prentice-Hall, 1988), pp. 80–93.

2. R. Dunn, *Software Defect Removal* (New York: McGraw-Hill Book Company, 1984), p. 60.

Risk Criteria	Risk Assessment	% Risk-Derived Resource Allocation

A project is **high** risk if two or more of the following criteria apply:

- Unique application

- Lack of up-to-date documentation

- Inexperienced development staff

- No schedule slack

- Uncertain requirements

- Multiple customers

- Subcontractor labor hours at least 50% of total development labor hours. Associated risks: less management flexibility, subcontractor rate increases.

- Software failure results in death, injury, or large financial loss to either the customer or seller.

A project is **medium** risk if the project is not high risk and if two or more of the following criteria apply:

- Application domain not well understood

- Documentation not up-to-date

- Some inexperienced development staff

- Little schedule slack

- Some major requirements uncertain

- First-time customer for seller

- Subcontractor labor hours between 25% and 50% of total development labor hours. Associated risks: reduced management flexibility, subcontractor rate increases

- Software failure results in high visibility within customer community

If the project does not match two of the medium-risk criteria above, the project is then assessed against the low-risk criteria. If the project does not match three of the low-risk criteria, the project is considered medium risk.

A project is **low** risk if the project is not high or medium risk and if three or more of the following criteria apply:

- Application domain well understood

- Up-to-date documentation

- Experienced development staff

- Flexible schedule

- Requirements certain

- Customer not new to the seller

- Software failure does not result in death, injury, or large financial loss to either customer or seller

High-Risk Project

High Risk: 15%, 20%, 65%

Medium-Risk Project

Medium Risk: 10%, 10%, 80%

Low-Risk Project

Low Risk: 10%, 5%, 85%

Legend: ■ Management □ Development ▨ Product Assurance

FIGURE 2–11 Assessing project risk during project planning is key to allocating dollar resources for risk-reduced project plan accomplishment. The risk criteria shown are examples illustrating the approach. They are a starting point for constructing your own criteria tailored to the needs of your environment.

risk product assurance percentage. It has been our general practice to allocate in the neighborhood of 10 percent of the project labor to management. This practice is reflected in the medium-risk pie chart. Consequently, 80 percent of the project labor is allocated to development.

■ In general, the high-risk criteria that are listed substantially increase project risk over the risks embodied in the medium-risk criteria. Thus, the high-risk product assurance percentage is determined by doubling the medium-risk product assurance percentage (i.e., 2*0.10 = 0.20). The high-risk management percentage is determined by increasing the medium-risk management percentage by 50 percent (i.e., 0.10*1.5 = 0.15). Consequently, 65 percent of the project labor is allocated to development.

■ The low-risk product assurance percentage is determined by halving the corresponding medium-risk percentage (i.e., 0.5*0.10 = 0.05). Since it has been our general practice to allocate 10 percent of the project labor to management, the low-risk management percentage is the same as the medium-risk management percentage (i.e., 0.10). Consequently, 85 percent of the project labor is allocated to development.

■ The more criteria that apply within a given category, the more firmly established is the risk for that category, and less leeway from the percentages shown should be considered. For example, if four high-risk criteria apply to an SOW, then the greater is the likelihood that the project may run into trouble. Consequently, the resource allocation should be in close conformance to the high-risk percentages shown. If, on the other hand, risk criteria apply to an SOW from more than one risk category, then more leeway should be allowed in allocating resources to management, development, and product assurance. For example, an SOW might have one high-risk criterion (e.g., unique application) and two medium-risk criteria (e.g., little schedule slack, some major requirements uncertain). Even though this SOW would be classified as medium risk, it may be prudent to allocate resources somewhere between the high-risk percentages and the medium-risk percentages.

It is important for the participants involved in the risk assessment process to achieve consensus. The purpose of the consensus is to allow differences that may result from the application of the risk criteria to be given visibility to all the participants. In this manner, all the participants evolve toward a joint understanding of the risk associated with completing the software systems development project on time, within budget, and in compliance with documented customer requirements. In general, resource estimating is, at best, educated guesswork. Despite the proliferation of resource-estimating models, estimating resources required to do a software systems development effort cannot be solely reduced to an exercise of plugging numbers into a set of formulas.

Figure 2–12 delineates our logic for applying risk criteria to a customer's SOW. The procedure for applying these criteria is the following:

■ The high-risk criteria are to be considered first. If any two of the listed criteria apply to the SOW, the project is categorized as high risk, and the high-risk pie chart applies. Consequently, 65 percent of the project labor dollars are to be assigned to development, 15 percent to management, and 20 percent to product assurance.

(Note: The high-risk criterion related to subcontractor labor hours is not known in detail until the project planning staff lays out the detailed development approach. However, in some cases, it is a priori known that subcontractor labor will be a majority of the development team labor. If the amount of subcontractor labor is not a priori known, then this criterion may be introduced in subsequent iterations of the cost estimates, particularly if it is uncertain whether a project should be classified as high risk or medium risk. A similar comment applies to the medium-risk criterion related to subcontractor labor hours.)

■ If the SOW is not determined to be high risk, then the medium-risk criteria are to be considered. If any two of the medium-risk criteria shown apply to the SOW, the project is categorized as medium risk and the medium-risk pie chart applies. Consequently, 80 percent of the project labor dollars are to be assigned to development, 10 percent to management, and 10 percent to product assurance.

■ If the SOW is not determined to be high or medium risk, then the low-risk criteria are to be considered. If any three of the low-risk criteria shown apply to the SOW, the project is categorized as low risk, and the

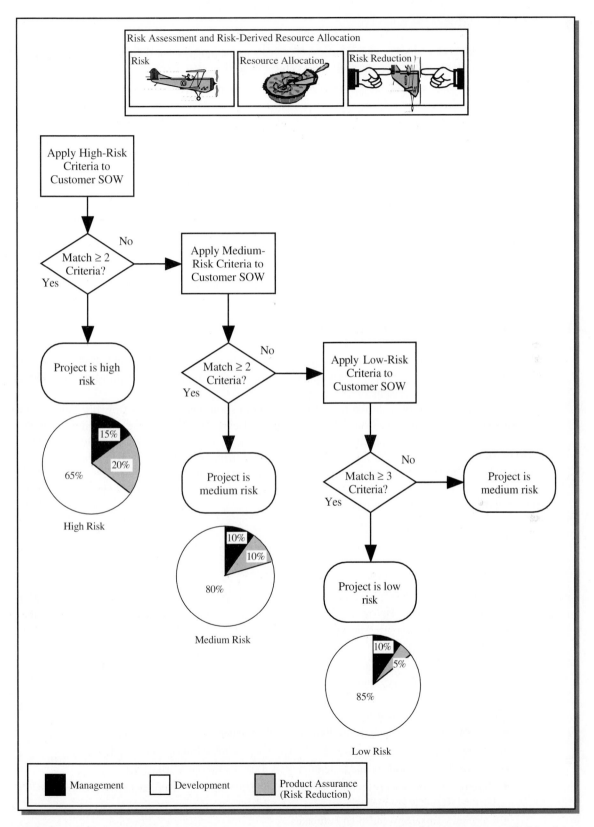

FIGURE 2–12 This logic illustrates how the risk criteria in the preceding figure can be applied to determine whether a project is high, medium, or low risk. This logic offers you insight into developing your own risk assessment approach on the basis of your own risk criteria. The assessed project risk is used to allocate resources among the management, product assurance, and development disciplines. The dollars allocated to product assurance serve to reduce project risk.

low-risk pie chart applies. Consequently, 85 percent of the project labor dollars are to be assigned to development, 10 percent to management, and 5 percent to product assurance.

■ If the preceding steps do not yield a criteria match, then the project is assumed to be medium risk, and the medium-risk pie chart applies.

This risk assessment logic can also be applied at the task level, sub-task level, etc. Furthermore, as the project unfolds, this logic can be applied on a periodic or event-driven basis as a part of your overall risk management approach.

Our risk assessment approach folds experience into rules of thumb designed to provide top-down, risk-derived resource allocation estimates. As subsequently explained, these risk-derived resource allocations are compared with bottom-up, detailed task-derived resource estimates. This top-down, bottom-up comparison typically involves several iterations to reconcile the scope of work within perceived budget constraints.

In the next section, we integrate the project planning concepts of life cycle, change management, risk assessment, and resource allocation, and discuss ideas on how to generate a project plan.

2.6 PROJECT PLANNING PROCESS

The purpose of this section is to provide you with guidance for developing an ADPE element that defines the project planning process for your organization. Our approach is to pull together the concepts discussed in preceding sections of this chapter.

The heart of your project planning ADPE element should be a process flow diagram. Figure 2–13 presents such a diagram based on the ideas discussed earlier. You can use this diagram as a starting point to define your project planning process. We walk you through this diagram to give you specific insight into how you can adapt this diagram to your environment. The discussion that follows is keyed to the numbers in the shaded boxes and the labeled arrows in the figure.

Figure 2–13 consists of the following responsible agents, major project planning process activities, and major communication paths:

■ **Responsible agents:**
  ■ Customer
  ■ Seller Senior Management
  ■ Seller Project Manager
  ■ Seller Development Manager
  ■ Seller Product Assurance Manager
  ■ Seller Business Manager
  ■ Seller Project Planning Staff consisting of Seller Development Manager, Seller Product Assurance Manager, and Seller Project Manager

■ **Major project planning process activities:**
  ■ Provides SOW Containing Work Requirements to Seller
  ■ Review SOW, Communicate with Customer, and Assemble Project Planning Team
  ■ Perform Risk Assessment and Determine Risk-Derived Resource Allocation
  ■ Develops Development, Product Assurance, and Management Approaches and Corresponding Task-Derived Resource Estimates
  ■ Calculates Task-Derived Dollar Estimates
  ■ Calculates Risk-Derived Dollar Estimates

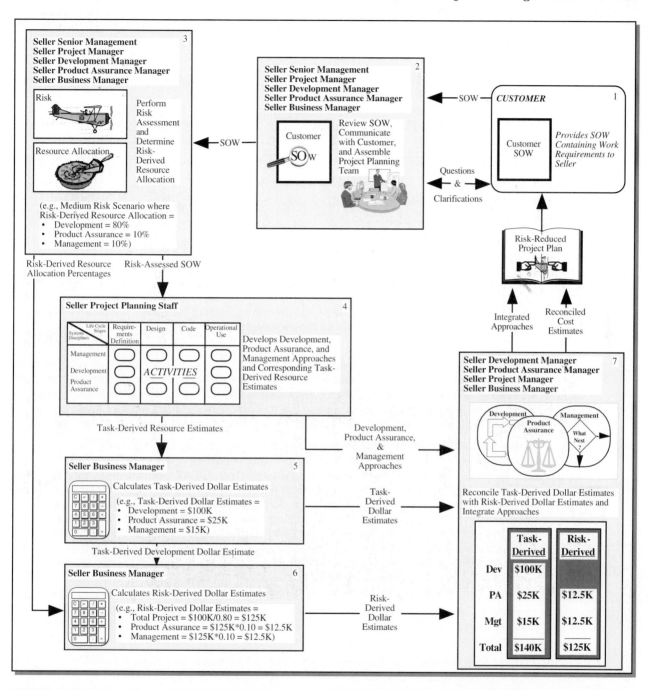

FIGURE 2–13 The software project planning process is risk-based and development driven. The planning process involves (1) assessing risks associated with meeting customer requirements, (2) defining resource percentages for development, product assurance, and management based on this assessment, (3) developing corresponding approaches and task-derived resource estimates, (4) reconciling task-derived and risk-derived resource estimates, and (5) integrating the approaches. The end result is a risk-reduced project plan with increased likelihood for successful accomplishment.

- Reconcile Task-Derived Dollar Estimates with Risk-Derived Dollar Estimates and Integrate Approaches.

- **Major communication paths:**
  - SOW (i.e., Statement of Work)
  - Questions and Clarifications
  - Risk-Derived Resource Allocation Percentages
  - Risk-Assessed SOW
  - Task-Derived Resource Estimates
  - Development, Product Assurance, and Management Approaches
  - Task-Derived Dollar Estimates
  - Risk-Derived Dollar Estimates
  - Integrated Approaches
  - Reconciled Cost Estimates
  - Risk-Reduced Project Plan

We walk you through Figure 2–13 in terms of the preceding elements and their interaction during the project planning process. Also, we provide a simple example to clarify key points.

1. **Provides SOW Containing Work Requirements to Seller.** The starting point for the project planning process is the statement of what the customer wants the seller to do. The customer's requirements are packaged into an *SOW* (i.e., statement of work). The customer provides the seller with an SOW in which the level of detail can vary from a list of simple one-line statements to a document spanning hundreds of pages. No matter where in this spectrum an SOW lies, it will generally precipitate questions from the seller.

2. **Review SOW, Communicate with Customer, and Assemble Project Planning Team.** The customer delivers the SOW to seller management. Depending on your organization, this management may be the (1) software project manager, (2) software project manager's boss, (3) manager responsible for generating business, (4) project planning manager, or (5) some combination of the preceding. This management carefully examines the SOW contents. In general, this examination will generate a list of *questions* that will require customer *clarifications* (e.g., what the meaning is of certain deliverables requested, what the customer is to furnish to the seller, where the work is to be performed, what is the schedule slack). Seller management needs to get answers to these questions before a realistic project plan can be written. Depending on the SOW size and complexity, seller management may have to iterate a number of times with the customer before SOW questions are answered.

   Generally, SOW examination is also coupled with the assembling of the project planning team, which is responsible for putting the words on paper. Depending on your organization, this team may consist of (1) individuals from a group dedicated to writing project plans, (2) individuals who will perform and manage the work called out in the project plan, or (3) some combination of the preceding.

3. **Perform Risk Assessment and Determine Risk-Derived Resource Allocation.** A candidate list of managers who make up this management is the (1) senior management (e.g., a corporate vice president), (2) project manager, (3) development manager(s), (4) product assurance manager, and (5) business manager (i.e., the manager responsible for contractual matters). Depending on your organization, more than one of these managers may be the same person.

   Earlier in this chapter, we showed you how to set up criteria for doing risk assessment. Your version of these criteria is to be applied here. The result of applying your risk criteria to the SOW is a *risk-assessed SOW*. The purpose of this risk assessment is to gauge the possibilities of *not* being able to accomplish the tasks (i.e., producing products with integrity) set forth in the SOW.

   Assume that you have performed the risk assessment and you have determined that the project is medium risk.

As we showed earlier, this risk assessment should be coupled to the percentage of project labor resources to be allocated respectively to the development, product assurance, and management disciplines. Your version of these percentages should be applied here to produce what we call *risk-derived resource allocation percentages*. As explained earlier, these percentages are used as top-down guidance that are compared with the development, product assurance, and management task-derived resource estimates in subsequent activities of the project planning process.

Before we proceed to the next project planning process activity, several observations are in order regarding the risk-derived resource allocation just described.

- If you are a seller, you need to ensure that the risk assessment criteria you use are reasonably unambiguous so that the application of these criteria by different people or organizations give repeatable results. Here, "repeatable" means that if the criteria are applied by different individuals or organizations, the results will cluster in one risk category. Earlier in this chapter, we gave you three sets of example criteria defining high-, medium-, and low-risk projects. These criteria are derived from actual project experience and did, indeed, produce repeatable results in the sense defined here.

- If you are a seller, you also need to ensure that you clarify for your customer what risk means in the preceding process. We have stated that risk here means the possibilities of not producing products with integrity. In your environment, you may want risk to mean something else. For example, you may want risk to mean the possibilities of not getting a good award fee from your customer (if you are working on a cost-plus-award-fee contract, or a contract with bonus incentives).

- If you are a buyer/user, you need to ensure that the seller clarifies for you what risk means. For example, you as a user/buyer may not be interested in spending money for product assurance if the seller's purpose for applying product assurance is to reduce the risk of getting a good award fee. You should note that there are circumstances in which applying product assurance to get a good award fee may not result in your getting a product with integrity. For example, there are dishonest sellers who may use the visibility afforded by product assurance to plug superficial fixes into a shoddy software product so that it can "pass" buyer/user acceptance testing.

Since our example project is assumed to be medium-risk, the risk-derived resource allocation percentages are assumed to be 80 percent for development, 10 percent for product assurance, and 10 percent for management. These percentages are used later in the cost estimation calculations to compare this resource allocation guidance with detailed planning estimates. The next step is to develop a development approach that is supported with product assurance and management activities.

4. **Develops Development, Product Assurance, and Management Approaches and Corresponding Task-Derived Resource Estimates.** This box includes the activities associated with putting the words on paper to generate the project plan document. The heart of this paper-generating activity is the formulating of the technical details of the (1) *development approach* the developers intend to follow to meet the customer's SOW requirements, (2) *product assurance approach* to support this development approach, and (3) *management approach* to guide the developers and effect synergism between them and the product assurance team. These three approaches are then used to develop *task-derived resource estimates* for accomplishing the approaches.

The seller project planning staff is responsible for these activities. Ideally, this staff should consist of the people who actually perform/manage the work set forth in the plan. In some organizations, this ideal may not be realized because some of these people are already performing on other projects. Some organizations in which work is periodically or continually coming in may have a cadre of people dedicated to project planning, or available on a part-time basis for project planning. Whatever the organizational set-up, the subprocess of writing the project plan consists of the following activities (although described sequentially, actual accomplishment of these activities may overlap depending on such factors as similarities between the project to be planned and previously accomplished projects):

4a. **Defines Development Approach and Development Task-Derived Resource Estimate.** The seller development manager defines the development approach by tailoring the generic four-stage life cycle to the SOW content as discussed earlier in this chapter. Remember, that the purpose of adopting a life cycle for the project is to bring to the fore a sequence of development tasks (and corresponding product assurance and management tasks) that need to be accomplished. The life cycle adopted is nothing more than a high-level task template.

We note that this tailoring process is not necessarily unique. That is, depending on how much visibility the seller and the customer may want into the development process, it may be desirable to slice one or more stages into multiple stages. For our simple example, Figure 2–13 shows a tailored life cycle consisting of four stages. This four-stage life cycle shows a single stage for requirements definition and a single stage for design. This four-stage breakout may be a perfectly logical way to address SOW content. However, if, for example, the software requirements are uncertain, it may be cost-beneficial to break this single stage into a Preliminary Requirements Definition Stage and a Detailed Requirements Definition Stage. With this approach, you can reduce the risk of spending too much time trying to settle on requirements specifics by first settling on broader requirements issues. It is generally counterproductive refining a multitude of capabilities to be incorporated into, say, a document processor containing sophisticated graphics-inclusion capabilities when all the customer really wants is a word processor with modest text-editing capabilities.

From the tasks called out in the development approach, the seller development manager generates a task-derived resource estimate. This estimate is typically expressed in terms of labor hours needed to accomplish the product development tasks. To standardize this resource estimation process, you may want to develop a set of worksheets that contains task names as rows and hours as columns, where the hours columns may depend on project risk. For example, for the development of a design document on a high-risk project, you may want to produce multiple drafts for review before going final, whereas on a low-risk project, a single draft may suffice. In your organization, you may break out these hours into various labor categories (e.g., analyst, senior designer, designer, trainer). Typically, each labor category has an hourly rate associated with it so that the hours can be converted to dollars or whatever unit of currency is used in your organization. The development approach becomes the driver for the product assurance and management approaches.

4b. **Defines Product Assurance (PA) Approach and PA Task-Derived Resource Estimate Based on Development Approach and Risk.** The seller product assurance manager defines the product assurance approach by using the SOW and the tasks identified in the development approach. In laying out this approach, this manager assures that all products called out in the development approach are reviewed. This manager uses the SOW as a double check on the developer's approach to ensure that no SOW requirements have been overlooked.

Like the seller development manager, the seller product assurance manager generates a task-derived resource estimate. Again, to standardize this resource estimating within your organization, you may want to develop a set of worksheets that contains product assurance task names as rows and hours as columns, where the hours columns may depend on project risk. For example, for a design document on a high-risk project, multiple drafts may be produced, each one requiring a product assurance review, whereas on a low-risk project, only one draft requiring product assurance review may be produced.

4c. **Defines Management Approach and Management Task-Derived Resource Estimate Based on Development Approach and Risk.** The seller project manager defines the management approach by using the SOW and the tasks identified in the development approach. In laying out this approach, this manager assures that all products called out in the development approach are given appropriate visibility through the development of an adequate number of drafts. As part of laying out this approach, the seller project manager needs to assure that the development approach calls out adequate drafts. Like the product assurance manager, the project manager uses the SOW as a double-check on the developer's approach to ensure that no SOW requirements have been overlooked.

Like the seller development manager, the seller project manager generates a task-derived resource estimate. Again, to standardize this resource estimating within your organization, you may want to develop a set of worksheets that contains management task names as rows and hours as columns, where the hours columns may depend on project risk. For example, for a high-risk project, you may want to have weekly CCB meetings, whereas on a low-risk project, monthly meetings may suffice for management visibility purposes. The project manager should ensure that the resource estimate includes project participation by the project manager's manager and other senior managers within the organization. Again, the extent of this senior management involvement is a function of project risk—the higher the risk, the greater the need for senior management involvement.

We stressed throughout this chapter the need to plan for anticipated, but unknown, change throughout project accomplishment. To address this need, all three managers involved with laying out the project plan must fold into their approaches CCB meetings throughout the project. In particular, when doing resource estimates, these managers need to ensure that they allocate hours for CCB participation and related activities such as minutes preparation and presentation of responses to action items. Furthermore, the project plan needs explicitly to address the role of the CCB in managing project change. For example, it can specify a suggested format for CCB minutes and call for the development of a CCB charter (or include the charter itself). One shortcut way of handling the CCB role is to cite an ADPE element governing CCB operation that your organization has incorporated into its engineering environment. Chapter 4 gives details on how such an element can be put together.

5. **Calculates Task-Derived Dollar Estimates.** This box includes the activities associated with converting the task-derived resource estimates from labor hours to labor dollars. This conversion to *task-derived dollar estimates* provides a common base for comparison, whereas labor hours by labor category do not.

   5a. **Calculates Task-Derived Development Labor-Dollar Estimate.** The seller business manager uses the development task-derived labor-hour estimate to calculate the development task-derived labor-dollar estimate. Assume that the development labor-dollar estimate is $100,000.

   5b. **Calculates Task-Derived Product Assurance Labor-Dollar Estimate.** The seller business manager uses the product assurance task-derived labor-hour estimate to calculate the product assurance task-derived labor-dollar estimate. Assume that the product assurance labor-dollar estimate is $25,000.

   5c. **Calculates Task-Derived Management Labor-Dollar Estimate.** The seller business manager uses the management task-derived labor-hour estimate to calculate the management task-derived labor-dollar estimate. Assume that the management labor-dollar estimate is $15,000.

At this point in our project planning process, the following has been assumed:

- the project is medium risk (development, product assurance, and management resource allocation percentages are 80 percent, 10 percent, and 10 percent, respectively);

- a four-stage life cycle is to be used for developing development, product assurance, and management approaches; and

- the development ($100,000), product assurance ($25,000), and management ($15,000) labor-dollar estimates total $140,000.

The next activity is to calculate *risk-derived dollar estimates* using the risk assessment resource allocation percentages and the development labor-dollar estimate.

6. **Calculates Risk-Derived Dollar Estimates.** This box includes the activities associated with using the risk-derived resource allocation percentages and the task-derived development labor dollars to calculate risk-derived dollar estimates.

   6a. **Calculates Total Risk-Derived Project Labor-Dollar Estimate Based on Development Labor Dollars.** The seller business manager simply divides the development labor-dollar estimate by the risk-derived development resource allocation percentage to calculate the total risk-derived project labor-dollar estimate.

   Using the $100,000 development approach example given above, the total risk-derived project labor-dollar estimate becomes $100,000/0.80 = $125,000. The risk-derived guidance indicates that the total labor resources needed for the project is the amount $125,000. This number does not include hardware, software, communication lines, etc., that may be needed to accomplish the SOW tasks.

   6b. **Calculates Risk-Derived Product Assurance Labor-Dollar Estimate.** The seller business manager simply multiplies the total risk-derived project labor-dollar estimate by the risk-derived product assurance resource allocation percentage to calculate the risk-derived product assurance labor-dollar estimate.

For the example just given, the risk-derived product assurance labor-dollar estimate becomes $125,000*0.10 = $12,500.

6c. **Calculates Risk-Derived Management Labor-Dollar Estimate.** The seller business manager simply multiplies the total risk-derived project labor-dollar estimate by the risk-derived management resource allocation percentage to calculate the risk-derived product assurance labor-dollar estimate.

For the example just given, the risk-derived management labor-dollar estimate becomes $125,000*0.10 = $12,500.

At this point in the project planning process example, it has been assumed that the task-derived dollar estimates versus the risk-derived dollar estimates are as follows:

- Development—$100,000 versus $100,000.

  At this point in the project planning process, both development estimates are always the same. As shown above, the task-derived development labor dollars and the corresponding risk percentage are used to calculate the overall risk-derived project labor-dollars. The total risk-derived project labor dollars are then multiplied by the product assurance and management risk-derived resource allocation percentages to account for assessed risk. As shown next, it may be necessary to revisit the development approach to rethink what needs to be done. Such revisits trigger adjustments to the product assurance and management approaches, as well as corresponding resource requirements.

- Product assurance—$25,000 versus $12,500.

- Management—$15,000 versus $12,500.

The next activity is to reconcile the differences between the task-derived estimates and the risk-derived estimates for product assurance ($25,000 versus $12,500) and for management ($15,000 versus $12,500).

7. **Reconcile Task-Derived Estimates with Risk-Derived Estimates and Integrate Approaches.** This activity integrates the work performed in the preceding steps. The responsible agents for performing this integration are the development manager, product assurance manager, project manager, and business manager. They review the approaches and remove inconsistencies. They harmonize development and product assurance approaches to ensure that all products developed are subjected to product assurance review—unless there are extenuating circumstances (such as tight schedules that only may permit cursory product assurance of some product drafts). They harmonize development and management approaches to ensure that on all tasks, management has insight into the status of the work through such activities as CCBs, scheduled audits, and project reviews.

   If the task-derived and risk-derived estimates are consistent (e.g., within 10 percent of each other), then the task-derived approaches and estimates are ready to be included in the project plan. However, your organization will need to agree on the definition of *consistent*. You may decide that consistency is described in absolute values, e.g., estimates within $5,000 of each other are considered consistent.

   In the example given, the product assurance task-derived estimate ($25,000) is 100 percent greater than the risk-derived estimate ($12,500). In addition, the management task-derived estimate ($15,000) is 20 percent greater than the risk-derived estimate ($12,500). Clearly in this example, there appears to be a misunderstanding of what needs to be done. The product assurance people may not fully understand what the developers are proposing. Perhaps, the product assurance people have had past experiences that they believe justify the $25,000.

   If the estimates are not consistent (as in the example), the following three alternatives are to be considered:

   7a. **Bring Task-Derived Estimates (and Corresponding Approaches) into Line with Risk-Derived Estimates.** In this case, the responsible managers need to reevaluate their respective approaches and their resultant resource estimates to attempt to resolve these differences. Resolution may include reconsideration of the risk-derived resource percentages. For example, if it turns out that application of the risk criteria leads to a project that is on the border between two risk categories (such as being just barely high risk because it satisfied the minimum number of criteria to place it in the high-risk category), it may be desirable to allow more leeway in the consistency check between risk-derived and task-derived estimates. If the responsible managers and the project planning staff cannot resolve their differences, then senior management should be brought in to break the deadlock.

7b. **Redo Development Approach and Corresponding Estimate and Iterate.** After careful consideration of the existing estimates, it may be necessary to revisit the development approach and iterate through the process to create a new development approach and corresponding new resource estimate. This rethinking process may help to clarify where the estimates significantly differ.

7c. **Combine Items 7a and 7b in Some Manner.** It may be necessary to combine some realignment of the task-derived and risk-derived estimates, with a revisit to the development approach.

Once there is agreement, the managers review the *integrated approaches* and coordinate the *reconciled cost estimates* for inclusion into the project plan.

The output of these seven activities is a *risk-reduced project plan*. This plan is then delivered to the customer. After customer review of the plan, one or more of the listed activities may have to be repeated—even though Activity 2 included interaction with the customer to clarify SOW issues. The following are typical reasons why several drafts of a project plan may have to be produced before the customer and the seller converge on project plan contents (part of this process may include SOW revision):

1. The customer may not understand the risk assessment process (e.g., Who or what is at risk—the seller's profit? The utility of the customer's products?)

2. The customer may not have sufficient money to buy the project plan's approach. In this case, the customer may have to revise the SOW to reduce its scope (e.g., remove deliverables).

3. The customer may not understand the value that the product assurance resources adds to the project and may therefore balk at paying for these resources.

A project planning development process output is the risk-reduced project plan. As is indicated in Figure 2–13, the project plan is a living contract between the customer and seller. The next section presents suggestions on what you may want to put into your project plan.

2.7 PROJECT PLAN CONTENTS

A project plan needs to respond to the customer's SOW. Some SOWs state the specific format, down to the font, font size, margins, spacing, etc., and some SOWs leave the project plan format up to the seller organization. Regardless of the SOW, we offer for your consideration the information content delineated in Figure 2–14. It should be noted that our concept of "project plan" encompasses the notion of "software development plan" in the U.S. defense community.

Consider the following suggested project plan contents:

- **Project Overview.** This section sets the project context.
  - *Purpose*—We recommend that you include a statement of the purpose for which the project is planned to accomplish. This helps to communicate your high-level understanding of the customer's requirements.
  - *Background*—Part of this understanding may be communicated in a historical summary of how and why the project came into being. We recommend that you include an overview graphic of the current software system, if appropriate.
  - *Project Goals*—To help highlight the specific goals to be achieved as a result of the project, we recommend that you include an overview graphic of the envisioned software system. In short, the graphic in the Background subsection and the graphic in the Project Goals subsection represent where the system is

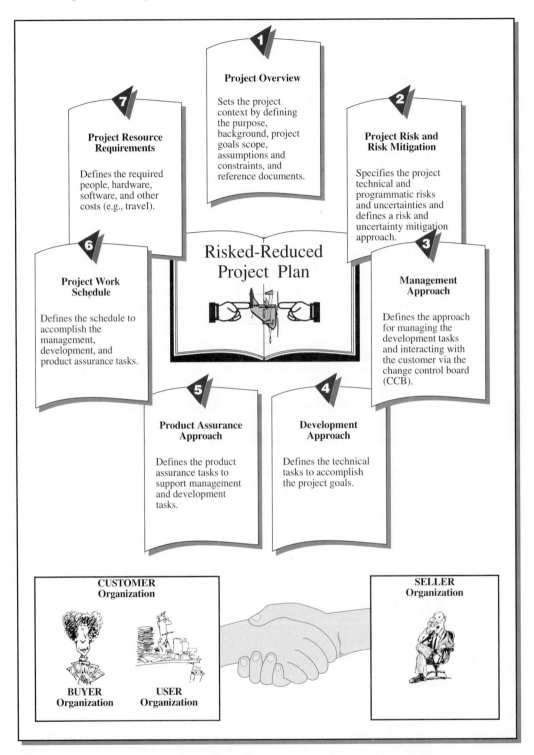

FIGURE 2–14 The project plan is a living contract between the CUSTOMER and SELLER that sets forth the work that the seller's management, development, and product assurance disciplines accomplish and the customer management approves. This figure shows suggested project plan topics and a suggested order for these topics.

today and where the system will be when you are done. Such before and after graphics helps the project team to think through what needs to be done. Such graphics also help to orient new staff.

- *Project Scope*—The project scope defines the project boundaries and interfaces with other entities, including other contractors and government agencies, if appropriate.
- *Assumptions and Constraints*—The assumptions and constraints are listed, discussed, and form, in part, the basis on which the project plan is written. For example, project deadlines depend upon the receipt of information and/or feedback in a timely fashion. If such an assumption does not hold, the plan may need to be changed to accommodate the change in schedule. Constraints dealing with such things as funding, time, and interfaces are also listed and discussed.
- **Project Risk and Risk Mitigation.** This section specifies the technical and programmatic risks identified as a result of your risk assessment.
  - *Identified Risks*—Each risk is listed, and an explanation of the potential impact it may have on the accomplishment of the SOW tasks is presented.
  - *Risk Mitigation*—A risk mitigation approach is presented for each of the identified risks. If appropriate, the mitigation approach may include customer actions that may require some negotiation.

The next three sections of the project plan define the seller's overall technical approach. As suggested in our risk assessment approach and project planning development process, the management, development and product assurance approaches are related to the perceived project risks in terms of the tasks to be performed and the resources required to perform them.

- **Management Approach.** This section defines the management oversight, coordination, and review activities for the project.
  - *Project Team Organization*—We suggest that an organization chart detailing the project team be included and described in terms of the specific organizational elements performing the work. Key personnel, rationale for their selection, and corresponding résumés are also recommended. If subcontractors are to be used, then their participation is identified and reporting channels are discussed. If appropriate, for positions that have not yet been staffed, identify the specific qualifications to be used in your selection process.
  - *Management Oversight and Reviews*—This section details the types and frequency of management reviews, status reports, and project meetings. For traditional systems engineering projects, management activities include monitoring project risk and progress, soliciting and monitoring customer feedback, and deciding whether the software system is ready to be shipped to the customer. For prototyping projects, management activities include obtaining end-user concurrence on human-to-computer interfaces, and domain expert concurrence on the software representation of the problem being solved, and customer acceptance of the prototyped system. For information engineering projects, management activities include reviewing the information needs of the software system users; the business and design models; and the module, system and acceptance test results. Regardless of project type (e.g., traditional, prototyping, information engineering), we recommend that you plan for a change control board (CCB) forum to help (1) manage product development and project change, (2) record associated decisions, and (3) manage expectations.
- **Development Approach.** This section defines how the development team tailored the generic four-stage life cycle to the SOW content. The development tasks drive the software systems development effort that need to be accomplished in order to respond to the customer's needs. Remember, that depending on how much visibility the seller and the customer may want into the development process, it may be desirable to slice one or more life cycle stages into multiple stages. Each stage can be described in terms of the tasks to be performed. We recommend that each task be described in terms of task objectives, techniques, and tools to be used. Also, specific milestones to be achieved and deliverables to be developed are detailed.

  For traditional systems engineering projects, development activities include developing operational system concepts, defining requirements, allocating requirements to hardware and software, describing data flow, conducting peer reviews, designing required databases, conducting code walkthroughs, providing training, and monitoring operational use.

For prototyping projects, development activities include describing initial prototype concepts, specifying prototype requirements, developing user interfaces, revising concepts and requirements, developing major prototyping functionality, specifying host environment modifications, and finalizing prototype concepts and requirements.

For information engineering projects, development activities include defining critical success factors, information needs, subject areas, entity types, entity relationships, processes and process dependencies, process action diagrams, procedure action diagrams, physical database models; and establishing cutover schedules.

Remember, the development approach becomes the driver for the product assurance and management approaches.

■ **Product Assurance Approach.** This section defines the product assurance approach by using the customer's SOW and the tasks identified in the development approach. The product assurance approach details the checks and balances to be used to help ensure that each developed software systems product satisfies the customer's requirements. Checks and balances are realized, in part, through quality assurance, verification and validation, test and evaluation, and configuration management. Product assurance responsibilities are detailed for and tied to the development tasks.

For traditional systems engineering projects, product assurance activities include examining the requirements for SOW congruency, testability, and consistency; preparing test plans; determining standards conformance; completing test procedures; conducting acceptance testing; baselining products; and archiving incident reports and change requests.

For prototyping projects, product assurance activities include defining test strategies and test data; comparing prototype requirements with the skeleton prototype; preparing acceptance test procedures; and performing acceptance testing.

For information engineering projects, product assurance activities include comparing the information strategy plan with a project standard; writing the test strategy; baselining the project documentation; comparing the entity relationship diagram with identified subject areas for consistency; comparing procedure action diagrams with process action diagrams for consistency; performing test procedures in the operational environment; and comparing the implementation plan with a project standard.

The product assurance approach supports the development approach and provides managers and developers with additional insight into the status of the development activities.

■ **Project Work Schedule.** This section contains the integrated schedule of the management, development, and product assurance approaches. A schedule of deliverables can be presented in a table.

■ **Project Resource Requirements.** This section identifies the resources required to perform the effort described by the management, development, and product assurance approaches. We recommend that your resource requirements take risk into account as just described.

A table detailing the staff hours by task can be provided. The required hardware and software can be detailed. In addition, other appropriate costs, such as travel, can be presented.

As shown in Figure 2–15, the project plan is based on the Buyer/User (i.e., customer) statement of work. Tailoring the generic four-stage life cycle to the specific situation helps you to plan what needs to be done and what resources are required.

As part of your organization's project planning process, we recommend you consider what systems disciplines (i.e., management, development, and product assurance) are needed during each tailored life cycle stage. This consideration helps to define the tasks to be accomplished during the software systems development.

2.8 PROJECT PLANNING SUMMARY

In this chapter, we focused on the concepts of life cycle, project disciplines, project players, risk assessment, and a project planning development process. We also discussed the contents of a project plan and suggested a plan outline. You can use this outline as a starting point for defining specific pro-

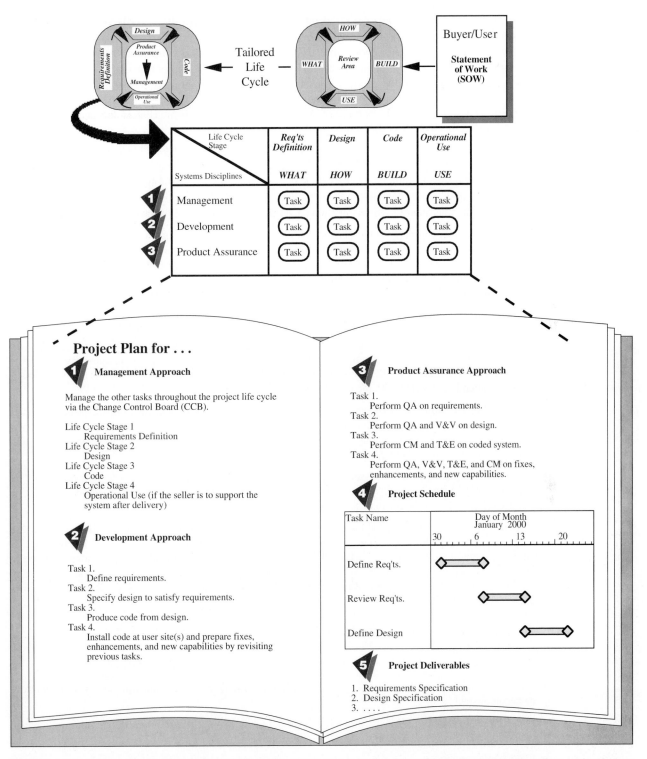

FIGURE 2–15 The project plan defines the seller's development, management, and product assurance tasks that respond to a buyer/user's statement of work (SOW). These tasks emerge by considering the intersection of each life cycle stage with each system discipline.

ject plans. These concepts can be integrated into an ADPE procedure that details your organization's project planning development process.

As illustrated in Figure 2–16, you can use the following annotated outline of an ADPE procedure as a starting point for defining your organization's project plan development process.

The project planning procedure may consist of the following sections:

- **Purpose.** This section states the purpose of procedure. The purpose sets the context and establishes the authority for the procedure. Specific purposes may include the following:
  - Activities performed by your organizational elements (e.g., your organization may have product test element that is responsible for what we call T&E).
  - Roles of your organization elements (e.g., your organization may have a training element that supplies people to a project who write user's manuals and give presentations to customers).
  - Guidance on time spent for project planning activities (e.g., target time for producing a project plan).

- **Background.** This section provides an overview of the project planning responsibilities, project plan structure, and possible project plan categories. These categories can help to establish the types of work done by your organization. For example, your organization may build only software systems using traditional systems engineering techniques or information engineering methodologies. Regardless, it is important to define the spectrum of project plans your organization develops or wants to develop.

- **Project Plan Development Process Overview.** This section provides an overview of the high-level activities of your project plan development process. We recommend that you develop an overview graphic that depicts the high-level activities, their inputs and output, and their interactions with one another. We also recommend that the detailed steps and individual responsibilities be presented in an appendix. Critical to successful implementation of the project plan development process is effective communication of the overall process that is supported with the necessary detail for implementation.

- **Project Plan Development Process.** This section provides the next level of detail of the project plan development process. We recommend that you develop a graphic that depicts this level of process activity. This section walks the reader through the entire process, but remember that the appendix can contain additional details and responsibilities.

- **Roles and Responsibilities.** This section provides a short description of the major organization units involved in the planning process. We recommend that a matrix detailing individual responsibilities by task be prepared. Depending upon the matrix size, you may want to make it an appendix.

- **Appendices.** Appendices are added as necessary. The main body of the procedure states the basics, and the appendices can add additional detail that embodies lessons learned or can provide tutorial information. As an organization matures in its engineering business processes, we recommend that the lessons be captured and incorporated into your ADPE elements. As people in your organization move on to other jobs, etc., their knowledge can be incorporated into your ADPE elements that serve, in some degree, as part of your organization's corporate memory.

Here are some project planning suggestions:

- Ensure that your project plan accounts for the resources required for revisits to other life cycle stages.

- Use a life cycle and your experiences to help you establish realistic project planning views of the work to be accomplished.

- Plan for a change control mechanism, such as a CCB, to help manage the anticipated, but unknown, change that accompanies any software systems development project.

- Include risk assessment in your project planning process, and collect meaningful data that help your organization increase its confidence in its resource estimates.

- Remember that risk assessment can be applied at the subtask level, as well as throughout the software systems development life cycle.

[Your Organization's Name and Logo]

Document #
Date

[Your Org.'s Name] Procedure
Project Plan Development Process

Document #
Date

1.0 PURPOSE

This section states the purpose of the element. The purpose is to delineate your organization's project planning process.

2.0 BACKGROUND

This section gives an overview of project planning responsibilities, project plan contents, and project plan types (e.g., traditional systems engineering or information engineering).

3.0 PROJECT PLAN DEVELOPMENT PROCESS OVERVIEW

This section presents a high-level overview of your organization's project planning process. The overview introduces the high-level steps involved with developing a project plan. It is important to stress that the steps may be performed sequentially, and/or concurrently, depending upon the particular planning situation.

4.0 PROJECT PLAN DEVELOPMENT PROCESS

This section defines, details, and walks through the high-level project planning steps. A figure detailing the high-level steps helps to explain how individual responsibilities and activities interact. Depending upon the level of detail appropriate for your organization, appendices can be used to explain the steps and responsibilities in greater detail.

5.0 ROLES AND RESPONSIBILITIES

This section presents the major organizational responsibilities for (1) preparing and reviewing the project plan and (2) negotiating with the customer prior to, during, and subsequent to project plan preparation to resolve SOW and project plan issues.

APPENDICES

Appendices can contain details for carrying through the instructions set forth in the body of the procedure. For example, appendices might include such things as (1) elaborations on one or more of the steps called out in Section 4 (for instance, if one step called out in Section 4 is "Do risk assessment," then an appendix might include the actual risk assessment procedure—such as the one described in this chapter), (2) a matrix indicating, for each step called out in Section 4, who has the primary responsibility and backup responsibility for performing that step (this matrix would be an elaboration of what is called out in Section 5 if this section did not delineate responsibilities down to the individual step level), and (3) example life cycles to be used for laying out product development approaches.

FIGURE 2–16   This illustration shows an annotated outline for getting you started defining an ADPE procedure for your project planning procedure.

- Educate your staff on your organization's project planning development process so that they can (1) understand what they are suppose to do and (2) contribute to and improve the process.

We have completed our discussion of the project planning development process in this chapter. The next chapter assumes that you have a software systems development project that is to produce software products. That chapter shows you how to define a process for moving products through your organization, with appropriate reviews, etc., for delivery to your customer.

Software Systems Development Process

All my life I've known better than to depend on experts. How could I have been so stupid, to let them go ahead?

—President John F. Kennedy, conversation with Theodore C. Sorensen concerning the Bay of Pigs.
Quoted in Sorensen, *Kennedy*, p. 309 (1965).

3.1 INTRODUCTION

One measure of successful software systems development is the ability to produce good products (i.e., products with integrity) with good processes (i.e., processes with integrity) *consistently*. Achieving this type of consistency depends primarily on the presence of the following two factors:

- **People with know-how**. As the cartoon on the left side in Figure 3–1 illustrates, having skilled people is critical. But having people with the necessary know-how to turn out good products is not sufficient if good products are to be turned out consistently.

- **An understanding of the "organizational way of doing business," that is, "process" of building software systems**. Left to their own devices, people do things their own way. *Consistency* requires an *organizational way* of doing things. Furthermore, from a long-term business viewpoint, understanding the software process cannot be limited to a few key individuals. Otherwise, as the cartoon on the right side in Figure 3–1 suggests, the way of doing business depends upon a few key individuals.

Successful software systems development is a delicate balance among (1) enabling people to grow professionally, (2) documenting processes embodying the experiences and knowledge of the people in the organization, (3) using know-how to apply such processes appropriately to a set of circumstances, and (4) refining processes based on the experience gained by applying the processes.

"With McBride here as our fall-back,
our systems are virtually fool-proof."
(© 1997 Bart Roozendaal.)

"'Be careful'! All you can tell me is 'Be careful'?"
(© 1997 by Sidney Harris.)

FIGURE 3–1   Successful software systems development projects depend, in part, on people.

What do we mean by "software process"? In this book, we define a *software process* as "a set of activities, methods, practices, and transformations that people use to develop and maintain software and the associated products (e.g., project plans, design documents, code, test cases, and user's manuals)."[1] Figure 3–2 illustrates people using a software process to develop and maintain software and associated products. However, many software development organizations do not follow a documented process or way of doing business. "Good" products can be produced. Nevertheless, without a documented process, it is difficult, if not impossible, for an organization to institutionalize a software process that consistently produces products that do what they are suppose to do, on time, and within budget.

Our concept of a software systems development process is tied to the concept of organization. In this book, *organization* means "an administrative and functional structure that operates to produce systems with software content." Figure 3–3 gives examples of this concept in terms of five software project combinations. A *software project* is "a planned undertaking whose purpose is to produce a system or systems with a software content."

Project combination number one represents an organization that consists of one software project, whereas combination number two consists of two projects. Combination number three represents a *program* that is "a collection of software projects bound by a common goal or a common customer/seller agreement." Combination number four represents an organization with multiple programs. Finally, combination number five represents an organization that may cut across company (or government agency) lines. In the case of companies, this cross-cutting situation can arise when multiple contractors support a program or project.

This chapter describes an example organizational software systems development process. You can use this example as a starting point to formulate (or enhance) a corresponding process for your environment. By *formulate* we mean "documenting a software systems development process that your organization may already use or would like to use."

---

[1]M.C. Paulk et al., "Capability Maturity Model for Software, Version 1.1," Software Engineering Institute Report CMU/SEI-93-TR-24, Carnegie Mellon University, Pittsburgh, PA, February 1993, p. 3.

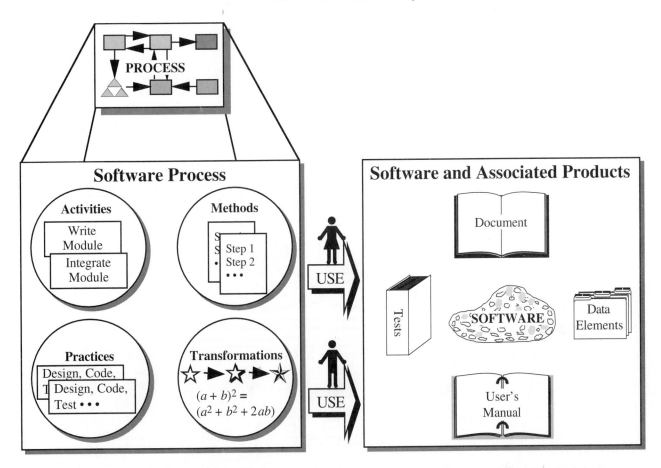

FIGURE 3–2 People use a software process to develop and maintain software and associated products.

Such an organizational process provides an integrating framework for developing and implementing a systems engineering environment (SEE). Once the process is documented in an Application Process Environment (ADPE) element and implemented, other elements can be developed to provide additional detail. For example, our example process includes a change control board (CCB), but this chapter's discussion does not contain the detailed guidelines one would expect for setting up and running a CCB. We recommend that detailed guidance be contained in another ADPE element, (e.g., a CCB guideline). Our example process also requires peer reviews, but this chapter's discussion does not contain detailed peer review guidance. The point is that once the organizational software systems development process is defined, additional detail can be provided in other ADPE elements.[2]

The plan for this chapter is the following:

- In **Section 3.2—Software Systems Development Process Nuggets**, we present the nuggets that you can expect to extract from this chapter.

- In **Section 3.3—Software Systems Development Process Overview**, we introduce key software systems development principles and a software systems development process. This process sets the context of dis-

---

[2]In this book, we provide additional insight into our example organizational software systems development process in other chapters. For example, Section 3.6 discusses the seller engineering group's responsibility for project planning. However, Chapter 2 provides the lower-level planning details and responsibilities. In effect, Chapter 3 is an ADPE element (i.e., Organizational Software Systems Development Process Policy) that is supported by a Chapter 2 ADPE element (i.e., Project Planning Procedure).

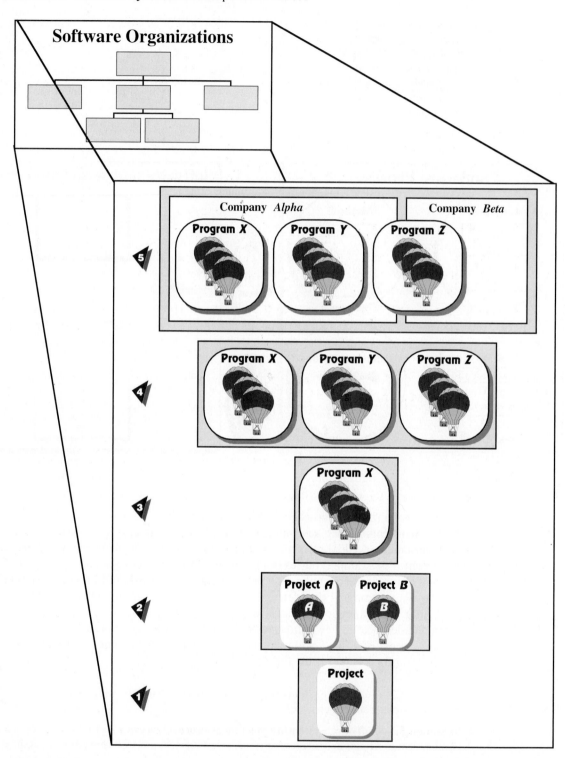

FIGURE 3–3   This figure shows five example software organizations based on software project groupings.

cussion for the rest of the chapter. The process offers you a starting point for developing a similar software systems development process for your place of business. Without a documented process, heroes make "it" happen. When the heroes move on, the organization generally regresses, and success becomes chancey until new heroes emerge. A documented process helps an organization avoid an overreliance on heroic efforts. The following major process elements are introduced: customer, seller process engineering group; customer/seller development team; change control board (CCB); seller senior management; and the major communication paths. Each of these elements is subsequently described in following sections.

- In **Section 3.4—Customer**, we provide tips for the buyer/user for writing a "good" statement of work (SOW) that tells a seller what the buyer/user wants. The SOW initiates the software systems development process. Writing a "good" SOW is not easy. "Goodness" is defined at the topmost level to mean "avoiding ambiguity and stipulating deliverables consistent with available time and money." Without a good SOW, a software systems development effort is in trouble at its inception. We call out issues for the buyer/user to consider when writing an SOW.

- In **Section 3.5—Seller Process Engineering Group**, we discuss how the organizational software systems development process is taken into account when the seller develops a project plan in response to a customer's SOW. This section augments the Chapter 2 discussion of the project planning process. We point out those seller activities that we believe should be planned for, regardless of specific life cycle. For example, regardless of life cycle, we believe the seller should conduct peer reviews for the evolving products.

- In **Section 3.6—Customer/Seller Development Team and Change Control Board (CCB)**, we focus the discussion on customer and seller communication and also on seller development team activities. We address the following:
  - Customer project manager
  - Seller development team activities that include communicating with the customer; evolving software products (i.e., documents, computer code, databases); conducting peer reviews; providing independent product assurance; performing technical editing; and performing project-level technical oversight
  - Product tracking form
  - Change control board (CCB)

  Some of these concepts are treated in more detail in subsequent chapters (e.g., Chapter 4 examines CCB mechanics).

- In **Section 3.7—Seller Senior Management**, we highlight the organizational software systems development process review and approval responsibilities of these managers.

- In **Section 3.8—Software Systems Development Process Summary**, we summarize the key points developed in the chapter. We include an annotated outline of an Application Development Process Environment (ADPE) policy for defining a software systems development process.

3.2 SOFTWARE SYSTEMS DEVELOPMENT PROCESS NUGGETS

Figure 3–4 lists the nuggets that you can expect to extract from this chapter. To introduce you to this chapter, we briefly explain these nuggets; their full intent will become apparent as you go through the chapter.

1. **If you are a buyer/user, specify in your request for proposal (RFP) that the seller define a software systems development process that involves you via a CCB-like mechanism.** You should structure your RFP to require the seller to define the particulars of the seller's software systems development process. Have the seller document this process in an ADPE element signed by you and the seller. This element should be revisited and updated no more frequently than every year.

2. **The software systems development ADPE element should contain the following: (1) generic activities performed by seller organizational elements (including the development, management, and product**

*Software systems development process
lessons learned (1 of 2)*

Nuggets

1   *If you are a buyer/user, specify in your request for
proposal (RFP) that the seller should define a software
systems development process that involves you via a
CCB-like mechanism.*

2   *The software systems development process ADPE
element should contain the following: (1) generic
activities performed by seller organizational
elements (including the development, product
assurance, and management activities) in
developing software products for delivery to the
customer and (2) the roles of the customer and
seller organizational elements in performing these
activities.*

3   *Include in the ADPE process element a figure
showing the process in terms of the (1) generic
activities, (2) major communications paths
connecting the activities, (3) organization(s)
responsible for performing each activity, and (4)
products produced.*

4   *Seller senior management should empower the project
manager to apply prescriptively the generic activities in
the ADPE process element.*

FIGURE 3–4   Successful software systems development is repeatable if an organization has a documented product development process that it follows. Without a documented process, the organization must rely on the heroics of individuals. Here are key process concepts explained in this chapter.

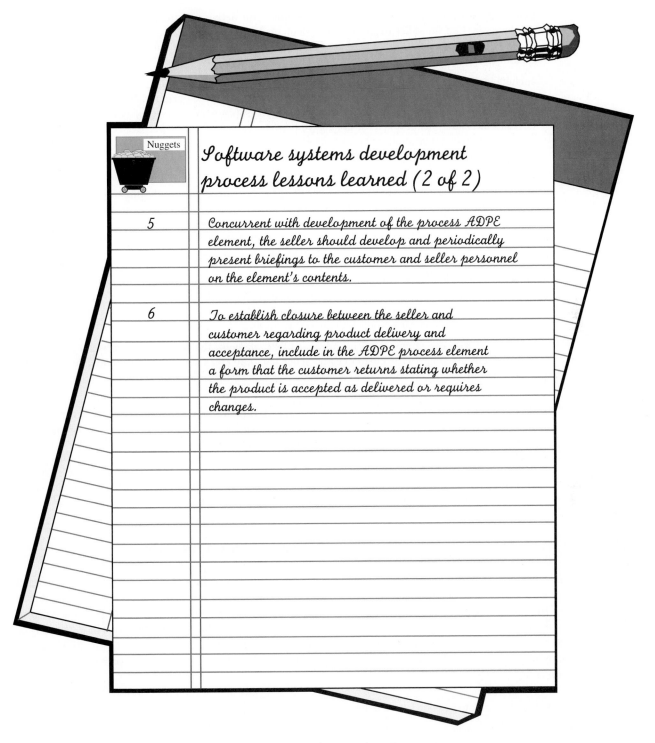

Software systems development process lessons learned (2 of 2)

Nuggets	
5	Concurrent with development of the process ADPE element, the seller should develop and periodically present briefings to the customer and seller personnel on the element's contents.
6	To establish closure between the seller and customer regarding product delivery and acceptance, include in the ADPE process element a form that the customer returns stating whether the product is accepted as delivered or requires changes.

FIGURE 3–4 *Continued*

assurance activities) in developing software products for delivery to the customer and (2) the roles of the customer and the seller organizational elements in performing these activities.** The generic activities should encompass the spectrum of activities from the receipt of a customer SOW to customer feedback on the delivered products.

3. **Include in the ADPE process element a figure showing the process in terms of the (1) generic activities, (2) major communications paths connecting the activities, (3) organization responsible for performing each activity, and (4) products produced.** The software systems development process figure establishes the "way" business is to be conducted between the buyer/user and seller. The explicit labeling of activities and communication paths and detailing organizational responsibilities defines the terms to be used by everyone. People understand what individual responsibilities are and how their particular contribution fits into the bigger picture.

4. **Seller senior management should empower the project manager to apply prescriptively the generic activities in the ADPE process element.** The software systems development process element should therefore be written so that it allows the project manager to perform the activities in the order and to the extent consistent with project schedules and available resources. The process ADPE element should not be written as a cookbook. There is no one way to build software. Step-by-step processes that are to be mechanically followed simply cannot account for the spectrum of contingencies that can arise during software systems development. People are the most important part of the process. However, the process helps to provide consistent software development. When people make a considered decision to apply prescriptively the documented process, the decision needs to be communicated so that everyone understands what resources the process requires and what products are to be produced.

5. **Concurrent with development of the process ADPE element, the seller should develop and periodically present briefings to the customer and seller personnel on the element's contents.** People need an opportunity to ask specific questions on how the software systems development process affects their day-to-day activities.

6. **To establish closure between the seller and customer regarding product delivery and acceptance, include in the ADPE process element a form that the customer returns upon product receipt and a form that the customer returns stating whether the product is accepted as delivered or requires changes.** Customer satisfaction is tied, in part, to customer feedback. Customer acceptance forms provide the customer (i.e., buyer/user) another opportunity to comment on the delivered product. As subsequently explained, we suggest that customer feedback concerning a delivered product can be expressed as (1) accepted as delivered, (2) accepted with minor changes, or (3) rejected.

3.3 SOFTWARE SYSTEMS DEVELOPMENT PROCESS OVERVIEW

As stated earlier, there is no one way to build software systems. If there were, software systems development would have been reduced to an assembly-line operation long ago. However, we believe there are fundamental development principles that help increase the likelihood of software systems development success. Software systems development principles provide the foundation for (1) examining an existing organizational software systems development process or (2) defining an organizational development process. As subsequently described, we believe the following principles provide this foundation:

- Plan the work to be done before doing it.
- Obtain agreement on defined responsibilities.
- Establish and empower self-directed work teams.
- Establish checks and balances.
- Maintain continual customer and seller interaction.
- Monitor project progress.

- Mentor project managers and train work teams.
- Provide interim review on project progress.
- Provide feedback on deliverables.
- Improve the software systems development process.

We believe these principles are fundamental to an organization's way of doing software systems development business.

In what sense does software systems development involve a "process" or "a way of doing business"? If an organization is in its beginnings or infancy, there may be an idea or concept of how to conduct the software systems development business, but the process may not be well-defined. However, the concept may be well understood by a few key individuals. As the organization matures, the development process may mature, and more individuals may understand the process. At the other end of the spectrum are well-established organizations. In such organizations, there may be a "defined" development process, but it may not be documented. Of course, there are organizations, both new and well established, that do have documented organizational software systems development processes. Regardless of what your particular situation may be, the concept of "process" can be viewed as a tool to communicate and explain the activities involved with consistently developing software systems that (1) are delivered on time, (2) are delivered within budget, and (3) do what the customers want the systems to do.

Figure 3–5 is an overview of our example organizational software systems development process. Our example process starts with a customer's statement of work (SOW) and ends with customer feedback regarding the delivered products (and supporting services). This process allows for the planning, evolving, and reviewing of products (i.e., documents, computer code, data) for delivery to the customer. The figure has round-edged rectangles, rectangles, and labeled arrows. The round-edged rectangles represent customer-related responsibilities, and the rectangles represent the seller-related responsibilities. The labeled arrows represent major communication paths and associated information.

As shown in Figure 3–5, our example organizational process consists of the following major elements:

- Customer.
- Seller Process Engineering Group.
- Customer/Seller Development Team (i.e., customer project manager, seller development team).
- Change Control Board (CCB).
- Seller Senior Management.
- Major communication paths.

Figure 3–5 also shows the following responsible agents and associated process activities:

- **Customer.** Prepares SOW, Negotiates Agreement, and Reviews Delivered Products for Acceptance.
- **Seller Process Engineering Group.** Plans the Work to Accomplish the Customer's SOW Tasks.
- **Customer Project Manager.** Communicates with Seller Project Manager.
- **Seller Project Manager.** Communicates with Customer Project Management and Evolves Software Product(s).
- **Lead Developer.** Establishes Project Files.
- **Lead Developer or Moderator.** Conducts Peer Reviews.

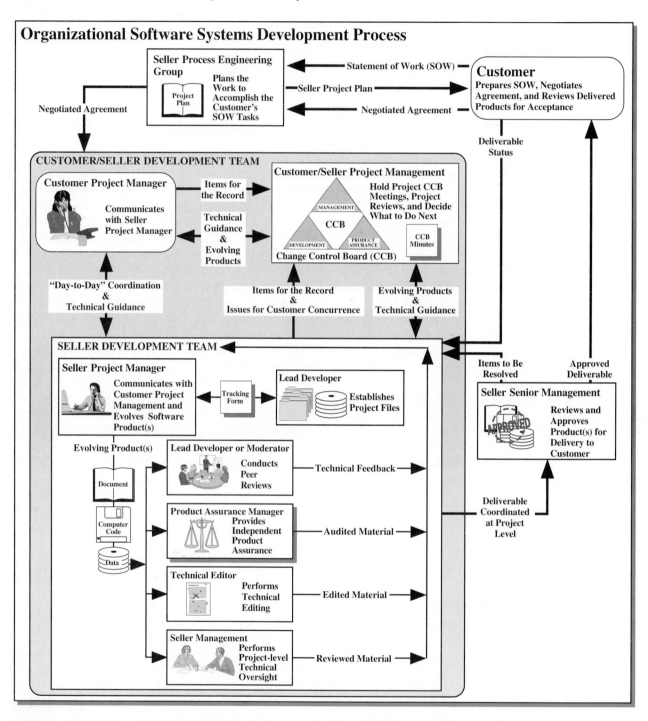

FIGURE 3–5 Our example organizational software systems development process is a closed-looped process that starts and ends with the customer.

- **Product Assurance Manager.** Provides Independent Product Assurance.
- **Technical Editor.** Performs Technical Editing.
- **Seller Management.** Performs Project-level Technical Oversight.

The software systems development process activities are linked together by the major communication paths. As shown in Figure 3–5, along each communication path information is transferred from one process element to another. The information transferred consists of the following items:

- Statement of Work (SOW).
- Seller Project Plan.
- Negotiated Agreement.
- Items for the Record.
- Technical Guidance and Evolving Products.
- "Day-to-Day" Coordination and Technical Guidance.
- Items for the Record and Issues for Customer Concurrence.
- Evolving Products and Technical Guidance.
- Tracking Form.
- Evolving Products (i.e., documents, computer code, or data).
- Technical Feedback.
- Audited Material.
- Edited Material.
- Reviewed Material.
- Deliverable Coordinated at Project Level.
- Items to Be Resolved.
- Approved Deliverable.
- Deliverable Status.

As shown in Figure 3–5, the process starts in the upper right-hand corner when the customer prepares a *statement of work (SOW)* that details what the customer wants. The seller's process engineering group "plans the work to accomplish the customer's SOW tasks" and provides the customer with a *seller project plan.* Upon mutual agreement, the customer provides the seller with a *negotiated agreement* which triggers the customer and seller development activities.[3] These activities involve management, development, and product assurance systems disciplines.

The seller project manager "communicates with the customer and evolves the software product(s)." Regardless of how the products evolve, the seller development team (1) establishes project files, (2) conducts peer reviews, (3) provides independent product assurance, (4) performs technical editing, and (5) performs project-level technical oversight. The seller development team evolves the products and communicates with the customer project manager to discuss issues that require customer concurrence.

---

[3]Notice that the customer/seller development team encompasses both customer and seller activities. We believe that both parties must actively participate in the development process. Without such joint participation, the risk of the project failing increases. The notion that a customer provides the seller with an SOW containing requirements and then checking on the project, say, six months later, is a prescription for disaster. At the same time, the customer needs to be careful not to get so involved that such involvement gets in the way of the seller doing the job.

The customer project manager "provides technical guidance to the seller project manager" as the project unfolds. Both the customer and the seller project managers "hold project CCBs, project reviews, and decide what to do next." After the project products are coordinated by the customer and seller project managers, the products are sent to the seller senior management for review and approval before being delivered to the customer.

The seller senior management may identify *items to be resolved* before the product is delivered to the customer. In this case, the seller development team resolves the items and resubmits the product to the seller senior management for approval. If all items are resolved, the *approved deliverable* is provided to the customer for acceptance. The customer provides feedback on the *deliverable status* with respect to its acceptability.

One question someone may ask is, "How could my existing organizational life cycle development activities and technologies fit into the example organizational software systems development process?" As shown in Figure 3–6, your existing life cycle development activities plug into the following seller development team activities:

- **Seller Process Engineering Group.** Plans the Work to Accomplish the Customer's SOW Tasks.
- **Seller Project Manager.** Communicates with the Customer Project Management and Evolves Software Product(s).

Our example organizational process is independent of a specific life cycle. The process requires, regardless of life cycle and supporting technology, that the preceding process activities be performed to some degree. Your existing life cycle may be traditional systems engineering, prototyping, or information engineering. As subsequently explained, regardless of the life cycle, as a minimum, the project plan and the corresponding negotiated agreement should take into consideration these process activities.

Each of the major elements, corresponding information, and their interaction with one another is detailed in the next four sections.

3.4 CUSTOMER

Our organizational software systems development process begins with the customer. As shown in Figure 3–5, the customer, among other responsibilities, prepares an SOW detailing what the customer wants the seller to do. In the software industry, the SOW can manifest itself in widely different ways. An SOW is called by a variety of different names, such as request for proposal, request for contractor services, or solicitation. In some environments, the SOW may be as short as one sentence or a couple of paragraphs. In other environments, the SOW can manifest itself as a detailed document consisting of hundreds or even thousands of pages. Other SOWs fall somewhere in between.

There are many types of SOWs. Specific SOW types include the following:

- Firm fixed price.
- Fixed price redetermination.
- Fixed price incentive.
- Fixed price level of effort.
- Time and material.
- Cost plus incentive fee.
- Cost plus award fee.
- Cost plus fixed fee.
- Letter contracts.

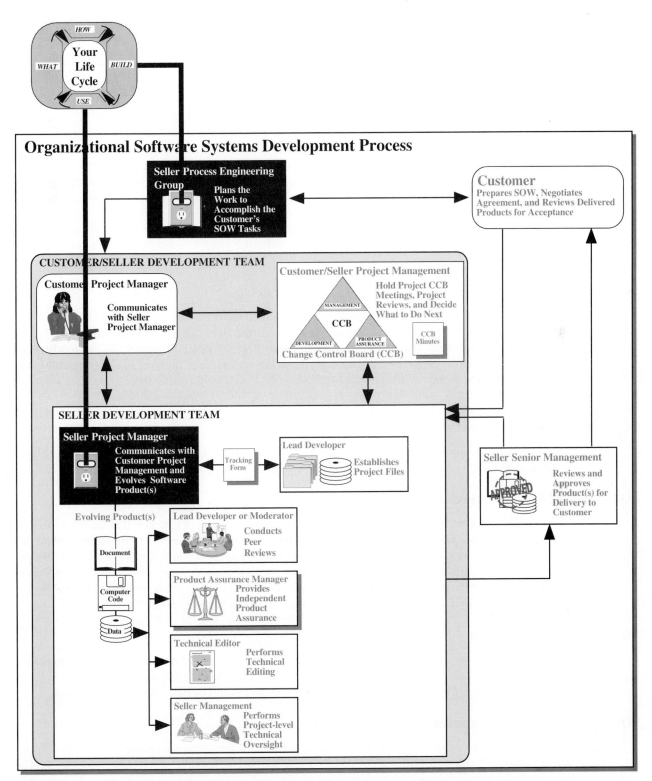

FIGURE 3–6 The software systems development process is independent of product development life cycle and specific product development technologies. The figure shows where you would introduce your life cycle(s) to adapt the process to your organization.

- Delivery order.
- Basic ordering agreement.
- Government owned, contractor operated.

Regardless of the type of SOW, in general, SOWs contain the same basic elements. Because of the varying risks associated with software systems development efforts, SOWs may specify different management approaches and incentives. However, writing a good SOW is difficult. It is difficult to know exactly what is needed. We all get smarter about what we are doing as we do it, but no matter how well an SOW is written, change happens. The flip side of this situation is that writing a corresponding project plan is also difficult. Therefore, depending upon the software systems development effort, the SOW can allow for change as the project proceeds by calling for revisits to tasks to update previously developed products.

Figure 3–7 summarizes twelve tips that are intended to help people who are writing SOWs to overcome the blank-page syndrome. These tips derive from lessons learned using SOWs to do project planning.

SOW Tip 1—Background

The first tip encourages the seller to provide background on the organization, its mission, policies, etc. Background establishes the authority for the work and lets the potential sellers know the SOW is probably real. The background also helps to set some context for the seller. However, as any experienced seller would say, if the SOW is the first time the seller understands the potential customer's background, the likelihood the seller will "win" the work is slim. It helps if the seller understands the potential customer.

SOW Tip 2—Points of Contact

The second tip is aimed at increasing effective communication between the customer and potential seller. Single points of contact help to reduce the confusion of what is really wanted and when.

SOW Tip 3—Task Specification

The third tip is the heart of *what* the customer wants the seller to do. Typically, it is useful if the customer specifies *what* is required and the seller responds with *how* the *what* is to be accomplished and with the dollar amount the customer is willing to spend. Allowing the seller to respond with *how* enables the seller to relate previous successful projects and software systems development processes to the work being requested. The customer can specify the degree of innovation the potential seller should propose or even suggest the criteria for evaluating the seller's proposal.

SOW Tip 4—SOW Writers

The fourth tip stresses the importance of the customer's internally coordinating buyer and user requirements. Such coordination takes time and can affect schedules. Many false starts in software systems development arise from inconsistent or uninformed understandings of what the customer wants.

SOW Tip 5—Task Deliverables

The fifth tip suggests that each task produce a deliverable or provide a supporting service. For example, a customer SOW task requires the seller to develop a requirements specification document. The customer also wants to review interim progress on the specification's evolution in terms of a topic outline and an annotated outline. The customer's dilemma, in part, is to balance visibility into the deliverable's progress with cost and schedule implications of requiring the seller to produce three deliverables

Customer
**Prepares SOW, Negotiates
Agreement, and Reviews Delivered
Products for Acceptance**

CUSTOMER
BUYER
Organization
USER
Organization

Statement of Work (SOW) Tips

1. **Background**—Give background on your organization to include mission, policies governing seller work, legislative commitments, level of understanding of seller software systems development practices.

2. **Points of Contact**—Specify points of contact, including who will be the customer [project]managers interfacing with seller personnel during work accomplishment. At a minimum, a point of contact who has decision-making authority during work accomplishment should be specified. This individual will participate in CCB meetings and will be empowered to provide direction to the seller during work accomplishment.

3. **Task Specification**—Specify the individual tasks that you want the seller to accomplish. Examples of such tasks are the following:

   – Develop and maintain a project plan
   – Write a requirements specification to include two drafts and one final draft
   – Prepare a user's manual
   – Write an acceptance test plan
   – Develop and execute acceptance test procedures.

4. **SOW Writers**—If the buyer and user are from two different organizations, ensure that they jointly prepare the SOW to reduce the likelihood of conflicting direction to the seller at project start-up.

5. **Task Deliverables**—Specify deliverables for each task. Such deliverables generally include both products and services. If the deliverable is a service, include a requirement for some written piece of correspondence that the seller sends you upon completion of service delivery.

6. **Due Dates**—Specify delivery dates for deliverables—but keep in mind that such dates should be subject to negotiation (via a CCB mechanism) as the project proceeds.

7. **SOW Value**—Give some indication of the size of how much you are willing to spend (in some environments, this information may be prohibited for inclusion in a SOW). Keep in mind that during the project planning activity you and the seller may have to iterate on cost versus work to be performed as both sides get a better understanding of what needs to be done.

8. **Life Cycle**—Give some idea of the type of life cycle you would like the seller to try to follow in accomplishing the work. For example, if your SOW is for a new system, indicate that you would like to follow a specific life cycle or let the seller propose one. When you lay out your tasks, allow for revisits to life cycle stages. For example, call for a requirements specification at month two and then call for a requirements specification update at month seven.

9. **Existing Seller Practices**—If the seller has established engineering practices (e.g., the seller has the analogs to ADPE elements that spell out these practices), reference these practices. Similarly, if your organization has policies and procedures that sellers are supposed to follow, reference these items. If, for some reason, the work you want done makes it impractical to use your organization's policies and procedures, indicate which ones are to be waived—and why.

10. **Change Control Board (CCB)**—Call for a CCB-like mechanism to be used throughout the work to maintain visibility into project progress, to provide a trace of this progress, to provide a catalyst for replanning, and to establish a channel for customer/seller dialogue and interaction.

11. **Risk Assessment**—Request the seller to assess the risk of accomplishing the work in your SOW. Request that the seller specify the risk assessment criteria. Also, ask the seller to specify risk mitigation strategies.

12. **SOW Revisions**—Recognize that your SOW may have to be revised one or more times before coming to closure with the seller.

FIGURE 3–7 The SOW (Statement of Work) is the customer's statement of what the customer wants the seller to do. The figure gives tips to help buyers/users write an SOW.

instead of one final deliverable. Many factors need to be considered when deciding how many deliverables should be required. In general, the greater the up-front visibility into a product, the greater the likelihood that once the final product is delivered it will not have to undergo significant change. However, with less visibility into the product, the greater the likelihood that there will be a gross disconnect in expectations and the deliverable will have to be reworked. To balance cost and visibility, perhaps some of the deliverables can undergo less, but mutually agreed upon, review and approval before delivery to the customer.

SOW Tip 6—Due Dates

The sixth tip is to set due dates for deliverables. However, this tip will also remind everyone that, as the project unfolds, there may be a requirement to adjust the due dates. For many contracts there may be only a few designated customer people (e.g., contracting official) who can legally bind the customer with a seller. Furthermore, there may be cases in which any changes to the negotiated agreement can be changed only by the contracting official. If the contracting official is responsible for multiple contracts, it may be impractical to get the contracting official to sign off on every schedule change. In such situations, we suggest that the customer and seller project managers mutually agree to a new schedule, record the agreement at a CCB, and subsequently report the change to the contracting official. We also suggest that project managers be given this authority if the (1) schedule change is not outside the overall negotiated agreement's period of performance and (2) overall contract value does not change.

SOW Tip 7—SOW Value

The seventh tip is aimed at trying to save everyone time and money. If it is possible, it is useful for the customer to give some approximation of the dollar value of the SOW. It makes little sense for a seller to give a million dollar answer to a hundred thousand dollar problem. Just as it is difficult to write a good SOW, it is also difficult to write a responsive proposal (e.g., project plan).

SOW Tip 8—Life Cycle

The eighth tip recommends that the seller either specify a preferred life cycle or let the seller recommend one. It is important that the seller explain how either life cycle fits into the seller organization's software systems development process or way of doing business.

SOW Tip 9—Existing Seller Practices

The ninth tip encourages the seller, if appropriate, to inform the customer of internal seller practices, particularly policies and procedures that are to be followed. If the customer does not want the seller to follow such practices, then the ones that are waived should be by mutual agreement. There are certain engineering practices that many sellers require their organizations to follow (this situation may be true for the customer as well). Not following recognized engineering practices may open the seller to possible criticism, but if the customer agrees, then there should not be a problem.

SOW Tip 10—Change Control Board (CCB)

The tenth tip encourages the use of a CCB to provide visibility into the project and a forum for dealing with the unknown, but anticipated, change that accompanies any software systems development project. In general, we suggest for projects of at least six months' duration, to establish a CCB meeting frequency of no less than monthly. At the beginning, it is preferable to meet more frequently—even weekly. Within these broad guidelines, allow meeting frequency to vary as project events dictate. For projects shorter than six months, CCB meetings held every two weeks is a good starting frequency for governing the project. As the project unfolds, you can adjust this frequency as project events dictate—but try to meet at least monthly. To maintain effective process control, CCB meetings must take place throughout a project.

SOW Tip 11—Risk Assessment

The eleventh tip suggests that the customer require the seller to perform a risk assessment for accomplishing the work specified in the SOW. The seller should explain the specific risk criteria and corresponding risk mitigation strategies.

SOW Tip 12—SOW Revisions

The twelfth tip is offered as a planning factor. Multiple SOW revisions may be necessary, as well as multiple proposals.

As explained in the next section, the SOW is eventually incorporated into a negotiated agreement that authorizes the seller to start working. The customer person responsible for overseeing the technical work to be performed is the customer project manager.

3.5 SELLER PROCESS ENGINEERING GROUP

As shown in Figure 3–5, the customer interacts with the seller process engineering group (PEG) that is responsible for planning the work to accomplish the customer's SOW tasks.[4] The PEG is also responsible for (1) assessing management, development, and product assurance methodologies, (2) establishing, coordinating, and implementing organization policies, guidelines, standards, and procedures within an systems engineering environment (SEE), and (3) providing technical training and project consultation.

Why give the PEG the responsibility for project planning? Would it not be better to make the (eventual) project manager responsible for planning the project? Centralized planning by the PEG (or the centralized coordination of the planning) enables the seller to develop and evolve consistent procedures for responding to customers' SOWs.[5] The PEG is in a position to look across multiple planning efforts and determine what works and what does not. Thus, the PEG can help set in place consistent practices for (1) performing planning start-up activities, (2) selecting the project team members, (3) determining the management, development, and product assurance approaches, (4) establishing the cost estimate, (5) preparing and reviewing the project plan for presentation to the customer, and (6) negotiating with the customer.

The PEG assembles a project planning team that uses the customer's SOW, the organizational software systems development process, and a life cycle to develop a project plan containing project-specific tasks for building the products the customer wants. The customer's SOW details **what** the customer wants in terms of product and services. The organizational process specifies processes that are to be performed during each project. For example, our organizational process states, in part, that each project should have a CCB-like mechanism. In addition, our process states that peer reviews, independent product assurance, technical editing, etc., are to performed during each project. The project plan specifies **how** the what is to be accomplished. Figure 3–8 presents an overview of this project planning concept and consists of the following three panels:

- **Project-Specific Process Planning**. The seller project planning team "prescriptively applies" the organizational software systems development process to the customer's SOW. Here, *prescriptively applies* means

---

[4]There are a number of factors influencing how an organization decides to perform project planning. Such factors include the following: how long an organization has existed, how experienced the people are in writing project plans, and how consistent each plan needs to be to be responsive to customers' SOWs. If your organization is relatively new or is new at project planning, then you may want to have your PEG (usually consisting of experienced people) be responsible for project planning as your organization starts up. Once the organization reaches critical mass and project teams settle into a routine with their customers, the PEG's emphasis can shift from planning the projects to providing guidance to project management and quality assurance oversight over project plans. As the organization matures, the project planning responsibilities can be reassessed.

[5]As an organization matures its project planning practices, it may decide to transition the actual project planning details to the individual project teams. The PEG can then serve as a (1) centralized coordinator of project planning, (2) quality assurance reviewer of each project plan, and (3) coach/mentor for project planners. In other words, as the organization matures, project planning responsibilities can be delegated to other organizational elements.

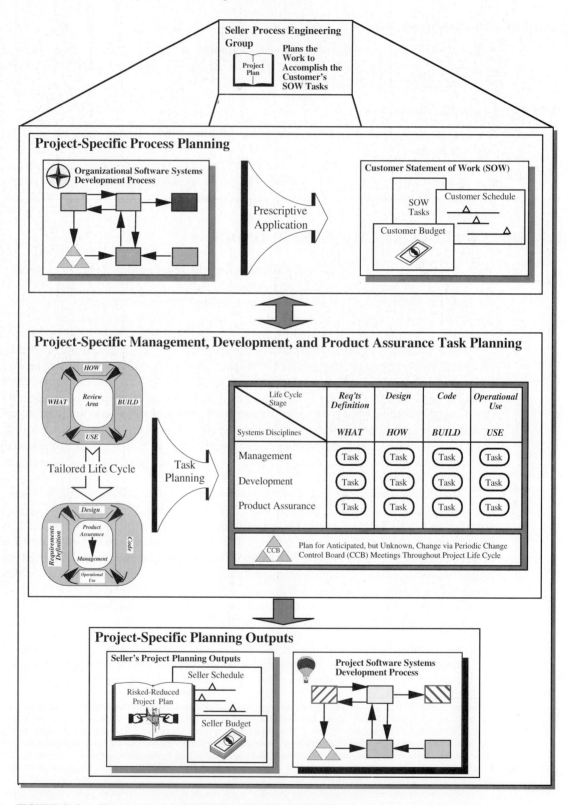

FIGURE 3–8 The customer's SOW, the organizational software systems development process, and the life cycle set the context for planning the project-specific work.

"adapting organizational process activities to project realities (e.g., budget and schedule constraints)." We use the qualifier "prescriptive" to convey that, once the SOW is examined and diagnosed, the project planning team sets the organizational process dosage (e.g., how many CCB meetings are needed, how many peer reviews are needed, how many product assurance reviews are needed, how much technical editing is needed, etc.).

- **Project-Specific Management, Development, and Product Assurance Task Planning**. Given the realities of the customer's SOW and an assessment of how much of the organizational process should be applied, the project planning team constructs the tasks to be performed. They lay out an appropriate life cycle and decide how to integrate the organizational process activities. The life cycle is tailored to project specifics for the management, development, and product assurance tasks necessary to produce the products and services the customer wants. The result of the task planning is two-fold: (1) a risk-reduced project plan and (2) a corresponding project software systems development process. Once a project plan is prepared, reviewed, and approved by seller senior management, the plan is delivered to the customer for consideration and subsequent negotiation.

- **Project-Specific Planning Outputs**. The risk-reduced project plan contains specific tasks with a proposed schedule and corresponding budget. The tasks express how the work is to be performed to produce products and services that the customer asked for in the SOW. The project software systems development process is embodied in the project plan and is consistent with the planned schedule, budget, and work to be accomplished.

As a result of the PEG planning the work (or coordinating the planning), the organizational process is adapted to an SOW to define management, development, and product assurance tasks appropriate to the SOW. This adaptation, defined in the project plan, details the specific life cycle steps, techniques, and tools needed to develop project-specific products. Once the customer receives the project plan, negotiations take place. Once the negotiations are concluded, a negotiated agreement (which embodies the project plan) is used by the customer/seller development team to guide the work to be done.

3.6 CUSTOMER/SELLER DEVELOPMENT TEAM AND CHANGE CONTROL BOARD (CCB)

As shown in Figure 3–5, the customer/seller development team consists of the customer project manager and the seller development team. Team members meet at the project change control board (CCB) to hold project reviews and decide what to do next. CCB meetings produce formal minutes that capture project decisions, action items, and discussion.

Customer Project Manager

The customer project manager is the counterpart to the seller project manager. Figure 3–9 shows how the customer and seller project managers interact with each other. The customer project manager coordinates on a "day-to-day" basis with the seller project manager and provides technical guidance to the seller development team, primarily through the seller project manager. This relatively informal day-to-day communication happens through conversations on the telephone or, for example, during a conversation when both people are standing around the coffee machine taking a break. Many times these "informal" communications affect project deliverables, schedule, and resources. Sometimes the customer project manager receives technical guidance or insight from the seller project manager and/or the development team. For example, the seller may provide the customer insight into the technical feasibility of using computer aided software engineering (CASE) technology. The customer may use this seller-provided technical guidance to assess the cost and schedule impact on the project.

The customer project manager also provides more formal communication to the seller through the CCB where specific action items, due dates, and responsibilities are assigned. The customer/seller development team holds CCB meetings to discuss specific items for the record. The customer may

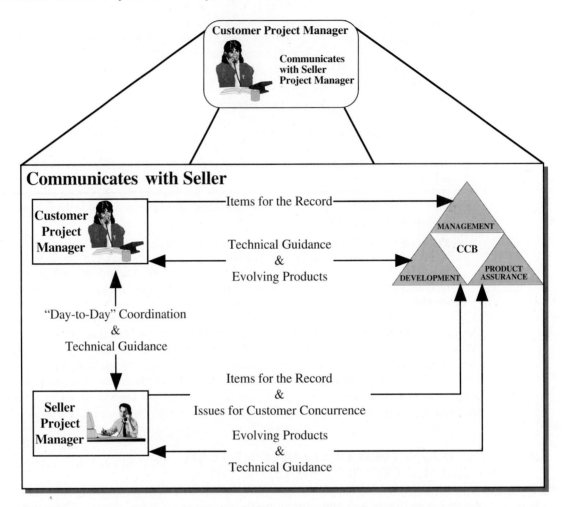

FIGURE 3–9 The customer project manager and the seller project manager constantly communicate with each other. Such communication includes technical guidance, day-to-day coordination on project activities, items for the record, and issues for customer concurrence. This type of manager-to-manager communication helps to increase the likelihood that the evolving products will embody what the customer wants.

provide technical guidance to the seller regarding, for example, required changes to the schedule. The customer project manager can also receive technical guidance or recommendations from the seller development team. For example, the seller may provide guidance to the customer regarding alternative approaches for meeting the new schedule requirements. The seller may also seek technical guidance from the customer regarding a particular product. For example, the seller may need clarification on specific requirements that are to be incorporated into the requirements specification. Furthermore, the CCB serves as a forum for the customer project manager to discuss seller (1) items for the record or (2) issues that require the customer's concurrence.

Regardless of the communication paths shown in Figure 3–9, it is important that customer/seller communications be captured and made a part of the project records. Informal communications can be simply written down in a short memo (handwritten is okay) and be incorporated into the more formal CCB meeting minutes.[6]

---

[6]Chapter 4 discusses the CCB mechanism in detail.

Seller Development Team

The seller development team is responsible for accomplishing the work specified in the negotiated agreement. The team includes the following roles: (1) a seller project manager, (2) a lead developer, (3) product assurance personnel, (4) a technical editor, and (5) management for the project manager. Depending upon the negotiated agreement, one team member may perform one or more roles. For example, if the project is relatively small, the seller project manager may also serve the role as the lead developer. The project team performs the following "generic" product development activities:

- Communicates with Customer Project Management and Evolves Software Product(s).
- Establishes Project Files.
- Conducts Peer Reviews.
- Provides Independent Product Assurance.
- Performs Technical Editing.
- Performs Project-level Technical Oversight.

We use the phrase "generic product development activities" for two reasons. First, as previously discussed, when the project is being planned, the seller's organizational software systems development process is prescriptively applied to the customer's SOW to account for budget and schedule realities. An appropriate life cycle is tailored to contain project-specific management, development, and product assurance tasks. The resulting project plan contains the specific life cycle steps, techniques, tools, and resources needed to evolve and deliver project-specific products. Second, the project plan then undergoes negotiation with the customer, and the result (hopefully!) is a negotiated agreement. This agreement contains the final project-specific details.

We now describe the generic activities that were just listed. Remember, our example organizational process requires that the generic product development activities are to be performed to some degree and in some order on any software systems development project. The degree and sequence of these generic activities are a function, in part, of the (1) project goals and scope and (2) resource and schedule constraints. These generic activities are designed to help reduce the risk inherent in any software systems development project. The following discussion provides additional detail on the generic activities.

Seller Development Team: Communicates with Customer Project Management and Evolves Software Product(s)   The seller project manager is the front-line manager responsible for carrying out the work specified in the negotiated agreement. The seller project manager (1) is the "day-to-day" primary point-of-contact with the customer project manager, (2) supervises the seller development team, (3) updates the project plan (e.g., revises schedules as the project unfolds) within the scope of the negotiated agreement, (4) works with the product assurance manager to define and implement product assurance plans, (5) maintains cost/schedule control of management and development resources,[7] and (6) is a participant in the evolution of the required software products.

The seller project manager is a proactive management position in which the manager takes the initiative to communicate with the customer as needed. The seller project manager frequently communicates with the customer to verify assumptions, clarify understandings of what needs to be done, and resolve known and/or anticipated risks. We use the term "frequently" to stress the point that the software products are not to be evolved without the participation of the customer. Again, the notion of the

---

[7]In our organizational software systems development process, the product assurance manager controls project product assurance resources and the scheduling of these resources. This control is one way of making product assurance "independent." In many organizations, the project manager controls *all* project resources, including product assurance.

customer throwing a list of requirements over a fence to the seller developers and then checking on progress, say six months later, is a prescription for failure. The seller project manager must be a proactive communicator.

The seller project manager also evolves the following software products:

- **Document**. Words and graphics on paper packaged into a document.
- **Computer code**. Computer code on magnetic media packaged into a system or system modification.
- **Data**. Data packaged into a database on magnetic media.

These products result from the accomplishment of the project-specific management, development, and product assurance tasks detailed in the negotiated agreement. Figure 3–10 illustrates the notion of evolving the software products.

A software product typically starts out as a concept or idea. As the project unfolds, the products take shape. For example, a requirements document evolves from a topic outline, to an annotated outline, to a detailed specification. As the requirements specification takes shape, the computer code also takes shape. Early in the project, there is a concept of what the computer code will do and how it may be organized. As the requirements specification evolves to a design specification, the computer code takes on additional shape. Equally important is the evolution of data. Simply stated, as the project unfolds, data evolve.[8]

Often complementing the software products are services. Example services include training the user community on the developed software product or providing hot-line support to users who have questions on how to use the product in an operational environment. Typically, a service is work that is required by the negotiated agreement and whose primary purpose is not to produce a software product. Figure 3–11 illustrates example services. Other example services include such things as conference support and demonstrations. If support materials (e.g., conference brochures) are not deliverables, they should still be peer reviewed, technically edited, etc. The seller project manager should give visibility to the preparation and delivery of services. Example ways to achieve visibility are (1) seller monthly progress reports, (2) letters informing the customer project manager that services were provided, and (3) CCB minutes.

Regardless of whether products are produced or services are provided, as the project unfolds, the customer and seller increase their understanding of what needs to be done in order to accomplish the project's tasks. Typically, this increased understanding results in changes to what was planned in the project plan and what was agreed to in the negotiated agreement. To accommodate these changes, the seller development team, in concert with the customer, make adjustments to the project management, development, and product assurance tasks. Figure 3–12 illustrates this point.

The seller project manager prescriptively applies the project software systems development process to the negotiated agreement. As a result, adjustments are made to task-level activities. For example, toward the end of the Design Stage, the product assurance personnel compare the design specification with the requirements specification to check for requirements traceability. It is discovered that the design (1) contains three requirements that are not in the requirements specification and (2) does not address two requirements that are in the requirements specification. Upon examination and discussion, the customer agrees with the seller that the new requirements are needed things the customer wants, but the customer still wants the seller to include the two "missing" requirements. In addition, the period of performance cannot be extended, the project budget cannot be increased, and, of course, the seller wants to keep the customer happy. (Set aside for the moment the issue of how three new re-

---

[8]When the customer writes the SOW, it is important for the customer to state how much of the product evolution should be customer-approved before the seller proceeds from one evolution to the next. For example, if the final product is a requirements specification, does the customer approve a topic outline before the seller proceeds to evolve an annotated outline? Customer approvals affect cost and schedule.

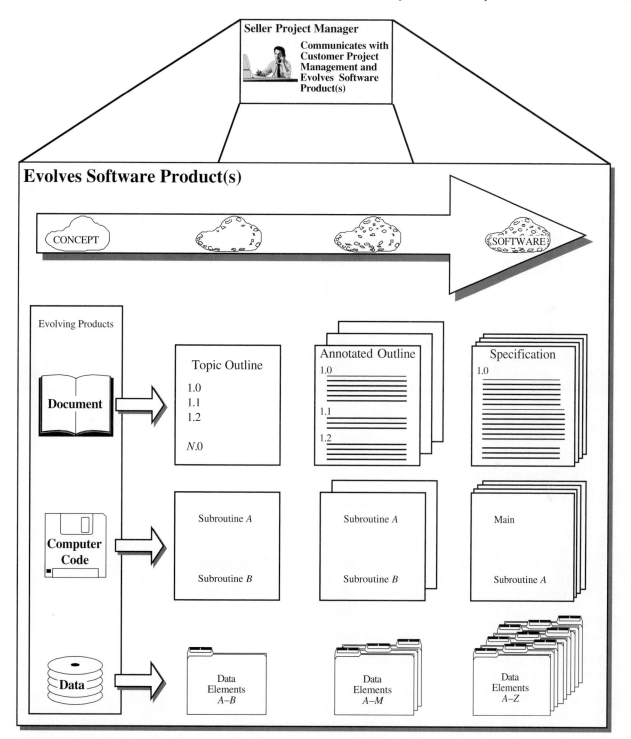

FIGURE 3–10 *Evolves software product(s)* means "applying the process activities that take a product from a vaguely defined concept to a completely filled-in product that embodies customer's requirements."

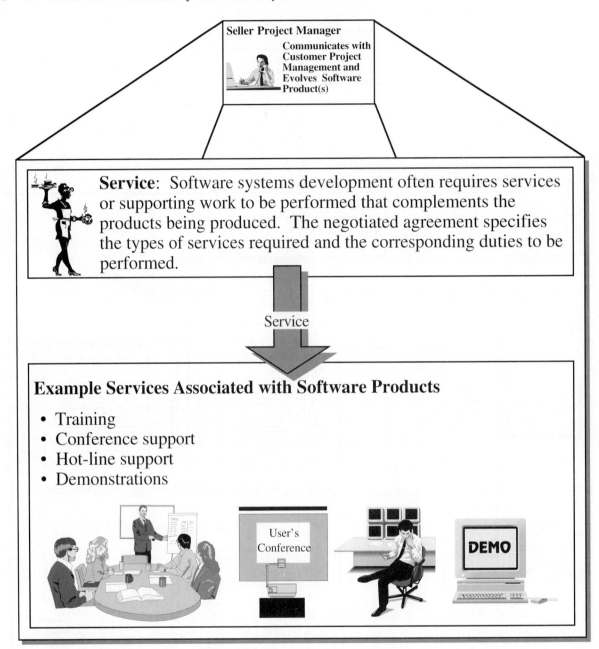

FIGURE 3–11 Services, like the products, are planned in accordance with the organizational software systems development process.

quirements found their way into the design.) Since the budget cannot be increased, the seller project manager proposes that some of the deliverables be combined into a single document. This potential solution keeps the schedule and budget intact but reduces the scope of the planned documents. Assuming that the proposal is acceptable to the customer, the work to be performed using the project development process is adjusted and the project proceeds. If the proposal is not accepted, additional discussion is necessary. Regardless, the project development process needs to be applied prescriptively to the negotiated agreement.

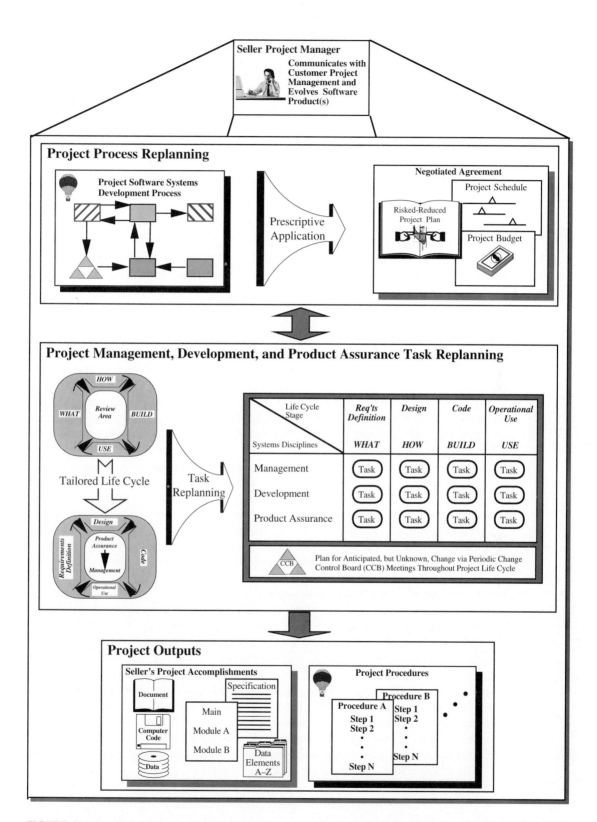

FIGURE 3–12   The seller development team prescriptively applies the project's development process to the negotiated agreement that embodies the seller's project plan. The results of this prescriptive application are the following: (1) products (and associated services) and (2) project-level development procedures that are consistent with the resource expenditures, completed work schedules, and work accomplished.

The seller project manager is also responsible for developing project-specific procedures or step-by-step instructions for performing recurring task activities. For example, as part of the organization's Application Development Process Environment (ADPE), there may exist a configuration management (CM) guideline delineating suggestions for implementing CM on a project. The seller project manager can use the guideline to help develop a project-specific procedure for CM.

Seller Development Team: Establishes Project Files   The lead developer for each deliverable product is responsible for establishing the project files. The minimum set of files required may or may not be specified in the negotiated agreement. However, establishing the product's project file is one of the first steps for ensuring that the product is properly formatted, coordinated, reviewed, and approved. To aid the lead developer performing the steps to deliver a product to the customer, we suggest the use of a product tracking form. Figure 3–13 presents an overview of a generic product tracking form that is tied to our example organizational software systems development process.

The form tracks the software product through the organizational process of peer reviews, product assurance support, technical editing, project-level and organization-level management review and approval, and customer receipt and acceptance. The lead developer is responsible for (1) conducting or establishing peer reviews, (2) coordinating with product assurance personnel, (3) coordinating with technical editor(s) when the product is a document, (4) ensuring that the product is ready for management review and approval, and (5) tracking the product throughout the software systems development process.

The form literally makes the process visible and, in effect, provides the lead developer with a self-auditing technique to help ensure that the process is followed. Hopefully not, but if the customer has a problem with a delivered product, the tracking form can help provide some insight into what was done and what was not done.

The form is particularly useful to project and senior management. It provides management with some insight into how and when the product was produced. For example, when the product and the tracking form are presented to the program manager for review and approval, the program manager knows who within the organization is involved with the development of the product. For those products produced by newer members of the organization, the program manager may decide to spend a little extra time to ensure that the product is ready for delivery to the customer. In those cases where the product may need some additional attention before delivery to the customer, the program manager may ask the project manager to improve the product. Subsequently, if appropriate, the program manager may decide additional training or mentoring is needed within the organization. Perhaps when the program manager is convinced that project managers understand what to do, the final approval authority for certain products may be delegated to the project managers.

Figure 3–14 shows an example tracking form linked to our example organizational software systems development process. To help you use this form, we explain how the tracking form is constructed. The form layout assumes an organization consisting of a collection of projects headed by a program manager. The program manager is supported by project managers who have front-line, day-to-day responsibility for the projects. The layout also assumes that the organization includes (1) a Deliverable Support Center (DSC) that provides document production support and a centralized product repository, (2) an independent product assurance organization, and (3) a process engineering group (PEG) responsible for defining and implementing a systems engineering environment (SEE).

The example form consists of the following sections:

- Project File Establishment at Deliverable Support Center (DSC).

- Technical Review of Product.

- Final Coordination with DSC.

- Project File Management.

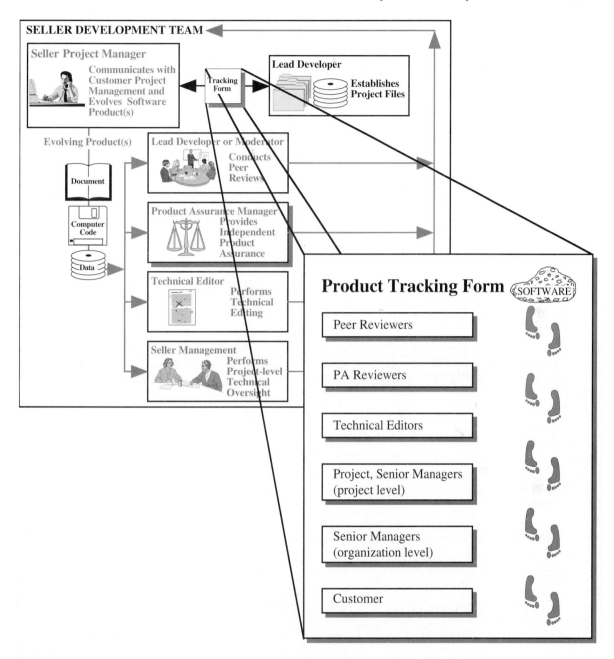

FIGURE 3–13 The lead developer of a product is responsible for establishing the necessary project files and tracking the product through the development process. The tracking form, as its name implies, is used, in part, to track a product as it progresses through the software systems development process.

- Comments/Issues.
- Management Review and Approval.
- Customer Receipt and Approval.

The tracking form corresponds to a product working its way through our software systems development process. As the tracking form indicates, establishing the project files is first, and receiving the

SELLER DELIVERABLE TRACKING FORM

PROJECT FILE ESTABLISHMENT at Deliverable Support Center (DSC)

Product Title: _____

Lead Developer(s): _____

Contributor(s): _____

Product Control Number: _____ Charge Number: _____

Contract Number/Name: _____

Date & Time Product Is Due to Customer: _____

TECHNICAL REVIEW of PRODUCT

_____   _____
Peer Reviewer or Moderator   Technical Editor (documents only)

_____   _____
Product Assurance Reviewer or Manager   Project-level Technical Oversight Management

FINAL COORDINATION with DSC

_____   _____
Deliverable Support Center Manager   Lead Developer

PROJECT FILE MANAGEMENT

Hardcopy filed at _____

_____
Lead Developer

Electronic copy filed at _____

COMMENTS/ISSUES

_____
_____
_____
_____
_____

MANAGEMENT REVIEW and APPROVAL

_____ ☐ concur   ☐ nonconcur   _____ _____
Project Manager   signature   date

_____ ☐ concur   ☐ nonconcur   _____ _____
Process Engineering Group Representative   signature   date

_____ ☐ concur   ☐ nonconcur   _____ _____
Business Manager (costing)   signature   date

_____ ☐ approved   ☐ other action   _____ _____
Program Manager   for release   signature   date

_____   _____ _____
Delivery and Distribution Representative   signature   date

CUSTOMER RECEIPT and APPROVAL

☐ Received Customer Receipt of Deliverable Form

☐ Received Customer Acceptance of Deliverable Form

Received written notification that deliverable requires additional work and notified Project Manager upon receipt ☐

[Form Number]   [Form Issue Date]

FIGURE 3–14   Here is an example of a seller deliverable tracking form that can be used with our organizational software systems development process.

customer's approval is last. However, there is no one way through the process, and therefore, there is no one way to use the tracking form. In addition, the way a product is tracked is tied, in part, to the product type. In general, the tracking form is used in its entirety to track a document. If the document is a seller project plan, then the process engineering group representative and business manager are required to concur or nonconcur before the plan is submitted to the program manager for approval. In general, the tracking form is used in its entirety to track the evolution of a computer code or database deliverable. However, certain signatures may not be required. For example, a technical editor does not review computer code or a database. Regardless, it is the lead developer's responsibility to work closely with other project and/or organization people to ensure that the product goes through the software systems development process. We briefly describe below each section of the form. This description also offers insight into what we mean by prescriptive application of the software systems development process.

Project File Establishment at Deliverable Support Center (DSC) Section

The seller project manager decides who the lead developer is for each required product. The lead developer obtains a tracking form from the DSC manager and establishes the required project files. This form section provides, in part, the DSC with the necessary information for coordinating activities with the lead developer as the product evolves. It is the lead developer's responsibility to (1) indicate on the form who is going to do what and in what order and (2) obtain the necessary signatures.

In general, a form action is completed when the indicated signatory signs the tracking form. For those form actions requiring concurrence or nonconcurrence, the action is completed when the indicated signatory checks the appropriate box and signs the form. We stress that when someone nonconcurs, the lead developer should try to resolve any issue with the person. If the situation cannot be worked out or if the lead developer is not available, the signatory is required to detail the reasons for the nonconcurrence in the comments/issues section. The tracking form is then forwarded to the next indicated person.

Technical Review of Product Section

The technical review of a product may proceed serially or in parallel, depending upon the particular situation. The peer reviewer signature indicates that one or more peer reviews were conducted. The technical editor signature indicates that a document underwent technical editing. The product assurance signature indicates that (1) a document has been audited or (2) computer code or a database has been tested according to the customer/seller agreed-upon set of procedures. If the testing is not done, the lead developer indicates in the comment section the reason for not testing and the corresponding risks. Project-level technical oversight is a seller management prerogative.

Final Coordination with DSC Section

Before the product is submitted to seller management for review and approval, the DSC manager and lead developer package the product in the form it is to be delivered to the customer. This final coordination provides an opportunity to specify last-minute delivery instructions.

Project File Management Section

The lead developer is responsible for indicating where the product can be located and ensuring that the product is filed appropriately.

Comments/Issues Section

Anyone involved in the product evolution writes explanatory information in this section. For example, the project manager may indicate to the delivery and distribution person that an extra copy is needed. The program manager may indicate that additional information is needed for a cover letter.

Management Review and Approval Section

This section implies a sequence. In general, the project manager reviews the product before submitting it to the program manager. Once the product is approved for release to the customer, the program manager gives the product to the delivery and distribution person. As indicated previously, when the product is a seller project plan, the process engineering group representative and the business manager review the product before submitting it to the program manager.

Customer Receipt and Approval Section

In addition to the product, the lead developer also provides the program manager with a cover letter, a customer receipt form, and a customer acceptance of deliverable form. The cover letter informs the customer of the specific product being delivered and any special circumstances surrounding the product's development. The customer receipt form is a self-addressed, return receipt that informs the seller that the product is received by the customer. Figure 3–15 provides an example receipt form.

The customer receipt form is used to establish closure between the customer and seller regarding product delivery. Such a form helps to reduce the likelihood of a product being delivered to the wrong individual. When the product is delivered to the customer project manager or designated representative, the customer signs the form. Upon receipt by the Deliverable Support Center (DSC), the designated DSC representative updates the tracking form in the central repository and informs the lead developer.

A customer acceptance of deliverable form is also delivered to the customer project manager. Figure 3–16 is an example of such a form.

The customer acceptance of deliverable form is used to establish closure between the customer and seller regarding the state of the delivered product. Such a form helps customer feedback. When the product is delivered to the customer project manager (or designated representative), the customer reviews the deliverable, decides the deliverable status, signs the form, and returns it to the seller. In this

---

CUSTOMER RECEIPT OF DELIVERABLE FORM

I acknowledge receipt of the following [**Project Name**] (Contract #) deliverable:

[**Title of Deliverable**]

Product Control Number: [**Actual product control or release number**]

Project Manager: [**Name of Project Manager**]

_____   _____
Customer Signature   Date of Receipt

[**Form Number**]   [**Form Issue Date**]

FIGURE 3–15 Here is an example of a customer receipt of deliverable form that can be used with our organizational software systems development process. The return address is on the reverse side.

CUSTOMER ACCEPTANCE OF DELIVERABLE FORM

To: **[Seller name and address, and, possibly, project/program name]**

Attn: **[Name of seller organization responsible for maintaining deliverable repository]**

The following deliverable, as required by **[customer/seller contract name/number]** has been received and reviewed in accordance with the negotiated agreement:

[Title of deliverable]
[Product control number]
[Name of seller project manager]

This deliverable:

☐ Is accepted as written.   ☐ Is accepted with minor changes as indicated below.

☐ Requires changes to be negotiated.

MINOR REQUIRED CHANGES: _____

_____

_____

_____

_____

_____

OTHER COMMENTS: _____

_____

_____

_____

_____

_____

_____   _____
Customer Signature   Date Signed
[Form Number]   **[Form Issue Date]**

FIGURE 3–16 Here is an example of a customer acceptance of deliverable form that can be used with our organizational software systems development process.

example, the deliverable status can be (1) accepted as written, (2) accepted with minor changes, or (3) requires changes to be negotiated. The time period for customer review is detailed in the negotiated agreement. The negotiated agreement also details what customer acceptance means. Regardless, upon receipt by the DSC, the designated DSC representative updates the tracking form in the central repository and informs the lead developer. If the customer indicates that there are required changes, then the DSC representative informs the lead developer, the seller project manager, and the seller program manager. The seller management then decides how to respond to the "required changes." The DSC representative then updates the tracking form in the central repository.

Figure 3–17 summarizes the seller DSC functions. The specific responsibilities vary with the way an organization is set up. For example, if your organization has only one project, you may decide that a DSC is really a project function. If on the other hand your organization has multiple projects and they range from one-person projects to twenty-person projects, you may decide that a DSC is a neces-

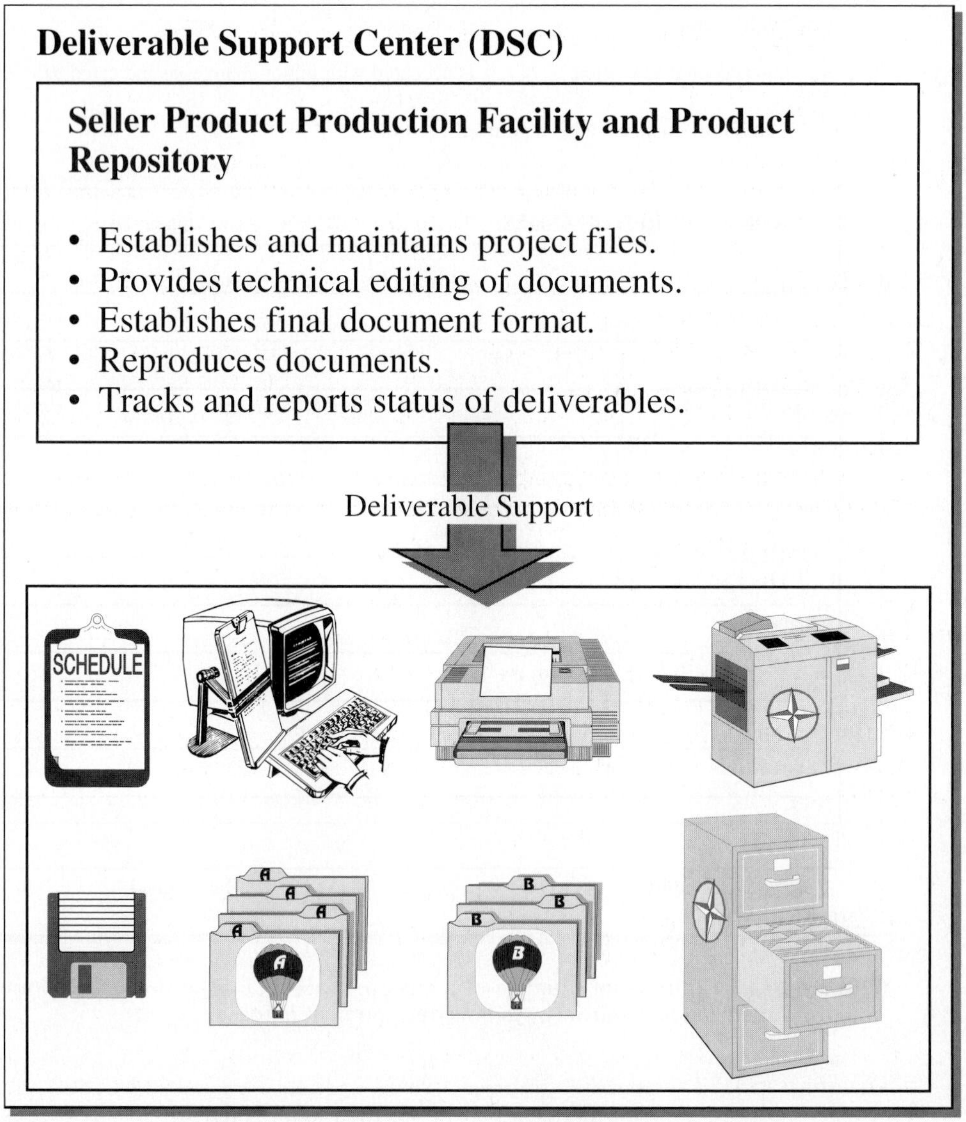

FIGURE 3–17 This figure shows our example seller Deliverable Support Center functions.

sity. Furthermore, the one-person projects generally cannot afford the cost of full-time personnel to provide technical editing, so the DSC could provide this service. The larger projects may have their own technical editors, and in this case, these project editors could follow the DSC guidelines for formatting documents.

Up to this point in our discussion of the seller development team generic activities, we have covered (1) communicating with the customer project management and evolving software products and (2) establishing project files. We now are going to describe the generic activity that deals with peer reviews.

Seller Development Team: Conducts Peer Reviews   The lead developer (or moderator) is responsible for ensuring that the evolving products are peer reviewed. As shown in Figure 3–18, peer reviews provide the lead developer with technical feedback that is used to refine the evolving product.

Peer reviews help the lead developer repeat successful approaches used by colleagues and avoid pitfalls. These insights serve to stabilize the developer's approach and help increase confidence that the product does what it is suppose to do. Time and resources should be planned for conducting peer reviews.

There are many types of peer reviews. For this organizational software systems development process, the lead developer conducts, as a minimum, either (1) one-on-one peer reviews or (2) scheduled peer reviews.

One-on-one peer reviews seek to increase the confidence that a product is complete and appropriate. A colleague who is familiar with the product or has similar experiences provides the lead developer with experienced-based insights. The lead developer and a colleague get together to discuss a portion of the product (e.g., a chapter of a document). As the lead developer provides the colleague with product details, the colleague asks questions and provides suggestions. Because of the limited scope of the review, one-on-one peer reviews do not require large blocks of time and can occur on a frequent basis. The lead developer is responsible for taking notes, following up on the reviewer suggestions, and keeping track of how much time is spent on each product. Such time tracking can be used to improve future planning estimates.

Scheduled peer reviews are larger in scope and usually only involve technical personnel. Depending upon the size of a project, scheduled peer reviews may require a moderator who is responsible for scheduling, organizing, and conducting the review. We recommend that the moderator be a project member. However, the moderator should not be the seller project manager or lead developer, because they could intimidate other reviewers and suppress candid remarks. Scheduled peer reviews should last from two to four hours and include three to six reviewers. The principal goal of the review is to identify technical issues, not to develop technical solutions. Checklists are useful tools to guide the review. The moderator can ask the project developers to prepare checklists for the review. In addition to administrative duties (e.g., reserving a meeting room, assigning the role of scribe to someone), the moderator is also responsible for developing a summary of the review and distributing it within two days. To improve future planning efforts, the lead developer should be responsible for keeping track of how much time is spent on peer-reviewing each product.

Seller Development Team: Provides Independent Product Assurance   The product assurance manager is responsible for providing the required independent product assurance support to the project. (Our organizational software systems development process assumes the organization has a product assurance manager who is responsible for providing product assurance support to all projects within the program.) The seller project manager is responsible for coordinating with the product assurance manager for support for each evolving product. Ensuring that the project has the appropriate amount of independent product assurance support requires clear communication between (1) the product assurance manager and the seller project manager and (2) the product assurance personnel and the seller development team developers.

"Independence" is a function of the following three dimensions:

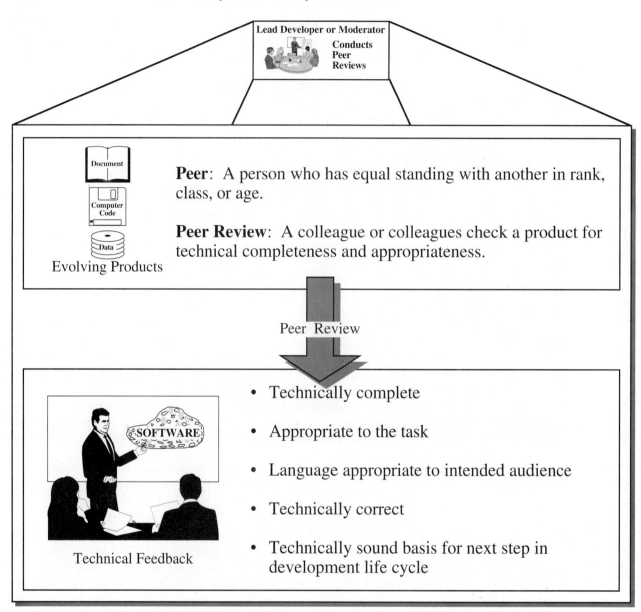

Evolving Products

Peer: A person who has equal standing with another in rank, class, or age.

Peer Review: A colleague or colleagues check a product for technical completeness and appropriateness.

Peer Review

Technical Feedback

- Technically complete

- Appropriate to the task

- Language appropriate to intended audience

- Technically correct

- Technically sound basis for next step in development life cycle

FIGURE 3–18 The peer review balances the product developer's approach with the insights of other people having applicable and comparable experience.

- **Organizational**. Organizational independence can vary from no independence (i.e., the product assurance manager reports to the seller project manager) to total independence (i.e., the product assurance manager reports to the highest levels of management within the organization).

- **Budgetary**. Budgetary independence can vary from no independence (i.e., the product assurance budget is completely controlled by the seller project manger) to total independence (i.e., the product assurance budget is completely controlled by the product assurance manger).

- **Product development**. Product development independence can vary from no independence (i.e., product assurance personnel expend labor helping to build a product, such as writing a section of a requirements specification) to total independence (i.e., product assurance personnel do not expend labor helping to build a product). However, not helping to build a product is not the same thing as not helping to shape a product. Product assurance can and should have a significant impact on how a product eventually turns out.

What do we mean by *independent* product assurance? "Independent" product assurance can vary greatly, and it should be accounted for during project planning. Figure 3–19 shows that product assurance helps to reduce project schedule and budget risks by conducting reviews of the evolving products.

The assigned product assurance personnel provide the planned-for support for each evolving product. Product assurance support consists of the integrated application of (1) quality assurance (QA), (2) verification and validation (V&V), (3) test and evaluation (T&E), and (4) configuration management (CM). The outputs of these activities are generally audited material that contains the results of comparing "what is expected" to "what is observed." The application of these product assurance activities helps to reduce risk, and provide an additional assurance that the product does what it is suppose to do.

Seller Development Team: Performs Technical Editing   The technical editor is responsible for ensuring that a document lacks ambiguity, uses language appropriate to the intended audience, is internally consistent, conforms to organizational standards, and contains no grammatical or spelling errors. As shown in Figure 3–20, technical editors work like the devil to improve the presentation of the document without materially changing the technical content. The technical editor also ensures that the document as a whole hangs together by checking that (1) text and figures are coordinated, (2) the table of contents matches document content, and (3) the index matches document content. Technical editing should be accounted for during project planning.

Seller Development Team: Performs Project-level Technical Oversight   Seller management is responsible for providing technical guidance to help ensure (1) consistent use of engineering principles, (2) reuse of existing documents, computer code, or databases, and (3) prescriptive application, at the project level, of management, development and product assurance disciplines, techniques, and tools. Figure 3–21 depicts this technical guidance.

Seller management, in effect, acts as a technical director by providing experienced-based guidance to the seller development team. For example, consider a situation in which the seller development team is helping the customer migrate a legacy system to a new software language, database management system, and platform. Although the development team members have relevant experience, they have never migrated a system as large or complicated. To help the team members scale up their experience, the seller project manager requests the seller program manager to review the current situation and provide a sanity check. The seller program manager reviews the project and makes some suggestions to the seller project manager and team members. In addition, the seller program manager seeks out a database expert whose particular expertise is in large-scale data conversion efforts. This expert comes on site for a few days to provide some guidance on how to recognize and avoid potential performance problems. The end result is that evolving products are reviewed, and the development team uses the corresponding feedback to stay on track.

Change Control Board (CCB)

The change control board (CCB) is a management support tool that provides a forum for discussing management, development, and product assurance activities. Our concept of a CCB extends far beyond the traditional configuration management (CM) control board concept. Simply stated, no matter how well the customer writes the SOW, no matter how well the seller writes a corresponding project plan, and no matter how well the customer and seller negotiate the final agreement, once the project begins, things start to change. Furthermore, changes persist throughout the project. Therefore, the CCB is a business forum where the customer and seller can discuss how to deal with this unknown, but anticipated, change. Figure 3–22 illustrates this concept.

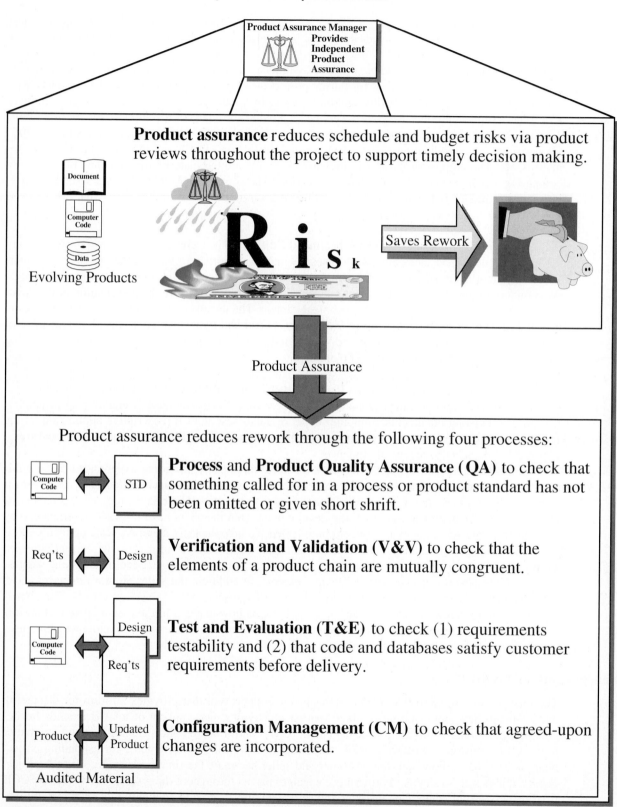

FIGURE 3–19 Independent product assurance is a key element of successful software systems development processes.

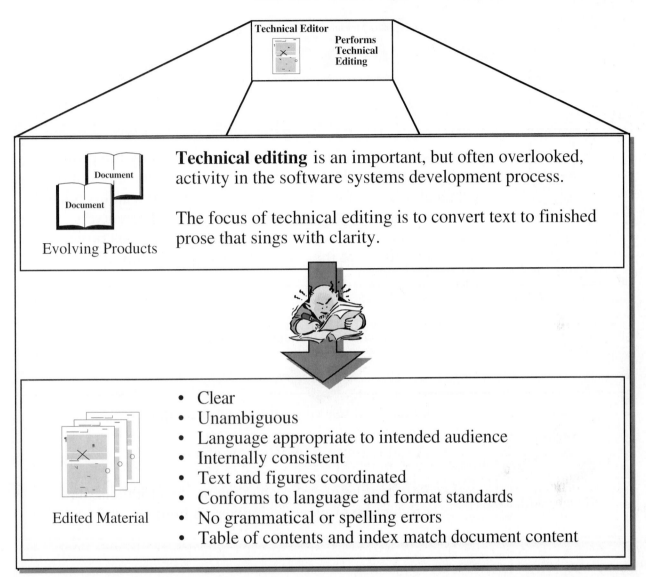

Evolving Products

Technical editing is an important, but often overlooked, activity in the software systems development process.

The focus of technical editing is to convert text to finished prose that sings with clarity.

- Clear
- Unambiguous
- Language appropriate to intended audience
- Internally consistent
- Text and figures coordinated
- Conforms to language and format standards
- No grammatical or spelling errors
- Table of contents and index match document content

Edited Material

FIGURE 3–20 Technical editing is an important, but often overlooked, activity in the software systems development effort.

CCB meetings help to foster effective communication between the customer and seller by acting as a catalyst to achieve closure between the parties regarding actions and decisions pertaining to product development. Discussions take place, action items are assigned, and decisions are recorded in CCB minutes. The CCB is a decision-making body where software systems development is conducted in an accountable and auditable manner.

In general, CCB meeting output consists of technical guidance and evolving products. The customer can provide technical guidance to the seller or vice versa. The seller provides the customer with evolving products for interim or final customer review and approval. Conversely, the customer provides the seller with a reviewed evolving product.

As shown in Figure 3–5, the overall result of the interaction between the customer/seller development team is a deliverable that has been coordinated at the project level. The deliverable product is now ready to be submitted to the seller senior management for review and approval.

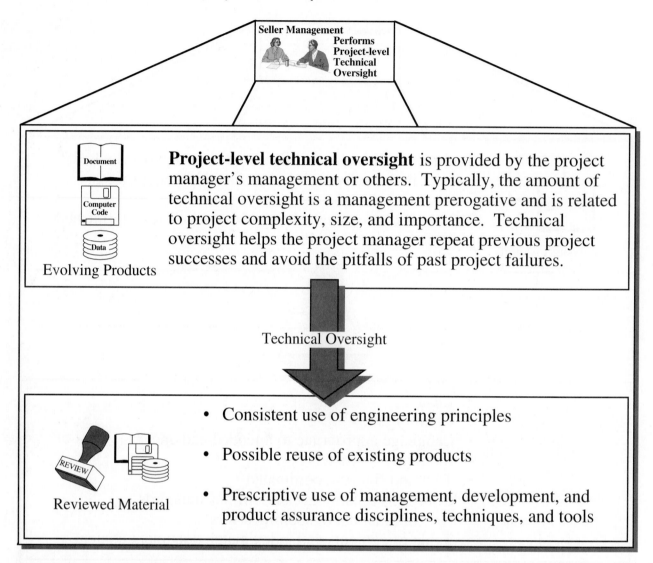

FIGURE 3–21 Project-level technical oversight helps the seller development team avoid potential problems by infusing the experience of others into the technical management of the project (i.e., the "I've been there" factor).

3.7 SELLER SENIOR MANAGEMENT

Seller senior management is responsible for reviewing the deliverable at the organizational level to confirm that there are no items to be resolved. If there are items to be resolved, seller senior management (in our example, the program manager) gets together with the seller development team, typically the seller project manager and the lead developer, to decide how to resolve the items.

The program manager ensures that the deliverable conforms to the systems engineering environment (SEE) policies, guidelines, procedures, and standards. We cannot stress enough this management responsibility. Successful implementation of an organizational process involves the participation, cooperation and support from everyone involved. However, senior management must set the tone. If senior management is not supportive, the task of implementing an organizational process is made more difficult. Typically, someone or some part of an organization is assigned the responsibility for imple-

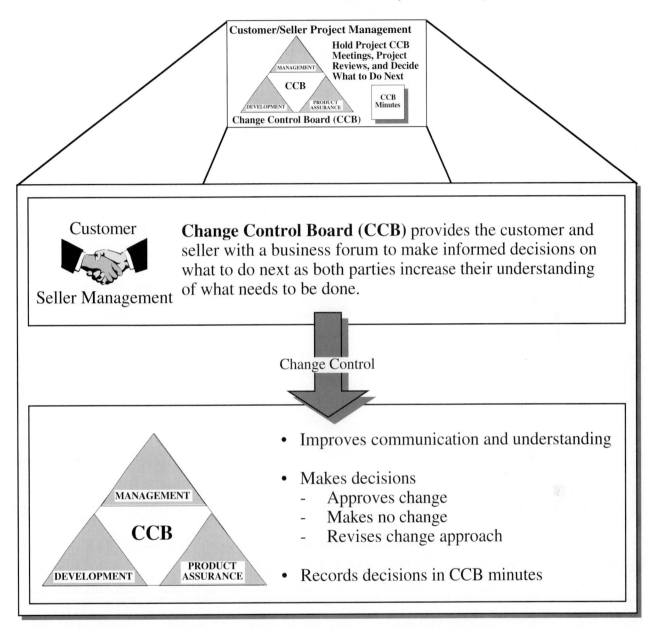

FIGURE 3–22   The CCB is a key element of successful software systems development processes.

menting an organizational process. Assigning someone or an organizational element (e.g., seller process engineering group) to be responsible is a good first step, but without the corresponding resources and authority, the task takes longer and costs more. Figure 3–23 illustrates the seller senior management responsibility.

When the deliverable is submitted to the program manager, it is packaged with its tracking form, cover letter, customer receipt of deliverable form, and customer acceptance of deliverable form. Remember, the tracking form consists of the following sections:

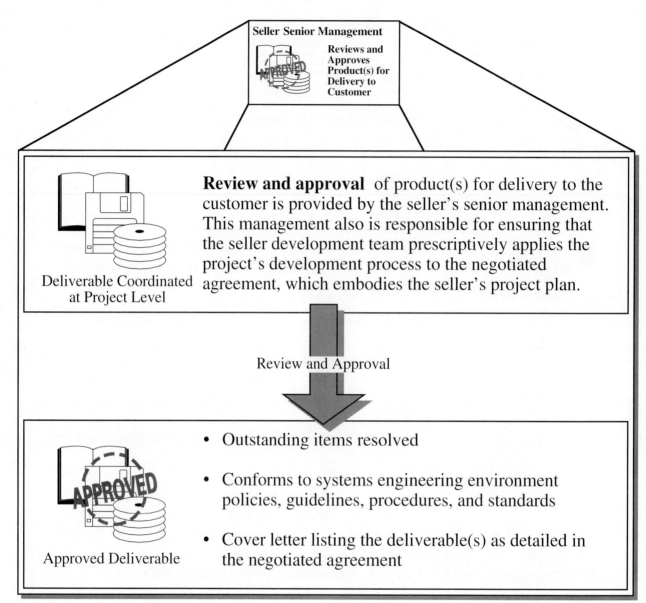

FIGURE 3–23 Seller senior management ensures, in part, that the seller development teams implement the organizational software systems development process.

- Project File Establishment at Deliverable Support Center (DSC).

- Technical Review of Product.

- Final Coordination with DSC.

- Project File Management.

- Comments/Issues.

- Management Review and Approval.

- Customer Receipt and Approval.

The program manager checks the sections to see how the product was tracked. The program manager reviews each of the tracking form sections (except the Customer Receipt and Approval because it has not yet been filled in) to determine how the product made its way through the development process. For example, if the product is a document, then the technical editor signature should appear in the technical review section. If the product is a document, computer code or a database, then the product assurance reviewer or manager signature should appear in the technical review section. If the product is computer code and there is no product assurance signature, the program manager checks the comments section to see if there is a reason for no testing. If the product is a project plan, the program manager checks, and double-checks, the cost estimate provided by the business manager. If the deliverable is a product assurance plan, the program manager checks to make sure that the product assurance manager and the seller project manager have technically reviewed and agreed to the plan. Assuming that there are items to be resolved, then the program manager gets together with the appropriate people to find out what the story is. Given that everything gets worked out, the program manager approves the product for delivery, signs the cover letter, and forwards the package to the person who is going to deliver the approved deliverable to the customer.

Upon receipt of the seller's approved deliverable, the customer signs the customer receipt of deliverable form and provides it to the seller. After the customer reviews the deliverable, the customer fills out the customer acceptance of deliverable form and provides the deliverable status to the seller.

3.8 SOFTWARE SYSTEMS DEVELOPMENT PROCESS SUMMARY

The organizational software systems development process defines the way an organization develops software systems. Although there is no one way to develop software systems, the following principles should be considered in any organizational process:

- Plan the work to be done before doing it.

- Obtain agreement on defined responsibilities.

- Establish and empower self-directed work teams.

- Establish checks and balances.

- Maintain continual customer and seller interaction.

- Monitor project progress.

- Mentor project managers, and train work teams.

- Provide interim review on project progress.

- Provide feedback on deliverables.

- Improve the software systems development process.

> The organizational process should be applied prescriptively to each project because no two projects are the same.

In this sense, the process provides a consistent approach to developing software systems and allows the particular circumstances of a project to influence how the work is to be done. For example, an organization's software systems development process may require that all computer code be tested before it is delivered to the customer. However, one potential customer is not willing to pay for such testing. In this case, the seller may decide not to take on the work because the risk is too high and the company's reputation could be seriously damaged if the project were to fail. On the other hand, the seller may be able to convince the potential customer to relieve the seller of the consequences for software failure, and so the seller decides to take on the work. Regardless of the particular situation, people's knowledge and experience should be used to help determine how much process is to be applied.

Two major factors govern organizational process definition: (1) level of detail and (2) organizational scope. Figure 3–24 shows a way to relate these two factors to one another.

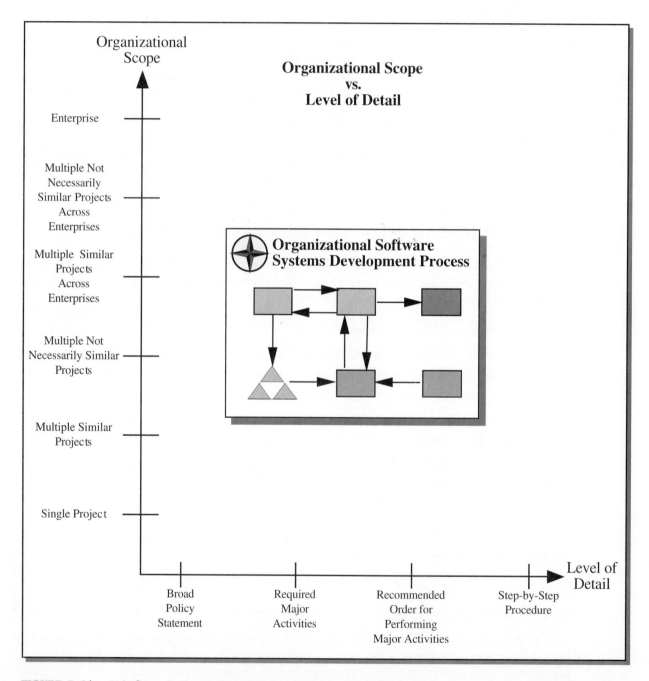

FIGURE 3–24   This figure indicates that the level of detail and organizational scope are two major considerations in defining a software systems development process in an Application Development Process Environment (ADPE) element.

The level of detail defining an organization's software systems development process may span a broad spectrum. In some organizations, it may make sense simply to define the major activities that all projects must perform and then leave it up to each project to apply prescriptively these activities. Here, *apply prescriptively* means "in a manner that makes sense in terms of factors such as project budget, project schedule, and the threat to human life that software failure may pose." In other organizations, the software projects may be so similar that it makes sense to define a detailed step-by-step procedure because "one size fits all."

Figure 3–24 also indicates that the scope of a software systems development process may or may not coincide with an organization within an enterprise. At one end of the spectrum, an organization may be a single project, and at the other end, an organization may be an entire enterprise. Therefore, an organizational process may be written for a single project, or for multiple similar projects, multiple not necessarily similar projects, projects spanning more than one enterprise, projects across entire enterprise, etc.

Considering these two dimensions helps to shape the organizational process. For example, the final review and approval responsibility can be vastly different for a single project organization versus an organization that cuts across enterprises and includes subcontractors working with a prime contractor. In the latter case, the process may allow the subcontractors to have certain limited responsibilities, but final release authority may be reserved for the prime contractor.

For those organizations that develop software systems embedded in larger systems, the software systems development process needs to plug into the systems development process. At a minimum, the software process should hook periodically into the system process to ensure that software product development is synchronized with the development of interfacing system components. One visible and accountable way of plugging into the systems development process is through CCB meetings involving the principals responsible for these interfacing components. Figure 3–25 illustrates this point.

In general, the software and systems processes should share common activities such as peer reviews, independent product assurance, and technical editing. One activity the systems process needs to account for that generally is not prominent in the software process is that of subsystem integration. This activity is concerned with making sure that the individual software process components fit and work together as prescribed in system-level specifications. Sometimes these specifications may include interface requirements and design specifications prescribing the what and how of the subsystem connections.

When defining the organizational software systems development process, you have to be careful not to turn the process into a paper drill. The process cannot take on the air of bureaucracy. If the staff members perceive that following the process covers them with paperwork, they will seek ways to circumvent the process. If the percentage of people circumventing the process is on the rise and/or is considerable (say, at least 30 percent), then the process may indeed be bureaucratic and needs to be changed. Remember that cries of bureaucracy are typical during the period immediately following process implementation and for weeks or even months thereafter. Before responding too quickly to the cries, it is important to let the process settle in. You need to track and respond to everyone's suggestions. In general, the larger the organization, the longer the settling-in period. Remember, too, that through prescriptive application of the process to individual projects, experienced staff will generate paperwork in amounts appropriate to the schedule and budget constraints of their projects. On the other hand, less experienced staff may either generate too little paperwork (because they are less certain about what to do and may be forced to shortcut some activities) or too much paperwork (because they are less certain about how much is enough). Mentoring of these individuals can facilitate the generation of the appropriate amount of paperwork across an organization.

To focus Application Development Process Environment (ADPE) development efforts, it is helpful to begin by defining the organizational software systems development process and capturing it in an ADPE element. This organizational element establishes the context for most subsequent elements. As shown in Figure 3–26, the subsequent elements serve to address in more detail one or more items called out in the ADPE organizational process element. For example, the organizational process may

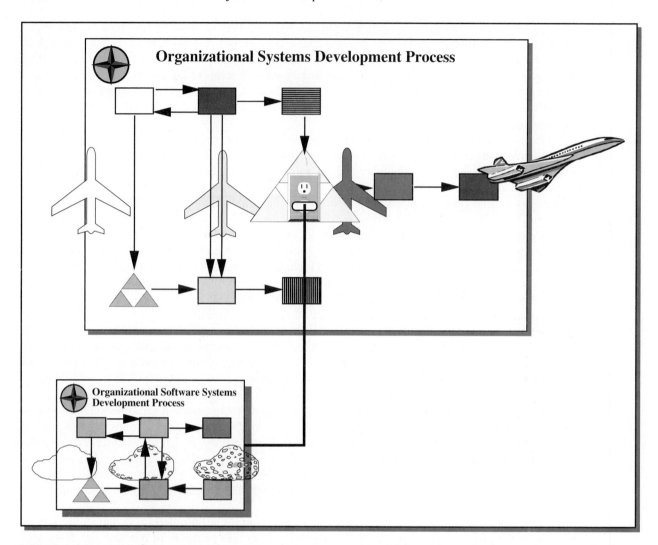

FIGURE 3–25 The software systems development process can plug into a systems development process via change control board meetings.

include a CCB. The mechanics of this item can then be addressed in an ADPE element on the CCB and/or on configuration management. The organizational software systems development process acts as an integrating agent for the other ADPE elements.

You can use the annotated outline of an ADPE policy shown in Figure 3–27 as a starting point for defining your organization's software systems development process.

The software systems development process policy may consist of the following sections:

- **Purpose.** This section states the purpose of the policy. The purpose sets the context and establishes the authority for the policy.

- **Background.** This section provides an overview of your organization, business, customers, and types of contractual vehicles (e.g., firm fixed price, time and material, cost plus fix fee, letter contract) that you use to conduct business.

- **Software Systems Development Process Overview.** This section describes your software systems development process. The key part of this section is a diagram showing this process. This diagram should delin-

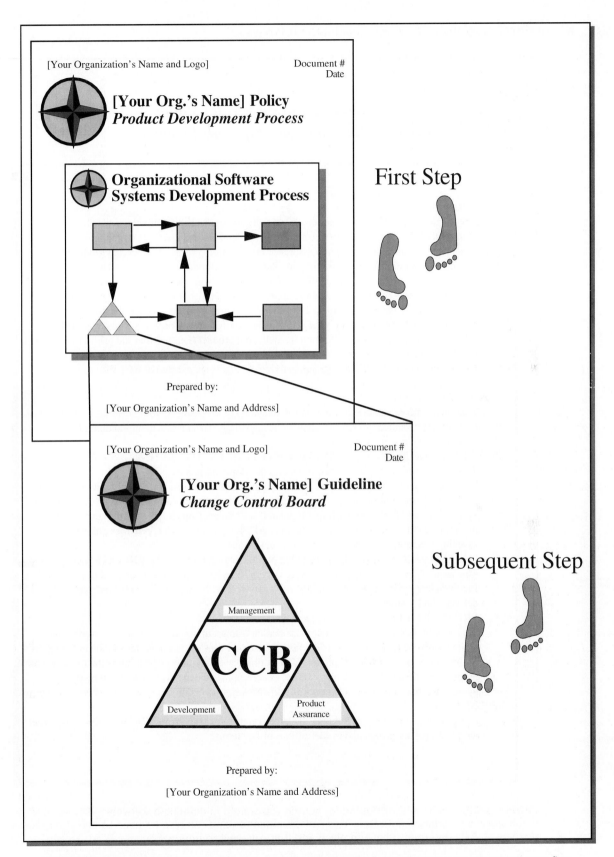

FIGURE 3–26   It is useful to define the organizational software systems development process first.

[Your Organization's Name and Logo]

Document #
Date

[Your Organization's Name] Policy
Software Systems Development Process

Document #
Date

1.0 PURPOSE

This section states the purpose of the element. This purpose is the following:

- Identify the generic activities performed by your organizational elements (e.g., project management organization, product assurance organization, process engineering group [PEG], training organization, deliverable support center) in developing a software product (i.e., documentation, computer code, database) for delivery to your customer

- Describe the roles of customer organizational elements and your organizational elements in performing these generic activities. The generic activities in this procedure should encompass the spectrum from SOW receipt by your organization to product delivery to the customer and feedback from the customer regarding the delivered product (i.e., whether the product is accepted or requires changes). The purpose of this element should *not* be a description of how to do various software product development activities (e.g., object oriented design, software requirements specification).

2.0 BACKGROUND

This section gives an overview of your organization, your business, your customers, and the types of contractual vehicles you use to conduct business (e.g., fixed price, memorandum of understanding, time and materials).

3.0 SOFTWARE SYSTEMS DEVELOPMENT PROCESS OVERVIEW

This section describes your software systems development process. The key part of this section is a diagram showing this process. This diagram, which should be walked through in this section, should delineate your organizational elements and those of your customer's involved in software systems development. Do not forget to include a CCB mechanism to manage change. This diagram should serve as the context for other ADPE elements. It thus provides guidance for evolving your entire ADPE in a self-consistent manner.

4.0 SOFTWARE SYSTEMS DEVELOPMENT ELEMENTS AND THEIR INTERACTIONS

This section describes how your software systems development elements defined in the preceding section interact with each other during software systems development, review and approval, delivery, and customer acceptance.

5.0 PROJECT FILES

This section describes the way your organization is to set up its files for tracking, storing, and maintaining your repository of deliverables. It should deal with such issues as the (1) definition of the project file concept, (2) project file location, (3) deliverable control numbers, (4) way that products are filed (in general, how "filing" is accomplished depends on product type (i.e., document, code, data base), (5) check-in and check-out procedures, and (6) project closeout.

APPENDICES

Appendices can contain such things as (1) deliverable tracking forms, (2) deliverable cover letter templates, (3) acronyms, and (4) definitions of key terms.

FIGURE 3–27 An annotated outline for getting you started in defining a software systems development process for your organization. This ADPE element outline can also be used to define a process that you already (informally) have in place and that you want to improve.

eate your organizational elements, as well as your customer's. Your process should contain a planning element, a change control mechanism, and customer feedback. The process provides guidance for evolving your entire ADPE in a self-consistent manner.

- **Software Systems Development Elements and Their Interactions.** This section describes all the elements and the way that they interact with one another during software systems development.

- **Project Files.** This section describes the way your organization is to set up its files for tracking, storing, and maintaining your deliverables. In addition to the issues listed in the figure, you should keep this system simple.

- **Appendices.** Appendices can contain examples of a tracking form, cover letter, customer receipt of deliverable form, and customer acceptance of deliverable form.

We have completed our discussion of our organizational software systems development process concept. The next chapter deals with the change control process and the change control board (CCB). As you will discover, our concept of a CCB extends far beyond the traditional configuration management (CM) control board.

chapter

4

Change Control Process

He who rejects change is the architect of decay. The only human institution which rejects change is the cemetery.

—Prime Minister Harold Wilson, speech to the Consultative Assembly of the Council of Europe,
Strasbourg, France, January 23, 1967. Text from *The New York Times*, January 24, 1967.

4.1 INTRODUCTION

Generally, the customer has *some idea* of what a software system is to do. However, the customer usually does not know *exactly* what a software system is to do. Probably the most fundamental aspect of software systems development is iteratively determining what the customer wants and then developing products to satisfy these wants. In this chapter, we turn our attention to describing controls that can be instituted on a software systems development project to achieve convergence between what the customer thinks the software system is to do and what the seller thinks the customer wants the software system to do—with the ultimate result that the seller produces what the customer wants (and can use).

The change control board (CCB) can be used to institute controls for achieving convergence between the customer and seller. This chapter details the CCB concept and provides you with guidance for setting up a CCB for your software systems development process. We believe that the CCB can effectively deal with customer (i.e, user/buyer) and seller communication issues dealing with software systems development. However, this is not to say that the CCB is the only effective mechanism for communicating with the customer.[1]

---

[1]As previously stated, our CCB concept extends far beyond the traditional configuration management (CM) control board concept. One aspect of software product development change control is certainly CM, but as you read this chapter, we present our expanded concept of change control.

THE WIZARD OF ID   Brant parker and Johnny hart

FIGURE 4–1 It is easy to miscommunicate. (*The Wizard of ID,* March 16, 1994. Reproduced by permission of Johnny Hart and Creators Syndicate, Inc.)

In this chapter, we show how the CCB can, and should, be used to address the communications problems that plague *any* software systems development project. As the comic strip in Figure 4–1 illustrates, communications misunderstandings plague everyday life.

In his opening remark to the to-be-debugged prisoner, the prison doctor shown in the first frame of the strip is undoubtedly unaware that he is miscommunicating his prescription to the inmate. In fact, in the absence of the remaining frames, most readers of the first frame would probably interpret the doctor's words as he had intended. Unfortunately, both the spoken and the written word are frequently misinterpreted.

It should not be surprising, then, that particularly in the world of software systems development, where the need for specificity is paramount, the consequences of misinterpretation can cause discomfort—or worse. For example, consider the comic strip in Figure 4–2. This comic strip models a typical interaction between a customer and a vendor of off-the-shelf software. The first frame of the comic strip intimates that the customer (peasant) seems to be sure of his requirements for a potion that the wizard is vending. This frame also makes it evident that the wizard seems to understand what the peasant really wants. Unfortunately, the third frame of the comic strip makes it evident that, at least from the perspective of the peasant, a misunderstanding has arisen. It is important to note from the frame that, from the perspective of the wizard, there is no misunderstanding.

WIZARD OF ID   BY BRANT PARKER & JOHNNY HART

FIGURE 4–2 Sometimes the customer believes that he effectively communicates his requirements, and the developer believes he understands what the customer communicated. Subsequent to developer implementation of the "requirements," the customer and developer may have vastly different perspectives regarding requirements satisfaction. (*The Wizard of ID,* October 11, 1984. Reprinted by permission of Johnny Hart and Creators Syndicate, Inc.)

In the real world of software systems development, the fact that the customer and seller can have diametrically opposite views of the state of a product can have overwhelming consequences. Consider, for example, the following statement from an actual software specification document:

"The exception information will be in the XYZ file, too."

Just as the wizard in Figure 4–2 interpreted the word "life" in the peasant's requirements statement to mean "age," the programmer interpreted "too" in the above specification to mean, "Another *place* the exception information appears is the XYZ file." Unfortunately, what the customer really wanted this statement to mean was, "Another *type* of information that appears in the XYZ file is the exception information." In fact, this information was not duplicated elsewhere. So, just as the peasant's "age" requirement misinterpretation led to an irreversible situation (assuming the wizard had no potion antidote), so the customer's "too" led to the loss of valuable and unrecoverable information. The cost of the lost information was about half a million dollars.[2]

Figure 4–3 generalizes the off-the-shelf software scenario in Figure 4–2 to the general case of software systems development. The king in the comic strip in Figure 4–3 is the archetypical software customer. The king has some idea of what he wants—but he does not know exactly. Perhaps the most fundamental aspect of software systems development is iteratively determining what the customer wants and then developing products to satisfy these wants.

Many system development efforts (whether or not they involve software) embody attempts to improve how things work without being precisely sure of what is wanted. This imprecision is perhaps implicit in Figure 4–3 in the broad-scoped question the king puts to the wizard, "Can you stop the rain?" Often, software systems development efforts begin with such customer thoughts as the following:

- Wouldn't it be nice if I could do such and such?
- What I really need is a system that will do. . . .
- Today I do processes *X, Y, Z, . . .* separately. It would be more efficient if I could integrate *X, Y, Z, . . .* into a single system.

FIGURE 4–3 A customer and a developer refine their understandings of what needs to be done to build a software system satisfying customer requirements. This mutual refinement of understanding continues throughout the development life cycle. The change control board (CCB) provides the wizard and king with a business forum to achieve this mutual refinement. The end result is successful software systems development. (*The Wizard of ID*, September 30, 1983. Reproduced by permission of Johnny Hart and Creators Syndicate, Inc.)

---

[2]This example is taken from D. C. Gause and G. M. Weinberg, *Are Your Lights On? How to Figure Out What the Problem Really Is.* (Boston: Little, Brown, and Company, 1982), pp. 73–74.

From the software systems developer's perspective, development, once initiated (by such customer thoughts as those just listed), may be pushed along by developer thoughts like the following:

- I think the customer would be happier if I could make his system do such and such instead of what it does now.

- Although the design I have developed meets customer needs, now I realize that there are other designs that will meet these needs more efficiently.

- I now have a better understanding of what the customer wants, so I think that I will implement his new capability as follows. . . .

The key point about these customer and developer thoughts and Figure 4–3 is related to time and money. For successful software systems development, the fourth frame in Figure 4–3 should really be merged with the first frame. Before a lot of time and money are wasted in taking the next step in a software systems development effort (the second and third frames in the figure encapsulate this presumably wasted time and money), the wizard needs an answer to his question, "What is it you really want?"

As illustrated in Figure 4–3, both the wizard and the king mutually progress in their understanding of what needs to be done as the project proceeds. Successful software systems development thus requires a mechanism that allows the wizard and king to process the changes that arise from this natural mutual refinement of understanding. That software systems development mechanism is the change control board (i.e., CCB). The CCB's primary purpose is to serve as a forum for managing these anticipated, but unknown, changes.

In this chapter, we describe a change control process critical to achieving convergence between what the king thinks he wants and what the wizard thinks the king wants. The ultimate result of the change control process, as embodied in the CCB, is that the wizard produces what the king wants (and can use).

The plan for this chapter is the following:

- In **Section 4.2—Change Control Process Nuggets,** we present the nuggets that you can expect to extract from this chapter.

- In **Section 4.3—Planned and Unplanned Change,** we define the scope of process change control. The section begins by asserting that achieving convergence between the buyer/user and seller is tantamount to saying the following:

  > A customer's wants migrate through a sequence of changes and ultimately become a product embodying the seller's (and hopefully the customer's) perceptions of these wants.

  The section then asserts that, in terms of a project's life cycle, this migratory process can be further described as a planned sequence of transitions from one life cycle stage to a subsequent one overlaid by unplanned transitions within stages or back to preceding stages or forward to succeeding stages.

- In **Section 4.4—The Processing of Changes,** we define for the seller the change control mechanics of the software systems development process. We step through the processing of product and programmatic changes using the CCB.

- In **Section 4.5—Examination of the Change Control Board,** we focus on the mechanics of the CCB itself. The preceding section focused on the role of the CCB in the overall product and programmatic change control process. In this section, we focus on who sits on the board, what decisions the board makes, and how the board operates.

- In **Section 4.6—Paperwork Support of the Change Control Board,** we discuss why paperwork is necessary in the change control process. We also show how to develop and use a set of change control forms. In addition, we provide a format for recording CCB minutes.

■ In **Section 4.7—Change Control Process Summary,** we summarize the key points developed in the chapter. It includes an annotated outline of an ADPE guideline for describing the workings of CCBs in the software systems development process. You can use this outline as a starting point for defining how CCBs are to be incorporated into your environment. This section also provides a transition to the next chapter.

4.2 CHANGE CONTROL PROCESS NUGGETS

Figure 4–4 lists the nuggets that you can extract from this chapter. To introduce you to this chapter, we briefly explain these nuggets. Their full intent will become more apparent as you go through the chapter.

1. **Every software systems development project should be governed by a board that meets periodically involving the buyer/user and seller.** Constitute this board with the disciplines of management, development, and product assurance. Remember, on some projects—particularly small ones—the same individual can represent more than one discipline. Give this board any name consistent with your business culture. In this book, we label this board the "Change Control Board (CCB)" because of its role in controlling the changes that inevitably arise on any software systems development project. This chapter offers you guidance for establishing CCBs in your organization.

2. **If product assurance is not part of your culture, use the CCB mechanism to foster the idea of the need for an independent agent providing alternative insight into project progress to support more effective decision making.** Use a project outsider initially to serve in this product assurance role. We believe that it is important to have an organization independent from the development organization in helping management make intelligent, informed decisions regarding how a software systems development project should proceed. This chapter shows you how, through the CCB, an independent product assurance organization acts as a decision-making catalyst.

3. **If you are a seller, develop a software systems development process that involves the buyer/user through a CCB-like mechanism.** If the buyer/user is reluctant to participate in a software systems development process, use the approach "try it, you might like it." As a seller, your role is to elevate software systems development to a businesslike proposition. The CCB establishes an accountability mechanism for both the seller and the buyer/user that enables software systems development to proceed in businesslike fashion. In addition, software systems development is susceptible to tinkering on the part of both sellers and buyers/users. This tinkering breeds a certain informality among the parties involved in software systems development. This chapter offers you guidance for elevating software systems development to a businesslike proposition to mitigate the risks that plague any software project. Since it is easy to change software, the urge to change software products can be almost overwhelming. In this chapter, we offer you suggestions for controlling such urges.

4. **If you are a buyer/user,** *mandate* **in your contract that the seller establish a CCB mechanism, involving you, that governs the software systems development project.** Only a few things should be mandated on any software systems development effort—the CCB is one of these. This chapter builds a case for why it is in the best interests of a buyer/user to direct the seller to establish a CCB mechanism involving both parties. We explain why a buyer/user (i.e., customer) cannot simply tell the seller what is wanted and when it is wanted, and then walk away until the seller delivers the developed software system to the buyer/user.

5. **Establish the CCB rules of engagement at project outset through a CCB charter.** This chapter offers you guidance for constructing a CCB charter.

6. **Record minutes of every CCB meeting.** At a minimum, these minutes should include (1) a summary of the issues discussed, (2) the decisions made, (3) the action items assigned, (4) the responsible agent for each action item, and (5) the date each assigned action is to be completed. The breadth and depth of CCB minutes should be iteratively and mutually determined by the involved parties. The basic guideline is "how much visibility do the involved parties need to manage change without getting bogged down in bureaucracy?" Key to elevating software systems development to a businesslike proposition is establishing seller

	Nuggets	Change control lessons learned
1		Every software systems development project should be governed by a board that meets periodically involving the buyer/user and seller.
2		If product assurance is not part of your culture, use the CCB mechanism to foster the idea of the need for an independent agent providing alternative insight into project progress to support more effective decision making.
3		If you are a seller, develop a software systems development process that involves the buyer/user through a CCB-like mechanism.
4		If you are a buyer/user, mandate in your contract that the seller establish a CCB mechanism, involving you, that governs the software systems development project.
5		Establish the CCB rules of engagement at project outset through a CCB charter.
6		Record minutes of every CCB meeting.
7		Some projects may be of sufficient complexity to require a hierarchy of CCBs to focus project decision making.
8		For projects of at least six months duration, establish a CCB meeting frequency of no less than monthly.
9		It is a good idea for buyers/users and sellers each to hold in-house CCB-like meetings throughout a software systems development project for purposes of reaching consensus before meeting with each other.
10		The minutes of each CCB meeting should explicitly indicate that the involved parties agreed to the content of the minutes.
11		Document in an ADPE element the CCB role in your environment.

FIGURE 4–4   Here are key change control concepts explained in this chapter.

and user/buyer accountability. This chapter offers you guidance for addressing this accountability issue through CCB minutes.

7. **Some projects may be of sufficient complexity to require a hierarchy of CCBs to focus project decision making.** Often, software to be developed is part of the development of other system components. This chapter offers you guidance for constructing a CCB hierarchy to target project complexity issues arising from this added complexity.

8. **For projects of at least six months' duration, establish a CCB meeting frequency of no less than monthly.** At the beginning, it is preferable to meet more frequently—even weekly. Within these broad guidelines, allow meeting frequency to vary as project events dictate. For projects shorter than six months, CCB meetings every two weeks is a good starting frequency for governing the project. As the project unfolds, you can adjust this frequency as project events dictate—but try to meet at least monthly. To maintain effective process control, CCB meetings must take place throughout a project. This chapter offers suggestions for regulating meeting frequency.

9. **It is a good idea for buyers/users and sellers each to hold in-house CCB-like meetings throughout a software systems development project for purposes of reaching consensus before meeting with each other.** The purpose of these "in-house CCB meetings" is to allow for the expressing of dissenting opinions while at the same time not compromising each party's business interests during "joint (i.e., buyers/users and sellers) CCB meetings." This chapter offers guidance for harmonizing in-house CCB meetings with joint CCB meetings.

10. **The minutes of each CCB meeting should explicitly indicate that the involved parties agreed to the content of the minutes.** It is a good idea to start each CCB meeting with a review of the minutes from the preceding meeting to allow for correction to the minutes in the presence of the involved parties. Software systems development success critically depends on all parties agreeing to be accountable for their decisions.

11. **Document in an ADPE element the CCB role in your environment.** This chapter gives you ideas for documenting the role of the CCB in the context of your organization's software systems development process.

4.3 PLANNED AND UNPLANNED CHANGE

Achieving convergence between the king and the wizard is tantamount to saying the following:

> A customer's wants migrate through a sequence of changes and ultimately become a product embodying the wizard's (and hopefully the king's) perception of these wants.

This migratory process can be further described as follows:

> The migratory process is a planned sequence of transitions from a life cycle stage to a subsequent stage overlaid by unplanned transitions within stages or back to preceding stages or forward to succeeding stages.

We refer to a planned transition from one life cycle stage to a subsequent stage as evolutionary change because such a change embodies the orderly (i.e., planned) growth of the software from one level of detail to a greater level of detail. We refer to the overlay of unplanned transitions within stages or back to preceding stages or forward to succeeding stages as revolutionary changes because each such change embodies an unanticipated alteration to the planned growth of the software. Figure 4–5 illustrates our concept of these two categories of change.

As shown in the upper half of Figure 4–5, planned change follows a direct path from one life cycle stage to a review area to another life cycle stage. For example, the planned software systems development activities transition from the (1) *WHAT Development Stage* to the (2) *Review Area* to the (3) *HOW Development Stage* to the (4) *Review Area* to the (5) *BUILD Development Stage* to the (6) *Review Area* to the (7) *USE Development Stage* to the (8) *Review Area*.

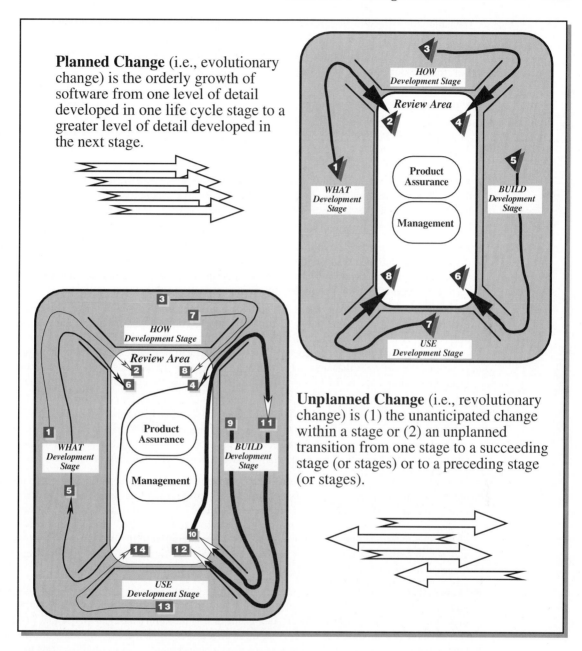

Planned Change (i.e., evolutionary change) is the orderly growth of software from one level of detail developed in one life cycle stage to a greater level of detail developed in the next stage.

Unplanned Change (i.e., revolutionary change) is (1) the unanticipated change within a stage or (2) an unplanned transition from one stage to a succeeding stage (or stages) or to a preceding stage (or stages).

FIGURE 4–5 Software systems development projects involve planned growth in greater levels of detail, and unplanned transitions within a life cycle stage or between stages.

In contrast, unplanned change follows an indirect path from one life cycle stage to a review area back to a life cycle stage, to a life cycle stage, etc. As shown in the lower half of Figure 4–5, the software systems development activities transition from planned changes (i.e., (1) to (2) to (3) to (4)) to unplanned changes as a result of review area activities that necessitate an unplanned revisit to the (5) *WHAT Development Stage*. The development continues on a planned path (i.e, (6) to (7) to (8) to (9) to (10)), and then as a result of review area activities, it is necessary to revisit the (11) *BUILD Development Stage*. The development then continues on a planned path (i.e, (12) to (13) to (14)). Regardless of the type of change, it is important to recognize the change and respond to it appropriately.

Consider the following examples of planned (i.e., evolutionary) and unplanned (i.e., revolutionary) change. The context for these examples is a six-stage life cycle: (1) requirements definition, (2) preliminary design, (3) detailed design, (4) coding, (5) production/deployment, and (6) operational use. However, these examples are not limited to a six-stage life cycle.

■ Suppose that a preliminary design specification for a software system, derived from a requirements specification for that system, listed the functions each of three software subsystems is to perform. Suppose that a detailed design specification describes how each of these functions is to be performed by computer code. This description of "how" is just an embodiment of the orderly growth of the software system and is thus an example of a planned change.

This example has two important points. First, the requirements specification did not have to be updated as the design took shape; therefore, resources did not have to be spent to update the requirements documentation. Second, since the design followed from the requirements, the design embodied the developers' perception of what the customer wanted.

■ Suppose that during the development of the detailed design specification in the preceding example it was discovered that a fourth subsystem (in addition to the three subsystems identified in the preliminary design specification) was incorporated into the detailed design because the developers thought this additional subsystem was needed to satisfy the intent of the requirements specification.

Presumably this fourth subsystem was not noticed during the development of the preliminary design specification because, for instance, the absence of design detail did not make manifest this requirements satisfaction issue. The modification (i.e., change) of the preliminary design specification to incorporate this fourth subsystem (presumably after the detailed design specification is approved) is an alteration to the orderly growth of the software that was not anticipated at the time the software was evolving from the Requirements Definition Stage to the Preliminary Design Stage. This modification is thus an unplanned change.

In contrast to the preceding example, the addition of the fourth subsystem resulted in expending additional resources to update the preliminary design. Achieving convergence between the customer and the seller resulted in a sequence of changes—planned and unplanned. Generally, sellers do not reflect all changes (or maintenance of software products) in their project plans or resource estimates. Also, note that it was not necessary to update the requirements specification; had it been necessary, even more resources would have been spent.

■ Suppose that computer code was developed from the detailed design specification in the preceding example, tested, and then deployed for operational use. Suppose further that sometime subsequent to this deployment, a malfunction was discovered in the computer code. This malfunction, which was not noticed during predeployment testing, resulted from a misinterpretation of the detailed design specification. Modification of the computer code to correct this malfunction is an alteration to the orderly growth of the software that was not anticipated at the time the software was evolving from the Coding and Production/Deployment Stages to the Operational Use Stage. This correction is thus an unplanned change.

■ Suppose that in the preceding example a review of the detailed design specification was scheduled to determine the feasibility of refining some of the functions in one or more of the software's subsystems (e.g., to make them operate more efficiently). As a result of this feasibility study, suppose that the detailed design specification was modified to incorporate these enhancements to the existing functions and that the computer code was also modified to incorporate these enhancements. These modifications to the detailed design specification and the computer code represent the orderly growth of the (already operational) software system and are thus examples of planned changes.

■ Suppose that the feasibility study referred to in the preceding example, in addition to specifying refinements to existing functions, revealed a logic flaw in the detailed design that had heretofore gone undetected during operational use of the computer code. As a result of this feasibility study, suppose that the detailed design specification was modified to correct this logic flaw (as well as incorporating the enhancements to the existing functions) and that the computer code was also modified to correct this logic flaw. These modifications to the detailed design specification and computer code to correct this latent logic flaw constitute alterations to the orderly growth of the software that were not anticipated at the time the software was evolving from the Detailed Design Stage to subsequent stages. These design and code modifications are thus examples of unplanned changes.

■ Suppose that, as a result of operational use of the computer code referred to in the three preceding examples, a need arose to add new functions to one or more of the existing subsystems. Suppose further that, as a result of this identified need, the requirements specification was augmented to incorporate these new functions and the preliminary design specification, detailed design specification, and computer code were correspondingly modified to incorporate these new functions. These modifications to these four software products represent the orderly growth of the (already operational) software system and are thus examples of planned changes. Alternatively, it could be argued that these modifications were not anticipated at the time the software was evolving prior to first operational use and thus are examples of unplanned changes. From this latter perspective, it thus follows that any new capabilities added to an operational system are unplanned.

Hopefully, these simple examples provide you with some insight into the migratory process of achieving convergence between the customer and seller. As the seller transitions from one life cycle stage to another, there may be unplanned transitions within stages or back to preceding stages or forward to succeeding stages. Software is malleable, and this intrinsic characteristic contributes to the ease with which software development projects can get into trouble. In this chapter we focus on techniques for establishing and maintaining control over this high susceptibility to change, thereby reducing the likelihood of encountering trouble during the life cycle. In describing these techniques, we frequently find it convenient to distinguish between planned and unplanned changes.

The distinction between planned and unplanned change is sometimes blurred, as the last example indicates. What difference does it make what kind of change it is? The prime reason that this distinction is important is to assure that all changes are given the requisite visibility and are handled in a unified way. Let us hasten to explain this somewhat paradoxical statement. Many people in the software development world do not recognize that the planned transitions of software from stage to stage are a form of change, i.e., that they are evolutionary changes as defined here. Lacking this perception, these people exercise little or no control over this evolving software. Consequently, instead of achieving convergence between the customer and seller, the opposite frequently happens. To illustrate this point, consider the following story based on the authors' actual experiences (names in this and other stories have been changed).

Why Control Planned Change?—A Story

Tom Smith was the seller's project manager for the development of a large management information system called ATLANTIS. He decreed that a succession of baselines was to be established, one at the end of each life cycle stage to serve as a point of departure for efforts in the next stage. However, Tom did not view this succession of baselines as planned changes to be controlled. He wanted his software engineers to be able to introduce different ideas easily "if they found a better way to do things."

Tom's engineers thus did not regard the preceding baseline as a rigid specification, and as a result the next baseline did not logically follow from its predecessor. There were plenty of surprises for everyone who read the current baseline. The customer's and seller's understanding of what the customer wanted were not converging.

In Tom's view, each baseline superseded its predecessor. His concept was strengthened by his contractual list of deliverables—the contract called only for a single delivery of each software product and did not suggest maintaining any software product. It is important to note that "maintaining" means that if, for example, when the design specification did not follow from the requirements specification, the requirements should be updated, or the design should be brought in line with the requirements. In addition, since the software engineers could introduce different ideas without customer agreement, the system being built did not reflect what the customer wanted, but rather what the engineers thought the customer might want.

Tom's logic was that not having to maintain the baselines saved him time and money and, from his viewpoint, increased the likelihood that his project would be completed on schedule and within budget. Tom's product assurance organization kept pointing out that he had no visibility into what was going to be in a baseline until it was produced. It was also pointed out that by allowing the software engineers to discard each baseline as its successor was produced, they had destroyed all traceability in his project. He had effectively lost all control over his project. The product assurance reports were an embarrassment to Tom, particularly when his senior management began asking questions about the reports. So Tom took the obvious step to solve what he perceived his problem to be—he disbanded his product assurance organization!

By this time, however, the customer was observing the fledgling system undergoing integration testing. The customer's observations told him that the project was going to be late and over budget. System ATLANTIS did not come close to solving his needs. Without hesitation, the customer terminated the contract to avoid further loss, and System ATLANTIS was never heard of again.

The moral of the story is that all change—both planned and unplanned—must be controlled (and maintained) in order to attain visibility and traceability in a project. We distinguish between the two categories of change primarily to assure that planned change is not omitted or overlooked.

A secondary reason for distinguishing between planned and unplanned changes is that they do have some different attributes. One such attribute is direction. Planned change always moves forward from baseline to a succeeding baseline, much the same way that human development evolves. Unplanned changes, on the other hand, may cause transitions either within a stage, back to a preceding stage, or forward to a succeeding one. Particularly important are the revisits to baselines resulting from unplanned changes, with the result that all project baselines are maintained, and visibility and traceability are retained.

Another attribute distinguishing these two types of change is that unplanned change processing is often more tightly time-constrained than planned change processing. This time constraint generally has an impact on some of the details of the change evaluation and approval steps, as we explain in subsequent sections.

4.4 THE PROCESSING OF CHANGES

In the preceding section, we divided software changes into planned change and unplanned change. Regardless of the category, changes are inevitable on any software project having more than one life cycle stage. As a project progresses through the life cycle, a baseline is created at the end of each stage. Each baseline embodies what was done during a given stage. This planned sequence of baselines represents the orderly growth of the software during the project life cycle. By our definition, each of these "orderly" baselines is a planned change.

Unplanned changes are also inevitable on any software project of any complexity. These changes arise from our fallibilities as human beings, from our general lack of complete experience, and from our inability to communicate perfectly among ourselves. Because of these limitations, it becomes necessary to make unplanned changes continually to correct misperceptions or misunderstandings. From stage to stage, we gain more insight and knowledge on a project and recognize the need to change the results of the current stage and of other stages. The larger and more complex the project, the larger and more convoluted the communications paths and the more likely the need for unplanned change.

Unplanned changes can also cause revisits to previous stages. These revisits precipitate baseline updates. Note that the update of a revisited baseline is an unplanned change. As a result of this change, baselines between the revisited baseline and the current baseline (i.e., intermediate baselines) must also be updated (as scheduled activities) to maintain visibility and traceability. Thus, the intermediate baseline updates are planned changes, according to our definition.

One final observation is in order before we present a short story about change on an actual software project. Unplanned changes often precipitate planned changes. If the unplanned changes are inevitable, then planned changes are also inevitable. It is important to acknowledge this inevitability of change on a software project.

Our objective in establishing and maintaining control of changes is not to prevent change but to control it. To understand why we adopt this objective, consider the following story.

The Inevitability of Change—A Story

As project manager on a new software development project, Mike Brown decided that success to him meant delivery of all software products on time and within budget. To this end he decreed that there would be absolutely no changes allowed on his project. A succession of baselines was to be developed during the life cycle. However, Mike did not consider these planned changes to be changes at all, but rather the normal progress of software development. He informed all his software engineers of his decision to prohibit change. He stated that each baseline would be a one-time delivery only, that is, a baseline would not be updated after issuance. Thus, not only did he save time and money by not processing changes, but also he conserved resources through elimination of document maintenance.

As the project went on, the software engineers found this rigid policy unworkable. During development and testing, the programmers discovered discrepancies in the current or preceding baselines (e.g., incongruities between the design document and the baselined requirements document). Several engineers had ideas for changes that they believed would have a beneficial effect on the final product. Since no changes were allowed on this project, the engineers had recourse to only two alternatives: (1) they could ignore the desirable or needed changes, or (2) they could ignore the strictures against making changes. Since the engineers were trying to solve the problems, most of them chose to make the changes without informing their manager. After all, they reasoned, it was easy to effect the changes in both documentation and code, and unit testing should uncover any problems arising from making code changes.

The project proceeded blissfully for a number of months. Mike was supremely confident that he had discovered the road to project success. Then the axe fell—integration of the code modules began. Unaccountably (to Mike at least), integration testing yielded a seemingly unending stream of reports of problems with the software code. At the same time, Mike's users, witnessing the integration tests, complained that the system performed functions they had not asked for and that it did not perform some functions they had requested. To his dismay, Mike watched helplessly while his project passed its delivery date and budget ceiling, with no certainty as to when a system satisfying his customers' needs could be obtained.

In this story, Mike Brown tried to prevent change. The result was disaster. As the software engineers acquired experience on the project, they saw things not previously perceived or recognized. These insights gave rise to the need for changes, which Mike had prohibited, with disastrous results. Since change on a software project is inevitable, we believe it makes better sense to acknowledge the existence of change and to attempt to control it.

Preventing all changes has the appeal of apparently not perturbing schedules and budgets, but as this story illustrates, there are substantial risks with this approach. The need for extensions of schedules and budgets is likely to become evident in the late stages of a project. Schedules and budgets may also change as a result of controlled changes, but in a controlled and visible manner.

To ensure that candidate software changes are processed in a visible and traceable manner, a controlling mechanism is needed to channel these candidate changes to the appropriate project participants. We call this controlling mechanism the change control board (CCB). In Figure 4–6, we portray the CCB as a control tower that controls the movement of software (1) from life cycle stage to life cycle stage for a six-stage life cycle (namely, Requirements Definition, Preliminary Design, Detailed Design, Coding, Production/Deployment, and Operational Use) and (2) in and out of the *Review Area*.

As we proceed through this example life cycle, the need arises to consider one or more candidate changes to the software product under development or to previously developed products. To address this need (which may occur at any point within a life cycle stage), we symbolically show a line from a life cycle stage to the CCB tower in the *Review Area* (e.g, from (4) Coding Stage to (5) CCB tower). In the *Review Area*, we assess the candidate changes, determine their impact on the software development effort, and make appropriate decisions. These decisions include specifying the following:

- What to do with the candidate changes—e.g., implement them, reject them, or hold them in abeyance.

- Which software products to modify—e.g., none, the one currently under development, products developed in previously visited life cycle stages.

- What revisits, if any, to make to other life cycle stages.

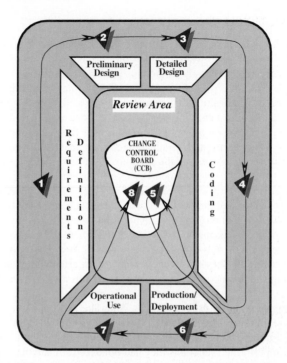

FIGURE 4–6   The change control board (CCB) is the forum for the control activity for the change process conducted during the review of changes.

Readers who have some background in configuration management will immediately recognize the CCB as the control organization historically used by the CM process to control modifications and enhancements to a system. On some projects, the CCB may also control changes to the computer code. In our context, the CCB performs the broader function of managing **all change** on a software project during all life cycle stages. This change management function encompasses both planned and unplanned change, and software in both textual (document) and coded forms.

Although Figure 4–6 shows a path from the outer loop into the *Review Area* near the end of each stage, this diversion path may occur anywhere within a stage. For planned changes, the diversion occurs whenever a software product is generated. If a product goes through several drafts, there is a diversion path for each draft. The end of each stage does not occur until the software product(s) comprising the baseline for that stage has (have) been approved.

For unplanned changes, the diversion path into the *Review Area* may connect to any point within the stage. For example, a developer at any point during the Coding Stage may detect a facet of the design omitted during the Detailed Design Stage. The designer submits a report of this omission, and the review process is initiated. Or during the Preliminary Design Stage a user may notice a requirement that has not surfaced before. The user immediately initiates the review process by submitting a request for change. Consequently, there can be a multitude of paths connecting any life cycle stage in Figure 4–6 to the *Review Area*.

The diversion down the path to the *Review Area* occurs whenever a change arises. That is, every change—whether planned or unplanned, large or small, of major or minor impact—is reviewed and evaluated by the change control process. The timing of the review and evaluation is set by your organization. For high-risk projects, you may decide to hold a CCB once a week. Regardless, the paths that a change takes during the change control process are controlled by the CCB. In Figure 4–7, we have magnified the *Review Area* to show generically how the change control process works in more detail, using the analogy of train tracks and switches.

The product that proceeds down the path into the *Review Area* may be an output of software development being proposed as a new baseline, such as a design document or the code for a software

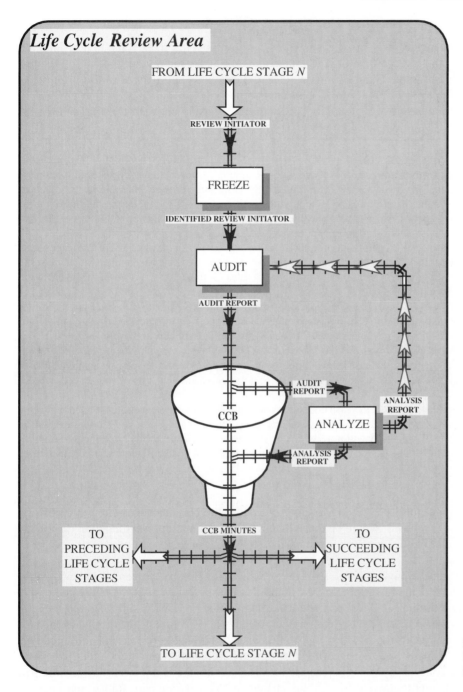

FROM LIFE CYCLE STAGE *N*

FIGURE 4-7 CCB control can be likened to the process of redirecting a train by switches.

module, or it might be a change request (CR) or an incident report (IR) defining a potential problem observed on the system. We refer to this product as a review initiator. If the review initiator is a new or updated software part, then the initiator contains the proposed change. A review initiator that is a CR or an IR usually does not specify a change, but rather the need for a change.

The review initiator passes through one or more of the following change control process actions: (1) freezing, (2) auditing, and (3) analyzing. The results of the analysis include (1) revisiting the audit action, (2) revisiting preceding life cycle stages, (3) proceeding to the next life cycle stage, or (4) going to a specific life cycle stage. Each change control process action is described below in the following paragraphs.

Change Control Process Action—*Freezing the Review Initiator*

The first action in the change control process shown in Figure 4–7 is to "freeze" the review initiator. The purpose of freezing the review initiator is to establish the basis for the review and control. Unless the software product initiating the change is frozen during the review, approval or disapproval of the change becomes meaningless. To understand why change becomes meaningless in the absence of freezing, consider the following story, which illustrates the relationship between freezing and change definition.

> In retail businesses, cash register operations are reviewed at the end of a shift or a workday. This review is conducted to verify that the cashier keeps an accurate accounting of transactions. Closeout of a cashier's drawer involves totaling the cashier's sales and counting the cash in the drawer. These amounts are reconciled against the preceding baseline for this audit, which is the amount of the money in the drawer at the start of the shift. That is, the cashier's sales plus the amount of money in the drawer at the start of the shift should equal the amount of money in the drawer at closeout.
>
> An important aspect of this closeout process is that the cashier must terminate all cash register operations during the closeout. That is, the cashier must make no sales, receive no payments, and make no change. Effectively, the contents of the cash drawer and the sales for that cashier are frozen while the closeout (review) is conducted.
>
> Consider the implications of trying to close out a cashier's drawer at a busy fast-food store while the cashier continues to make sales, receive payments, and make change. The checker determines and records the total sales at the beginning of the closeout. Of course, the cashier will add to these sales as the cash is being counted, but the checker will not have a record of their amount. As the checker is counting the amount of cash in the register, the cashier is adding to and subtracting from the various denominations in the drawer, both counted and uncounted. Modifications to the counted amounts are, of course, not recorded by the checker.
>
> When the checker completes the cash count, the checker calculates the sum of the cash amount at the beginning of the shift plus the total sales. The checker expects this sum and the cash count to be equal for successful closeout, but the checker will not find that to be true so long as the cashier continues to do business. Redetermining the total sales or recounting the current cash will change the amounts compared but will not change the end result—the inequality will persist as long as the cashier continues to do business, i.e., as long as the checker does not freeze the operation of the register and the contents of the cash drawer.

Imagine the frustration and futility of trying to close out under the circumstances cited in this story. Any count of the cash in the drawer would be meaningless—it would not represent the total cash in the drawer at any moment in time. Under these circumstances, conduct of a closeout would be a waste of time.

Similarly, as indicated in Figure 4–7, a software product must first be "frozen" if its review is to be meaningful. For example, the result of a review might be the establishment of the software product initiating a review as a baseline. If the product has meanwhile been modified substantially, then the baselined product does not represent the current product. And if the CCB directs the originator to make certain specific modifications to the product, the originator may be unable to respond fully and correctly if the product has already been changed in the specified portions that were to be modified.

The choice of the concept of freezing is deliberate. The action here is not to cast a software part in concrete, that is, to attempt to prevent forever any change to that software part. Rather, our intent in freezing is to control change. When a change becomes necessary and is approved, the software item can be thawed, changed, and then refrozen. In this manner, we can accommodate change while still maintaining continuous visibility into the current state of the software and traceability of the software from one change to subsequent ones.

A part of the freezing process is the identification function. Each software product and its contents should be identified at the time of freezing the product. It is not significant which organization (e.g., the development or the product assurance organization) performs this identification. Since identification is largely a subjective exercise, one organization should perform all identification throughout the life cycle. In this manner, consistency is achieved in application of the identification standards prescribed for a project.

Identification entails attaching a label to the review initiator itself and to each part of the review initiator. These labels provide visibility into the planned or unplanned change being reviewed. Without these labels, people are reduced to referring to software as, for example, "the second paragraph of the latest version of the preliminary design" or "that piece of code that failed last Tuesday." Such references are often not specific enough to be useful in communicating among project members. In fact, nonlabeled references could be extremely misleading. Consider, for instance, the "latest" version of a preliminary design. Two people attempting to discuss the second paragraph of their latest version of a preliminary design may each be discussing a different entity. It is entirely possible that a person might not receive an issue of a document. It is even more likely that a person receiving an unidentified document would confuse it with other unidentified issues of the document. The person might, as a result, ignore the new document (considering it to be the same as the old document) or subsequently consult the old document because the person does not recognize that a newer edition exists.

Change Control Process Action—*Auditing the Review Initiator*

The second action in the change control process shown in Figure 4–7 is to audit the identified review initiator. Because Chapter 5 discusses auditing in detail, we only touch upon the subject here. Auditing entails comparing the review initiator with one or more other items. These items could be a set of standards, a preceding baseline, a preceding draft of the identified review initiator, or the software requirements specification. Those items used in the comparison are a function of the nature of the review initiator, as we illustrate later in this section. The objective of auditing is to make visible the discrepancies between the identified review initiator and the items with which it is compared. These discrepancies are documented in an audit report, which along with the identified review initiator itself is submitted to the CCB for consideration.

Change Control Process Action—*Analyzing the Review Initiator*

We next consider the "control tower" in Figure 4–7 labeled "CCB." The CCB represents the decision-making body that determines the disposition of each change. Its function is analogous to the control tower in a railroad switching yard, determining the destination of the rolling stock by using switches.

The first determination that the CCB makes is whether further analysis of the identified review initiator is needed prior to CCB determination of its disposition. Generally, the CCB would bypass this analysis only for small problems with evident solutions that can be quickly implemented. For example, presented with a preliminary design specification and an audit report listing discrepancies observed in the preliminary design specification, the CCB may decide that the discrepancies in the audit report make the changes required obvious enough so that no further analysis is needed. For example, a discrepancy might state that the preliminary design is incomplete in that it has not addressed one of the functions in the requirements specification. On the other hand, the CCB may consider that further analysis of a discrepancy should be conducted to define sufficiently the change needed. For example, a section in the detailed design is ambiguous or cannot be understood, or a discrepancy indicates that the preliminary design specification and the requirements specification are inconsistent in that the design is based on achieving a substantially faster response time than was required.

Figure 4–7 shows that the analyze function supports the CCB but is not part of the CCB meeting. When the CCB decides that analysis of the identified review initiator is needed, it effectively turns the switch in Figure 4–7 to route the identified review initiator to the organization doing the analysis. Upon completion of the analysis, that organization generally returns the identified review initiator and the results of its analysis to the CCB.

The nature of the analysis differs according to the type of change proposed and the directions provided by the CCB. The analysis might consist of one of the following:

- A complete investigation into the impact of the change and the resources required to implement it (e.g., for a change request).

- A formulation of the precise change to be made (e.g., for an incident report that clearly requires a code change, or for a discrepancy in an audit report that points to ambiguous text).

- A determination of the scope of the problem and the exact changes required to implement a solution (e.g., for an incident report whose cause is not immediately obvious, or whose solution may require changes in a number of different software parts).

The CCB may, of course, direct that other analyses of a problem or a proposed change be performed.

When the CCB directs that a proposed change be analyzed, the analysis is often conducted by the seller's development organization, although on occasion other organizations may be involved in the analysis. For example, the buyer's product assurance organization may analyze a proposed change to a product assurance plan. When the analysis is completed, the results are presented to the CCB for further consideration of the proposed change.

The identified review initiator, the audit report, and the analysis report are the technical inputs to the CCB for determination of the disposition of the change. The analysis report formulates the proposed change (if the change is not already indicated on the identified review initiator) and assesses its impact.

For planned changes, the audit report records discrepancies between the proposed change (a proposed new or updated baseline) and the requirements specification and between the proposed change and the predecessor baseline. Other considerations affecting the CCB's decisions may be political (e.g., assuagement of a user who may feel that he or she has been ignored), schedule (e.g., the effect of making changes to the date that the system becomes operational), or economic (e.g., the amount of money remaining to effect changes). Based on these considerations, the CCB decides on a disposition of each change. This decision is analogous to throwing a switch to determine the path in the software life cycle subsequently taken. For example, if the CCB accepts a software product developed during a given life cycle stage (a planned change) and establishes it as a baseline, the path chosen leads to the beginning of the next life cycle stage. The CCB may decide that a software product requires reworking before it is acceptable; in this case, the path selected returns to the current life cycle stage.

When the CCB approves an unplanned change, revisits to one or more life cycle stages may be necessary. For example, a change request may cause a return to the Requirements Definition Stage to amend the requirements specification, with subsequent revisits to the other stages in succession as the change is implemented in a sequence of planned changes. As another example, approval of an incident report arising during acceptance testing may cause a revisit to the Detailed Design Stage to modify the design, followed by coding of the change and its testing. In some circumstances, the CCB may direct a revisit to a succeeding stage. For example, an incident report written on an operational system may result in a revisit to the Detailed Design Stage to correct the problem. While performing that correction, a coding error is discovered, and the CCB, in approving its resulting code correction, may specify a revisit to the Coding Stage.

The decisions that the CCB makes are documented in CCB meeting minutes. These minutes allow management and project participants to see what is happening on a project, and make software changes manifest and traceable from their origination to their archiving.

The alternative path in Figure 4–7 from the analysis process to the audit process (indicated by dashed arrow heads) might be considered for use in some circumstances. For example, suppose the audit of a draft preliminary design document reveals that a section of the design has been stated ambiguously. The development organization rewrites the section and normally presents its proposed resolution to the CCB. The CCB might approve the proposed resolution, and the approved change would be made to the preliminary design document. But suppose the revision to the section in the preliminary design document does not solve the problem (e.g., the section is still ambiguous) or introduces a new problem (e.g., the revised section is inconsistent with a later chapter in the document). These defects in the revision may not be evident to the CCB, particularly if the revision is substantial in scope or depth.

If the CCB baselines the document as revised, false starts may occur as the project proceeds from its faulty baseline, thereby wasting considerable resources.

How does the CCB become aware of such defective revisions? Following the normal path shown in Figure 4–7 (i.e., indicated by the solid arrow heads), the CCB may not become aware of these defects until the design document is next updated or until the software produced in the next stage is audited. At this point, considerable time and money may have been wasted. To avoid such waste, the alternate path shown with dashed arrow heads in Figure 4–7 could be used. In this case, the development organization, on completion of its analysis, provides its proposed resolution directly to the audit organization. The auditors would reaudit the revised section of the preliminary design document and send both the revised section and the audit results to the CCB for its consideration. Any remaining ambiguities, inconsistencies, or other discrepancies are made manifest to the CCB before it determines the disposition of the proposed change. Through the use of the alternative path rather than the normal path, discrepancies may surface earlier in the life cycle, thereby avoiding subsequent wastage. Of course, conducting the reaudit will cost money and take time, but it potentially will save much more money and time. Using the alternative path is a specific instance of the philosophy of "pay now versus pay much more later."

Now that we have described the change control process shown generically in Figure 4–7, we illustrate this process with the following three specific examples:

- **Planned change.** Presentation of a draft detailed design specification at the end of the Detailed Design Stage.

- **Unplanned change.** Submission at any point in the life cycle of a proposed amendment to the requirements.

- **Unplanned change.** Submission by a user of an incident report while the system is in operational use.

Change Control Process Example of Planned Change—*Change Control for a Draft Detailed Design Specification*

For this example, we assume that a project has been in the Detailed Design Stage of the life cycle in Figure 4–6 and that the development organization has just produced a draft of the detailed design specification. The draft detailed design specification has been diverted into the *Review Area*. The processing of this planned change is shown in Figure 4–8.

The draft detailed design specification is first frozen by placing a copy under the control of the product assurance organization. In other words, from this point on, the draft detailed design specification cannot be changed without CCB action. If the draft detailed design specification exists on an electronic medium, copies of both the electronic medium form and the hard-copy form are placed under control. At this time, the draft detailed design specification is also identified by the product assurance organization if it was not identified by the development organization. Identification entails labeling both the document itself and its contents.

The draft detailed design specification is next presented to the auditors in the product assurance organization,[3] who compare it with the following three documents:

- The CCB-approved requirements specification (on this project, this document has been established as the Requirements Baseline).

- The approved preliminary design specification (on this project, this document is the predecessor baseline to the draft detailed design specification).

- The standards established for this project.

---

[3]It is not mandatory that a separate product assurance organization conduct this audit. We advocate an independent product assurance organization for performing this and other audits, but alternatives are possible. It is essential that the audits be conducted, regardless of what organization conducts them. However, the organization conducting the audits should be objective and unbiased.

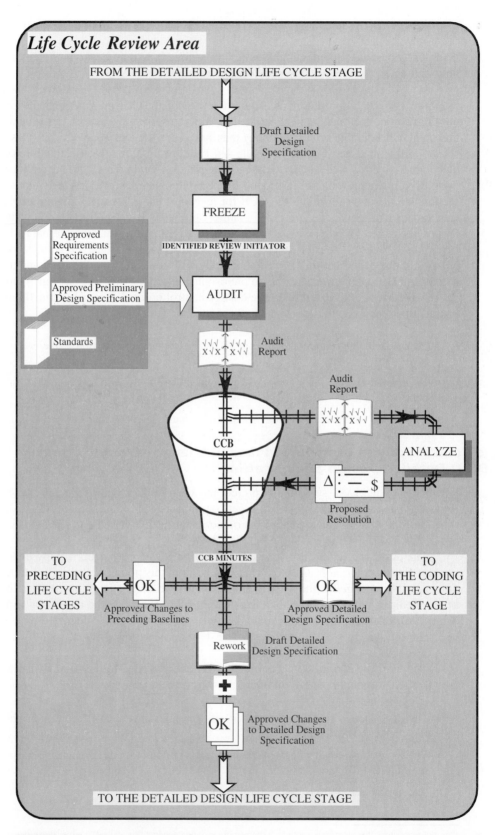

FIGURE 4–8 Change control of a planned (i.e., evolutionary) change—submission of a draft detailed design specification.

As a result of this comparison process, the auditors produce an audit report describing their findings in terms of the discrepancies observed in the course of the comparisons.

The draft detailed design specification and the audit report are presented to the CCB for its consideration. Each discrepancy in the audit report is considered individually. The first decision the CCB makes on a discrepancy is whether the discrepancy must be analyzed to provide further information on which the CCB can base its decision. If analysis is necessary, the discrepancy is sent to the organization designated by the CCB (typically the development organization), which determines the cause of the discrepancy, assesses its impact on the project, and proposes a resolution to the discrepancy (i.e., the precise change proposed). This information is provided by the analyzing organization to the CCB.

The CCB considers the resolution recommended for each discrepancy and either approves the resolution, rejects it, or returns it to the analyzing organization for further investigation.

When all the discrepancies have been considered and resolved, the CCB considers whether to baseline the draft detailed design specification in light of the (1) audit report on it, (2) CCB's own perusal of the document, and (3) approved resolutions to the audit report discrepancies. The CCB makes one (or, in some circumstances that are subsequently discussed, more than one) of the following decisions relative to the detailed design specification, resulting in an exit from the review area to the life cycle stages as shown by the three-way switch in Figure 4–8 and as indicated with bold text in the following list:

- The CCB approves the draft detailed design specification and establishes it as the Detailed Design Baseline. With this baseline established, the project can proceed **to the Coding Life Cycle Stage**. It is not necessary for the audit report to show no discrepancies for this decision to be made. The CCB may decide to establish the Detailed Design Baseline with discrepancies still outstanding, if the discrepancies were considered sufficiently small in number and impact.

  Such outstanding discrepancies would subsequently be resolved by the CCB. These resolutions might, among other things, require that changes be made to the Detailed Design Baseline, i.e., that the baseline be updated. The review process for this proposed update to the Detailed Design Baseline would be identical to that shown in Figure 4–8, except that the detailed design baseline would be used for the audit instead of the approved Preliminary Design Baseline.

- The CCB sends the draft detailed design specification back to the developers for reworking, along with a list of discrepancies and their resolutions. In this case, the CCB decision is to proceed **to the Detailed Design Life Cycle Stage**. The approved resolutions are implemented, and the draft detailed design specification is updated. When the draft detailed design specification has been updated in response to the discrepancy list, the updated draft detailed design specification is again subjected to the review illustrated in Figure 4–8.

- The CCB approves changes that require updates to preceding baselines. These baselines might be, for example, the Requirements Baseline or the Preliminary Design Baseline. The need for such changes might arise from discrepancies observed during the audit. The proposed resolution of a discrepancy may reveal that the cause of the discrepancy lies not in the draft detailed design specification but in one of the preceding baselines. As a result of the CCB decision to change one or more of the preceding baselines, the path is taken to the stage where each baseline to be updated was originally developed (i.e., **to Preceding Life Cycle Stages**). (A result of this revisit to a life cycle stage could be that it triggers more revisits. These subsequent revisits might be forward in the life cycle, or backward, or might skip stages.) As each baseline is updated, it is reviewed in the same fashion as shown in Figure 4–8. Note that this CCB decision may be made in addition to one of the two decisions just given.

The preceding example is representative of the change control process as it applies to planned changes. The names of your specific software products and life cycle stages may vary from those in Figure 4–8, but the basic process remains the same.

A question that arises after consideration of the preceding example is "What does the development organization do while this review process is in progress?" After all, the review process must take some time for the conduct of an audit, for analysis of discrepancies, and for the considerations of the

CCB. Does the development organization simply mark time (at considerable expense) during this review period? The answer to the question is that the developers should not be idle during this review period following development of a draft software product. There are usually a number of productive things they can do. If there are incomplete portions of the draft software product currently under review, the developers can finish those portions and have them ready for the next issue of the software product. They can assist in the completion of other software products being developed in the current life cycle stage. They can start their planning and preliminary work for the subsequent life cycle stage. Through informal liaison and discussions with the auditors, the developers can find out about discrepancies uncovered by the auditors in the software product under review, investigate them, and be prepared with recommended resolutions when they are formally received. And usually the developers are involved in the analysis of discrepancies and in the deliberations of the CCB.

We now illustrate the Figure 4–7 change control process for two revolutionary changes—first for a proposed amendment to requirements, and second for a user report of unexpected behavior in an operational system.

Change Control Process Example of Unplanned Change—*Change Control for a Proposed Amendment to Requirements*

An amendment to the requirements on a project can be originated at any time during the life cycle. Whenever it is originated, the amendment is submitted for review as shown in Figure 4–9. The proposed amendment to requirements is first frozen by the product assurance organization. This action entails assigning an identification label and placing a copy of the proposed amendment under control by putting it in a master file of proposed amendments to requirements.

The auditors next compare the proposed amendment with the following items:

- The requirements specification (i.e., the Requirements Baseline), to determine whether the amendment is truly a change to the requirements and to ascertain which of these requirements the proposed amendment affects.

- Previously submitted amendments to requirements, to determine whether the proposed amendment has previously been proposed (i.e., whether the proposed amendment duplicates one previously considered or currently being processed).

The proposed amendment is then submitted to the CCB, whose first decision is to determine whether the proposed amendment should be analyzed. In general, the proposed amendment is assigned to an investigating organization (typically the development organization) for analysis in a specified time frame. However, the CCB might bypass this step if it were not considered necessary. For example, if the audit determines that a proposed amendment is a duplicate of one previously considered by the CCB, there is no need to analyze the proposed amendment a second time—the CCB has already made its decision relative to this proposed amendment. In such a case, the CCB might proceed directly to reject the more recent submission of the proposed amendment. This rejection is unrelated to the CCB decision on the first submission of the proposed amendment and merely reflects that the CCB will not consider the later submission.

If the CCB decides that the proposed amendment to requirements needs to be analyzed, the investigating organization performs the analysis and prepares an impact assessment. This impact assessment contains the following information:

- An assessment of the impact of the proposed change on the project software products, i.e., what must be changed and how.

- An assessment of the impact of the proposed change on project resources such as time, manpower, and costs.

- A delineation of the benefits and liabilities of possible alternatives to the proposed change.

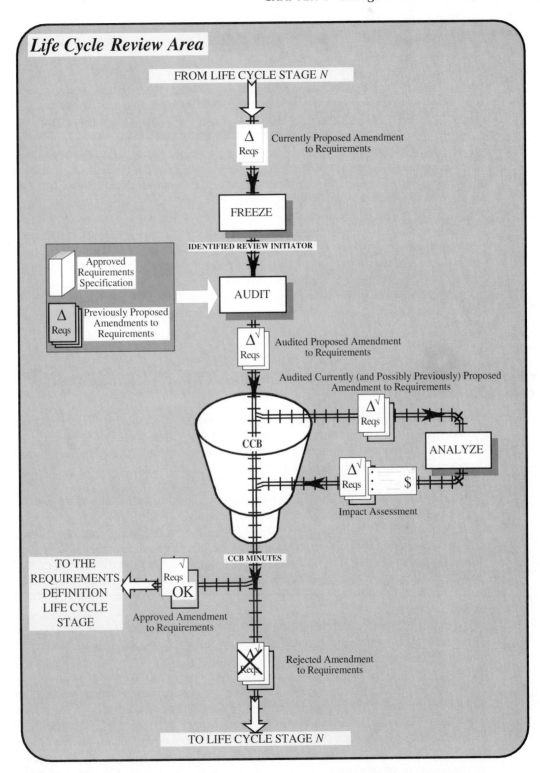

FIGURE 4–9 Change control of an unplanned (i.e., revolutionary) change—a proposed amendment to requirements.

With the impact assessment in hand, the CCB determines the disposition of the proposed amendment to requirements. As shown in Figure 4–9, the CCB throws the switch in one of the two following directions:

- The CCB may approve the amendment to requirements. When this decision is made, the path **to the Requirements Definition Life Cycle Stage** is taken. There the developers implement the approved change to the requirements by updating the Requirements Baseline. Note that all other established baselines will usually also have to be updated to maintain congruence among the baselines.

- The CCB may reject the proposed amendment to requirements. In this case, the originator of the proposed amendment is informed of the decision, the proposed amendment is archived (for reference in case the same amendment is proposed again), and the project continues the path **to the Life Cycle Stage** N (where stage N is decided by the CCB).

Observe in the foregoing example that an amendment to requirements (an unplanned change), when approved, gave rise to a set of updates to currently established baselines (planned changes). Note also that the process shown in Figure 4–9 is independent of whatever life cycle stage the project is in when the proposed amendment to requirements is originated.

Our second example on unplanned change deals with an incident report. We discuss an incident report from a user of an operational system, describing an abnormal or unexpected behavior of the system.

Change Control Process Example of Unplanned Change—*Change Control for an Incident Report*

The change control process in this example is initiated by an incident report (IR) generated by a user actually using the system during the Operational Use Stage. As in our preceding two examples, the first step in the review process is to freeze the review initiator, i.e., the IR. The product assurance organization assigns a label to the IR and places a copy of the IR under control by putting it in a master file of incident reports.

The auditors conduct an audit at this point by checking the archive to see whether the incident reported in the IR has previously been reported and/or resolved. If the IR is a duplicate of a pending IR (one that has not yet been resolved), the CCB, at its first decision point, may decide to reject the IR (the project team is currently trying to resolve the incident under another IR), to dispense with further processing of the IR, and to return to the Operational Use Stage. If the IR is not a duplicate or is a duplicate that was thought to be previously resolved (it appears that the previous resolution did not resolve the incident), the CCB generally sends the IR to an investigating organization (typically, the development organization) for analysis.

In this example, as shown in Figure 4–10, the analysis determined that a correction to the code was necessary to resolve the incident. The development organization prepares a proposed code change, but rather than sending it back to the CCB, it uses the alternative route (indicated with dashed arrow heads) by sending the proposed code change to the system test team to be audited.

The test team, a group independent from the development organization (e.g., product assurance organization), audits the proposed change by conducting system tests of the provisionally changed software code. That is, the test team takes the changed software code, integrates it with the existing code, and tests the resulting system in a live or nearly live environment. The purpose of these tests is to ascertain whether the reported incident is successfully resolved by the code change and whether any deterioration of other system capabilities results from the change. The test team reports its findings to the CCB.

The CCB, using its switch capabilities, can direct the IR along the following three paths, shown in Figure 4–10:

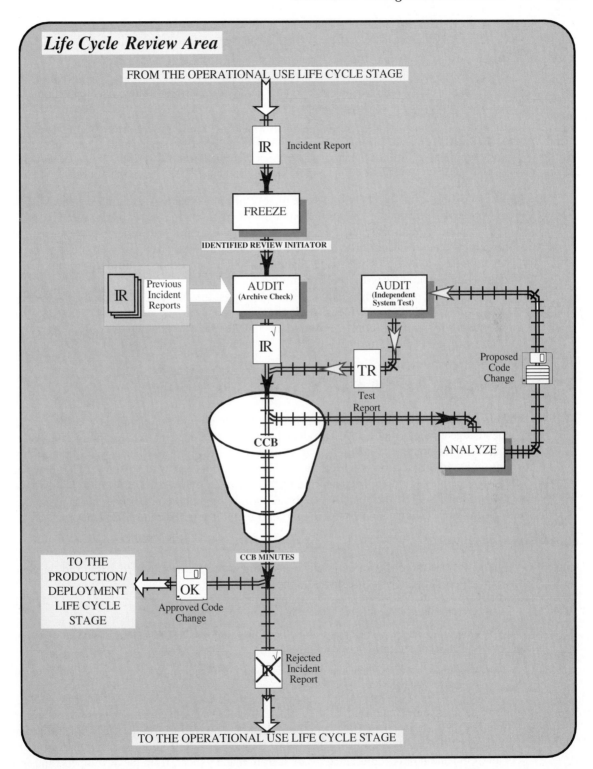

FIGURE 4–10 Change control of an unplanned (i.e., revolutionary) change—a user-submitted incident report.

- If the test report indicates that the incident has not been satisfactorily resolved, the CCB may direct that the investigating organization **reanalyze the IR** and prepare a new proposed change.

- If the test report indicates that the proposed code change has satisfactorily resolved the incident without harmful side effects (i.e., without introducing problems in other system capabilities), the CCB may approve the proposed change and route it **to the Production/Deployment Life Cycle Stage** for production and dissemination of the modified software.

- The CCB may decide to reject the IR, in which case return is made **to the Operational Use Life Cycle Stage** and the originator is informed of the action. Such an action might be taken if the IR is a duplicate of a pending IR or if the IR does not represent a problem with the software code (e.g., it may have resulted from an operator error or from a user's misperception of the system's capabilities).

The foregoing example shows only one of several routes that an IR might take during the change control process. For example, the resolution of the IR might be to modify one or more baselines, to amend the software requirements, or to modify one of the other project products (say, a user's manual). We have looked at the change control process in some detail. Our discussion and illustrations show that the focal point of this processing is the change control board. It is now time to explore the CCB in more depth—to ascertain what it is and how it works.

As a final note for this section, we point out that the change control process discussed in this section—with the CCB as the focus of all change processing—is not the only way to process software changes. When you are implementing your change control process, you need to assess the risk of not channelling all changes through a CCB-like mechanism.

4.5 EXAMINATION OF THE CHANGE CONTROL BOARD

In the preceding section, we showed that the change control board (CCB) was the central element in the change control process. We introduced the CCB as a decision-making body establishing baselines, approving discrepancy resolutions, directing revisits to life cycle stages, and authorizing updates of baselines. In this section, we focus on this board and discuss who sits on it, what decisions it makes, how it operates, what is contained in a CCB charter, and how a CCB meeting is conducted. The purpose of this in-depth examination is to bring to light the important considerations associated with planning for, establishing, and sustaining this central element in the change control process.

CCB Composition—*Who Sits on the CCB?*

The following three software systems development disciplines that contribute to the achievement of software product integrity should sit on the CCB:

- **Management.** Including both senior and project management.

- **Development.** Including analysis, design engineering, production (coding), unit and subsystem testing, installation, documentation, and training.

- **Product assurance.** Including quality assurance, verification and validation, test and evaluation, and configuration management.

Because the synergistic efforts of these three disciplines are needed to achieve software products with integrity and because the CCB is the forum that is central to the product assurance function of change control, it seems only reasonable that the CCB should include all three disciplines in its membership. The CCB should have representatives on it from management, from the developers, and from the product assurance practitioners. However, this does not mean that a CCB should be permanently staffed with a representative from each subfunction just mentioned. For example, a CCB does not have to be permanently staffed with a coding representative and a training representative, among others. Many CCB meetings are not concerned with coding or training. The CCB should be permanently staffed with at least one representative from management, from development, and from product assurance, with additional representation provided according to the subject matter under consideration at any particular meeting. Remember that the CCB is a forum for the exchange of information, whose purpose is to make change control decisions. It is essential to this purpose to have representation from and interaction among all concerned parties relative to whatever matter is under consideration.

In this discussion of representation on the CCB, we have not said which archetypical project participant (i.e., user, buyer, and seller) provides the representatives. After all, user, buyer, and seller project participants may have its own project management, as well as its own development and product assurance staffs. Which archetypical participant should provide representatives to the CCB? We believe they all should. Ideally, the CCB should include management, development, and product assurance representatives from the user, from the buyer, and from the seller. It may not always be practical to have all these representatives (for example, the user may be many thousands of miles away from the buyer and seller), but to the extent possible the CCB should be established as an integrated one. What better forum exists for interaction of the user, buyer, and seller in the control of change on a project? Such a CCB greatly increases the visibility of the changes under consideration and of the viewpoints of all project participants. The result should be better change control decisions.

Up to this point, we have discussed the CCB as if it were a single board managing all change. In practice, many projects will have more than a single CCB to manage change within a project. Several factors are involved in the decision regarding how many CCBs to establish on a project, as discussed in the following paragraphs.

One of these factors is the individual and collective needs and concerns of the user, the buyer, and the seller. Figure 4–11 shows the effect of this factor on the establishment of CCBs. The figure shows how organizational units of the user, the buyer, and the seller, encompassing the disciplines of management, development, and product assurance, can meet together to form an integrated CCB. The shadings in the figure indicate various combinations of the user, buyer, and seller joining in an integrated CCB:

- **User/buyer CCB.** A user/buyer CCB might meet to consider baselining the requirements specification, prior to its delivery to the seller for fulfillment.

- **User/seller CCB.** A user/seller CCB might consider the resolution of incidents arising in operational software, provided the incidents had no impact on cost and schedule. If such incidents did impact cost and/or schedule, the buyer would be most interested in participating in the discussion.

- **Buyer/seller CCB.** A buyer/seller CCB might be convened, for example, to consider a draft detailed design document, in which the user would have a minor interest.

- **User/buyer/seller CCB.** We consider this CCB the preferred option.

Some people may argue that creating a CCB consisting of buyer and seller personnel is inherently unworkable. Project managers, either buyer or seller, would generally rather not have unpleasant or unfavorable news (such as the need to make a large number of changes to a software product that should be near the end of its development) divulged in a public forum. It is human nature to put off public disclosure of an organization's problems in the expectation that timely solutions to the problems can be developed within the organization. If such solutions can be found, there is no need to make the problems public. On the other hand, if such solutions are not forthcoming, the problems may have to be surfaced publicly at some later date, when they generally would be more difficult and costly to solve. The CCB provides a forum where such problems can be made visible and where the entire project team can focus on their solution. The earlier in the life cycle that problems are introduced to the CCB, the more likely it is that a software product with integrity can be achieved. The authors have seen numerous cases in which joint buyer/seller CCBs have proven quite workable in resolving problems.

In some circumstances, one of these organizations (i.e., user, buyer, or seller) may validly wish to convene a CCB comprised only of members of its own organization. For example, the seller may

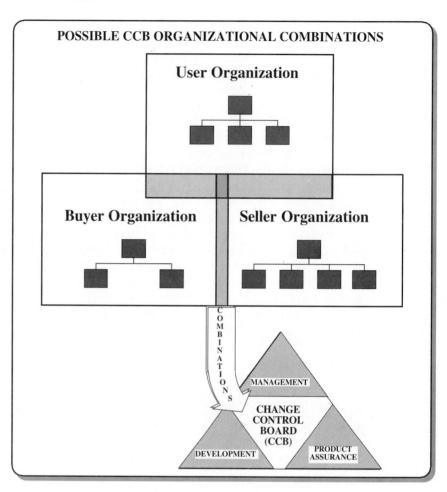

FIGURE 4–11 CCBs provide forums for units of each organization within the user/buyer/seller triumvirate—or for pairs of these organizations, or for all three organizations—to interact continually and effectively on a software development project for the purpose of managing change.

wish to hold a CCB meeting with only seller personnel present to consider the first draft of a document that will eventually be baselined. This CCB would increase the likelihood that the document had product integrity before it was presented to the buyer and user. When this seller CCB is satisfied with the document, it would be presented to an integrated buyer/seller CCB for consideration as a baseline.

CCB Hierarchies—*How Many CCBs?*

A second factor in determining the number and kind of CCBs to establish is the system development issues that might be faced on a project. Figure 4–12 shows a hierarchy of system development issues, along with a sample of each issue and a CCB that might be established to handle the issue. The hierarchy shown is not unique; we use it here for expository purposes. In the figure, the level of hierarchy is indicated by appropriate indentation. Within every project, there are system issues and, in many projects, system external interface issues to be addressed. Within the system, there are subsystem issues and inter-subsystem interface issues to be considered (for systems having major, identifiable subsystems). Within each subsystem, there are hardware, software, and internal (hardware/software) interface issues to be resolved.

Sample issues like those suggested in Figure 4–12 exist for almost every project, but all the CCBs shown in the figure would not necessarily be established on every project. Which ones should be established for a project vary from project to project. The key elements to consider when deciding whether an issue is significant enough to merit creation of a separate CCB include project size and

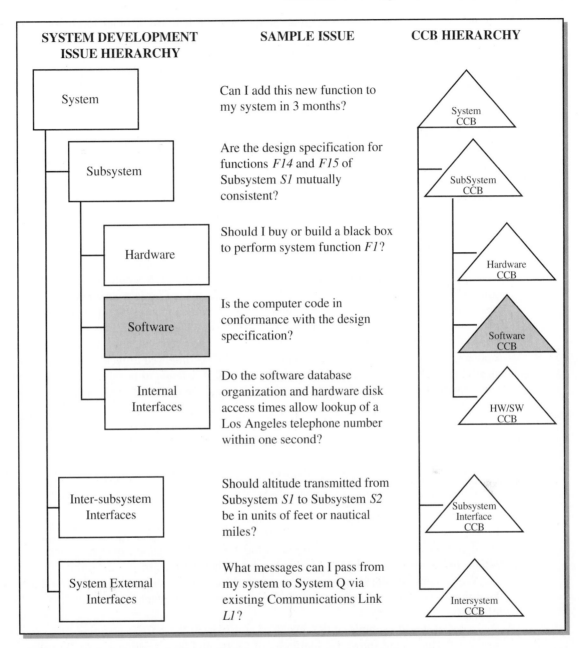

FIGURE 4–12 A CCB hierarchy generally derives from the hierarchy of issues associated with system development and their perceived significance.

complexity, and criticality and importance of the issue within a project. Those issues for which CCBs are not established are subsumed by the next highest issue in the hierarchy for which a CCB is established. For example, on a small project, only a System CCB might be established. All the issues shown in Figure 4–12 would be considered by this System CCB. Consider, on the other hand, a very large project where each subsystem is an operational system in itself. In this case, the full spectrum of CCBs shown in Figure 4–12 might be constituted.

Because the focus of this book is on software, we have shaded the software issue in the hierarchy and the Software CCB in Figure 4–12. Most software issues are handled at this level. However, you should be aware that some software-related issues are handled at other levels in the issue hierarchy. For instance, see the sample issue for subsystem in Figure 4–12—the consideration of design specifications clearly has software-related aspects as well as hardware-related aspects. On some projects, the software issue is refined into subissues for which separate CCBs are established. The authors are familiar with a project, for example, in which a Software Incident Report CCB and a Software Change Request CCB were established.

A third factor to consider in planning for the establishment of CCBs is the level of expertise needed for each CCB. Consider a CCB whose members are managers of the various organizations represented at the CCB. Such a CCB would have difficulty making informed decisions on issues involving the technical details of the project. The management-oriented members of the CCB may not have the technical background to understand the problems or resolutions presented to them. A similar difficulty arises if the CCB consists of engineers and staff personnel and is faced with making decisions concerned with project policy. This latter CCB probably would not have the expertise or the authority in policy concerns to make proper decisions.

A solution to these difficulties is to staff the CCB with both managers and technical personnel from the management, development, and product assurance disciplines. This solution carries the disadvantage that, for some period of time, every member of the CCB would be noncontributing. Each situation needs to be evaluated so that there is an effective use of project personnel.

Another solution is to create several CCBs, each having a restricted area of decision making and a membership with the appropriate level of expertise. One approach that we have seen function successfully using such levels is to constitute a CCB composed of managers from the management, development, and product assurance disciplines, and a CCB composed of technical personnel from the three disciplines. The scope of the management-level CCB extends to resource allocation, budgets, schedules, and policies; technical details are not considered. On the other hand, the technical-level CCB concentrates on the detailed technical aspects of the project. Matters arising at a CCB meeting that do not fall within the appropriate level of expertise of that CCB are referred to the other CCB.

In planning for the CCBs to use on a project, at least three factors should be considered:

- Involvement of the user, buyer, and seller.

- System development issues to be handled.

- Levels of expertise required.

Applying these factors to their extreme could lead to the creation of a bewildering array of CCBs, whose prime effort would probably be deciding what the area of responsibility for each CCB should be! We certainly do not suggest going to an extreme. We are suggesting that these three factors should be rationally considered in the context of each project when planning the establishment of a hierarchy of CCBs.

A real-world example of the results of considering these CCB planning factors is shown in Figure 4–13. This figure shows the hierarchy of CCBs and their relationship to the seller's development and product assurance staffs on a large project. This project is a "system of systems." Each subsystem is a large, independently operating system, interfacing with the other subsystems via high-speed data links. The CCB hierarchy consists of a buyer/user management-level system CCB and a buyer/seller technical-level software CCB for each subsystem.

Note in Figure 4–13 that the relationship between the Software CCB for Subsystem Y and the seller's development and product assurance staffs for Subsystem Y is one of technical guidance and is not a line of authority. Note also that the domains of concern for the two levels of CCB overlap—the management-level CCB addresses some technical issues, and the technical-level CCB addresses some managerial issues.

But not every product assurance manager is faced with large-sized projects. You might well ask for an example of a CCB hierarchy for a medium-sized or small-sized project. Figure 4–14 is a modi-

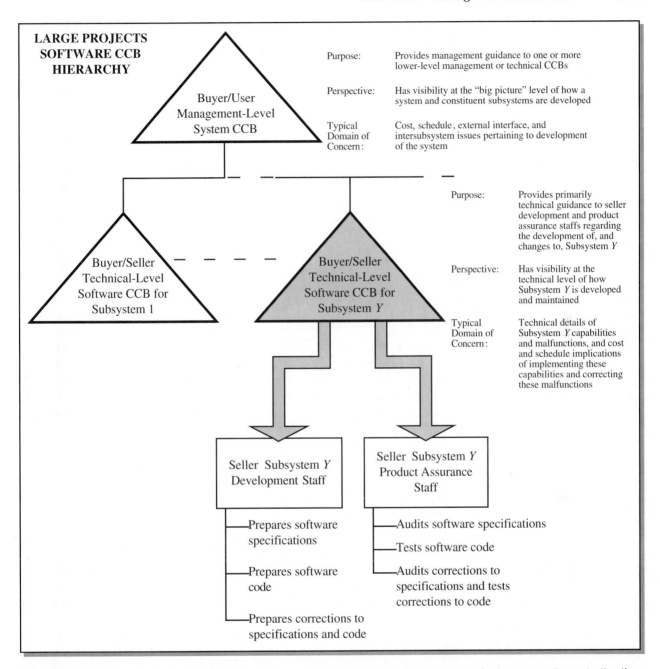

FIGURE 4–13 Sample (software) CCB hierarchy organized along management/technical and user/buyer/seller lines illustrating how management and technical CCB guidance effects and affects software change.

fied version of the CCB hierarchy for large-sized projects and represents a hierarchy for medium/small-sized projects that the authors have planned and implemented.

The CCB hierarchy for large-sized projects has been modified in the following ways:

- All subsystem CCBs have been removed, except for that for Subsystem *Y*.
- The retained Subsystem *Y* CCB has been labeled as the Software CCB (for the entire system).

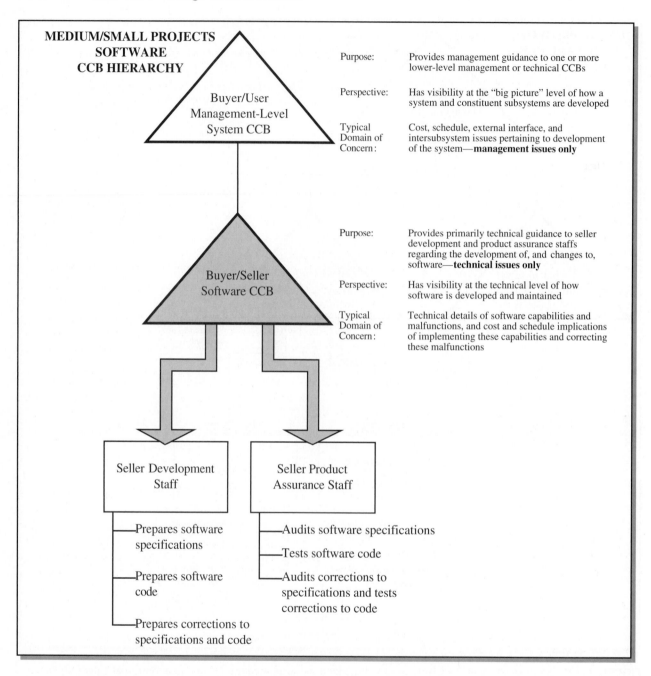

FIGURE 4–14   Sample (software) CCB hierarchy for medium-sized or small-sized projects.

■ The domains of concern of the two remaining CCBs have been redefined so that the management-level CCB does not address any technical issues and the technical-level CCB does not address any management issues.

However, do not be misled by these two examples. Many variations are possible and have been implemented to satisfy particular project needs. Some variations may employ only a single CCB; others may use numerous CCBs. The number of possible CCB hierarchies is great, affording the opportunity to tailor a hierarchy that is suitable for each particular project.

Thus far in this section we have examined CCB composition and hierarchies of CCBs. We now turn our attention to CCB operation. Here we consider the types of decisions a CCB makes, the voting mechanism it uses to arrive at a decision, and the person who should chair the CCB. (Although in the following discussion we refer to "the" CCB, we intend for the discussion to apply to any appropriate CCB in a hierarchy.)

CCB Decisions—*What Types of Decisions Are Made?*

The CCB is a decision-making body. As the change control organization, its primary functions are to establish baselines and to resolve discrepancies, change requests, and incident reports that come before it. When considering a draft baseline, the CCB may elect either to (1) accept the draft and establish a baseline, (2) establish a baseline subject to later resolution of outstanding discrepancies, or (3) reject the draft baseline. Acceptance is not necessarily predicated upon there being no outstanding discrepancies against the draft baseline. Although such a goal is desirable, practical considerations often dictate that the CCB establish a baseline and postpone resolution of any outstanding discrepancies to some later agreed-upon date. Rejection of a draft baseline could be based on its noncongruence with its predecessor baseline or its requirements, or on other discrepancies, such as its internal inconsistency or its failure to satisfy specified standards. When the CCB rejects a draft baseline, it provides a list of approved changes to the draft baseline. The development organization reworks the draft baseline to incorporate the changes and submits the revised draft baseline to the CCB for approval.

The CCB can make basically the same decisions relative to discrepancies, change requests, and incident reports. As shown in Figure 4–15, these decisions are to (1) approve a change, (2) make no change, and (3) revise the change approach. The individual nuances of these decisions relative to discrepancies, change requests, and incident reports are discussed in the following paragraphs. Note in Figure 4–15 that the decision process is initiated by submission of a change control form.

Let us consider first the decisions that the CCB can make relative to the resolution of a discrepancy uncovered by an audit. A *discrepancy,* quite simply, is "an incongruity (i.e., a difference) observed as a result of comparing (i.e., an audit) a software product with the ground truth." The CCB can approve the proposed resolution of the discrepancy to change the draft baseline or another baseline. It can reject the proposed-resolution and order the reanalysis of the discrepancy by the investigating organization. Finally, the CCB can close out the discrepancy with no action being required. This latter decision could be based on several circumstances. The discrepancy could be a duplicate of another discrepancy that had already been resolved. The discrepancy could have resulted from a misunderstanding by the auditor. For example, if the auditor is uncertain about a point, the auditor may write a discrepancy to prompt the CCB to consider whether a problem indeed exists. If the CCB decides no problem exists, the CCB closes out the discrepancy with no action being required.

Regarding a change request, the CCB can make one of three decisions: it can (1) accept it (and have the change implemented), (2) reject it (in which case the originator is notified and the change request is archived), or (3) require its reanalysis. The decision to accept the proposed change may mean that the next life cycle stage is entered. Rejection of the proposed change may result with continuation of the current life cycle stage, when the originator of the change request is informed of the decision and project work continues. If the change request must be reanalyzed, it is returned to the investigating organization. The investigators will return the change request to the CCB after completing its reanalysis, and the CCB will again consider it for approval.

Next we consider CCB decisions relative to incident reports. Observe how Figure 4–15 applies here. The CCB can decide to (1) approve a change that resolves the incident, (2) reject an incident as requiring no action to be taken, or (3) require reanalysis of the incident by the investigating organization. An approved change can take several forms. To correct the problem that the incident reported, a

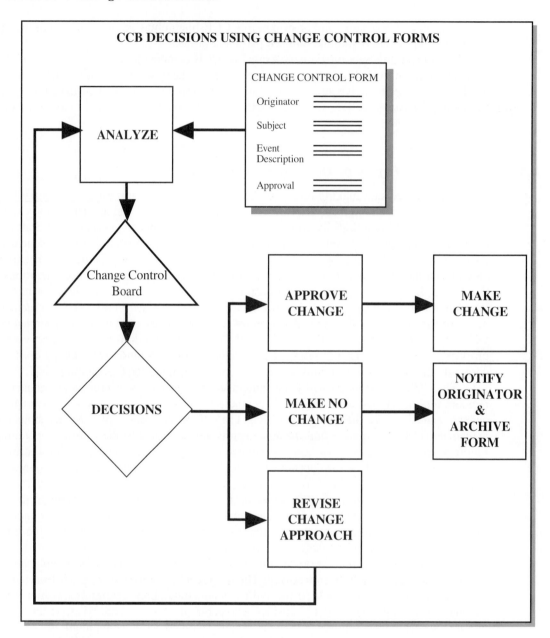

FIGURE 4–15 The decisions that the CCB can make relative to a change control form.

change to the software code and/or to one or more of the documents previously developed on the project can be required. These documents could be either software documents or software-related documents (e.g., a user's manual). An approved change could also require an enhancement to the software. Such a change would be made to the Requirements Baseline.

For a variety of reasons, an incident report (IR) can be rejected with no requirement for any action to be taken. A similar incident report may have been previously considered and rejected or approved for a change that has not yet been implemented, or a similar IR may have been previously submitted and be under consideration currently. The duplicate incident report in these three instances would not be considered further; the originator of the incident report would be notified of the CCB decision and the incident report archived. Another reason for rejecting an IR with no action to be taken is that the incident report could be the result of operator or user error. It could have resulted from a misunderstanding of the software operation on the part of the user who originated it.

CCB Operations—*How Does the CCB Decide What to Do Next?*

Having discussed the decisions that the CCB may make, we now consider how the CCB arrives at those decisions (i.e., CCB voting mechanisms). Such mechanisms include the following:

- One-person-one-vote.
- One-organization-one-vote.
- Consensus vote.
- Single-person vote.

One choice for a CCB voting mechanism is to give each board member one vote and to specify that the majority effects a decision (what constitutes a majority must be specified in the directive establishing the CCB). To those of us raised in a democratic tradition, this voting mechanism has obvious appeal: all views are considered equally, and everyone is a part of the decision process (and therefore probably more interested in the proceedings). But watch out! This form of voting mechanism could lead to stacking the vote by one organization. For example, if the seller's entire development organization came to a CCB meeting, it might outvote the rest of the membership and make all the decisions conform to its organization's wishes. Another disadvantage of the one-person-one-vote voting mechanism is that politics could be introduced into the voting process. "If I vote to approve items *A* and *B* that you are interested in getting approved, will you vote to approve items *C* and *D* that I am interested in getting approved?" The result is CCB decisions based on vote trading and not on the technical merits of each item considered.

A possible modification to the one-person-one-vote voting mechanism would be to give a vote to each organization represented on the CCB rather than to each individual. This method loses some of its democratic appeal—indeed, it is a republican process. (Note that both "democratic" and "republican" begin with a lower-case letter!) But it still keeps everyone involved in the decision process. The possibility of politicking still exists in this method, but the ability to stack the vote is prevented—the number of votes remains constant, regardless of how many members of one organization attend a meeting.

Another voting mechanism to consider is to achieve a consensus among the board members on each item under consideration. By *consensus* we mean "the informal agreement (no vote counting) of most of those present at a meeting." This method permits the expression of all viewpoints and retains the interest of all board members. It is more expeditious than voting by individuals or organizations, and it tends to inhibit politicking. But what if the CCB cannot achieve consensus? No decision can be made in such a case, unless a mechanism to break deadlocks has been included in the CCB's charter. Such an escape mechanism might be to give all the votes to a single person when it is necessary to break a deadlock.

Giving all the votes to a single person (say, for the moment, the chairperson of the CCB) could be the voting mechanism used by a CCB under all circumstances. Such a method certainly fosters decision-making, but it may quickly stifle the interest of the other board representatives. If the chairperson never considers their views, listens to their comments, or consults with them prior to making a decision, they will have little interest in the CCB proceedings or even in attending the meetings. The chairperson must recognize his or her potential for limiting participation and take positive measures to encourage input and discussion from all CCB members. The chairperson needs the visibility that their input provides if he or she is to make good change control decisions.

CCB Leadership—*Who Should Be the CCB Chairperson?*

We need to say a few words here about the chairperson of the CCB. The selection of this person is especially important when he or she has all the votes. Under the other voting mechanisms, the selection of the chairperson is less critical, the primary duties of the chairperson in these cases being to keep the board on track with its agenda and to keep discussion focused on the issues. So let us consider possible choices for CCB chairperson when all the votes for the board are given to that person. To enlarge the scope of the selection, let us further assume that the CCB is composed of buyer and seller representatives. Table 4–1 shows for several candidates some considerations pertinent to the selection of a CCB chairperson.

You can observe from that table that there are advantages and disadvantages to selecting any of the candidates listed there. On each project, you must weigh the considerations given in this and the preceding paragraphs and in Table 4–1 in selecting a CCB chairperson and a CCB voting mechanism for making decisions.

CCB Charter—*What Is Contained in a CCB Charter?*

A CCB charter spells out the specific scope of CCB activities. The following discussion provides a recommended charter outline, suggested boilerplate wording for sections 1 and 3, and guidance for other sections (enclosed within brackets). The CCB charter may contain the following sections:

- **1.0 CCB PURPOSE.** The purpose of the *[Project Name]* Change Control Board (CCB) is to ensure that *[Project Name]* product changes and related programmatic changes (i.e., consideration of proposed cost and schedule changes) are processed in a visible and traceable manner. The CCB is the forum in which (1) *[Project Name]* project participants get together to discuss what needs to be done, (2) responsible agents are assigned for performing agreed-upon work, and (3) decisions and assigned actions are recorded.

- **2.0 CCB MEMBERSHIP.** [This section lists organizational titles of management, the product development organization, and the product assurance organization who are to be regular attendees at the CCB. All these organizations are required. If the CCB is to include third parties, their organizational titles are listed. The minimum requirement for seller management representation is the seller project leader, and for the

TABLE 4–1   Advantages and Disadvantages of Candidates for CCB Chairperson.

CCB Chairperson Candidate	Advantage(s)	Disadvantage(s)
Seller's project manager	■ Responsible for project development and maintenance ■ Probably most technically competent of managerial personnel	■ May not have the buyer's interests at heart
Buyer's project manager	■ Bears the prime responsibility to the user for product integrity ■ Puts up the money to fund the project	■ May not be technically competent to render reasonable decisions regarding software changes
Seller's product assurance (PA) representative	■ Change control is one of PA representative's prime responsibilities	■ May be biased toward seller's interests at the expense of the buyer ■ May be too technically oriented, slighting management considerations
Buyer's product assurance (PA) representative	■ Change control is one of PA representative's prime responsibilities	■ May not be sensitive to certain project issues that may affect the feasibility of implementing changes approved
Seller's and buyers project managers, serving jointly	■ Buyer and seller equally represented ■ Buyer and seller bear the prime responsibility for the project within own organizations	■ Has potential for deadlock

customer, the customer project leader. This section also contains a statement that other organizations may be invited by the seller and/or customer project leaders on an as-needed basis. In addition, this section indicates the organization responsible for documenting the meeting. As an option, this section can indicate that the chairperson will designate someone from the seller project team on a rotating basis to be responsible for documenting the meeting.]

- **3.0 CCB CHAIRPERSON.** The chairperson is *[indicate one of the following: customer project manager, seller project manager, or alternates; if there are to be joint chairpersons, indicate some combination of these entities].* The chairperson will manage the meeting in such a manner that input and discussion are encouraged from all attendees. Product and programmatic decision authority rests with the chairperson and is made a matter of record in the meeting documentation.

- **4.0 CCB ACTIVITIES.** [This section lists the activities that the CCB is to perform. This section also specifies the CCB meeting frequency. The minimum requirement for this frequency is monthly. The specification of CCB activities can be as detailed as management desires. Examples of such activities are listed below. This list is intended to be a starting point for defining CCB responsibilities. In general, a particular CCB will have some subset of these responsibilities or adaptations of these responsibilities.

  - Reviewing a schedule of software and data product deliverables to determine whether these deliverables are being produced on time and within budget.
  - Prioritizing efforts to be undertaken.
  - Reviewing proposed changes to a requirements or design or database specification, or some other product.
  - Considering a customer or internal proposal to alter the work called out in a project plan.
  - Approving patch code (i.e., an emergency repair that permits continued use of operational software capabilities until a permanent change can be implemented).
  - Logging incident reports (IRs) that product assurance has prepared describing the difference between a product under review and related predecessor products and/or standards governing the development of that product.
  - Deciding on a labeling scheme (i.e., configuration identification) for products (i.e., documentation, computer code, and databases [draft and final]).
  - Reviewing a product (such as a design document) to determine whether previously approved changes have been incorporated.
  - Approving a product assurance plan.
  - Reviewing a product assurance report that documents inconsistencies between a product and a predecessor product (e.g., inconsistencies between a software design specification and a software requirements specification).
  - Reviewing the results of an acceptance test showing discrepancies between output generated by the code and output specified in requirements and design documentation from which the code was presumably developed.
  - Approving a documentation standard that is to govern the format and content of products to be produced on a project.
  - Recording CCB minutes.
  - Reviewing CCB minutes from the previous CCB meeting to confirm their accuracy.
  - Reviewing a dry run of a presentation of project status that is eventually to be given to senior management.
  - Reviewing, approving, and, if necessary, recording changes to the documentation of the preceding CCB meeting.]

- **5.0 CCB MEETING DOCUMENTATION.** [This section specifies the information to be recorded at the CCB meeting. At a minimum, the following information is required:

  - Meeting date, time, and duration.
  - List of attendees (first and last name of each) and their organizations.

- Discussion (documentation of this discussion can be as detailed as management desires; at a minimum, it should provide the context for associated decisions made and action items assigned during the meeting).
- Existing action items (i.e., open action items and ones closed during the meeting being documented; each action item should be described in at least one complete sentence).
- New action items (the guidance for existing action items apples here, too).
- Summary of action items (running list of all items to date showing the responsible individual{s}, status, date assigned, date due).
- Decisions made.

The types of change control forms that are to be used to define, track, and manage changes should be indicated. It is helpful to include sample forms as attachments to the charter.

In addition to the minimum information required, other information bearing on discussions, decisions, and action items can be attached to the meeting documentation. For example, such information may include the following: screen designs, memorandum for the record, and E-mail messages.]

CCB Meeting Conduct—*How Is a CCB Meeting Conducted?*

The specific manner in which a CCB meeting is to be conducted depends on its purpose and scope as defined in the CCB charter. However, there are several general considerations for conducting a CCB meeting. These considerations are addressed in the following paragraphs.

Prior to a CCB meeting, the chairperson may choose to prepare an agenda. Once the CCB becomes institutionalized on a project, this activity may be unnecessary. In particular, the CCB minutes format, once it has stabilized, serves as a general agenda for a CCB meeting. Experience shows that after two or three meetings, the participants generally agree upon a minutes format that is satisfactory for supporting CCB operation.

The chairperson may choose to run the meeting or designate someone else to perform this function. The meeting should begin with review of the minutes from the preceding meeting. To expedite this review, the chairperson may choose to distribute copies of these minutes to attendees prior to the meeting. Following the review, attendees should be given the opportunity to offer changes to the minutes. If these changes are agreed to by others, they should be made a matter of record in the minutes of the current meeting. The minutes of the current meeting should then reflect that (1) the minutes of the preceding meeting were approved with the changes cited or (2) in the case that no changes were made, the minutes were approved as written.

Next, the actions cited in the minutes of the preceding meeting that were to be accomplished by the current meeting should be individually addressed. Decisions reached regarding these actions should be recorded. New actions resulting from these decisions should be recorded and individuals responsible for these actions should be assigned, as well as dates when these actions are to be completed. The discussion pertaining to CCB actions should be incorporated into the minutes. The record of this discussion should be as detailed as mutually agreed to by CCB participants or as directed by the CCB chairperson. New action items should recorded, and the information on outstanding action items resulting from CCB actions should be updated.

Next, new business (e.g., new change proposals, and depending on the CCB scope, programmatic changes such as revised product delivery dates, changes in CCB participants, [proposed] changes in personnel assignments impacting product development) should be addressed and made a matter of record. New action items resulting from this new business discussion should be recorded.

If two different projects require coordination, the CCB meeting should also consider issues requiring coordination of the activities of CCBs for each project. To coordinate the activities of these two CCBs, it may be necessary to ensure that participants in one CCB attend the other CCB at appropriate times. This coordination activity should be given visibility in the CCB minutes through the assignment of action agents and corresponding due dates. Alternatively, the next scheduled meeting of these two CCBs may be designated as a joint CCB involving participants from both CCBs. The meeting should be closed by specifying the time and place of the next CCB meeting. Copies of the CCB minutes should be distributed to all CCB attendees and nonparticipants desiring visibility into the project (e.g., management). It is also useful to send a copy to a centralized project file.

Regarding the amount of detail to include in CCB meeting minutes, the following considerations apply:

- The basic purpose of the minutes is to provide the CCB decision makers the information needed to make intelligent, informed decisions regarding how the program should proceed. Since memories tend to fade over time, the amount of detail needed depends, in part, on CCB meeting frequency—more frequent meetings generally imply a need for less detail.

- The seller project manager, in concert with the customer project manager, may choose to use CCBs as a forum for doing some product development (e.g., specify user-friendly requirements in testable terms). In this case, the CCB minutes can contain considerable detail. Such detail often expedites product completion, since these details can be directly coordinated with the customer at the CCB. Then, this agreed-upon material can be directly incorporated into the product to be delivered.

- For programs that are planned to span a year or more, the amount of detail included in CCB minutes should be governed by the risks associated with personnel turnover. More detailed minutes will facilitate transitions associated with seller project turnover and will lessen the impact of technical staff turnover.

This discussion completes our examination of the CCB. We have now discussed the types of changes on a project, the process of change control, and the organization at the focus of this process. To complete our study of software change control, we need only discuss the paperwork supporting the change control process. The next section addresses this topic. Strictly speaking, paperwork support of the CCB is a bookkeeping function. The software change control portion of the bookkeeping function is included in the current chapter because it is an integral part of the change management process.

4.6 PAPERWORK SUPPORT OF THE CHANGE CONTROL BOARD

Paperwork! The very mention of the word probably makes you grimace. Yet the paperwork support of the change control board (CCB) is essential if the change control process is to be visible and traceable. Our definition of "paperwork" encompasses both hard copy and electronic copy. Your organization will need to decide the appropriate mix of hard copy and electronic copy to support your change control process.

In this section, we discuss why paperwork is necessary in change control and then show you how to develop and use a set of change control forms and CCB minutes. We take this approach (rather than presenting "the" forms or minutes that you must use) because you will want to tailor your change control forms and minutes to your particular project and environment. To this end, we first derive a typical set of forms needed to support the CCB. We provide guidelines on forms design, and then lead you through the design of one of these forms, the incident report. We show you examples of the other needed forms—software change notice, change request, and an impact assessment. We present three general scenarios covering all the situations that could precipitate a software change and illustrate the use of the sample forms in these scenarios. We conclude the section with a discussion of CCB minutes and how they can be used with or in lieu of change control forms.

CCB Paperwork—*What Forms Are Needed?*

Is paperwork really necessary to support the change control process? The authors have not met anyone who would not agree that some paperwork is necessary to control change. Paperwork appears to be widely viewed as a "necessary evil." Perhaps it would seem less evil if one considered that the alternative (no paperwork) might well lead to statements by the project participants such as the following:

- Exactly what change am I being asked to approve?

- I've got an angry user on the telephone. Does anyone remember what problem she reported last month?

- No, I haven't made that change—I didn't know it had been approved.

- I'm ready to make the change now, but I forget the details of the elegant solution that our recently departed guru recommended. Does anyone know how I can reach him?

- You were right—this problem is the same one we had last fall. I've found the report of the old problem, but I can't find out how we solved it. I guess I'll have to solve it all over again.

Statements like these indicate a lack of visibility and traceability in the change control process. Forms make manifest the visibility and traceability that the CCB provides to the change control process. The use of a form to record a problem, to recommend that a change be made, or to indicate a CCB decision immediately captures that event and makes it uniformly visible to all project participants. Instead of becoming the subject of guesswork, the event is made concrete.

Capturing the event and using cross-references between forms provides traceability between events connected with the change control process. Figure 4–16 illustrates the concept that forms (in conjunction with the CCB) give visibility and traceability to the change control process.

In the figure, a change control **Event p** (e.g., the occurrence of an incident at a user site) has been recorded on **FORM TYPE A**. A subsequent **Event q** (e.g., the promulgation of a notice announcing an approved change) causes form **TYPE B** to be generated. The act of recording **Events p** and q has made the change control process more visible. Visibility between the forms is symbolically shown in the figure by the arrow connecting forms **TYPE A** and **TYPE B**.

In the figure, **Event q** is related to **Event p**. For example, **Event p** could be an incident, while **Event q** could be the promulgation of the resolution to the incident. Traceability between **Events p** and q is symbolically shown in the figure by the arrow connecting the two-way reference between the forms. On the actual forms that we discuss later in this section, traceability between these events is attained by a pointer to **FORM TYPE B** placed on **FORM TYPE A**, and by a pointer to **FORM TYPE A** placed on **FORM TYPE B**.

Note that this figure does not imply that every project event is recorded on a form. Indeed, the opposite is true—many events on a software project are not recorded on forms (e.g., a meeting of a CCB).

The fundamental questions to ask yourself include the following:

- What forms are needed?

- How are change control visibility and traceability achieved?

- How should existing forms be used?

- How should unplanned and planned changes be processed?

To answer these fundamental questions, we suggest that you consider the following categorization of changes that includes one more level of depth than unplanned and planned change. This categorization we characterize by the following three questions:

- **Unplanned Change.** Do we want something not already in the software or something that extends what is already there? Briefly stated: Do we want something new or different?

  Is something in the software at variance with the requirements specification? Briefly stated: Is something wrong?

- **Planned Change.** Should we establish this product as a new or updated baseline? Briefly stated: Should we baseline this product?

We contend that this categorization includes all possible changes to the software in a system.

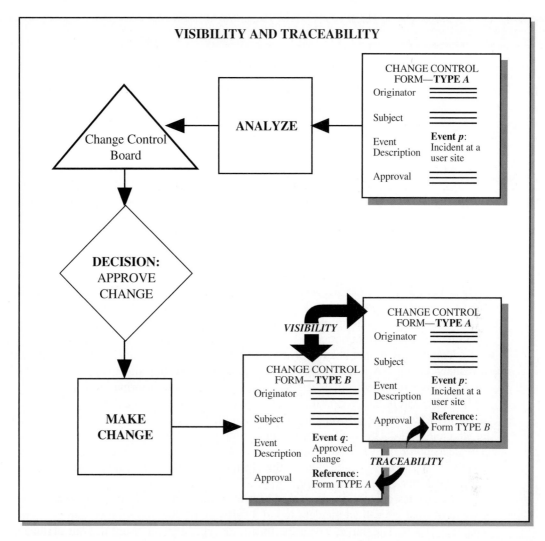

FIGURE 4–16 Forms, in conjunction with the CCB, give visibility and traceability to the change control process.

Next you need to choose a set of forms to support the change control process. We do not recommend that you construct the change control process to match existing forms, but rather the reverse. Table 4–2 lists the basic events in the change control process events (i.e., initiation, freezing, audit, analysis, decision, and implementation), and some information to be recorded about each event. All these events shown in the table result in providing information relative to a pending change. However, the information obtained from an audit is generally recorded in an audit report (possibly a collection of other change control forms), and no separate change control form is needed to support this event. The information gathered from the change control process events listed in Table 4–2 is captured on change control forms.

You can derive a set of forms by allocating the basic change control process events to various forms as you answer the following questions presented earlier:

■ Do we want something new or different?

■ Is something wrong?

■ Should we baseline this product?

Table 4–2	**For each event in the change control process, information must be recorded to provide visibility and traceability to the process.**

Event	*Information to Be Recorded*
Initiation	Identification of the originator and of the environment, statement of the problem
Freezing	Identification of the problem
Audit	Discrepancies uncovered
Analysis	Cause, impact, and recommended resolution
Decision	CCB action
Implementation	Statement of what is to be changed

Note that each change control process event for a category must be recorded either (1) on one of the forms you decide to use or (2) in some other established place, such as CCB minutes. Table 4–3 shows a set of forms resulting from one of our allocations of the change control process events.

Observe from the table that we chose not to record the implementation event on any form used to answer the question, "Do we want something new or different?" This omission is deliberate—when the CCB approves a change to add something new or different, the implementation almost always initially involves the updating of the requirements specification. The republication of the requirements specification is sufficient notice of the implementation of the unplanned change.

You usually do not need a form to provide visibility and traceability to the process of baselining a planned change. A form is not needed simply because the information that would be recorded on such a form is recorded someplace else. The initiation event information is found within the change itself, that is, within the proposed new or updated software baseline. The identification of the change is generally added to the software baseline during the freezing event. The results of the audit are recorded in an audit report. The analysis of the audit findings is recorded and presented to the CCB in a report. The decision of the CCB is recorded in the CCB minutes. Implementation of the change—when the change is approved—is indicated on the change itself. Therefore, no additional forms are required to support baseline change processing.

The names given to these change control forms vary widely in the industry. For example, others may term what we call an incident report a software trouble report, a system problem report, or a discrepancy report. The names given the forms are typically important to your organization. We prefer, for example, the term "incident report" (IR) because of its less pejorative connotations.

Similarly, the set of forms in Table 4–3 is not unique—that is, it is not the only set of forms that could be specified to support the software change control process. For example, the U.S. Department of Defense uses a form called an engineering change proposal (ECP) that is a combination of our change request and impact assessment forms. You might want to designate for each of your projects your own set of forms based on a different allocation of process events to forms. The set that we propose is provided primarily for exemplification purposes, although in our experience it has proven to be a workable and effective set.

Table 4–3	**A set of forms to support the change control process.**	
Category	*Form*	*Process Events Recorded*
Do we want something new or different?	▪ Change Request (CR)	▪ Initiation, freezing, decision
	▪ Impact Assessment (IA)	▪ Analysis
Is something wrong?	▪ Incident Report (IR)	▪ Initiation, freezing, analysis, decision
	▪ Software Change Notice (SCN)	▪ Implementation
Should we baseline this product?	▪ No additional forms	

CCB Paperwork—*How Do You Design Change Control Process Forms?*

We now describe how you can design your change control process forms. For this purpose, we work through a sample problem of how to design the IR form. We then present you with examples of the other forms in the set we specified in Table 4–3. You might want to design your own forms for your particular project and its environment, or you might tailor the sample forms that we provide to suit your project and environment.

In designing forms, keep in mind the following considerations. Most important is that the various forms capture the data you need to record. Of almost as great importance is consideration for the people who will be filling out the forms. Each form should be simple to fill out. It should be easy to read and should clearly label each item as to what is wanted. The form should indicate acceptable values if a range of values or a code is used. Make it easy for the person filling out the form, and you will be rewarded with complete and correct data entry. Make it difficult for the person filling out the form, and you will get inaccurate, incomplete, and invalid data entered.

As shown in Table 4–4, generally, every change control form should contain information about the following categories:

- **Originator.** Includes information not only on the initiator of the form but also on each person who fills out a part of the form in response to an event.

- **Subject.** Concerned with identifying what the form is addressing, whether it is documentation or software code. The subject is the same for all events recorded on a form. Therefore, subject information need be placed on a form only once, regardless of how many events are recorded on the form. Event description is recorded for every event covered by a form.

- **Event description.** List the specific data elements used to describe the event description. The elements can vary widely, depending upon the event recorded and the desires of each project's management.

- **Approval.** May not be needed for all events and should be placed on the form only for events that do require them, as specified in project policy directives.

If a form records data on more than one event, information in some categories must be recorded for each event (e.g., the originator category or the event description category). The specification of data elements and layout of a change control form depend upon the project and the software environment in which the form will be used. To show you how Table 4–4 can be applied to the design of a form, we next develop (in a sample problem) the design of an incident report.

Table 4–4	Generic content of a change control form.
Category	*Content*
Originator	Information in this category must identify the person filling out the form and the person's organization and telephone number, so that the person can answer questions relative to the data the person enters. If the form records several events, each person filling out a part of the form must be identified.
Subject	The subject of the form, be it document, computer code, or database, must be precisely identified, including its environment if appropriate, so that a reader can locate it or reconstruct it, if necessary.
Event description	This category contains the information that is to be recorded about each event. It might describe a problem, the impact of an incident, the recommended resolution of an incident, or the approved disposition of a proposed change.
Approval	Some events may require the approval of one or more authorities before further action can occur. For such events, the form must record these approvals.

Designing an Incident Report Form—*A Sample Problem*

Background and Problem   As part of the seller's product assurance planning group at the beginning of a medium-sized project,[4] you have decided to implement a set of forms for supporting the change control process. One of these forms is an incident report (IR). This form is to be used to record data for the unplanned change control events of initiation, freezing, analysis, and decision when something in the software is apparently wrong (see Table 4–3). When designing this IR form, you should give at least one reason for each item included on the form.

Solution Approach   The IR form we are designing will record data for four change control process events (i.e., initiation, freezing, analysis, and decision). We first decide on each content element for each event, using Table 4–4 as a guideline. For example, the initiation event includes the following content elements: name, organization, and telephone number of the incident originator. Then we lay out these content elements so that the format is understandable, easy to use, and well organized. Figure 4–17 is the result of this form-design process.

We now explain in detail how we arrived at the figure.

- **Initiation Event.** The name, organization, and telephone number of the incident originator are placed on the IR form so that the originator may be contacted should questions arise. Organization and full telephone number are important here, since the IR may be originated by anyone in the user's, buyer's, or seller's organization.

  Next, the IR form should record the subject of the incident, that is, the document or computer code involved in the incident and its environment. This information allows a reader of the IR to locate its subject or to reconstruct it, as may be necessary to analyze or audit the IR. The form records the date and time of the incident for traceability. The incident could result from a problem in the documentation or in the executable code. For a document, the document name, label, page, and paragraph number are required to locate the subject of the incident. For the executable code, we want the release number and the version number to pinpoint which code is involved in the incident. If the incident arose while executing a test procedure, the test procedure label, test case number, and test step label must be provided.

  The IR form must provide for a full description of the incident—this element states what is perceived to be wrong. The originator should be able to indicate an urgency desired for incident resolution (high, medium, or low) and, if desired, a suggested resolution to assist and guide the incident analyst. For executable code incidents, the IR form should indicate whether the incident could be duplicated during a run, after a restart, or after a reload. In case the description of the incident or the suggested resolution exceeds the size of the space allocated, a box should be provided to indicate that initiation event data are continued on another page. A box should also be provided to indicate the presence of attachments, such as listings or printouts. All this information helps the analyst resolve the incident. No approvals are generally required for this event. In some environments, project management might require approval of an IR by the originator's supervisor, to prevent unnecessary or improper IRs from being initiated.

- **Freezing Event.** The only element on the IR form required to support this event is the IR control number. This number is important in referencing the incident (visibility) and in tracking the incident (traceability). It consists of the last two digits of the current year, followed by a hyphen and a four-digit sequence number. This labeling assignment is generally performed by a member of the product assurance organization, and it is not necessary to record the identity of the person performing that task.

- **Analysis Event.** Since the subject was identified in the initiation event section of the IR form, there is no need to repeat it here. However, the IR form must indicate the name of the person filling out the analysis-event section of the form, since the analyst is in general not the same individual as the incident initiator. Because this project is medium-sized, we assume that the number of seller project personnel is small enough that we can omit the analyst's organization and merely include her or his telephone extension.

---

[4]By a *medium-sized* project, we mean a project having roughly ten to twenty persons working on it full-time.

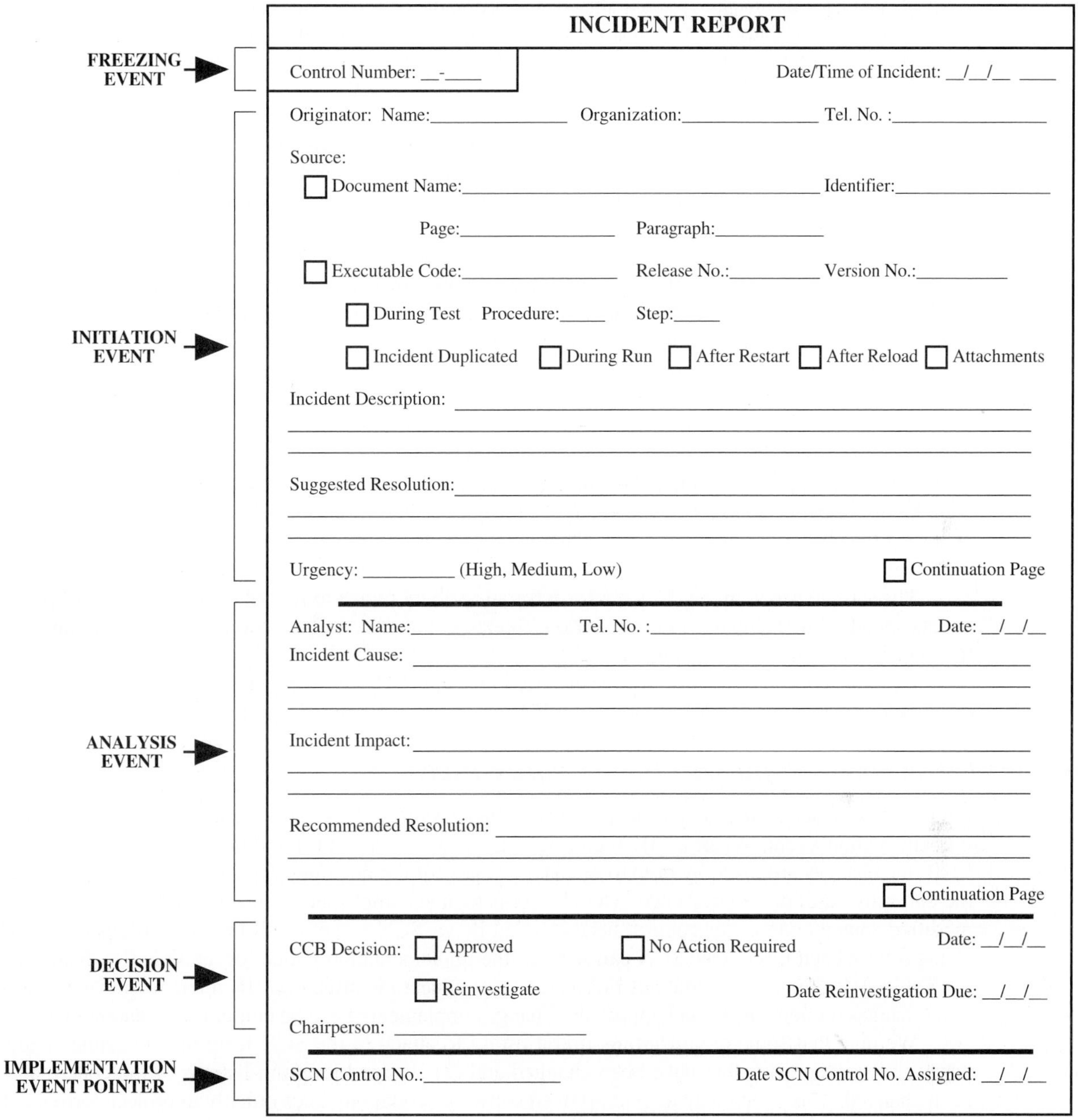

FREEZING EVENT ▶

INITIATION EVENT ▶

ANALYSIS EVENT ▶

DECISION EVENT ▶

IMPLEMENTATION EVENT POINTER ▶

INCIDENT REPORT

Control Number: __-____   Date/Time of Incident: __/__/__ ____

Originator: Name:_____ Organization:_____ Tel. No. :_____

Source:

☐ Document Name:_____ Identifier:_____

        Page:_____   Paragraph:_____

☐ Executable Code:_____ Release No.:_____ Version No.:_____

    ☐ During Test   Procedure:_____   Step:_____

    ☐ Incident Duplicated ☐ During Run ☐ After Restart ☐ After Reload ☐ Attachments

Incident Description: _____
_____
_____
_____

Suggested Resolution:_____
_____
_____
_____

Urgency: _____ (High, Medium, Low)   ☐ Continuation Page

Analyst: Name:_____   Tel. No. :_____   Date: __/__/__
Incident Cause: _____
_____
_____
_____

Incident Impact: _____
_____
_____

Recommended Resolution: _____
_____
_____
                                                    ☐ Continuation Page

CCB Decision: ☐ Approved   ☐ No Action Required   Date: __/__/__

            ☐ Reinvestigate   Date Reinvestigation Due: __/__/__

Chairperson: _____

SCN Control No.:_____   Date SCN Control No. Assigned: __/__/__

FIGURE 4–17   Example of an incident report (IR) form and associated events that it documents.

The analyst must indicate on the IR form the analysis of the incident cause and of the incident's impact on the project, and a recommended resolution of the incident. This resolution may recommend that a change be made or that no action be taken as a result of the IR. If a change is recommended, the precise change recommended should be included in the recommended resolution. Provision should be made for a continuation sheet for the event description, if necessary. No approvals are generally required for this event. In some environments, approval of the analyst's work by his or her supervisor might be required.

■ **Decision Event.** In our approach to change control processing, the CCB is always responsible for this event. Thus, no entry on the IR form is needed to indicate who fills out this section. The subject can also be omitted from this section, since it already appears on the IR form. The event description is the CCB decision. The allowable CCB decisions are the following: change approved, no action required, or reinvestigate (with reinvestigation due date stipulated). The signature of the CCB chairperson is needed on the IR form for approval of the decision.

In addition to using data elements for the four events served by the IR form, we add for traceability one data element—a possible cross-reference to an SCN—from the implementation event. This information is generally recorded by a member of the product assurance organization. No originator, subject, or approval data are recorded for this event, because they are recorded on the SCN referenced.

Using the foregoing data elements and adding elements for the dates of change control events for traceability purposes, we developed the IR form shown in Figure 4–17. The figure also shows the change control events that the form documents. Since different people usually fill out the elements for each event, the form has been organized and ruled into a separate part for each event.

The sample problem shows how the generic content specified in Table 4–4 was applied as appropriate to each of the events covered by the form. The form was also specifically tailored to the project for which it was designed. This latter feature is very important. Organizations usually redesign their change control forms from project to project, even when the project team remains relatively the same. Generally, such changes are made because each project is organized somewhat differently, or the software environment is changed, or the change control process is modified. Such changes may necessitate changing the change control forms too. That is why we do not give you the only forms that should be used, but instead give you examples and guidelines on how to develop your own forms.

The sample problem developed a form for an incident report to record the change control process events specified in Table 4–3 (i.e., initiation, freezing, analysis, and decision). The IR form answered the question "Is something wrong?"

Examples of the remaining forms specified in Table 4–3 (i.e., software change notice, change request, and impact assessment) are shown in Figures 4–18, 4–19, and 4–20, respectively.

Change Control Form—*Software Change Notice (SCN)*

Figure 4–18 presents an example of a software change notice. This form records information from the implementation event. When an IR requiring changes to document(s) and/or code is approved by the CCB, the changes are made by preparing change pages for the document(s) and by modifying a copy of the currently baselined source code. The change is then accomplished by placing the change pages and modified source code under control, accompanied by an SCN to notify all project participants that the changes have been made. One SCN can serve as the implementation notice for multiple IRs. Notice that, per Table 4–4, Figure 4–18 contains originator data, subject identification (IR reference), event description (changes implemented), and approvals. Changes implemented can be continued on another page.

We note that some organizations find it useful to attach to the SCN form the (1) actual changed pages of the documents that have been changed and (2) changed program listings of the code that has been changed. This is one way to get approved software product updates quickly to project participants.

Change Control Form—*Change Request (CR)*

Figure 4–19 is an example of a change request form. The CR records the initiation of a request for a change, as well as the freezing and decision events. A CR is initiated whenever something new or different is desired by any project participant. The CR describes the change desired, the justification for making the change, and the impact on the use and operation of the system of implementing the requested change.

Notice from Figure 4–19 that a CCB-approval decision could be adjudged as either within the scope of existing contracts or out of scope of existing contracts (thus requiring modification of those contracts). In addition to incorporating into the CR data elements for the initiation, freezing, and decision events, we include for traceability a cross-reference to the impact assessment form for this CR

SOFTWARE CHANGE NOTICE

Control Number: __-____

Date: __/__/__

Originator: Name:_____ Organization:_____ Tel. No. :_____

Change Implemented:

Software Name	Software Identifier	Version/ Revision	Type of Software (Doc. or Code)	Incident Report (IR) Control No.

☐ Continuation Page

Approval:

Software Development Manager:_____ Date: __/__/__

Product Assurance Manager:_____ Date: __/__/__

Project Manager:_____ Date: __/__/__

FIGURE 4–18 Example of a software change notice (SCN) form.

from the analysis event. The form is organized and ruled into separate parts for each person filling out the form. Provision has been made to continue initiation event data on a separate page.

Change Control Form—*Impact Assessment (IA)*

Figure 4–20 shows an example of an impact assessment form. This form records the results of the analysis event of the unplanned change control process when something new or different is desired. The IA is filled in as a result of a CR.

The event description on the IA form is composed of three parts:

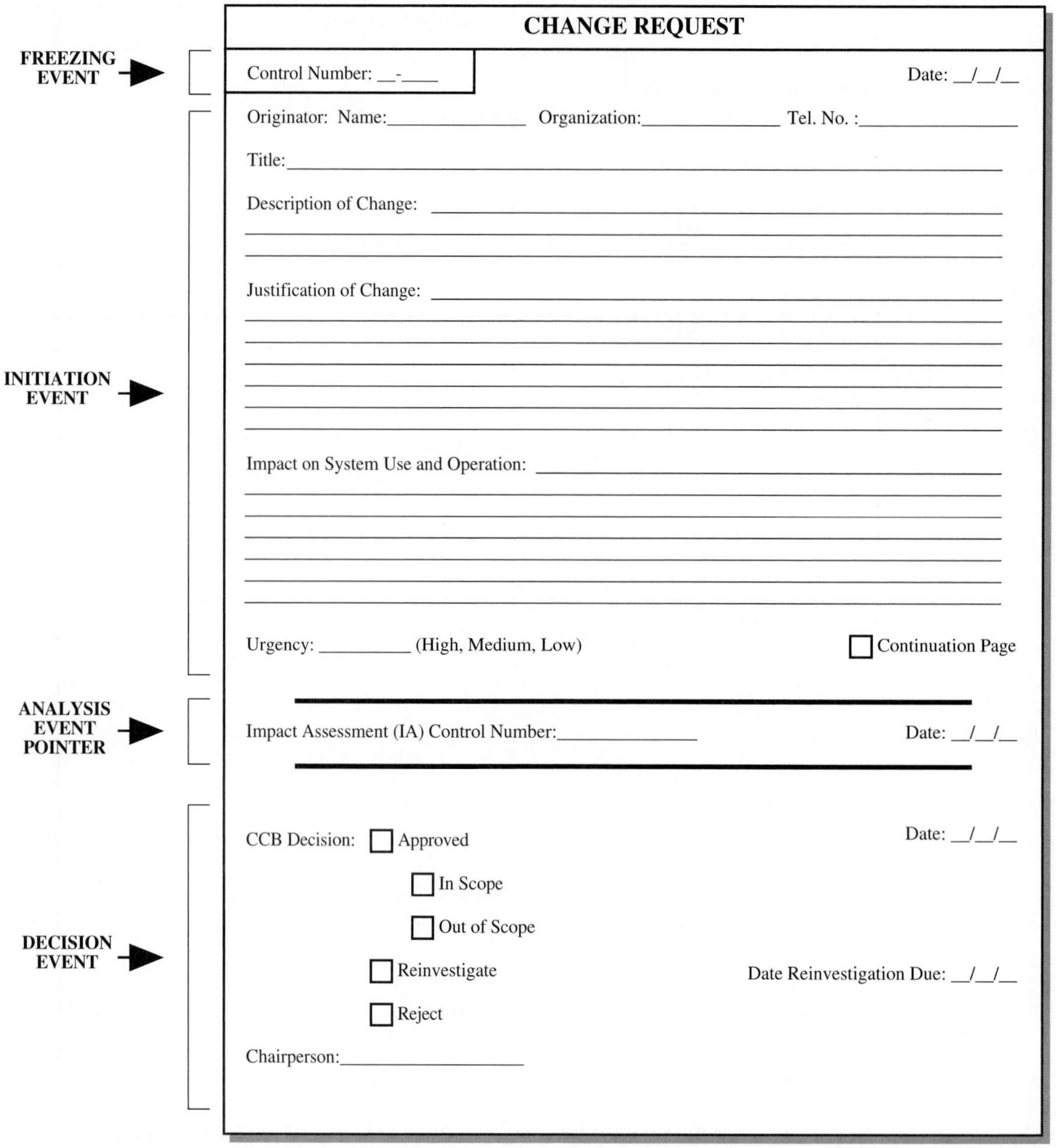

FREEZING
EVENT ►

INITIATION
EVENT ►

ANALYSIS
EVENT
POINTER ►

DECISION
EVENT ►

CHANGE REQUEST

Control Number: __-____   Date: __/__/__

Originator: Name:_____ Organization:_____ Tel. No. :_____

Title:_____

Description of Change: _____
_____
_____

Justification of Change: _____
_____
_____
_____
_____
_____
_____
_____

Impact on System Use and Operation: _____
_____
_____
_____
_____
_____
_____

Urgency: _____ (High, Medium, Low)   ☐ Continuation Page

Impact Assessment (IA) Control Number:_____   Date: __/__/__

CCB Decision: ☐ Approved   Date: __/__/__

                ☐ In Scope

                ☐ Out of Scope

        ☐ Reinvestigate   Date Reinvestigation Due: __/__/__

        ☐ Reject

Chairperson:_____

FIGURE 4–19 Example of a change request (CR) form and associated events that it documents.

■ **Technical analysis.** The approach to be used in designing the proposed change, the software (documentation and code) affected by making the change, and the approach to be used in testing the system after the code has been changed.

■ **Impact analysis.** Considerations of schedule, labor, and costs to implement the proposed change.

■ **Alternatives.** A brief discussion of alternatives to the proposed change, with benefits and liabilities provided for each alternative.

Each part may be continued on another page.

```
┌─────────────────────────────────────────────────────────────────────┐
│                          IMPACT ASSESSMENT                            │
├──────────────────────────────────┬────────────────────────────────────┤
│  Control Number: __-____         │              Date: _/_/_          │
├──────────────────────────────────┴────────────────────────────────────┤
│  Analyst:  Name:_____    Organization:_____   Tel. No. :_____
│
│  Change Request (CR) Control No.: _____
│
│  Title: _____
│
│  Technical Analysis:
│    Design Approach:_____
│    _____
│    _____
│    _____
│
│    Documentation Affected:_____
│    _____
│    _____
│    _____
│
│    Code Affected:_____
│    _____
│    _____
│    _____
│
│    Testing Approach:_____
│    _____
│    _____
│    _____
│                                              ☐ Continuation Page
│  Impact Analysis:
│    Schedule Considerations:_____
│    _____
│
│    Labor Considerations:_____
│    _____
│
│    Cost Considerations:_____
│    _____
│                                              ☐ Continuation Page
│
│  Alternatives:_____
│    _____
│    _____
│    _____
│    _____
│    _____
│                                              ☐ Continuation Page
└─────────────────────────────────────────────────────────────────────┘
```

FIGURE 4–20 Example of an impact assessment (IA) form.

Now that we have a sample set of forms, let's take a look at how they might be used in an organization's change control process. In Figure 4–21, we present scenarios showing the use of the change control process forms and the interaction of the forms with the CCB. Each of these scenarios deals with one of the three following questions (recall Table 4–3) related to unplanned and planned change:

- Do we want something new or different?

- Is something wrong?

- Should we baseline this product?

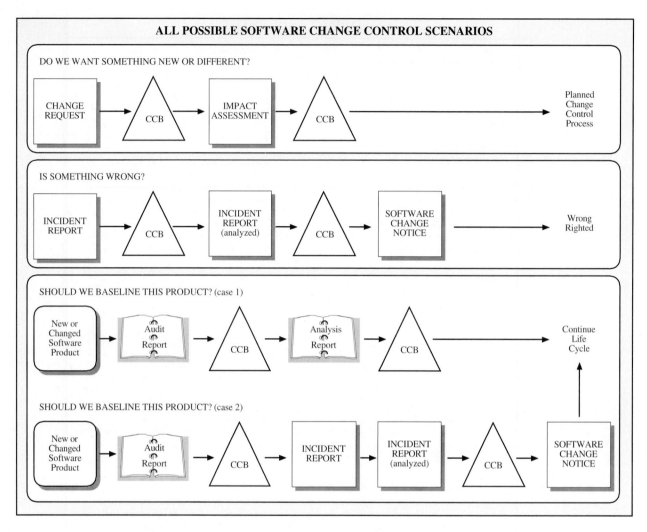

FIGURE 4–21   Scenarios showing the use of the change control forms.

To illustrate how an organization's change control process may work, we describe each of the three scenarios. We also provide examples of filled-out change control forms in Figures 4–22 through 4–25.

Change Control Process Scenario One—*Do We Want Something New or Different?*

The first scenario is initiated by a desire for something not already in the software or something that extends what is already there. (This change control process is introduced in Figure 4–9.) As illustrated in Figure 4–22, the originator, Tom Green, initiates this unplanned change by describing the change as follows:

> Provide the capability to add foods (and their associated data) to the database. A capacity of up to 500 additional foods should be provided.

Tom fills out the rest of the upper part of the CR. This CR is presented to the CCB, which assigns it to an analysis group. The product assurance organization fills out the middle part of the CR for traceability by assigning the IA Control No. of 98-0012 on March 20, 1998.

Completed by
Product Assurance
when CR received

Completed by
change requester

Completed by Product
Assurance when CCB
directs that IA be
prepared

Completed at
CCB Meeting

⊕ **CHANGE REQUEST**

Control Number: *98–0019*   Date:15 March 98

Originator: Name:___Tom Green___ Organization:___National Meals___ Tel. No. : _909/555-9567_

Title:__MEAL PLANNER Database Update Capability_____

Description of Change : __Provide the capability to add foods (and their associated data) to the database._
_A capacity of up to 500 additional foods should be provided._____

_____

Justification of Change : __The capability is needed for two reasons:_____

a.   We need to be able to use local and regional names for foods currently in the database (e.g., "snap
       beans" for "string beans").
b.   We need to be able to use local and regional foods not currently in the database (e.g., she-crab
       soup).

Impact on System Use and Operation: _Our nutritionists can use local names and foods, avoiding manual_
_labor and need to remember unfamiliar names._____

_____

_____

_____

_____

Urgency : ___High___ (High, Medium, Low)   ☐ Continuation Page

Impact Assessment (IA) Control Number:___*98–0012*___   Date: *20 Mar 98*

CCB Decision: ☒ Approved   Date: *March 24, 1998*

                    ☐ In Scope

                    ☒ Out of Scope

                    ☐ Reinvestigate   Date Reinvestigation Due: __/__/__

                    ☐ Reject

Chairperson:_*Mary White*_____

FIGURE 4–22   Example of a completed change request (CR) form, showing the use of the form in answering the question "Do we want something new or different?"

As shown in Figure 4–23, the assigned analyst, Hugh Brown, documents the results of the analysis in an IA, which is then submitted to the CCB. Hugh documents the technical and impact analysis.

With the IA in hand, the CCB makes a decision on the disposition of the CR. As shown in Figure 4–22, the results of this decision are added to the bottom part of the CR. Notice that the CCB considers this change to be out of scope of the existing contract. The contract will thus have to be changed prior to the actual implementation of the change. Since, in our example, the CCB decision was to approve the proposed change, the planned change control process is initiated (after the contract is modified) as

---

IMPACT ASSESSMENT

Completed by Product Assurance when CCB directs that IA be prepared

Control Number: *98-0012*

Date: *20 Mar 98*

Analyst: Name: *Hugh Brown*   Organization: *Development*   Tel. No. : *8197*

Change Request (CR) Control No.: *98-0019*

Title: *MEAL PLANNER Database Update Capability*

Technical Analysis:

Design Approach: *Create an additional subsystem for database update. Include data entry, data validation, and database update functions. Modify current user interface.*

Documentation Affected: *System Specification, Requirements Specification, Design Specification, User's Manual*

Code Affected: *Code for additional subsystem will be all new. MMI (Man-Machine Interface) Subsystem will need to be modified for this capability.*

Completed by analyst in development organization

Testing Approach: *Updated product must be acceptance tested by our company T&E Group. Particular attention must be focused on user interface, storage capacity limits, and system performance.*

☐ Continuation Page

Impact Analysis:

Schedule Considerations: *5 months, starting about 1 May 1998*

Labor Considerations: *18 person-months*

Cost Considerations: *$150,000*

☐ Continuation Page

Alternatives: *Users could inform us of the database modifications needed. We could update the database and send them a new database. This alternative would cost less, but may not be satisfactory to users in terms of responsiveness and their dependence on our company for database updates.*

☐ Continuation Page

FIGURE 4–23 Example of a completed impact assessment (IA) form for the change request (CR) 98-0019.

the now-approved change is reflected in successive baseline updates, starting with the system specification.

Change Control Process Scenario Two—*Is Something Wrong?*

The second scenario is initiated by the question of something being at variance with the requirements specification. (This change control process is introduced in Figure 4–10.) As illustrated in Figure 4–24,

---

INCIDENT REPORT

*Completed by Product
Assurance when IR
received*

Control Number: *99-0012* Date/Time of Incident: *990122/0900*

Originator: Name: *Jane Black* Organization: *Nutrition, Ltd.* Tel. No. : *210/555-2467*

*Completed by
user*

Source:

☐ Document Name:_____ Identifier:_____

  Page:_____ Paragraph:_____

☒ Executable Code:_____ Release No.: *98-2* Version No.: *1.2*

  ☐ During Test Procedure:_____ Step:_____

  ☒ Incident Duplicated ☒ During Run ☐ After Restart ☐ After Reload ☒ Attachments

Incident Description: *Whenever, a quantity in grams is entered in MEALPLANNER, all the output numbers are outlandishly high. See attached listing for the results of entering "steak, 225 grams."*

Suggested Resolution: *Correct gram-to-out converter.*

Urgency: *Medium* (High, Medium, Low) ☐ Continuation Page

---

*Completed by
analyst in
development
organization*

Analyst: Name: John Blue Tel. No. : 8226 Date: 990130

Incident Cause: The subroutine to convert grams to ounces (GRAMTOOZ) is scaled incorrectly—100 times too high.

Incident Impact: For a single food entry, user must divide results by 100. For meals entered in grams, the user must calculate results manually.

Recommended Resolution: In module GRAMTOOZ, change line 85 to
QUOZ=0.03527 * QUGR

☐ Continuation Page

---

*Completed by
CCB chairperson*

CCB Decision: ☒ Approved ☐ No Action Required Date: *990214*

  ☐ Reinvestigate Date Reinvestigation Due: _/_/_

Chairperson: *Bob Redman*

*Completed by Product
Assurance*

SCN Control No.: *99-0030* Date SCN Control No. Assigned: *990217*

FIGURE 4–24 Example of a completed incident report (IR) form, showing use of the form in answering the question "Is something wrong?"

the originator, Jane Black, initiates this (potentially) unplanned change by describing the incident as follows:

> Whenever a quantity in grams is entered in MEAL PLANNER, all the output numbers are outlandishly high. See attached listing for the results of entering "steak, 225 grams."

Jane, who can be any project participant, fills out the rest of the upper part of the IR.

This scenario is initiated when any project participant fills out the upper part of an IR. The IR is introduced to the CCB, which assigns it to an analysis organization. As shown in Figure 4–24, the analyst, John Blue, fills out the middle portion of the IR with his analysis of the IR, and returns it to the CCB. John documents the incident cause and impact, and recommended resolution. When the CCB makes its decision, the decision portion of the IR is filled out. The example change in this scenario was approved by the CCB. The developers prepare the approved change, and when the change is ready for implementation, an SCN is issued. Figure 4–25 is an example of a filled-out SCN that might result from the IR shown in Figure 4–24. With the change made, the original wrong has been righted in a visible, traceable, and hence manageable manner.

There is a variation to this scenario that arises occasionally at certain user installations. A number of such installations must operate around the clock. Many of these installations are operated by the government, but increasingly more of them operate in the private sector (for example, some mail-order systems and some point-of-sale systems). For these installations, a failure in their computer-based systems can have serious consequences. When something goes wrong with their software, these users have an emergency situation. Is the change control process bypassed for such emergencies? Not at all. A procedure that is responsive to the emergency situation and yet maintains control should be developed in the product assurance plan for systems at such installations.

One procedure to handle such situations that we have observed in successful operation is as follows: When a site liaison representative of the seller (responsible for continued system maintenance) is notified by site personnel of an emergency situation, the representative contacts the appropriate software analyst. The analyst evaluates the problem to ensure that there is sufficient data to repair it, that the problem is not the result of improper system usage by the operator, and that the problem is not a duplicate of an incident report. The analyst then proceeds to resolve the problem by the most expedient means available. When the analyst has a solution, the analyst contacts, by telephone, at least one member of the CCB (using teleconferencing facilities, if possible) to obtain approval prior to disseminating the solution. When approval is obtained, the analyst sends the necessary corrections to the site having the problem. No attempt is made to obtain a solution that is elegant or efficient or that will last beyond the time required to develop a permanent correction. What is desired is a solution that quickly returns the site to operational status and that prevents further system degradation.

When the solution has been sent to the site, the analyst fills out an IR on the incident and on the next working day submits the IR (to obtain a permanent solution) and the temporary solution (other sites may need the same temporary fix) to the CCB.

In this procedure, notice that the basic change control process is abbreviated but not omitted. Even in these emergency circumstances, a CCB meeting of sorts is convened. Visibility and traceability are maintained under all circumstances.

Change Control Process Scenario Three—*Should We Baseline This Product?*

This scenario deals with planned change and is initiated by the question of establishing a product as a new or updated baseline. (This change control process is shown in Figure 4–8.) The change control process is initiated by presentation of the draft of a software product proposed as a new or updated baseline. This product is audited, and an audit report is provided to the CCB. The CCB assigns an analysis organization (usually the development organization) to analyze the discrepancies contained in the audit report. The results of this analysis are presented to the CCB in a report that provides a recommended resolution of each discrepancy. The CCB makes a decision on how to resolve each discrepancy and then decides whether to baseline the software product. Once the product is baselined, the project continues along its life cycle.

This scenario has a variation that is used by some organizations (case 2 in Figure 4–21). In this variation, when the CCB receives the audit report on a proposed new or updated baseline, it does not have every discrepancy in the audit report analyzed and reported upon (with a recommended resolu-

---

	SOFTWARE CHANGE NOTICE

Control Number: *99-0030*   Date: *980217*

Originator: Name: *Nancy Greenfield* Organization: *Product Assurance* Tel. No. : *2194*

Change Implemented:

Software Name	Software Identifier	Version/ Revision	Type of Software (Doc. or Code)	Incident Report (IR) Control No.
GRAMTOOZ	*4.2.1.14*	*3.4*	*Code*	*99-0012*

Completed by Product Assurance when IR received

☐ Continuation Page

Approval:

Software Development Manager: **Bill Blackburn**   Date: **17 Feb 99**

Product Assurance Manager: *Jim Brownlee*   Date: *990218*

Project Manager: *Ann Whitemarsh*   Date: Feb. 21, 1999

FIGURE 4–25 Example of a competed software change notice (SCN) for the incident report (IR) 99-0012.

tion) in an analysis report. A certain number of discrepancies can be easily and quickly resolved at the CCB meeting. For example, an inconsistency in the spelling of the software system name or an ambiguous term that is readily clarified can be quickly resolved. For such discrepancies, there is no need to spend additional resources to analyze the problem and to document a recommended resolution—the CCB can make an immediate decision on each.

In this variation, when the CCB receives the audit report, it considers each discrepancy in turn. If a discrepancy can be readily resolved, the CCB makes an immediate decision on it. If a discrepancy is not readily resolvable at the CCB meeting, the CCB directs that an IR be created describing the discrepancy. This IR is processed just as any other IR is processed. As shown in Figure 4–21, the IR is analyzed (typically, by the development organization) and returned to the CCB with the results of the analysis indicated as IR (ANALYZED). If the CCB approves a change as a result of this IR, an SCN is issued when the change is implemented.

Another important facet of CCB operation is the production and maintenance of formal minutes for every CCB meeting. Let us now describe and illustrate this important bookkeeping task in detail.

CCB Minutes

The minutes of a CCB meeting are essential to provide an accurate, precise, and thus visible account of the proceedings of the CCB, both for the CCB members and for other project participants. The minutes provide a recorded view into what was said and decided at a CCB meeting. The minutes record the status of software products and changes and each action decided upon. For each action, responsibility is assigned and a schedule for its accomplishment is established. The series of CCB meeting minutes forms a trace of the functioning of the CCB over the project life cycle.

Have you ever left a meeting feeling that you understood what had been decided at the meeting, only to discover in a later discussion with a colleague that the colleague's understanding differed from yours? Have you ever known a meeting decision to be overlooked and forgotten because it was not written down? If you are a senior manager, have you ever wondered whether a project under your cognizance was progressing satisfactorily? These situations can be corrected by publication of meeting minutes. To convince you further of the benefit of publishing CCB meeting minutes, we provide you with the following story, which is an adaptation from an actual project.

Lack of Visibility of Project Meetings—A Story

Paul Little, the seller's project manager on Project PQR, was familiar with CCBs but did not believe in their value. He authorized the leader of his development group, Peter Anderson, to make changes in computer code (deviating from the design specifications) as Peter saw fit. Paul met frequently with the user/buyer; usually Paul was the only person from the seller's company present. No record of any of the meetings with the customer was ever made.

Near the beginning of Project PQR, a lengthy meeting between the user/buyer (i.e., customer) and seller was held (at the customer's request) to ensure that the requirements for the project were clearly understood. The requirements review meeting was attended by most of the seller's project staff and by a number of users. During the meeting, a question was raised about the briefly stated requirement that "all data entries shall be fully validated." A user stated that the Project PQR system was to perform all the data entry validation checks performed by the existing system (which Project PQR was replacing), plus several new and more complex data validation checks that were urgently needed. Unfortunately, the current system was not well documented, and no list of the current data validation checks existed. The user agreed to "dig out" from current computer source code all the current data validation checks and to inform the seller what these checks were. No minutes were kept of this meeting on user needs.

A week later, the user orally presented to Peter (the seller's development group leader) a number of data entry validation checks for the current system. Peter noted these items but did not see fit to publish the list or to keep any written record of his meeting with the user. He followed up the meeting by assigning data validation checks to appropriate development group members. A month later, Peter suddenly resigned from the company to accept an opportunity with another company.

Mary Rose, head of the seller's test team (who was not present at the requirements review meeting), was unable to obtain a list of the data validation checks to be performed by the Project PQR system. In frustration, she designed tests to ascertain that the system performed data validation checks that seemed reasonable to her. (Unfortunately, what her tests ascertained fell far short of the user's needs in this area.)

On the day before the Project PQR system was to be demonstrated to the user prior to delivery, Paul told his (new) development group leader, Sally Vines, that at his meeting with the user that morning, the user said he was anxiously awaiting demonstration the next day of one of the new, complex data validation checks (first introduced at the requirements review meeting). Sally was surprised. She told Paul that she had never heard of the requirement and certainly had not programmed it. Paul was aghast. He told Sally that two months before, at one of his meetings with the user, the user had asked whether that specific capability would be in the delivered system. Paul had confidently told the user that the desired capability would be in the first delivery of software code.

Frantically, Sally and her group set about to add the missing capability in the few hours still left. Regrettably, they did not succeed in getting the new capability to work properly at the next morning's demonstration. In fact, at the demonstration it soon became evident that their frantic efforts had caused several other previously checked-out data validation checks to work improperly. Concerned by the improper performance of the system, the user requested additional demonstration of all the data entry validation checks that he needed. This demonstration revealed that none of the new capabilities had been coded and that a number of capabilities used by the current system had been omitted. The user was greatly upset and refused to accept the software. With much chagrin, the seller's project team went back to work and a few months later delivered to the user a software system that the user found acceptable. Paul, the project manager, had departed one month earlier to seek employment elsewhere.

In our story, it turned out that no one remembered the data entry validation checks introduced at the requirements review meeting. Everyone assumed that the list of validation checks the user gave Peter contained all the checks that the user desired. Since the list of validation checks that the user gave to Peter was never written down, but rather was passed along orally, some checks got lost in the oral transfers. The abrupt departure of Peter caused loss of the only information the seller had about data entry validation checks to be incorporated in the new system. These problems could have been avoided if minutes of each meeting had been recorded and published. The developers would have had visibility into what to develop. The testers would have had visibility into what to test. The user would have had visibility into what he would be receiving in his completed system. The departure of the development group leader would not have had an impact on this visibility. The production of minutes here would have saved considerable time and money for the project.

We now turn our attention to the mechanics of keeping track of what the CCB does. Let us consider first who should record the minutes of a CCB meeting. Some people consider taking minutes to be a purely clerical job and would use a person trained in secretarial skills (e.g., shorthand) for this task. Such a person would generally not be involved in the discussion within the CCB and therefore could devote full attention to keeping the minutes. A CCB secretary with shorthand skills could produce a verbatim transcript of a CCB meeting if required. On the negative side, a person with secretarial skills generally is not technically cognizant of the CCB discussion and therefore might not know when CCB decisions had been reached.

Another possible CCB secretary would be a member of the development staff responsible for implementing CCB-approved changes. Such a person would be most knowledgeable on the software and possible changes to it, i.e., in understanding what the CCB discusses and decides. However, that very understanding would probably involve the person in the subjects under discussion and distract her or him from the secretarial duties. Further, the person's organizational allegiance may bias her or his recording.

A member of the product assurance organization could serve as CCB secretary. This person certainly would be technically cognizant of the CCB discussions and decisions. The PA practitioner may well get involved in the CCB discussion, but such involvement is usually focused on the CCB reaching a decision rather than on the decision itself. Since the product assurance practitioner is not involved in implementing software changes, the practitioner is likely to have a dispassionate viewpoint of the proceedings. This neutral viewpoint should be reflected in the recording of the minutes.

What should be recorded in the CCB minutes? The most fundamental items to record are the results of discussions of agenda items, action assignments, and decisions of the CCB. These items could be quite wide-ranging (depending upon the CCB charter for a project). However, the most important subjects relative to its change control responsibilities are software products and software changes. The status of each item discussed and the action taken on each must be recorded in the minutes. Other subjects that should be recorded include the results of audits and of tests, the establishment of baselines, and the implementation of software products and changes. At the end of the minutes, a summary of actions to be taken is included, with responsibility for action and due date explicitly stated. A suggested format for CCB minutes is presented in Figure 4–26.

Memorandum   Date: __/__/__
Identification Number

To: Distribution [see bottom]
From: [Typically, the memo is from the CCB secretary]
Subject: Minutes of System XYZ Change Control Board (CCB) Meeting
Reference: [Typically, the minutes from the preceding CCB meeting are cited here]

1.0   [Date of Meeting]

2.0   [List of meeting attendees and their organizational affiliation]

      2.1   [List of organizations not represented at the meeting who typically participate]

3.0   CCB Actions

[The subparagraphs under this paragraph contain a record of what happened at the meeting to include things such as the following:

- Approval of and changes, if any, to the minutes of the preceding CCB meeting (or meetings)

- Presentation and/or disposition of IRs, SCNs, CRs, IAs, TIRs

- Discussion of audit (including test) findings and decisions regarding how discrepancies are to be resolved

- Presentation (or overview) of a candidate software baseline (i.e., a draft product such as a draft design specification in conjunction with a design review)

- Turnover of computer code from the development organization to the product assurance organization for (acceptance) testing

- Discussion of new issues (such as a new capability for which a CR has not yet been formulated)]

4.0   Action Items

[This paragraph lists the who/what/when resulting from the items addressed in paragraph 3.0 as assigned during the meeting, typically by the CCB chairperson:]

Number	Action Item	Action Agent	Due Date	Paragraph Reference
[Action item identifier]	[Brief description of action]	[Organization of individual responsible for the action]	[Date action is to be completed]	[Pointer to subparagraph in paragraph 3.0 that gives the context for the action]

5.0   [Time and place of next CCB meeting]

Distribution:
[Listed here are the individuals or organizations that are to receive copies of the minutes. This list typically includes all individuals listed in paragraph 2.0 and management personnel who desire visibility into the status of System XYZ.]

FIGURE 4–26 Format for CCB minutes.

Rationale for including some of the items shown in Figure 4–26 follows:

- An **identifier and date**—to give visibility to the minutes and to make them traceable.

- A **list of attendees and their organizational affiliation**—to record who participated in the decision-making.

- A **list of organizations not represented at the meeting**—to record whose viewpoints were not considered in the decision-making.

- The **status of the minutes of the preceding meeting**, including any necessary corrections—to assure that the trace of CCB minutes is correct and accurate.

- The **time and place of the next meeting**—to give visibility to the schedule for the next meeting.

- A **list of people receiving copies of the minutes**—to inform each recipient who else has received the information contained in the minutes (and to expand project visibility outside the CCB meeting participants, if desired).

Recording the status of the minutes of the preceding meeting is particularly important for traceability purposes. The minutes should show that the preceding meeting minutes were correct as recorded or that they needed specific corrections and were approved as corrected.

A copy of the minutes should be distributed to every person who attends the meeting. Copies should also be sent to each member of the CCB who was not present at the meeting and to appropriate senior managers. These minutes let them know exactly what happened at the meeting. The presence of the names of senior managers in the distribution list of the minutes contributes to making management visible to project participants.

Next, let us briefly consider the mechanics of a CCB meeting relative to the keeping of minutes. The first item of business at every CCB meeting is to consider the minutes of the preceding meeting. Any corrections desired are introduced, considered, and either approved or disapproved. If there are no corrections, the minutes are approved without correction. Otherwise, the minutes are approved as corrected.

As each item on the agenda is discussed and a decision is made, the CCB secretary records that decision. When the secretary is not sure what decision has been reached by the CCB, the secretary should stop the proceedings and ascertain precisely what was decided. At the end of the CCB meeting, the secretary should summarize the decisions made by the CCB and the actions to be taken.

To close out this section, we present and discuss minutes of four different types of CCBs. The minutes follow the format shown in Figure 4–26. The four types of meetings are as follows:

- A software CCB considering a planned change (see Figure 4–27).

- A software CCB considering unplanned changes (see Figure 4–28).

- A test incident CCB considering the results of an acceptance test (see Figure 4–29).

- A software turnover CCB considering the results of resolving TIRs[5] (see Figure 4–30).

Note that these example CCB minutes have representatives from the user, the buyer, and the seller. For clarity, instead of using fictitious organizations in these figures, we indicate each person's organization by his/her affiliation (user, buyer, or seller) and group (management, development, or product assurance). We also indicate in brackets information as to position (e.g., manager, secretary, chairperson) for some of the CCB members in order to show how these positions relate to the CCB. The bracketed information would not normally appear in CCB minutes.

---

[5]A test incident report (TIR) is a special case of an incident report. TIRs can be generated by a test team when they execute a set of test procedures constructed from a test plan and specification documentation (e.g., requirements and design specifications). The expected results specified in the test documentation are compared with the observed results obtained from computer code execution. If the expected results do not match the observed results, the tester generates a TIR detailing the differences.

✦	**Memorandum**	June 1, 1998 MPCCB - 98/8

To: Distribution
Thru: Mary White, MEAL PLANNER CCB Chairperson
From: Jim Limerick, MEAL PLANNER CCB Secretary
Subject: Minutes of MEAL PLANNER CCB Meeting
Reference:(a) MEAL PLANNER CCB minutes MPCCB - 98/7 dated May 22, 1998

1.0   Date of Meeting: May 29, 1998

2.0   Attendees:

    Tom Green   User/Management

    Mary White   Buyer/Management [chairperson]
    Polly Lemonsky   Buyer/Development
    Jim Limerick   Buyer/Development [secretary]
    Ned Rosebud   Buyer/Development
    Stan Tanbrook   Buyer/Product Assurance

    Ann Whitemarsh   Seller/Management [project manager]
    Bill Blackburn   Seller/Development [manager]
    Hugh Brown   Seller/Development
    Jim Brownlee   Seller/Product Assurance [manager]
    Walt Silverstone   Seller/Product Assurance

  2.1   Organizations Not Represented: none.

3.0   CCB Actions

  3.1   Reference (a) was approved as published.

  3.2   Action items from previous meetings resolved: none.

  3.3   Hugh Brown presented an overview of Version 1.4 of MP-01, Software Requirements Specification for System MEAL PLANNER. This version is the result of applying CR 98-0019 to the previous version. CR 98-0019 added the capability to update the MEAL PLANNER database.

  3.4   Stan Tanbrook presented an audit report documenting the results of auditing Version 1.4 of MP-01. After considering the audit report, the board made the following disposition of the audit report findings:

    3.4.1 Findings 1, 3, 4, 5, 8, 10, 11, 14, 17, 19, and 20 had recommended resolutions proposed by the auditor or by a board member. These resolutions were approved by the board for implementation (i.e., revision of Version 1.4 of MP-01). These approved changes are identified as IR 98-0097.

    3.4.2 Findings 6, 7, 9, 12, 15, and 16 require further analysis. IRs 98-0098, 98-0099, 98-0100, 98-0101, 98-0102, 98-0103, respectively, will be originated by the Seller/Product Assurance Group for these findings. The IRs assigned to the Seller/Development Group for investigation and analysis.

    3.4.3 Findings 2, 13, and 18 require no action to be taken. After discussion, the board decided that these findings represented misunderstanding by the auditor and that no problems existed.

FIGURE 4–27   Minutes of a software CCB meeting considering a planned change.

Figure 4–27 shows the minutes of a CCB considering a planned change, namely, CR 98-0019 to System MEAL PLANNER. This change request had previously been approved by the CCB. Hugh Brown (from the development organization) presented an overview of a draft of the revised version of the MEAL PLANNER Software Requirements Specification. Hugh was followed by Stan Tanbrook (from the buyer's product assurance group) who presented an audit report on the draft software product. The CCB considered all the findings in the audit report. For eleven of these findings, the CCB felt no need for further analysis and approved them for implementation. These findings resulted in changes

3.0 CCB Actions (continued)

3.5 Ned Rosebud raised the issue as to whether the user had a need to delete foods from the database. (CR-98-0019 asked only for the capability to add foods to the database.) Tom Green, the originator of CR 98-0019, stated that, while he only asked specifically to add foods, he implied in the title of the CR (". . . database update capability") that he also had a need for the capability to delete foods. The board moved to add this capability to Version 1.4 of MP-01, identifying this change as approved IR 98-0104.

3.6 The board took no action on baselining Version 1.4 of MP-01, pending the resolution of IRs 98-0098 through 98-0103, and the implementation of approved IRs 98-0097 and 98-0104.

4.0 Action Items

Number	Action Item	Action Agent	Due Date	Paragraph Reference
98-212	Implement IR 98-0097	Seller/Development	July 1, 1998	3.4.1
98-213	Analyze IRs 98-0098 through 98-0103	Seller/Development	July 8, 1998	3.4.2
98-214	Implement IR 98-0104	Seller/Development	July 15, 1998	3.5
98-215	Baseline MEAL Planner Requirements Specification Version 1.4	MPCCB	July 16, 1998	3.6

5.0 Next Meeting: Monday, June 8, 1998, at 2:00 p.m. in the Main Conference Room.

Distribution:
All attendees
Tim Graystone [Buyer/General Manager]
Al Plumtree [Seller/President]

FIGURE 4–27 *Continued*

to be made to the software requirements specification. An incident report (IR 98-0097) was written to cover this set of approved changes, in order to give them visibility and accountability (i.e., to enable them to be tracked until implemented). The CCB decided that six of the audit report findings required further analysis before the CCB made a decision. Incident reports were originated for each of these findings. The CCB decided that no action was required on three of the audit report findings. The auditor may have been unsure about whether discrepancies existed, and so gave the issues visibility by reporting them as findings. The broad representation on the CCB, with its range of viewpoints, was able

◆	**Memorandum**	February 12, 1999 MPCCB - 99/6

To: Distribution
Thru: Bob Redman, MEAL PLANNER CCB Chairperson
From: Jim Limerick, MEAL PLANNER CCB Secretary
Subject: Minutes of MEAL PLANNER CCB Meeting
Reference: (a) MEAL PLANNER CCB minutes MPCCB - 99/5 dated February 5, 1999

1.0   Date of Meeting: February 12, 1999

2.0   Attendees:

      Jim Limerick   Buyer/Product Assurance [secretary]
      Bob Redman   Buyer/Management [chairperson]
      Harriet Rose   Buyer/Product Assurance

      Bill Blackburn   Seller/Development [manager]
      John Blue   Seller/Development
      Jim Brownlee   Seller/Product Assurance [manager]
      Nancy Greenfield Seller/Development
      Walt Silverstone Seller/Product Assurance
      Ann Whitemarsh Seller/Management [project manager]

     2.1   Organizations Not Represented: Buyer/Development Group
                                        User/Management

3.0   CCB Actions

     3.1   Reference (a) was approved with the following modification:

         3.1.1 Paragraph 3.3: Add Nutrition, Ltd., to the list of sites to which Release 99-3 will be delivered.

     3.2   Action item from previous meeting was resolved as follows:

         3.2.1 Action item #99-0032, second installation of Release 99-3: Bill Blackburn stated that the installation of Release 99-3 at National Meals was completed with only a few minor problems. The installation notes remain the only item to be completed for the installation. Delivery of the installation notes will be carried as an action item for the Seller/Development Group; action due by March 15, 1999.

     3.3   Harriet Rose stated that an emergency incident had been reported by Diet Plus, Inc., two days ago. It was assigned control number IR 99-0015. The incident involved the calculation of the total calories in a meal. John Blue, with the concurrence of Ann Whitemarsh and Bob Redman, had sent a patch to Diet Plus, Inc., by wire, but did not test the patch. The board moved that the Seller/Product Assurance Group test the patch immediately, and that the Seller/Development Group determine a permanent fix by February 17.

     3.4   Recommended resolutions to the following IRs were presented to the board and the following decisions were made:

IR No.	Presenter	Disposition	Action	Action Agent	Due Date
99-0010	Nancy Greenfield	No action required	Notify originator	Seller/Product Assurance	Feb 17, 1999
99-0012	John Blue	Approved	Submit SCN	Seller/Development	Feb 18, 1999

FIGURE 4–28   Minutes of a software CCB meeting considering unplanned changes.

to resolve these issues as not being discrepancies. One of the buyers raised the issue of an apparent inconsistency, not previously observed, in change request CR 98-0019. The CCB decided that a capability desired by the user was missing from the software requirements specification and directed that it be added (identifying the change as IR 98-0104 for visibility and traceability).

    Figure 4–28 shows the minutes of a CCB considering an unplanned change. Notice that a correction has been made to the minutes of the previous meeting (paragraph 3.1.1). Whether corrected or not, minutes of the previous meeting should always be approved by the CCB. Under paragraph 3.0, the

3.0   CCB Actions (continued)

    3.4   Recommended resolutions to the following IRs were presented to the board and the following decisions were made:

IR No.	Presenter	Disposition	Action	Action Agent	Due Date
99-0013	John Blue	Reinvestigate	Reanalyze IR	Seller/ Development	Feb 19, 1999
99-0014	Nancy Greenfield	Approved	Submit SCN	Seller/ Development	Feb 18, 1999

4.0   Action Items

Number	Action Item	Action Agent	Due Date	Paragraph Reference
99-0046	Deliver installation note to National Meals.	Seller/Development	Mar 15, 1999	3.2.1
99-0047	Test patch for IR 99-0015	Seller/Product Assurance	Feb 10, 1999	3.3
99-0048	Analyze IR 99-0015	Seller/Development	Feb 17, 1999	3.3
99-0049	Notify originator of IR 99-0010 no action required.	Seller/Product Assurance	Feb 17, 1999	3.4
99-0050	Submit SCNs for IRs 99-0012 and 99-0014	Seller/Development	Feb 18, 1999	3.4
99-0051	Reanalyze IR 99-0013	Seller/Development	Feb 19, 1999	3.4

5.0   Next Meeting: Friday, February 19, 1999, at 10:00 a.m. in the Main Conference Room.

Distribution:
    All attendees
    Tim Graystone [Buyer/General Manager]
    Tom Green [User/Management]
    Polly Lemonsky [Buyer/Development]
    Al Plumtree [Seller/President]

FIGURE 4–28   *Continued*

CCB minutes document the (1) handling of an action item from a previous meeting, (2) consideration of an emergency incident that occurred two days before, and (3) processing of four incident reports. Notice that all these items resulted in the generation of additional action items, which are summarized in paragraph 4.0. As shown in paragraph 3.4, IR 99-0012 was approved, and a software change notice needs to be submitted. An SCN would be prepared and submitted by one of the seller development staff. Note that the approval should also be indicated on the actual IR. Observe in paragraph 2.1 that representatives of two groups normally present at the CCB meeting did not attend this one. In the distribution list at the end of the minutes, the names of the missing representatives are included so that they can be apprised of the meeting results.

CCB meetings generally are not held solely to discuss one type of change. In general, a CCB considers both planned and unplanned changes at the same meeting.

The minutes shown in Figures 4–29 and 4–30 relate to consecutive CCB meetings that might occur during an acceptance testing cycle. The interaction of a Test Incident CCB and a Software

---

	Memorandum	November 13, 2000 SCCB - 2000/40

To: Distribution
Thru: Sally Plum, SHAPES CCB Chairperson
From: Helen Gray, SHAPES CCB Secretary
Subject: Minutes of SHAPES CCB Meeting
Reference: (a) SHAPES CCB minutes SCCB - 2000/39 dated November 5, 2000

1.0   Date of Meeting: November 10, 2000

2.0   Attendees:

    Jane Black   User/Management
    Bill Blackburn   Seller/Development [manager]
    Amy Blue   Buyer/Product Assurance
    Hugh Brown   Seller/Development
    Jim Brownlee   Buyer/Product Assurance [manager]
    Helen Gray   Seller/Product Assurance
    Nancy Greenfield   Seller/Development
    Jack Lemon   Seller/Development
    Sally Plum   Buyer/Management [CCB chairperson]
    Peter Rose   Buyer/Product Assurance
    Ann Whitemarsh   Seller/Management [project manager]

    2.1   Organizations Not Represented: Buyer/Development Group

3.0   CCB Actions

    3.1   Reference (a) was approved as published.

    3.2   Action items from previous meetings resolved: none.

    3.3   Release 2000-3, Version 2.1 was turned over to the Seller/Development Group.

    3.4   Amy Blue [Buyer/Product Assurance test leader] presented to the board 105 TIRs (numbered 2000-1006 through 2000-1110). There was extensive discussion of TIRs 2000-1024 through 2000-1032, which describe problems related to the new menus defined in the SHAPES Detailed Design Specification. Bill Blackburn [Seller/Development manager] indicated that he would have his staff give particular attention to this set of problems.

    3.5   It was agreed that the Seller/Development Group would return the Release 2000-3 software code to the Buyer/Product Assurance Group on November 20, 2000, for additional testing.

4.0   Action Items: none.

5.0   Next Meeting: November 20, 2000, at 3:00 p.m. in the Auxiliary Conference Room.

Distribution:
    All attendees
    Tim Graystone [Buyer/General Manager]
    Sue Pinkerton [Buyer/Development]
    Al Plumtree [Seller/President]

FIGURE 4–29   Minutes of a Test Incident CCB meeting.

	Memorandum	November 13, 2000 SCCB - 2000/40

To: Distribution
Thru: Sally Plum, SHAPES CCB Chairperson
From: Helen Gray, SHAPES CCB Secretary
Subject: Minutes of SHAPES CCB Meeting
Reference: (a) SHAPES CCB minutes SCCB - 2000/39 dated November 3, 2000

1.0   Date of Meeting: November 10, 2000

2.0   Attendees:

Jane Black	User/Management
Bill Blackburn	Seller/Development [manager]
Amy Blue	Buyer/Product Assurance
Hugh Brown	Seller/Development
Jim Brownlee	Buyer/Product Assurance [manager]
Helen Gray	Seller/Product Assurance
Nancy Greenfield	Seller/Development
Jack Lemon	Seller/Development
Sally Plum	Buyer/Management [CCB chairperson]
Peter Rose	Buyer/Product Assurance
Ann Whitemarsh	Seller/Management [project manager]

    2.1   Organizations Not Represented: Buyer/Development Group

3.0   CCB Actions

    3.1   Reference (a) was approved as published.

    3.2   Action items from previous meetings resolved: none.

    3.3   Release 2000-3, Version 2.2 was turned over to the Buyer/Product Assurance Group.

    3.4   Of the 105 TIRs turned over at the CCB meeting on November 10, 2000, 100 TIRs have been corrected via code changes (TIRs 2000-1006 through 2000-1085 and 2000-1091 through 2000-1110).

    3.5   Bill Blackburn stated that TIR 2000-1086 was the result of the improper operation of the system by the Buyer/Product Assurance Group and therefore no corrective action was required. Jim Brownlee said that he would correct the pertinent test procedure to provide appropriate clarification to the testers.

    3.6   Bill Blackburn submitted TIRs 2000-1111 through 2000-1130. He indicated that solutions and associated code had been developed for TIRs 2000-1111, 2000-1123, and 2000-1127 through 2000-1130. He also indicated that resolutions for the remaining new TIRs have not yet been developed. There was some discussion about TIR 2000-1124, which Bill Blackburn felt may not really be a problem because the SHAPES Requirements Specification was vague in the area of concern. Bill Blackburn stated that he wrote TIR 2000-1124 to obtain clarification on the matter. The board decided that the issue raised in TIR 2000-1124 was indeed a problem.

    3.7   It was agreed that the Buyer/Product Assurance Group would return Release 2000-3. Version 2.2 to the Seller/Development Group on November 29, 2000.

    4.0   Action Items: none.

    5.0   Next Meeting: November 29, 2000, at 3:00 p.m. in the Auxiliary Conference Room.

Distribution:
    All attendees
    Tim Graystone [Buyer/General Manager]
    Sue Pinkerton [Buyer/Development]
    Al Plumtree [Seller/President]

FIGURE 4–30   Minutes of a Software Turnover CCB meeting.

Turnover CCB provide visibility into the acceptance testing cycle used to determine whether a software product is ready to be delivered to a customer.

Figure 4–29 shows that the 105 TIRs were written in the testing period prior to the Test Incident CCB, and Figure 4–30 shows that the code was developed in response to 100 TIRs prior to the Software Turnover CCB. A traceability thread can be seen linking the minutes in Figure 4–29 (paragraph 3.4) and the minutes in Figure 4–30 (paragraph 3.4).

In all the minutes shown in Figures 4–27 through 4–30, note that senior management of both the buyer and the seller is included in the distribution of the minutes. From these minutes, senior management gains visibility into the progress of the project. These sample minutes complete our discussion of the important bookkeeping task of keeping and publishing CCB minutes.

This discussion completes our examination of the forms that support the change control process. In this section, we have shown that paperwork is necessary to provide visibility and traceability in the change control process. We discussed how you could develop the forms that you might need on a project. We also provided a set of forms as examples and illustrated their use. Finally, we provided a sample format for CCB minutes and several examples of how you may decide to record CCB decisions and actions.

4.7 CHANGE CONTROL PROCESS SUMMARY

In this chapter, we focused on the mechanics of change control. After presenting the two broad classes of change that are continually occurring on a software project (planned change and unplanned change), we discussed in depth the process of change control, the organization and procedures to accomplish it, and the paperwork to support it. We pointed out and illustrated that the focal point of the change control process is the CCB. This most important organization is the control activity for the entire change control process.

The role we defined for the CCB in this chapter is broader in scope—regarding planned change control and unplanned document change control—than is generally granted to it by others. Perhaps some readers would be more comfortable in referring to this group as a committee—the title used is immaterial. What is important is that a group like the one we have here called a CCB be established to control the change process in a disciplined, visible, and traceable manner.

We have presented the CCB as a decision-making body controlling software changes. The CCB must consider each planned or unplanned change. But how does the CCB know whether to approve, disapprove, reanalyze, etc., each change? To formulate an answer to this question, recall our discussion of the technical inputs to the CCB—the review initiator, the audit report, and the analysis report.

As illustrated in Figure 4–31, you can use the following annotated outline of an ADPE CCB guideline as a starting point for defining how CCBs may be incorporated into your software systems development environment.

The CCB guideline may consist of the following sections:

- **Purpose.** This section states the purpose of the guideline. The purpose is to provide guidance for establishing CCBs, defining the role of CCBs in project efforts, and conducting CCB meetings. Specific purposes of the guideline may include:
  - Your organization's CCB concept
  - Definition of CCB participants
  - Methods for documenting CCB meetings
  - Guidance for developing a CCB charter
  - Guidance for conducting CCB meetings
- **Background.** This section provides an overview of the software systems development organization, and the types of products and services the organization provides to its customers.

[Your Organization's Name and Logo]

Document #
Date

[Your Org.'s Name] Guideline
Change Control Board (CCB)

Document #
Date

1.0 PURPOSE

This section states the purpose of the element. The purpose is to provide guidance for establishing CCBs, defining the role of CCBs in project efforts, and conducting CCB meetings. Specific purposes of the guideline may include CCB concept and participants, methods for documenting CCB meetings, and guidance for CCB charters and for conducting CCB meetings.

2.0 BACKGROUND

This section gives an overview of the software systems development organization and the types of products and services that the organization provides to its customers.

3.0 CHANGE CONTROL BOARD OVERVIEW

This section presents an overview of the CCB concept. This material contains some tutorial information (e.g., how the CCB can help the customer and seller organizations better communicate with each other) and representative decisions, action items, or discussions. Management, development, and product assurance disciplines are presented and discussed in terms of the skills each disciplines provides to a project.

4.0 CCB IMPLEMENTATION CONSIDERATIONS

This section defines and walks through the process of establishing a CCB. CCB scope of activities are discussed in terms of (1) programmatic issues, (2) product development issues, (3) product change issues, and (4) product assurance issues. It is useful to present examples of possible issues. The ground rules for interaction between the seller and customer are defined.

The section also defines the methods for documenting CCB meetings and internal project meetings. A sample format for a CCB charter and a sample format for CCB minutes are provided. How a CCB meeting is conducted is also detailed.

APPENDICES

Appendices can contain details for carrying through the guidance set forth in the body of the guideline. For example, appendices might include such things as templates for CCB minutes and CCB charters.

FIGURE 4–31   An annotated outline for getting you started in defining a CCB guideline.

- **Change Control Board Overview.** This section presents an overview of the CCB concept. This material contains some tutorial information, and lessons learned by members of seller and customer staff. Management, development, and product assurance disciplines are presented and discussed in terms of the skills each discipline provides to a project. It is important to present a definition of what type of meeting constitutes a CCB meeting. Remember, not every project meeting with the customer needs to be a CCB. A project meeting may be defined as a CCB meeting when some combination of the following items affects project success: (1) decisions (affecting project deliverables, schedule, or resources) are made, (2) action items are assigned, and/or (3) issues are discussed. Representative project decisions, action items, and discussions may be presented. For example,

  - Decisions changing a deliverable due date, specifying deliverable format and content, directing that no more product assurance testing is required.

  - Actions items to prepare a document outline by a due date, to investigate the impact on product delivery using relational database technology versus object-oriented technology.

  - Discussions regarding the ability to complete a task within the remaining project resources, proposed changes to the project plan, test incident reports generated during acceptance testing.

  The section also details what organizational units are CCB participants. This discussion defines what specific organizational elements make up the management, development, and product assurance groups. For example,

  > . . . the product assurance group is assigned the responsibility for providing management with insight into product status. The product assurance group is an independent organization and provides the following skills: (1) quality assurance, (2) verification and validation, (3) acceptance test and evaluation, and (4) configuration management. . . .

- **CCB Implementation Considerations.** This section defines and walks through the process for establishing a CCB. CCB scope of activities are discussed in terms of (1) programmatic issues, (2) product development issues, (3) product change issues, and (4) product assurance issues. Examples of the possible issues are presented. The ground rules for interaction between the seller and customer are defined.

  The section also defines the methods for documenting CCB meetings and internal project meetings. A sample format for a CCB charter and a sample format for CCB minutes are provided. How a CCB meeting is to conducted is also detailed.

- **Appendices.** Appendices are added as necessary. The appendices provide the place where you can add additional detail without breaking up the text in the main body. For example, you may want to have an appendix that contains an annotated CCB charter outline. In the main body you can simply make your point about the charter and refer the reader to the appendix for the details. Appendices can also contain change control processes, such as the one we discussed in the chapter, and supporting change control forms.

We have completed our discussion of the change control process in this chapter. However, in discussing the change control process, we made frequent reference to the audit function. The allusions to auditing in the context of change control in this chapter should make you better prepared to appreciate the importance of the audit function discussed in the next chapter.

Product and Process Reviews

chapter

5

> *Asking a working writer what he thinks about critics is like asking a lamp-post what it feels about dogs.*
>
> —Christopher Hampton (b. 1946), British playwright.

5.1 INTRODUCTION

The captain who went down with the *Titanic* was informed—so history tells—that his ship was in iceberg-infested waters. Although he (and his crew and passengers) may have indeed felt that the *Titanic* was unsinkable, would he (and his crew and passengers) not have been better off knowing where the icebergs were and how big they were, so that he had an option of navigating around them?

We believe that each software systems development project should be approached with the candid realization that each project is a voyage through iceberg-infested waters. No matter how well customers and/or sellers believe they understand what is needed to be done, there are unknown icebergs (e.g., unsatisfied requirements, schedule slippages, and cost overruns). Customers and/or sellers need to be able to see such icebergs and steer clear of them to the extent prudently possible.

This chapter focuses on how customers and/or sellers can gain visibility into project icebergs associated with software systems development processes and the resultant products. As shown in Figure 5–1, the purpose of product and process reviews is to give decision makers and other software systems development project participants visibility into the project state of affairs. These reviews serve to lessen guesswork on what to do next.

Just as the captain of the *Titanic* and his crew needed iceberg detectors, the captain of the software project ship and the captain's crew need product and process state detectors. Figure 5–2 suggests that customer and/or sellers with such detectors can better anticipate the project future—and reduce the likelihood of shocking surprises.

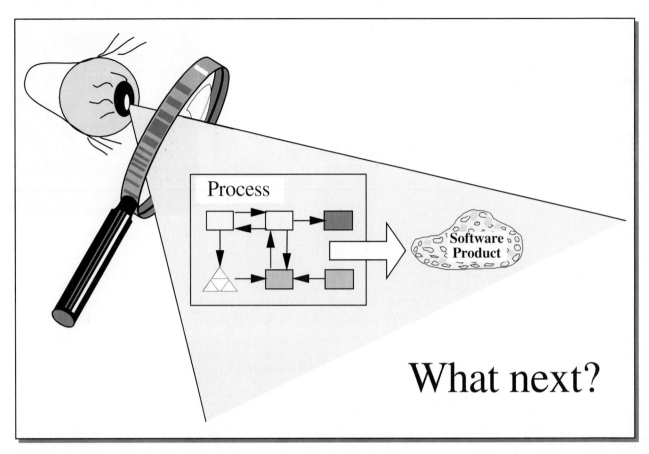

FIGURE 5–1 Reviews give visibility into processes and resultant software products. With this visibility, management, development, and product assurance personnel can make intelligent, informed decisions regarding what to do next on a software project.

"How do you want it—the crystal mumbo-jumbo or statistical probability?"

© 1997 by Sidney Harris.

"I just wanted to get your reaction to that."

© Leo Cullum 1996.

FIGURE 5–2 Product and process reviews serve to give decision makers and other project participants visibility into the project state of affairs—so that they can better anticipate the project future. Moreover, this visibility serves to reduce the likelihood of shocking surprises regarding product state.

This chapter presents techniques for detecting and steering clear of project icebergs. We label these techniques "software product reviews" and "software systems development process reviews."

At the most fundamental level, a review is a comparison of an entity against a ground truth pertaining to that entity. As a result of this comparison, discrepancies between the entity and the ground truth may be uncovered. Figure 5–3 depicts this concept for products and processes.

Ground truth is an established benchmark against which, by comparison, change is detected. If the ground truth is found to be faulty, it needs to be corrected and then reestablished as the new ground truth. We use the following two classes of ground truth:

- **Product ground truth** includes standards, requirements, predecessor products, design, the product itself, and some combination of products. For example, a software detailed design specification can be compared against the following product ground truth:
  - A documentation standard that was used to develop the specification.
  - A previously developed and approved requirements specification that was used as the WHAT for the design.

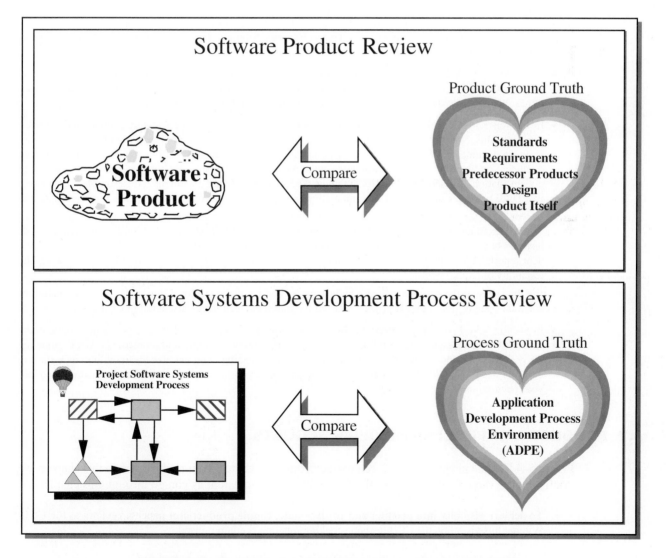

FIGURE 5–3   The heart of product and process reviews is ground truth.

- A previously developed and approved preliminary design specification that specified at a top level how the WHAT in the requirements specification is to be implemented.

- Itself

Regarding self-comparison, a product can be compared against itself for inconsistencies, ambiguities, grammatical weaknesses, spelling errors, TBDs (to be determined). Regarding comparison against standards, a product can be compared against standards governing the product format and/or content (i.e., a quality assurance comparison).

- **Process ground truth** includes, in this book, one or more application development process environment (ADPE) elements. For example, a project's peer review process can be compared against guidance provided in an ADPE Peer Review element. As another example, a project's CCB operation can be compared against guidance offered in an ADPE CCB element.

This chapter details reviews that are limited to the project level. It is at this level that visibility into product and process state is of prime importance. However, many of the review concepts that we address can also be applied at other organizational levels.

The plan for this chapter is the following:

- In Section 5.2—**Product Reviews and Process Reviews Nuggets**, we present the nuggets that you can expect to extract from this chapter.

- In Section 5.3—**A Taxonomy of Product and Process Reviews**, we present a set of software product and project process review concepts organized by management, development, and product assurance disciplines. We illustrate the review concepts with examples drawn from the real world.

- In Section 5.4—**Combining Reviews for Software Audits**, we introduce software product and software process audits. We present the software product audit concept and then provide two audit examples using software documents. We also discuss how audits are used in conjunction with the CCB. The first software document audit example (i.e., Automatic Donut-Making System) stresses how requirements and design documentation are used during a product audit. The second software document audit example (i.e., System PREDICT) stresses how project documentation is used to uncover discrepancies that represent potential icebergs.

  We then examine two more software product audit examples. The first example (i.e., System SHAPES) illustrates how a requirements specification, a design specification, a test plan, test procedures, and test incident reports (TIRs) are used to test a system. The second example (i.e., System LOOKOUT) stresses the testability of requirements.

  We then present the software process audit concept and set the stage for a more in-depth examination of software systems development processes using measurement techniques discussed in Chapter 6.

- In Section 5.5—**Product and Process Reviews Summary**, we summarize the key points developed in the chapter. We include annotated outlines for an (1) ADPE policy for product assurance, (2) ADPE guideline for peer reviews, and (3) ADPE procedure for acceptance testing. You can use these outlines as a starting point for developing ADPE elements addressing product and process reviews that can be incorporated into your environment.

5.2 PRODUCT AND PROCESS REVIEWS NUGGETS

Figure 5–4 lists the nuggets that you can extract from this chapter. To introduce you to this chapter, we briefly explain these nuggets. Their full intent will become apparent as you go through this chapter.

1. **To achieve visibility into product and project state, couple product and process reviews to the CCB.** Without this visibility, the CCB decision-making function is compromised.

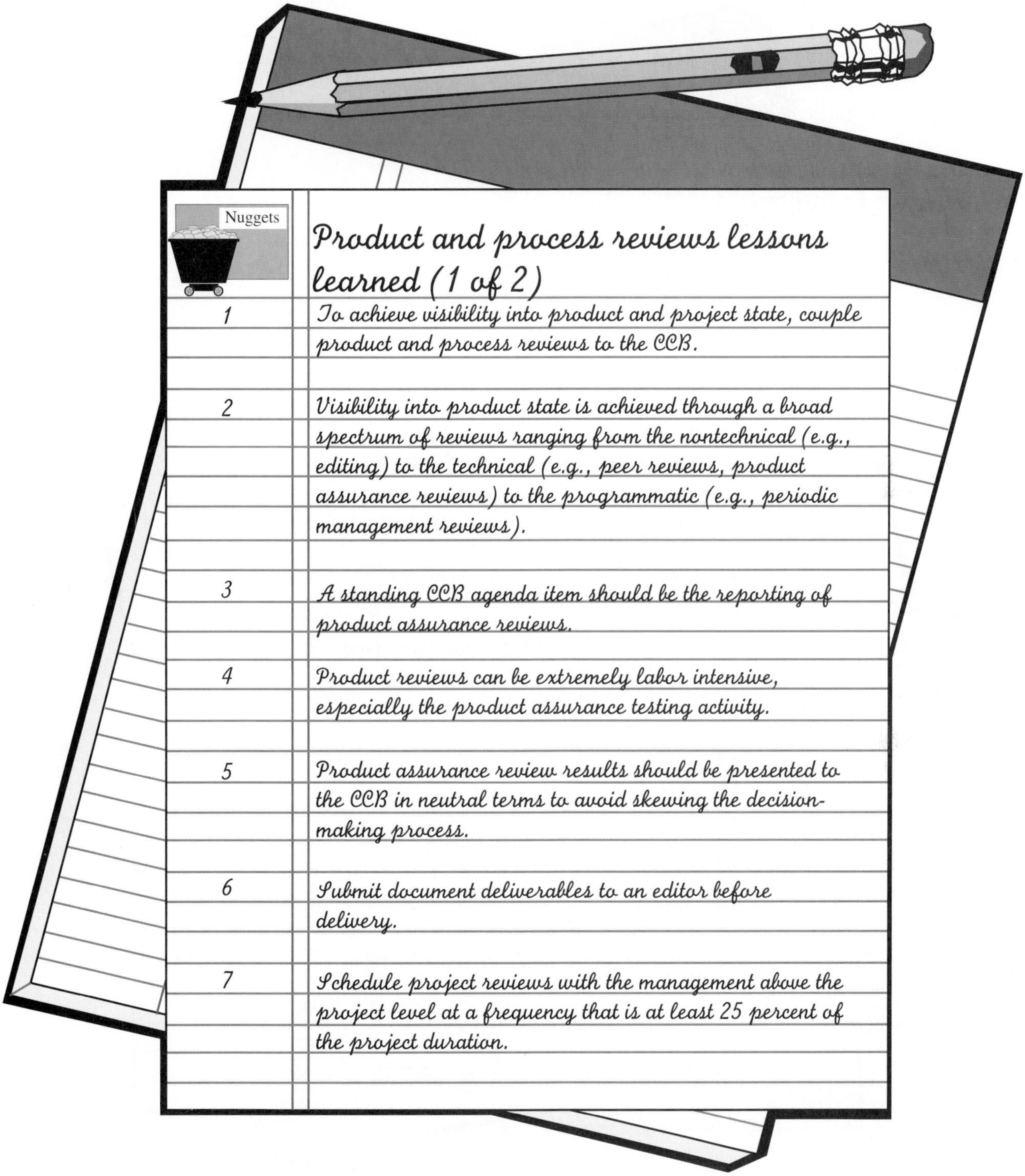

Nuggets

Product and process reviews lessons learned (1 of 2)

1	To achieve visibility into product and project state, couple product and process reviews to the CCB.
2	Visibility into product state is achieved through a broad spectrum of reviews ranging from the nontechnical (e.g., editing) to the technical (e.g., peer reviews, product assurance reviews) to the programmatic (e.g., periodic management reviews).
3	A standing CCB agenda item should be the reporting of product assurance reviews.
4	Product reviews can be extremely labor intensive, especially the product assurance testing activity.
5	Product assurance review results should be presented to the CCB in neutral terms to avoid skewing the decision-making process.
6	Submit document deliverables to an editor before delivery.
7	Schedule project reviews with the management above the project level at a frequency that is at least 25 percent of the project duration.

FIGURE 5–4   Product and process reviews help the seller develop products that conform to the customer's requirements. These nuggets are your guide to keeping your software systems development process and resultant products on track.

Product and process reviews lessons learned (2 of 2)

8	Management should ensure that peer reviews are incorporated into the software systems development process. In general, management should not participate in the reviews.
9	Seller management should establish policy regarding what review information is appropriate for disclosure to the buyer/user at a CCB.
10	At a minimum, document in an ADPE element the product assurance role in your environment.

FIGURE 5–4   *Continued*

2. **Visibility into product state is achieved through a broad spectrum of reviews ranging from the non-technical (e.g., editing) to the technical (e.g., peer reviews, product assurance reviews) to the programmatic (e.g., periodic management reviews).**

3. **A standing CCB agenda item should be the reporting of product assurance reviews.** This item can range from a brief mention that a review took place to a consideration of each incident report that product assurance generates.

4. **Product reviews can be extremely labor intensive, especially the product assurance testing activity.** The payoff for this labor expenditure is reduced risk of doing things over again. Our project planning guidance is not to skimp on resources for product review. Cursory (or rubber-stamp) product review is generally wasted effort.

5. **Product assurance review results should be presented to the CCB in neutral terms to avoid skewing the decision-making process.** Product assurance should make sure each incident report is reasonably self-contained to facilitate decision making.

6. **Submit document deliverables to an editor before delivery.** Misspellings and poor grammar can quickly deflate seller credibility in the eyes of the customer, even if the work is sound technically. However, some misspellings and grammatical errors can undermine technical content.

7. **Schedule project reviews with the management above the project level at a frequency that is at least 25 percent of the project duration.** Project reviews help to ensure that senior management has visibility into a project.

8. **Management should ensure that peer reviews are incorporated into the software systems development process. In general, management should not participate in the reviews.** Management should work with the technical staff to reach an agreement as to what information resulting from peer reviews should be made available to what level of management. Peer reviews are primarily intended for candid technical interchange among developers. This comment is not meant to imply that management can never participate in a peer review. Each organization decides what is best for its particular situation.

9. **Seller management should establish policy regarding what review information is appropriate for disclosure to the buyer/user at a CCB.** Balance must be achieved between maintaining customer confidence in seller candor and customer use of review results to bash the seller.

10. **At a minimum, document in an ADPE element the product assurance role in your environment.** In this element, you may want to include some guidance regarding other reviews such as peer reviews, editing, and managements reviews. Alternatively, you may want to address these reviews in separate ADPE elements.

5.3 A TAXONOMY OF PRODUCT AND PROCESS REVIEWS

The reviews described in this chapter are primarily associated with the seller development team. As indicated by the areas highlighted in black in Figure 5–5, product and process reviews involve the seller project manager, the lead developer, the product assurance manager, the technical editor, seller management, and the change control board (CCB).

Because many of the product and process reviews support CCB activity, the customer also is involved in these review activities. Furthermore, because these reviews should be integrated with any software systems development process, buyers/users reading this chapter may want to incorporate these concepts into their requests for seller services.

There is no unique way to categorize product and process reviews. Figure 5–6 shows that we choose to categorize the software product and project process reviews along the lines of the three systems disciplines introduced in Chapter 1—i.e., management, development, and product assurance.

Our review taxonomy addresses the visibility issues to reduce software systems development risk. Each of the reviews in our taxonomy provides insight into the state of the software development

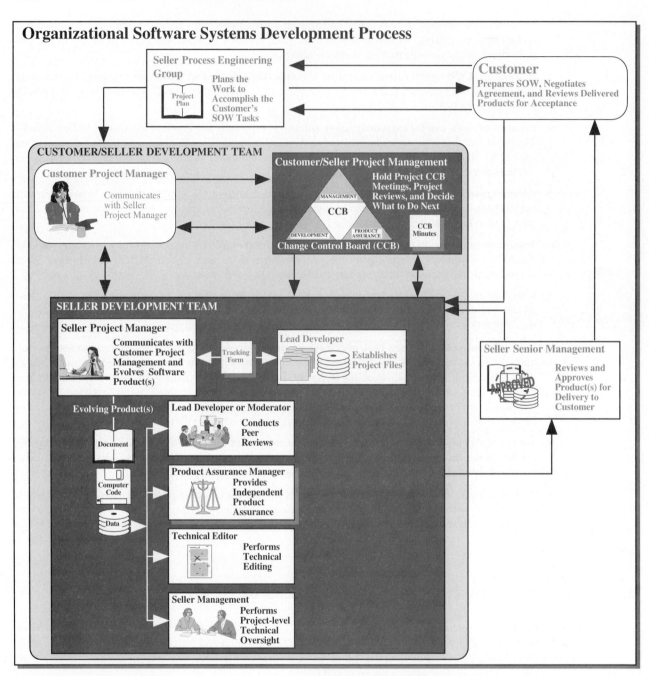

FIGURE 5–5 This chapter's discussion focuses on key software product and software systems development process reviews. The seller development team performs these reviews at the project level.

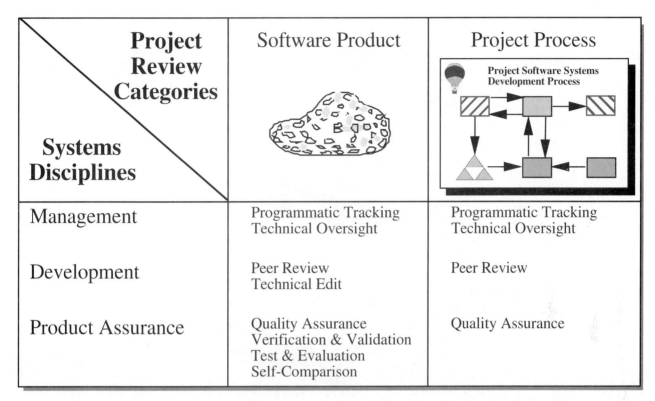

Project Review Categories / Systems Disciplines	Software Product	Project Process
Management	Programmatic Tracking Technical Oversight	Programmatic Tracking Technical Oversight
Development	Peer Review Technical Edit	Peer Review
Product Assurance	Quality Assurance Verification & Validation Test & Evaluation Self-Comparison	Quality Assurance

FIGURE 5–6 This chapter describes key management, development, and product assurance reviews at the project level. The reviews fall into two major categories—product and process.

project. This insight helps the customer and/or developer make intelligent, informed decisions on what to do next.

As shown in Figure 5–7, software product reviews involve complementary management, development, and product assurance viewpoints. For example, management may ask a programmatic tracking question such as the following—"Is the product being developed on time and within budget?" Developers may examine the technical details of a software product at a peer review and provide suggestions to the lead product developer. Product assurance reviewers may examine whether a software product conforms to established standards. Each review serves different visibility needs.

Just as the different types of product reviews offer complementary views of a product, the different types of process reviews offer complementary views of the project's software systems development process. As suggested by the questions in Figure 5–8, these views serve different visibility needs.

We present both the product and process reviews from management, development, and product assurance viewpoints in the following sections.

Management Reviews

Management provides the following types of programmatic tracking and technical oversight for a specific software product:

- A project manager tracks the cost and schedule of product development. This programmatic tracking gives visibility to cost and schedule issues surrounding the development of a product. A project manager asks questions such as the following: Is product development falling behind? Have unplanned costs emerged that will impact the budget for delivering the product on time?

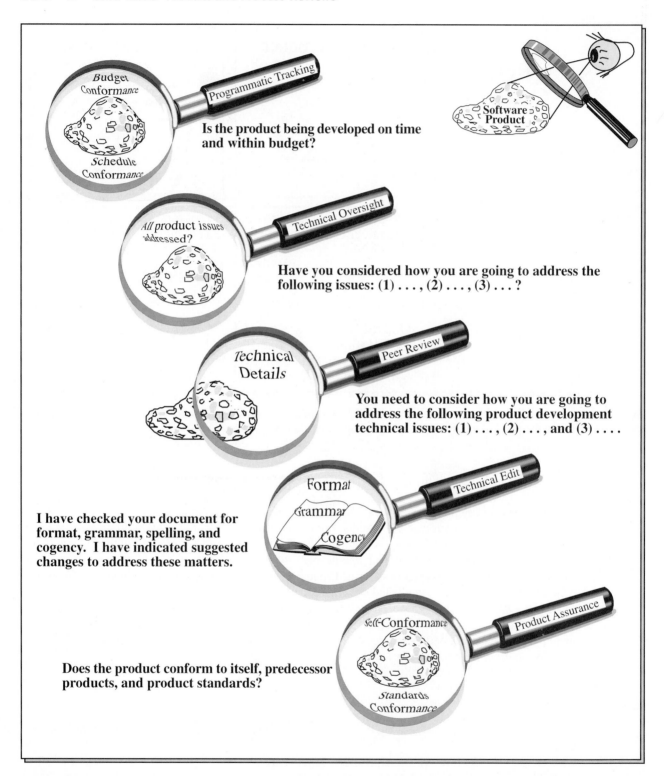

FIGURE 5–7 Software product reviews address programmatic, technical, editorial, and conformance questions.

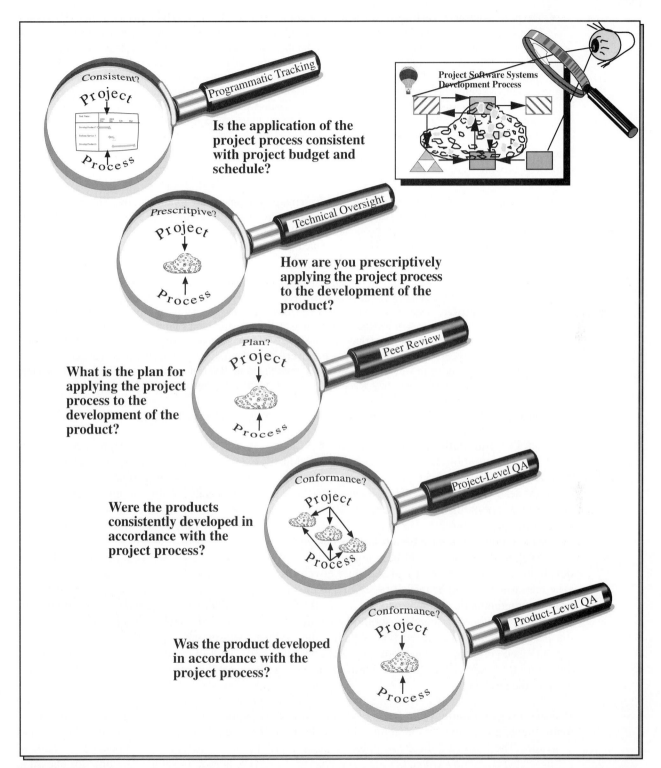

FIGURE 5–8 Project software systems development process reviews address programmatic, technical, and conformance questions.

- The project manager's management (or other senior management) periodically provides technical oversight for a specific software product. Senior management becomes involved with product development to mentor the project manager to anticipate product development adversities (e.g., requirements creep induced by a customer who has difficulty focusing on product specifics or misunderstandings by seller developers of what the customer wants). The amount of technical oversight is a management prerogative and is related to a product's complexity, size, and importance. This oversight helps the project manager repeat previous successes. For those cases in which the project has more than one layer of management, the project manager provides technical oversight to task leaders (i.e., the next lower management layer).

Management provides the following types of programmatic tracking and technical oversight of the project's software systems development process:

- A project manager tracks project software systems development programmatically. The programmatic tracking gives visibility to cost and schedule issues surrounding the entire project (versus product-specific issues). A project manager asks questions such as the following: Is the project falling behind? Am I consistently late with my deliverables? Have unplanned costs emerged that will impact the budget for delivering the project's remaining products on time?

- The project manager's management (or other senior management) periodically provides technical oversight for a specific project. Management becomes involved with a project to mentor the project manager to anticipate project software systems development adversities (e.g., analysis paralysis induced by blind adherence to the development process, or the lack of effective and timely communication between the developers and the buyer/users). The amount of technical oversight is a management prerogative and is related to a project's complexity, size, and importance. This oversight helps the project manager repeat previous successes. For those cases in which the project has more than one layer of management, the project manager provides technical oversight to task leaders (i.e., the next lower management layer).

Examples of management product and process reviews are presented in the sections that follow.

Product Programmatic Tracking   Figure 5–9 addresses the following type of product programmatic tracking question: Is the product being developed on time and within budget? Two examples of programmatic tracking discrepancies are shown. One discrepancy involves a schedule slippage because the lead developer was called away from the office. Fortunately, in this example, the product's delivery was not on the project's critical path, and the delivery could be slipped one week without impacting the overall project. The second discrepancy involves a schedule acceleration due to peer reviews and product assurance reviews of the design specification.

Such discrepancies might be reported (or uncovered) during the comparison of a product under development against the cost and schedule governing the development of that product. The cost and schedule, which should be initially specified in the project plan, serve as programmatic standards. This product programmatic check provides a means for determining whether (1) the standards should be adjusted (i.e., whether the schedule should be changed or the budget should be changed, or both) or (2) the product should be adjusted (i.e., whether the product requirements should be augmented or cut back). When performed throughout a project and when performed in conjunction with other reviews, these programmatic checks help to achieve convergence between customer and seller expectations regarding the product.

Process Programmatic Tracking   Figure 5–10 addresses the following type of process programmatic tracking question: Is the application of the project process consistent with project budget and schedule? The following three examples of process programmatic tracking discrepancies are shown: (1) projected budget overruns, (2) schedule change, and (3) reduction in scope. The timeline shown is for a four-month segment of the project involving two products and one service; the timeline indicates *planned* schedules. The discrepancy reports shown are assumed to be written sometime during December 1999, before the completion of Product 5.

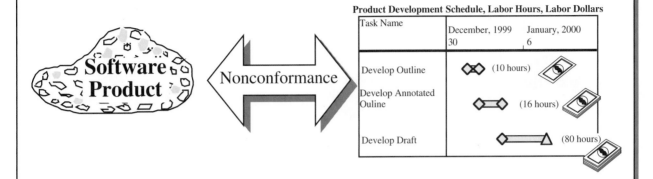

Product Programmatic Tracking

The project plan calls for a draft of the requirements specification to be delivered to the customer in one week. The product lead developer was unexpectedly called away from the office for a week. The project is currently understaffed so that no backup exists. The delivery of the draft requirements specification will thus be delayed one week. There is no impact on the project budget resulting from this schedule slippage.

At the project CCB meeting held this week, the customer and the project manager agreed that acceptance testing could begin a week earlier than stipulated in the project plan. This schedule acceleration resulted from the solid design specification delivered two months ago. Because this specification was thoroughly peer reviewed, and because product assurance cross-checked in detail this specification against the requirements specification, development of the computer code proceeded more rapidly than originally planned. In addition, the resources allocated to development of this computer code were underrun by 25 percent. This underrun will be put towards next year's project budget.

FIGURE 5–9 Product programmatic tracking helps provide insight into planned versus actual schedule and resource product development issues.

Such discrepancies might be reported (or uncovered) during the comparison of project in progress against the cost and schedule governing that project. The cost and schedule, which should be initially specified in the project plan, serve as programmatic standards. This process programmatic check provides a means for determining whether (1) the standards should be adjusted (i.e., whether the schedule should be changed or the budget should be changed, or both) or (2) the project should be adjusted (i.e., whether the project scope should be augmented or cut back). When performed throughout

Process Programmatic Tracking

Segment of Project Schedule, Labor Hours, Labor Dollars

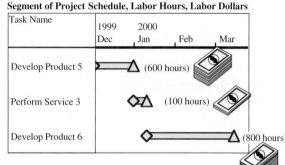

The development of Product 5 is currently scheduled to be completed by the end of December for 600 hours of labor. To date, 500 hours have been expended because of two false starts precipitated by a misunderstanding of customer requirements. To complete the development of Product 5 on time will require 300 additional hours that have currently not been included in the project budget. If the budget is not augmented, the development of Product 6 will be impacted.

At the project CCB meeting held this week, the customer and the project manager agreed that the performance of Service 3 should be delayed one month so that the development of Product 6 could begin two weeks earlier than currently planned. This schedule adjustment will not require adjustment to the project budget.

The project is currently three weeks ahead of schedule but 10 percent over budget. The customer is in the process of sending an SOW amendment reducing the scope of Product 6 to allow the product to be developed within the budget.

FIGURE 5–10   Process programmatic tracking helps to provide insight into planned versus actual schedule and resource issues involved with the overall project.

a project, these project-level programmatic checks help to achieve convergence between customer and seller expectations regarding the overall project.

Product Technical Oversight   Figure 5–11 addresses the following type of product technical oversight question: Have you considered how you are going to address the following issues: (1) . . . , (2) . . . , and (3) . . . ? Two examples of product technical oversight are shown. Such remarks might be

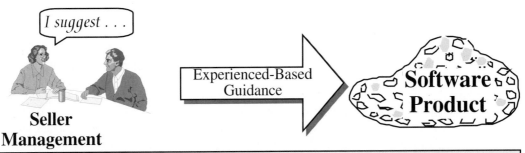

Product Technical Oversight

I suggest . . .

Seller Management

Experienced-Based Guidance

Software Product

> *Upon reviewing the data conversion requirements document, I offer the following suggestions:*
>
> - *Data conversion concepts included in the writeup are generally defined in easy-to-understand terms. However, the concepts should be illustrated with specific examples because the intended audience for this document is not familiar with the technical details of data conversion. For instance, the concept of the translate function should be augmented with one or more examples showing how the source data are to be changed in terms of length, type, and/or precision.*
>
> - *A figure showing the overall conversion process does exist in the document, but the figure is not explained. Suggest that words be included that walk the reader through the process, from start to finish.*

> *Upon reviewing the draft project plan, I offer the following suggestion:*
>
> - *There does not appear to be a balance between the planned resources and the number of deliverables. Suggest you revisit the deliverables and see if you can combine them in some fashion so that they are more in balance with the resource estimate.*

FIGURE 5–11 Here are some example remarks that a senior manager might pass along to a project manager or to a project team member on the context or orientation of a software(-related) product.

discussed after the seller management has an opportunity to review the products, but before the products are shown to the customer.

The management remarks are based primarily on personal or known experiences that have been successful or unsuccessful. The example remarks concerning the data conversion requirements document suggests that the team may understand the conversion process, as evidenced by the reference to the figure showing the overall conversion process. However, management is suggesting that the figure should be described in more detail so that the reader (e.g., a customer) clearly understands what is going to happen. Such explanation may result in the developer's discovering something that was overlooked or the customer's pointing out something that was not previously discussed with the seller. In this example, one intent of the product technical oversight is to remove any ambiguities in what is needed to be done before the data are converted.

Regarding the second management comment on the overall conversion process in the data conversion requirements document, the suggestion is made to explain a figure. The developers may think that figures included in documents are self-evident. Here, management is bringing to bear its experience in working with customers to ensure that a product clearly communicates.

The seller management remarks concerning the draft project plan suggest that the planning team may understand the technical side of the planning problem but does not fully appreciate the resources required to produce the deliverables. The seller developers on the planning team are engineers who think in terms of computer code. Sometimes they may read "Cadillac" where buyer/user intended "Chevrolet." Here, the seller management is suggesting that the developers rethink their approach and see if they can balance the number of deliverables with the planned resources.

Process Technical Oversight   Figure 5–12 addresses the following type of process technical oversight question: How are you prescriptively applying the project process to the development of the product? One example of process technical oversight is shown. In this example, the seller management offers suggestions regarding the project's software development process.

In this example the seller senior manager suggests that the development team keep track of how long the peer reviews are taking. In the future, the development team can use this historical information to help it better plan required resources. In addition, the seller senior manager suggests that the CCB meetings be modified to track "new" requirements as they are discovered. As indicated in the manager's remarks, the schedule cannot be slipped; therefore, implementing new requirements may mean that additional resources are needed. However, additional resources are not always the solution to implementing more requirements. Other approaches include "phased implementation"—that is, putting some requirements in one product and addressing the remainder in a follow-on product.

Development Reviews

Development product and process reviews include peer reviews and technical editing. Peer reviews can range from "one-on-one" sessions between the lead developer and a peer (or a couple of peers) to "formal scheduled" sessions during which materials are distributed to the reviewers (e.g., three to six reviewers) in advance of the scheduled time. As discussed in the following paragraphs, the reviews are technical in nature. Generally, management does not directly participate but should be informed about the reviews.

Development conducts the following types of peer reviews of the evolving product and technical edits of documents:

- Product peer reviews involve detailed technical interchange among developers to help the lead developer better implement what the customer wants. For example, the peer review can help the lead developer present material consistent with the product's intended audience. If the audience consists of novices, then the material should include explanations of fundamental or basic concepts. On the other hand, if the audience consists of experts, the material does not have to devote so much attention to the basics.

- Technical editing helps to ensure that the document content is communicated unambiguously to the targeted audience and that the product conforms to accepted documentation standards. Technical editing focuses on technical content *presentation* to ensure that the product is cogent and unambiguous.

Development conducts the following type of peer reviews of the project's software systems development process:

Process Technical Oversight

Upon reviewing the project-level process, I offer the following suggestions:

- *When conducting your peer reviews, I suggest that you keep track of how long they take so that you can use this information in future project planning.*

- *Having participated in a series of CCB meetings, I have observed that the customer's technical people have a tendency to introduce new requirements or changes to existing requirements. Since the project schedule cannot be changed, I suggest that you talk to the seller project manager about what requirements can and cannot be fulfilled within the existing budget and schedule. I understand that new requirements will be discovered, but you'll never get there if you cannot get agreement on what is to be included for this first release. You can offer to track the new requirements or changes for future releases.*

- *It appears that the customer is not reviewing the delivered products in a timely fashion. Unfortunately, the customer does not have enough people or time to respond. I believe you need to modify your project process. I suggest that you talk to the seller project manager and offer to brief the seller staff within 5 working days after you deliver a product. At this briefing your staff can walk the customer staff through the deliverable contents, and the customer staff can provide your staff with the necessary feedback.*

FIGURE 5–12   Here are some example remarks that a senior manager might pass along to a project manager or to a project team member regarding the project-level software systems development process.

■ Project process peer reviews involve detailed technical interchange among developers to help the lead developer detail the steps necessary to develop a software product within the context of the project's software systems development process. For example, the peer review can help the lead developer decide on the appropriate mix of process review activities (e.g., product peer reviews, technical edits, and/or product assurance reviews) to apply to a software product.

Examples of development product and process reviews are presented in the following paragraphs.

Product Peer Reviews   Figure 5–13 addresses the following type of product peer review statement:

> You need to consider how you are going to address the following product development technical issues: (1) . . . , (2) . . . , and (3) . . . .

Example product peer review comments are shown for (1) a software document, (2) a software-related document, (3) computer code, and (4) data.

The lead developer gets together with one or more peers to discuss a product or some portion of a product. As suggested in Figure 5–13, the peers ask questions and provide suggestions to the lead developer. For example, the peers suggest that the response time requirement in the requirements specification is not testable. The peers point out that the requirement does not define a time interval over which response time is to be measured. Note that the issue of testability is occurring during requirements specification. In this example, the seller developers are trying to ensure closure with the customer on what the customer wants by making sure each requirement is testable.

Process Peer Reviews   Figure 5–14 addresses the following type of process peer review question: What is the plan for applying the project process to the development of the product? Three examples of process peer review comments are shown: (1) requirements specification development, (2) computer code development, and (3) database development.

The lead developer gets together with one or more peers to discuss the software development process or some portion of the process. As suggested in the figure, the peers ask questions and provide suggestions to the lead developer. For example, the peers suggest that the lead developer use information engineering techniques and tools to develop the database. Specific recommendations are made regarding the process of detailing subject areas in terms of entity types, their relationships, and then attributes. The seller developers are also trying to ensure closure with the customer by suggesting the lead developer obtain customer acceptance of what has been done and what needs to be done as the project proceeds through its life cycle.

Technical Editing of Software and Software-Related Documents   Figure 5–15 addresses the following type of technical edit statements: I have checked your document for format, grammar, spelling, and cogency. I have indicated suggested changes to address these matters. A number of technical edits are illustrated.

A technical editor must be careful not to change the meaning of the author's words. However, a technical editor should give visibility to uncertainties by raising questions. Note the last technical edit at the bottom of the figure. There is a world of difference between "now" and "not." Some technical edits can have earth-shaking consequences.

Figure 5–16 lists some technical editing tips. These tips derive from lessons learned editing hundreds of documents.[1]

In some situations, time does not permit a thorough technical edit. It is therefore a good idea to prioritize items such as those shown in the figure. What is critical to your organization regarding documents should be at the top of the list. For example, if you have a customer who has certain "trigger"

---

[1]We thank Peter Keefe for allowing us to incorporate the material in Figure 5–16 in this book.

Product Peer Review

Lead Developer

Peers

Software Document—Requirements Specification

Section six, paragraph five, of the requirements specification lists performance requirements for the man-machine interface. In particular, the response time requirement, as currently written, is not testable because it does not define a time interval over which response time is to be measured.

Software-Related Document—User's Manual

The manual needs to include figures showing sample screen displays for all the functional capabilities shown in Section 6.

Computer Code

The module that calculates automobile fuel economy does not contain comments indicating the formulas being programmed.

Data

The data model specifies an entity type VIDEO_STORE. Attributes are not specified for this entity type.

FIGURE 5–13   Here are examples of product peer review comments for a software document, software-related document, computer code, and data.

Process Peer Review

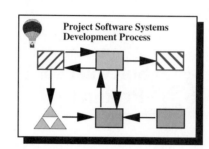

Lead Developer

Peers

Requirements Specification Development

To reduce the likelihood of false starts, it is suggested that you plan for a development sequence that allows for an outline, an annotated outline, a draft, and a final version of the specification. Be sure to account for peer reviews, technical editing, and product assurance reviews.

Computer Code Development

Remember that our project software systems development process requires that each module is subject to code walkthroughs and unit testing. Also, the results of your unit test walkthroughs need to be recorded in your software development folders.

Database Development

Suggest that you use information engineering techniques and tools to develop the database. Start with subject areas and then detail each area with the entity types, their relationships, and attributes. Be sure to get customer acceptance at each stage to avoid going down the wrong path.

FIGURE 5–14   Here are examples of process peer review comments for the development of a requirements specification, computer code, and a database.

Technical Editing

Checks that document (text and figures) conforms to document format standards, uses cogent and unambiguous language, and contains no spelling errors.

Software Requirements Specification for System ABC

Eighty-seven

1.0   Introduction

~~Four score and seven~~ years ago Company *BBB* started. The company desires to enter the information technology age; System ABC is the company's entree into this age. This document specifies the functional capabilities to be supported by the software subsystem of System ABC.

2.0   System overview

The purpose of System ABC is to help Company <u>BBB</u> administrative staff prepare monthly status reports. More specifically, this system will provide the following capabilities:

—shall

- •   •   •   •

Nuclear Weapon's User Manual

- •   •   •   •

3.0   Weapon Deployment

- •   •   •   •

Is this word spelled correctly? The preceding context seems to suggest that the word should be "not."

Enter A = NOGO
The following message will be displayed on the screen:

Nuclear weapons may (now) be deployed

- •   •   •   •

FIGURE 5–15   Here are examples of technical edits for two types of software(-related) documents.

Technical Editing Tips

Items to Check

√ All required elements of a complete deliverable document are present
√ Cover letter follows template
√ Acceptance of deliverable and receipt of deliverable forms have correct document title
√ Front cover follows document template format
√ Title page information is consistent with front cover and cover letter
√ Contents and figure lists have correct page references
√ All pages are printed and are numbered correctly
√ All figures, tables, photographs, and other diagrams are included
√ Header information is correct and appears on the correct pages

Scan for Format Errors

• Incorrect or incorrectly placed headers (check landscape pages carefully)
• Widow and orphan lines
• Incorrect numbering sequence
• Wrong bullet format
• Incorrect spacing between paragraphs and sections
• Too much white space
• Unacceptable illustrations (e.g., cannot read text, poor placement on the page)
• Nonstandard margins

Line-by-Line Edit

• Does the document read well?
• Do the sentences flow one to the next in a logical, "connected" manner?
• When applicable, has the document template been followed?
• Are abbreviations, acronyms, symbols, and numbers used correctly?
• Are there misspellings?
• Are document titles italicized?
• Are *i.e.* and *e.g.* used properly and not overused?
• Are bulleted lists in a parallel style?
• Are one-word, two-word, and hyphenated terms like *database* consistently used?
• Is the capitalization of titles, proper names, and project-specific terms consistent in the document?
• Is capitalization used judiciously and not overdone?
• Are sentences complete?
• Are verb tenses correct?
• Is there agreement between subjects and verbs (e.g., "minutes" is a plural noun)?
• Are compound adjectives hyphenated when necessary for readability?
• Are "that" and "which" used correctly?
• Do sentences have end punctuation?
• Is punctuation used correctly with quotation marks (e.g., in the United States, periods always go inside)?
• Are hyphens, em-dashes, and en-dashes used correctly?
• Is the serial comma used correctly? [Note: Practices vary. Reference or develop a style guide to set the practice for your organization.]
• Is the semicolon used between phrases containing commas?
• Is the apostrophe used correctly to show possessions and contractions?

Note: If meaning is uncertain, consult with the document author before editing the uncertainty!

FIGURE 5–16   This figure presents a starting point for constructing a set of technical editing tips for documents.

words or phrases (e.g., "execute the tasks" should be replaced with something like "perform the tasks") that the customer always reacts to in a negative way, you may want to develop a checklist to be used when editing the customer's documents. Such a checklist is particularly useful when you are rushing to get something to the customer.

Product Assurance Reviews

Product assurance product reviews include quality assurance (QA); verification and validation (V&V); test and evaluation (T&E); and self-comparison. Product assurance for a product supports timely management decision making by answering questions such as the following:

- Is the product under development conforming to the product standards? (i.e., product quality assurance [QA] check)

- Does the product under development (1) logically follow from the predecessor product and (2) conform to customer requirements? (i.e., verification and validation [V&V] check)

- Is the software system code congruent with the requirements and design specifications? (i.e., test and evaluation [T&E] check)

- Does the product have the following characteristics: (1) internally consistent, (2) unambiguous, (3) free of grammatical weaknesses, (4) free of spelling errors, and (5) free of "to be determined" items? (i.e., self-comparison check)

Product assurance process reviews include QA at a product level (i.e., using one product to check a project's software systems development process) and project level (i.e., using more than one product to check a project's software systems development process). Product assurance for a project's software systems development process supports timely management decision making by answering questions for a specific product (i.e., product level) or a collection of products (i.e., project level). Such questions include the following:

- Is the development of the product conforming to the project's software systems development process? (i.e., process quality assurance [QA] check at the product level)

- Is the development of the project's products conforming to the project's software systems development process? (i.e., process quality assurance [QA] check at the project level)

Both product and process reviews often provide discrepancy reports that are given to project decision makers, such as the project manager. To facilitate decision making and to avoid biasing the decision process, the reports should provide context and use neutral language. Sufficient detail should be provided to (1) clarify issues to be decided and (2) make it easy to obtain additional information pertaining to these issues.

Examples of product assurance product and process reviews are presented in the following sections.

Product Quality Assurance   When performing a software product quality assurance (QA) check, the software product is compared with product standards (i.e., various ground truths) established for a project. The software product is assessed as to its conformance with each standard in this set. This type of QA comparison (audit) may result in considerable savings in resources due to a timely audit. For example, assume that an apparent design error is uncovered prior to commencement of coding. It is cheaper to fix the design, than to fix the computer code and the design.

Figure 5–17 presents two examples of product quality assurance (QA) discrepancy examples: (1) design document and (2) requirements specification. The design document discrepancy is reported in terms of a module missing an error exit. The requirements document discrepancy is reported in terms of nonconformance with the documentation standard.

Product Quality Assurance (QA)

Subsection 4.2 of the design document defines the five software modules that make up Subsystem S2. Four of these modules are specified as having error exits. No error exits, however, have been specified for module MS2(3) of this subsystem. Paragraph 7.3.4 of the programming standard stipulates that all modules should have error exits. This apparent discrepancy between the description of module MS2(3) and the programming standard should be resolved for compliance.

The System ABC Requirements Specification does not conform to paragraph 2.1.6 of the company's documentation standard. Paragraph 2.1.6 of the documentation standard stipulates that every requirements specification must state its database backup and restoration needs. The System ABC Requirements Specification is silent on this issue. For completeness, this apparent omission should be addressed.

FIGURE 5–17 Here are examples of product quality assurance (QA) discrepancies that might be uncovered during the comparison of a product under development against one or more standards governing the development of that product.

Product Verification and Validation   When performing a product verification and validation (V&V) check, the software product is compared against a ground truth composed of two items—the predecessor software product and the requirements specification. The comparison of a software product with a predecessor software product is labeled as verification, and the comparison of a software product with the requirements specification is labeled as validation. A special case of this comparison process exists when the predecessor product of a software product being audited is the requirements specification. The requirements specification is the only item in the ground truth in this case, and the comparison of the software product with the requirements specification is both a verification and validation.

Figure 5–18 presents two verification and two validation (V&V) discrepancy examples. The verification discrepancies show how a detailed design document does not logically follow from the preliminary design document. For example, the detailed design document refers to Subsystem S_{13}, but the preliminary design specification makes no reference to Subsystem S_{13}. Somehow this subsystem made its way into the detailed design specification. This discrepancy is an example of how a document does not logically follow from its predecessor document. Furthermore, the validation discrepancies show how requirements and design specifications can be inconsistent with one another.

For both verification and validation, the comparison determines whether the two products are congruent. As we discuss in the next section, determining congruency is a two-step process. The auditor first must find software parts in both products that match as to subject, and then must determine whether those software parts match in content. For example, suppose an auditor is comparing a preliminary design specification (PDS) with a requirements specification (RS). Assume that the auditor finds a paragraph in the requirements specification on the subject of drawing circles. The auditor searches the preliminary design specification for material on that subject and finds an entire section devoted to drawing circles. Having found a match in subject between the two products, the auditor next compares the paragraph in the RS with the section in the PDS to see whether they have the same content. If the only difference between these two software parts is the greater detail that is anticipated in the PDS, the auditor has located a pair of congruent parts in the two products. That is, if a software part or parts in one product matches in subject and content a software part or parts in the other product, then the software parts are congruent. If a software part in one product does not match in subject any software part in the other product, then an incongruity exists. An incongruity also exists if a software part or parts in one product matches in subject a software part or parts in the other product, but does not match in content. These and all other incongruities are reported as discrepancies. Finding software parts that match in subject is generally not a trivial task. Congruence between software products can be a one-to-one, a many-to-one, or a one-to-many relationship. Further, where incongruities exist, there may be parts in one product that have no match in subject in the other product.

Product Test and Evaluation   Figure 5–19 presents three test and evaluation (T&E) discrepancy examples. The first example presents a T&E discrepancy in which the expected results of the circle command did not match the observed results. In fact, in this case, an ellipse was drawn instead of a circle. This type of error may not be as easily discovered by examining the source code. However, when the tester executes the test steps and tries to match the expected result with the observed result, the discrepancy is easily discovered.

The second product T&E discrepancy example deals with another discrepancy of expected results versus observed results. In this case, an error message was expected, but instead, the tester observed a bar graph. Again, this discrepancy is easily discovered by executing the test procedures.

The third product T&E discrepancy deals with a user's manual discrepancy. The manual describes the word processor's hyphenation capability. When the user actually used the hyphenation capability, the word processor's functionality was different from what was described in the manual. As shown in Figure 5–19, the word *mission* was broken in the wrong place, and no hyphen was inserted.

Product Self-Comparison   Figure 5–20 presents six self-comparison examples that include the following discrepancy types:

Product Verification and Validation (V&V)

Verification Discrepancies

Subsection 1.3 of the detailed design document (System Architecture) provides a summary description of each of the system's subsystems. This description includes a reference to Subsystem S13. Section 2.2 of the preliminary design specification, which specifies the system's subsystems, makes no reference to a Subsystem S13. This apparent discrepancy should be resolved for consistency.

Subsection 3.6 of the detailed design document (System Displays) defines the format and content of each of the displays that can be generated at a user terminal. In describing the time that may elapse to generate displays, this section contains the following statement: "The amount of time required to generate the display shown in figure 3.6-3 depends in part upon the scale specified by the user for the map background. If this scale is greater than fifty (50) miles to the inch, the software will require at least five (5) seconds to generate and display the map following completion of the user input requesting generation of the display." This statement appears to be inconsistent with the response time performance requirement specified in subsection 3.1 of the preliminary design specification, viz., the response time between entry of a display request and the display of a response must be less than 4 seconds. (This performance requirement is derived from paragraph 6.7 in the requirements specification.) This apparent discrepancy should be resolved for consistency.

Validation Discrepancies

The detailed design specifies that the search algorithm in module S4.8 will sequentially search the tray table to determine which trays are currently lined up at their discharge chutes (and therefore must be tilted to discharge their contents). This design logically follows from the preliminary design specification, which stated in paragraph 3.4.2 that subsystem S4 would, for each increment of tray sorter travel, tilt all trays aligned with their discharge chutes. However, analysis indicates that a sequential search would be too slow to satisfy paragraph 5.2.2 of the requirements specification, which specified that the system must be capable of tilting all 980 trays of the tray sorter on any one increment of tray sorter travel. This apparent discrepancy should be resolved for conformance.

Paragraph 6.2 of the requirements specification states that the system must be available 24 hours per day, 7 days per week. The preliminary design specification does not address this requirement. This discrepancy should be resolved for completeness.

FIGURE 5–18 Here are examples of product verification and validation (V&V) discrepancies that might be uncovered during the comparison of a product under development against a predecessor product and the requirements for that product.

Product Test and Evaluation (T&E)

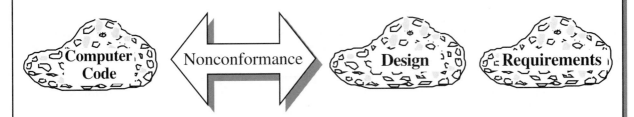

In step 16 of test procedure 4-2, the expected response to the terminal command "CIRCLE (8, 10.4,5)" was that a circle would be drawn on the terminal display at coordinates (8, 10.4) with a radius of 5 units. The actual result of the entry of this command was the display of an ellipse on the terminal, centered at coordinates (8, 10.4) with a minor axis of 10 units and a major axis of 14 units.

Upon entry of the command "GRAPH (BAR)" at step 98 of test procedure 6A (having previously entered the parameters for a bar graph in preceding test steps), a bar graph was displayed on the terminal with alternate bars going up and down with bar magnitudes 200 times larger than the values previously entered. What was expected at this step was the display of an error message stating that negative values were not allowed in drawing bar graphs.

Page 109 of the word processor user's manual indicates that to turn on hyphenation, choose Auto Hyphenation from the Text menu. The manual also indicates that, per Section 7.2 in the word processor design specification, this choice causes words to be automatically hyphenated using the hyphenation points contained in the word processor's dictionary. When Auto Hyphenation was selected, the word "mission" appearing at the end of a line was broken as follows:

mi
ssion.

That is, per Section 4 in the word processor requirements specification that cites the dictionary to be incorporated into the word processor, the word was broken in the wrong place, and no hyphen was inserted.

FIGURE 5–19 Here are examples of product test and evaluation (T&E) discrepancies that might be uncovered during the testing of computer code.

Product Self-Comparison

{ Internal inconsistencies
Ambiguities
Grammatical weaknesses
Spelling errors
TBDs }

Paragraph 4.3.4.5 (Number of Terminals to Be Supported) of the requirements specification indicates that the system is to be capable of supporting up to fifty (50) terminals. This paragraph appears to be inconsistent with the discussion in section 1 that suggests that between one (1) and fifteen (15) users will be able to access the system simultaneously. This apparent discrepancy should be resolved for consistency.

Section 1 of the design document (System Overview) contains several different spellings of the same system name (e.g.,FRAMAS, FRAMUS, FRUMAS). These discrepancies should be corrected for consistency.

Subsection 3.1 of the requirements specification (Performance Requirements) contains the following statement: "The system response time to a user query input at a terminal device shall not exceed three (3) seconds." The definition of "system response time" does not appear to be specified anywhere in the document. Does it mean, for example, "the time that elapses between the instant the user presses the RETURN key on the terminal device at the end of his query until the instant the system's response to the query first appears on the terminal's display device"? This point should be clarified.

The second sentence of the fourth paragraph of section 1 of the design specification is not understood. This issue should be addressed for the sake of clarity.

Section 2 of the requirements specification (System Overview), which contains a discussion of the system capabilities to be automated (i.e., capabilities to be supported by software functions), does not contain a corresponding discussion of the capabilities to be supported by computer hardware and communications equipment. For completeness, this issue should be addressed.

Section 5 of the requirements specification is entitled "Performance Requirements." Subsection 5.4 (Response Time Requirements) is listed as To Be Determined (TBD). For completeness, this discrepancy should be addressed.

FIGURE 5–20 Here are examples of product self-comparison discrepancies that might be uncovered during the comparison of a product under development against itself.

- **Internal inconsistencies.** The top shaded box describes a discrepancy dealing with the number of terminals that can be supported by the system. One paragraph states 50 terminals and another paragraph suggests that up to 15 users can be supported at the same time.

  Another consistency example is briefly described in the second shaded box. The description points out the fact that the system name has several different spellings within the same document. The discrepancy report points out that this inconsistency needs to be resolved.

- **Ambiguities.** The third shaded box deals with ambiguities associated with a requirements specification. The phrase "system response time" is not defined in the document. The definition can have a significant impact on the design of the system. Such a discrepancy should be clarified.

  Another example of an ambiguity is pointed out in the fourth shaded box. A particular paragraph in a design specification is not understood. As stated in the discrepancy report, this ambiguity should be resolved so that there is no misunderstanding of how things are suppose to work.

- **Completeness.** The fifth shaded box describes a discrepancy in a requirements specification dealing with system capabilities that are to be automated. It appears that one section of the requirements specification states that certain system capabilities are to be supported by software. However, the specification is silent as to what software capabilities are to be supported by hardware and communications equipment. This issues should be resolved for completeness.

- **Spelling errors.** Although the figure does not show a speling error,[2] such errors can substantially reduce the credibility of a document.

- **TBDs.** The bottom shaded box shows how To Be Determined (TBD) can be used to highlight the fact that something needs to be resolved. By using a TBD, the item is not loss or forgotten. However, like all discrepancies, TBDs need to be resolved as well.

To aid in product self-comparison activities, checklists can be developed to help the reviewer catch different types of discrepancies. Again, for those customers who may have particular hot buttons, the checklists can help to increase customer satisfaction.

Process Quality Assurance at Product Level   Figure 5–21 presents two process quality assurance (QA) discrepancies at a product level. The first process QA discrepancy shows how a seller's software systems development process was not followed for a product (i.e., a requirements specification) that was delivered to the customer. The second example indicates that part of a software systems development process was not followed but that another part of the process helped to identify potential problems.

A project-specific process is adapted from the organizational process, presumably during project planning. The process QA check provides a means for determining whether the standards should be adjusted (i.e., whether the process should be changed—either at the project level or at the organizational level) or, if the product is still under development, whether the product should be adjusted (e.g., through more peer reviews).

Process Quality Assurance at Project Level   Figure 5–22 presents two process quality assurance (QA) discrepancies at a project level. The first process QA example deals with a review of a project's files that indicate that deliverables are consistently delivered late. Several actions may result from this process QA check across the project. First, the seller and customer did not come to closure on the requirements. It is also apparent that the seller project staff may need training specific to the types of products required. Finally, additional project planning training may be necessary.

The second process QA example deals with a project that is not holding recommended CCB meetings with the customer, but the project's deliverables seem to be acceptable to the customer. In this case, it may be that the organization's recommendation for a CCB monthly meeting may need to

---

[2]We know that "speling" error should be "spelling" error.

Process Quality Assurance (QA) at a Product Level

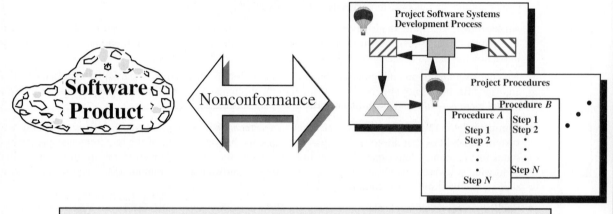

The requirements specification that was delivered to the customer last month was returned for a major rewrite because it did not address human interface issues. A review of the product tracking form and project CCB minutes showed that no peer reviews were conducted on the document, even though project procedures mandate that at least one peer review be conducted on any deliverable. The project peer review checklist for requirements specifications contains a check for human interface issues.

Release 4.1 of System QUICK was delivered on time, within budget, and met customer requirements as confirmed on the acceptance of deliverable form received last week from the customer. The development of the computer code and its testing complied with all process activities established for the project—except that no code walkthroughs were conducted. Apparently, the extensive unit and integration testing that was conducted brought to light logic flaws that were fixed prior to acceptance testing. This latter testing brought to light several misunderstandings regarding customer requirements. These misunderstandings were resolved with the customer at acceptance testing CCB meetings.

FIGURE 5–21 Here are examples of process quality assurance (QA) discrepancies that might be uncovered (or reported) during the comparison of a product under development (or that has finished development) against the project-specific software systems development process.

Process Quality Assurance (QA) at a Project Level

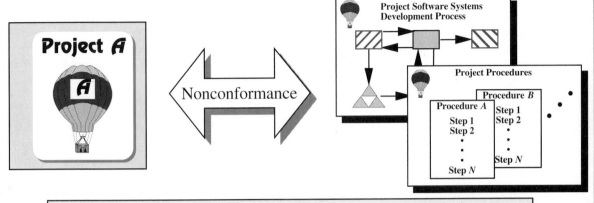

A review of the project files for Project A shows that deliverables are consistently delivered late. A review of the correspondence surrounding the development of the Project A Project Plan indicates that the customer requirements were cited as being highly uncertain. This review also indicated that the project staff, including the project manager, had little experience in developing products in the Project A application area. The product delivery dates cited in the project plan did not appear to have accounted for the impact on product development pace stemming from the uncertain customer requirements.

The organizational software systems development process mandates that each project shall have a CCB that meets with the customer at least monthly. An audit of the files of the recently completed Project A indicates that either (1) no CCB meetings took place or, if such meetings were held, (2) no minutes were prepared. The audit also shows that all deliverables specified in the Project A Project Plan were delivered on or before the dates specified in the project plan. The project files contain completed acceptance of deliverable forms for five of the project's eight deliverables. These forms indicate that the five deliverables were accepted as delivered. The status of the remaining three deliverables is unknown.

FIGURE 5–22 Here are examples of process quality assurance (QA) discrepancies that might be uncovered (or reported) during the comparison of a project against the project-specific software systems development process.

be reconsidered. It may be that every other month is frequent enough for CCB meetings. However, before changing the recommended CCB meeting frequency, the process QA check should be performed for similar projects. Depending on the results, then consideration should be given to see whether the recommended CCB meeting frequency should be changed.

A project-specific process is adapted from the organizational process, presumably during project planning. The process QA check at the project level (i.e., across the project's deliverables versus just one product) provides a means for determining whether the standards should be adjusted (i.e., whether the process should be changed—either at the project level or at the organizational level) or confirming that the process is working (i.e., consistently producing products with integrity). When performed across projects, these process QA checks help to improve the organizational software systems development process and the resultant products.

5.4 COMBINING REVIEWS FOR SOFTWARE AUDITS

In Chapter 3, we discussed how reviews (i.e., peer reviews, technical editing, independent product assurance, and management technical oversight) can be a part of an organization's software systems development process. In this chapter, we have expanded upon the Chapter 3 reviews by presenting and discussing the following taxonomy of product and process reviews:

- Management Reviews
  - Product Programmatic Tracking
  - Process Programmatic Tracking
  - Product Technical Oversight
  - Process Technical Oversight

- Development Reviews
  - Product Peer Reviews
  - Process Peer Reviews
  - Technical Editing of Software and Software-Related Documents

- Product Assurance Reviews
  - Product Quality Assurance
  - Product Verification and Validation
  - Product Test and Evaluation
  - Product Self-Comparison
  - Process Quality Assurance at Product Level
  - Process Quality Assurance at Project Level.

As we have previously discussed, these product and process reviews can be performed individually. Now we want to illustrate the value of combining these reviews. We refer to these combined reviews as a "software audit." As with most concepts in this book, there is no one way for combining these reviews for software audits.[3] We discuss one approach to provide you with a starting point for combining these reviews in a way that makes sense for your organization. We have chosen to subdivide software audits into the following two types:

- **Software product audits.** During a software systems development project, the seller develops a product. The seller compares the product against what the customer asked for. If the comparison yields discrepan-

---

[3]The scope of an audit depends on many factors. Consequently, an audit could consist of a single product or process review.

cies, then the product (and/or what the customer asked for) is changed until the discrepancies are resolved. Comparing software products against one another to determine whether these products are being developed logically and are congruent with what the customer asked for is what we term "software product audits."

As discussed in the next section, software product audits consist of some combination of the four software product reviews performed by product assurance—namely, Product Quality Assurance, Product Verification and Validation, Product Test and Evaluation, and Product Self-Comparison. We discuss how software product audits are coupled to the CCB.

■ **Software process audits.** The seller uses software systems development processes to develop the project's required products. As the project unfolds, the seller can compare the project's software systems development processes against organizational processes. Also, the seller can compare project processes against what was said in the negotiated agreement with the customer. These comparisons are what we term "software process audits."

As discussed in the next section, software process audits consist of some combination of the four process reviews performed by management, development, and product assurance—namely, Process Programmatic Tracking, Process Technical Oversight, Process Peer Review, and Process Quality Assurance. We discuss how software process audits are coupled to the software development organization and the process engineering group.

Software Product Audits

Software product auditing begins whenever a draft software product, a software-related product, a change request (CR), or an incident report (IR) is produced and frozen. The auditing process ends with the delivery of an audit report to the CCB.

Figure 5–23 illustrates how software(-related) product audits for *documents* are coupled with the CCB.[4] Note that this process is independent of any particular life cycle model. This draft software document is presented to the product assurance organization[5] for comparison (i.e., audit) against the document's ground truth. The audit itself compares the draft software product against the ground truth.

The ground truth for a software document consists of an approved requirements specification, an approved life cycle stage N-1 product (i.e., predecessor product), and product standards. Notice that the ground truth can be used for quality assurance checking (i.e., software product compared with product standards), and verification and validation checking (i.e., software product compared against predecessor product and requirements). In addition, comparison of a software document to itself is also routinely performed in a software product audit. You can combine QA, V&V, and self-comparison techniques to conduct software product audits.

As a result of this comparison, discrepancies between the draft software product and the ground truth may be uncovered. These discrepancies are documented in a software product audit report, which is presented to the CCB for its disposition. Figure 5–24 delineates a suggested format for a software product audit report.

The product audit report consists of the following sections: Introduction, References, Procedure, Findings, Conclusions, and Recommendations. Notice in the audit report that the auditor's objective findings (i.e., Section 4) are clearly separated from any of the auditor's subjective opinions (i.e., Sections 5 and 6). Also observe that, in addition to discrepancies uncovered by quality assurance, verifica-

---

[4]CRs and IRs follow the same software product auditing process. Refer to Chapter 4 for the detailed discussion of how CRs and IRs are coupled to the CCB.

[5]The independent product assurance organization is our recommended choice for performing the comparison of the product against the ground truth. If your organization does not have an independent product assurance organization, this comparison should be performed by an individual or organization that did not construct the product.

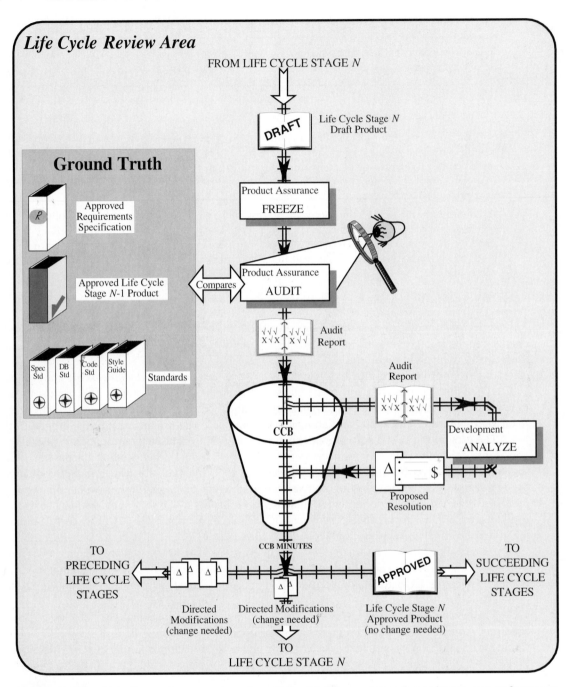

FIGURE 5–23 This figure shows an overview of the auditing process for software and software related products.

	Software Product Audit Report Title	Date Document Number

Section 1. Introduction

  1.1 **Purpose**. State the purpose of the audit report, which is to provide the results of an audit of a particular software product for a particular project.

  1.2 **Identification**. Identify the software that was audited, the date the software audit was completed, and the auditors' names.

  1.3 **Project references**. Provide a brief summary of the references applicable to the history and development of the project under which the audit was conducted.

  1.4 **Overview**. Provide a brief overview of the report contents.

Section 2. References

  List all the references applicable to the report.

Section 3. Procedure

  Describe the procedure used to conduct the audit. Reference the specific documents or entities used in the process. List any assumptions made or any constraints imposed relative to the audit.

Section 4. Findings

  Present the **objective** findings uncovered during the audit organized as shown below.

  4.1 **Conformance to standards**. Report the findings of the quality assurance check in terms of structure, format, content, or methodology. (The applicable standards may be externally imposed, such as government [buyer/user] standards imposed on a contractor [seller], and/or internally imposed, such as corporate or project management guidelines and/or ADPE elements.)

  4.2 **Software identification**. Present the results of identifying the software parts. A representation of the configuration of the parts may be provided here or placed in an appendix. List any difficulties in labeling the parts.

  4.3 **Traceability matrix**. Show the traceability between the requirements specification and the software product. Detail disconnects between the requirements specification and the software product, and between the preceding baseline and the software product.

  4.4 **Results of verification**. Present the discrepancies observed as a result of verifying the software product (i.e., comparing it against a predecessor product or products).

  4.5 **Results of validation**. Present the discrepancies observed as a result of validating the software product (i.e., comparing it against the requirements for the product). [In some circumstances, it may be useful to consolidate 4.3, 4.4, and 4.5 to avoid repetition.]

  4.6 **Results of self-comparison**. Present the discrepancies uncovered from comparing the software product against itself to assess the clarity, consistency, completeness, and testability (if applicable) of the product.

  4.7 **Bookkeeping**. List the software parts that were changed as a result of an update to the software product. Also list the approved changes (i.e., the change requests and incident reports) incorporated into the software product.

Section 5. Conclusions

  Present the conclusions formulated by the auditors based upon the audit findings. It should be noted that the conclusions represent the auditors' judgment and are thus primarily subjective, as contrasted to the objective findings given in Section 4.

Section 6. Recommendations

  Provide the auditors' recommendations as a result of conducting the audit. This section represents the auditors' judgment and is thus primarily subjective.

FIGURE 5–24 Here is a suggested format for a software product audit report.

tion and validation, and self-comparison processes, various discrepancies may be uncovered as a result of the development of a traceability matrix.[6]

The first action that the CCB takes upon receipt of the audit report is to process the discrepancies uncovered. Approaches in which the CCB can record and process the discrepancies include the following:

- Assign the entire product audit report to the development organization for analysis; the resulting analysis report provides recommended resolution for every discrepancy.

- Categorize discrepancies into those whose resolution is apparent and those whose resolution is not apparent; process the former category immediately; create an IR for every discrepancy in the latter category; process the IRs.[7] Selectively creating IRs provides better visibility and traceability than processing the audit report without creating IRs. However, there is a price to pay for this increased visibility and traceability: increased resources are required to handle and process the IRs.

- Create an IR for every discrepancy in the product audit report; process the IRs. These IRs are handled and processed just like those IRs created as a result of incidents resulting from use of a deployed system. A product audit report is still prepared in this method, but there is no need to report the discrepancies uncovered in the audit. Here, the product audit report simply summarizes and categorizes the discrepancies as IRs. Again, for the increased visibility and traceability afforded by this method, there is an increased price to pay for handling and processing the IRs. Note that the processing of every IR requires time and money, even if the discrepancy documented by the IR has small impact and its resolution is immediately obvious.

These three approaches are listed in ascending order of visibility, traceability, cost, and time. If human life is at stake and/or large financial losses are a possibility, you may want to use some form of the third approach where an IR is created for every discrepancy. At the beginning of a project, the CCB should carefully weigh the benefits and liabilities of these three approaches when establishing its mode of operation.

Once an approach is chosen, the discrepancies are analyzed and subsequently the analyzers present to the CCB a recommended resolution for each discrepancy. With a recommended resolution available from the analysis report, the CCB proceeds to make its decision on each discrepancy in the product audit report. Such decisions are recorded in the minutes of the CCB.

The CCB decides, as a result of the product audit report and analysis by the developers, either that no changes are needed for the draft product or that the draft product does need changing. If no changes are needed or only a few changes with relatively minor impact still remain unresolved, the draft product for life cycle stage N is approved and established as a baseline.[8] If changes are needed, the modifications directed by the CCB are made in the current stage to the draft product for life cycle stage N, or previous stages are revisited to change software documents in the ground truth, namely, either the requirements specification or approved products from previous stages. When changes are made to the draft product for stage N, the draft product, when changed, will be reintroduced to the product auditing process. When a revisit to a previous stage is directed, the approved product for that stage is updated and the product auditing process for the revisited stage is initiated. Such revisits cost time and money, but these revisits are what maintainability is all about. A draft product cycles through the product audit and control process as many times as necessary until the CCB decides that no

---

[6]A traceability matrix is a document that traces each software part in a requirements specification to its corresponding software part(s) in each subsequent software product and to the test documentation whose execution validates the requirements embodied in the software part.

[7]The change control process for incident reports (IRs) is discussed, in part, in Chapter 4 using Figure 4–10. The developers complete the analysis portion of the IR, the CCB makes its decision, and if a change is approved, a software change notice (SCN) is used to promulgate the change.

[8]IRs may require minor or major changes to the draft product. The CCB may decide that the draft product does not need to be changed for the moment. Regardless, the IRs and corresponding changes need to be tracked. Eventually, each IR needs to be resolved—e.g., the CCB decides to make the change (because of an IR), the CCB decides to make the change in the future, or the CCB decides that the change will never be made.

changes to the draft product are needed or that the remaining unresolved discrepancies are few enough and of minor impact. In either case, the product is baselined.

Software product auditing applies to all software products, whether the software is documentation or computer code. However, there are differences in the details of the process, depending upon whether the software is documentation or code. These differences are addressed in the following examples. Before we present software product audit examples, we discuss in more detail the nature of product discrepancies that might be discovered.

It must be noted that a product discrepancy does not necessarily represent something that is wrong with a software product. A discrepancy, quite simply, is an incongruity[9] observed as a result of comparing a software product with the ground truth. It is possible, of course, that a discrepancy represents something that is wrong in the software product. But a discrepancy could also represent something that is wrong with the ground truth. If the ground truth is incorrect, it must be corrected and then be reestablished as the ground truth. Furthermore, a discrepancy could result from a misunderstanding or an invalid assumption derived from the ground truth. In this case, the ground truth should be clarified and the software product modified to reflect the clarification of the ground truth. Finally, it is possible that a discrepancy does not really represent an incongruity between a software product and the ground truth. Upon analysis of the discrepancy, it is determined that there was a misunderstanding of the ground truth and/or the software product. The discrepancy is not a discrepancy, it is a mistake.

Consider the situation where an auditor is not sure whether an incongruity exists. If the auditor does not report this possible incongruity and it does indeed exist, an incongruity would not be made visible. Therefore, the auditor faced with this situation should report the possible incongruity. Other project personnel in the CCB forum should be able to resolve whether the discrepancy exists. If it does not exist, it is simply rejected by the CCB. This approach of "when in doubt, report" is designed to prevent discrepancies from slipping through the cracks. However, this approach should not be carried to extremes. The introduction of an excessive number of frivolous discrepancies wastes time and money.

Managers particularly should be aware that every discrepancy does not necessarily represent something wrong with the software product being audited. We have often seen busy managers base their evaluation of a new software product purely upon the number of discrepancies uncovered in a software product audit, as if every discrepancy represented an error in the new product. The preceding paragraph shows how unfair such an evaluation may be—the discrepancies might represent problems with the new product, problems with the ground truth, or no problems at all. A manager can make a better evaluation if the manager bases it not on the number of discrepancies in the audit report but on the decisions the CCB makes on the discrepancies uncovered by the audit. Analysis of such decisions would reveal how many and how substantial are the changes to be made to the software product and to the ground truth. This information would provide a better evaluation of the new software product than would a count of the discrepancies in the audit report. Discrepancies that result in no changes being made to any product should not be considered in evaluating either the software product or the ground truth.

A discrepancy should be reported in specific, objective, and neutral terms and should contain the rationale for addressing the discrepancy. A discrepancy should be specific in designating the software part(s)—in the software product being audited and/or in the ground truth—that are incongruous and in stating what the incongruity is. The report of a discrepancy should objectively state facts and should neither express opinions nor make assumptions. A discrepancy report should be neutral in that it does not assert that either the software product or ground truth is wrong, but only that they differ. A properly worded discrepancy would **not** include statements such as these:

- "Section 1 of the document is poorly worded and is therefore difficult to understand."
- "The reliability requirement is nonsensical. Whoever wrote it obviously has no understanding of how software operates."

---

[9]An incongruity is an absence of congruence; that is, an incongruity is a part in a software product that cannot be associated with any part in another, related software product or itself.

■ "Although the design meets all its requirements, the design of the database retrieval capability, in my opinion, is too cumbersome to function in an optimum manner."

Software product auditing seeks to determine (1) whether each part in a software product has an antecedent in a predecessor product, and, conversely, (2) whether each part in this predecessor product has a subsequent part in the software product. Through this two-way comparison, auditing establishes the extent to which the two products are congruent.[10]

There are several ways for an auditor to determine these antecedent/predecessor part matches. One way is to search the entire predecessor product for each software part in the software product to locate **all** subject matches. Since the predecessor product is searched from beginning to end for each software part in the software product, this method is thorough because this method finds all subject matches. However, this method can be extremely time-consuming and expensive. This high resource expenditure generally makes searching the entire predecessor product for each software product part not feasible for software products of some size. A practical alternative part-matching method is shown in Figure 5–25.

In this alternative part-matching method, the following two comparisons are made:

■ **Antecedent comparison.** Each part in the software product is compared with the predecessor product to locate a part that matches in subject. Notice that the search does not necessarily have to cover the **entire** predecessor product for each software product part—the search continues only until the first matching part is found. For example, in the upper panel of Figure 5–25, part p is compared with the predecessor product until a subject match is found. Then part q and part r are similarly matched. Notice that parts q and r both match to the same part in the predecessor product. This relationship is a one-to-many relationship in terms of the predecessor product (one) to the software product (parts q and r).

■ **Subsequent comparison.** This comparison for finding subject matches is the converse of the antecedent comparison. Each part in the predecessor product is compared with the software product to locate a part that matches in subject. For example, in the lower panel of Figure 5–25, part x is compared with the software product until a subject match is found. Then part y is similarly matched. Notice in this case that parts x and y both match to the same part in the software product. This relationship is a many-to-one relationship in terms of the predecessor product (parts x and y) to the software product (one).

This two-way comparison finds, in a nominal amount of time, all one-to-one, many-to-one, and one-to-many relationships. Predecessor product disconnects (parts in the predecessor product that have no subject matches in the software product) and software product disconnects (parts in the software product that have no subject matches in the predecessor product) are also identified. It is considerably less time-consuming than searching the entire predecessor product for each software product part.

To clarify the foregoing concepts, consider the following examples. These examples describe the audit of highly simplified software products. The overall purpose is to explain how software product auditing, as we define it, is actually done. The software products used in the examples are simplifications of real software products.

Software Document Audit Example—Automatic Doughnut-Making System   Assume that you have been designated to audit the software design specification for an automated doughnut-making system (ADMS) that is under development. Figure 5–26 shows the operational concept for the ADMS. Essentially, ADMS enables a person to make doughnuts. The person is walked through the process by following a set of instructions that are displayed on a monitor. Once the instructions are completed, ADMS combines and processes the ingredients to produce the doughnuts that are requested. When completed, ADMS is to consist of a set of hardware components that can be programmed via a set of

---

[10]This two-way comparison can also be applied when one or both of the products are software-related products (e.g., a requirements specification [software product] and a user's manual [software-related product]).

Software Product Auditing

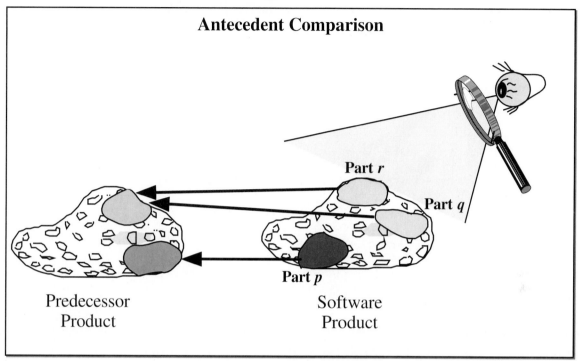

Antecedent Comparison

Part *r*

Part *q*

Part *p*

Predecessor
Product

Software
Product

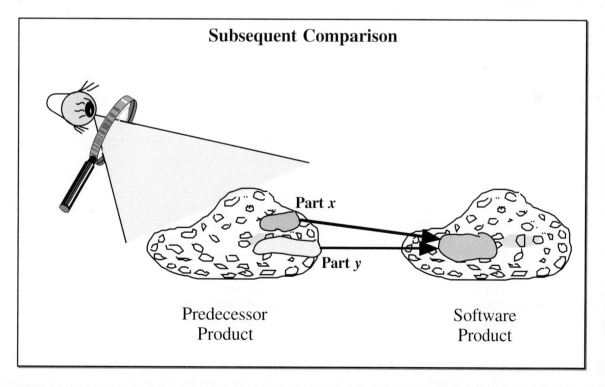

Subsequent Comparison

Part *x*

Part *y*

Predecessor
Product

Software
Product

FIGURE 5–25 Software product auditing establishes the extent to which the two products are congruent.

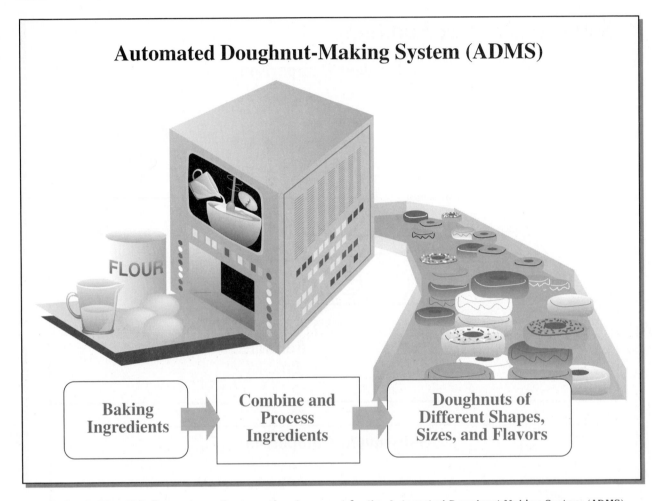

Automated Doughnut-Making System (ADMS)

FLOUR

| Baking Ingredients | → | Combine and Process Ingredients | → | Doughnuts of Different Shapes, Sizes, and Flavors |

FIGURE 5–26   This figure shows the operational concept for the Automated Doughnut-Making System (ADMS).

software instructions to (1) take as input baking ingredients, (2) combine and process these ingredients, and (3) produce doughnuts of different shapes, sizes, and flavors as output.

A functional requirements specification for the software for this system has been produced and baselined. A highly simplified version of this requirements specification is shown in Figure 5–27.

A draft of the software design specification has just been produced and is now ready for audit. This software design specification is partially shown in Figure 5–28.

Remember, a software product audit involves antecedent comparison (software product compared against predecessor product) and subsequent comparison (predecessor product compared against software product). In this simplified example, the requirements specification represents the predecessor product, and the design specification represents the software product to be audited. Therefore, for the purposes of this example design audit, the antecedent comparison consists of comparing the design specification with the requirements specification; and the subsequent comparison consists of comparing the requirements specification with the design specification.

Now, on the basis of the requirements and design specifications provided, what discrepancies might you observe as you audit the design specification?

First, you would determine the matches in subject between the requirements specification and the design specification. Even though these specifications are simplified products, you can use the two-way comparison method described earlier to locate subject matches. The antecedent and subsequent

**Functional Requirements Specification for the Programmable
Subsystem of the Automated Doughnut-Making System (ADMS)**

1.0 INTRODUCTION

This document specifies the functions that the programmable (i.e., software) subsystem of the Automated Doughnut-Making System (ADMS) performs. ADMS takes baking ingredients as input and, through user-selectable functions, combines and processes these ingredients to output doughnuts of different shapes, sizes, and flavors.

2.0 SYSTEM OVERVIEW

ADMS consists of the following two subsystems:

a. Hardware Subsystem (requirements separately documented)

b. Software (Programmable) Subsystem that allows the user to select functions to be performed through a hardware control panel.

3.0 SOFTWARE SUBSYSTEM FUNCTIONS

The Software Subsystem shall perform the functions listed in the subparagraphs below.

3.1 Input Processing Function

This function shall drive all hardware components that receive doughnut ingredients.

3.2 Recipe Processing Function

This function shall combine and process doughnuts in accordance with hardware-resident recipe templates selected from a control panel [future ADMS versions may provide a capability to input recipe templates resident on compact disks]. The following set of primitive control panel instructions shall be accommodated [recipe template selection shall be handled through the Hardware Subsystem]:

3.2.1 Add. Add the ingredients specified to the bowl.

3.2.2 Mix. Mix the ingredients in the bowl at the speed and for the time specified.

3.2.3 Roll. Roll out the mixture on the cutting board.

3.2.4 Cut. Cut out the dough for either regular (with hole) or filled doughnuts.

3.2.5 Bake. Bake the doughnuts for the time and at the temperature specified.

3.2.6 Fill. Fill doughnuts with ingredients specified.

3.2.7 Dust. Dust doughnuts with ingredients specified.

3.3 Output Processing Function

This function shall drive all hardware components that package the baked doughnuts.

FIGURE 5–27 Here is a simplified functional requirements specification for the Programmable Subsystem of the Automated Doughnut-Making System. This specification is the ground truth for the audit of the design specification for this system.

Date
Document Number

Design Specification for the Programmable Subsystem of the Automated Doughnut-Making System (ADMS)

•   •   •

2.0 SOFTWARE SUBSYSTEM ARCHITECTURE

•   •   •

2.2 Ingredient Receipt Component

•   •   •

2.3 Recipe Processing Component

•   •   •

2.3.1 Mix Module.

a. Purpose. This module will alternately add specified ingredients to the mixing bowl and mix the contents of the bowl for specified times.

•   •   •

2.3.2 Roll Module.

•   •   •

2.3.3 Cut Component.

a. Purpose. This component will cut out doughnuts. It consists of the following two modules:

1. **Regular Cut Module.** This module cuts doughnuts with a hole in each one.

2. **Fill Cut Module.** This module cuts doughnuts without holes.

•   •   •

2.3.4 Bake Module.

•   •   •

2.3.5 Fill Module.

•   •   •

2.3.6 Glaze Module.

•   •   •

2.4 Doughnut Packaging Component

•   •   •

FIGURE 5–28 Here is a partial design specification for the Programmable Subsystem of the Automated Doughnut-Making System.

comparisons yield results shown in Figure 5–29. This method locates all the subject matches that exist in this case, as can be verified by a quick scan of the two specifications (feasible only because the specifications are so simple). Notice the following results:

- **Antecedent comparison.** In the design specification, the Cut function is found in 2.3.3 (i.e., this component will cut out doughnuts), 2.3.3a.1 (i.e., this module cuts doughnuts with a hole in each one), and 2.3.3a.2 (i.e., this module cuts doughnuts without holes).

  In the requirements specification, the Cut function is found in 3.2.4 (i.e., Cut out the dough for either regular [with hole] or filled doughnuts).

  Therefore, this example antecedent comparison picks up the one-to-many relationship connected with the Cut function—in other words, the one reference in the predecessor product to the many references in the software product.

- **Subsequent comparison.** In the requirements specification, the Add function is found in 3.2.1 (i.e., Add the ingredients specified to the bowl), and the Mix function is found in 3.2.2 (i.e., Mix the ingredients in the bowl at the speed and time specified).

  In the design specification, the Add and Mix functions are found in 2.3.1 (i.e., this module will alternately add specified ingredients to the mixing bowl and mix the contents of the bowl for specified times).

  Therefore, this subsequent comparison picks up the many-to-one relationship connected with the Add and Mix requirements with the Mix design—in other words, the many references in the predecessor product to the one reference in the software product.

Also notice that two disconnects are located. The antecedent comparison reveals that the Glaze module in the design specification (i.e., 2.3.6) has no match in the requirements specification. Evidently a developer (probably expressing his or her personal taste, no pun intended) added a capability to the design to produce glazed doughnuts, a capability not contained in the requirements. This disconnect would be reported as a discrepancy. The CCB must decide whether this glaze capability is not desired and thus should be removed from the design specification, or whether this capability, initially overlooked, is indeed desired, in which case the requirements specification would be amended to incorporate this capability.

The other disconnect becomes evident with the subsequent comparison. The design specification does not address the requirement to dust doughnuts (i.e., 3.2.7). This omission is also a discrepancy to be reported to the CCB.

Your next step in the audit process is to determine whether the parts of the design specification and the requirements specification that match in subject also match in content. In this example, we provide little content in the specifications. However, in the content that is provided, there is one incongruity. When requirements specification paragraph 3.2.2 for mixing is compared with design specification paragraph 2.3.1 a, you should observe that the requirement that mixing be done at specified speeds is omitted from the design specification. This omission would be reported as a discrepancy.

This example illustrates the mechanics of determining the congruence of two software products using antecedent and subsequent comparisons. You should not be misled by the ease with which our deliberately simple software products could be audited. In the real world, auditing of voluminous specifications is a labor-intensive task. Although auditing can consume considerable resources, it potentially saves even more resources through early detection of problems. Auditing is another example of the concept of "pay now versus pay much more later."

This task of assessing congruence between software products can be simplified by the developer of the products. The developer might include in each software part of each product the labels identifying the matching software parts in the predecessor product and in the requirements specification. Alternatively, the developer might produce a traceability matrix, linking software product part labels to part labels in the predecessor product and in the requirements specification. For either comparison method, the auditor should verify the accuracy and the completeness of the information provided.

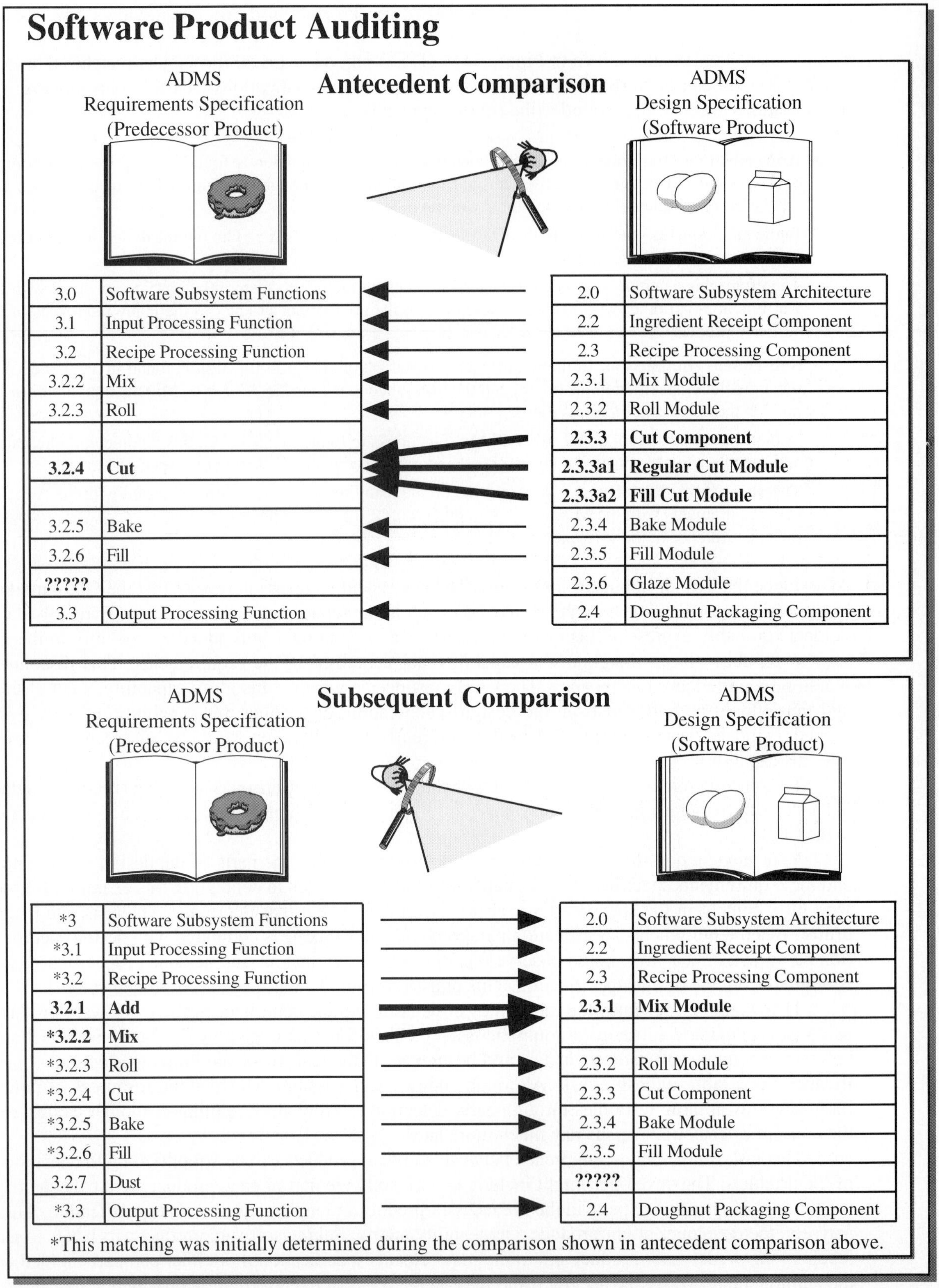

Software Product Auditing

Antecedent Comparison

ADMS Requirements Specification (Predecessor Product)

ADMS Design Specification (Software Product)

3.0	Software Subsystem Functions	←	2.0	Software Subsystem Architecture
3.1	Input Processing Function	←	2.2	Ingredient Receipt Component
3.2	Recipe Processing Function	←	2.3	Recipe Processing Component
3.2.2	Mix	←	2.3.1	Mix Module
3.2.3	Roll	←	2.3.2	Roll Module
			2.3.3	**Cut Component**
3.2.4	**Cut**	←	**2.3.3a1**	**Regular Cut Module**
			2.3.3a2	**Fill Cut Module**
3.2.5	Bake	←	2.3.4	Bake Module
3.2.6	Fill	←	2.3.5	Fill Module
?????			2.3.6	Glaze Module
3.3	Output Processing Function	←	2.4	Doughnut Packaging Component

Subsequent Comparison

ADMS Requirements Specification (Predecessor Product)

ADMS Design Specification (Software Product)

*3	Software Subsystem Functions	→	2.0	Software Subsystem Architecture
*3.1	Input Processing Function	→	2.2	Ingredient Receipt Component
*3.2	Recipe Processing Function	→	2.3	Recipe Processing Component
3.2.1	**Add**	→	**2.3.1**	**Mix Module**
***3.2.2**	**Mix**	→		
*3.2.3	Roll	→	2.3.2	Roll Module
*3.2.4	Cut	→	2.3.3	Cut Component
*3.2.5	Bake	→	2.3.4	Bake Module
*3.2.6	Fill	→	2.3.5	Fill Module
3.2.7	Dust		**?????**	
*3.3	Output Processing Function	→	2.4	Doughnut Packaging Component

*This matching was initially determined during the comparison shown in antecedent comparison above.

FIGURE 5–29 This figure illustrates the results of doing a two-way comparison of the ADMS requirements and design specifications. As shown, each comparison yields a disconnect (i.e., **?????**).

Software Document Audit Example—System PREDICT   To close out this discussion of software document audits, we present an example that illustrates the concepts of uncovering and reporting discrepancies. The example is cast in the form of a product audit of a system preliminary design specification for a software system called System PREDICT. This system is to predict the point differential of a football game based on information pertaining to the two teams involved in a game. Instead of presenting the entire audit report, only the findings of the audit have been included.

Figure 5–30 shows a one-page requirements specification for System PREDICT. Assume that this specification constitutes the requirements baseline for this software development effort. In addition to this requirements specification, there is a preliminary design specification for System PREDICT. Figure 5–31 shows a draft of the preliminary design specification.

Assume that you are an auditor whose task is to audit this preliminary design specification draft against the System PREDICT Requirements Baseline shown in Figure 5–30. Also, assume you are to submit your findings to a CCB whose function is to determine whether this draft preliminary design specification should become the System PREDICT Preliminary Design Baseline. In addition, assume that this baseline will be used to develop a detailed design from which computer code will be developed. Finally, assume that an auditor should ideally be a neutral, objective reporter of discrepancies, that the auditor should be as specific as possible in reporting discrepancies, and that the auditor should offer rationale to justify why each discrepancy should be addressed. With these assumptions and with the information contained in Figures 5–30 and 5–31, what discrepancies between the documents shown in these figures might you, as an auditor, report to the CCB?

Figure 5–32 contains findings of the software product audit. In the following discussion, we comment on these findings to provide insight into (1) the way in which an audit might be conducted and (2) the specifics of what an audit might uncover.

In the auditor's finding 1, the auditor goes through each of the seven classes (i.e., a, b, c, d, e, f, and g) of information listed in Figure 5–30 and comments on what has been done in carrying them through to preliminary design. Here are explicit examples of how an auditor addresses the question of whether a software product logically follows from a predecessor product and whether a software product embodies what the customer asked for. In performing these comparisons, we see how the auditor sheds light on the following discrepancies:

- **Potential ambiguities in the requirements baseline.** For example, finding l.c points out that the requirements baseline is silent as to the quantitative relationship between the point differential in previous games played by the two teams and its contribution to the point differential of the game to be played.

- **Potential omissions in the preliminary design specification.** For example, finding l.e points out that the preliminary design specification does not appear to deal with the possibility that one or both teams may be playing under weather conditions that one or both have not played under previously. In addition, finding 1.f points out that the requirements baseline, and thus the preliminary design specification, does not address the possibility that some games may be played at a neutral location.

Much of what the auditor has to say in finding 1 exemplifies the classical argument "Where do requirements end and where does design begin?" However, the auditor raises issues for the CCB that it may not have considered when it approved the Requirements Baseline and that the CCB may wish to address in the Requirements Baseline before design proceeds much further (and requirements ambiguities become more difficult to resolve). Thus, the auditor provides the vital function of raising the visibility of the software development process to a level where apparently significant development issues can be dealt with at a time when their resolution may cause little or no schedule or resource impact. This example illustrates the "pay now versus pay much more later" message.

Now, let's look at the auditor's second finding. In finding 2, the auditor points out an apparent disconnect between requirements and design (i.e., something called for in the Requirements Baseline appears to have been omitted in the design). The auditor then points out that the requirement omitted from the design may need to be reconsidered because it is unclear how any design developed can be

March 15, 1998
PRED-S1
Version 1.1

Requirements Specification for System PREDICT

1.0 INTRODUCTION

This requirements specification delineates the capabilities for a system called PREDICT. The overall purpose of this system is to predict the point difference of a football game based on certain information regarding the two teams involved in the game. This information is delineated in section 2.

2.0 SYSTEM INFORMATION REQUIREMENTS

System PREDICT shall require the following information to compute point differential predictions:

a.   The overall won-lost record of each time in all regular season games played prior to the game whose outcome is to be predicted.

b.   The total number of scored and allowed by each team in all regular season games prior to the game whose outcome is to be predicted.

c.   The scores of any previous regular season games involving the two teams.

d.   Injuries to key players on each team.

e.   The likely weather conditions at game time and the previous performance of each team under similar conditions.

f.   Which team is playing at home.

g.   The effect of the game on each team's playoff chances.

3.0 SYSTEM FUNCTIONS

System PREDICT shall, given the information in section 2, predict the point differential between the two teams to within 25 percent of the actual point differential.

FIGURE 5–30   Here is a simplified functional requirements specification for System PREDICT. This specification is the ground truth for the audit of the preliminary design specification for this system.

Preliminary Design Specification for System PREDICT

1.0 INTRODUCTION

This specification sets forth the preliminary design for System PREDICT, whose overall purpose is to predict the point differential of a football game based on certain information regarding the two teams playing the game. This specification thus delineates the algorithm for computing this point differential in terms of the seven factors specified in the System PREDICT Requirements Specification.

2.0 SYSTEM PREDICT ALGORITHM

Using the values from Table PRED-D1-1, compute point differential, *PD*, by (1) subtracting the Team 2 value in the table from the corresponding Team 1 value, (2) multiplying this difference by a weighting factor, and (3) summing these results over all seven factors. That is, *PD* is computed from the following mathematical formula:

$$PD = \sum_{j=1}^{7} [(Factor\ Team\ 1)_j - (Factor\ Team\ 2)_j]w_j$$

where

$w_j = 1$ for $j = 1, 2, 4, 5, 7$
$w_j = 2$ for $j = 3$
$w_j = 3$ for $j = 6$.

If *PD* is greater than zero, Team 1 is predicted to beat Team 2 by *PD* points; otherwise, Team 2 is predicted to be the winner (unless $PD = 0$, in which case the game is rated a tossup).

Table PRED-D1-1

Factor #	Factor Definition	Team 1	Team 2
1	If the team won-lost record is at least 0.500, give the team 1 point; otherwise, give the team 0.	$(Factor\ Team\ 1)_1$	$(Factor\ Team\ 2)_1$
2	If the total number of points scored by the team minus the total number of points allowed by the team in all previous regular season games is greater than zero, give the team 1 point; otherwise, give the team 0.	$(Factor\ Team\ 1)_2$	$(Factor\ Team\ 2)_2$
3	Let *X* be the average of the point differential in any previous regular season game involving the two teams (computed by subtracting Team 2's from Team 1's score and divided by the number of games played). If *X* is greater than zero, give Team 1, 1 point and Team 2, –1 point; otherwise, give Team 2, 1 point and Team 1, –1 point.	$(Factor\ Team\ 1)_3$	$(Factor\ Team\ 2)_3$
4	If *N* is the number of key players on the team who will miss the game because of injury, give the team –*N* points.	$(Factor\ Team\ 1)_4$	$(Factor\ Team\ 2)_4$
5	If the weather conditions at game time are *C* and the team has won more often than it has lost under these conditions during the regular season, give the team 1 point; otherwise, give the team –1 point.	$(Factor\ Team\ 1)_5$	$(Factor\ Team\ 2)_5$
6	If the team is playing at home, give the team 1 point; otherwise, give the team 0.	$(Factor\ Team\ 1)_6$	$(Factor\ Team\ 2)_6$
7	If the team is in playoff contention, give the team 1 point; otherwise, give the team 0.	$(Factor\ Team\ 1)_7$	$(Factor\ Team\ 2)_7$

FIGURE 5–31 Here is a draft of the preliminary design specification for System PREDICT.

April 21, 1998
PRED-D1
Draft XXX

Discrepancies Uncovered from an Audit of the System PREDICT Preliminary Design Specification

An audit of draft XXX of the System PREDICT Preliminary Design Specification (PDS) against the Requirements Baseline (RB) has been performed. The following discrepancies between the two items were uncovered during the audit:

1. The RB lists seven classes of information that are to be used to predict the point differential. For each of these classes, the PDS appears to make some assumptions regarding how the in formation in the class is to contribute to the point differential. These assumptions are listed below. Therefore, to ensure that the requirements set forth in the RB are being properly interpreted, it is suggested that these assumptions be reviewed, and if deemed appropriate, be reflected in the RB. Also listed below are some apparent discrepancies between the RB and PDS. It is suggested that these discrepancies be resolved.

   a. The PDS assumes that the intent of the RB regarding a team's won-lost record is that, if it has a non-losing record, then the team is given 1 point in computing the point differential. The RB is silent as to the quantitative relationship between a team's won-lost record and its contribution to the point differential (i.e., in contrast to the PDS, another possible interpretation of the RB requirement is that the larger the difference between a team's wins and its losses, the greater should be the contribution to the point differential [assuming the team's wins exceed its losses]).

   b. The PDS assumes that the intent of the RB regarding a team's point differential is that, if a team has scored more than it has allowed, then the team is given 1 point in computing the point differential. As was the case with the won-lost information class, the RB is silent as to the quantitative relationship between a team's point differential and its contribution to the predicted point differential of the game (e.g., in contrast to the PDS, another possible interpretation of the RB requirement is that the larger the difference between the number of points the team has scored and the number of points it has allowed, the greater should be the contribution to the predicted point differential of the game [assuming the points scored exceed the points allowed]).

   c. The PDS assumes that the intent of the RB regarding the scores of any previous regular season games involving the two teams is that, if the average of the point differential of these scores is greater than zero, then Team 1 is given 1 point in computing the point differential of the game to be played and Team 2 is given –1 point. As was the case with the preceding two information classes, the RB is silent as to the quantitative relationship between the point differential in previous games played by the two teams and its contribution to the point differential of the game to be played (e.g., in contrast to the PDS, another possible interpretation of the RB requirement is that the most recent game played between the two teams should count more than previous encounters, which is not reflected in a simple average over previous scores [it should be noted that the RB is somewhat ambiguous in that it does not indicate whether previous regular season games are restricted to the current season or include previous seasons, and, if so, how many previous seasons; from the PDS, it would appear that the designer interpreted the RB to encompass games played in the current and previous seasons, because the two teams generally meet at most only twice during a regular season, so that, if the intent of the RB was to include only the current season, there would be no need to perform the average indicated in the PDS]). It should also be noted that the PDS is silent on what value is to be assigned to the predicted point differential if the average point differential in previous games is exactly zero. The PDS should cover this contingency so that programmers can specify this logical possibility in the code they will write for System PREDICT.

FIGURE 5–32 Findings of an audit of the System PREDICT Preliminary Design Specification against the System PREDICT Requirements Specification.

d. The PDS assumes that the intent of the RB regarding injuries to key players is that there is a linear relationship between the number of key players injured and the number of points to be subtracted from the point differential. The RB is silent as to this relationship, and other relationships are, of course, possible (e.g., ones that take into account who the injured player is—for example, a quarterback may be worth twice as much to a team as a key defensive player).

e. The PDS assumes that the intent of the RB regarding (predicted) weather conditions at game time is that, if a team won more games than it lost under similar weather conditions in the past, then 1 point is given to that team in computing the point differential. The RB is silent as to the quantitative relationship between weather conditions and previous performance under such conditions. Many other interpretations of the RB are of course possible. Furthermore, the PDS does not appear to deal with the possibility that one or both teams may be playing under weather conditions that one or both have not played under previously (e.g., a team may be in its first season and may come from the South where snow never falls, and may be playing a team in blizzardlike conditions).

f. The PDS assumes that playing at home is worth 1 point in the predicted point differential. The RB is silent as to how much playing at home should be worth. Furthermore, the RB, and thus the PDS, do not address the possibility that some games may be played at a neutral location (i.e., where no team would be considered "home" in terms of fan support). For completeness, this possibility should be addressed in the RB and PDS.

g. The PDS assumes that if a team is in playoff contention, then it is given 1 point in computing the point differential. The RB is silent as to how much being in playoff contention is worth in terms of computing predicted point differential. Of course, many other quantitative relationships are possible (such as one that takes into account whether the game being played will determine if one or both teams will be eliminated from postseason play).

h. The PDS assumes that, to compute the predicted point differential, the results obtained from each of the seven information classes are to be summed and weighted with the weighting factors specified in the PDS. The RB offers no guidance as to how the information classes are to be weighted with respect to one another. For completeness, such guidance should probably be included in the RB.

2. The RB stipulates the following performance requirement for System PREDICT:

> "System PREDICT shall . . . predict the point differential between the two teams to within 25 percent of the actual point differential."

This performance requirement does not appear to be addressed in the PDS. That is, the PDS is silent as to the estimated error associated with the mathematical formula given in the PDS for computing predicted point differential. More fundamentally, it is not clear how the performance can be proven a priori to be satisfied (e.g., it is not clear how it can be proven that any mathematical relationship relating, say, injuries to key players and the effect of these injuries on the score of a game, is accurate to within so many percentage points). It is therefore suggested that the RB performance requirement cited above be reviewed to determine whether it can be verified with respect to any formula that may be proposed in the PDS. Is it the intent of the user to "verify" the formula by applying it to historical data (for example, the scores involving all teams in the league for the past ten years) and adjusting the formula parameters until agreement with these historical data is obtained with the desired degree of accuracy? If so, then perhaps the RB should be modified to reflect this intent to provide a more specific basis for design work.

FIGURE 5–32 *Continued*

proven to satisfy the omitted requirement. To help the CCB deal with this issue, the auditor offers some suggestions as to how the requirement may be stated in terms that designers and coders can deal with. Again, it should be noted that in this finding the auditor raises the visibility of the software development process to a level where the CCB can deal with significant requirements issues long before they become deeply embedded in design (and code).

Notice that the auditor's findings are expressed in objective terms, using noninflammatory language. The findings are generally specific (in most cases supported by example) and supported by rationale. The overall result is that the auditor has probably provided the CCB with the information that it will need to make intelligent, informed decisions about what should be done with draft XXX of the preliminary design specification and whether the Requirements Baseline should be updated.

This example illustrates typical discrepancies uncovered during a software product audit and how to report them. The product audit report makes explicit the assumptions used by the software developers in creating a design, so that the CCB can confirm whether the assumptions are valid.

Software Systems Acceptance Testing Audits

In the preceding section, we described the auditing process for software in the form of documentation. We now turn to the complementary auditing process for software in its other form—when the software is computer code. The generic model of the auditing process that we have just described in Figure 5–23 still applies when computer code is being audited. In this case involving computer code, a life cycle product (i.e., code) is compared with its ground truth (i.e., design and requirements specifications). Discrepancies observed during the comparison are reported to the CCB. However, the details of the computer code auditing process are substantially different from the documentation auditing process.

We begin by looking at the preparations made prior to the conduct of the computer code audit. This discussion is followed by an example that illustrates how to construct a test procedure. We next look at the auditing process in detail and observe how the auditing (testing) cycle causes software code to converge to a product with no or few discrepancies. This product then can be delivered to the user.

When the life cycle software product to be audited is code, we term the process test and evaluation (T&E). T&E is system level testing and is user oriented. T&E is an assessment of whether software code is congruent with requirements and design specifications. But in T&E we do not generally determine this congruency by comparing source code listings (a document form of code) directly with the requirements and design specifications. Rather, computer code is put in its executable form and, through execution in a live or nearly live environment, is indirectly compared with the two specifications through use of test plans and procedures. Figure 5–33 illustrates this T&E concept.

This figure shows the connectivity between the product development world and product assurance world. Both worlds come together during acceptance testing. In the development world, requirements and design specifications provide the basis for coding. They also provide the basis for an acceptance test plan that, in turn, serves as the basis for test procedures.

Each test procedure specifies the results expected from performing specific operations on computer code. When the specific operations are executed on code, the actual results observed are recorded and compared with the expected results contained in the test procedures. Any differences between the expected and observed results are reported as discrepancies. Thus, the requirements and design specifications are the ground truth for this audit but are involved in the audit comparison only indirectly (i.e., through the test plans and procedures).

We stated before that T&E was conducted in a live or nearly live environment. By *live or nearly live environment* we mean "an environment that is identical to or closely approximates the environment in which the user operates." The actual testing occurs before the software system is delivered to the customer. This testing is referred to in the literature by several names; we refer to it as acceptance testing, because it usually occurs just before the customer accepts the system for operational use. The

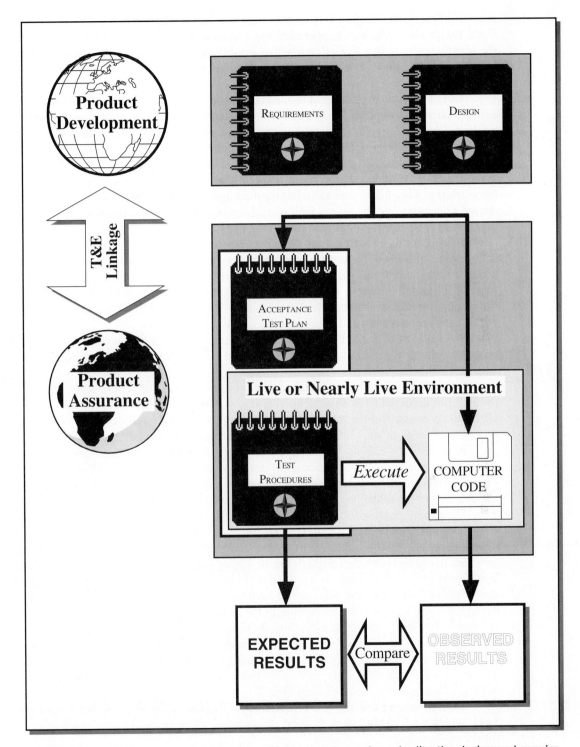

FIGURE 5–33 T&E assesses the extent to which computer code embodies the design and requirements.

purpose of acceptance testing is to demonstrate that operating computer code satisfies the user's needs. Since the user's needs include operating the system in the user's own environment, we must conduct the acceptance tests in a live or nearly live environment. Performing the tests in some other environment (e.g., the development environment) would not demonstrate that the computer code satisfies the user's needs.

T&E activity is not confined to the coding and subsequent stages of the life cycle. In fact, T&E activity extends throughout the life cycle. T&E generally begins (1) right after the requirements specification is baselined or (2) in parallel with requirements specification development, with the initiation of efforts to develop a test plan. A test plan is concerned with such items as test organizations, test schedules, test resources, test personnel and their responsibilities, the approach to be used to test the system, and, most important for our current consideration, a list of tests to be executed during acceptance testing. This list is derived from the requirements, with one or more tests planned to be conducted to demonstrate the satisfaction of each requirement.[11] Thus, the test plan links tests to specific requirements. Figure 5–34 delineates an annotated outline for a test plan.

Subsequent to the baselining of the detailed design specification, each test listed in the test plan is developed into a step-by-step test procedure that demonstrates satisfaction of the requirements specified for the test in the test plan. The steps in the procedures are designed to assess whether the requirement(s) to be demonstrated by the procedures have been satisfied by computer code. Figure 5–35 shows an annotated test procedure format that builds in traceability back to development documentation such as requirements and design specifications, and test plans.

The OPERATOR ACTION and EXPECTED RESULTS columns are the most important test procedure elements and are shaded for this reason. The information in these columns links the acceptance testing process to the development process.

Information on actions to be taken or commands to be used within a test step, as well as on the results to be expected from those actions or commands, is obtained from the design specification. The set of test procedures reflects both the requirements and the design of the software system. Each test procedure should contain within it a pointer to the requirement(s) that the procedure tests.

With this five-column format, there is traceability among the four documents concerned with T&E: (1) requirements specifications, (2) design specifications, (3) test plan, and (4) test procedures. The requirements and design specifications are the ground truth for the audit, and the test plan and procedures are the specifications for the conduct of the acceptance tests.

The requirements specification establishes a list of functions that the software is to perform. Software designers translate these requirements into a design specification that designates subsystems and modules needed to satisfy the requirements. The requirements specification and design specification are often traced to each other through use of a traceability matrix. The test plan, as already described, lists the tests to be performed during T&E and links each test to one or more requirements. This linkage is usually added to the traceability matrix, so that there is traceability from the requirements through the specification documentation to the tests that demonstrate that computer code satisfies the requirements. Finally, each test procedure should contain pointers to the requirement(s) that the procedure tests and to the portions of the detailed design that were used in the creation of the test procedures. This traceability is important in determining that all requirements have been accounted for in the test procedures, and, when differences are observed between the expected and actual results, in determining which requirements are unsatisfied.

We recommend that the test procedures be written in the five-column format shown in Figure 5–35, which we have successfully used on a number of projects. The elements of the test procedure format are as follows:

■ **Header.** This section of the test procedure provides identification of the test, states the objective of the test, gives the long title of the test, and provides notes on how to conduct the test, on the estimated duration of

---

[11]Note that a single test could be used to demonstrate the satisfaction of more than one requirement.

	Date
Test Plan Title	Document Number

Section 1. Introduction

This section gives introductory information regarding the project, the system to be tested, and the testing approach as indicated in sections 1.1–1.4 below.

1.1 **Purpose**. Identify the project and stipulate the test plan purpose by indicating what the document contains (e.g., organizational responsibilities, test approach, test schedule—that is, tell them what you are going to tell them.

1.2 **Scope**. Specify the project software releases/versions encompassed by the plan. For example, a project may extend over several years with one or more software releases/versions scheduled per year. In this case, section 1.2 specifies which of these releases the plan addresses.

1.3 **System Overview**. Describe the system to be exercised by the testing approach specified in the plan. This overview serves to identify aspects of the system operation that will be the focus of the plan's testing approach (e.g., man-machine interface, data conversion accuracy and completeness). This section should include a conceptual diagram showing how the system operates, including its external interfaces.

1.4 **Testing Approach Overview**. Give an overview of the approach specified in section 3. This overview is often of particular interest to management, especially senior management (both seller and customer), who may have neither the time nor the inclination to read section 3. For example, if section 3 spells out a multilevel approach to testing, section 1.4 should briefly indicate the objective and scope of each of the test levels. This overview should be linked to the conceptual diagram included in section 1.3. Sometimes, it may be desirable to eliminate this section and put the testing approach overview in (1) an executive summary (for senior and other interested management) and/or (2) the beginning of section 3.

Section 2. Applicable References

List all the references applicable to the test plan. In general, these references include project standards (such as ADPE elements), a product assurance plan that establishes the context for project testing, and software specification documents (such as requirements, design, and data base specifications from which the code and data bases to be tested are developed).

Section 3. Testing Approach

Describe the approach (but not the detailed test steps—this information belongs in test procedures) to be used to test the system described in section 1.3. This description includes specifying the *types* of tests to be performed (such as tests designed to exercise system functions one by one without regard to how these functions may be used operationally, tests designed to exercise sequences of functions that approximate operational use of the system, tests designed to stress the system to its design and requirements limits and possibly beyond these limits). This description lists the specific tests to be performed (but, again, not the test steps). For each of these tests, give it a name and specify its objective. Describe how the test procedures for these tests are to be specified (e.g., the five-column format described elsewhere in this chapter). Describe how test incidents are to be reported and CCB activity in connection with test incidents. For completeness, it is often desirable to describe how this testing approach—which should be prepared and performed by a group independent from the product development group—complements the testing approach that the product developers will use to ready the code and databases for system-level testing by the independent test (product assurance) group. Product developers typically perform unit and integration testing for this purpose. "Unit testing" is the exercising of a unit (a separately compilable sequence of code statements to ascertain whether it meets design specifications; "integration testing" is the exercising of progressively larger collection of units to check out the integrated operation of each collection of units; the final step in integration testing is the exercising, as a single entity, of all the units in the system under development.

FIGURE 5–34 Here is a suggested format for a software test plan.

Test Plan Title

Date
Document Number

Section 4. Test Management Requirements

Indicate how the testing described in section 3 is to be managed including a delineation of the responsibilities of each project organization involved with testing (remember to include customer organizations if, as we recommend, you decide to include customer participation in the testing process). Describe the CCB roles in test management [see subsequent discussion in this chapter regarding these roles].

Section 5. Personnel Requirements

Delineate the responsibilities of those individuals who are to perform the testing (such as the test director, test witnesses, and test operators). Remember to include customer personnel if, as we recommend, you decide to include the customer in the testing process (e.g., as test witnesses, as CCB participants).

Section 6. Hardware Requirements

Describe the hardware (including communications and network equipment) needed to support testing. Describe the configuration of hardware components on which the software and databases to be tested are to operate. Include any hardware needed to support test procedure development and execution, and other hardware tools (such as simulators that model the operation of external systems interfacing with the system to be tested).

Section 7. Software Requirements

Describe the software (including communications and network equipment) needed to support testing. Include the software code and databases that are the objects of the testing. Also include software tools such as compilers, CASE instruments (such as information engineering tools used to automatically generate code and databases from data and process models), and simulators that may be used to model the user's operational environment if the testing is not to be performed in the user's operational environment.

Section 8. Schedule

Specify the schedule for testing activities. Generally, the schedule should span the period between test plan publication and the publication of a test report that gives the results of test procedure execution. Allow for updates to the test plan and test procedures.

Section 9. Cost

Delineate the cost associated with the requirements called out in sections 4–7. Generally, an estimate of this cost should appear in the project plan. If there is a product assurance plan that provides context for the T&E activity, this cost may be delineated there, in which case section 9 can be omitted (or can simply point to the product assurance plan or other sources containing the cost estimate). Even if other sources already contain a T&E cost estimate, it may still be a good idea to include this section. Usually, the information contained in this section is more refined than estimates rendered elsewhere because, in contrast to these other sources, the focus of this document is on T&E.

Appendices

Include in these optional appendices such things as acronyms, definitions of key terms, and process flow diagrams bearing upon the testing approach. For example, if the plan is addressing the testing of a program to convert data from, say, a flat file environment to a relational environment, an appendix describing the data conversion functions to be tested (such as *moving* data unchanged, *translating* from one field length to another, *transforming* data from one set of units to another via mathematical formulas) might be useful. Also, if it is decided to incorporate test procedures into the test plan (as opposed to publishing them separately), it may be useful to house these procedures in appendices.

FIGURE 5–34 *Continued*

Test *XX.Y*

OBJECTIVE: This area contains a statement that defines the objective of Test *XX.Y*. This statement should come from the test plan.

TITLE: This line contains the long title of the test procedure. This title should come from the test plan.

NOTES: This area provides general notes concerning the test procedure. Such notes might include comments on how to execute the test procedure, an estimate of the test duration, the specification of the requirements the procedure tests, or a statement of resources (people, equipment) needed for this test.

STEP	OPERATOR ACTION	PURPOSE	EXPECTED RESULTS	COMMENTS
N	Describes the actions taken by the person executing the test procedure. The language in this column is usually in computerese (e.g., it may be the entering of a command according to some computer language syntax).	Describes the reason for the step. The language in this column is an explanation in the vernacular of the operator action in column 2 (i.e., in terms that the customer can understand).	Describes the expected response of the system being tested to the action specified in the OPERATOR ACTION column. This expected response is generally derived from requirements and design specifications (and sometimes user's manuals) or some other written documents that attest to what the customer and seller agreed that the system is to do and how it is to do it. The person executing the procedure compares the system response to the Operator Action with the information in this column. If they do not match, the person writes a TIR. In this way, execution of the test is a formal demonstration of whether the system is doing what the customer and seller said the system is to do.	Contains additional information such as boundary data, dependencies among test steps, an estimate of elapsed time associated with executing this step, suggested excursions from the test step, a discussion of the rationale for the step or operator action, or the test underlying the step, and the overall objective of a subset of the test steps in the entire procedure. May also contain pointers to requirements and/or design documentation and/or other documentation bearing on the system being tested.

[Document No.]
[Release/Version No.]
[Page No.]   [Date]

FIGURE 5–35 Here is a test procedure format that builds in traceability back to predecessor product development documentation such as requirements and design specifications, and test plans.

the test, on requirements tested, and on test resources (e.g., test data) needed for the test. The information for the identification of the test and the objective of the test comes from the test plan. This information provides explicit traceability between the test procedure and the test plan.

- **STEP.** This column provides a (usually sequential) identifying number for each step.

- **OPERATOR ACTION.** This column specifies the precise action taken by the tester (e.g., entering a keyboard command, pressing a function key, selecting a pull-down menu choice, turning a computer on/off, plugging in a compact disk device) in executing a particular step. The information in this column comes from the detailed design specification. Typically, the information is described in computerese.

- **PURPOSE.** This column explains why the tester took the action specified in column 2—that is, what the tester expects to accomplish by the tester's actions. Typically, the information is described in plain language used by the customer. The PURPOSE should also be reviewed by the customer to help ensure that the seller is implementing what the customer wants.

- **EXPECTED RESULTS.** This column describes the response of the system to the action taken by the tester in column 2. The information in this column comes from the requirements and the detailed design specifications. When the test is performed, the information in this column is compared with observed results as each test step is executed in order to uncover any discrepancies.

- **COMMENTS.** This column contains a variety of information that may be useful to the tester. Figure 5–35 provides a number of suggestions for information to put in this column.

Note particularly the linkages of the test procedure to the requirements specification and the detailed design specification in the header (under Notes) and in the Comments column of Figure 5–35.

Having introduced a test procedure format, we now illustrate in the following example how to construct a test procedure using that format. Test procedures are a key element in performing T&E. If a test procedure is not properly constructed, the test procedure may not achieve its purpose of demonstrating that operational computer code satisfies some specified requirement(s).[12]

Acceptance Test Procedure Example—System SHAPES   This section discusses preparations for an audit of a software product that is computer code. This discussion presents an example that illustrates how to construct a five-column test procedure that demonstrates the traceability among the (1) requirements specifications, (2) design specifications, (3) test plan, and (4) test procedures. Remember, the requirements and design specifications are the ground truth for the audit, and the test plan and procedures are the specifications for the conduct of the acceptance tests.

Figure 5–36 shows a one-page extract from a requirements specification for a software system called SHAPES. This system is to permit a user sitting at a computer terminal with a display device to construct various geometric shapes. In the discussion that follows, we show how to construct a test procedure to exercise the circle-drawing capability.

The second document used to construct the five-column test procedure is a design specification. Figure 5–37 shows a portion of the System SHAPES Design Specification.

This specification and the requirements specification are needed to describe (1) how the tester is to interact with System SHAPES during the test and (2) what the tester expects to see as a result of this interaction.

Assume that these two specifications constitute respectively the Requirements Baseline and the Detailed Design Baseline for System SHAPES. Also assume that you are a tester whose task is to perform acceptance testing on System SHAPES. Assume further that you have already prepared a test plan for this purpose and that Figure 5–38 shows an extract from this test plan that defines tests for exercising the SHAPES circle-drawing capability.

---

[12]Note: This example contains some mathematics, in particular some elementary analytic geometry. It is not necessary to understand the mathematics in the following example to understand the T&E issues dealt with. The mathematics has been included for completeness.

Requirements Specification for System SHAPES

The purpose of System SHAPES is to permit a user sitting at a computer terminal with a display device to construct various geometric shapes. To achieve this purpose, the system shall perform the following functions:

1. Draw complete geometric shapes on a display in response to user-supplied inputs. The shapes that shall be accommodated are those listed in Table 1 below, which shows the corresponding user-supplied input.

Table 1. Geometric Shapes to Be Constructed from User-Supplied Input

SHAPE		INPUT
1. Circle		1. Radius, center of circle
2. Square		2. Length of side, center of square
3. Equilateral triangle		3. Length of side, center of triangle
4. Circular arc		4. Arc (1) radius, (2) angular width, and (3) center
5. Ellipse		5. Ellipse (1) semimajor axis, (2) semiminor axis, and (3) center

2. The border of geometric shapes shall be one of the following as selected by the user:

  a. Solid line

  b. Dashed line

  c. Dotted line

FIGURE 5–36 Here is a portion of the SHAPES requirements specification that is one input to SHAPES test procedure construction.

Design Specification for System SHAPES

• • •

2.2 Circle-Drawing Subsystem

This section describes the design of the Circle-Drawing Subsystem of System SHAPES. The purpose of this subsystem is to draw circles on a display device based on a user-supplied (1) circle radius, (2) circle center, and (3) code specifying the type of border (namely, solid line, dashed line, or dotted line).

2.2.1 Computational Procedure

The following processing steps specify the operation of this subsystem:

1. Let the user-defined border codes be defined as follows:

   A = solid line
   B = dashed line
   C = dotted line

2. If (x_0, y_0) are the coordinates of the circle center and R is the circle radius, then a point (x, y) on the circle is given by the following formula:

$$(x - x_0)^2 + (y - y_0)^2 = R^2$$

3. The above formula shall be used to compute the coordinates of a point on the circle. There are three cases to consider—one for each border desired. The processing steps for each case are specified below.

   • • •

2.2.2 User Interface

To access the SHAPES Circle-Drawing Subsystem, the user shall utilize the following command:

   CIRCLE (RADIUS, X, Y), CODE

where

   RADIUS = user-supplied radius in the format *NN.NN*, where *NN.NN* must lie in the range 0.50 to 10.00 inclusive. The first *N* is optional.

   X = user-supplied abscissa of the circle center in the format ± *N.NN,* where *N.NN* must lie in the range 0.00 to 5.00 inclusive.

   Y = user-supplied ordinate of the circle center in the same format and having the same range as X.

[Note: The center of the display device is assumed to lie at (X,Y) = (0.00,0.00); the width of the device is assumed to be 25.00 units and its height is assumed to be 22.00 units.]

   CODE = user-supplied border code whose allowable values are A, B, or C as defined in 2.2.1 above.

FIGURE 5–37 Here is the circle-drawing portion of the design specification for System SHAPES.

2.2.3 Error Conditions

Table 2.2-1 below defines the error diagnostics that shall be generated using the algorithms specified in Appendix C whenever the command specified in 2.2.2 above is not used as indicated there.

Table 2.2-1. Circle-Drawing Subsystem Error Diagnostics and Their Causes

DIAGNOSTIC CODE	DIAGNOSTIC	CAUSE(S)
CE1	COMMAND SYNTAX ERROR	Command name misspelled (e.g., CIRCEL) Command string parameter mistake or punctuation error [e.g., CIRCLE(3.50,0.50,),A]
CE2	RADIUS OUT OF RANGE	Value of parameters out of range [e.g., CIRCLE(11.09,0.50,0.00),B]
CE3	CENTER ABSCISSA AND/OR ORDINATE OUT OF RANGE	Value of parameter X and/or Y out of range [e.g., CIRCLE(5.67,0.50,7.05),C]
CE4	BORDER CODE NOT A, B, OR C	Value of border code out of range [e.g., CIRCLE(3.00,0.50,0.50),D]

• • •

FIGURE 5–37 *Continued*

• • •

3.3 Circle-Drawing Tests

This section defines the tests for exercising the circle-drawing capabilities of System SHAPES. All tests are intended to be performed at a computer terminal with a display device. The computer terminal will accept tester-supplied inputs, and the display device will show the SHAPES response to these inputs. Two tests are defined—Test CD.1, which exercises the command CIRCLE with in-range values as defined in section 2.2.2 of the design specification; and Test CD.2, which exercises the error diagnostics defined in section 2.2.3 of the design specification.

3.3.1 Test CD.1 (Command CIRCLE Parameter Check)

The objective of this test is to verify that command CIRCLE draws circles when proper command parameter values are input. Selected in-range values of the command parameters will be input, and the displayed circles will be viewed to determine whether they are constructed according to section 2.2.2 of the design specification as illustrated below.

CIRCLE(RADIUS,X,Y),CODE

3.3.2 Test CD.2 (Command CIRCLE Error Diagnostic Check)

The objective of this test is to verify that the error diagnostics appearing in Table 2.2-1 of section 2.2.3 of the design specification are produced when command CIRCLE is improperly used. Selected out-of-range values of the command parameters will be input, and the display will be viewed to determine whether the diagnostics specified in Table 2.2-1 appear.

• • •

FIGURE 5–38 Here is an extract from a test plan for System SHAPES showing circle-drawing tests based on the SHAPES design specification.

This extract shows the following two tests to be performed: (1) Test CD.1 (Command CIRCLE Parameter Check) and (2) CD.2 (Command CIRCLE Error Diagnostic Check). Using the five-column format shown in Figure 5–35, how would you construct a test procedure for Test CD.1 defined in Figure 5–38?

In constructing this test procedure, keep in mind that it is to be part of a test procedures document and that the execution of these test procedures is to be used to test and retest the SHAPES software code until the CCB decides that this code is ready for operational use.

Figure 5–39 shows the first three steps of a test procedure designed to implement Test CD.1 as defined in the SHAPES Test Plan extract given in Figure 5–38.

The layout is based on the five-column format previously introduced. Any format is okay as long as it contains the information shown in the OPERATOR ACTION and EXPECTED RESULTS columns. This information is the linkage between product development activity and product assurance activity. The resultant tester comparison of the system response to the OPERATOR ACTION with the EXPECTED RESULTS provides decision makers with the means for determining whether the computer code and supporting databases are doing what the customer wanted.

In the following discussion, we comment on Figure 5–39 to provide you with insight into the specifics of how a test procedure is constructed from a test plan and from design and requirements specifications.

At the top of the procedure in Figure 5–39, the overall objective of the test is stated. This statement is essentially the same statement that appears in subsection 3.3.1 of the test plan shown in Figure 5–38. Thus, this statement provides explicit traceability between the test procedure and the test plan. It also provides quick insight into the intent of the test. This quick insight is particularly helpful when a test consists of hundreds of individual steps. Under such circumstances, it is difficult to perceive, by looking at such a long list of steps, what system design aspects or requirements the procedure is trying to test. The statement of test objective appearing at the top of the procedure helps alleviate this difficulty. In a test procedure document consisting of hundreds or thousands of tests (not uncommon for systems of even moderate complexity), the absence of an objective for each test can make the comprehension of the set of test procedures impossible. Particularly in these circumstances, a statement of the overall objective of each test is essential for proper interpretation and use of the document.

Below the statement of objective in the test procedure, the title of the test appears (i.e., Command CIRCLE Parameter Check in Figure 5–39). This title generally augments the test identifier (i.e., Test CD.1 in Figure 5–39) shown to the left of the statement of objective. The title provides insight into the nature of the test (which in this case is a check of the parameters appearing in a user command). As such, the test title complements the statement of objective appearing above it.

Below the test title are two notes that provide amplifying comments on the test as a whole. Specifically, the notes in Figure 5–39 address the following points:

- The first note essentially defines the scope of the test (namely, that only proper parameter values are to be input). This note also points to another test (using the test identifier CD.2) which will deal with improper (i.e., out-of-range) parameter values. The former type of test is often termed positive testing, while the latter type of test is often termed negative testing.

- The second note suggests some excursions from the written procedures that should be performed. The excursions are for the purpose of extending the breadth and depth of the test. The development of written test procedures is generally an extremely labor-intensive activity. Consequently, it is often simply not possible to write down all the test steps needed to exercise comprehensively all or even most aspects of a requirement (or a set of requirements) or a design (or sections of a design) that is the object of a particular test. To strike some sort of compromise between this real-world constraint stemming from limited resources and the need to perform thorough testing, a test procedure write-up often includes suggestions (such as the one in the second note) for performing test steps that are not explicitly shown in the write-up but that are straightforward variations or extensions of test steps shown. In the context of the test procedure depicted in Figure 5–39, an example of such variations might be the following:

System SHAPES Test Procedure

Test CD.1

OBJECTIVE: The objective of this test is to verify that command CIRCLE draws circles when proper command parameter values are input.

TITLE: Command CIRCLE Parameter Check

NOTES: 1. No improper parameter values are to be input (see Test CD.2).

2. In addition to the parameter values used in the test steps below, other (proper) values should also be input to extend the breadth and depth of the test.

STEP	OPERATOR ACTION	PURPOSE	EXPECTED RESULTS	COMMENTS
1.	Enter CIRCLE(1.00,0.00,0.00),A	To draw a circle of radius 1.00 centered at (0.00,0.00) with a solid-line border.	A circle of radius 1.00 appears at the center of the display with a solid-line border.	The display has background markings that allow the tester to determine visually the x and y values of the center and the value of the radius.
2.	Enter CIRCLE(5.00,0.00,0.00),B	To draw a circle of radius 5.00 centered at (0.00,0.00) with a dashed-line border.	A circle of radius 5.00 appears at the center of the display with a dashed-line border.	Steps 1–10 explicitly exercise section 2.2.2 of the SHAPES Design Specification, which implements the capabilities specified in the first line of Table 1 in the SHAPES Requirements Specification and in paragraph 2 of that specification.
3.	Enter CIRCLE(10.00,–0.50,–0.50),C	To draw a circle of radius 10.00 centered at (–0.50,–0.50) with a dotted-line border.	A circle of radius 10.00 centered at (–0.50,–0.50) (i.e., slightly below and to the left of the center of the display) appears on the display with a dotted-line border.	
4.	● ● ● ● ● ● ● ● ●			

ABC-TProc-SHAPES1-33/R1
SHAPES Release 1.0

December 7, 1999

CD.1-1

FIGURE 5–39 Here is a portion of a System SHAPES test procedure derived from the System SHAPES Test Plan extract (i.e., Test CD.1).

The purpose of the first test step shown in the figure is to draw a circle of radius 1.00 in the center of the display with a solid border. The purpose of the second step is to draw another circle with a different radius also in the center of the display but with a dashed-line border. The purpose of the third step is to draw another circle with a radius that differs from the radii used in steps 1 and 2. Also, this third circle is to be centered somewhere other than in the center of the display, and, in contrast to the first two circles, it is to have a dotted-line border. It is thus clear from these steps that the strategy of test CD.1 is exactly that prescribed in subsection 3.3.1 in the test plan shown in Figure 5–38. Namely, the strategy is to use selected in-range values of CIRCLE parameters to construct different circles. From the comments appearing in the Comments column in Figure 5–39, it appears that this strategy is also followed in steps 4 through 10 (which are not shown in the figure). Now, from subsection 2.2.2 of the SHAPES Design Specification, it is evident that there are many more in-range combinations of parameter values for the CIRCLE command than can be incorporated into ten steps in the manner indicated in Figure 5–39. On the other hand, these combinations are clearly variations of the steps shown. Thus, for example, one set of such variations of step 1 might be the following:

$$\text{CIRCLE}(R, 0.00, 0.00), \text{ A}$$

where R is allowed to vary from 0.50 to 10.00—the minimum and maximum values respectively for this parameter (as indicated in the design specification)—in increments of, say, 0.1. Such an excursion from step 1 in the written procedure would represent a fairly thorough testing of the capability to draw solid-line circles centered at the center of the display whose radii completely cover the allowable range for this parameter.

The information in each of the three test steps shown is based primarily on subsection 2.2.2 of the design specification (as noted in the Comments column in Figure 5–39). For example, the information in the OPERATOR ACTION column (i.e., what the tester has to input to elicit a response from the code being tested) is a particular realization of the command format specified in that subsection. Also, the information in the EXPECTED RESULTS column is derived directly from the design specified in that subsection. This heavy reliance on design documentation occurs frequently in test procedure development work. The primary reason is that test procedures are generally written at the "button-pushing" level of detail and that such detail is often not found until the Detailed Design Stage of the life cycle.

A comment is in order before we describe the COMMENTS column. What happens if the information needed for the OPERATOR ACTION and EXPECTED RESULTS columns is not present in the requirements specification and/or design specification? The people putting the test procedures together (e.g., product assurance) will need to ask the developers questions in order to obtain the needed information. This interaction is an example of product assurance acting as a forcing function on the development process. By *forcing,* we mean "the tester forces the developer to think through what the system is suppose to do." This forcing function helps *everyone* to think through the implementation of the requirements and design.

Now, let us return our discussion to the COMMENTS column in Figure 5–39. In addition to linking test steps back to the design specification, the COMMENTS column also links the steps back to the requirements specification. Thus, through this linkage, it is possible after test step execution to determine in specific terms the extent to which customer requirements (in this case, the capability to draw circles on a display) are embodied in the computer code. This information is precisely what a CCB needs to determine whether computer code needs to be modified before it is delivered to the customer for operational use.

Regarding the information in the EXPECTED RESULTS column, note that this information needs to be expressed in terms that permit a tester to observe the response of the system so that the tester can effect a meaningful comparison between this information and the actual system response. This comparison is the heart of the test execution activity, because from this comparison come discrepancies. These discrepancies provide the basis for CCB action regarding the release of the code for operational use.

The preceding discussion gives some idea how a test procedure can be constructed from a test plan and specification documentation. From this discussion, you should now be able to construct a test procedure for Test CD.2 defined in subsection 3.3.2 of the test plan shown in Figure 5–38.[13]

Constructing a test procedure is not a mechanical exercise. There is a careful balance of many factors that include the following: the (1) number of steps to include, (2) time available to build and then exercise the test procedures, (3) available resources, (4) criticality of the system (e.g., Could system failure involve the loss of life?), (5) available documentation, and (6) agreement between the seller and customer regarding what the system is suppose to do. Figure 5–40 summarizes our discussion on a way to build acceptance test procedures.

The figure shows the linkage among the requirements specification, design specification, and test procedures. For example, the requirements specification can be used to fill in some of the EXPECTED RESULTS column. Section 3.4 of the requirements specification states the requirement that the system shall display happy and sad faces in response to facial feature input. The design specification can be used to fill in some of the OPERATOR ACTION and EXPECTED RESULTS columns. Section 7.2 of the design specification details the command the operator uses to construct a happy face. It is important to note that the specifications do not necessarily have to be bound documents. The specifications could be any correspondence that a project deems official, such as CCB minutes or memoranda between the customer and seller project managers. Regardless, the five-column acceptance testing format helps explicitly to link software products and the customer/seller agreed-upon system capabilities. The information in this figure is typically used to populate a traceability matrix.

The set of test documentation discussed—test plan and test procedures—is not the only set possible. For example, the federal government often adds an intermediate document. This document, the test specification, outlines each test procedure prior to formulation of the procedure steps. Other variations of test documentation include the use of different names for test entities (e.g., a test procedure may be known as a test case) or the use of a hierarchy of tests (e.g., test groups/test procedures/test cases). None of these variations modifies the primary concept we are discussing—that specific written test documentation derived from appropriate sections of the requirements and design specifications must be developed prior to the beginning of acceptance tests.

Now that we have looked at the preparation of the test plan and test procedures—activities that must precede the actual audit of the code—we are in a position to discuss the auditing process itself. This process, which we term "acceptance testing" is shown in Figure 5–41.

The focal point of the acceptance testing process is acceptance test procedure execution. The figure shows how test procedure execution couples (1) what the requirements and design specification say a software system is to do with (2) what the software system actually does. When the tester executes a test step, the tester observes the system's response and compares this response with what appears in the EXPECTED RESULTS column. If the results do not match, the tester writes a TIR and then executes the next test step. If the results do match, the tester executes the next test step. For example, the EXPECTED RESULTS column in the figure shows a happy face. However, as shown in the figure, when the tester executes the test step, the tester observes a scowling face on the computer screen. The tester compares the EXPECTED RESULTS (happy face) with the observed results (scowling face). In this case, since the results do not match, the tester writes a TIR and then executes the next test step.

The output of test procedure execution is thus a set of TIRs that document discrepancies between specified operation and observed operation. It is then up to customer and seller management to decide how these discrepancies are to be resolved before the seller delivers the system to the customer. The customer and seller management make this decision at a CCB.

In the following paragraphs we examine the TIR form in detail. However, before turning our attention to this form, we examine how to manage acceptance testing. For this purpose, we take the view

---

[13]Creating test procedures is not an academic exercise. In constructing a test procedure for CD.2, you will discover that the requirements specification is silent on a key point that results in a design specification ambiguity.

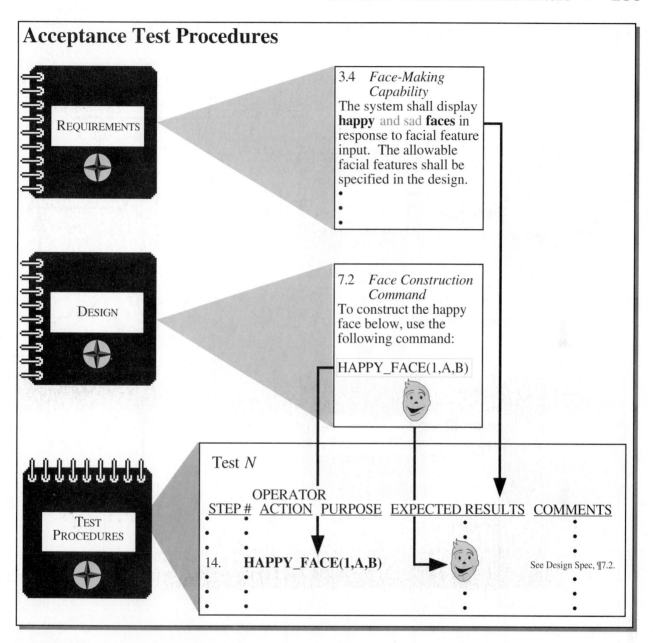

FIGURE 5–40 To demonstrate formally that a software system to be delivered does what the customer and seller agreed to, acceptance test procedures should be explicitly linked to the system development activities that yielded products reflecting this agreement.

that acceptance testing is a cycle governed by two types of CCBs—Software Turnover CCB and Test Incident CCB. As we proceed through the testing cycle, we will see how these two CCBs help to provide visibility into the computer code at every step in the testing cycle. This visibility is captured through (1) CCB minutes, (2) TIRs, (3) written test procedures, and (4) documented baselines. With this visibility, we can trace the baseline changes and test incident reports. Visibility and traceability are particularly important during the acceptance testing cycle. Generally, the scheduled software code delivery date is rapidly approaching. The software code is being changed frequently and rapidly. Without

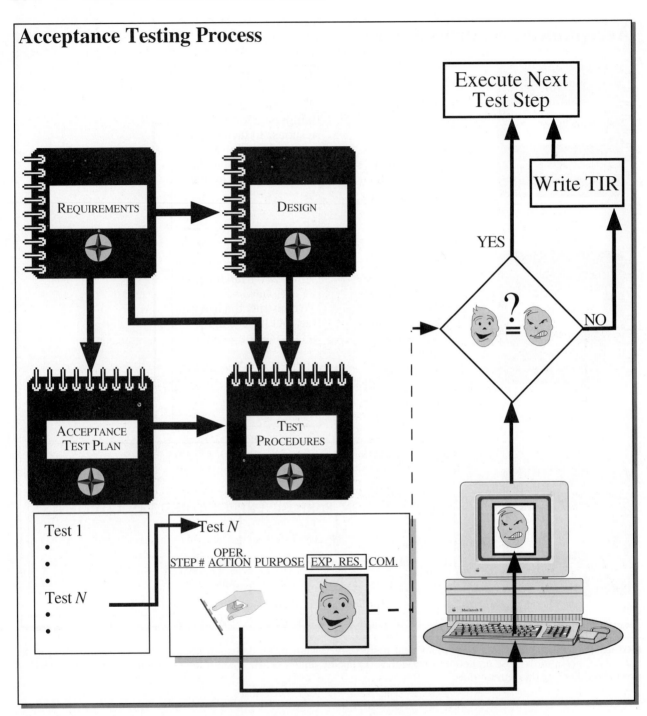

FIGURE 5–41 This figure presents an overview of the acceptance testing process.

good visibility and traceability, it is easy to lose control over the software. Test incidents may be overlooked or go unreported; they may be misplaced and never addressed. TIR resolutions requiring code corrections may be found, but the code may not be corrected. Corrected code may never be retested, and harmful side effects from code changes or improper corrections may never be uncovered. The set of code being tested may not converge to a set suitable for delivery to the customer, but may actually diverge with an increasing number of test incidents from testing cycle to testing cycle. Visibility and traceability are essential if the seller development team is to achieve convergence with what the customer wants.

Figure 5–42 shows the acceptance testing cycle that we now walk through. Notice that the focal points of the cycle are the Software Turnover CCB and the Test Incident CCB. As we discuss, these CCBs are special cases of the CCB concept discussed in Chapter 4. These CCBs are simply tailored to focus on the determination of whether a software system is ready to be shipped to the customer.

The starting point in our walkthrough of the acceptance testing cycle occurs when the seller development team provides the software system to be tested and the supporting material to the product assurance personnel at a Turnover CCB. Let us assume that the software system is a new system, that is, one that has not yet had any acceptance testing. However, as we walk through the acceptance testing cycle, we also discuss software systems that have had some acceptance testing.

What exactly is turned over at the CCB? There are a wide variety of answers in response to this question. This variety may be a reflection of the variety of organizations involved in software development and the variety of change control procedures used by those organizations. In the following list, we state the items that we believe should be turned over at the Software Turnover CCB meeting:[14]

- **Source code.** This product is created by the developers and is subsequently changed in the event that the resolution of a TIR requiring a change to the code is approved by the CCB. The computer source code must therefore be placed under configuration control at this point. Other source code derivative products, such as a computer source code listing or computer object code, can be generated from computer source code.

- **Build instructions.** These instructions detail how to transform the source code modules into an entity that constitutes the software system. These build instructions enable the system builder (in the product assurance organization) to assemble the source code modules into a system for testing.

- **Known problems.** Problems associated with the turnover software become baseline discrepancies that are documented as TIRs. Their submission to the CCB provides visibility as to the software status and averts unnecessary testing.

- **Unit and integration test results.** The development organization conducts unit and integration tests[15] and records the results in test reports. These reports indicate how these tests were conducted and details the test outcomes—including problems encountered and whether these problems were corrected. Such unit and integration test results increase the visibility of the state of the software code.

- **Calibration data.** These data consist of a set of input test data and a corresponding set of output results data. For example, assume that the software computer code adds two numbers together and produces a result. Input test data are the numbers 4 and 5. The corresponding output results data would be the number 9. Before the testers begin their testing, they want to make sure that they are going to test the software computer code that the development organization provided to the testers at the Software Turnover CCB. The testers use the build instructions to assemble the source code modules into a system for testing. Once the system is built, the testers would use the calibration data (i.e., input test data [4,5] and output results data [9]) to exercise the built system. If the testers input the numbers 4,5 and the system produced the result of 12, then the testers would know that they do not have the system they think they have.

---

[14]We believe that this turnover list is independent of project organization. Note that this discussion is also applicable to databases.

[15]By *unit testing,* we mean "the exercising of a unit (a separately compilable sequence of code statements) to ascertain whether it meets design specifications." By *integration testing,* we mean "the exercising of progressively larger collections of units to check out the integrated operation of each collection of units. The final step in integration testing is the exercising, as a single entity, of all units in the system under development."

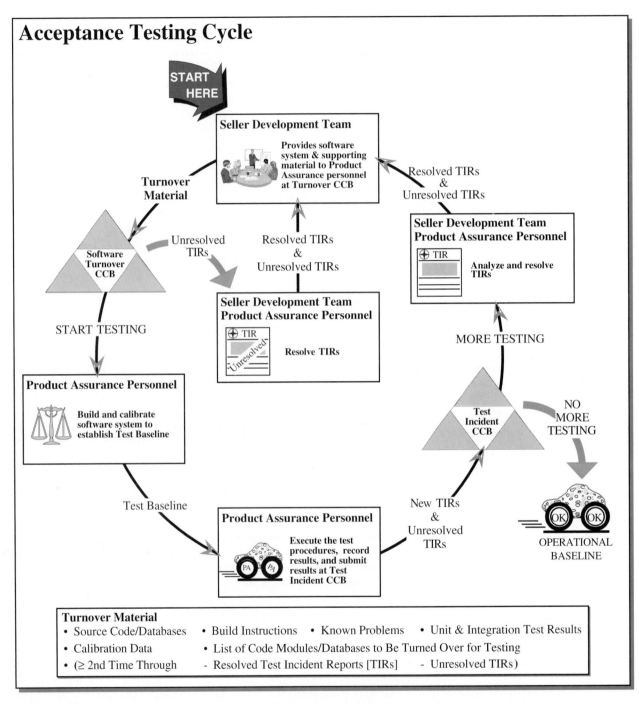

Acceptance Testing Cycle

START HERE

Seller Development Team

Provides software system & supporting material to Product Assurance personnel at Turnover CCB

Turnover Material

Resolved TIRs & Unresolved TIRs

Software Turnover CCB

Unresolved TIRs

Resolved TIRs & Unresolved TIRs

Seller Development Team Product Assurance Personnel

⊕ TIR

Analyze and resolve TIRs

START TESTING

Seller Development Team Product Assurance Personnel

⊕ TIR Unresolved

Resolve TIRs

MORE TESTING

Product Assurance Personnel

Build and calibrate software system to establish Test Baseline

Test Incident CCB

NO MORE TESTING

Test Baseline

Product Assurance Personnel

Execute the test procedures, record results, and submit results at Test Incident CCB

New TIRs & Unresolved TIRs

OK OK

OPERATIONAL BASELINE

Turnover Material
- Source Code/Databases • Build Instructions • Known Problems • Unit & Integration Test Results
- Calibration Data • List of Code Modules/Databases to Be Turned Over for Testing
- (≥ 2nd Time Through - Resolved Test Incident Reports [TIRs] - Unresolved TIRs)

FIGURE 5–42 The interaction of the Software Turnover CCB and the Test Incident CCB during the acceptance testing cycle raises the software system's visibility and infuses it with traceability. The cycle continues until the customer and seller mutually agree that the software system is ready to be released (i.e., "accepted by the customer").

The testers know that some software part is missing (e.g., it may not have been turned over at a Software Turnover CCB) or it has been changed or the build instructions may be incorrect. Basically, something that worked before no longer works. Software could be missing parts or could be changed and not be detected by this calibration test. The purpose of the calibration data is to obtain a degree of comfort that the testers are reading from the same sheet of music as the development organization—*before the testers expend resources executing the test procedures.*

Calibration data are not used to test the software (the test procedures provide an independent set of data for testing) but to calibrate the software system. It is important to calibrate the system before you expend resources testing the wrong system.

- **A list of code modules to be turned over for testing.** This list identifies the software parts delivered.

- **(≥ 2nd time through: resolved test incident reports [TIRs] and unresolved TIRs).** Resolved and unresolved TIRs come into play during the second and subsequent times through the testing cycle. Resolved TIRs become part of the software system that is built by the product assurance personnel for acceptance testing. Unresolved TIRs that are provided to the Software Turnover CCB may have to be resolved before testing begins, may not be resolved until later, or may be converted to incident reports (IRs) or change requests (CRs).

The minutes of the Software Turnover CCB meeting should specify what was turned over at the meeting, list the known software problems,[16] establish priorities for testing the software, and set a date when the testers will end their testing and submit any TIRs they generate to the test incident CCB.

Following the Software Turnover CCB meeting, the software configuration management personnel (of the product assurance organization) place the delivered source code modules under control. This controlled set of code is given the name "Development Baseline" to signify that this code is what the developers handed over for testing. Then, the product assurance organization, using the build instructions provided at the turnover meeting, build an executable software system that is given the name "Test Baseline." The product assurance testers then first execute the built system using the calibration data to see whether they obtain the same outputs included with the calibration data that they received at the turnover meeting. If not, the modules in the Development Baseline need to be checked (presumably by the developers) to see whether they were indeed the ones the developers used to generate the output calibration data. If the product assurance testers are able to reproduce the output calibration data, they use their previously written test procedures to exercise the Test Baseline in a live or nearly live environment. As a result of this testing, they may generate new TIRs.

The product assurance personnel execute the test procedures, record the results, and then submit the results at a Test Incident CCB. Before we describe the role of the Test Incident CCB, we first discuss how TIRs are used during testing. An example TIR form is shown in Figure 5–43.

The TIR form shown is an example only, designed to match our other change control forms that we have discussed. This TIR form is a simplification and amalgamation of the IR and SCN forms already presented. We chose this design for this form because the test incident report process is basically a simplified version of answering the question "Is something wrong?"

When a tester executing the test procedures observes a discrepancy, the tester fills out the initiation event portion of the TIR and gives it to the bookkeeper[17] in the product assurance organization. The bookkeeper assigns a control number to the TIR in the freezing event portion of the TIR and presents all accumulated TIRs to the Test Incident CCB. At that meeting, the CCB might decide that no action is required on the TIR or might decide to convert the TIR either to an IR or a CR. Conversion to

---

[16]As the seller development team members prepare the turnover material, they may find a problem with the software code. The developers can record this newly discovered problem on a TIR and include it as part of the turnover material. TIRs are usually generated by the testers, but in this case the developers generate the TIR.

[17]The bookkeeping role can be performed in a variety of ways. For example, the bookkeeper can be the tester or a member of the configuration management (CM) staff. When the testing activity involves a lot of testers, it may be preferable to have a member of the CM staff serve as the single point of contact for collecting TIRs. This approach increases the likelihood that all TIRs will be properly accounted for.

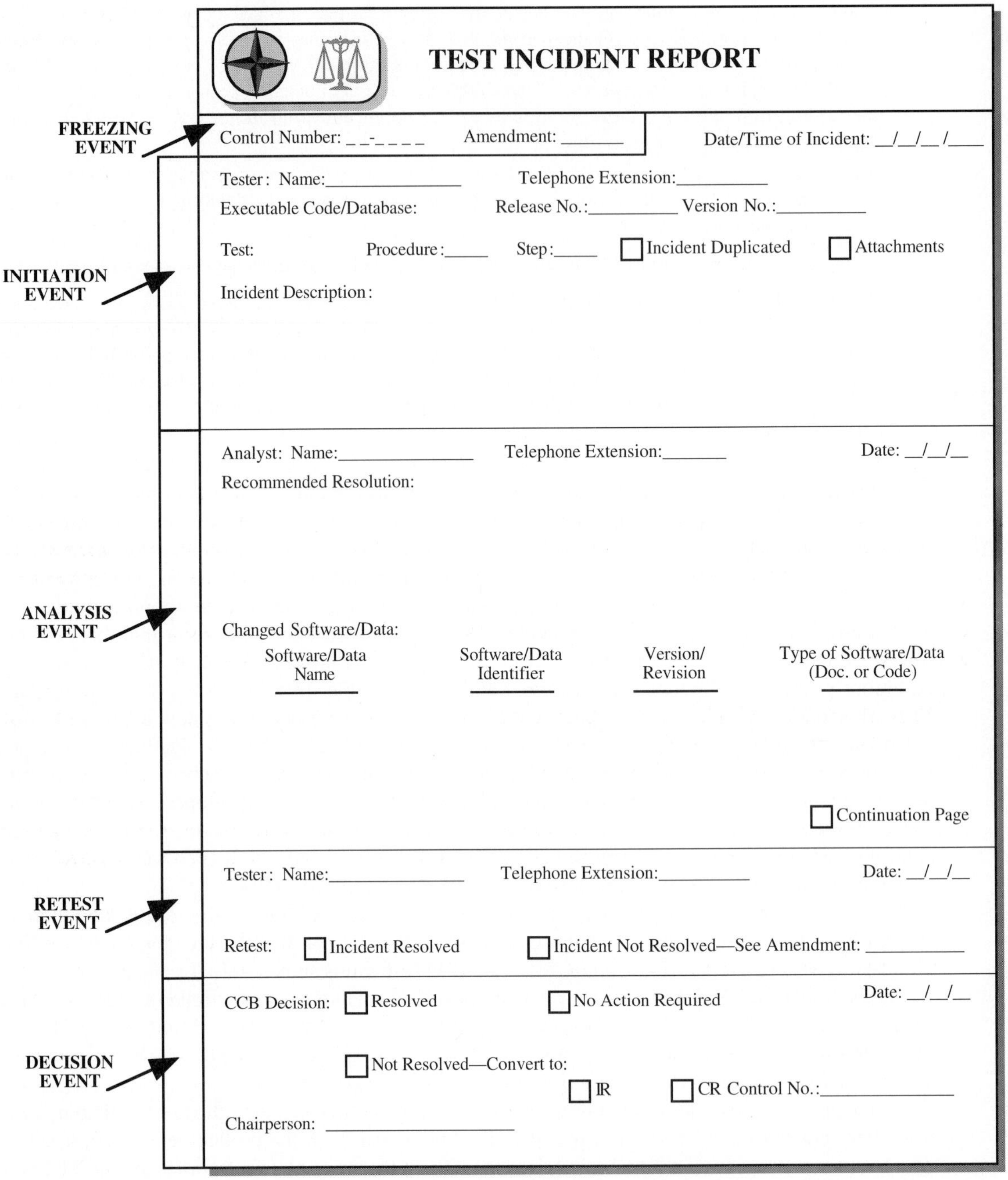

FREEZING
EVENT

INITIATION
EVENT

ANALYSIS
EVENT

RETEST
EVENT

DECISION
EVENT

TEST INCIDENT REPORT

Control Number: _ _-_ _ _ _   Amendment: _____   Date/Time of Incident: __/__/__ /___

Tester : Name:_____   Telephone Extension:_____

Executable Code/Database: Release No.:_____ Version No.:_____

Test: Procedure :_____   Step :_____   ☐ Incident Duplicated   ☐ Attachments

Incident Description :

Analyst: Name:_____   Telephone Extension:_____   Date: __/__/__

Recommended Resolution:

Changed Software/Data:

Software/Data Name	Software/Data Identifier	Version/ Revision	Type of Software/Data (Doc. or Code)

☐ Continuation Page

Tester : Name:_____   Telephone Extension:_____   Date: __/__/__

Retest: ☐ Incident Resolved   ☐ Incident Not Resolved—See Amendment: _____

CCB Decision: ☐ Resolved   ☐ No Action Required   Date: __/__/__

☐ Not Resolved—Convert to:

☐ IR   ☐ CR Control No.:_____

Chairperson: _____

FIGURE 5–43   Example of a test incident report (TIR) form and associated events that it documents.

an IR might occur if the CCB establishes the Operational Baseline[18] at a subsequent CCB—any residual TIRs are converted to IRs at that time. For any one of these three decisions, the CCB chairperson fills out the decision event portion of the TIR. If the CCB decides to send the TIR to the developers for resolution, no entry is made in the decision event portion of the TIR.

---

[18]We use the term "Operational Baseline" to signify that the tested code is now ready for operational use.

The developer assigned to process a TIR fills out the analysis event portion of the TIR. The developer adds a recommended resolution to the TIR and a list of the software parts in the Development Baseline that the developer has changed. At the subsequent Software Turnover CCB, all the TIRs that were completed through the analysis event are reviewed. The CCB might decide that no action is required on the TIR or that it should be converted to a CR. For these decisions, the bottom portion of the TIR would be filled out by the CCB chairperson. Otherwise, the Software Turnover CCB forwards the TIR to the testers for retest. A tester retests the software system to determine whether the incident has been resolved. The tester retests the system by reexecuting the test procedure indicated on the TIR and observing at the TIR-specified test step whether the observed and expected results now agree. If no discrepancy appears, the tester indicates in the retest event portion of the TIR that the incident has been resolved. At the next Test Incident CCB, the chairperson indicates that the test incident has been resolved in the decision event portion of the TIR, and the TIR is closed. However, if the tester still finds a discrepancy as a result of retest, the tester indicates that fact in the retest event portion of the TIR and initiates an amendment to the TIR (amendments are labeled sequentially starting with the letter A). The amendment is written on another TIR form and attached to the original TIR. The tester fills in the incident description item of the TIR amendment according to the tester's observations during retest. The development analyst fills in the analysis section of the TIR amendment, and the tester completes the retest event on the amendment. The TIR can continue around the acceptance testing cycle a number of times, with the TIR and its amendments providing visibility as to what occurred during each cycle and traceability from event to event. The TIR is closed out eventually when the CCB approves the resolution of the test incident, converts it to an IR or a CR, or requires no code or document changes to be made.

To further explain the TIR form, assume that the TIR shown in Figure 5–44 was generated. The context for this TIR is the previously discussed System SHAPES. Assume further that we are using SHAPES to draw ellipses on a map of the earth's surface. The tester fills out the initiation event portion of the form and submits it to the product assurance bookkeeper, who assigns it the control number 99-1066.

TIR 99-1066 and all other TIRs written during this test period are submitted to the next meeting of the Test Incident CCB. At this meeting, each TIR is discussed in turn; if the CCB can resolve a TIR at the meeting, it does so and closes the TIR. For example, if the TIR is a duplicate or if it results either from a misunderstanding by the tester or from an error in the test procedures, the CCB usually decides to take no action on a TIR, and the TIR is closed. In the case of an error in a test procedure, the testers correct the errant test procedure and rerun the test. The CCB might also decide that a TIR represents a capability not currently contained in the requirements specification. Such a TIR may be converted by the CCB to a change request, i.e., the CCB will consider amending the requirements after an impact assessment has been made. The TIR is closed, and the CR is processed. The CCB may also decide that it will not change the requirements to respond to the TIR, in which case the TIR is closed and the originator notified.

At this particular Test Incident CCB meeting, TIR 99-1066 is recognized as a problem and is sent to the development organization for analysis. This analysis provides insight into the question "Is something wrong?" The outcome of this analysis can be one of the following:

■ Something is wrong with the software system. Something needs to be fixed, and the developers believe that it can be fixed before the next Software Turnover CCB.

As the developers attempt to fix the software system, it becomes apparent that the system cannot be fixed before the next Software Turnover CCB. In this case, the seller development team explains at the next Turnover CCB that the effort required to fix the system was considerably more than what was thought to be case at the previous Test Incident CCB. At the Turnover CCB, the decision makers can make decisions that include the following:

■ The TIR needs to be resolved. In this particular case, the software system needs to be fixed before the Operational Baseline is established. The developers are directed to fix the system.

TEST INCIDENT REPORT

System Shapes

Control Number: 99-1066 Amendment: ______

Date/Time of Incident: 11/10/99/2130

Tester: Name: Amy Blue Telephone Extension: 2174

Executable Code/Database: Release No.: 99-3 Version No.: 2.1

Test: Procedure: El 2 Step: 49 [X] Incident Duplicated [ ] Attachments

Incident Description:

Expected ellipse to be drawn with semimajor axis oriented north-south. When ellipse with semimajor axis = 5000 miles was drawn, semimajor axis was oriented northeast-southwest.

Analyst: Name: Jack Lemon Telephone Extension: 1492 Date: 11/15/99

Recommended Resolution:

Register overflow. Use double precision arithmetic whenever semimajor axis greater than 2000 miles.

Changed Software/Data:

Software/Data Name	Software/Data Identifier	Version/ Revision	Type of Software/Data (Doc. or Code)
ELIPCALC	5.2.1	1.6	Code
ELIPDRAW	5.2.4	2.1	Code

[ ] Continuation Page

Tester: Name: Peter Rose Telephone Extension: 8214 Date: 11/18/99

Retest: [X] Incident Resolved [ ] Incident Not Resolved—See Amendment: ______

CCB Decision: [X] Resolved [ ] No Action Required Date: 11/19/99

[ ] Not Resolved—Convert to: [ ] IR [ ] CR Control No.: ______

Chairperson: Sally Plum

FIGURE 5–44 Example of a completed test incident report (TIR) showing an incident resolved by changing code. The first retest of the code demonstrated that the recommended code changes were correct.

- The TIR is converted to an IR. In this particular case, the software system does not need to be fixed before the Operational Baseline is established.

- Something is not wrong with the software system. In this case, the seller development team determines that no products need to be fixed. This situation generally arises when a TIR is misunderstood at the Test Incident CCB.

The minutes of this Test Incident CCB should include a list of all TIRs submitted, a list of resolved and unresolved TIRs, the designation of any software capabilities that should be given particular attention because of the number or impact of TIRs pertinent to those capabilities, and the date of the next Software Turnover CCB meeting, at which the development organization will turn the software back over to the product assurance organization for further testing.

The development organization analyzes and attempts to resolve as many TIRs as possible in the time period allotted. The analysis event portion of each TIR resolved is filled out at this time. In the case of TIR 99-1066 two modules were adjudged to be faulty by the analyst (from the development organization), ELIPCALC and ELIPDRAW. The developers obtain a copy of each of these two modules from the software development library and correct them to resolve the test incident.

At the subsequent Software Turnover CCB meeting, all resolved TIRs are presented to the CCB. For TIRs requiring changes to code modules (such as TIR 99-1066), the corrected source code modules (including ELIPCALC and ELIPDRAW) are also turned over to the product assurance organization. In the process of resolving TIRs, the development organization often uncovers additional discrepancies. It is important to note that such discrepancies might include areas of uncertainty in the various specifications for the project. These discrepancies are reported as TIRs and introduced at this Software Turnover CCB meeting. The minutes of this CCB meeting should document all TIRs returned to the CCB and their resolutions, all new TIRs introduced at the meeting, and the date when the Test Incident CCB would be held.

After this meeting, the product assurance organization substitutes the corrected source code modules in the Development Baseline. The software system (Test Baseline) is rebuilt to include the corrected code modules. Then the testers exercise the Test Baseline again, using their test procedures. During this testing period, particular attention is paid to the procedure test steps where resolved TIRs were first observed. If a discrepancy still exists at a particular test step, an amendment to the TIR is prepared and attached to the TIR. With regard to TIR 99-1066, the tester found no discrepancies at step 49 of procedure EL2, and so indicated that the incident was resolved in the retest section of the TIR. At the next meeting of the Test Incident CCB, the decision makers, noting that TIR 99-1066 had been resolved on retest, marked the decision event section to indicate that the incident had been resolved and then closed the TIR.

The Test Incident CCB also decides when the testing cycle terminates. Ideally, the cycle terminates when no TIRs result from the execution of the test procedures and no residual unresolved TIRs exist. However, we live in a far from ideal world and must have other mechanisms to allow us to exit the testing cycle. Even if TIRs are outstanding at the end of a cycle, the CCB may elect to terminate the cycle if the number of outstanding TIRs is relatively few and the impact of the TIRs on system operation is relatively minor. Another consideration is whether the software has tended toward stability in the last few cycles. If the number of TIRs outstanding at the end of each cycle is steadily decreasing, the system appears to be stable and is converging to the Operational Baseline. Other considerations regarding when to terminate the testing cycle include the arrival of the required delivery date of the system to the customer and the exhaustion of funds available to conduct testing. These last two considerations often override any other considerations as to when to terminate the testing cycle.

Regardless of the reason for terminating the acceptance testing cycle, all outstanding TIRs should be converted to incident reports. These IRs are processed as discussed in Chapter 4. It should be noted that when the testing cycle is terminated, the system often has outstanding discrepancies. Although this situation is less than ideal, the way IRs are processed provides a mechanism for resolving them in a visible, traceable manner. This processing increases the likelihood that the delivered product is readily maintainable. These observations should provide some peace of mind to the user receiving this software. At least the user knows what problems the user might face and that someone is working on their solution.

Contrast the foregoing situation to a situation in which no testing cycle (with its audit and control functions) is provided. On most projects, a testing period is planned between the completion of coding/unit testing/integration testing and the date of delivery of the software code to the customer. The delivery date is usually fixed; it is generally very difficult to change a delivery date. On the other hand, the date of completion of coding/unit testing/integration testing frequently tends to slip toward the delivery date. The net result of such slippage is a reduction of the testing period. Usually there are no plans to pass through the testing period more than once. The testing period is often viewed as a "kick-the-tires" final inspection just before delivery, from which at most only a few discrepancies are expected. With this concept, no recycling through a testing period is necessary. If there are only a few discrepancies in the computer code, this approach works satisfactorily. But if there are any substantial number of discrepancies, the testing period could become chaos without any systematic way (i.e., defined acceptance testing cycle) of executing the test procedures, recording the results, filling out TIRs, and presenting the TIRs to a Test Incident CCB. The testing period could become a time of frenzied activity—testing, correcting code in response to test incidents, and retesting all going on in parallel in a period of time that usually has been abbreviated because of slippage of the completion date of the computer code. Reports of test incidents could be misplaced, corrected code could be overlooked, code changes could counteract other code changes. When the delivery date arrives (and delivery will occur on the specified delivery date), the state of the software is unknown. What discrepancies still exist? What discrepancies have been overlooked? In the period of frenzied testing activity, there is no time to document the changes made to the code or even to record which modules were changed. Under these circumstances, maintenance of the software becomes very difficult.

In this section, we looked in detail at the auditing process as it applies to computer code. We showed how this audit of code against requirements and design specifications is accomplished by executing code operating in a live or nearly live environment using written test procedures, the process we call T&E. We pointed out how product assurance gives visibility during the acceptance testing cycle to the state of the Development and Operational Baselines through CCB minutes, TIRs, and written test procedures, and how it provides traceability during the transition from the Development Baseline to the Operational Baseline.

Requirements Testability Example—System LOOKOUT   From the seller's perspective, the bottom line of the software systems development process is to demonstrate formally that what the customer asked for is indeed embodied in the computer code and supporting databases to be delivered. In this book, we call this formal demonstration "acceptance testing." A fundamental premise of acceptance testing is that the functional capabilities that the customer wants (i.e., functional requirements) are testable. A "testable requirement" is one that satisfies the following criteria:

- The requirement is sufficiently defined to permit writing test procedures that demonstrate whether or not the capability or capabilities defined by the requirement are embodied in the computer code and/or supporting databases.

- The test procedures are executable in a cost-effective manner.

Strictly speaking, a statement of functional capability that is not testable is not a requirement. If the presence or absence of such capability cannot be formally demonstrated, then it lies in an engineering netherworld. A key software systems development process challenge then is determining requirements testability so that the process can be brought to a successful conclusion.

Determining that a requirement is testable is, in general, a nontrivial endeavor. As we have reiterated, both the seller and customer progress in their understanding of what needs to be done as a project proceeds. This increased understanding often has a direct impact on establishing requirements testability as we now explain.

Elaborating on the preceding testability criteria, we say that a software requirement is testable if we can describe a cost-effective exercise of the requirement that can be performed on the computer hosting the software code and databases to be tested. Presumably such an exercise can then be broken down into a set of test steps that a tester can perform and a corresponding set of expected results that a tester can compare with the observed operation of the software code. As we have explained, the test procedure steps are accompanied by a set of expected results. When the tester executes the test steps, the tester compares the result of software code operation against these expected results. If the results of this code operation do not agree with the expected results, the tester writes a test incident report to document this discrepancy. To illustrate in specific terms what is involved with establishing requirements testability, we examine a requirements specification. The purpose of this examination is to focus on what is involved with conceptualizing such test exercises. Of course, strictly speaking, until such exercises are converted to performable test steps, requirements testability has not been formally demonstrated. Because test procedure development does not generally occur until some time after requirements are presented (and documented), demonstrating requirements testability is, in fact, an open issue until test procedures are written. Frequently, it is not until test procedure writing begins that testability nuances surface—again, because of the increased understanding of what needs to be done that naturally emerges when people are forced to think through how to demonstrate capability.

To give you how-to-do-it insight into how to assess requirements testability from a requirements specification (before test procedure writing), we look at a requirements specification. This look will help you anticipate certain testability issues. However, keep in mind the previously mentioned caveat—until test procedure writing begins, the contents of the requirements specification may still need to be reworked to transform previously considered testable statements into testable statements. It should be noted that the requirements specification that we consider is adapted from an actual specification that contained testability issues that were dormant for years until the project adopted a formal approach to testing that included preparing written test procedures derived from requirements (prior to adopting the formal testing approach, the project used a cursory, "kick-the-tires" approach).

Figure 5–45 shows a two-page document entitled "Subsystem Requirements Specification for Earth Surface Areas." As section 1 of the document indicates, a computer subsystem is supporting the operations of the meteorological satellite system LOOKOUT. Among other things, LOOKOUT monitors weather activity over various parts of the earth. In support of this monitoring, the computer subsystem includes the capability to allow its users to define rectangles on the earth's surface (called "spherical rectangles") that serve as reference areas for weather observations (e.g., to observe what percentage of the time the area is cloudless).

Section 3 of the requirements specification (page 2) defines six capabilities (paragraphs 3.a to 3.f) regarding the spherical rectangles (as Figure 2 in the requirements specification indicates, these rectangles are three-dimensional, being defined on the earth's curved surface). We analyze whether each of these capabilities is testable. If a capability is not testable, we consider ways in which the capability should be formulated so that it can be tested.

We stress at the outset that the testability issues that we address are precisely the types of issues that the organization responsible for acceptance testing (which we suggest should be an independent product assurance organization) should address during software systems development. We also stress that, just as requirements definition is an activity that continues throughout a software project, so too is requirements testability assessment an activity that continues throughout a software project.[19]

In the following discussion, we describe an exercise that might be performed and what a tester might look for to determine whether computer code embodies each of the six section 3 requirements.

- For requirements *a* and *e* (see Figure 5–45), the tester could define a rectangle by entering the latitude and longitude of its northeast and southwest vertices. The tester could then observe on the display device the re-

---

[19]Some parts of the subsequent discussion require knowledge of spherical trigonometry to be completely understood. However, it is not necessary to understand the mathematical details of this discussion completely to understand the testability issues addressed. The mathematics has been incorporated into the discussion to illustrate in specific terms the types of mathematical issues that testers may face in the real world. The mathematical issues discussed are derived from the authors' actual software project experience.

Subsystem Requirements Specification
for
Earth Surface Areas

1 December 1998
LOOKOUT-SP-109/R3

1. BACKGROUND AND PURPOSE

The meteorological satellite LOOKOUT monitors weather activity over various parts of the earth. The LOOKOUT System Specification details the capabilities of this satellite. In support of this monitoring, the LOOKOUT System Specification identifies a computer subsystem that allows the users of the LOOKOUT System to define certain types of areas (defined below) on the earth's surface. These areas serve as references for weather observations (e.g., to observe what percentage of the time the area is cloudless). The purpose of this subsystem requirements specification is to specify the capabilities for defining areas on the earth's surface.

2. SUBSYSTEM OVERVIEW

The user defines earth surface areas by inputting data via a keyboard. The areas are four-sided figures. The top and bottom sides lie along lines of constant latitude; the left and right sides lie along lines of constant longitude. The result of keyboard entry is the display of the area on a CRT device. The area is displayed overlaid on a map background showing land masses. The map background will show lines of constant longitude as parallel straight lines and lines of constant latitude as parallel straight lines intersecting the longitude lines at right angles.

The user is also provided a mouse that controls the position of a cursor on the CRT device. The user can continuously display the latitude and longitude of the cursor.

As a user option, the user can display latitude and longitude lines on the map background. The spacing between these lines is user specified (e.g., the user can specify that latitude lines appear every 30' [thirty minutes] and longitude lines appear every 1.0° [one degree]). The user can obtain hardcopy of the screen display from a printer. Figure 1 shows an example display of an area overlaid on a map with latitude and longitude lines explicitly shown.

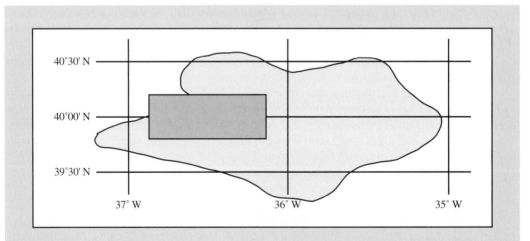

Figure 1. Four-Sided Area Displayed on Map Background with Latitude/Longitude Grid Lines

FIGURE 5–45   This requirements specification provides the backdrop for illustrating the concept of requirements testability.

3. SURFACE AREA REQUIREMENTS

To support quantitative analysis of weather observations made from the LOOKOUT satellite, the subsystem shall provide the capability to define four-sided areas on the surface of the earth. These areas shall conform to the following specifications and limitations:

a. Each area shall be oriented such that the north and south sides lie along lines of constant latitude, and the east and west sides lie along lines of constant longitude. (Note: These areas are spherical rectangles; the north and south sides in this type of rectangle are, in general, of unequal length. See Figure 2. When projected onto a flat surface where longitudes are parallel lines, a spherical rectangle appears to have equal north and south sides. See Figure 1.)

b. The maximum dimension of any side shall not exceed 80 nautical miles. (Note: If any side exceeds this maximum, the user shall be informed with a diagnostic.)

c. The maximum area of any rectangle shall not exceed 3600 square nautical miles. (Note: If the area exceeds this maximum, the user shall be informed with a diagnostic.)

d. All areas shall lie between 75° North and 75° South. (Note: If an area lies outside this region, the user shall be informed with a diagnostic.)

e. Each area shall be defined by specifying the latitude and longitude of its northeast and southwest vertices (see Figure 2).

f. The LOOKOUT database shall be capable of storing 200 areas (i.e., 200 pairs of vertices, with each vertex consisting of a latitude and a longitude—see Figure 2). (Note: If an attempt is made to store more than 200 areas, the user shall be informed with a diagnostic.)

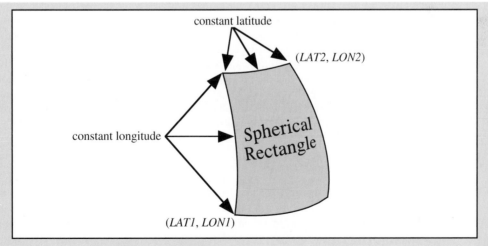

Figure 2. A rectangular area on the earth's surface, whose north and south sides lie along lines of constant latitude and whose east and west sides lie along lines of constant longitude, is defined by its southwest vertex at latitude *LAT1* and longitude *LON1* and its northeast vertex at latitude *LAT2* and longitude *LON2*.

FIGURE 5–45   *Continued*

sultant figure to see whether its borders lie along the latitudes and longitudes defined by the vertices (see Figure 1 in the requirements specification). This observation can be quantified by using the following capability cited in the second paragraph in section 2 of the specification:

> The user is also provided a mouse that controls the position of the cursor on the CRT device. The user can continuously display the latitude and longitude of the cursor.

Thus, the tester can use the mouse to move along the rectangle's borders and observe whether the north and south sides lie along lines of constant latitude and whether the east and west sides lie along lines of constant longitude, where the latitudes and longitudes are those specified in the input vertices.

The preceding discussion thus represents a test of the requirements *a* and *e* in that it describes an exercise that a tester can perform to confirm that a rectangle can be constructed that lies along lines of constant latitude and longitude as defined by the latitude and longitude of the rectangle's northeast and southwest vertices. These two requirements are thus testable.

To illustrate further some potentially latent testability issues regarding requirements *a* and *e*, we observe the following:

- The tester exploits the capability to display latitude and longitude values continuously using a mouse. Now, unless the tester has a very firm hand, and depending on the sensitivity of the mouse/readout mechanism, the readout of a scan along a rectangle border may show small changes in values (e.g., running the mouse along the northern border that is supposed to lie, say, at 30°N may show readings varying between 29 degrees and 59 minutes and 30 degrees and 1 minute). No accuracy requirements are stipulated in the requirements specification. Thus, presumably such small variations may have no significance in confirming border constancy. However, when a test procedure is written along the lines just described to confirm the presence of the capabilities in requirements *a* and *e*, an accuracy requirement may emerge when the test procedure is reviewed by others.

- Had there been no latitude/longitude readout capability, and had there not been the user option to display latitude and longitude lines on the map background as indicated in paragraph 3 of section 2, then it may have been necessary for the tester to instrument the code being tested so that it displays such a background or otherwise indicates where the figure lies on the surface of the earth. The need to instrument code itself creates a testability issue. When the code is instrumented, the issue arises that the code being tested is not the code that is to be delivered to the customer, since the instrumentation code will be removed from the system to be delivered. Thus, when instrumenting code for testing purposes, it becomes necessary to demonstrate that this code does not change the system operation. That in itself can become a significant challenge. Often what is done for display-oriented systems such as LOOKOUT, is to rely on visual comparison of screen displays and/or printouts of these displays with and without the instrumentation code to demonstrate that the presence of the instrumentation code has no perceptible effect on the operation of the system. This visual comparison can be facilitated by printing out transparencies of the screen displays. The transparencies of a display with and without the instrumentation code can then be overlaid on one another to demonstrate that all parts of the display not including output from the instrumentation code coincide.

- An ancillary issue that often arises in testing systems involving map displays (and that is implicit in testing LOOKOUT) is the following:

> How do you know that the display of maps (e.g., the display of land masses and associated latitudes and longitudes as shown in Figure 1 of the LOOKOUT Subsystem Requirements Specification) is correct?

- This issue can be restated as follows:

> What is the ground truth for the maps to be displayed?

- One way to address this issue is to have the customer supply paper maps explicitly showing the map projection(s) and the map scale(s) that the customer wants displayed. Then, using this map-projection and map-scale information, transparencies of map displays at these projections and scales can be printed and then overlaid on the customer-supplied maps. If the printout of land masses and associated latitude and longitude lines coincide with the land masses and associated latitude and longitude lines on the customer-supplied maps, then, by definition, the display of maps is correct. Again, accuracy considerations may come into play when determining how closely the computer printouts have to match the customer-supplied maps.

■ For requirements *b* and *c* (see Figure 5–45, section 3), it is necessary to perform mathematical computations in order to determine expected results. To do these computations, it is necessary to know what model is being used for the shape of the earth. This model is not indicated in the requirements specification. Requirements *b* and *c* are therefore untestable.

To see the significance of the need to prescribe an earth model, assume that the requirements specification indicates elsewhere that the earth is a sphere of radius $R = 3440$ nautical miles. With this assumption, it is then possible to write down the distance and area formulas shown in Figure 5–46 that could be used to check requirements *b* and *c*. Using these formulas to compute rectangle side lengths and rectangle areas (in a manner like that shown at the bottom of Figure 5–46), the tester could then define various rectangles by specifying their northeast and southwest vertices such that (1) some of these rectangles have one or more sides that exceed 80 nautical miles, (2) some of these rectangles have no sides exceeding 80 nautical miles, (3) some of these rectangles have an area exceeding 3600 square nautical miles, and (4) some of these rectangles have an area less than 3600 square nautical miles. The tester could thus enter these vertex pairs and then observe on the display device the result of entering these pairs. In those cases where the vertex pairs yield rectangle side lengths no greater than 80 nautical miles and an area no greater than 3600 square nautical miles, the display would presumably show the rectangles corresponding to the vertex pairs input; otherwise, as section 3 of the requirements specification indicates, the display would presumably respond with some error diagnostic indicating the offending length and/or area.

To illustrate further other testability issues regarding requirements *b* and *c*, we observe the following:

■ If the earth is not assumed to be a sphere (but, say, an ellipsoid), the distance and area formulas shown in Figure 5–46 may have to be modified or replaced to account for deviation from sphericity. The extent to which modification or replacement may be required depends, in general, on the accuracy required; that is, for completeness the requirements specification should probably indicate the accuracy required for distance and area computations.

■ The requirements specification does not indicate that the LOOKOUT CRT is to display the rectangle side length values and the area value. Strictly speaking, then, the tester does not have to check for these values; the tester only has to check whether a rectangle is or is not accepted by LOOKOUT. However, consider what might happen as the tester begins writing test procedures to check requirements *b* and *c*. The tester need to compute these values may plant the seed in the minds of the LOOKOUT software system developers and, eventually, the customer that it may be desirable to augment these requirements to include the display of rectangle side lengths and areas. If these requirements were augmented in this way, the tester would then have to compare the values the tester computes from formulas such as those shown in Figure 5–46 with the values appearing on the LOOKOUT CRT.

■ It should be pointed out that the mathematical detail shown in Figure 5–46 would not need to be included in the requirements specification. For testability purposes, it would be sufficient for the requirements specification in Figure 5–45 to indicate (1) whether the earth model to be used were spherical, ellipsoidal, or something else and (2) where the particulars on the earth model to be used could be found (e.g., a standard reference on earth parameters). From this information, the tester (and the software system developers) could find or otherwise derive the formulas or algorithms for computing spherical rectangle side lengths and areas.

■ If the requirements specification were silent on the earth model to be used but the tester and the developers recognized that an earth model is needed to proceed with development and test preparation, some interesting situations could arise if the developers assumed one earth model and the tester assumed another model. This situation actually arose in connection with the requirements specification upon which the LOOKOUT specification is based. The tester used a spherical earth model with a radius $R = 3440$ nautical miles (a value often used to approximate a nonspherical earth; this value is determined by making the volume of a sphere equal to the volume of an ellipsoid that approximates the actual earth shape having a polar radius of 3432 nautical miles and an equatorial radius of 3444 nautical miles). The developers used a spherical earth model with a radius $R = 3437.74677\ldots$ nautical miles (a value that is used to define the nautical mile; this model is used to simplify navigational calculations). Figure 5–47 shows a spherical rectangle one degree on each side in the region of the equator. The figure also shows the computation of

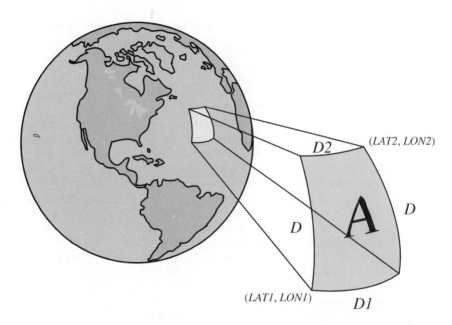

Spherical Rectangle Mathematical Relationships

D $= R(LAT2 - LAT1)$ = great circle distance of east or west side of rectangle
$D1 = R(LON1 - LON2)\cos(LAT1)$ = small circle distance of south side of rectangle
$D2 = R(LON1 - LON2)\cos(LAT2)$ = small circle distance of north side of rectangle
A $= R^2(LON1 - LON2)[\sin(LAT2) - \sin(LAT1)]$ = area of rectangle

R = earth radius
cos = cosine function
sin = sine function

All angles are measured in radians.
One radian = $180°/\pi$ = 57.2957795131 . . . degrees, π = 3.14159265359 . . . .

Latitudes above the equator are positive (e.g., 30°N = +0.5236 radians).
Latitudes below the equator are negative (e.g., 30°S = −0.5236 radians).
Longitudes to the west of the prime meridian are positive (e.g., 30°W = +0.5236 radians).
Longitudes to the east of the prime meridian are negative (e.g., 30°E = −0.5236 radians).
The above sign conventions assure that the distance and area formulas given above yield positive values for any point on the earth's surface.

Examples:

  1. $(LAT1, LON1)$ = (30°S, 1°E) = (−0.5236, −0.0175), $(LAT2, LON2)$ = (29°S, 2°E) = (−0.5061, −0.0349), R = 3440 nautical miles

    D = 3440 (−0.5061 + 0.5236) = 60.2 nautical miles
    $D1$ = 3440 (−0.0175 + 0.0349) cos(−0.5236) = 51.8 nautical miles
    $D2$ = 3440 (−0.0175 + 0.0349) cos(−0.5061) = 52.4 nautical miles
    A = $(3440)^2$ (−0.0175 + 0.0349) [sin(−0.5061) − sin(−0.5236)] = 3128 square nautical miles

  2. $(LAT1, LON1)$ = (29°N, 2°W) = (0.5061, 0.0349), $(LAT2, LON2)$ = (30°N, 1°W) = (0.5236, 0.0175), R = 3440 nautical miles

    D = 3440 (0.5236 − 0.5061) = 60.2 nautical miles
    $D1$ = 3440 (0.0349 − 0.0175) cos(0.5061) = 52.4 nautical miles
    $D2$ = 3440 (0.0349 − 0.0175) cos(0.5236) = 51.8 nautical miles
    A = $(3440)^2$ (0.0349 − 0.0175) [sin(0.5236) − sin(0.5061)] = 3128 square nautical miles

FIGURE 5–46 This figure shows how to convert positions on the earth's surface expressed as latitude/longitude pairs to lengths and areas on that surface. The formulas shown are for a spherical earth model.

the area of this rectangle for these values of the radius. As the figure indicates, from the tester's perspective, the area of the rectangle in question is too large to be accepted by the system (i.e., its area is a little more than one square nautical mile larger than the maximum value stipulated in requirement c). As the figure also indicates, from the developers' perspective the rectangle is not too large, having an area slightly less than 3600 square nautical miles. As it turned out, when the tester ran a test of requirement c, the system accepted the rectangle. The tester thus wrote a TIR, because the tester expected, on the basis of the calculation shown in Figure 5–47 for $R = 3440$ nautical miles, that this rectangle had an area larger than the requirement c maximum. When this TIR was brought to the attention of the developers, the developers took exception to it. It then came to light that (1) each side was using different earth models and (2) the requirements specification was silent on what earth model was to be used. More significantly, however, it also came to light that underlying the rectangle parameters listed in the requirements specification was the "requirement" to ensure that *all* rectangles one degree on a side were to be accepted by the system. Because no formal testing had been conducted for years, this implicit requirement and the earth model testability issue had been dormant for years.

In summary regarding requirements b and c, in order to test these requirements, it is necessary to know the model being used for the shape of the earth. The details of this shape depend on the accuracy required for distance and area computations (e.g., required computational accuracies may be such that it is sufficient to assume that the earth is a sphere, because changes to distance and areas that would result by assuming a nonspherical earth would be smaller than the required accuracies of the values of these quantities). Consequently, unless the requirements specification were augmented to address earth-model (and computational-accuracy) issues, requirements b and c would have to be considered untestable.

■ For requirement d ("all areas shall lie between 75° North and 75° South"), the tester could extend the scope of the tests used to exercise requirements a and e by including rectangles whose northern borders lie above 75° North latitude and other rectangles whose southern borders lie below 75° South latitude. As section 3 of the requirements specification indicates, vertex pairs defining such rectangles would presumably cause the software to respond with some error diagnostic indicating the offending border(s). However, there is a potential ambiguity in the statement of the requirement. The potential ambiguity arises from the word "between." Sometimes this word is used in the inclusive sense so that in the case of requirement d, the value "75" would be included; sometimes this word is used in the exclusive sense so that in the case of requirement d, the value "75" would be excluded. Unless this sense is understood, a tester is unable to determine the expected result for a rectangle whose northern border lies on 75°N or for a rectangle whose southern border lies on 75°S. Of course, this potential ambiguity could be removed by rewording the statement of the requirement in one of the two following ways:

All areas shall lie between 75° North and 75° South inclusive.

All areas shall lie between 75° North and 75° South exclusive.

Thus, with the one caveat regarding the interpretation of the word "between," requirement d can be considered testable.

■ For requirement f, the tester could again extend the scope of the tests used to exercise requirements a and e by entering up to 200 pairs of acceptable vertices (vertex pairs that do not violate requirements b, c, and d). It should be noted that, for repeatability, accomplishment of the testing of requirement f would probably benefit from automated support. For example, it may be useful to store the (up to) 200 vertex pairs on some mass storage device (say, a disk). Then, through a keyboard-entered command, these pairs could be read into the system, each pair (quickly) generating a figure on the display device and storing the figure on a mass storage device for subsequent reproduction on a printer, so that the resultant hardcopy could be carefully analyzed subsequent to test execution to explicitly check that (at least selected) rectangles corresponding to the vertex pairs input were properly generated. Following this exercise, the tester would attempt to create additional rectangles in excess of 200 by entering additional vertex pairs. As indicated on page 2 of the requirements specification in Figure 5–45, when the number of rectangles stored on the mass storage device exceeds 200, the system would presumably respond with some error diagnostic indicating that the system limit of 200 stored rectangles has been exceeded. Thus, the preceding discussion indicates that requirement f is testable. This discussion also indicates that testing this requirement would probably be greatly facilitated by at least automating the process of entering test data.

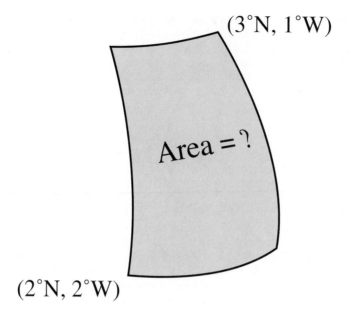

(3°N, 1°W)

Area = ?

(2°N, 2°W)

Does this rectangle satisfy requirement *c* (i.e., is its area ≤ 3600 square nautical miles)? The answer depends on the earth model.

For *R* = 3440 nautical miles,

$$\text{Area} = (3440)^2 \ (0.0174532925 \ldots) \ [\sin(3°) - \sin(2°)] = 3601.24409 \ldots \text{ square nautical miles}$$

For *R* = 3437.74677 . . . nautical miles,

$$\text{Area} = (3437.74677 \ldots)^2 \ (0.0174532925 \ldots) \ [\sin(3°) - \sin(2°)] = 3596.5279 \ldots \text{ square nautical miles}$$

The nautical mile is defined such that the (great circle) distance between two points lying on the same longitude separated by one degree of longitude is 60 nautical miles. The value of the earth radius yielding this definition is 60/(1 degree expressed in radians) = 60/(0.0174532925 . . .) = 3437.74677079 . . . nautical miles. One nautical mile equals 1852 meters exactly, which equals 6076.11548556 . . . international feet (= 1852/0.3048 international feet exactly).

FIGURE 5–47 This figure shows calculations for two spherical earth models—one for a model whose radius is 3440 nautical miles and one for a model whose radius is used to define the nautical mile.

To illustrate further other testability issues regarding requirement *f*, we observe the following:

■ It would perhaps have been preferable to reword requirement *f* along the following lines:

The LOOKOUT database shall be capable of storing between 1 and 200 areas inclusive.

Wording such as the above more precisely reflects the operational need for the system. With a statement such as the above, the tester can prepare, in the manner described earlier, any number of areas between one and 200 inclusive to demonstrate that the system is doing what the requirement stipulates it should do. With the wording as given in Figure 5–45, the tester would simply prepare 200 areas and see if they could be stored. But, perhaps through some glitch in the computer code logic, trying to store, say, 167 areas might (erroneously) cause an error diagnostic to be issued. This anomaly could potentially be overlooked. (It is also true that this anomaly would be overlooked if the wording were as above and the tester chose not to test every number of areas between one and 200, but rather chose a subset of these cases.) While it might be argued that many would interpret the wording of requirement *f* as it appears in Figure 5–45 along the lines given above, some (including the customer) might interpret it some other way (e.g., "the LOOKOUT database shall be capable of storing at least 200 areas"). To avoid such potential misinterpretations, it is preferable to word required capabilities in terms that can be translated into unambiguously defined exercises of the capabilities. The following are additional examples of variations to the wording of requirement *f* that present some testing (and, hence, testability) difficulties:

> The LOOKOUT database shall be capable of storing a maximum of 200 areas.

> The LOOKOUT database shall be capable of storing a minimum of 200 areas.

In the first example, what should happen if 201 areas are stored? Should the system issue an error diagnostic? Should the tester prepare just two sets of input data—one with exactly 200 areas and one with some number of areas greater than 200? Should the tester, as we argued earlier, prepare additional sets of input data with the number of areas varying between 1 and 200? If so, then isn't the tester acting as if the requirement were, in fact, stated as we said earlier, namely,

> The LOOKOUT database shall be capable of storing between 1 and 200 areas inclusive.

In the second example, should the tester simply prepare just one set of input data—namely, 200 areas? Or does the tester have to prepare progressively larger numbers of areas since the requirement is open-ended? Also, in an actual operational setup, how does a database start out with 200 entries? Should an error diagnostic be issued if, at any time, the contents of the database fall below 200 areas?

When we introduced the definition of testability, we noted that the second criterion for testability was the following:

> The test procedures are executable in a cost-effective manner.

Sometimes this cost-effectiveness criterion places limitations on the testing approach. In discussing the testability of requirement *f*, we hinted at a limitation when we suggested that testing this requirement would probably be greatly facilitated by at least automating the process of entering test data. Now, suppose that, instead of the number 200, requirement *f* contained a much larger number—say, 20,000 or 200,000. A testing approach that may have been cost-effective for 200 areas may not be cost-effective for 20,000 or 200,000 areas. It was intimated that manually entering vertex pairs defining even 200 rectangles may be time-consuming—how much the more so for 20,000 or 200,000 vertex pairs? Automated support may not be *necessary* for the case of 200 because it may not take an inordinate time to prepare manually this many data ("inordinate" is, of course, a relative term; what may be inordinate in one environment may be acceptable in another); however, manually preparing one hundred or one thousand times this many data may simply not be feasible, let alone cost-effective. Thus, if 200 were replaced by a much larger number, the brute force testing approach of manually generating and examining the 200 rectangles discussed earlier would have to be replaced by some other approach if the requirement were to be testable (e.g., statistical sampling where, for instance, the database were automatically populated with 20,000 rectangles, and then, say, 100 of these rectangles were randomly selected from the databases to see whether they matched items that were in the list of 20,000 generated).

Figure 5–48 summarizes our discussion regarding the testability of the six LOOKOUT software requirements listed on page 2 of the requirements specification in Figure 5–45. Figure 5–48 also gives a graphical depiction of each requirement. The boxes showing the two untestable requirements (i.e., *b* and *c*) are shaded in dark grey; the box showing the requirement that may or may not be testable (i.e., *d*) is shaded in light grey.

We close this discussion of the important topic of requirements testability with the following remarks reiterating and expanding upon key points from this discussion:

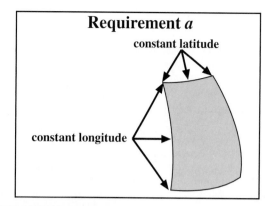

Requirement a

constant latitude

constant longitude

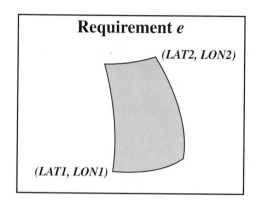

Requirement e

(LAT2, LON2)

(LAT1, LON1)

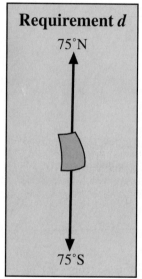

Requirement d

75°N

75°S

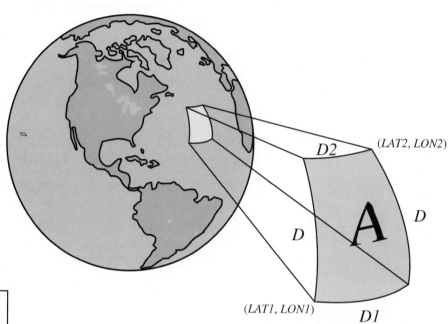

(LAT2, LON2)

D2

D

D

A

(LAT1, LON1)

D1

Requirement f

Database

200

Requirement b

$D \le 80$ nautical miles
$D1 \le 80$ nautical miles
$D2 \le 80$ nautical miles

Requirement c

$A \le 3600$ square nautical miles

Requirement	Testable?	Reason/Comments
a	Yes	Mouse can trace borders to give latitude/longitude readout
b	No	No earth model specified
c	No	No earth model specified
d	Maybe	Meaning of word "between" may be ambiguous
e	Yes	Mouse can give readout of vertex values for displayed rectangle
f	Yes	Replication of requirements *a* and *e* rationale/test

FIGURE 5–48 A summary of the testability of LOOKOUT software requirements.

1. The bottom line of the software systems development process is to demonstrate formally that what the customer asked for is indeed embodied in the computer code and supporting databases to be delivered. We call this formal demonstration "acceptance testing." Thus, requirements testability lies along the critical path towards achieving successful software systems development.

2. We said that, for a requirement to be testable, it must satisfy the following two criteria:
   ■ The requirement is sufficiently defined to permit writing test procedures that demonstrate whether or not the capability or capabilities defined by the requirement are embodied in the computer code and/or supporting databases.
   ■ The test procedures are executable in a cost-effective manner.

   As we explained, the first criterion contains a catch-22. Test procedures are generally not written until design activity is under way. Until the "how" to do the "what" in the requirements specification is defined in the design specification, the tester cannot, in general, completely specify the expected results in test procedures. Thus, the testability of a requirement may not be fully known until long after requirements specifications have been baselined and rebaselined. However, as we illustrated in connection with several of the LOOKOUT requirements, questions raised by testers as early as the initial formulation of requirements serve to drive out testability issues. Because the tester is in constant pursuit of being able to write down what is to happen when the tester takes a certain action (i.e., what are the expected results of this action), this pursuit acts as a forcing function on the development process to highlight things the developers may not have considered as they mold design from requirements. Thus, determining requirements testability is an activity that, in many cases, continues through the acceptance testing process itself. For, even as test procedures are executed and system behavior is observed, the participants in the testing process may see things that they had not previously anticipated. Often, these new observations bring to the fore testability nuances. We illustrated in our discussion of the LOOKOUT requirements how some of these nuances can appear long before test procedure execution (e.g., what does "between" mean?)—how much the more so during and after test procedure execution?

3. Allied with the observations in item 2 is the issue of determining how much detail to incorporate into the requirements specification and what properly belongs in the design domain. This issue has no unique resolution. The simple response to this issue is the following:

   > Include enough detail to respond to questions that are raised. If you do not know the answers to some of the questions, include them as TBDs ("to-be-determined") in the requirements specification or document (e.g., in CCB minutes) that they are design issues.

   For example, as Figure 5–48 reminds us, LOOKOUT requirements *b* and *c* are not testable because no earth model is specified in the requirements specification. When discussing these requirements, we pointed out that it would be sufficient to cite a standard reference in which the earth model to be used was defined to make these requirements testable. There would be nothing wrong in pulling some of the material from that reference into the requirements specification—such as the earth model parameters (e.g., earth radius) and the associated mathematical formulas for calculating lengths and areas on the surface of that model. There would also be nothing wrong in putting the mathematical formulas into a design specification since, strictly speaking, these formulas specify the "how" of doing the "what" embodied in requirements *b* and *c*. Regarding requirements *a* and *e*, there is an issue regarding side lengths that we did not consider when we discussed the testability of these two requirements. This issue has to do with the case $LAT1 = LAT2$ and/or $LON1 = LON2$. The requirements specification is silent on these degenerate cases (i.e., when the rectangle collapses to a line or a point). Of course, the LOOKOUT user probably has no interest in these situations. But, in fact, these situations may arise in practice because, for example, the user may have inadvertently made a data entry error by setting the latitudes equal to one another and/or setting the longitudes equal to one another. Strictly speaking, such considerations impact on the testability of requirements *a* and *e*. These considerations fall into the domain of what is often referred to as "negative testing"—that is, testing how the system responds when a capability is misused. Often such considerations are put off until the design stage when the issue of error diagnostics is addressed. It is preferable, however, to address such issues earlier. In fact, as Figure 5–45 shows and as we mentioned, the LOOKOUT requirements specification does address *some* of these system misuse considerations.

Another requirements versus design specification testability issue regarding requirement *e* is that of data entry order. The requirements specification does not explicitly indicate whether the first vertex entered is the southwest corner or the northeast corner. The labeling in Figure 5–45 could be construed to imply that the southwest corner is to be entered first since it is called (*LAT1*, *LON1*); on the other hand, the wording in paragraph 3.e mentions the northeast vertex first. It could be argued that this information is a "how" and not a "what" so that it properly belongs in a design specification. Wherever it belongs, the tester needs this information to specify expected results—and to do negative testing (which, in this case, would be to enter the vertices in reverse order).

4. The discussion of the testability of requirements *b* and *c* brings to light a challenge that typically faces a tester. If a tester does not have specific expertise in an area to be tested, it may be necessary for the tester to do some detailed analysis of the implications of testing that area. Thus, in the case of requirements *b* and *c*, the tester, if not conversant with computations on the surface of a sphere, would need to dust off his or her mathematics books to locate formulas that would help him or her generate expected results. In general, a good tester need not be an expert on the technical details of what he or she is to test. The tester does, however, have to be able to invoke his or her analytical skills to seek answers to questions raised by the capabilities he or she is to test.

Complementing software product audits are software process audits, which are described in the next section.

Software Process Audits

The purpose of a software process audit is threefold:

- To ascertain the extent to which an organization is doing what it signed up to do.
- To identify those process activities that may need to be improved.
- To provide the customer and seller visibility into the software development process.

As we have discussed, many times the software development processes may be in the heads of a few of the organization's gurus. Although the gurus' processes may not be documented, the processes are used. Many times the products produced by the undocumented processes are well received by the customer. However, in this book, we have also discussed that one measure of successful software systems development is the ability to produce good products (i.e., products with integrity) with good processes (i.e., processes with integrity) *consistently*. It is hard, and some would say impossible, to achieve such consistency over the long term without documenting "the organization's way of doing business."

Additionally, we have discussed how successful software systems development is a delicate balance among (1) enabling people to grow professionally, (2) documenting processes embodying the experiences and knowledge of the people in the organization, (3) using know-how to apply such processes appropriately to a set of circumstances, and (4) refining processes based on the experience gained by applying the processes.

We take the approach that a systems engineering environment (SEE) houses, in part, the processes embodying the experiences and knowledge of people in the organization. To refresh your memory, the SEE consists of the following two complementary components:

- **Application Development Process Environment (ADPE).** The set of those policies, guidelines, procedures, and standards defining the *processes* for developing products (i.e., documents or computer code or databases). The ADPE is a framework for bringing about consistent product development.

- **Application Development Technology Environment (ADTE).** The *technology* as embodied in hardware and software development tools, and associated procedures for their use, required to develop products.

Software process audits use ADPE elements as part of the ground truth. A software process audit is the review of a process as it is being exercised, or after it has been exercised, to determine whether it conforms to standards defining processes. In this book, the "standards" are the ADPE elements defining an organization's way of doing the business of software systems development and the negotiated agreement. Figure 5–49 illustrates an overview of this audit process for a project's software systems development process.

Figure 5–49 shows the auditing process beginning at life cycle stage N (i.e., while the software development process is being followed), but a process audit could take place after all or part of the software development process has been exercised. An auditor conducts the process audit by comparing the software systems development process against the ground truth. Process audits can be conducted by seller management, the lead developer, an independent product assurance organization, or some combination of these entities.[20]

In our discussion of software product audits, ground truth includes (1) the approved requirements specification, (2) the approved life cycle stage N-1 product, and (3) standards (recall Figure 5–23). As we discussed, the software product ground truth can be used in product reviews and product audits. The same types of statements can be made with respect to software process audits. However, ground truth for software process audits includes (1) ADPE elements and (2) the negotiated agreement. As was the case with product reviews, you can combine various process reviews when you perform process audits. For example, process ground truth can be used for process comparison techniques that include process programmatic tracking, process technical oversight, process peer reviews, and process quality assurance at a product and project level. Combining these comparison techniques is an example of combining process reviews for software process audits.

As a result of process audits, discrepancies between the project's software systems development process and the ground truth may be uncovered. These discrepancies are documented in a process audit report, which is presented to the seller's software organization for its disposition. Depending upon the seller's organization, the audit report may be presented to the program manager who oversees several projects. Alternatively, the audit report may be presented to the head of the seller's software process engineering group. Certain audits may be called for by the seller's project manager or the customer's project manager. Also, audits may be conducted by an outside organization to determine whether your organization is conforming to your business practices. A potential customer may require such an outside audit before the customer decides to do business with the seller. Regardless, Figure 5–50 delineates a suggested format for a software process audit report.

The software process audit report is similar to the software product audit report. For example, the auditor's objective findings (i.e., Section 4) are presented separate from any of the auditor's subjective opinions (i.e., Sections 5 and 6). Also observe that, in addition to discrepancies uncovered by checking the conformance to the ADPE elements, various discrepancies may be described as a result of the prescriptive application[21] of the ADPE elements to the project's software systems development processes. For example, an ADPE element describing the organization's peer review process may recommend at least two peer reviews for each product. When the auditor checks how the project is implementing this guidance, the auditor observes that the project is conducting at least four reviews per product. The project believes that the increased number of peer reviews helps to identify potential problems early. In this case, a corresponding recommendation may be that the organization's peer review guidance be changed to increase the number of peer reviews per product.

---

[20]Chapter 8 discusses how the seller deliverable tracking form introduced in Chapter 3 can be coupled to the measurement approach described in Chapter 6 to gain insight into how a project is following the organization's software systems development process at the project level.

[21]Remember, in Chapter 1 and elsewhere, we described "prescriptive application" as the practical application of software systems engineering principles. By *practical,* we mean "application of techniques consistent with available time and resources." We do not believe that software systems development is a cookie-cutter exercise (i.e., reduced to a simple set of step-by-step instructions). Skills in applying management, development, and product assurance techniques are key ingredients to achieving software systems development success.

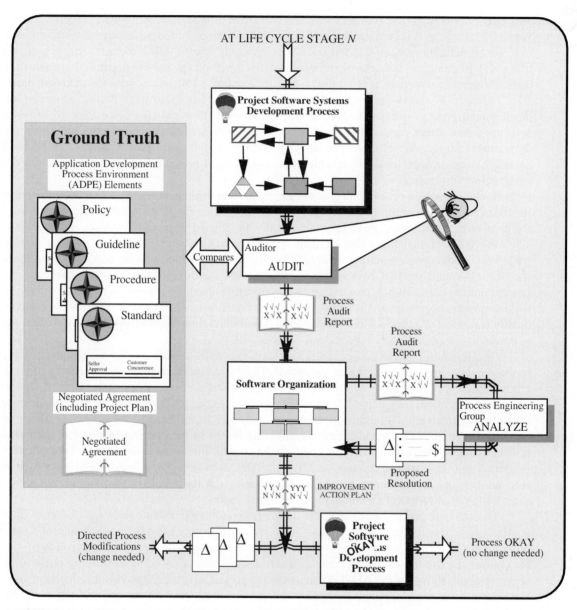

FIGURE 5–49 This figure shows an overview of the auditing process for software systems development processes.

Other findings can be the result of the following comparisons:

■ **Qualitative comparison.** Qualitative process audits combine process programmatic tracking, process technical oversight, process peer reviews, and process quality assurance at a product and project levels. Qualitative process audits can use checklists to record that a given process activity is or is not being performed.

■ **Quantitative comparison.** Quantitative process audits involve defining, collecting, using, and communicating software systems development process measurement. Quantitative process audits can use metrics to calculate the extent to which each process activity is being performed.[22]

---
[22]Chapter 6 deals with quantitative techniques in detail.

Section 1. Introduction

1.1 **Purpose**. State the purpose of the audit report, which is to provide the results of an audit of a particular software systems development process for a particular project.

1.2 **Identification**. Identify the software systems development process that was audited, the date the software process audit was completed, and the auditors' names.

1.3 **Project references**. Provide a brief summary of the references applicable to the history and development of the project under which the audit was conducted.

1.4 **Overview**. Provide a brief overview of the report contents.

Section 2. References

List all the references applicable to the report (e.g., the improvement action plan).

Section 3. Procedure

Describe the procedure used to conduct the audit. Reference the specific documents or entities used in the process. List any assumptions made or any constraints imposed relative to the audit.

Section 4. Findings

Present the **objective** findings uncovered during the audit organized as shown below.

4.1 **Conformance to Application Development Process Environment (ADPE) elements**. Report the findings of the programmatic tracking, technical oversight, peer review and/or quality assurance checks in terms of structure, format, content, or methodology.

4.2 **Prescriptive application**. Describe the prescriptive application of the ADPE element(s) to the project's software systems development process(es). Detail disconnects between the elements and the software process.

4.3 **Results of qualitative comparison**. Present the discrepancies observed as a result of comparing the software systems development process against a simple checklist of process activities.

4.4 **Results of quantitative comparison**. Present the discrepancies observed as a result of comparing the software systems development process against the process activity value scales.

4.5 **Bookkeeping**. List the software systems development process changes that were incorporated as a result of an update to the software systems development process. Also list the approved changes (i.e., the as detailed in the improvement action plan) incorporated into the software systems development process(es).

Section 5. Conclusions

Present the conclusions formulated by the auditors based upon the audit findings. It should be noted that the conclusions represent the auditors' judgment and are thus primarily subjective, as contrasted to the objective findings given in Section 4.

Section 6. Recommendations

Provide the auditors' recommendations as a result of conducting the audit. This section represents the auditors' judgment and is thus primarily subjective.

FIGURE 5–50 Here is a suggested format for a software process audit report.

As illustrated in Figure 5–51, both qualitative and quantitative comparisons use the ADPE as the ground truth. Qualitative and quantitative process audit comparisons may be used to determine whether an organization is following its business practices in developing its products. In addition, process audits may be used to provide insight into which business practices need to be added, removed, and/or improved.

To clarify the foregoing concepts, consider the following simple example. First, let's take a quick look at a qualitative comparison involving an organization's software systems development process. Assume the software systems development process to be audited is the process that we discussed in Chapter 3. Recall that a form is used to track a software product working its way through the software systems development process activities. An auditor can use this form as a simple checklist to compare qualitatively the project's use of the organizational software systems development process. The auditor checks a series of these tracking forms and records the qualitative observations on the example summary form shown in Figure 5–52.

The auditor assigns a control number when the software organization (e.g., program manager, head of seller's software process engineering group, seller project manager, customer project manager) directs that an audit is to be conducted. The auditor fills in the auditor's name, organization, project being audited, and the auditor's telephone number. Then, as the auditor reviews each of the deliverable tracking forms, the auditor records the observations in the appropriate column on the qualitative software process audit form, which becomes an attachment to the process audit report.

For example, assume that the auditor checks ten tracking forms and observes that no peer reviews have taken place. This observation would be noted in the software process audit, and a possible recommendation may be to start conducting peer reviews. The auditor should also check the negotiated agreement to see whether peer reviews were specifically excluded from this project, and adjust from the observations as appropriate. Such situations might arise when a customer requests a waiver from the seller's business practices. In this case, the seller should inform the customer of the attendant risks associated with such a waiver.

To gain more insight regarding the extent to which each organizational process activity is being performed by the project, a quantitative comparison is needed. As just stated, quantitative comparison involves the use of metrics. The subject of metrics is presented in detail in Chapter 6. To introduce the concept of quantitative comparison, we briefly present the following possible quantitative outcomes:

- If the process audit shows that the process is being followed but that the resultant products consistently lack integrity (e.g., are delivered late, do not do what they are supposed to do), then the process should probably be altered.

- If the process audit shows that the process is not being followed but that the organization is consistently producing products with integrity, then the practices that *are* being used need to be folded into the organization's process.

- If the process audit shows that the process is not being followed and that the resultant products consistently lack integrity, then steps should be taken to get the organization to follow the process consistently.

- If the process audit shows that the process is being followed and that the resultant products have integrity, then the organization has a "good" process that, at most, may need fine-tuning.

The details of the quantitative process audits will become more apparent after you read Chapter 6. For the time being, we will simply state that process measurement is a part of continual software systems development process improvement. The software process audit helps to identify needed process improvement areas.

Upon reviewing the software process audit report, the software organization processes the discrepancies uncovered. Approaches in which the software organization can process the discrepancies include the following:

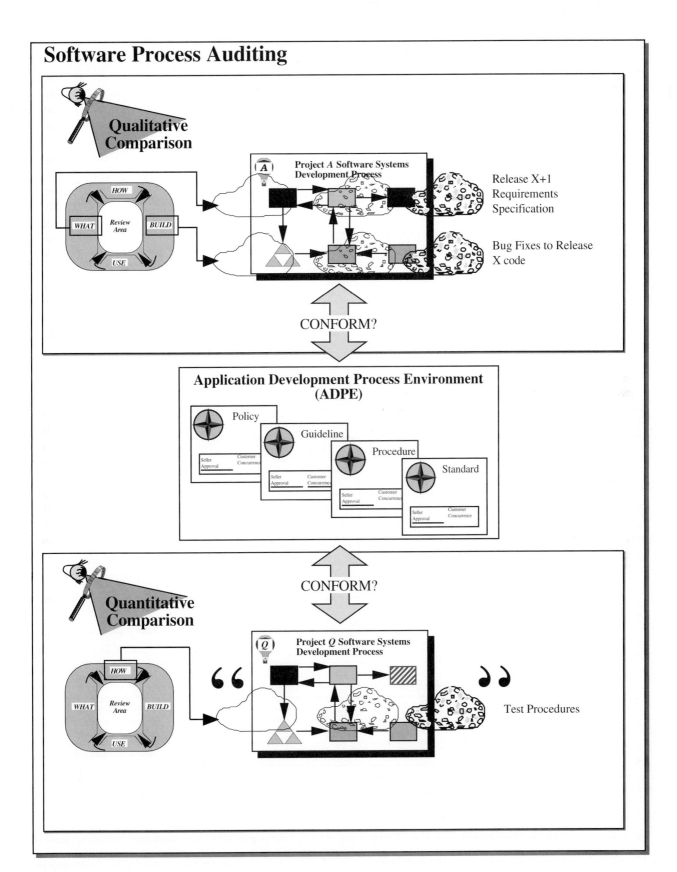

FIGURE 5–51 Software process auditing establishes the extent to which project processes are congruent with organizational processes documented in the ADPE.

QUALITATIVE OBSERVATIONS
OF
SELLER DELIVERABLE TRACKING FORMS

Control Number: _____-_____

Date: __/__/____

Auditor:_____   Organization:_____   Project:_____   Tel. No. :_____

Product Control Number (PCN)	Product Type: -Document -Code -Database	Peer Review Held?	Product Assurance Review?	Techncial Edit?	Project-level Technical Oversight?	Final Coordination with DSC?	Product Filed?	Product Reviewed and Approved?	Customer Receipt Received?	Customer Acceptance Received?	Notification of Additional Work Received?
1.											
2.											
3.											
4.											
5.											
6.											
7.											
8.											
9.											
10.											

COMMENTS/ISSUES

[Form Number]   [Form Issue Date]   ☐ Continuation Page

FIGURE 5–52   Here is an example qualitative software process audit form that can be used with our organizational software systems development process.

- Assign the entire process audit report to the process engineering group for analysis, that will result in a report providing recommended resolutions for every discrepancy.

- Categorize discrepancies into those whose resolution is apparent and those whose resolution is not apparent. Apparent discrepancies are resolved immediately. The remaining discrepancies are assigned to the process engineering group for analysis that results with a report detailing recommended resolutions for every discrepancy.

- Treat each discrepancy as a suggestion for improving the organizational processes, and process each suggestion in accordance with the organizational continuous improvement process that is a part of the ADPE.

These three approaches provide the software organization with visibility into potential process improvement areas. When the software organization decides on which approach or combination of approaches to use, an improvement action plan is prepared by the appropriate organizational entities. Either process change is needed or no process change is needed. If changes are needed, the modifications are made in accordance with the organizational continuous improvement process. Whether change is needed or not, getting the people in the organization to follow the processes may also be needed.

5.5 PRODUCT AND PROCESS REVIEWS SUMMARY

Product and process reviews help to uncover discrepancies in software products and software systems development processes, respectively. Before the CCB can approve changes to attain and maintain software products with integrity, the CCB must know the state of software products as they evolve, as they are being built, and after they are delivered. Likewise, before the software organization (e.g., program manager, head of seller's software process engineering group, seller project manager, customer project manager) can approve changes to attain and maintain software processes with integrity, the organization must first know whether the processes are being used and to what extent the processes are being used. This knowledge is acquired through product and process audits that uncover discrepancies.

To help you define (or refine) your organization's software engineering environment, we offer annotated outlines for independent product assurance, peer reviews, and acceptance testing. First, let us highlight product assurance. As illustrated in Figure 5–53, you can use the following annotated outline of an ADPE policy as a starting point for defining your organization's independent product assurance program. This outline consists of the following sections:

- **Purpose.** This section states the purpose of the element. The purpose sets the context, defines the product assurance (PA) processes (i.e., QA, V&V, T&E, and CM), and delineates the implementation responsibilities for the policy. These responsibilities are key because they are shared by the entire organization, not just some independent "quality" organization that is not involved with the day-to-day development activities and customer interactions. *This element should stress that independent PA reduces risk; it is not risk elimination.*

- **Background.** This section provides an overview of your organization, business, customers, and types of contractual vehicles that you use to conduct business. Your organization's PA concept can be presented, along with the types of products and processes that the PA organization is to review.

- **Policy and Implementation Guidance.** This section presents specific PA policy elements and guidance for carrying them out. This section can include the following:
  - PA organization
  - PA processes
  - PA and project planning
  - Project PA plans
  - PA resource management

[Your Organization's Name] Policy
Independent Product Assurance

1.0 PURPOSE

This section states the purpose of the element. This purpose is the following:

- Define your organization's statement of principles governing independent product assurance activities
- Define product assurance processes and explain how they reduce software systems development risks
- Delineate the policy implementation responsibilities of organizational elements and/or individuals and, if desired, your customer(s).

This element should stress that independent product assurance, in general and reviews, in particular, provide insight (i.e., visibility) into the (technical) state of a product so that customer and seller management can make informed decisions regarding what to do next to evolve a product. By doing so, product development risk is reduced because less rework is required to produce a product that complies with customer requirements, thereby adding value to product development.

2.0 BACKGROUND

This section gives an overview of your organization, your business, your customers, and the types of contractual vehicles you use to conduct business (e.g., fixed price, memorandum of understanding, time and materials). It should explain in general terms your organization's product assurance concept. It should also explain the classes of products your organization develops (e.g., documents, computer code, databases) that product assurance will focus on.

3.0 POLICY AND IMPLEMENTATION GUIDANCE

This section presents the specific elements of your product assurance policy and guidance for carrying them out. Example elements include the following:

- **Product Assurance Organization**—indicate whether PA support is to be (1) centralized within a single organization or (2) part of each project team or (3) some other arrangement; indicate who is in charge of product assurance and the management reporting chain for that individual (i.e., indicate what "independent" means in your organization).
- **Product Assurance Processes**—indicate the processes that PA is to perform in your organization (e.g., QA, V&V, T&E, and CM defined elsewhere in this book); indicate whether PA processes extend to the software systems development process (e.g., process QA as defined elsewhere in this book).
- **Product Assurance and Project Planning**—indicate the (quantitative) relationship between PA and risk reduction in allocating project resources in the project plan; indicate whether PA support is required for each project and, if not, indicate the PA exemption criteria (e.g., the customer has a product assurance organization or contractor).
- **Project Product Assurance Plan**—indicate your organization's requirement for a project product assurance plan (e.g., the first project deliverable, an appendix to the project plan, informal agreement between the PA manager and project manager).
- **Product Assurance Resource Management**—indicate who is responsible for managing project PA resources (e.g., project manager, someone other than the project manager); this policy element is for some organizations a dimension of what "independence" means.
- **Product Assurance Reporting**—indicate PA reporting requirements (e.g., in objective terms only regarding discrepancies between a product and the ground truth for that product, or in subjective terms not necessarily related to the ground truth, or in some combination); indicate whether PA reports have the organizational clout to prevent a product from being released to the customer.

Figure 5–53 An annotated outline for getting you started defining an independent product assurance policy for your organization.

[Your Organization's Name] Policy
Independent Product Assurance

3.0   POLICY AND IMPLEMENTATION GUIDANCE *(continued)*

- **Product Assurance Membership in Change Control Boards (CCB)**—indicate whether or not PA members are to be assigned permanently to each project CCB and what "assignment to a project CCB" means in terms of things such as attending CCB meetings, receiving copies of CCB minutes, raising product-related issues at CCB meetings (e.g., requirements testability).
- **Product Assurance Acceptance Testing**—indicate who is responsible for conducting the testing that your organization uses to determine that a software system and supporting databases can be released to the customer (in this book, this activity is called "acceptance testing"); indicate the role the CCB plays, if any, in the acceptance testing process (e.g., Turnover CCB and Test Incident CCB as discussed in this book); indicate the relationship, if any, between assessed project risk and the acceptance testing process (e.g., CCBs are mandatory for high-risk projects); indicate who is responsible for determining whether requirements are testable (e.g., product developers, product assurance staff).
- **Product Assurance Audits**—indicate the way in which product and process audits will be integrated with the software systems development process (e.g., audits will be made a matter of record in project CCB minutes, the manager of project managers will authorize periodic reviews of project files to give visibility to the extent of project conformance to the organization's software systems development process).
- **Product Assurance Procedures**—indicate the means by which the organization responsible for product assurance will document its methods for carrying out the policy (e.g., procedure documenting how to perform a document audit).
- **Incident Report Resolution**—indicate the means to be used when management and the product assurance organization cannot resolve a PA incident report.
- **Applicability and Authorized Deviations**—indicate the scope of applicability of the policy (e.g., all projects in your organization); indicate the means for obtaining authorization to deviate from the policy.

4.0   PRODUCT ASSURANCE POLICY IMPLEMENTATION RESPONSIBILITIES

This section delineates the responsibilities of each agent within your organization (e.g., project manager, manager of project managers, manager of the process engineering group, product assurance manager, product assurance analysts) for implementing the policy elements set forth in Section 3. With customer approval, it may also be desirable to delineate the responsibilities of customer agents (e.g., customer project manager) for policy implementation.

APPENDICES

Appendices can contain such things as (1) a discussion of the various checks and balances that are part of your organization's software systems development process in addition to independent product assurance (e.g., the reviews discussed in this chapter—peer reviews, technical editing, and project-level technical oversight), (2) an elaboration of the organization's product assurance processes defined in the body of the policy (e.g., definition of acceptance testing documentation, explanation of what V&V of a database means), and (3) project planning steps for estimating management, development, and product assurance resources based on risk assessment.

Figure 5–53   *Continued*

- PA reporting
- PA membership in CCBs
- PA acceptance testing
- PA audits
- PA procedures
- Incident report resolution
- Applicability and authorized deviations.

- **Product Assurance Policy Implementation Responsibilities.** This section delineates the individual responsibilities within your organization for implementing the PA policy elements. For example, the seller project manager's responsibilities might include the following:

  - Disseminate project product assurance policy to all project members within the scope of the project manager's responsibility.

  - Provide required direction and guidance to the seller development team to support implementation of internal and external product assurance functions.

  - Interact directly with designated product assurance personnel throughout the development effort as defined by the project plan and ADPE policies, guidelines, procedures, and standards.

- **Appendices.** Appendices can contain examples of the various types of product and process reviews that are part of your organization's software systems development process. More detailed explanation can be provided for the product assurance processes and the way that they influence your project planning process.

The second annotated outline deals with peer reviews and is shown in Figure 5–54. This outline consists of the following sections:

- **Purpose.** This section states the purpose of the guideline. You can highlight your organization's peer review approach that may include a delineation of implementation responsibilities, possible checklists, and corresponding instructions. This element should stress that peer reviews (1) provide a controlled mechanism for refining products and processes, (2) provide technical feedback to the lead developer or software organization, and (3) are not a measure of the lead developer's performance.

- **Background.** This section provides an overview of your organization, business, customers, and types of contractual vehicles that you use to conduct business. Your organization's peer review concept can be presented and should include, as a minimum, informal and formal (scheduled) reviews.

- **Peer Review Guidance.** This section presents guidance for preparing for and conducting the organization's peer reviews. Topics to be discussed include peer review roles, preparation guidance, kinds of reviews, duration of the reviews, checklists, and forms.

- **Appendices.** Appendices can contain examples of various types of sample review forms and checklists. Example checklists include peer review readiness, requirements review, and design review. Example forms include peer review invitation and peer review comments.

The third annotated outline deals with acceptance testing and is shown in Figure 5–55. This outline consists of the following sections:

- **Purpose.** This section states the purpose of the procedure. This element should stress that acceptance testing formally demonstrates that customer and seller agreed-upon capabilities are embodied in the to-be-delivered software code and supporting databases.

- **Background.** As with other ADPE elements, this section provides an overview of your organization, business, customers, and types of contractual vehicles that you use to conduct business. This section introduces your organization's acceptance testing concept and the test documentation to be used.

- **Acceptance Testing Steps and Associated Organizational Responsibilities.** This section presents specific elements of your acceptance testing steps and guidance for performing the steps. The acceptance testing process, steps, and organizational responsibilities should be presented.

[Your Organization's Name] Guideline
Peer Reviews

1.0   PURPOSE

This section states the purpose of the element. This purpose is the following:

- Define your organization's approach [and, possibly, procedures] for preparing for and conducting product reviews primarily involving product developer and product assurance peers
- Delineate responsibilities for preparing for and conducting peer reviews
- Provide checklists and forms to facilitate and standardize peer review preparation and accomplishment
- Provide instructions for completing checklists and forms provided.

This element should stress that peer reviews (1) provide a *controlled* mechanism for refining products, (2) provide *technical* feedback to the lead developer, and (3) are *not* a measure of the lead developer's performance. In the literal sense, in a peer review, a colleague or colleagues check a product for technical completeness and appropriateness. This review balances the product developer's approach with the insights of others having applicable and comparable experience. These insights serve to stabilize the developer's approach, thereby increasing confidence that the product does what it is supposed to do. This element should also establish organizational policy regarding management participation in peer reviews. The trade-off here is the need for management visibility into product development progress versus the need for uninhibited technical exchange among peers.

2.0   BACKGROUND

This section gives an overview of your organization, your business, your customers, and the types of contractual vehicles you use to conduct business (e.g., fixed price, memorandum of understanding, time and materials). It should explain in general terms your organization's need for peer reviews (e.g., to reduce product rework thereby increasing product integrity) and the types of peer reviews that the organization will use to meet this need. At a minimum, the following two types should be called out:

- **Informal One-on-One**—generally involve two product developers, do not require a scheduling or meeting protocol, but must be recorded and made part of project records.
- **Formal (Scheduled)**—generally involve multiple product developers, possible participation by experts from outside the organization and/or from other projects, product assurance staff, and possible participation by technical managers and/or the project manager and/or other managers; are scheduled so that invited participants can prepare and attend.

Sometimes, peer reviews are further categorized by format—meeting or walkthrough. The purpose of a peer review meeting may be to address such things as (1) internal progress with respect to one or more products, (2) requirements issues, and (3) resolution of schedule problems. The purpose of the walk-through is to go through a product or part of a product in a structured manner to identify insufficiencies in things required for completion (*not* to correct the insufficiencies). Insufficiencies are of two major kinds—(1) those that, if not corrected, would prevent the item under review from conforming to its ground truth and (2) those of an engineering aesthetic nature (e.g., an elegant computational approach versus a brute force approach, a typographical error, a symmetric placement of buttons on a screen).

3.0   PEER REVIEW GUIDANCE

This section presents guidance for preparing for and conducting (1) informal one-on-one peer reviews, (2) formal (scheduled) peer reviews, and (3) other types of peer reviews that your organization may need. Topics to be addressed should include (1) peer review roles, (2) preparation guidance (e.g., package to distribute to reviewers, review time estimates), (3) guidance on project factors governing the types and kinds of peer reviews applicable (e.g., project size, risk, consequences of software failure), (4) guidance on conducting peer reviews (e.g., duration, order of peer review activities, checklists and forms, review follow-up activities). The peer review roles listed below, which have been more or less institutionalized within the software industry, should be addressed. Also shown are some typical associated responsibilities.

FIGURE 5–54   An annotated outline for getting you started defining a guideline explaining how to prepare for and conduct peer reviews as part of your organization's software systems development process.

[Your Organization's Name] Guideline
Peer Reviews

3.0   PEER REVIEW GUIDANCE *(continued)*

- **Moderator**
  - Conducts peer review
  - Steps through material calling for comments
  - Maintains order and professional atmosphere
  - Keeps review focused on stated objectives (in particular, preventing discussion of how to correct identified insufficiencies)
  - Documents review results (e.g., using a form)

- **Recorder**
  - Records (all) comments (e.g., using a form)
  - Records all insufficiencies uncovered during the review (e.g., using a form)
  - Finalizes recorded comments and insufficiencies following review completion
  - Delivers finalized recorded comments and insufficiencies to previously designated individuals

- **Product Developer**
  - Enlists reviewers
  - Prepares and distributes review packages
  - Schedules review in coordination with management and resolves scheduling conflicts
  - Listens *nondefensively* and assimilates comments
  - Implements appropriate changes in the item under review

- **Reviewer(s)**
  - Reviews materials thoroughly
  - Evaluates technical content
  - Marks up review materials with complete, legible comments
  - Completes review checklist (if applicable)
  - Provides comments, raises questions, and identifies insufficiencies in a *professional*, *nonoffensive* manner

- **Independent Product Assurance**
  - Checks that review preparation and conduct process is followed
  - Tracks all review action items to closure

APPENDICES

Appendices can contain such things as (1) sample review forms and checklists, (2) instructions for completing forms and checklists, (3) detailed procedures for conducting reviews to supplement the Section 3 guidance. Examples of types of forms and checklists that might be included are the following:

- Peer Review Invitation Form
- Peer Review Comments Form
- Peer Review Readiness Checklists
- Requirements Review Checklist
- Design Review Checklist
- Database Design Checklist
- Computer Code Walkthrough Checklist
- Test Plan Review Checklist
- Test Procedure Review Checklist
- Document Outline Review Checklist
- Document Review Checklist

FIGURE 5–54   *Continued*

[Your Organization's Name] Procedure
Acceptance Testing Cycle

1.0 PURPOSE

This section states the purpose of the element. This purpose is the following:

- Define your organization's statement of principles governing acceptance testing activities
- Define the steps in the acceptance testing processes
- Delineate the procedure implementation responsibilities of organizational elements and/or individuals and, if desired, your customer(s).

This element should stress that acceptance testing formally demonstrates that customer and seller agreed-upon capabilities are embodied in the to-be-delivered software code and supporting databases.

2.0 BACKGROUND

This section gives an overview of your organization, your business, your customers, and the types of contractual vehicles you use to conduct business. It should explain in general terms the organization's acceptance testing concept. It should also explain the names, types, and hierarchy of test documentation to be used. You may use the following three-tiered hierarchy:

- **Test Plan**—specifies the test organization, test schedule, allocation of resources, the assignment of responsibilities, and the set of tests to be executed.
- **Test Procedure**—produced from the test plan by translating each test called out in the plan into a sequence of instructions to a tester.
- **Test Incident Report (TIR)**—is used during the acceptance testing process described in the procedure to track discrepancies between what was expected, as recorded in a test procedure, and what was observed during test procedure execution.

3.0 ACCEPTANCE TESTING STEPS AND ASSOCIATED ORGANIZATIONAL RESPONSIBILITIES

This section presents the specific elements of your acceptance testing steps and guidance for carrying them out. Example elements include the following:

- **Acceptance Testing Process Overview**—presents the overall purpose of the steps in the acceptance testing cycle.
- **Acceptance Testing Steps**—describe the detailed steps in the acceptance testing process. Detailed steps include the following:
  1. Development team prepares computer code and/or databases to be tested.
  2. CM organization assists development team with the status accounting of development baseline.
  3. Development team conducts software/database turnover CCB.
  4. CM organization builds turned over code and/or databases into test baseline.
  5. Test organization exercises test baseline using previously approved test procedures.
  6. Test organization submits TIRs to test incident CCB for resolution.
  7. Development team corrects TIRs by changing source code, databases, design, etc.
- **Organizational Responsibilities**—This section delineates the responsibilities of each agent within your organization for implementing the acceptance testing steps. With customer approval, it may also be desirable to delineate the responsibilities of customer agents for procedure implementation.

4.0 TEST PROCEDURE FORMATTING INSTRUCTIONS

This section explains how to format test procedures. Each test step should include tester actions, purpose of step, expected results, and comments.

5.0 TEST INCIDENT REPORT (TIR) INSTRUCTIONS

This section provides instructions for filling out the TIR. These instructions are linked to the acceptance testing cycle steps and organizational responsibilities.

APPENDICES

Appendices can contain such things as examples of test procedures, test incident reports, turnover CCB minutes, and TIR CCB minutes.

FIGURE 5–55 An annotated outline for getting you started defining an acceptance testing cycle procedure for your organization.

- **Test Procedure Formatting Instructions.** This section explains how to format test procedures. We recommend that your organization adopt the five-column format that includes test step number, tester actions, test step purpose, expected results, and comments.

- **Test Incident Reporting (TIR) Instructions.** This section provides instructions for filling out a TIR.

- **Appendices.** Appendices should be added as necessary. For instance, appendices can contain examples of test procedures and test incident reports.

We have completed our discussion of software product reviews and software systems development process reviews. The next chapter deals with measurement, and it details how you can set up metrics for products and processes. The chapter provides you with guidance for measuring the "goodness" of products and the "goodness" of the processes that produced the products. The focus of the chapter is on how to use measurement to achieve *consistent* product and process "goodness."

chapter
6

Measurement

There is no such thing as absolute value in this world. You can only estimate what a thing is worth to you.

—Charles Dudley Warner, "Sixteenth Week," *My Summer in a Garden* (1871).

6.1 INTRODUCTION

Measurement for measurement's sake is a waste of time and money. As illustrated in Figure 6–1, some people view measurement as a meaningless exercise.

We present measurement techniques that enable you to measure software products and software systems development processes in everyday terms familiar—and therefore meaningful—to your organization.[1] We believe that understanding how to define, collect, use, and communicate measurement is a significant contributor to successful software projects. Furthermore, we believe that successful software systems development is a continual improvement exercise. Measurement is a means for effecting this improvement.

Figure 6–2 illustrates this chapter's focus on two concepts to improve the understanding of measuring software development. These two concepts are product integrity and process integrity. Product integrity can be defined in terms of product attributes and attribute value scales. For each of the product attributes, an attribute value scale is defined in everyday terms familiar to your organization. Similarly, process integrity can be defined in terms of process components, component activities, and activity value scales. The revolving arrows represent the interaction between product and process measurements. Understanding such interactions helps refine your measurement activities. As ex-

---

[1]The product/process integrity measurement approach presented is actually a general approach to quantifying almost any object. We call this approach "object measurement," or **OM**[SM]. **OM**[SM] is a service mark owned by Scott E. Donaldson and Stanley G. Siegel.

"Can you settle a bet, Wellman? Herb says 53% of all statistics are meaningless and I say it's 56%."

© Leo Cullum 1996.

"It's my fervent hope, Fernbaugh, that these are meaningless statistics."

© Leo Cullum 1996.

FIGURE 6–1   Measurements need to be expressed in everyday terms that are familiar to the organization; otherwise, they may be of little value.

plained in this chapter, measuring product integrity and process integrity enables you to measure the "goodness" of the products and the "goodness" of the software systems development process used to develop the products.

In this section, we set context for the subject of software process and product measurement. We first discuss whether software process improvement may even be applicable to your organization. We then briefly review some measurement fundamentals.

The primary purpose of measurement is to bring about product and process improvement so that your customers are satisfied with your products. This purpose assumes that the product and process are worth improving. When an organization seeks to achieve orders of magnitude improvement, Business Process Reengineering (BPR)[2] technology is often considered. Typically, a business seeks to restructure its processes when it is losing money, or worse, threatened with going out of business.

As illustrated in Figure 6–3, in many businesses, the software systems development process is part of a much larger business process. It is often not clear whether the overarching business process may prevent meaningful software systems development process improvement. If such is the case, then no amount of tinkering with the software systems development process will be useful until the larger business process is first improved—or, in the extreme, reengineered.

The catch-22, then, is the following:

> How do you know whether the software systems development process needs to be improved if you don't know whether the larger business process is the real impediment to software systems development success in your business?

At the risk of oversimplification, this question translates into the following process improvement/ reengineering analogy:

> A process that uses a hammer to drive screws cannot generally be improved by redesigning the hammer; the process needs to be reengineered by replacing the hammer with a screwdriver.

Certain techniques grounded in common sense should bring about software process improvement. If it turns out that applying these techniques does not bring improvement, then the problems lie elsewhere in the business. In such instances, BPR may need to be invoked in a context far larger than your software systems development process. Thus, if by applying the techniques we present in this chapter you do not realize process improvement, you may need to look upward within your business to get at the real

---

[2]For a detailed discussion of BPR, see M. Hammer and J. Champy, *Reengineering the Corporation* (New York: HarperBusiness, 1993).

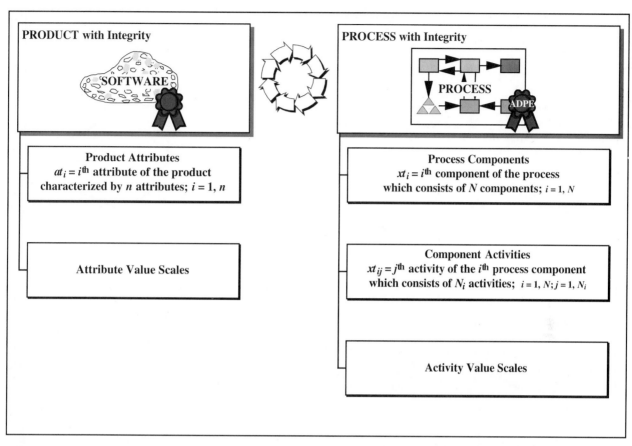

FIGURE 6–2 This figure shows our conceptual framework for product and process measurement. Product measurement involves identifying product attributes (at_i) and corresponding value scales of interest to the organization. Process measurement involves an additional layer of decomposition. Processes are decomposed into components (xt_i) and component activities (xt_{ij}). Value scales are defined for each activity in terms that are meaningful to the organization.

source of the problem standing in the way of successfully producing software systems. For example, your software systems development process may indeed be completing the development of software systems on time and within budget. However, these systems may not get into the hands of the customers until much later because of convoluted business processes associated with miles of paper pushing. Clearly, in such circumstances, no amount of tinkering with the software systems development process is going to solve the overarching business process problem of on-time delivery of the systems to the customers.

One additional observation is in order here regarding BPR versus software development process improvement. Improvement begins with a definition of the software systems development process. This definition provides the overall context for more detailed processes. From the BPR perspective, if a business has no defined and documented software systems development process, then the definition of such a process and its implementation constitute a form of BPR. Putting the software systems development process in place is the first step in bringing order to a presumably ad hoc or chaotic situation. Once some order has been established, it then makes sense to begin thinking about improving what has been put in place.

This chapter deals with the concept of measurement as it applies to software products and the process used to develop these products. Frequently, when the software engineering literature addresses measurement, it uses the term "metric." IEEE Standard 610.12-1990 defines *metric* as follows:

A quantitative measure of the degree to which a system, component, or process possesses a given attribute.

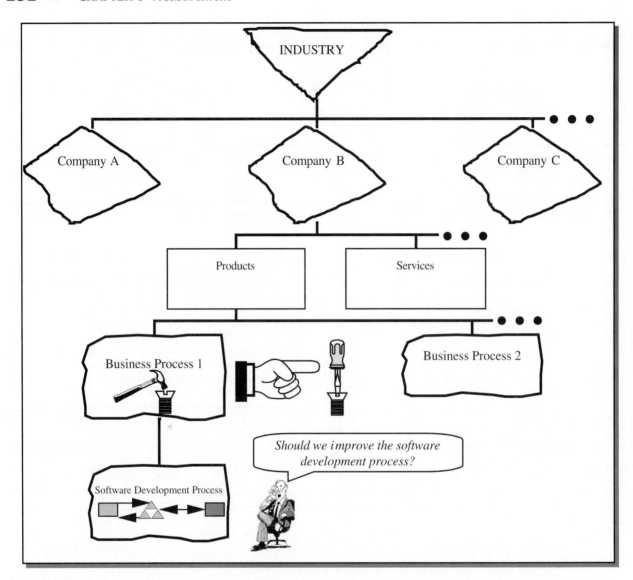

FIGURE 6–3   Software systems development process improvement is tied to the state of your overall business process.

In truth, the term "metric" is used in various ways. For example, Baumert and McWhinney, in the Software Engineering Institute Technical Report CMU/SEI-92-TR-25, "Software Measures and the Capability Maturity Model" (September 1992), offer the following definitions for the related terms "measure," "measurement," and "metric" (p. B-2):

> **Measure** *n.*—A standard or unit of measurement; the extent, dimensions, capacity, etc. of anything, especially as determined by a standard; an act or process of measuring; a result of measurement. *v.* To ascertain the quantity, mass, extent, or degree of something in terms of a standard unit or fixed amount, usually by means of an instrument or process; to compute the size of something from dimensional measurements; to estimate the extent, strength, worth, or character of something; to take measurements.

> **Measurement**— The act or process of measuring something. Also a result, such as a figure expressing the extent or value that is obtained by measuring.

> **Metric**—In this document, metric is used as a synonym for measure.

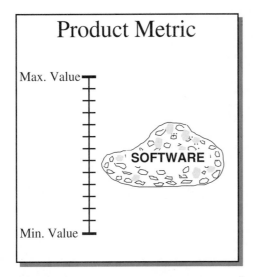

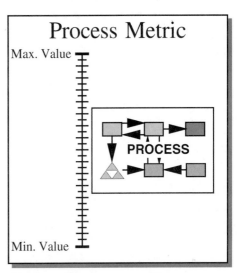

FIGURE 6–4   The term "metric" is used in a variety of ways in the software engineering literature. We use *metric* to mean "(1) a standard or unit of measurement, or formula used to quantify something and/or (2) the values that the standard or formula may assume."

To improve a software product or a process that produces the product, measurement is needed. Figure 6–4 presents our concept of product and process metrics. As stated in the figure caption, we use *metric* to mean "(1) a standard or unit of measurement, or formula used to quantify something, and/or (2) the values that the standard or formula may assume." For example, in the nonsoftware world, "foot" is a standard of measurement used to quantify the length of something. The formula "area = length × width" is used to quantify the region that a rectangle of a specified length and width occupies. The number calculated when an actual length and width are substituted into the formula is also a metric.

Also note that the value scales are generally different for product and process, but both scales range from a minimum value to a maximum value. In this chapter, we look at the analogues to length, width, and area for software development processes and resultant products. The challenge is to establish units of measurements (or, equivalently, value scales) and a relatively painless way to make measurements based on these value scales. In addition, your measurements need to have benchmarks. As shown in Figure 6–5, everyday measurements, such as a person's weight, the time to run a certain distance, and the number of calories a person needs to consume daily, have meaning only when they can be related to certain standards, or benchmarks, for those measurements.

For example, running a mile in less than four minutes is considered to be "fast" even for the most highly trained runners. The 4-minute-mile benchmark has been established through many measurements made over many years during athletic events. This cumulative measurement experience gives meaning to the number "4-minute-mile" for people who are familiar with track and field events. Likewise, if process and product measurements are to be meaningful, benchmarks need to be established. Here, *meaningful measurements* means "the measurements can be used to determine whether and where the product or process needs to be improved." For example, to determine that a project's development process is "good," it is necessary to determine (1) whether "good" products are being produced and (2) whether the project's process "conforms" to the organization's development process, as defined in the organization's application development process environment (ADPE).

As we explain in this chapter, if a project is not conforming to the organization's process but is producing "good" products, then the organization may need to (1) reconsider the development process definition, (2) work with the project to conform to the defined, organizational process so that consistent practices across projects can be achieved, or (3) reconsider the organizational questions being an-

FIGURE 6–5 To be meaningful, measurements must have benchmarks. Benchmarks need to be established for software products and software development process measurements, and the relationship between the product and process measurements.

swered by the metrics. Figure 6–6 illustrates the point that measurement is tied directly to questions that are important to the organization.

Customers want products that do what they are suppose to do. Customers also want to have the products delivered on time and within budget. As shown in Figure 6–6, software systems development measurement should address fundamental questions such as the following:

- Am I producing "good" products? The name of the game is to produce "good" products that satisfy the customer. Whether or not you are in business to make a profit, your customer needs to be satisfied with your products. The measurement challenge is to determine what a "good" product means. Consequently, as shown in the upper panel of the figure, the "goodness" values are established from the customer's viewpoint.

- Is my process consistently producing "good" products within budget? Whether or not you are in business to make a profit, your process needs consistently to produce "good" products. If you are in a profit-making situation, then your process should enable you to make your profit. If you are not in a profit-making situa-

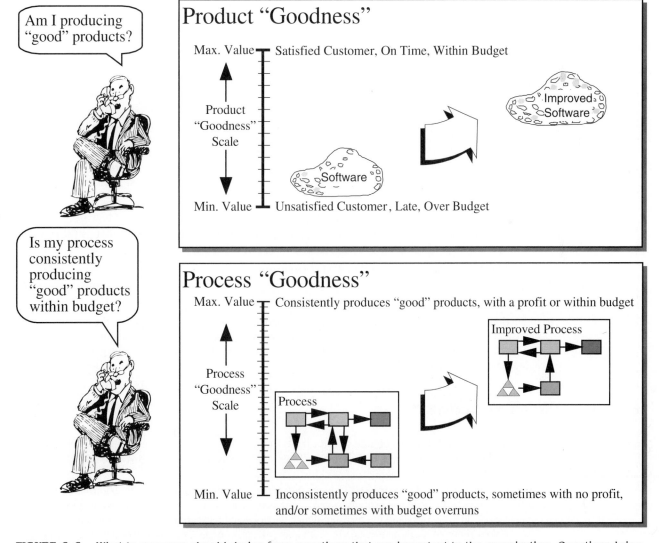

FIGURE 6–6   What to measure should derive from questions that are important to the organization. Questions bring to the fore (1) quantities to be measured and (2) value scales pertinent to these quantities. Measurements can be used to help improve software development processes and the resultant products.

tion, then your process should enable you to meet your budget. In either situation, the measurement challenge is to determine what a "good" process means to your organization. Consequently, as shown in the lower panel of the figure, the "goodness" values are established from the seller's viewpoint.

In this context, software process improvement becomes an exercise in evaluating product "goodness" and process "goodness." As Figure 6–6 illustrates, a product is "good" if it does what it is supposed to do and is delivered on time and within budget—so that the customer is satisfied. If the product is not "good," then the product, the process that produced the product, or both need improvement. A process is "good" if it consistently yields good products such that the seller can make a profit or stay within a budget. If the process is not "good," then the process needs improvement. Measurement needs to (1) be expressed in everyday terms so that the results make sense to the organization and (2) integrate seller and customer perspectives.

The plan for the rest of this chapter is the following:

- In **Section 6.2—Measurement Nuggets**, we present the nuggets that you can expect to extract from this chapter.

- In **Section 6.3—Product Integrity**, we show you how to quantify software product attributes to help determine whether a customer is satisfied with seller results. Our intent is to explain to you one approach for assessing customer satisfaction in terms of an index that assigns a value to the integrity (i.e., completeness) of each product that comes out of the software systems development process.

- In **Section 6.4—Process Integrity**, we show you how to measure the activities that make up your software systems development process to determine the correlation between these activities and producing products with integrity. This correlation provides insight into the extent to which these activities are, or are not, contributing to "good" products. Those activities not contributing are candidates for modification or elimination. These modifications and/or eliminations define what "process improvement" means. The discussion in this section is tied to the software systems development process described in Chapter 3. The purpose of this tie is to show you in specific terms how to measure the software development process in terms of its process components and activities. However, the measurement approach is general and can be applied to your development process.

- In **Section 6.5—Capability Maturity Model[SM] for Software (CMM[SM])**, we describe how the product integrity and process integrity concepts can be applied to the Software Engineering Institute's (SEI) widely known framework for improving software development, the CMM for Software.

- In **Section 6.6—Other Process-Related Measurements**, we give you ideas for defining process-related metrics, other than the product and process integrity indexes. Our objective is not to be comprehensive, but rather to be suggestive of supplementary ways that you can attack software measurement.

- In **Section 6.7—Measurement Summary**, we summarize the key points developed in the chapter. We include an annotated outline of an ADPE guideline to help you define an organizatinal approach for product and process measurement. As explained in the chapter, our approach to measurement is general in that it is independent of development technologies and tools.

6.2 MEASUREMENT NUGGETS

Figure 6–7 lists the nuggets that you can extract from this chapter. To introduce you to this chapter, we briefly explain these nuggets. Their full intent will become apparent as you go through this chapter.

1. **Measurements need to be expressed in everyday terms that are familiar to the organization; otherwise, they may be of little use.** Simply stated, if the people doing the day-to-day software systems development work do not understand the measurements, the collected measurement data may be counterproductive to your improvement activities. This chapter offers you an approach for defining meaningful measurements for your organization.

Nuggets		Measurement lessons learned
	1	Measurements need to be expressed in everyday terms that are familiar to the organization; otherwise, they may be of little use.
	2	Keep the measurement process simple—otherwise, it will die quickly. "Simple" means "easy-to-collect data and easy-to-interpret information resulting from these data."
	3	Establish benchmarks to give meaning to measurements. Without context, process measurement is a waste of time.
	4	Measure product integrity by (1) selecting product attributes to measure, (2) defining value scales for each product attribute, (3) recording observed attribute values, and (4) combining the recorded attribute values into a single number called a product integrity index.
	5	Measure process integrity by (1) selecting the software development process components to measure, (2) selecting component activities to measure, (3) defining values scales for each component activity, (4) recording observed activity values, and (5) combining the recorded activity values into a single number called a process integrity index.
	6	Customer satisfaction is the ultimate measure of software systems development process value. If the process fails to yield products satisfying the customer, the process needs repair.
	7	Measure customer satisfaction by incorporating customer feedback on delivered products into the process.
	8	Measurements should be a part of the software systems development process.
	9	Document in an ADPE element the measurement process and the items to be measured.

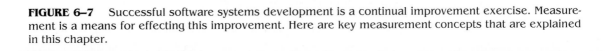

FIGURE 6–7 Successful software systems development is a continual improvement exercise. Measurement is a means for effecting this improvement. Here are key measurement concepts that are explained in this chapter.

2. **Keep the measurement process simple—otherwise, it will die quickly.** *Simple* **means "easy-to-collect data and easy-to-interpret information resulting from these data."** Our experience shows that many good-intentioned process measurement programs do not survive because (1) data collection is too onerous a task and (2) the data collected are difficult to relate to process improvement. This chapter offers suggestions for blunting these classical causes of measurement program failure.

3. **Establish benchmarks to give meaning to measurements. Without context, process measurement is a waste of time.** This chapter offers you ideas for establishing a framework for interpreting the measurements you make and collect. Many of us at one time or another have been concerned about our weight. It is easy to measure our weight. However, the resultant measurement is generally of little value if, for example, our objective is to gain or lose weight. We need weight benchmarks to know whether we are underweight, okay, or overweight. Similarly, we need process benchmarks that can tell whether the process that we have measured is underweight, okay, or overweight with respect to, say, the integrity of delivered products that the process yields. This chapter offers you ideas for constructing such benchmarks.

4. **Measure product integrity by (1) selecting product attributes to measure, (2) defining value scales for each product attribute, (3) recording observed attribute values, and (4) combining the recorded attribute values into a single number called a product integrity index.** Many of our conventional measures, such as the "foot," have their origin in objects that most people could recognize. A challenge in the software process measurement game is to find analogues to such easily recognized units of measure. This chapter offers you ideas for such analogues. This chapter also offers you ideas for converting the multidimensional product integrity concept into a one-dimensional index. These ideas will, at the same time, give you insight into how you can measure individual product integrity attributes or combinations of these attributes—whatever attributes you may choose to quantify product "goodness."

5. **Measure process integrity by (1) selecting the software development process components to measure, (2) selecting component activities to measure, (3) defining value scales for each component activity, (4) recording observed activity values, and (5) combining recorded activity values into a single number called a process integrity index.** This chapter offers you ideas for converting the multidimensional process integrity concept into a one-dimensional index, and ideas about how this index is related to the product integrity index. We explain how process integrity is a generalization of the product integrity concept.

6. **Customer satisfaction is the ultimate measure of software systems development process value. If the process fails to yield products satisfying the customer, the process needs repair.** This chapter offers you ideas for measuring customer satisfaction and linking this measure to process activities. Through this linkage, we offer you ideas for modifying process activities to increase customer satisfaction.

7. **Measure customer satisfaction by incorporating customer feedback on delivered products into the process.** How can you get insight into what the customer thinks your software systems development process is delivering? This chapter offers you ideas for integrating within the process customer feedback on delivered products. We offer suggestions on how to measure this feedback in terms that can be linked to process activities.

8. **Measurements should be a part of the software systems development process.** Defining, collecting, using, and communicating measurement data should be integrated into the development process and used, in part, to improve the organization's products and processes. However, measurement for measurement's sake is a waste of time and resources. This chapter presents ideas on how to establish measurements that can be integrated into your organization's software development activities.

9. **Document in an ADPE element the measurement process and the items to be measured.** A measurement process is an organized way of effecting software systems development process improvement. This chapter gives you ideas for documenting the measurement process, thereby helping you organize your approach to software systems development process improvement.

6.3 PRODUCT INTEGRITY

Like other organizations, you want your organization to stay in business. It is axiomatic that "staying in business" is strongly tied to customer satisfaction, which can be expressed in many ways. The purpose of this section is to explain how the product integrity concept can be used to quantify "customer satisfaction."

Our approach in this section is the following:

■ We use an example set of attributes to define an example product integrity index.

■ We use the example index to generate values for several different products to show you how to do product "goodness" measurement using the index.

■ We then give you a general formula for computing the index.

■ The worked-out examples and the general formula enable you to apply straightforwardly our product integrity measurement approach to your environment.

Figure 6–8 depicts the example set of attributes. We have chosen the five attributes shown because they are often of interest to management and product developers. These attributes are defined more specifically as follows:

at_1 Fulfills specified customer needs (i.e., does what it is supposed to do as recorded and agreed to by the customer and the seller).

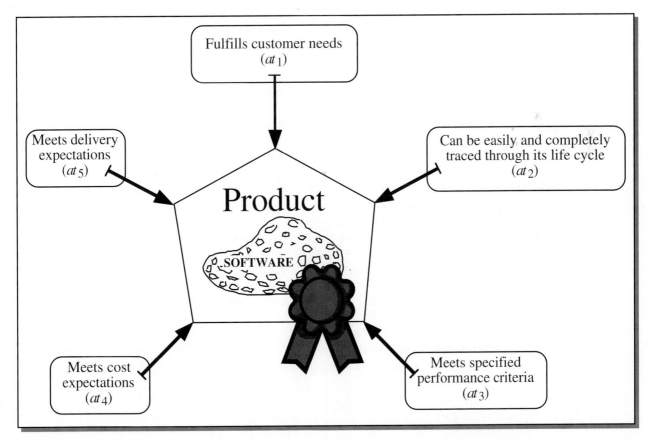

FIGURE 6–8   Here is an example of a way to define product integrity in terms of attributes that are often of interest to both management and product developers.

at₂ Can be easily and completely traced through its life cycle (i.e., is "maintainable"—it can be easily updated to (1) incorporate new things, (2) revise existing things, and (3) get rid of things no longer deemed needed by the customer).

at₃ Meets specified performance criteria (e.g., How many? How often? How long?; these criteria are sometimes considered special cases of customer needs—the first product integrity attribute).

at₄ Meets cost expectations (i.e., costs what the customer and the seller agreed that it should cost as expressed in a project plan or updates to the plan).

at₅ Meets delivery expectations (i.e., is delivered in accordance with schedules agreed to by the customer and the seller in a project plan or updates to the plan).

Product integrity is thus a multidimensional concept that associates attributes with a product. To use product integrity to quantify customer satisfaction, we need a convenient way to quantify something with multiple dimensions (here, something with five dimensions). The discussion that follows offers an approach that can be used to quantify any multidimensional entity. This discussion also makes it evident how any subset of the five product attributes we discuss, or any set of attributes you want to use, can be used to measure customer satisfaction. The following treatment thus provides a general approach to using product integrity as a basis for measuring customer satisfaction. Through experimentation with this general approach, you can define a preferred approach to apply in your environment.

The mathematical and scientific disciplines often handle multidimensional quantities with entities known as "vectors." The scientific discipline of physics, for example, uses vectors to describe many quantities (displacement, velocity, acceleration, force, momentum—to name a few). To illustrate from this list, the change of position of a particle is called a "displacement." When we go to work in the morning, we displace ourselves from our home to our place of work. We can represent this displacement as an arrow on a map drawn from the place on the map that is our home to a place on the map where our office is. This arrow represents the (straight-line) distance from our home to our office and the direction of this distance with respect to, say, some reference frame, such as that used to define the four compass points. Figure 6–9 shows the concept of displacement in one, two, three, and *n* dimensions.

Figure 6–9 also shows how the length of the vector is calculated to determine the magnitude of the displacement. For example, we represent displacements in three-dimensional space by specifying a triple of numbers (x_1, x_2, x_3), which defines the displacement of a point with respect to three mutually perpendicular axes. These axes establish a scale of values in this space.

We use this notion of displacement in space to derive the idea of a product integrity index. The space of interest is product attribute space. That is, the axes in product integrity space are product attributes. Figure 6–10 illustrates a three-dimensional product integrity space, where the attribute axes are the quantities at_1, at_4, and at_5 defined earlier.

By extension, then, if we want to quantify product integrity as it is defined by the example set of five attributes introduced earlier, we can think of product integrity as an entity in five-dimensional space. One axis in this space shows how much a product "fulfills customer needs"; a second axis shows how the evolution of the product "can be easily and completely traced through its life cycle"; and so forth for the other product integrity attributes (unfortunately, since we live in a three-dimensional world, we cannot draw the five-dimensional extension to Figure 6–10).

To understand how we can use these vector-related ideas for quantifying the concept of product integrity as a means for measuring customer satisfaction, consider the following five-dimensional vector:

$$PI = \frac{\begin{bmatrix} a_1 \\ a_2 \\ a_3 \\ a_4 \\ a_5 \end{bmatrix}}{N} = \frac{\begin{bmatrix} CustNeeds \\ Traceable \\ PerfCrit \\ WithinBudget \\ OnTime \end{bmatrix}}{N} \qquad (6.3\text{–}1)$$

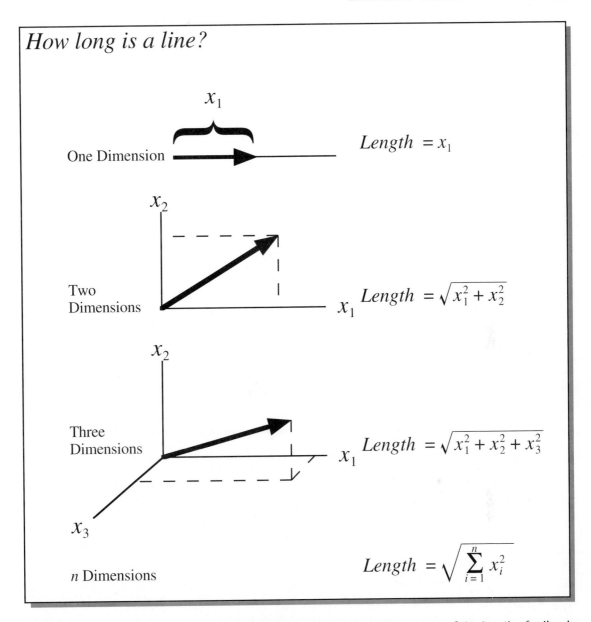

How long is a line?

One Dimension $\qquad$ *Length* $= x_1$

Two Dimensions $\qquad$ x_1 *Length* $= \sqrt{x_1^2 + x_2^2}$

Three Dimensions $\qquad$ x_1 *Length* $= \sqrt{x_1^2 + x_2^2 + x_3^2}$

n Dimensions $\qquad$ *Length* $= \sqrt{\sum_{i=1}^{n} x_i^2}$

FIGURE 6–9 The idea for a product integrity index derives from the concept of the length of a line in space. The figure shows how the length of a line can be portrayed in spaces of various dimensions as the magnitude of a vector representing a displacement. The tail of the vector represents the starting point, and the head of the vector represents the destination point. The length of the vector represents the distance between the starting point and the destination point. Similarly, the **product integrity index** is simply the length of a line in product attribute space.

In Equation 6.3–1, **PI** is a vector in five-dimensional product integrity space whose components, at_i, are the example product integrity attributes defined earlier. The quantity N is a normalization factor that establishes a "product goodness scale." As we subsequently explain, we choose N so that the length of **PI** is restricted to the range from zero to one.

Now, to turn Equation 6.3–1 into a measurement tool, we consider the following questions:

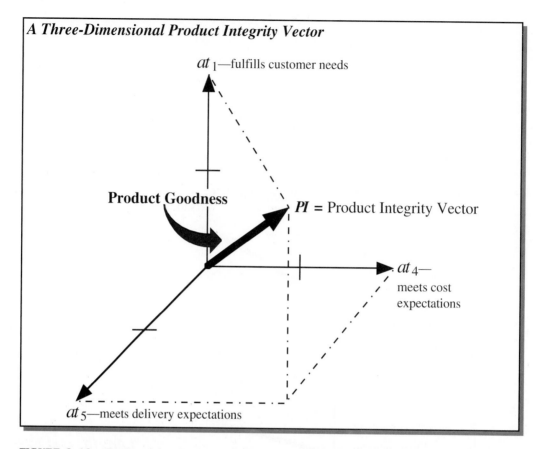

FIGURE 6–10   Product integrity is a multidimensional concept associating a number of attributes with a product. A vector is one way simply to represent a multidimensional concept. The figure shows a three-dimensional product attribute space made up of three members from the example set of five attributes introduced earlier. A vector in this space is the product integrity vector. Its length is what we will use to measure product "goodness." Our approach to measuring product "goodness" is thus an exercise in measuring the length of the product integrity vector.

- How can we convert a five-dimensional quantity into a single quantity to simplify measurement interpretation?
- What scales do we establish for the attributes?
- What relative weights do we assign to the attributes?
- How can we assign a scale of values for the single quantity?

Clearly, there are many sensible ways to address these questions.

The first question deals with simplifying measurement. As Equation 6.3–1 indicates, multidimensional expressions of product integrity are possible. However, for simplicity, we have chosen to restrict ourselves to a one-dimensional quantity to express product integrity quantitatively. Recalling Figure 6–10, that quantity is the length of the product integrity vector **PI** (i.e., it is the five-dimensional extension to the three-dimensional case shown in the figure).

As Figure 6–10 indicates, each product attribute dimension contributes to the "length" of the vector **PI**. To convert the five-dimensional quantity in Equation 6.3–1 into a single quantity (to represent "quality" or "completeness"), we calculate the "length" of the vector. We call the length of **PI** the Product Integrity Index, or *PIindex*. As subsequently explained, this product integrity vector length,

PIindex, is simply the square root of the sum of the weighted (w_i) squares of the attributes at_i divided by the normalization factor *N*.

The second question deals with attribute scales. Many people find it useful and convenient to quantify things in terms of percentages. Thus, a convenient range for an attribute scale goes from zero to one. Again, for simplicity, we take the approach of limiting the attribute scales to the range zero to one.[3]

The third question deals with relative weights for product attributes. If we assign the same scale to each attribute (namely, zero to one), we are weighting each attribute equally. For simplicity, we will take this approach. However, you may wish to emphasize one attribute more than the others. For example, if you wanted to give "meets delivery expectations" double the importance of any of the other attributes, you could set its scale to run from zero to two and set the scales of the other attributes to run from zero to one. Equivalently, you can keep all the scales the same and give prominence to selected attributes through the use of weighting factors (w_i). We show you how to introduce such weighting factors.

The fourth question deals with establishing a value scale for the length of **PI**. We select a scale for the magnitude of this vector by choosing a value for the normalization factor *N*. Arguing as we did before, we simply select a scale that ranges from zero to one. For equally weighted attributes, the value of *N* then becomes the square root of the sum of the squares of the maximum values that the attributes at_i can take on. For the case in which a product has five attributes each with a maximum value of one, the value of *N* thus becomes the square root of 5. We also show you how to compute *N* if the attributes are not equally weighted.

On the basis of the preceding discussion of one way to address the four questions previously introduced, we can now define a product integrity index, *PIindex*, that ranges from zero to one as follows:

$$PIindex = \frac{\sqrt{\sum_{i=1}^{n} w_i^2 at_i^2}}{\sqrt{\sum_{i=1}^{n} w_i^2 (\text{maximum}[at_i])^2}}$$

(6.3–2)

where at_i = product integrity attribute
n = number of product integrity attributes
w_i = weighting factor for attribute at_i
maximum $[at_i]$ = maximum value of at_i.

Figure 6–11 presents three examples of how Equation 6.3–2 can be used. Example 1 represents our software product represented by five attributes. Example 2 represents the case in which the attribute, at_1—fulfilling customer requirements, is considered twice as important as the other attributes. Example 3 represents the case in which attributes at_2 and at_3 are suppressed.

The product integrity index, *PIindex* is normalized to one (i.e., restricted to the range of zero to one). If you want to remove this normalization, then remove the denominator.

To illustrate how this Equation 6.3–2 works, we need to define value scales for each of our example software product attributes at_i. There is a multiplicity of ways such assignments can be made. Figure 6–12 shows one way to set up value scales for these attributes.

This example is explained below as follows, and it provides insight into ways that you can make such assignments that are relevant to your organization.

- For at_1 (fulfills specified customer needs), we set up a three-value scale based on an acceptance of deliverable form[4] as follows:

[3]Note that we are mapping our attribute values to dimensionless scales. This mapping allows us to combine the attribute values into a single quantity.

[4]We explained in Chapter 3 that, as part of our software systems development process, we use an acceptance of deliverable form to obtain, in part, customer feedback. For this example, we have assigned discrete values for the three possible customer evaluations.

Example 1—Equal weighting factors

$n = 5$, all $w_i = 1$, all maximum $at_i = 1$

$$PIindex = \frac{\sqrt{\sum\limits_{i=1}^{5} at_i^2}}{\sqrt{5}}$$

Example 2—One attribute is twice as important as any other attribute

$n = 5$, all $w_i = 1$ except for $w_1 = 2$ (fulfilling customer requirements twice as important as any other attribute), all maximum $at_i = 1$

$$PIindex = \frac{\sqrt{4at_1^2 + \sum\limits_{i=2}^{5} at_i^2}}{\sqrt{8}}$$

Example 3—One or more attributes are suppressed

$n = 5$, all $w_i = 1$ except for $w_2 = w_3 = 0$ (i.e., the traceability and performance requirements attributes are excluded), all maximum $at_i = 1$

$$PIindex = \frac{\sqrt{\sum\limits_{i=1,4,5} at_i^2}}{\sqrt{3}}$$

FIGURE 6–11   This figure illustrates three ways in which the general formula for the product integrity index, *PIindex*, can be used.

- $at_1 = 1$ if the customer returns the form indicating "accepted as delivered."
- $at_1 = 0.5$ if the customer returns the form indicating "accepted with minor changes."
- $at_1 = 0$ if the customer returns the form indicating "changes to be negotiated."

If we wanted to provide more insight into the percentage of requirements fulfilled, we could count such requirements appearing in the product and compare them against some ground truth showing what this number of requirements should be ("shalls" in the language of requirements analysis). For example, suppose the product were a requirements specification, and suppose CCB minutes indicated that 40 requirements should be addressed in the document but only 30 actually appeared when the document was delivered (as determined by the customer). Then, for this example, if we chose to use this counting approach to assign a value to at_1, that value would be $(30/40) = 0.75$.

- For at_2 (can be easily and completely traced through its life cycle), the situation can become complicated. Depending on the product, traceability may involve more than the product itself. For example, if the product is computer code, then traceability involves the existence of predecessor products such as design and requirements specifications. If the product is a requirements specification, then traceability typically involves documents that a customer may supply, such as congressional legislation or corporate policies. More generally, traceability involves such things as product decisions recorded at CCB meetings, internal project meetings, and recorded seller and customer management conversations and E-mail between these two parties. To keep things simple, we set up a crude three-value scale based on the existence of records showing how the product evolved, as follows:

  - $at_2 = 0$ if nothing other than a customer-prepared statement of work (SOW) exists calling for the development of the product.
  - $at_2 = 0.5$ if written records exist for some part of the project's life cycle showing how the product contents are what they are.
  - $at_2 = 1$ if detailed written records exist throughout the life of the project showing how the product contents are what they are.

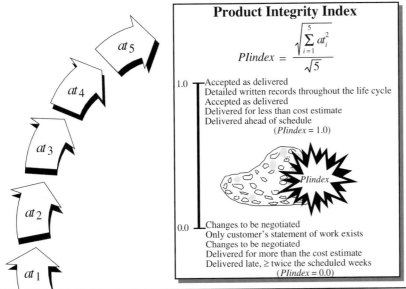

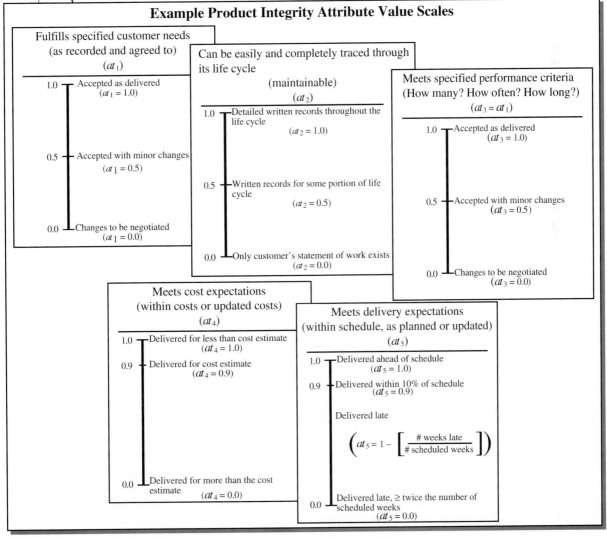

FIGURE 6-12 This figure illustrates value scales for each of the five example product integrity attributes (at_i) discussed. You will want to set up attributes and value scales that make sense for your organization.

- For at_3 (meets specified performance criteria), we simply set $at_3 = at_1$, since performance criteria are often lumped with customer needs (if such is not the case in your environment, then you can follow the suggestions previously offered for the attribute at_1). That is, we use the following scale:
  - $at_3 = 1$ if the customer returns the form indicating "accepted as delivered."
  - $at_3 = 0.5$ if the customer returns the form indicating "accepted with minor changes."
  - $at_3 = 0$ if the customer returns the form indicating "changes to be negotiated."

- For at_4 (meets cost expectations), we set up a three-value scale as follows:
  - $at_4 = 1$ if the product was delivered for less than the cost specified in the project plan or as modified in CCB minutes.
  - $at_4 = 0.9$ if the product was delivered for the cost specified in the project plan or as modified in CCB minutes.
  - $at_4 = 0$ if the product was delivered for more than the cost specified in the project plan or as modified in CCB minutes.

  Clearly, this scale places a slight premium on delivering for less than planned cost. The scale also ranks a deliverable delivered for $1 more than planned cost the same as a deliverable delivered for $3,000 more than planned cost. Again, in your environment, you may not wish to place a premium on delivery below cost—but the preceding example gives the idea for how you can establish such premiums (this remark applies also to the attribute at_5 [meets delivery expectations] in the following).

- For at_5 (delivered on time), we set up a scale as follows:

  $at_5 = 1$ if the product was delivered before the delivery date specified in the project plan or before the delivery date as modified in CCB minutes.

  $at_5 = 0.9$ if the product was delivered with no more than a 10 percent schedule slippage. Here, "percent slippage" is calculated by taking the length of time allocated in the project plan for preparing the product or as modified in CCB minutes and dividing that time into the slippage time and multiplying by 100. For example, if the product was scheduled to be delivered 10 weeks after project start, but it was actually delivered 11 weeks after project start, then $at_5 = 0.9$ because the slippage was $(1/10) \times 100 = 10$ percent.

  $at_5 = (1 - X)$, where X is the fraction of schedule slippage as just calculated. For example, if the product was scheduled to be delivered 10 weeks after project start, but it was actually delivered 13 weeks after project start, then $at_5 = (1 - [3/10]) = 0.7$. For all schedule slippages greater than or equal to the original length of time to produce the deliverable, $at_5 = 0$ (for example, if a deliverable was to be developed over a 10-week period, any delays greater than or equal to 10 weeks result in $at_5 = 0$).

  This scale places a slight premium on delivering early. Also, it favors on-time product delivery while allowing for some planning leeway.

We now illustrate how to calculate *PIindex* in Equation 6.3–2 using the preceding scales for the following example products: (1) a requirements specification, (2) a new release of legacy software system, (3) an updated user's manual, and (4) a new project plan.

Example 1—*PIindex* Calculation for a Requirements Specification

The product is a requirements specification. After delivery, the customer sent back the acceptance of deliverable form showing "accepted with minor changes." Thus, $at_3 = at_1 = 0.5$. The product was delivered on time so $at_5 = 0.9$. The project plan called for 300 hours to be expended on the task to produce the document, but only 275 hours were expended. Thus, $at_4 = 1$. Written records consisting of CCB minutes showing decisions underlying the document's content exist for some part of the project. Thus, $at_2 = 0.5$. The product integrity index, *PIindex*, for this requirements specification is therefore the following:

$$PIindex = \frac{\sqrt{0.5^2 + 0.5^2 + 0.5^2 + 1^2 + 0.9^2}}{\sqrt{5}} = 0.72.$$

Figure 6–13 shows how this requirements specification example can be graphically presented.

The top panel displays how *PIindex* is calculated given the recorded data, and summarizes the product integrity attributes. The bottom panel provides additional detail into the attributes, their scales, and the recorded data. The bottom panel displays the observed attribute values on a Kiviat-like diagram. This diagram gives the next level of insight into the nature of the product being measured. In particular, it shows the recorded value of each product integrity attribute plotted on the scale for that attribute.[5]

Example 2—*PIindex* Calculation for a New Release of a Legacy Software System

The product is a new release of a legacy software system. After delivery (which was preceded by acceptance testing), the customer sent back the acceptance of deliverable form showing "accepted as delivered." Thus, $at_1 = at_3 = 1$. The product was supposed to be delivered 20 weeks after project start, but was delivered 5 weeks late so $at_5 = (1 - [5/20]) = 0.75$. The project plan called for 3000 hours to be expended on the task to produce the system upgrade, but only 2900 hours were expended. Thus, $at_4 = 1$. No requirements or design specifications exist. However, each code module has a header containing key information about the module's contents and a version number. In addition, written records consisting of CCB minutes showing decisions underlying the code module changes exist throughout the acceptance testing cycle. Thus, $at_2 = 0.5$. The product integrity index, *PIindex*, for this new release of the legacy system is therefore the following:

$$PIindex = \frac{\sqrt{1^2 + 0.5^2 + 1^2 + 1^2 + 0.75^2}}{\sqrt{5}} = 0.87.$$

Example 3—*PIindex* Calculation for an Updated User's Manual

The product is an update to a user's manual for a new release of a software system that the seller maintains. The customer was uncertain about many things that the manual should contain and constantly wanted to change its contents (even up to the last minute). After delivery, the customer sent back the acceptance of deliverable form showing "changes to be negotiated." Thus, $at_3 = at_1 = 0$. Because of the customer uncertainty and the many changes to the document, the manual, which was supposed to be delivered 10 weeks after project start, was delivered 5 weeks late, so $at_5 = (1 - [5/10]) = 0.50$. The project plan called for 300 hours to be expended on the task to produce the user's manual, but, because of

---

[5]It is important to note that, in general, when you are dealing with unequally weighted attributes (which is not the case with the example shown in Figure 6–13), this situation can affect the way you display your measurements. When you have unequally weighted attributes (i.e., all w_i are not equal), there are several possible ways of using the Kiviat-like diagram to display what is going on. Some of these ways are the following:

■ *You can plot unequally weighted observed values.* In this case, the length of a value scale in your display ranges from the weight (w_i) times the minimum attribute value (minimum [at_i]) to the weight (w_i) times the maximum attribute value (maximum[at_i]). For example, suppose that attribute at_1 in Figure 6–13 had twice the weight as any of the other attributes (i.e., $w_1 = 2$ and all the other $w_i = 1$). In this case, the length of the at_1 value scale would run from a minimum value of zero (i.e., [w_1] times [minimum {at_1}] = 2 times 0) to a maximum value of the two (i.e., [w_1] times [maximum {at_1}] = 2 times 1), while the other attribute value scales would run from zero (i.e., [w_i] times [minimum{at_i}] = 1 times 0, for i = 2, 3, 4, 5) to one (i.e., [w_i] times [maximum{at_i}] = 1 times 1, for i = 2, 3, 4, 5)

■ *You can plot equally weighted observed values.* Each scale in this case would run from zero to one (including the scale for at_1). To show that at_1 has twice the weight as any of the other attributes, you could annotate the Kiviat-like diagram with a statement to this effect.

■ *You can plot unequally weighted and equally weighted observed values.*

The bottom line here is to set up the display (Kiviat-like or otherwise) in a way that makes sense for your organization.

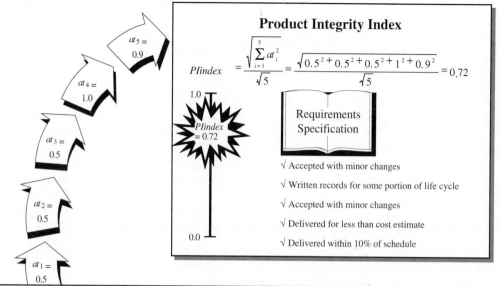

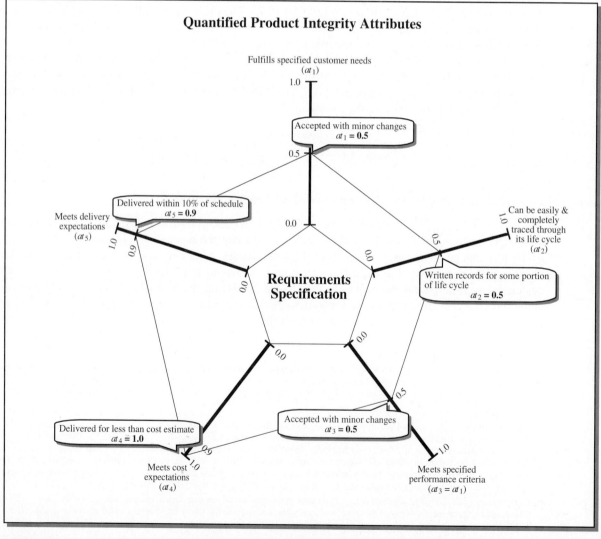

FIGURE 6–13 This figure illustrates one way to display the results of quantifying the integrity of a software product (e.g., a requirements specification). For the attribute values shown, *PIindex* = 0.72.

the numerous changes and schedule slippages, 360 hours were expended. Thus, $at_4 = 0$. Written records consisting of CCB minutes showing the change track record of the document exist. These records also indicate that the customer was alerted to potential schedule slippages and cost overruns because of the document's unsteady state. Thus, $at_2 = 0.5$. The product integrity index, *PIindex*, for this user's manual update is therefore the following:

$$PIindex = \frac{\sqrt{0^2 + 0.5^2 + 0^2 + 0^2 + 0.5^2}}{\sqrt{5}} = 0.32.$$

Example 4—*PIindex* Calculation for a New Project Plan

The product is a new project plan for the development of a software system. The process engineering group, which is responsible for project planning, estimated that the plan, with one revision, would cost $3000 and would take 20 working days to deliver to the customer. The plan was actually delivered 24 working days after start, so that $at_5 = (1 - [4/20]) = 0.80$. The actual cost to produce the plan was $2700, so that $at_4 = 1$. Besides the SOW, the customer supplied needed reference material that was (1) referenced in the plan, (2) used to construct a current system concept, (3) used to construct a system concept after plan accomplishment, and (4) used to construct the technical approach. Thus, $at_2 = 1$. The plan resulted in a contract, which implies that the plan fully responded to the customer requirements stipulated in the SOW. In addition, the contract implies customer acceptance of the project plan and is therefore equivalent to the customer sending back the acceptance of deliverable form showing "accepted as delivered." Thus, $at_3 = at_1 = 1$. The product integrity index, *PIindex*, for this project plan is therefore the following:

$$PIindex = \frac{\sqrt{1^2 + 1^2 + 1^2 + 1^2 + 0.8^2}}{\sqrt{5}} = 0.96.$$

Figure 6–14 summarizes the *PIindex* calculations for the preceding examples.

As we stated at the outset of this chapter, it is easy to measure our weight. However, the resultant measurement is generally of little value if, for example, our objective is to gain or lose weight. We need weight benchmarks to know whether we are underweight, okay, or overweight. Similarly, we need benchmarks for *PIindex*. For example, we can use the product integrity index to establish norms for "product quality" or "completeness." As you gain experience with this index, you can establish goals for various types of products, projects, and seller periods of performance. For example, you can establish goals such as the following:

- Each release of a legacy system for which little or no documentation exists shall have a product integrity index not less than 0.75.

- Each deliverable for each project whose ultimate objective is to produce a new software system shall have a product integrity index not less than 0.85.

The examples discussed deal with calculating *PIindex* after a product is delivered to the customer. However, *PIindex* can also be used to quantify a product's integrity during its development, as well as after its delivery. As shown in Figure 6–15, to apply *PIindex* during product development, (1) think of the product development process as building a sequence of interim products leading up to the delivered product (e.g., outline, annotated outline, rough draft, etc.), and (2) measure the integrity of each of these interim products in a way similar to the way that the integrity of the delivered product is measured.

Assessing the integrity of these interim products can help the project manager and the product development staff appropriately focus efforts to increase the integrity of the to-be-delivered product.

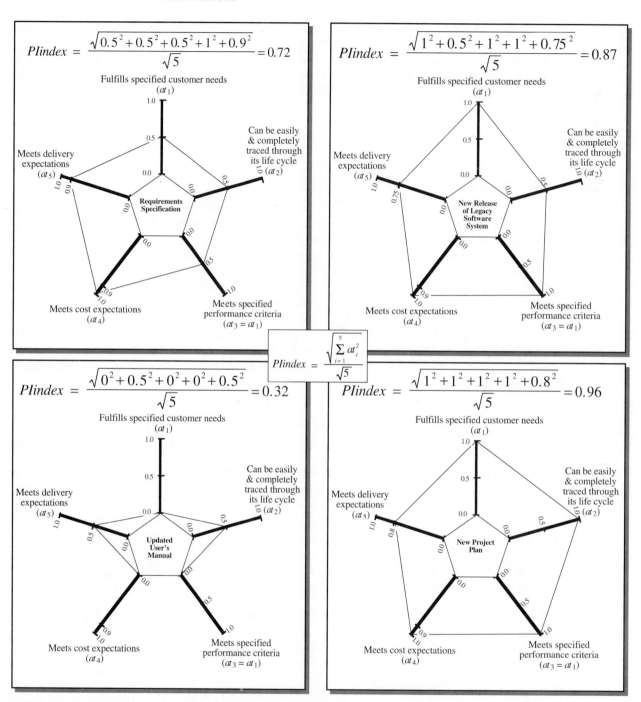

FIGURE 6–14 This figure illustrates *PIindex* for four software products. *PIindex* was calculated after the customer received each product and returned the acceptance of deliverable form.

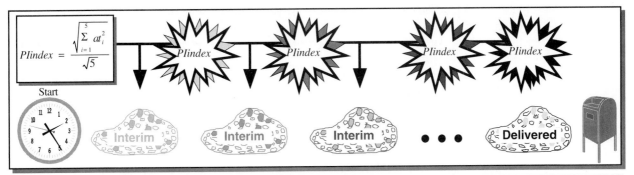

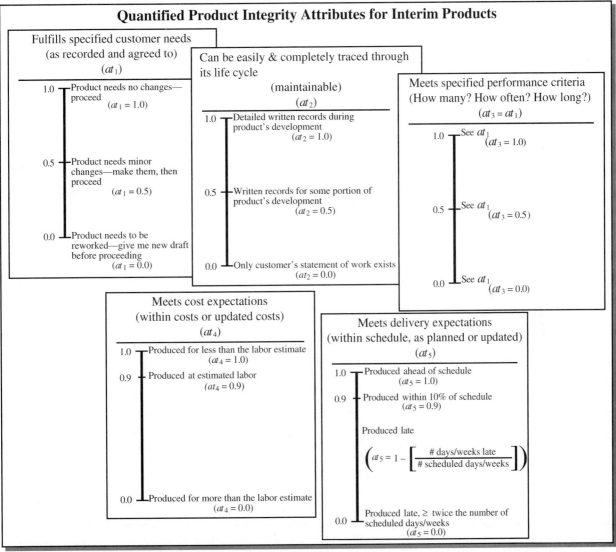

FIGURE 6–15 The product integrity index, *PIindex*, can be used to quantify a product's integrity during its development, as well as after its delivery to the customer.

The figure shows how each of the product integrity attributes can be interpreted for interim products. These interpretations are based on the interpretations given to these attributes for the to-be-delivered product. You can set up a similar correspondence for whatever interpretations you choose to give to your product integrity attributes.

To aid in tracking the evolution of a product, it may be useful to plot the interim *PIindexes*. Figure 6–16 illustrates this idea for a requirements specification. *PIindex* and each of the product attributes (at_i) are plotted. Such juxtaposed plots can help the project manager to ensure that a product is evolving as planned. These plots can also give the customer quantitative visibility into the evolution of the deliverable.

As shown in the top panel of Figure 6–16, there are six reporting periods before the requirements specification is scheduled for delivery to the customer. During the first reporting period, the requirements specification *PIindex* was reported to be near 0.9. Looking down the period-1 column, you can see the following:

at_1 The specified customer's needs were met with an outline that was approved.

at_2 Only the customer's SOW existed at the start of the project, which is what you would expect.

at_3 Performance criteria are set equal to customer's needs.

at_4 Cost expectations were exceeded.

at_5 Delivery expectations were met.

The project seems to be going well, so the project manager told the team to skip the next reporting period and report progress in period 3. To the project manager's surprise, when *PIindex* was reported in period 3, the value had fallen below 0.5. Looking down the period-3 column, you can see the following:

at_1 The specified customer's needs were not met with an annotated outline that was not approved.

at_2 The approved outline and CCB minutes existed, but other hallway and telephone conversations with the customer were not reflected in the CCB minutes.

at_3 Performance criteria are set equal to customer's needs.

at_4 Cost expectations were exceeded.

at_5 Delivery expectations were not met.

When *PIindex* dropped, it acted as an indicator that the project was not progressing as desired. Upon inspecting the attribute values, the project manager was able to gain some insight into the situation. The project manager then assembled the appropriate team members for a meeting to discuss the particulars and make decisions about what to do next. The project manager decided to have the team rework the annotated outline and discuss the results with the customer. The interaction with the customer was to be documented so that "what" the customer was saying would (1) not be forgotten and (2) could be incorporated into the outline. The project manager also decided to bring in a more senior person who had specific experience that could help the team work the annotated outline. Finally, the project manager, in concert with the team, decided to submit the reworked outline ahead of schedule, so that if there were any last minutes issues, they could be addressed before formal delivery to the customer. As can be seen in the period-4 results, the decisions made resulted in an increase in *PIindex*. The story goes on, but the point is that the *PIindex* value, the attributes, the attribute value scales, and the display of the collected information help to focus attention on those areas of interest to the customer and the seller. Such focus helps to reduce project risk and increase success.

Such juxtaposed plots can also help the project manager's bosses gain visibility into project progress. Such insight is particularly useful when these bosses have responsibility for multiple pro-

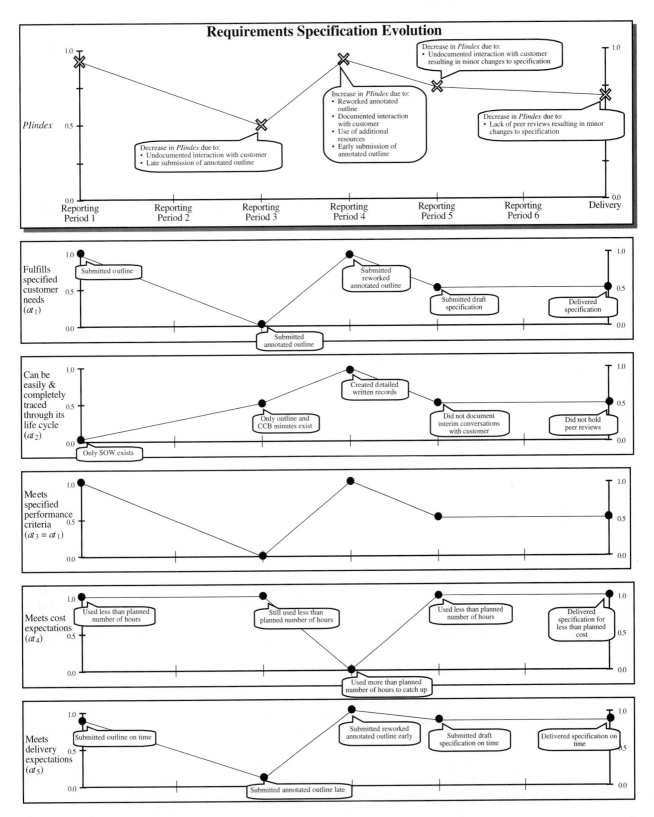

FIGURE 6–16 This figure illustrates how the product integrity index concept can be used to track the integrity of a product as it evolves from the start of its development to the time it is delivered to the customer.

jects. By periodically reviewing such plots, managers (and others) help to drive out what really matters to the customer and the organization. Once a project or organization settles on what is important (as reflected in the value scales), then the product integrity index can help the project or organization follow a structured approach to improving the products it develops. We illustrate this fundamental idea as follows for an organization that consists of a number of projects and which produces, say, tens of deliverables a month:

- By looking at monthly reports of interim or final *PIindex* values, the head of the organization (the program manager) can quickly see which of the tens of deliverables (1) to be shipped out or (2) shipped out may be falling short. Those deliverables with values near 1 probably do not need the program manager's attention. By definition, those deliverables embody what the organization thinks is important. It is only the deliverables with values far away from 1 that need attention. However, how far is "far away" will be determined by the organization as it becomes more comfortable working with *PIindex*. For those deliverables needing attention, the program manager can use Kiviat diagrams such as those shown in Figure 6–14 to see quickly why those products fell short. Thus, using *PIindex* to track product development can help management at all levels further pinpoint product shortfalls—before they become big headaches.

- Over time, as the database of *PIindex* values grows, the program manager and others in the organization can observe trends in the "goodness" of products being delivered. Trend analysis can help pinpoint those areas where the organization can improve—and by how much. This insight can be used to decide on corrective actions. For example, if such trend analysis shows that most products with low *PIindex* values are that way because they are delivered over budget, then the organization can take steps to improve its resource-estimating procedure with some confidence that this corrective action is the right thing to do. In addition, if the program manager finds that on-time delivery is averaging less than 0.50, this statistic may be a signal that project planning estimating techniques need improvement.

Regardless of which form of the *PIindex* formula you decide on for your organization, compiling statistics based on *PIindex* can help you gain insight into areas for product development process improvement.

We summarize our product measurement discussion in Figure 6–17, which lists five steps to follow when setting up and collecting product metrics. Our recommendation is to start simple and try a pilot measurement program.

After you have decided on what questions you want answered and what products you want to measure, you need to decide on the granularity of your product measurements. We recommend that you do not select too many product attributes at first. You do not want the measurement program to take on a life of its own. You need to collect data and determine what attributes are worth measuring. As the number of product attributes increases, each attribute's contribution to the measurement is reduced accordingly, but you do not want too few, else you may not gain significant insight into the answers to your questions. The key point here is that the steps in Figure 6–17 provide (1) a structured way of quickly focusing in on product weaknesses and (2) a structured way of taking corrective action to correct these weaknesses.

We want to make one final point in this section. How do you know when you have improved the software systems development process? As shown in Figure 6–18, one way is to measure the average value of the *PIindex* for products over a period of time.

On the basis of the analysis of the *PIindex* attributes, you can make adjustments to your development process, and then measure the average value of *PIindex* for products developed by the changed process. If the average value has increased, then the process has been improved. In contrast to this *indirect* method of measuring process improvement, the next section discusses how you can *directly* measure your software systems development process for the purposes of improving it.

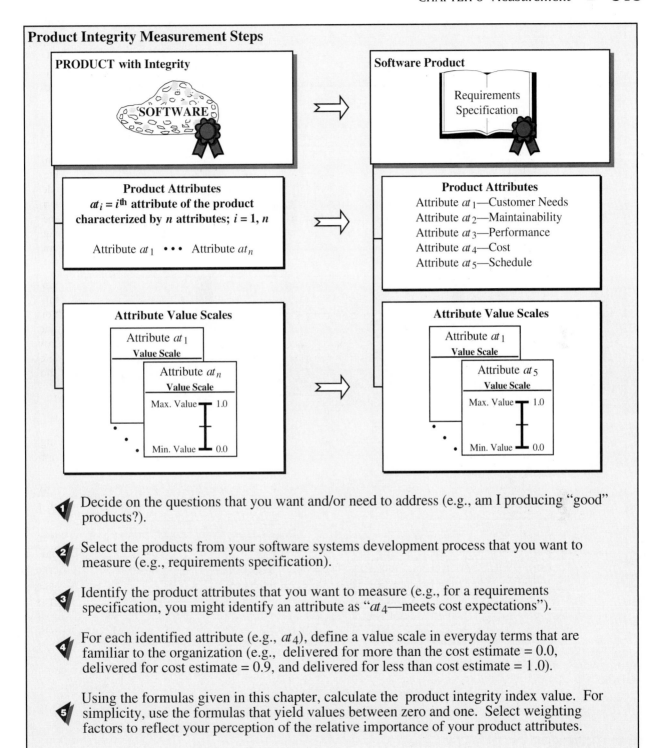

Product Integrity Measurement Steps

PRODUCT with Integrity

SOFTWARE

Software Product

Requirements
Specification

Product Attributes
$at_i = i^{th}$ attribute of the product
characterized by n attributes; $i = 1, n$

Attribute at_1 • • • Attribute at_n

Product Attributes
Attribute at_1—Customer Needs
Attribute at_2—Maintainability
Attribute at_3—Performance
Attribute at_4—Cost
Attribute at_5—Schedule

Attribute Value Scales

Attribute at_1
Value Scale

Attribute at_n
Value Scale

Max. Value ┳ 1.0

Min. Value ┻ 0.0

Attribute Value Scales

Attribute at_1
Value Scale

Attribute at_5
Value Scale

Max. Value ┳ 1.0

Min. Value ┻ 0.0

1. Decide on the questions that you want and/or need to address (e.g., am I producing "good" products?).

2. Select the products from your software systems development process that you want to measure (e.g., requirements specification).

3. Identify the product attributes that you want to measure (e.g., for a requirements specification, you might identify an attribute as "at_4—meets cost expectations").

4. For each identified attribute (e.g., at_4), define a value scale in everyday terms that are familiar to the organization (e.g., delivered for more than the cost estimate = 0.0, delivered for cost estimate = 0.9, and delivered for less than cost estimate = 1.0).

5. Using the formulas given in this chapter, calculate the product integrity index value. For simplicity, use the formulas that yield values between zero and one. Select weighting factors to reflect your perception of the relative importance of your product attributes.

FIGURE 6–17 This high-level procedure helps you through the product measurement steps based on the concepts and examples introduced so far in this chapter.

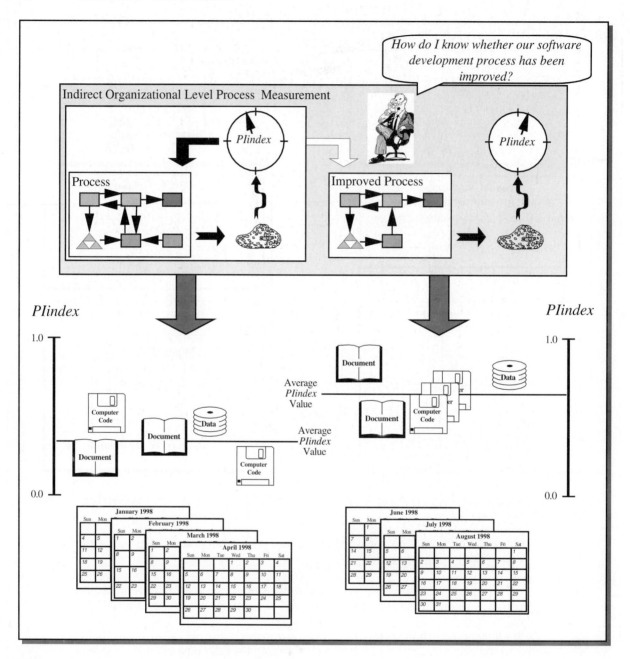

FIGURE 6–18 *PIindex* can be used indirectly to measure improvements in the organizational software development process.

6.4 PROCESS INTEGRITY

The purpose of this section is to give you guidance for defining a set of process metrics that can be used in conjunction with the product integrity index discussed in the preceding section. Process integrity metrics can provide you with input for improving your software systems development process.

As previously stated, one dictionary definition of *process* is the following:

A series of actions or operations leading to an end.

Chapter 3 described how to define our example software systems development process. There, we showed you how to define the actions (activities) and their relationships whose purpose is to produce software products (i.e., documents, computer software systems, and/or databases). Here, we show you how to measure that software systems development process in terms of its process components and component activities. Before we measure our example process, we need to define process integrity.

Process integrity is defined as follows:

A process, when performed as part of software product development, has integrity if the process components and associated component activities are performed as part of product development in accordance with ADPE element content.

As shown in Figure 6–19, by analogy to the product integrity index, *PIindex*, we define a process integrity index, *ProcIindex*. The figure shows that process integrity is more complicated than product integrity. Simply stated, *PIindex* is two layers deep, and *ProcIindex* is three layers deep. At the first level, the process is decomposed into components. At the second level, each process component is decomposed into activities. At the third level, value scales are defined for each activity.

The form of the process integrity equations is similar to the form of the product integrity equation (i.e., Equation 6.3–2). At the first level, the process component (xt_i) replaces the product attribute

---

Process Integrity Index

$$ProcIindex = \frac{\sqrt{\sum_{i=1}^{N} w_i^2 \, xt_i^2}}{\sqrt{\sum_{i=1}^{N} w_i^2 (\text{maximum } [xt_i])^2}}$$

N = number of organizational process components
w_i = weighting factor for process component xt_i
xt_i = the ith process component
maximum $[xt_i]$ = maximum value of xt_i

$$xt_i = \frac{\sqrt{\sum_{j=1}^{N_i} w_{ij}^2 xt_{ij}^2}}{\sqrt{\sum_{j=1}^{N_i} w_{ij}^2 (\text{maximum} [xt_{ij}])^2}}$$

N_i = number of activities making up process component xt_i
w_{ij} = weighting factor for activity xt_{ij} of process component xt_i
xt_{ij} = the jth activity of the ith process component
maximum $[xt_{ij}]$ = maximum value of xt_{ij}

FIGURE 6–19 This figure presents the general formula for the process integrity index, *ProcIindex*, that is normalized to one.

(at_i) in the numerator. "Maximum value of xt_i" replaces "maximum value of at_i" in the denominator. At the second level, the process component (xt_i) is analogously defined in terms of process component activities (xt_{ij}).

To explain *ProcIndex* further, we discuss how to measure the software systems development process described in Chapter 3. As shown in Figure 6–20, this process consists of the following four process components (xt_i):

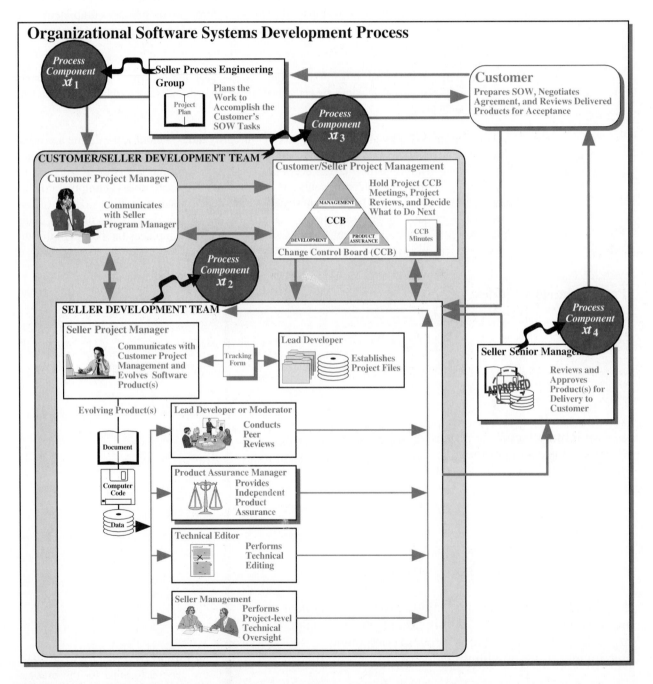

FIGURE 6–20 The software systems development process can be measured by assessing specific process components. In this example, four process components are shown.

xt_1 Seller Project Planning—The Seller Process Engineering Group is responsible for planning the work to be accomplished based on a customer's statement of work (SOW).

xt_2 Seller Development Team—This team is responsible for accomplishing the work specified in the project plan.

xt_3 Customer/Seller Development Team—This team is responsible for coordinating project activities with one another.

xt_4 Seller Senior Management—This management level is responsible for reviewing and approving project products for delivery to the customer.

There are seven process integrity measurement steps. To set the stage for explaining these steps, Figure 6–21 depicts how we define *ProcIindex* for our example software systems development process. Now we will walk you through the seven process integrity measurement steps.

Process Integrity Measurement Step 1

The first process measurement step is to decide on the questions we want and/or need to address. Here, we are addressing the following question:

Is the organizational software systems development process producing "good" products?

Process Integrity Measurement Step 2

The second process measurement step is to select the process components from the organizational software systems development process that we want to measure. We have selected the following four process components as previously described: (xt_1) Seller Project Planning, (xt_2) Seller Development Team, (xt_3) Customer/Seller Development Team, and (xt_4) Seller Senior Management. These four process components are the first layer of the process metric calculation. Figure 6–22 illustrates how the process integrity index, *ProcIindex*, is calculated by using these four process components.

Process Integrity Measurement Step 3

Before we calculate each process component, we need to identify the process component activities that we want to measure. Each process component (xt_i) needs to be defined in terms of specific activities (xt_{ij}). For example, Seller Project Planning (xt_1), is defined by its six process activities:

xt_{11} Seller reviews SOW, communicates with customer, and assembles project planning team.

xt_{12} Seller performs risk assessment.

xt_{13} Seller Project Planning Team develops task-derived resource estimates.

xt_{14} Seller Business Manager calculates task-derived dollar estimates.

xt_{15} Seller Business Manager calculates risk-derived dollar estimates.

xt_{16} Seller Management reconciles task-derived dollar estimates with risk-derived dollar estimates.

These six activities represent the second layer of process metric calculation for a process component. Figure 6–23 gives a complete list of process activities for each of the four process components. Measuring activities can help to identify those activities that are, or are not, contributing to customer satis-

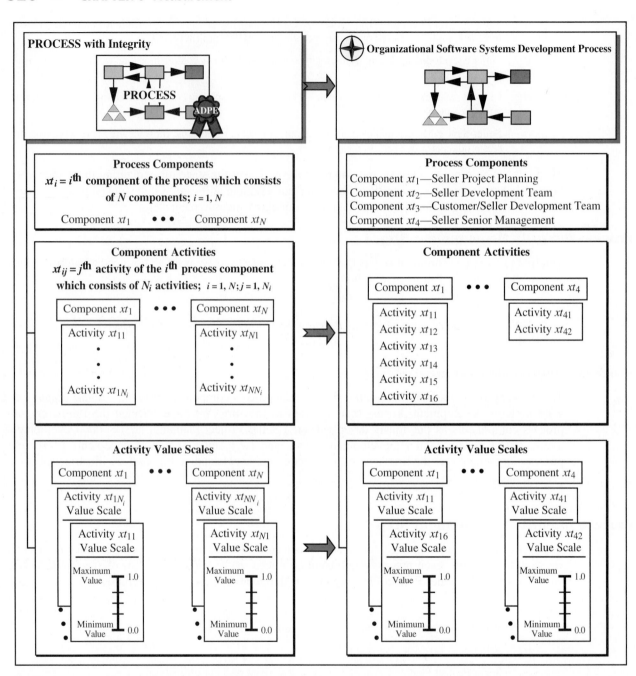

FIGURE 6–21 The left-hand side of this figure represents our process measurement framework that is used to decompose a process into its components and activities. Activity value scales are defined in terms meaningful to the organization. The right-hand side of this figure represents how our example organizational software systems development process maps to our framework.

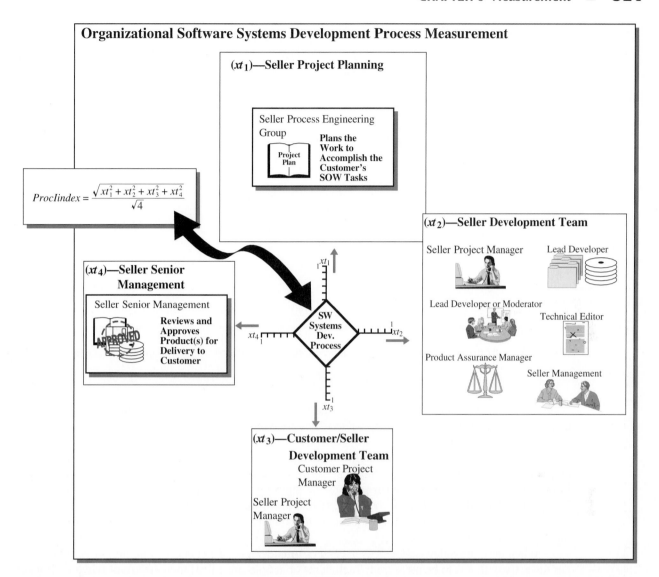

Organizational Software Systems Development Process Measurement

(xt_1)—Seller Project Planning

Seller Process Engineering Group

Project Plan

Plans the Work to Accomplish the Customer's SOW Tasks

$$ProcIindex = \frac{\sqrt{xt_1^2 + xt_2^2 + xt_3^2 + xt_4^2}}{\sqrt{4}}$$

(xt_4)—Seller Senior Management

Seller Senior Management

APPROVED

Reviews and Approves Product(s) for Delivery to Customer

SW Systems Dev. Process

(xt_2)—Seller Development Team

Seller Project Manager   Lead Developer

Lead Developer or Moderator

Technical Editor

Product Assurance Manager

Seller Management

(xt_3)—Customer/Seller Development Team

Customer Project Manager

Seller Project Manager

FIGURE 6–22   This figure illustrates how the process integrity index, *ProcIindex*, is calculated by using four process components—(xt_1) Seller Project Planning (which includes risk assessment), (xt_2) Seller Development Team (which includes peer reviews), (xt_3) Customer/Seller Development Team (which includes CCB activity), and (xt_4) Seller Senior Management (which includes review and approval activities).

faction. Those activities that are not contributing directly to customer satisfaction may be candidates for modification or elimination. We categorize such modifications as process improvement activities.

Figure 6–24 illustrates how the process integrity index, *ProcIindex*, is further defined and calculated by using the process activities for each of the four components. As shown in the figure, Seller Project Planning and Seller Development Team each consists of six activities; Customer/Seller Development Team and Seller Senior Management each consists of two activities.

Process Integrity Measurement Step 4

Before measurement data can be collected, the third layer of the process metric calculation needs to be performed. Specifically, the fourth process measurement step is to define an activity value scale for

---

Organizational Software Systems Development Process Components and Associated Activities

(xt_1)—Seller plans work based on customer's SOW

(xt_{11})—Seller reviews SOW, communicates with customer and assembles project planning team

(xt_{12})—Seller performs risk assessment

(xt_{13})—Seller Project Planning Team develops task-derived resource estimates

(xt_{14})—Seller Business Manager calculates task-derived dollar estimates

(xt_{15})—Seller Business Manager calculates risk-derived dollar estimates

(xt_{16})—Seller Management reconciles task-derived dollar estimates with risk-derived dollar estimates

(xt_2)—Seller Development Team accomplishes work specified in the project plan

(xt_{21})—Seller Project Manager communicates with customer and evolves software products

(xt_{22})—Seller Lead Developer establishes project files

(xt_{23})—Seller Lead Developer conducts peer reviews

(xt_{24})—Seller Product Assurance Manager provides product assurance support

(xt_{25})—Seller Technical Editor performs technical editing

(xt_{26})—Seller Management performs project-level technical oversight

(xt_3)—Customer/Seller Development Team members coordinate project activities with one another

(xt_{31})—Customer Project Manager provides technical guidance to Seller Project Manager

(xt_{32})—Seller and Customer Project Managers hold project CCBs

(xt_4)—Seller Senior Management reviews and approves project products for delivery to customer

(xt_{41})—Seller Senior Management reviews project products to determine if products conform to ADPE

(xt_{42})—Seller Senior Management approves products for delivery to customer

---

FIGURE 6–23 Example activities for our organizational software systems development process.

each process activity. Figures 6–25, 6–26, and 6–27 present example activity value scales for each of the component activities. The activity value scales are expressed in everyday terms.

Some of the activity value scales shown have only two values, while others have three or four values. The values on the scale help to influence the direction the organization wants to go. For example, in Figure 6–25, activity (xt_{12})—Seller performs risk assessment—has two values (i.e., 0.0 and 1.0). In this example, the organization (or perhaps the buyer) places importance on risk assessments, and it is expected that this activity is to be done. If risk assessment does not happen, a value of 0.0 is assigned. As will be shown, when this value is plotted on a Kiviat-like diagram, it is readily apparent that this activity has not been done.

When defining value scales, it is necessary to understand what specific item(s) or action(s) trigger the activity that is to be measured. Such items or actions are called **measurement triggers**. For example, for "Seller performs risk assessment," value scales can be defined as "Seller did not perform risk assessment on **customer's SOW** = 0.0," and "Seller performed risk assessment on **customer's SOW** = 1.0." You can use measurement triggers to help assign values to process activities.

Activity value scales may provide an opportunity to show more gradual improvement in performing a specific activity. For example, in Figure 6–26, activity (xt_{23})—Seller Lead Developer conducts peer reviews—has four values (i.e., 0.0, 0.25, 0.75, and 1.0). In this example, the organization may have some projects that routinely use peer reviews, and they have found them to be useful. Therefore, the organization wants to change its development culture such that all projects have peer reviews. However, it is recognized that it may take some time to get everyone up to speed on how to conduct and to document peer reviews. In some instances, some developers may be reluctant to have their work reviewed, or some customers may not want to pay for such reviews. Changing the culture may take time; therefore, the scale can accommodate incremental improvements, rather than an all-or-nothing approach.

Activity value scales can be established to measure customer, as well as seller activities. For example, in Figure 6–27, activity (xt_{31})—Customer Project Manager provides technical guidance to Seller Project Manager—attempts to measure customer communication. In an effort to be responsive

Organizational Software Systems Development Process Measurement

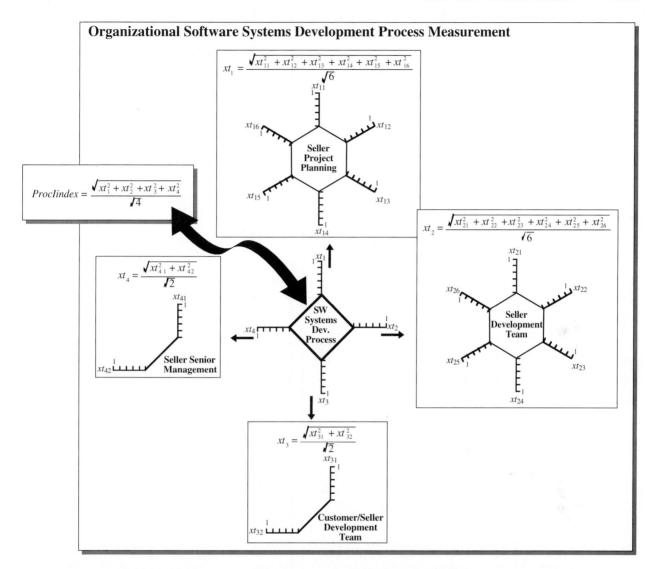

$$xt_1 = \frac{\sqrt{xt_{11}^2 + xt_{12}^2 + xt_{13}^2 + xt_{14}^2 + xt_{15}^2 + xt_{16}^2}}{\sqrt{6}}$$

$$ProcIndex = \frac{\sqrt{xt_1^2 + xt_2^2 + xt_3^2 + xt_4^2}}{\sqrt{4}}$$

$$xt_2 = \frac{\sqrt{xt_{21}^2 + xt_{22}^2 + xt_{23}^2 + xt_{24}^2 + xt_{25}^2 + xt_{26}^2}}{\sqrt{6}}$$

$$xt_4 = \frac{\sqrt{xt_{41}^2 + xt_{42}^2}}{\sqrt{2}}$$

$$xt_3 = \frac{\sqrt{xt_{31}^2 + xt_{32}^2}}{\sqrt{2}}$$

FIGURE 6–24 To compute *ProcIndex*, each process component is decomposed into specific activities.

to customer needs, potential confusion (with respect to what needs to be done next, or what the "real" requirements are, etc.) can occur if clear communication channels are not established. This value scale is set up to reward customer and seller communication, but it emphasizes that the customer and seller management should to be talking with one another. The customer manager tells the seller manager what is needed, and the seller manager supervises and directs the seller development team members. Another example is activity (xt_{32})—Seller and Customer Project Managers hold project CCBs. This value scale is set up to measure if agreed-upon communication channels and decision making are being followed. The seller has established an ADPE element for making decisions at CCBs, and the customer has agreed to this mechanism. This value scale is set up to reward holding project CCBs in accordance with the ADPE guidance. If the customer and seller do hold CCBs in accordance with the guidance but are not happy with how the CCBs are working, then the ADPE guidance can be changed. There is no one way to hold the CCB. However, if the customer and seller do not try to follow the guidance that is based on their experiences, then it will be difficult, if not impossible, to effect consistent practices or improvement to the practices.

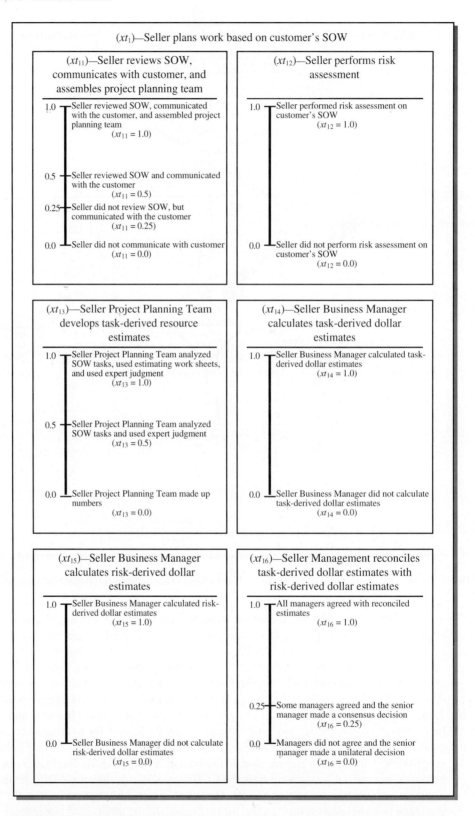

FIGURE 6–25 Example activity value scales for the Seller Project Planning component of the organizational process.

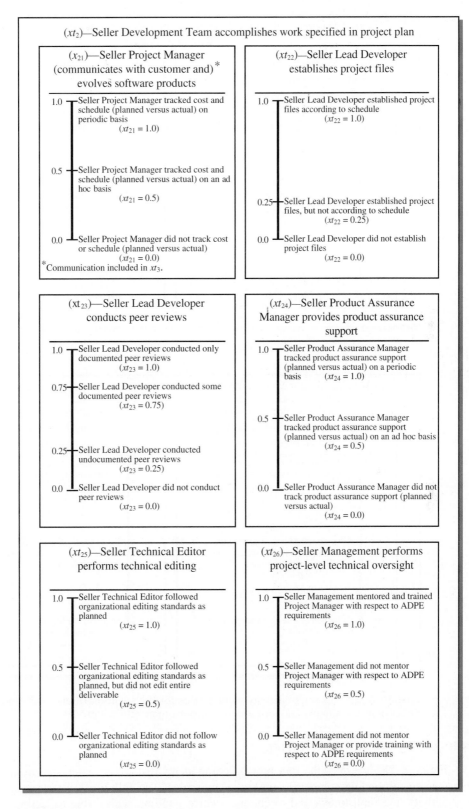

FIGURE 6–26 Example activity value scales for the Seller Development Team component of our organizational process.

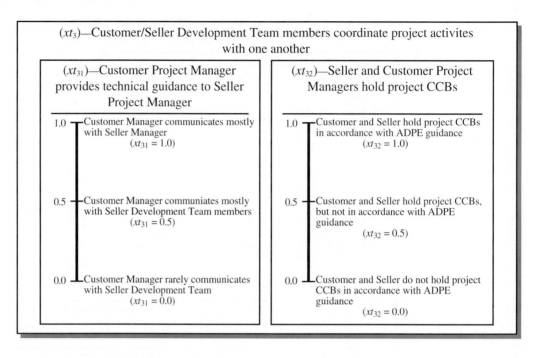

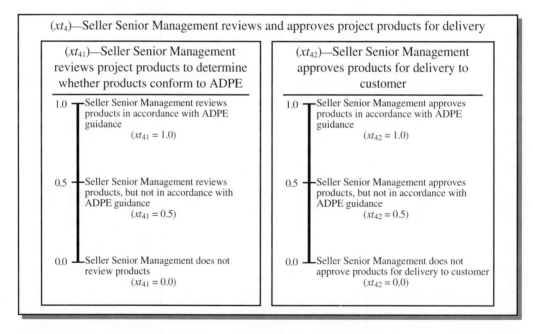

FIGURE 6–27 Example activity value scales for the Customer/Seller Development Team and Seller Senior Management components of our organizational process.

Process Integrity Measurement Step 5

Figure 6–28 illustrates the four process components that we are interested in measuring, and the sixteen corresponding component activities and scales. The fifth process measurement step is to observe activity accomplishment and to choose a corresponding scale value reflecting that accomplishment. For example, for "Seller performed risk assessment," we observe that the customer's SOW was as-

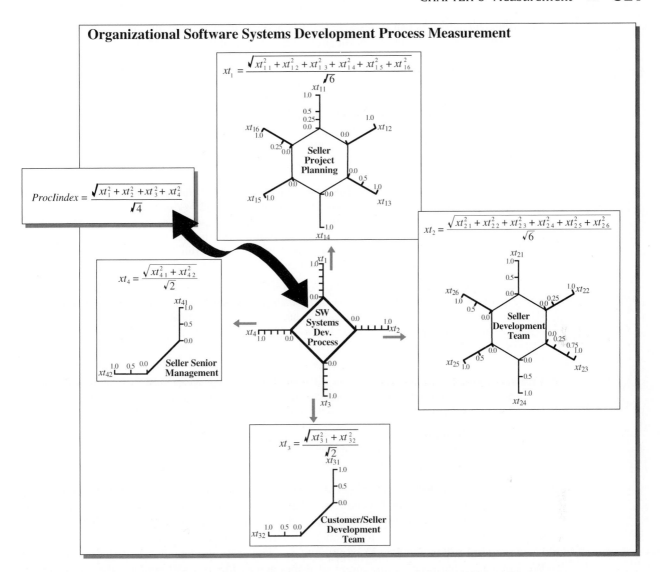

FIGURE 6–28 *ProcIndex* is defined and calculated in terms of process components, component activities, and activity value scales.

sessed for risk according to our organization's risk assessment procedure. Thus, the observed activity accomplishment is "Seller performed risk assessment on customer's SOW," and consequently the corresponding scale value reflecting that accomplishment is 1.0.

Remember, the measurement trigger can be different for each activity. Thus, to measure an entire process, a number of triggers are generally needed.

Process Integrity Measurement Step 6

The sixth process measurement step is to use the formulas given in this chapter to calculate the process component value based on the activity values. For simplicity, we use the formulas that yield values between zero and one. We also select weighting factors that reflect our perception of the relative importance of our process component activities. For our example, we set all weighting factors to one.

Electronic spreadsheets can be established to capture the measurement data, calculate the metrics, and display the results. Figure 6–29 illustrates an example of what the results may look like.

Process Integrity Measurement Step 7

Once all the activity values have been assigned, the seventh process measurement step is to combine the process component values into a process integrity index. In this example, the results are input into the *ProcIndex* equation. As shown in the top panel of Figure 6–29, *ProcIndex* is equal to 0.59. By examining the details in the lower panel of the figure and referring to the corresponding value scales, the following observations are made:

- **Seller Project Planning** $(xt_1) = $ **0.85.** The seller reviewed the SOW, communicated with the customer to discuss any questions, and assembled a project planning team. A risk assessment was performed, and the planning team used its expert judgment to develop task-derived resource estimates. The seller business management calculated the task-derived and risk-derived dollar estimates so that the management team could compare the top-down risk estimate with the bottom-up task estimate. The seller managers got together to discuss the estimates, and they could not agree. The senior manager made a decision.

- **Seller Development Team** $(xt_2) = $ **0.56.** The cost and schedule were tracked on an ad hoc basis. The person who was assigned the Lead Developer position established project files but did not do it according to the schedule. The Lead Developer held peer reviews but they were not documented. The independent product assurance support was tracked on a periodic basis. The project documentation was only partially edited. Because of several concurrent projects, the seller management did not mentor the seller project management.

- **Customer/Seller Development Team** $(xt_3) = $ **0.50.** The customer management communicated with the seller developers, and there was some confusion regarding requirements. This confusion was fostered by the fact that the CCBs that were held did not document decisions regarding the requirements.

- **Seller Senior Management** $(xt_4) = $ **0.35.** The seller management was overloaded with work and did not take the time to review the work before approving it for delivery to the customer.

At this point, we need to decide on whether our question—Is the organizational software systems development process producing "good" products?—has been answered. We suggest meeting with the appropriate people to examine the observations and discuss how to address the corresponding results. This measurement process helps to focus on what activities the organization needs to address. We would also suggest looking at the corresponding *product* integrity results.

We summarize our process measurement discussion in Figure 6–30, which lists seven steps to follow when setting up and collecting process metrics. Our recommendation is to start simple and try a pilot measurement program.

After you decide on what questions you want answered, the process components, and the process component activities you want to measure, you need to decide on the granularity of your process measurements. We recommend that you do not select too many process component activities at first. You need to collect data and determine what activities are worth measuring. If you have many activities, each activity's contribution to the measurement is reduced accordingly (unless weighting factors are used). However, you do not want to measure too few activities, else you may not be gaining insight into whether or not your process is consistently producing products that satisfy your customer.

As a result of reviewing the preceding measurement observations, decision makers can focus their attention (and potentially, resources) on those activities that may need improvement or on questions that need to be answered. The decision might be to take more measurements and review them carefully. Perhaps, the software development process needs to be more closely followed; maybe the process needs to be changed, or maybe the management is overcommitted. Regardless, these measurements are expressed in everyday terms to be used consistently to achieve customer satisfaction in terms of value scales that make sense for your organization.

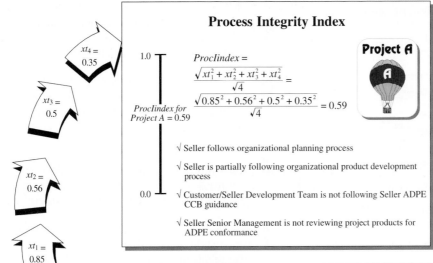

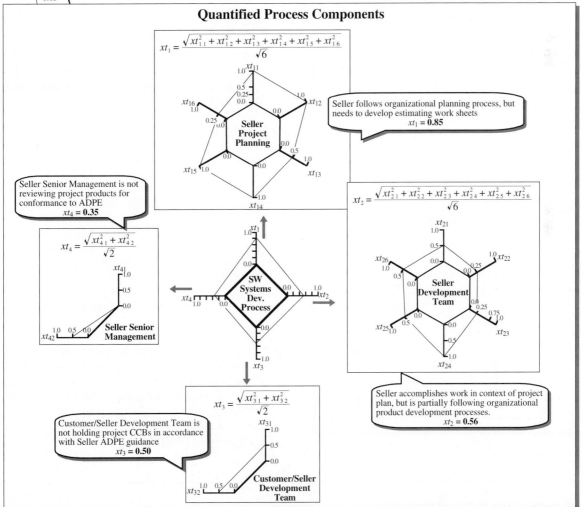

FIGURE 6–29 This figure illustrates one way to display the results of quantifying a software development process. On the basis of the example measures, the process integrity index, *ProcIndex*, equals 0.59.

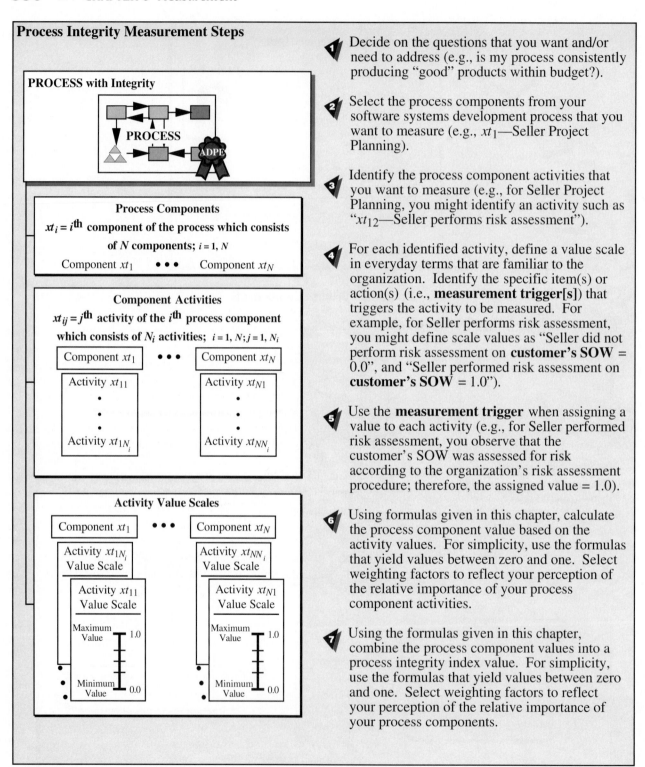

Process Integrity Measurement Steps

PROCESS with Integrity

PROCESS

ADPE

Process Components

$xt_i = i^{th}$ component of the process which consists of N components; $i = 1, N$

Component xt_1 • • •   Component xt_N

Component Activities

$xt_{ij} = j^{th}$ activity of the ith process component which consists of N_i activities; $i = 1, N; j = 1, N_i$

Component xt_1 • • •   Component xt_N

Activity xt_{11} ⋮ Activity xt_{1N_i}

Activity xt_{N1} ⋮ Activity xt_{NN_i}

Activity Value Scales

Component xt_1 • • •   Component xt_N

Activity xt_{1N_i} Value Scale

Activity xt_{11} Value Scale

Maximum Value — 1.0

Minimum Value — 0.0

Activity xt_{NN_i} Value Scale

Activity xt_{N1} Value Scale

Maximum Value — 1.0

Minimum Value — 0.0

1 Decide on the questions that you want and/or need to address (e.g., is my process consistently producing "good" products within budget?).

2 Select the process components from your software systems development process that you want to measure (e.g., xt_1—Seller Project Planning).

3 Identify the process component activities that you want to measure (e.g., for Seller Project Planning, you might identify an activity such as "xt_{12}—Seller performs risk assessment").

4 For each identified activity, define a value scale in everyday terms that are familiar to the organization. Identify the specific item(s) or action(s) (i.e., **measurement trigger[s]**) that triggers the activity to be measured. For example, for Seller performs risk assessment, you might define scale values as "Seller did not perform risk assessment on **customer's SOW** = 0.0", and "Seller performed risk assessment on **customer's SOW** = 1.0").

5 Use the **measurement trigger** when assigning a value to each activity (e.g., for Seller performed risk assessment, you observe that the customer's SOW was assessed for risk according to the organization's risk assessment procedure; therefore, the assigned value = 1.0).

6 Using formulas given in this chapter, calculate the process component value based on the activity values. For simplicity, use the formulas that yield values between zero and one. Select weighting factors to reflect your perception of the relative importance of your process component activities.

7 Using the formulas given in this chapter, combine the process component values into a process integrity index value. For simplicity, use the formulas that yield values between zero and one. Select weighting factors to reflect your perception of the relative importance of your process components.

FIGURE 6–30   This high-level procedure helps you through the process measurement steps based on the concepts and examples introduced in this chapter.

6.5 CAPABILITY MATURITY MODEL (CMM) FOR SOFTWARE

The purpose of this section is to show how the process integrity concept and formulas discussed in the preceding sections can be applied to a widely known framework for improving software systems development—the Capability Maturity Model (CMM) for Software developed by the Software Engineering Institute (SEI).[6] We assume that you are familiar with the CMM, and you can skip this section without loss of continuity. However, to set context and to link with the previous discussion of process measurement, we present a brief summary of the model. A complete description of Version 1.1 of the model can be found in the following publications (see the bibliography at the end of this book for a brief description of each of these documents):

- Paulk, M. C., B. Curtis, M. B. Chrissis, and C. V. Weber, "Capability Maturity Model for Software, Version 1.1," Software Engineering Institute and Carnegie Mellon University Technical Report CMU/SEI-93-TR-24, February 1993.
- Paulk, M. C., C. V. Weber, S. M. Garcia, M. B. Chrissis, and M. Bush, "Key Practices of the Capability Maturity Model, Version 1.1," Software Engineering Institute and Carnegie Mellon University Technical Report CMU/SEI-93-TR-25, February 1993.
- Paulk, M. C., and others. *The Capability Maturity Model: Guidelines for Improving the Software Process.* Reading, MA: Addison-Wesley Publishing Company, 1995.

The CMM for Software (hereafter referred to as the CMM) summary given in the following paragraphs is adapted from the first two documents in the list.

The CMM is a five-level road map for improving the software process. The CMM is a *guide* (not a cookbook) for evolving toward a culture of software engineering excellence. It is a model for *organizational* improvement. The CMM provides a framework for improving software engineering practice. The CMM not only provides guidelines for improving process management but also provides guidelines for introducing technology into an organization. Furthermore, the CMM is an underlying structure for consistent software process improvement efforts. An organization can perform these exercises on itself to assess its capability to produce good software products consistently. Customers can perform corollary evaluation exercises on prospective software development vendors to help assess the risk of doing business with those vendors. Figure 6–31 depicts the five maturity levels—(1) Initial, (2) Repeatable, (3) Defined, (4) Managed, and (5) Optimizing.

As indicated in the figure, Level 1 organizations produce software by some amorphous process that is only known to a few individuals or heros. During the course of the project, the project leader ends up saying something like the following:

We only have a few weeks before delivery. Kiss your spouses, boy friends, girl friends, dogs, cats, whatever, goodbye for the next three weeks. By the way, that includes nights and weekends, as well. That's what it is going to take to get it done.

With luck, the work somehow gets done. However, even in the best of circumstances, it is difficult to account for everything that is needed for successful software development to take place. Therefore, the SEI defines each maturity level as a layer in the foundation for continuous process improvement. A maturity level is a well-defined evolutionary plateau[7] on the path toward becoming a mature

---

[6]See the bibliography for a brief description of the SEI mission.

[7]We have shown the levels to be parallel because we believe that most organizations operate at multiple levels, at the same time. In contrast, the SEI literature presents the levels in a staircase-like fashion to indicate that an organization needs to establish itself at one level before moving up to the next level.

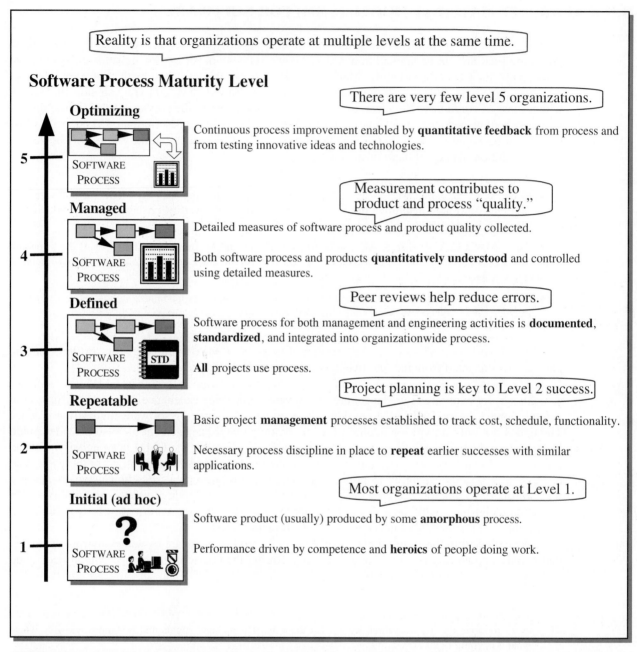

Reality is that organizations operate at multiple levels at the same time.

Software Process Maturity Level

There are very few level 5 organizations.

Optimizing

5 —

SOFTWARE PROCESS

Continuous process improvement enabled by **quantitative feedback** from process and from testing innovative ideas and technologies.

Measurement contributes to product and process "quality."

Managed

4 —

SOFTWARE PROCESS

Detailed measures of software process and product quality collected.

Both software process and products **quantitatively understood** and controlled using detailed measures.

Peer reviews help reduce errors.

Defined

3 —

SOFTWARE PROCESS   STD

Software process for both management and engineering activities is **documented**, **standardized**, and integrated into organizationwide process.

All projects use process.

Project planning is key to Level 2 success.

Repeatable

2 —

SOFTWARE PROCESS

Basic project **management** processes established to track cost, schedule, functionality.

Necessary process discipline in place to **repeat** earlier successes with similar applications.

Most organizations operate at Level 1.

Initial (ad hoc)

1 —

SOFTWARE PROCESS

Software product (usually) produced by some **amorphous** process.

Performance driven by competence and **heroics** of people doing work.

FIGURE 6–31   The Software Engineering Institute's Capability Maturity Model for Software is a five-level road map for improving an organization's software systems development process. Each maturity level is a well-defined evolutionary plateau on the path toward becoming a "mature" software organization.

software organization. Associated with each maturity level (except Level 1) is a "software process capability" that describes the range of expected results from following a process.

As indicated in Figure 6–31, the software process is essentially ad hoc and generally undisciplined for a Level 1 organization. A Level 1 organization's process capability is unpredictable because the software process is constantly changed as the work progresses. Level 1 performance depends on the individual capabilities of the staff and managers and varies with their innate skills, knowledge, and motivations. Level 2 organizations focus on project management. The process capability of an organization has been elevated by establishing a disciplined process under sound management control. In contrast to a Level 1 organization, at Level 2 a repeatable process exists for software projects. At Level 3, the focus shifts to establishing organizationwide processes for management and engineering activities. Level 3 processes evolve from the processes and success while achieving Level 2. At Level 2, one or two projects may have repeatable processes, but at Level 3 all projects use the processes. At Level 4 the measurements that have been put in place at Level 2 and Level 3 are used to understand and control software processes and products quantitatively. At Level 5, continuous process improvement is enabled by quantitative process feedback and technology insertion.

Each maturity level consists of "key process areas (KPAs)" that are defined by "key practices."[8] Key process areas identify the issues that must be addressed to achieve a maturity level. KPAs are a cluster of related activities that, when performed collectively, achieve a set of goals considered important for enhancing process capability. KPAs are defined to reside at a single maturity level.[9] For example, as shown in Figure 6–32, associated with Level 2 are six KPAs—(1) Requirements Management, (2) Software Project Planning, (3) Software Project Tracking and Oversight, (4) Software Subcontract Management, (5) Software Quality Assurance, and (6) Software Configuration Management.

Associated with each of these six KPAs is a set of goals. For example, associated with the Software Project Planning KPA are three goals, one of which is the following: "Software estimates are documented for use in planning and tracking the software project." Goals are associated with key practices which are the policies, procedures, and activities that contribute most to the effective institutionalization and implementation of a goal (and therefore a KPA). A key practice can be associated with more than one goal.

Key practices are grouped into five common features—(1) Commitment to Perform, (2) Ability to Perform, (3) Activities Performed, (4) Measurement and Analysis, and (5) Verifying Implementation. The key practices that make up the common features represent the "what" needs to be done or simply stated the requirements. Although many practices contribute to success in developing effective software, the key practices were identified because of their effectiveness in improving an organization's capability in a particular key process area. Implementation of the key practices is the "how" part of institutionalization of KPAs.

With the preceding as background, we present the following simplified example of how process integrity can be computed for each of the SEI maturity levels or KPAs. This example is presented using the seven process measurement steps:

Process Measurement Step 1

Decide on what questions you want and/or need to address. Is my project performing activities associated with the Level 2 KPAs?

Process Measurement Step 2

Select the process components from your software systems development process that you want to measure. As shown in Figure 6–33, we select the Level 2 KPAs as the process components to be measured.

---

[8]Regarding the use of the word "key" here and elsewhere in the model, the description of the CMM includes the following statements:

> The adjective "key" implies that there are process areas (and processes) that are not key to achieving a maturity level. The CMM does not describe all the process areas in detail that are involved with developing and maintaining software. Certain process areas have been identified as key determiners of process capability; these are the ones described in the CMM.

> Although other issues affect process performance, the key process areas were identified because of their effectiveness in improving an organization's software process capability. They may be considered the requirements for achieving a maturity level.

[9]This constraint may be removed in future versions of the model. The measurement approach subsequently discussed in this section is not tied to this constraint.

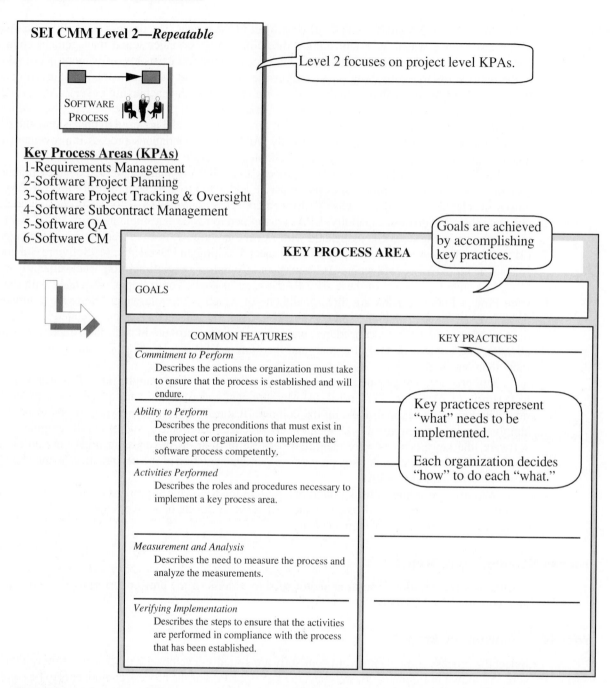

FIGURE 6–32 Each maturity level consists of "key process areas (KPAs)." Each KPA is characterized, in part, by "goals" and "key practices."

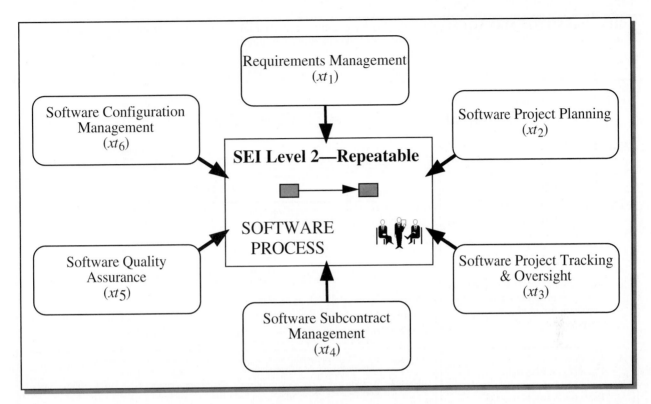

FIGURE 6–33 A repeatable software process that has integrity is one that has the following six process components shown above—(xt_1), (xt_2), (xt_3), (xt_4), (xt_5), and (xt_6).

Process Measurement Step 3

Identify the process component activities that you want to measure. For each Level 2 KPA, we identify the Activities Performed common feature as the process component activities to be measured. For simplicity of explanation, Figure 6–34 shows only the detail for the Requirements Management KPA.[10] The process component activities to be measured for Requirements Management correspond to the activities labeled RM.AC.1, RM.AC.2, and RM.AC.3. Other process component activities would be measured for the remaining Level 2 KPAs.

Process Measurement Step 4

For each identified activity, define a value scale in everyday terms that are familiar to the organization. Figure 6–35 shows our activity value scale definitions for the Requirements Management activities. The (xt_{11}) activity value scale is continuous and is based on a percentage of the requirements reviewed by the engineering group.[11] The (xt_{12}) activity value scale has three discrete values designed to encourage review and incorporation of changes to agreed-upon requirements before they are incorporated into the project. The (xt_{13}) activity value scale reflects either "yes" or "no." This activity value scale was designed to stress whether or not the activity is being performed.

---

[10]In Figure 6–34, the term "allocated requirements" is used in the CMM to denote those system requirements that are set apart (i.e., allocated) for implementation through software code.

[11]In the language of our book, "engineering group" is an organizational element encompassing development disciplines.

REQUIREMENTS MANAGEMENT—Establish a common understanding between the customer and the software
(Level 2 Key Process Area) project of the customer's requirements

Capability Maturity Model for Software, Version 1.1, February 1993
CMU/SEI-93-TR-24, ESC-TR-93-177

GOALS

RM.GL.1—System requirements allocated to software are controlled to establish a baseline for software engineering and management use. | RM.CO.1 | RM.AB.1 | RM.AB.2 | RM.AB.3 | RM.AB.4 | RM.AC.1 | RM.ME.1 | RM.VE.1 | RM.VE.2 | RM.VE.3 |

RM.GL.2—Software plans, products, and activities are kept consistent with the system requirements allocated to software. | RM.CO.1 | RM.AB.3 | RM.AB.4 | RM.AC.2 | RM.AC.3 | RM.ME.1 | RM.VE.1 | RM.VE.2 | RM.VE.3 |

COMMON FEATURES	KEY PRACTICES
Commitment to Perform Describes the actions the organization must take to ensure that the process is established and will endure.	RM.CO.1—The project follows a written organizational policy for managing the systems requirements allocated to the software.
Ability to Perform Describes the preconditions that must exist in the project or organization to implement the software process competently.	RM.AB.1—For each project, responsibility is established for analyzing the system requirements and allocating them to hardware, software, and other system components. RM.AB.2—The allocated requirements are documented. RM.AB.3—Adequate resources and funding are provided for managing the allocated requirements. RM.AB.4—Members of the software engineering group and other software-related groups are trained to perform their requirements management activities.
Activities Performed Describes the roles and procedures necessary to implement a key process area.	RM.AC.1—The software engineering group reviews the allocated requirements before they are incorporated into the software project. RM.AC.2—The software engineering group uses the allocated requirements as the basis for software plans, work products, and activities. RM.AC.3—Changes to the allocated requirements are reviewed and incorporated into the software project.
Measurement and Analysis Describes the need to measure the process and analyze the measurements.	RM.ME.1—Measurements are made and used to determine the status of the activities for managing the allocated requirements.
Verifying Implementation Describes the steps to ensure that the activities are performed in compliance with the process that has been established.	RM.VE.1—The activities for managing the allocated requirements are reviewed with senior management on a periodic basis. RM.VE.2—The activities for managing the allocated requirements are reviewed with the project manager on both a periodic and event-driven basis. RM.VE.3—The software quality assurance group reviews and/or audits the activities and work products for managing the allocated requirements and reports the results.

FIGURE 6–34 The Requirements Management process component (i.e., key process area) can be measured using the three activities labeled RM.AC.1, RM.AC.2, and RM.AC.3.

Similarly, to compute integrity values for the other five KPAs, value scales for each of the activities associated with each KPA would be defined. The resulting process "goodness" scale is shown in Figure 6–36.

Process Measurement Step 5

For each identified activity, observe activity accomplishment and choose a corresponding scale value reflecting that accomplishment. Observations are made, values are assigned, and values are recorded using a software spreadsheet program.

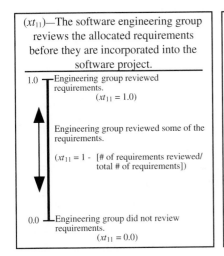

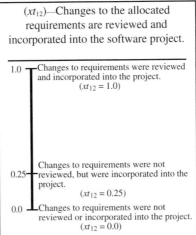

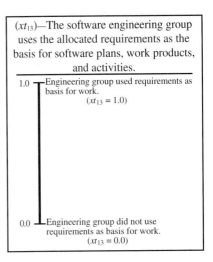

FIGURE 6–35 Example activity value scales for the three activities making up the Requirements Management key process area.

Process Measurement Step 6

Using the formulas given in this chapter, calculate the process component value based on the activity values. For simplicity, use the formulas that yield values between zero and one. Select weighting factors to reflect your perception of the relative importance of your process components.

As shown in Figure 6–37, the generalized process integrity index formula is used to establish the formulas necessary to measure the activities associated with the Level 2 KPAs. As indicated in the figure, the formulas are normalized so that the calculated values will fall between zero and one, and the weighting factors are set equal to one.

Process Measurement Step 7

Using the formulas given in this chapter, combine the process component values into a process integrity index value. For simplicity, use the formulas that yield values between zero and one. Select weighting factors to reflect your perception of the relative importance to your organization.

A formula for rolling the KPA integrity values up into a Level 2 integrity index is shown in Figure 6–37. For the Requirements Management KPA (xt_1), there are 3 activities; hence, the square root of 3 in the denominator. For the Software Project Planning KPA (xt_2), there are 15 activities; hence, the square root of 15 in the denominator for the formula. For the Software Project Tracking and Oversight KPA (xt_3), there are 13 activities; for the Software Subcontract Management KPA (xt_4), there are 13 activities; for the Software Quality Assurance KPA (xt_5), there are 8 activities; and for the Software Configuration Management KPA (xt_6), there are 10 activities. Thus, in terms of determining an organization's compliance with Level 2 KPAs and underlying practices, the process integrity vector resides in a space of 62 dimensions (3 + 15 + 13 + 13 + 8 +10). A similar approach can be used to compute process integrity indices for the other CMM levels.

6.6 OTHER PROCESS-RELATED MEASUREMENTS

In addition to product integrity and process integrity measurements, it may be useful to establish other process-related measurements tied to one or more components of the software systems development process. Again, the question is, "What attributes of the software systems development process are of

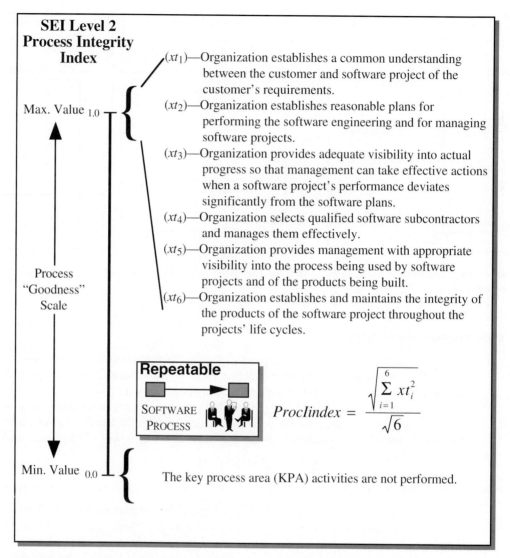

SEI Level 2 Process Integrity Index

Max. Value 1.0

(xt_1)—Organization establishes a common understanding between the customer and software project of the customer's requirements.

(xt_2)—Organization establishes reasonable plans for performing the software engineering and for managing software projects.

(xt_3)—Organization provides adequate visibility into actual progress so that management can take effective actions when a software project's performance deviates significantly from the software plans.

(xt_4)—Organization selects qualified software subcontractors and manages them effectively.

(xt_5)—Organization provides management with appropriate visibility into the process being used by software projects and of the products being built.

(xt_6)—Organization establishes and maintains the integrity of the products of the software project throughout the projects' life cycles.

Process "Goodness" Scale

Repeatable

SOFTWARE PROCESS

$$ProcIndex = \frac{\sqrt{\sum_{i=1}^{6} xt_i^2}}{\sqrt{6}}$$

Min. Value 0.0

The key process area (KPA) activities are not performed.

FIGURE 6–36 The Level 2 process "goodness" scale ranges from a minimum value of 0.0 (i.e., activities not being performed in any KPA) to a maximum value of 1.0 (i.e., all activities being performed in each KPA).

interest to measure?" In part, the answer is tied to determining which activities contribute to "staying in business," which is strongly tied to "customer satisfaction." "Customer satisfaction" can be expressed in many ways. In this section, we show you how to effect process improvement, using an approach other than product and process integrity indexes. Our approach consists of the following two steps:

■ The application of metrics to the software systems development process activities to provide insight into the extent to which these activities are, or are not, contributing to customer satisfaction (as expressed in terms of the five product integrity attributes[12]).

---

[12]Remember, in Section 6.3, we explained the concept of product integrity in terms of the following product attributes: (at_1) fulfills customer needs, (at_2) can be easily and completely traced through its life cycle, (at_3) meets specified performance criteria, (at_4) meets cost expectations, and (at_5) meets delivery expectations.

Process Integrity Index

$$ProcIndex = \frac{\sqrt{\sum_{i=1}^{N} w_i^2\, xt_i^2}}{\sqrt{\sum_{i=1}^{N} w_i^2 (\text{maximum}[\,xt_i])^2}}$$

N = number of organizational process components
w_i = weighting factor for process component xt_i
xt_i = the ith process component
maximum $[xt_i]$ = maximum value of xt_i

$$xt_i = \frac{\sqrt{\sum_{j=1}^{N_i} w_{ij}^2\, xt_{ij}^2}}{\sqrt{\sum_{j=1}^{N_i} w_{ij}^2 (\text{maximum}[\,xt_{ij}])^2}}$$

N_i = number of activities making up process component xt_i
w_{ij} = weighting factor for activity xt_{ij} of process component xt_i
xt_{ij} = the jth activity of the ith process component
maximum $[xt_{ij}]$ = maximum value of xt_{ij}

SEI Level 2—Repeatable *ProcIndex*

$N = 6$, all $w_i = 1$, all maximum $[xt_i] = 1$

$N_1 = 3$, $N_2 = 15$, $N_3 = N_4 = 13$, $N_5 = 8$, $N_6 = 10$, all $w_{ij} = 1$, all maximum $[xt_{ij}] = 1$

xt_1 = Requirements Management, xt_2 = Software Project Planning, xt_3 = Software Project Tracking and Oversight, xt_4 = Software Subcontract Management, xt_5 = Software Quality Assurance, and xt_6 = Software Configuration Management

$$ProcIndex = \frac{\sqrt{\sum_{i=1}^{6} xt_i^2}}{\sqrt{6}} = \frac{\sqrt{xt_1^2 + xt_2^2 + xt_3^2 + xt_4^2 + xt_5^2 + xt_6^2}}{\sqrt{6}}$$

$$xt_1 = \frac{\sqrt{\sum_{j=1}^{3} xt_{1j}^2}}{\sqrt{3}} \qquad xt_2 = \frac{\sqrt{\sum_{j=1}^{15} xt_{2j}^2}}{\sqrt{15}} \qquad xt_3 = \frac{\sqrt{\sum_{j=1}^{13} xt_{3j}^2}}{\sqrt{13}}$$

$$xt_4 = \frac{\sqrt{\sum_{j=1}^{13} xt_{4j}^2}}{\sqrt{13}} \qquad xt_5 = \frac{\sqrt{\sum_{j=1}^{8} xt_{5j}^2}}{\sqrt{8}} \qquad xt_6 = \frac{\sqrt{\sum_{j=1}^{10} xt_{6j}^2}}{\sqrt{10}}$$

FIGURE 6–37 The process integrity index for CMM Level 2 can be defined using the activities for each of the six Key Process Areas. For example, there are three activities for Requirements Management (i.e., xt_1), fifteen activities for Software Project Planning (i.e., xt_2), etc.

- Those activities that are not contributing to customer satisfaction will be modified (or eliminated) until they do. These modifications are what "process improvement" means.

We now explain how to apply these two steps to derive a set of process metrics. The context for this discussion is our example organizational software systems development process. This process is sufficiently general so that you will be able to adapt it to your own environment.

The discussion that follows assumes that the organizational process is used to govern a number of projects unfolding, more or less, in parallel. We measure things on individual projects and then average these things over one or more projects. From these averages, we derive findings about the underlying software systems development process to effect its improvement.

In order to preform actual measurements of software systems development processes, the preceding considerations need to be tempered by practical considerations. Measurement involves collecting data and putting the data into a meaningful form for process improvement purposes. These tasks cannot be onerous because they will get in the way of software systems development work—and measurement will not be performed. Thus, as we stressed in preceding sections, the metrics must be simple to collect and analyze. The price for this simplicity is that the metrics are limited regarding the insight they provide into process workings. For the near term, your approach should be to collect some simple metrics to see if they help highlight activities that should be changed to effect process improvement. Through this experience, you can then determine whether you need more sophisticated measurement techniques.

The simplicity criterion just mentioned means in a metrics context that we simply count the number of times specific software systems development activities are performed. To bring in customer satisfaction, we use the receipt of deliverable and acceptance of deliverable forms. The Acceptance of Deliverable form provides customer feedback regarding each product delivered according to the following three degrees of "customer satisfaction" (in descending order of this satisfaction):

- The product is accepted as delivered

- The product is accepted with minor changes needed

- The product requires changes to be negotiated.

Clearly, the data on the acceptance of deliverable form do not provide detailed insight into the extent to which the product fulfills specified customer needs (i.e., product integrity attribute at_1) or meets specified performance criteria (i.e., product integrity attribute at_3). In terms of overall process improvement, these detailed considerations are not pertinent. For instance, our example organizational software systems development process mandates that, before computer code is delivered to the customer, it must be acceptance tested. This acceptance testing activity does address the details of the product integrity attributes at_1 and at_3 for that computer code product. In fact, if acceptance testing does demonstrate the presence of these attributes, customer confirmation on the acceptance of deliverable form is a foregone conclusion. The point is that (1) counting these forms, (2) putting these counts into the three bins of degrees of customer satisfaction just listed, and then (3) relating these counts to the number of times certain activities are carried out, does provide gross insight into the effectiveness of these activities in the overall software systems development process.

To relate the preceding discussion to actual process measurement, we discuss some specific process-related metrics. We begin with a general process-related metric and then illustrate it with specific examples. This general metric and the associated examples are a starting point for defining a set of process-related metrics to provide some insight into the state of your software systems development process and to effect its improvement. We also consider other metrics to illustrate additional process-related measurement ideas.

The general process-related metric is the following:

$$M1_q = \frac{\sum_{i=1}^{\#Del}(NProcActivity_{q\,i})}{\#Del} \qquad (6.6\text{--}1)$$

$M1_q$ is the average number of times it takes to perform activity q in the organizational software systems development process in producing the ith deliverable before delivery. The quantity $NProcActivity_{q\,i}$ is the number of times the qth process activity is performed on the ith deliverable before delivery. The quantity $\#Del$ is the number of deliverables to include in the average. This number may apply to a specific project or to a group of projects. For example, $\#Del$ may be the number of deliverables produced on a project over a three-month period. As another example, the quantity $\#Del$ may be the number of deliverables produced on all projects under the supervision of a particular seller senior manager. Examples of the quantity $NProcActivity_{q\,i}$ are the following:

- Number of CCB meetings where the ith deliverable was discussed
- Number of peer reviews to produce the ith deliverable
- Number of product assurance reviews to produce the ith deliverable
- Number of technical edits to produce the ith deliverable
- Number of management reviews of the ith deliverable

The metric $M1_q$ can indicate the following, depending on $\#Del$ included in the sum:

- The extent to which the qth organizational software systems development process activity is being used to produce deliverables
- The average number of times activity q is required to get a deliverable to the customer
- The trend in the average number of times activity q is required to get a deliverable to the customer (this trend would be measured by collecting and reporting the metric, for example, every month for a given value of $\#Del$)

To illustrate $M1_q$, let $NProcActivity_{q\,i} = NPeer_i$, the number of peer reviews required to produce the ith deliverable. Then, we define the metric $MPeer$ related to the organizational software systems development process peer review activity as follows:

$$MPeer = \frac{\sum_{i=1}^{\#Del}(NPeer_i)}{\#Del} \qquad (6.6\text{--}2)$$

This metric is the average number of peer reviews required to produce deliverables for delivery. If, for example, the sum in Equation 6.6–2 is restricted to a single project, this metric indicates the following:

- The extent to which the peer reviews are being used on the project
- The average number of peer reviews required to get a deliverable to the customer for that project
- If this metric were collected and reported, say monthly, the trend in the average number of peer reviews required to get a deliverable to the customer for that project

If similar statistics were compiled for other projects, then we could determine for subsequent project planning purposes how many peer reviews to include in the cost and schedule of project plans. This information would serve to improve the project planing process called out in your organizational software systems development process because it would help to refine the costing and scheduling algorithms.

However, the metric in Equation 6.6–2 does not explicitly address product integrity attributes. The following metric, which is an adaptation of Equation 6.6–2, illustrates how connection to these attributes can be made:

$$MPeerACC = \frac{\sum_{i=1}^{\#DelAcc}(NPeer_i)}{\# DelAcc} \tag{6.6–3}$$

This metric is the average number of peer reviews required to produce deliverables that are accepted by the customer (i.e., the customer returns the acceptance of deliverable form indicating "the product is accepted as delivered"); the *#DelAcc* is the number of such deliverables. If, for example, the sum in Equation 6.6–3 is restricted to a single project, this metric indicates the following:

- The average number of peer reviews required to get a deliverable accepted by the customer for that project
- If this metric were collected and reported, say monthly, the trend in the average number of peer reviews required to get a deliverable accepted by the customer for that project

If similar statistics were compiled for other projects, then we could see whether there is a correlation between the number of peer reviews and customer acceptance. Of course, other organizational software systems development process activities influence customer acceptance. It is thus admittedly an oversimplification to say that there is a single value for this average that should be applied across all projects to enhance the likelihood of customer acceptance of products. For example, certain projects might involve the development of complex products that by their nature would require more peer reviews than less complex products would.

But the preceding metric could provide some insight into the correlation between the peer review activity and customer satisfaction as expressed on the acceptance of deliverable form, as follows:

Suppose several projects have a track record of consistent product acceptance by the customer. Suppose also that the value of *MPeerACC* obtained by averaging over these projects is, say, 3.5 (i.e., three to four peer reviews are used to produce deliverables on these projects). Furthermore, suppose that (1) several other projects have a track record of consistent deliverables requiring "changes to be negotiated" and (2) the value of *MPeerACC* averaged over these projects is, say, 0.5 (i.e., one or no peer reviews are used to produce deliverables on these projects). Then, *other organizational software systems development process activities being equal* (admittedly, a big "if," but this "if" could be examined by applying the instantiations of the metric $M1_q$ for these activities), it could be surmised that there is some correlation between the peer review activity and customer acceptance of products.

Of course, things generally turn out to be far more complicated than the simple situation just illustrated. To get a sense of such complications, we modify the situation so that it reads as follows:

Suppose several projects have a track record of consistent product acceptance by the customer. Suppose also that the value of *MPeerACC* averaged over these projects is, say, 3.5 (i.e., an average of three peer reviews are used to produce deliverables on these projects). Furthermore, suppose that (1) several other projects have a track record of consistent deliverables requiring "changes to be negotiated" and (2) the value of *MPeerAcc* averaged over these projects is, say, 4.5. Then, if other organizational software systems development process activities were being applied consistently across both sets of projects (which could be determined by applying the instantiations of the metric $M1_q$ to these activities), the organizational software systems development process peer review activity would need to be examined from perspectives such as the following: (1) Are there fundamental differences between the way peer reviews are being utilized on one set of projects versus the other set (e.g., are the peer reviews on the project set with *MPeer ACC* = 4.5 less formal with no written record of what was accomplished?)? (2) Are the two sets of projects fundamentally different in terms of the nature of their products so that it is not meaningful to say that, because it takes more peer reviews on these projects, the peer review process is less effective? For (1), the process improvement response might be to modify the way that set of projects performs its peer reviews so that it mirrors the way the other set of projects performs peer reviews. If this modification brings *MPeerACC* in line with the value of this metric for the other set of projects, then the effectiveness of the peer review activity would be demonstrated. For (2), the process improvement response might be to modify the organizational software systems development process to call out two approaches to peer reviews—one for projects that mirror the one project set and the other that mirror the other project set. The result of this organizational software systems development process modification would be process improvement.

It should be noted that an assumption underlying this analysis is that if there is a correlation between doing an activity *N* times and customer product acceptance, then doing the activity much less than *N* or more than *N* is less desirable. This assumption helps simplify the analysis. It is not possible to make general statements about the validity of this assumption. You will need to see what makes sense for your organization. For example, you may need to specify the number of times a given activity is to be performed. Then, you can observe the effect on customer acceptance of products and make adjustments accordingly.

Metrics such as the one defined in Equation 6.6–3 can be extended to encompass more than one organizational software systems development process activity. This approach may be useful if it proves too difficult to correlate a specific activity with customer satisfaction. For example, it may be more useful to lump peer reviews and independent product assurance reviews into a single metric. This metric might provide insight into the correlation between detailed technical product reviews (which these activities are intended to address) and customer satisfaction. Extending the Equation 6.6–3 idea, such a metric might be the following:

$$MTRevACC = \frac{\sum_{i=1}^{\#DelAcc}(NPeer_i + NPA_i)}{\#DelAcc} \tag{6.6–4}$$

This metric is the average number of peer reviews and independent product assurance reviews required to produce deliverables that are accepted by the customer (i.e., the customer returns the acceptance of deliverable form indicating "the product is accepted as delivered"). As was the case in Equation 6.6–3, $NPeer_i$ is the number of peer reviews required to produce the ith deliverable accepted by the customer. Similarly, NPA_i is the number of independent product assurance reviews required to produce the ith deliverable accepted by the customer. If, for example, the sum in Equation 6.6–4 is restricted to a single project, this metric indicates the following:

- The average number of detailed product technical reviews (i.e., peer reviews and independent product assurance reviews) required to get a deliverable accepted by the customer for that project

- If this metric were collected and reported, say monthly, the trend in the average number of detailed product technical reviews required to get a deliverable accepted by the customer for that project

If similar statistics were compiled for other projects, then we could see if there is a correlation between the number of detailed product technical reviews and customer acceptance.

In addition to activity-specific metrics such as those just discussed, there are metrics that can address product integrity attributes by simply counting the number of deliverables over a specific period of time. For example, the following metric addresses the product integrity attribute of "at_5—meets delivery expectations":

$$\%DelOnTime = \left[\frac{(\# \, DelOnTime)}{\# \, Del} \right] \times 100 \tag{6.6–5}$$

This metric gives the percentage of deliverables delivered on time to the customer during a specific period for certain projects, where "on time" is according to delivery dates specified in project plans or CCB minutes. The quantity *#Del* is the number of deliverables delivered during a specific period for specific projects. The quantity *#DelOnTime* is the number of these deliverables delivered on time. For example, *#Del* may be the number of deliverables delivered during a particular month for all projects active during that month. As another example, *#Del* may be the number of deliverables on a specific project during the entire period the project was active. The preceding metric provides insight into how well the organization is meeting planned schedules. This insight, in turn, provides insight into the effectiveness of the project planning activity in scheduling deliverables and the effectiveness of the CCB activity in updating project plan schedules. Ideally, the organization should strive to have *%DelOn-Time* = 100 (all deliverables are delivered on time) for whatever *#Del* encompasses. If *%DelOnTime* encompasses all projects and if the value of this metric is significantly less than 100 (say, 50), then this statistic would be used to investigate whether (1) certain organizational process activities should be accomplished in less time and/or (2) the project planning activity needs to be revised to set more realistic schedules. This investigation, in turn, may precipitate changes to the activities in question—the end result being organization process improvement.

Regarding the project planning activity, this activity precedes actual organization product development work. Yet, there are product integrity issues regarding this activity. Sometimes the customer pays for the product resulting from this activity—namely, the project plan. If the cost of this activity has been a major customer concern in the past, one metric that can possibly help in this area is the following:

$$AvPPlan\$ = \frac{\sum_{i=1}^{\# \, Projects} (PPlan\$_i)}{\# \, Projects} \tag{6.6–6}$$

The metric *AvPPlan$* is the average cost to produce a project plan resulting in a project. *PPlan$$_i$* is the cost to produce the i^{th} project plan resulting in a project. *#Projects* is the number of projects to include in the average. This average can be computed over any period. Thus, for example, *#Projects* could be the number of projects in a six-month period. By computing this average periodically (e.g., monthly), the trend in this average can be determined (e.g., the average cost to produce a project plan has declined at a rate of 10 percent per month for the last six months). Also, the project plans to include in the sum can be limited by defining *#Projects* appropriately. Thus, for example, the metric in Equation 6.6–6 can be used to compute the average cost to produce a project plan for a specific customer by limiting *#Projects* and *PPlan$$_i$* to customer "ABC Corporation" projects. This metric can also be used to define the average cost of project plans for various categories of projects. For example, by limiting *#Projects* and *PPlan$$_i$* to "O&M" projects, we can compute the average project planning cost for O&M work. The metric *AvPPlan$* can also help set customer expectations regarding the cost of the organization's project planning process.

Embedded in the last metric is the number of iterations required to produce a project plan before it results in a project. The following metric can give visibility into these iterations and thereby provide additional insight into how to control project planning cost (and thereby increase the integrity of the project planning part of the organization way of doing business):

$$Av\# \, PPlan\Delta = \frac{\sum_{i=1}^{\# \, Projects} (PPlan\Delta_i)}{\# \, Projects} \tag{6.6–7}$$

The metric *Av#PPlanΔ* is the average number of drafts required to produce a project plan resulting in a project. *PPlanΔ$_i$* is the number of drafts required to produce the ith project plan resulting in a project. *#Projects* is the number of projects to include in the average. This average can be computed over any period. Thus, for example, *#Projects* could be the number of projects in a six-month period. By computing this average periodically (e.g., monthly), the trend in this average can be determined (e.g., the average number of drafts required to produce a project plan has declined at a rate of 10 percent per month for the last six months). Also, the project plans to include in the sum can be limited by defining *#Projects* appropriately. Thus, for example, the metric in Equation 6.6–7 can be used to compute the average number of drafts required to produce a project plan for a specific customer, by limiting *#Projects* and *PPlan$$_i$* to customer "ABC Corporation" projects. This latter statistic could be used to determine whether there was a shortcoming in the project planning process or a difficulty with a particular customer (or some combination of these two considerations). The metric in Equation 6.6–7 can also be used to determine the number of drafts required to produce project plans for various categories of projects. For example, by limiting *#Projects* and *PPlan$$_i$* to "O&M" projects, we can compute the average number of drafts required to produce project plans for O&M work. This statistic, in turn, can help refine the project planning activity through scheduling algorithms that depend on the type of work that the organization is being requested to do. For example, if *Av#PPlanΔ* turns out to be 3.5 for O&M work and 1.5 for the development of new software systems, and other factors being equal (e.g., there are no customer dependencies), then we can inform customers that three to four meetings between the customer and the organization will probably be required to finalize an O&M project plan, while one to two meetings between the customer and the organization will probably be required to finalize a new-systems-development project plan.

One organizational software systems development process activity often given special attention is acceptance testing.[13] Unless specifically dictated by the customer, software systems should not be delivered to the customer without acceptance testing. Furthermore, customer involvement in the acceptance testing CCBs is an effective way of assuring that the software system to be delivered does what it is supposed to do, i.e., fulfills specified customer needs and/or meets specified performance criteria. The following two metrics can be used to assess respectively the extent to which (1) software systems are being acceptance tested before delivery and (2) the customer participates in acceptance testing CCB activity:

$$\%SystemsAccTested = \left[\frac{(\# AccTestedSystemsDel)}{\# SystemsDel} \right] \times 100 \qquad \textbf{(6.6–8)}$$

$$\%SysAccTestedwithCustomer = \left[\frac{(\# AccTestedSystems \text{ with } Customer)}{\# SystemsAccTested} \right] \times 100 \qquad \textbf{(6.6–9)}$$

In Equation 6.6–8, the metric *%SystemsAccTested* gives the percentage of software systems accepted tested during a specific period for certain projects. The quantity *#SystemsDel* is the number of software systems delivered during a specific period for specific projects. The quantity *#AccTestedSystemsDel* is the number of these systems acceptance tested. For example, *#SystemsDel* may be the number of software systems delivered during a particular month for all projects active during that month. As another example, *#SystemsDel* may be the number of systems delivered on a specific project during the entire period that the project was active. Ideally, the organization should strive to have *%SystemsAccTested* = 100 (all software systems are acceptance tested before delivery) for whatever *#SystemsDel* encompasses. If *%SystemsAccTested* encompasses all projects and if the value of this metric is significantly

---

[13]As discussed in chapter 5, acceptance testing is the system-level testing that the seller performs before delivering the system to the customer. We recommend that the customer be involved in the acceptance testing process. In this way, what the customer receives at delivery is what the customer expects.

less than 100 (say, 50), then this statistic would be used to investigate why acceptance testing is not being performed. The reasons uncovered may precipitate changes to one or more organizational process activities. If, for example, a reason uncovered was that senior customer management issued edicts—at the eleventh hour—that no acceptance testing be performed, then it may be necessary to clarify the organizational software systems development process to ensure seller senior management involvement with customer senior management prior to planned acceptance testing. The end result of such changes to the activities in question is organizational process improvement.

In Equation 6.6–9, the metric *%SystemsAccTestedwithCustomer* gives the percentage of the acceptance testing activity conducted with customer participation in acceptance testing CCBs, during a specific period for certain projects. The quantity *(#SystemsAccTested with Customer)* is the number of software systems delivered during a specific period for specific projects where the customer participated in acceptance testing CCBs. The quantity *#SystemsAccTested* is the number of systems acceptance tested during this period for the specific projects in question. Ideally, the organization should strive to have *%SystemsAccTestedwithCustomer* = 100 (all software systems are acceptance tested with customer involvement before delivery) for whatever *#SystemsAccTested* encompasses. The presumption here is that, when test incident report (TIR) resolution involves the customer, our first and third product integrity attributes are satisfied by definition.

Another potentially useful approach to assessing process effectiveness at a gross level (i.e., independent of any particular organizational process activity) is to do simple counts on the contents of the acceptance of deliverable form. The following metric illustrates this approach for the case in which the contents of the form indicates "Accept as Delivered" (analogous metrics can be defined for the other two-form content possibilities):

$$CustomerSatisfied = \left[\frac{\#FormAcc + \#Unknown}{\#DelKnown + \#DelUnknown} \right] \times 100 \qquad \textbf{(6.6–10)}$$

This metric offers a variety of interpretations depending on how the factors in the numerator and denominator are used. The scope of the metric depends on the scope of the factors in the denominator. The quantities in this equation are defined as follows:

- *#FormAcc* is the number of deliverables for which the organization has received an acceptance of deliverable form indicating "Accept as Delivered."

- *#Unknown* is the number of deliverables for which the organization has not yet received an acceptance of deliverable form and for which an assumed value will be assigned.

- *#DelKnown* is the number of deliverables for which the organization has received an acceptance of deliverable form.

- *#DelUnknown* is the number of deliverables for which the organization has not yet received an acceptance of deliverable form.

- *CustomerSatisfied* is the percentage of deliverables for which the customer has indicated "Accept as Delivered" and thus is a gross measure of positive customer perception of the organization.

The following example illustrates how this metric can be used:

Suppose we are interested in customer perception of the organization for a two-month period across all projects. Suppose further that during this period the organization delivered 100 deliverables and received 50 acceptance of deliverable forms, 25 of which indicated "Accept as Delivered." In this case, *#DelKnown* = 50, *#DelUnknown* = 50, and *#FormAcc* = 25. Regarding the 50 deliverables for which the forms have not yet been received, suppose we conjecture that none of them will come back with "Accept as Delivered" (a highly undesirable case for these outstanding deliverables, the worst case being that all the forms come back indicating "Changes to Be Negotiated"). With this conjecture, *#Unknown* = 0, and the value of *CustomerSatisfied* becomes 25 percent. If, on the other hand, we conjecture that they all will come back with "Accept as Delivered," *#Unknown* = 50, and the value of *CustomerSatisfied* becomes 75 percent. These values then have the global interpretation that, for the two-month period in question, the degree of customer satisfaction with organization products across all projects is no worse than 25 percent and no better than 75 percent. If, in fact, there is a good likelihood that indeed most of the outstanding acceptance of deliverable forms will come back with other than "Accept as Delivered" indicated (as can be determined by querying the responsible project managers), then the 25 percent figure would be more representative of the state of organization affairs regarding customer perceptions. In this case, a detailed look at other metrics would be called for to see why the approval rating is so low. Equation 6.6–10 can also be used to assess customer satisfaction solely on the basis of the known status of the deliverables. For this assessment, the quantities *#UnKnown* and *#DelUnknown* are both set to zero. Using the numbers just given, the value of *CustomerSatisfaction* for the two-month period in question would then become 50 percent. This value would have the following interpretation: "For the two-month period in question, half the deliverables for which the customer returned acceptance of deliverable forms were judged acceptable as delivered."

The preceding discussion focused on metrics pertaining to organization process improvement in a product integrity context. Other quantities, although not directly related to process improvement, may offer insight into organization work profiles that could eventually be used to effect process improvement. Regarding these profiles, questions such as the following might be asked:

- What is the average size project?
- What is the average project cost?
- How is the work distributed across the customer's organization?

Regarding the first question, a metric such as the following, patterned after the metric in Equation 6.6–6, might be helpful:

$$AvProjectPersSize = \frac{\sum_{i=1}^{\#Projects}(ProjectPersSize_i)}{\#Projects} \tag{6.6-11}$$

The metric *AvProjectPersSize* is the average number of organization employees working on an organization project. *ProjectPersSize_i* is the number of organization employees working on the ith project. *#Projects* is the number of projects to include in the average. This average can be computed over any period. Thus, for example, *#Projects* could be the maximum number of projects active in a six-month period. By computing this average periodically (e.g., monthly), the trend in this average can be determined (e.g., the average project size has declined at a rate of two people per month for the last six months). Such trends, when coupled to trends derived from other metrics such as *CustomerSatisfied* in Equation 6.6–10, may indicate general failure (or success) of the organization process. For example, declining project size coupled with increased customer satisfaction during the same period may indicate process success because the organization is able to do good work with fewer people. On the other hand, declining project size coupled with declining customer satisfaction for the same period may indicate process failure because the customer's organization is taking its business elsewhere.

The project types to include in the Equation 6.6–11 sum can be limited by defining *#Projects* appropriately. Thus, for example, Equation 6.6–11 can be used to compute the project size for a specific customer by limiting *#Projects* and *ProjectPersSize_i* to ABC Corporation projects. This metric can also be used to define the average project size for various categories of projects. For example, by limiting *#Projects* and *ProjectPersSize_i* to "O&M" projects, we can compute the average project size for O&M work. Again, coupling these metrics to other metrics can provide insight into failure (or success) of the organization process in particular spheres. For example, by limiting *#Projects* and *ProjectPers-Size$_i$* to "O&M" projects, and by limiting the inputs to the *CustomerSatisfied* metric in Equation 6.6–10 to O&M deliverables, we can gain insight into how well, or poorly, the process may be working for O&M work. For instance, a trend in O&M project size showing a decline and a customer satisfaction trend for these projects for the same period showing an increase may indicate process success for O&M work. That is, these two trends may indicate that the organization is able to do good O&M work with fewer people.

The following are some counting issues that need to be considered when using the metric in Equation 6.6–11:

- Should product assurance personnel be included in *ProjectPersSize$_i$*?
- Should support personnel (e.g., technical editors) be included in *ProjectPersSize$_i$*?

A global response to these issues is that values quoted for the metric should indicate what *ProjectPers-Size$_i$* includes.

The second question in the list—what is the average project cost?—can be addressed by a metric analogous to the one given in Equation 6.6–11, namely

$$AvProject\$ = \frac{\sum_{i=1}^{\#Projects}(Project\$_i)}{\# Projects} \tag{6.6–12}$$

The metric *AvProject$\$$* is the average cost of an organization project. *Project$\$_i$* is the cost of the ith project. *#Projects* is the number of projects to include in the average. This average can be computed over any period. Thus, for example, *#Projects* could be the maximum number of projects active in a six-month period. By computing this average periodically (e.g., monthly), the trend in this average can be determined (e.g., the average project cost has declined at a rate of $10,000 per month for the last six months). Such trends, when coupled to trends derived from other metrics such as *CustomerSatisfied* in Equation 6.6–10, may indicate general failure (or success) of the organization process. For example, declining project cost coupled with increased customer satisfaction during the same period may indicate process success because the organization is able to do good work at reduced cost.

The project types to include in the Equation 6.6–12 sum can be limited by defining *#Projects* appropriately. Thus, for example, Equation 6.6–12 can be used to compute the project cost for a specific customer by limiting *#Projects* and *Project$\$_i$* to ABC Corporation projects. This metric can also be used to define the average project cost for various categories of projects. For example, by limiting *#Projects* and *Project$\$_i$* to "O&M" projects, we can compute the average project cost for O&M work. Again, coupling these metrics to other metrics can provide insight into failure (or success) of the organization process in particular spheres. For example, by limiting *#Projects* and *Project$\$_i$* to "O&M" projects and by limiting the inputs to the *CustomerSatisfied* metric in Equation 6.6–10 to O&M deliverables, we can gain insight into how well, or poorly, the process may be working for O&M work. For instance, a trend in O&M project cost showing a decline and a customer satisfaction trend for these projects for the same period showing an increase may indicate process success for O&M work. That is, these two trends may indicate that the organization is able to do good O&M work at less cost.

The third question in the list—how is the work distributed across the customer's organization?—can be addressed, for example, by using the metrics in Equations 6.6–11 and 6.6–12. As already discussed, these metrics can be used to compute the average size and cost of projects for Office *X*. If we perform these computations across all customer offices that the organization does business with, we generate a cost and manning profile of work across the customer's organization. By observing trends in these profiles and by coupling these trends to the corresponding trends in the *CustomerSatisfied* metric in Equation 6.6–10, we can gain insight into how well (or poorly) the organization is serving different client communities. We can use this insight to sharpen the organization's client focus and thereby increase its business base. For example, if the trends in these metrics indicate that the organization is serving the ABC Corporation poorly, the organization can give added attention to staffing its projects with, for example, more experienced personnel than might otherwise be considered.

Table 6–1 summarizes this section by listing the metrics formulas and their definitions.

6.7 MEASUREMENT SUMMARY

Software systems development processes produce software products, such as requirements specifications and computer code. A product can be measured by assessing product attributes, and a process can be measured by assessing its process components and corresponding activities. As shown in Figure 6–38, product and process measurements can be used to help improve software systems development. However, numbers can be used to prove almost anything. As Mark Twain once said, "There are three kinds of lies: lies, damned lies, and statistics."[14]

When you set out to establish your product and process metrics program, it is important to think through ahead of time what the measurements are going to be used for. With this purpose in mind, a measurement program can be based on values that are significant to both the seller and the customer.

A word of warning—be sensitive to the concern within your organization that people may view product and process measurements as measuring them. Asking such questions such as, "What is Sam's productivity? Is he turning out as many lines of code as Roger or Sally?" is tricky business. In fact, we recommend that you avoid such direct questions. We suggest questions that probe the product or process may be more acceptable. Questions such as, "Can we consistently produce products that satisfy our customer? Do we have a development process that produces products that satisfy our customer and make a profit?" may be of more value. Measurements must answer questions that are important to the organization—otherwise, they are not worth collecting. As Figure 6–39 illustrates, there are multiple viewpoints when measuring products and process. These views apply to any organization that consists of more than one software project. That is, the organization has a process that each project adapts to its special needs to accomplish its tasks. The organization is aiming to improve its software systems development process and resultant products, while the project is aiming to improve task-level performance and corresponding products. The project measurements can be used as a feedback mechanism to improve the organizational process. Figure 6–40 summarizes the possible relationship between the product integrity index, *PIindex*, and the process integrity index, *ProcIindex*.

Your actual results depend on your specific set of circumstances. You need to examine your measurements to understand how the results may guide your product and process improvement activities. It is recommended that the data be collected, reviewed, and discussed on a routine schedule. Data collection is a part of everyday work. Figure 6–41 illustrates this point.

An analog to integrated process measurement is the measurements that occur as an automobile moves. Such integrated measurements include speed, available fuel, engine temperature, and oil level. Among other things, these measurements indicate how well the automobile is functioning. These measurements also indicate when the automobile's performance may need to be improved. Example performance improvement measurements include measuring the miles traveled between stops for gas to

---

[14]Mark Twain, on page 246 in his autobiography published in 1924, quotes this as a remark attributed to Benjamin Disraeli (1804–1881), a British statesman. For background on this oft-used quote, see S. Platt, ed., *Respectfully Quoted: A Dictionary of Quotations from the Library of Congress* (Washington, DC: Congressional Quarterly Inc., 1992), p. 333.

TABLE 6–1   Summary of Organization Process Improvement Metrics.

Metric Formula	Definition
$$M1_q = \dfrac{\sum\limits_{i=1}^{\#Del}(NProcActivity_{qi})}{\#\,Del}$$	The average number of times it takes to perform activity q in the organization software systems development process in producing the ith deliverable before delivery
$$MPeer = \dfrac{\sum\limits_{i=1}^{\#Del}(NPeer_i)}{\#\,Del}$$	The average number of peer reviews required to produce deliverables for delivery
$$MPeerACC = \dfrac{\sum\limits_{i=1}^{\#DelAcc}(NPeer_i)}{\#\,DelAcc}$$	The average number of peer reviews required to produce deliverables that are accepted by the customer (i.e., the customer returns the acceptance of deliverable form indicating "the product is accepted as delivered")
$$MTRevACC = \dfrac{\sum\limits_{i=1}^{\#DelAcc}(NPeer_i + NPA_i)}{\#\,DelAcc}$$	The average number of peer reviews and independent product assurance reviews required to produce deliverables that are accepted by the customer (i.e., the customer returns the acceptance of deliverable form indicating "the product is accepted as delivered")
$$\%DelOnTime = \left[\dfrac{(\#\,DelOnTime)}{\#\,Del}\right] \times 100$$	The percentage of deliverables delivered on time to the customer during a specific period for certain projects, where "on time" is according to delivery dates specified in project plans or CCB minutes
$$AvPPlan\$ = \dfrac{\sum\limits_{i=1}^{\#Projects}(PPlan\$_i)}{\#\,Projects}$$	The average cost to produce a project plan resulting in a project
$$Av\#\,PPlan\Delta = \dfrac{\sum\limits_{i=1}^{\#Projects}(PPlan\Delta_i)}{\#\,Projects}$$	The average number of drafts required to produce a project plan resulting in a project
$$\%SystemsAccTested = \left[\dfrac{(\#\,AccTestedSystemsDel)}{\#\,SystemsDel}\right] \times 100$$	The percentage of software systems accepted tested during a specific period for certain projects
$$\%SysAccTestedwithCustomer = \left[\dfrac{(\#\,AccTestedSystems\ with\ Customer)}{\#\,SystemsAccTested}\right] \times 100$$	The percentage of the acceptance testing activity conducted with customer participation in acceptance testing CCBs, during a specific period for certain projects
$$CustomerSatisfied = \left[\dfrac{(\#\,FormAcc + \#\,Unknown)}{\#\,DelKnown + DelUnknown}\right] \times 100$$	The customer perception of the seller organization
$$AvProjectPersSize = \dfrac{\sum\limits_{i=1}^{\#Projects}(ProjectPersSize_i)}{\#\,Projects}$$	The average number of seller organization employees working on a customer's project
$$AvProject\$ = \dfrac{\sum\limits_{i=1}^{\#Projects}(Project\$_i)}{\#\,Projects}$$	The average cost of a project

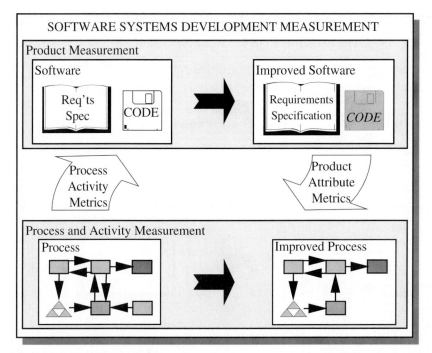

SOFTWARE SYSTEMS DEVELOPMENT MEASUREMENT

Product Measurement

Software

Req'ts Spec

CODE

Improved Software

Requirements Specification

CODE

Process Activity Metrics

Product Attribute Metrics

Process and Activity Measurement

Process

Improved Process

FIGURE 6–38 Measurements can be used to help improve software systems development processes and the resultant products.

provide insight into fuel economy which, in turn, offers insight into which parts of the automobile may need to be serviced.

In Figure 6–42, we summarize the product and process measurement steps, and the possible relationships between the measurements. This figure can be used as a guideline for setting up, observing, collecting, and analyzing your measurements.

You can use the annotated outline of an ADPE guideline in Figure 6–43 as a starting point for defining your organization's measurement program. This outline consists of the following sections:

- **Purpose**. This section states the purpose of the guideline. The purpose sets the context and establishes the authority for the guideline.

- **Background and Measurement Issues.** This section provides an overview of your organization, business, customers, and types of contract vehicles (e.g., fixed price, time and materials) that you use to conduct business. Measurement issues are identified and expressed in terms of specific questions that the organization or project wants or needs to have addressed.

- **Product and Process Improvement Approach.** This section defines how the product and process measurement steps introduced in this chapter are to be used. The section defines, details, and walks through the measurement steps. It is recommended that high-level figures be used to explain the steps. Depending upon the level of detail appropriate for your organization, appendices can be used to explain the steps and responsibilities in more detail.

- **Product and Process Measurements.** This sections defines the specific formulas to be used to answer your specific set of questions. Example calculations can be given to show how to use the equations. Suggested reporting formats may also be included.

- **Roles and Responsibilities.** This section presents the major organizational responsibilities for the measurement program.

- **Appendices.** Appendices are added as necessary. The main body of the guideline states the basics, and the appendices can add additional detail that embodies lessons learned, or provide tutorial information. As an

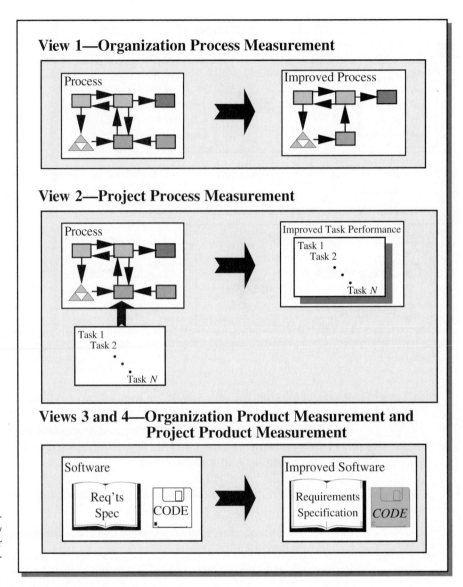

View 1—Organization Process Measurement

Process → Improved Process

View 2—Project Process Measurement

Process → Improved Task Performance

Task 1
Task 2
⋮
Task *N*

Task 1
Task 2
⋮
Task *N*

Views 3 and 4—Organization Product Measurement and
Project Product Measurement

Software → Improved Software

Req'ts Spec   CODE

Requirements Specification   CODE

FIGURE 6–39 The product integrity index or process integrity index can be implemented for organization and project perspectives.

organization matures in its engineering business processes, we recommend that the lessons be captured and incorporated into your ADPE elements. As people in your organization move on to other jobs, their knowledge can be incorporated into your ADPE elements, which serve, in part, as part of your organization's corporate memory.

In closing our discussion of integrity measurements, we want to offer some additional remarks concerning (1) how our measurement concept can be extended to arbitrary levels of detail and (2) the static viewpoint of process measurement.

Extending Measurement Formulas   The formulas for the product and process integrity indexes can be extended, if desired, to arbitrary levels of detail. For example, regarding the process integrity index, if it is desired to partition activities into subactivities, this extension can be accomplished as follows:

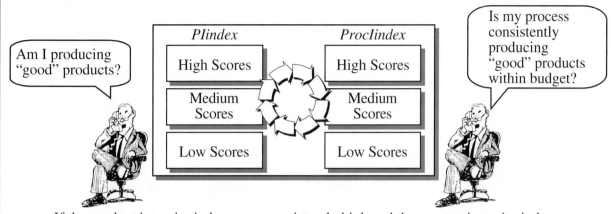

If the product integrity indexes are consistently high and the process integrity indexes are consistently low, it may mean that you are not following your process but that you are producing "good" products. Possibly, the development team is relying on the heroics of a few people. If your goal is to have "good" products consistently produced by a "good" process, then you may need to reconsider your process or goal.

If the product integrity indexes are consistently low and the process integrity indexes are consistently high, look to change your process. This situation may mean that you are following your process but that you are not producing "good" products.

If both integrity indexes are consistently low, it may be that you are not following significant parts of your process.

If both integrity indexes are consistently high, then you may have to fine-tune your process to push the indexes to one.

If both integrity indexes are consistently in the medium range, then you may have to make changes to your process to elevate the indexes.

FIGURE 6–40 What is the relationship between your product and process integrity indexes? This figure suggests some possible interpretations.

$$xt_{ij} = \frac{\sqrt{\sum_{k=1}^{N_{ij}} w_{ijk}^2 \, xt_{ijk}^2}}{\sqrt{\sum_{k=1}^{N_{ij}} w_{ijk}^2 (\text{maximum}[xt_{ijk}])^2}} \qquad (6.7\text{–}1)$$

where

N_{ij} = number of subactivities making up activity xt_{ij}, the jth activity of process component xt_i

W_{ijk} = weighting factor for subactivity xt_{ijk} of activity xt_{ij}

maximum[xt_{ijk}] = maximum value of xt_{ijk}

i is the process component label

j is the component activity label

k is the subactivity label

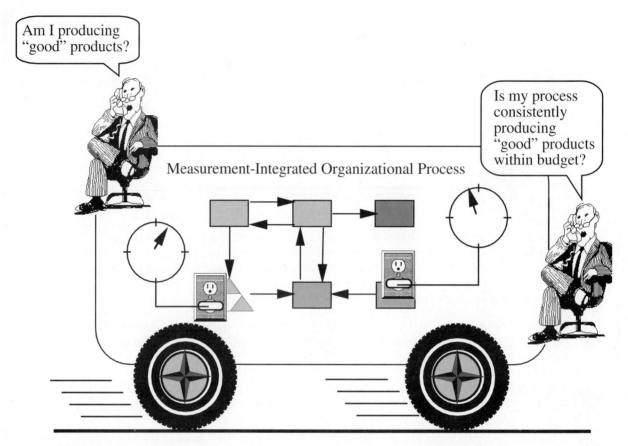

FIGURE 6–41 Applying metrics to the software systems development process should be part of the process itself.

The subactivities are measured directly by setting up value scales for each subactivity. Then, the contribution of each process component xt_i to the process integrity index is computed from the xt_{ij} using the formula previously given. And, finally, *ProcIndex* is computed from the xt_i using the formula previously given.

Corresponding comments apply to the product integrity index. For example, each product attribute can be partitioned into subattributes (at_{ij}). The subattributes are measured directly by setting up value scales for each subattribute. Then, the contribution of each product attribute at_i to the product integrity index is computed from the at_{ij} using a formula like the one given for computing xt_i from xt_{ij}. And, finally, *PIindex* is computed from the at_i using the formula previously given.

One final comment is in order regarding the process integrity index. We suggest, that until you acquire experience using the formulas given down to the activity level, you restrict your measurements to this level. Remember, for processes of even moderate complexity, the number of activities will generally be ten or more (the process considered earlier had sixteen activities). Thus, unless some activities are heavily weighted, no one activity will make a dominant contribution to the index. Thus, if you partition the activities into subactivities, the contribution of any particular subactivity to *ProcIndex* will not be dominant unless it is heavily weighted. Similar comments apply to the use of subattributes to determine a product integrity index.

We say that a product has integrity if it manifests the attributes at_i that we have chosen for it. If we were not interested in quantifying these attributes, then we would say that a product lacks integrity if one or more of the chosen attributes is missing. When we quantify these attributes (as we have done

Product Integrity Measurement Steps

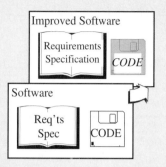

- Decide on the questions that you want and/or need to address (e.g., am I producing "good" products?).
- Select the products from your software systems development process that you want to measure (e.g., requirements specification).
- Identify the product attributes that you want to measure (e.g., for a requirements specification, you might identify an attribute as "at_4—meets cost expectations").
- For each identified attribute (e.g., at_4), define a value scale in everyday terms that are familiar to the organization (e.g., delivered for more than the cost estimate = 0.0, delivered for cost estimate = 0.9, and delivered for less than cost estimate = 1.0).
- Using the formulas given in this chapter, calculate the product integrity index value. For simplicity, use the formulas that yield values between zero and one. Select weighting factors to reflect your perception of the relative importance of your product attributes.

Process Integrity Measurement Steps

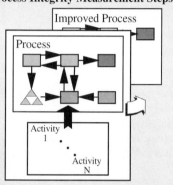

- Decide on the questions that you want and/or need to address (e.g., is my process consistently producing "good" products within budget?).
- Select the process components from your software systems development process that you want to measure (e.g., xt_1—Seller Project Planning).
- Identify the process component activities that you want to measure (e.g., for Seller Project Planning, you might identify an activity as "xt_{12}—Seller performs risk assessment").
- For each identified activity, define a value scale in everyday terms that are familiar to the organization. Identify the specific item(s) or action(s) (i.e., **measurement trigger[s]**) that triggers the activity to be measured. For example, for Seller performs risk assessment, you might define scale values as "Seller did not perform risk assessment on **customer's SOW** = 0.0", and "Seller performed risk assessment on **customer's SOW** = 1.0").

- Use the **measurement trigger** when assigning a value to each activity (e.g., for Seller performed risk assessment, you observe that the customer's SOW was assessed for risk according to the organization's risk assessment procedure; therefore, the assigned value = 1.0).
- Using formulas given in this chapter, calculate the process component value based on the activity values. For simplicity, use the formulas that yield values between zero and one. Select weighting factors to reflect your perception of the relative importance of your process component activities.
- Using the formulas given in this chapter, combine the process component values into a process integrity index value. For simplicity, use the formulas that yield values between zero and one. Select weighting factors to reflect your perception of the relative importance of your process components.

Possible Measurement Results

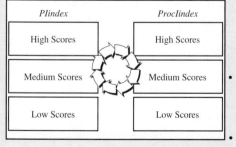

- If the product integrity indexes are consistently high and the process integrity indexes are consistently low, it may mean that you are not following your process but that you are producing "good" products. Possibly, the development team is relying on the heroics of a few people. If your goal is to have "good" products consistently produced by a "good" process, then you may need to reconsider your process or goal.
- If the product integrity indexes are consistently low and the process integrity indexes are consistently high, look to change your process. This situation may mean that you are following your process but that you are not producing "good" products.
- If both integrity indexes are consistently low, it may be that you are not following significant parts of your process.

- If both integrity indexes are consistently high, then you may have to fine-tune your process to push the indexes to one.
- If both integrity indexes are consistently in the medium range, then you may have to make changes to your process to elevate the indexes.

FIGURE 6–42 This high-level procedure is to help you through the product and process measurement steps based on the concepts and examples introduced in this chapter.

[Your Organization's Name and Logo]   Document #
                                                                                            Date

[Your Organization's Name] Guideline
Software Systems Development Process Metrics

Document #
Date

1.0 PURPOSE

This section states the purpose of the element. This purpose is the following:

- Identify the measurements to be performed to (1) quantify where your organization is product- and process-wise, (2) quantify differences from this baseline assessment, (3) establish quantitative process and product goals, and (4) quantify progress toward achieving these goals.
- Define the approach for incorporating process and product improvements based on the measurement activity.

2.0 BACKGROUND AND MEASUREMENT ISSUES

This section gives an overview of your organization, your business, your customers, and the types of contractual vehicles that you use to conduct business (e.g., fixed price, memorandum of understanding, time and materials). It also identifies measurement issues that your organization needs to address to improve the way it does software systems development business. One way to structure these issues is to use the multiple views introduced in this chapter. Example issues are the following:

- What is the likelihood of producing products with integrity?
- Is the product delivered on time?
- Is the product delivered within budget?
- Does the product do what the customer wants it to do?
- How maintainable is the product?
- How long does it take to get through our organizational development process?
- How are product integrity attributes quantified?
- How are process component activities quantified?

3.0 PRODUCT AND PROCESS IMPROVEMENT APPROACH

This section describes how the product and process measurement steps introduced in this chapter are to be used.

4.0 PRODUCT AND PROCESS MEASUREMENTS

This section describes your responses to the Section 2 issues in terms of measurements to be performed, including any mathematical formulas and other algorithms to be used to generate numbers. This chapter provides you with a starting point for defining measurements for your organization (e.g., product integrity index, process integrity index). This section can also include example measurements using the mathematical formulas introduced in the section.

5.0 ROLES AND RESPONSIBILITIES

This section presents the major organizational responsibilities for performing and managing product and process measurement activities.

APPENDICES

Appendices can contain such things as (1) mathematical derivations and other details underlying any formulas introduced in the main body, (2) alternative measurements, (3)limitations of Section 4 measurements , (4) acronyms, and (5) definitions of key terms.

FIGURE 6–43   An annotated outline for getting you started in defining a product and process measurement approach for your organization. This ADPE element can also be used to refine a measurement approach you already (informally) have in place.

in this chapter), the product integrity index that we calculate from these quantified attributes is a way of saying how much integrity a product has. Thus, for example, if we evaluate *PIindex* on a scale ranging from zero to one and if *PIindex* = 0.60, then we say that the product is sixty percent along the way toward manifesting the attributes chosen for it (or, equivalently, the product is lacking in integrity by forty percent).

Regarding process integrity, we say that a process, *when performed* as part of software product development, has integrity if the components and associated activities that make up the process are performed as part of product development *in accordance with ADPE element content.* By assigning value scales to the activities (and, thus, by implication, to the components) and measuring the extent to which the ADPE element activities are performed as part of product development, when we calculate *ProcIindex* we are making a statement about the extent to which the ADPE element activities and components are performed as part of product development. Thus, for example, if *ProcIindex* is set up to measure the project planning process component consisting of, say, ten activities as specified in an ADPE element, and if by measuring these activities while we are producing a project plan it turns out that *ProcIindex* = 0.75 (on a scale ranging from zero to one), then we say that the ADPE process used to produce the plan lacked integrity by twenty-five percent. By examining the associated Kiviat diagram or the activity values themselves, we would obtain quantitative insight into the extent to which each project planning activity was carried out.

As we discussed, there are various combinations of *PIindex* and *ProcIindex* that can arise in practice. By analyzing these combinations, an organization can get insight into whether (1) ADPE processes need to be changed because following the processes (i.e., the processes had high integrity values) leads to products with low integrity values, or (2) the organization is falling down in performing certain ADPE activities and the resultant products have low integrity values, or (3) the ADPE processes are okay because they are being followed and products with high values of integrity are being produced.

Static Viewpoint of Process Measurement   Our previous discussion of process measurement is in terms of process components, component activities, and activity value scales. We stressed the importance of observing and recording the degree to which component activities were performed. We showed you how to set up various types of value scales (e.g., binary, discrete, continuous) and suggested how you might use the observed results to improve software systems development processes. We chose to introduce our process measurement concept from this dynamic or performance-based viewpoint. However, we did not want to leave you with the impression that the performance-based viewpoint is the only way to implement process measurement.

We believe that there is a static or nonperformance-based viewpoint that deserves your consideration when setting up a process measurement program. Our car analogy in Figure 6–41 introduced the idea that performance-based process measurements can indicate when the automobile's performance may need to be improved.[15] However, there are times when performance does not reflect the automobile's primary value. For instance, when the automobile designer sits down to improve the existing car line or to create a new car line, the value of the automobile can be expressed in static terms. Here, we might stress the importance of observing and recording the degree to which the automobile and supporting infrastructure exists. Is the design done? Is the design approved? Is the assembly line in place and ready to manufacture the automobile? Has documentation been prepared for the automobile dealers and their service departments? Once the automobiles are shipped to the dealerships, then the performance-based viewpoint might be more appropriate. After the automobile is ready for the junk yard, nonperformance-based measurements might be more useful than performance-based measurements. At this point in the automobile's life, the value might be expressed in terms of automobile components that are still of value. From the junk-yard owner's viewpoint the automobile may have valu-

---

[15]Remember, the moving automobile represents software systems development processes at work and the gauges represent measurement of that work.

able parts that can be salvaged (e.g., the new set of tires you just bought before the car died). From the automobile designer's viewpoint there may be valuable lessons learned that can be incorporated into the next automobile design.

The point is that there is a temporal dimension that impacts the value of the automobile. As a result, the automobile's value can be expressed in terms of performance, nonperformance, or some combination.

Just as the automobile's value can be expressed in different terms, so can a process's value be expressed in different terms. For example, as an organization is implementing an improved or new process, the value of the process may be reflected by its design, approval, documentation, and associated training. The design value scale values may be set up, for instance, as follows:

- 0.0 if the process design is not completed

- 0.5 if the process design is completed, but not approved

- 1.0 if the process design is completed and approved

Such a nonperformance-based value scale reflects the process's early life. As the process is implemented, then performance-based value scales, as we have previously presented, can be constructed to reflect whether or not the process is being followed. And as the process reaches its useful life, its value scales can change yet again. Regardless of how you choose to set up your measurement program, we suggest you start simple.

We have completed our discussion of product and process measurement. The next chapter is concerned with the human issues dealing with an organization undergoing a cultural change. The chapter presents cultural change issues from the following perspectives: (1) the organization responsible for developing and promulgating process elements, (2) seller project participants and project managers, (3) buyer/user project management, (4) buyer/user senior management, and (5) seller senior management.

chapter

7

Cultural Change

Culture itself is neither education nor law-making; it is an atmosphere and a heritage.
—*H. L. Mencken,* Minority Report, *p. 360 (1956).*

7.1 INTRODUCTION

Recall the following definition of culture introduced in Chapter 1; this definition is drawn from the field of psychology:

> *Culture* is a pattern of basic assumptions invented, discovered, or developed by a given group as it learns to cope with its problems of external adaptation and internal integration, that has worked well enough to be considered valid and therefore is taught to new members as the correct way to perceive, think, and feel in relation to those problems.[1]

For this chapter, it is not important to settle on a precise definition of culture. This definition offers a *sense* of what the term may mean. With this admittedly squashy baseline established, we have a point of departure for talking about how cultural change is a part of any attempt to change the way an organization develops software systems. Figure 7–1 suggests that cultural change takes time and teamwork.

Redirecting the way that an organization develops software systems is part of a cultural change process.[2] Getting software systems development processes on paper is a challenge. Changing the way

---

[1]E. H. Schein, "Organizational Culture," *American Psychologist*, vol. 45, no. 2 (February 1990), p. 111.

[2]The discussion of the cultural change process in this chapter's Introduction section is adapted from a workshop entitled *Managing Innovation*, Strategic Performance Solutions Corporation, Silver Spring, MD. Used by permission of Gary Donaldson, President.

"A JOURNEY OF A THOUSAND MILES BEGINS WITH A SINGLE STEP."

© 1994 CHARLES BARSOTTI

© 1994 H L SCHWADRON

"We're all team players here, Furgis. Miss Parmenter will break you in."

© Charles Barsotti 1996.　　　　　© Harley L. Schwadron 1996.

FIGURE 7–1　Changing an organization's software systems development culture takes time and teamwork.

people approach the software development can prove to be even more difficult. When starting the journey toward cultural change, it is important to anticipate difficulties that may be encountered. Understanding the underlying dynamics goes a long way towards easing the transition.

Change in the basic ways of perceiving, problem solving, and behavior requires adopting a new frame of reference. New frameworks are frequently viewed with a cautious, hesitant, and questioning attitude. This behavior is commonly labeled as resistance. At the risk of oversimplification, this resistance operates on two levels—visible and invisible.[3]

At the visible level, people resist *change*; at the invisible level people resist *loss.* At the visible level, other people can observe the *resistance;* at the invisible level, other people cannot observe the *losses, doubts,* and *fears* (real or imagined) that reside in each individual (and within the group). Furthermore, at times, the individual who is resisting may not recognize the real source of his or her resistance. When this multilevel aspect of resistance is not recognized, there is a tendency to project negative motives onto those who do not embrace a new proposal. This misunderstanding can lead to a nonproductive cycle by all parties.

Pushing people to accept change does not work in the long term. Pulling people with a vision of a better future works more effectively. To reach the stage where people are open to a new, shared vision requires working through the more basic emotional issues of fear, uncertainty, and loss. This "working through" requires patience, support, and understanding, not blame. Endorsing a proposal for change will not occur until there is a feeling by key stakeholders that individual needs and concerns are understood and will be addressed. Figure 7–2 lists some losses, doubts, or fears that people may struggle with when they are faced with change.

People commit to change for their own reasons, not for someone else's. No amount of rational discussion builds commitment. Change is not embraced without the perception of personal gain and the opportunity to participate in shaping the outcome. When establishing (or fine-tuning) your organization's process for evolving your software systems development environment, it is important to allow individuals from all levels of the organization to have a say in the development practices.

---

[3]Resistance operates at many levels. For the purposes of our discussion, we have simplified our treatment of resistance to two levels—visible and invisible. This simplification is sufficient for the engineering issues addressed in this book.

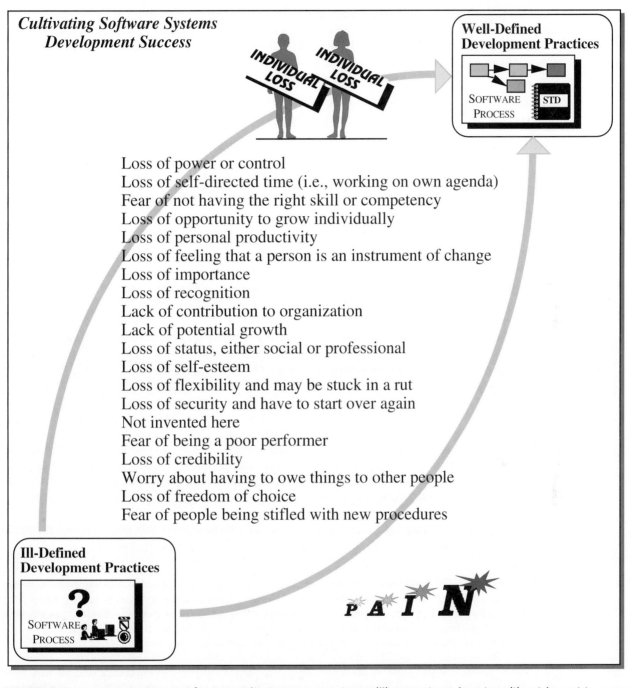

Loss of power or control
Loss of self-directed time (i.e., working on own agenda)
Fear of not having the right skill or competency
Loss of opportunity to grow individually
Loss of personal productivity
Loss of feeling that a person is an instrument of change
Loss of importance
Loss of recognition
Lack of contribution to organization
Lack of potential growth
Loss of status, either social or professional
Loss of self-esteem
Loss of flexibility and may be stuck in a rut
Loss of security and have to start over again
Not invented here
Fear of being a poor performer
Loss of credibility
Worry about having to owe things to other people
Loss of freedom of choice
Fear of people being stifled with new procedures

FIGURE 7–2 Losses, doubts, and fears contribute to a person's unwillingness to make a transition (change) to a new way of doing things. Often people view transition as a painful experience.

People may view the change (transition) as a losing proposition. By focusing on a win-win situation you can go a long way towards easing the transition to a new way of doing business. To design a win-win strategy requires both understanding and addressing the underlying concerns most people have regarding any new proposal. The underlying concerns range from trying to understand why the change is necessary through questions related to gains and losses that will be experienced. It is human nature to anticipate the worst before giving credence to the new.

The losses (real or imagined) listed in Figure 7–2 can be found at all levels of an organization. As implied in the figure, the organization may want to cultivate its ill-defined development practices into well-defined development practices, but people want to understand how their making this change (transition) affects them. People basically want to know the answers to the following questions:

- What will change, remain the same, or be deleted?
- How pervasive and irreversible will the change be?
- What will be the personal impact?
- What will be lost?
- What will be gained?
- How fast will it happen?
- What control, support, and guarantees will everyone be given?

Honest answers to these questions will promote trust. False or misleading information used to coat over unpleasant feelings will sabotage commitment. Everyone's main concern is that individual circumstances and needs will be fairly addressed, even if it means hearing difficult news and not getting what one wants.

As a change agent you might ask, How can a perceived loss be reframed as a net gain? To achieve this objective partially, a change agent needs to listen actively to what people say, explicitly and implicitly. For example, a person may be arguing a technical point about a software system design issue, yet may really be concerned about the impact of the proposed changes on that person's skill set. A change agent draws out the underlying concern, restates the concern as a question that needs to be addressed, and facilitates an understanding of how the issue will be addressed to the benefit of the person. It is important to accomplish this redirection without doing all the work for the person (i.e, the person needs to contribute to the discussion). Change agents often try to convince someone that the proposed change is the right thing to do—trying to convince someone can be a frustrating experience. A more effective and powerful approach is for the change agent to help the other person develop ownership of the situation. Facilitating ownership is accomplished, in part, by helping the other people to discover their own truths.

Consider the following brief story about a manager's resistance (visible and invisible) to adopting a new way of doing business and a suggested way to create a win-win situation:

A manager, who is a valuable contributor to the organization's success, is asked to help implement a change in the way software systems are being developed. The change is not a radical departure from the existing practice, but the change is not the manager's idea. The manager believes that adopting the new business practices will result in a loss of power or control (in addition to other losses, doubts, and fears listed in Figure 7–2).

As a result of these beliefs (real or imagined), the manager resists adopting the new business practices. The manager communicates this resistance, directly and indirectly, to the manager's staff. The end result is that the manager's part of the organization only partially implements the change (i.e., the new business practices). People view the manager's actions as "resistance to the change" when, in fact, the manager is "resisting the loss of power or control." That is, the manager's invisible resistance to loss translates into a visible resistance to new business practices. The visible resistance is what people see (no pun intended).

Consequently, some people implement the change, and some do not. This manager's visible resistance is a subtle and frequently unconscious form of side-stepping change. This resistance undercuts the organization's goal to implement a change that is intended to improve the way the organization does business.

When a change agent asks the manager why there is so much resistance, the manager avoids the question and responds by proudly talking about the success the manager has achieved by applying cutting-edge technologies. The manager makes several references to the successful contributions of the next lower layer of technical management, all of whom are 15 to 20 years younger than the manager. The change agent actively listens to the manager and concludes that the manager has lots of pride and has a self-image as a high-tech leader.

A potential way to overcome some of the manager's resistance is to sit down and talk to the manager about how the manager views the change. It is important to get the manager to talk about the change and how the manager perceives that the change will affect day-to-day activities. The discussion should include details involving the manager's role as a result of the change. The change agent should ask the manager for suggestions on how to implement the new development process. One area that can be explored is whether the manager would be willing to mentor the organization's younger staff on the new practices. The change agent can ask the manager for support to implement the changes. Such an interaction may be perceived as a win-win for the manager and the change agent.

Of course, the entire story is more complicated, but the point is that change is emotional. People do not always directly communicate what is on their minds, nor are they self aware of their own motivations. These facts need to be dealt with as part of the cultural change journey.

People are more likely to contribute when they feel that they have a hand in creating the new order. Most people want to contribute to the well-being of the organization. Sometimes they need a helping hand to see how their contributions will make a difference. Pride of authorship drives motivation and reduces anxiety as the pieces of the puzzle come together. Feeling a loss of control over one's destiny is crippling. Taking time to have the staff contribute to the design and implementation of new initiatives serves as a powerful mechanism to overcome resistance.

Stakeholders are more at ease in accepting new ways of working when there is (1) an understanding regarding the purpose of the change; (2) a picture of the alternative way of operating; (3) a work plan to reach the goal; and (4) a designated part each person can play in both the change process and the new way of operating. Stakeholders need a clear picture and shared vision of how the future ways of operating work together. A vision pulls a stakeholder forward. Painting a shared vision reduces anxiety, fear, and resistance when facilitating change.

Stakeholders are more likely to support major change when they have a clear sense of why the change is being proposed. They need to understand the driving forces and purpose. There needs to be a connection between the new way of doing business and a compelling argument for the need for change. Most people are not in touch with the urgency to change unless a crisis situation exists. Proactive change is typically more difficult to sell because many stakeholders live in the present and may not see any immediate need. An effective strategy is to involve as many key people in gathering and analyzing data that suggest change is required. Sharing findings with peers enhances the probability of success more than having management dictate actions.

It is important to recognize that not all change is the same. There are two basic levels of change: continuous and discontinuous. Continuous change represents a fine-tuning and/or augmentation of existing traditions (e.g., introduction of peer reviews into an existing software systems development process). Discontinuous change requires a break from past traditions (e.g., introduction of a software systems development process where no such process existed before). Moving from a continuous state to a discontinuous state requires a repositioning of thinking regarding values, assumptions, and behaviors. Many people confuse continuous change with discontinuous change. To achieve cultural transformation requires a full commitment to discontinuous change. The level of change that is going to take place affects the strategies for implementing the change.

Continuous change gives power and dominance to operational management strategies, where the focus is on "here and now" practical, production needs. Discontinuous change places more emphasis on strategic leadership and transitional management. The focus in on the future. More emphasis is placed on these two opposing perspectives. "Here and now" has a way of commanding attention because it is in the moment, it is concrete and tangible, whereas a vision of the future state is less well defined.

If there is not unequivocal commitment and support from top management, the "here and now" forces will win, and the best that can be achieved is modification to existing beliefs without fundamental change. Balancing the demands of these competing forces is the role of leadership and management. Successful initiatives will fail if the frontline supervisors are not in line with senior management. It is all too common that change initiatives become frozen between the upper and middle echelons of the organization.

The Software Engineering Institute (SEI) and other organizations committed to fostering software process improvement recognize that the capability to engineer software systems successfully involves much more than talented people and good technology. An important ingredient is a willingness of the people to change the way that they do things for the greater good of the organization. One way to effect this change is through what the SEI refers to as mastering team-based practices.[4] If people are to build software systems by applying their engineering skills in a team environment, they must also know how to get along with one another. Establishing this interpersonal harmony is a key ingredient to leveraging the application of engineering skills. The individual who focuses on self and one's own needs, giving little attention to the needs of others on the project team, can more than cancel out the value of the application of that person's engineering skills. We believe this statement to be true—even if that person has proven unparalleled skills in one or more engineering areas such as analysis, design, coding, product assurance, and training. We illustrate this key point with the brief story that follows.

Jan Talent was an experienced, bright, and talented technical manager who understood the value of disciplined software systems development. But Jan had difficulty putting group needs above her own. More specifically, Jan balked at accepting alternative engineering ways that she had not adopted herself.

Jan managed a number of software project managers; and she reported to a program manager who managed several managers like Jan. The program manager headed an organization that consisted of these first- and second-line managers, a product assurance organization, and a process engineering group (PEG) responsible for developing ADPE elements[5] in concert with other managers. The PEG was headed by a manager who reported to the program manager. When the PEG promulgated ADPE elements, Jan chose to ignore those processes in the elements that did not conform to her way of doing things. She specifically directed her project managers to do things her way. For example, if the PEG, in concert with input from other members of the organization, established as policy that product assurance was to be a standing member of a project's CCB, Jan chose to direct her managers to bar product assurance from participating in CCB meetings. The end result of Jan's recalcitrance was that it contributed to the fracture of the overall organization.

When the other managers at Jan's level saw what Jan was doing, some of them also chose to put group needs on the back burner and ignored to varying degrees the way of doing business as defined in the ADPE elements. They chose this course of action, in part, because their customers were used to doing business in a less structured way than that defined in the ADPE elements. These managers, along with Jan, would use this argument with the program manager to gain relief from doing business the ADPE way. This end-run approach naturally created tensions among the PEG manager and Jan and some of the other managers at Jan's level. These tensions bred mutual disrespect among these managers. Furthermore, this disrespect reached all the way down to the working-level troops. Rather than sign up to the ADPE way of doing business, these troops adopted the self-preservation approach and signed up to the business way promulgated to them by Jan and their project managers. The end result of this state of affairs was that instituting the ADPE culture was severely hampered. More significantly from a business standpoint, this situation did not go unnoticed by the customer.

As illustrated by the preceding two short stories, the people part of cultural change is important. The processes that people use to develop software systems are also important. The level of change being implemented is important. Figure 7–3 illustrates these points by depicting a cultural evolution process that accounts for people, processes, and the level of change being implemented.

There is no one way to evolve an organization's software systems development culture, but we believe that you can use the depicted process to analyze; evolve; implement; and refine (i.e., continu-

---

[4]B. Curtis, W. Hefley, and S. Miller, "People Capability Maturity Model^SM," Software Engineering Institute and Carnegie University Mellon Technical Report CMU/SEI-95-MM-02 (September 1995), p. L4–31.

[5]Remember, the SEE consists of two complementary components—an application development process environment (ADPE) and an application development technology environment (ADTE).

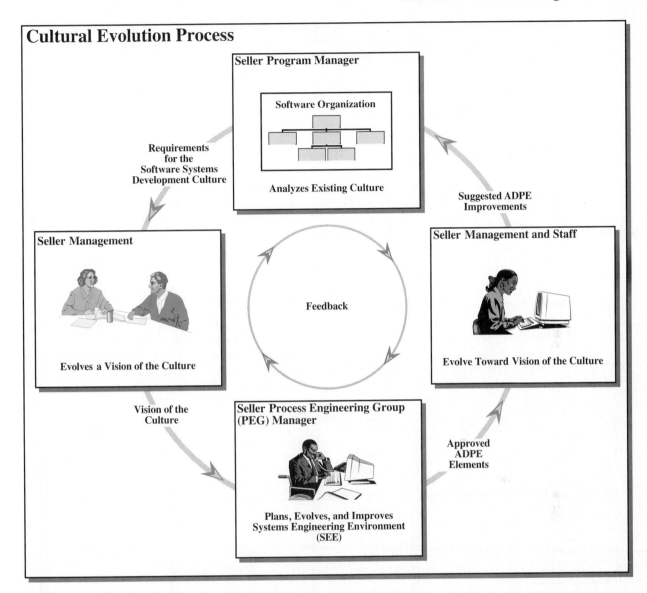

FIGURE 7–3 Changing a software systems development environment starts with establishing an understanding of the organization's overall existing culture.

ous change) or transform (i.e., discontinuous change) your organization's software development culture. This ongoing process enables an organization to implement either continuous and discontinuous change or some combination.

Figure 7–3 has four rectangles that represent the following four responsible agents and their associated process phases:

- Seller Program Manager—Analyzes Existing Culture.

- Seller Management—Evolves a Vision of the Culture.

- Seller Process Engineering Group (PEG) Manager—Plans, Evolves, and Improves System Engineering Environment (SEE).

- Seller Management and Staff—Evolve Toward Vision of the Culture.

These four phases are linked together by the major communication paths and associated information. As shown in Figure 7–3, along each communication path information is transferred from one process phase to another. The information transferred consists of the following items:

- Requirements for the Software Systems Development Culture.
- Vision of the Culture.
- Approved SEE Elements.
- Suggested ADPE Improvements.

As with most processes, feedback is present. We represent feedback with the set of continuous arrows in the center of the figure. Each of the four phases is discussed in the following paragraphs.

Seller Program Manager—Analyzes Existing Culture

Ideally, the cultural evolution process in Figure 7–3 starts when the Seller Program Manager decides it is time for the software organization to analyze the existing software systems development culture. Part of this self-examination involves establishing how the software systems development culture fits into its higher-level organizational culture. There are many ways to describe the different types of higher-level organizational cultures. We have chosen to summarize culture types in terms of the following eleven characteristics: time frame, focus, planning, change mode, management, structure, perspective, motivation, development, communication, and leadership.[6] Figure 7–4 lists the following four higher-level organization cultures in terms of these eleven characteristics:

Culture Type / Characteristics	**Reactive** - survive - protect - find fault - worry about self	**Responsive** - set goals - plan action - solve problems - build teams	**Proactive** - set mission and objectives - plan long-range - manage performance - develop organization	**High Performance** - identify potentials - navigate strategically - manage evolution - create metasystems
Time Frame	past	present	future	flow
Focus	diffused	output	results	excellence
Planning	justification	activity	strategy	evolution
Change Mode	punitive	adaptive	planned	programmed
Management	fix blame	coordination	alignment	navigation
Structure	fragmented	hierarchy	matrix	networks
Perspective	self	team	organization	culture
Motivation	avoid pain	rewards	contribution	actualization
Development	survival	cohesion	attunement	transformation
Communication	force-feed	feedback	feed forward	feed through
Leadership	enforcing	coaching	purposing	empowering

FIGURE 7–4 This figure summarizes four types of organizational cultures. It is important for you to understand what your culture is and what you want your culture to be before you begin planning a transformation.

---

[6]L. Nelson, and F. Burns, "High performance programming: A framework for transforming organizations," *Transforming Work* (Alexandria, VA: Miles River Press, 1984).

- **Reactive Culture.** A culture in which people worry about themselves and justify their existence. The organization is fragmented, diffused, and bureaucratic. Management is constantly trying to fix blame for why something did not work out right. Management spends a lot of time defending the status quo.

- **Responsive Culture.** A culture in which people build teams. The organization solves problems and sets goals. Management and people pay attention to trends in the industry and try to adjust organizational activities accordingly. Management helps to coordinate activities and resources.

- **Proactive Culture.** A culture in which people develop the organization. The organization plans for the long term and is results-oriented. Management helps to align the organization's resources with its mission and objectives.

- **High Performance Culture.** A culture in which people and performance outcomes are in rhythm with the organization's mission. The organization runs smoothly. The organization constantly strives to achieve excellence. Management and people try to anticipate what industry trends will be. Management navigates the organization through its evolution.

To exemplify the four culture types in Figure 7–4, we offer the following four organizational behaviors associated with the "Change Mode" characteristic:

- **Reactive Culture—Punitive Behavior.** Change is punished, both on the individual and on the project level.

- **Responsive Culture—Adaptive Behavior.** The organization is constantly trying to keep up-to-date in its business practices. People are trained in the classroom and at seminars. The organization funds internal support groups that discuss ways to improve business practices.

- **Proactive Culture—Planned Behavior.** The organization plans for the future and tries not to react to the present. The proactive culture takes the responsive culture another step up the maturity ladder and tries to anticipate what the future may hold and then devises appropriate strategies.

- **High Performance Culture—Programmed Behavior.** The organization is constantly learning from what it is doing and feeding this knowledge back into what it does so that it can do better.

Now, consider the following four organizational behaviors associated with the "Leadership" characteristic:

- **Reactive Culture—Enforcing Behavior.** The individual will perform the business practices the organization's way—the company's way or the highway.

- **Responsive Culture—Coaching Behavior.** Management coaches/mentors individuals or teams. Coaches/mentors help to guide development of skills and improvement in performance.

- **Proactive Culture—Purposing Behavior.** The organization defines its purpose for existing and the value added services/products it provides to its customer community.

- **High Performance Culture—Empowering Behavior.** The organization has a self-directed workforce whose members are coowners in the organization's mission.

With an understanding of the organization's overall culture, the software organization can better develop a statement of the requirements for the software systems development culture. If the reality is that the organization's overall culture is predominantly reactive, then it may be unrealistic for the software organization to specify culture requirements that reflect the characteristics of a high performance culture to be implemented in a year's time frame.

Seller Management—Evolves a Vision of the Culture

Given that a set of requirements for the software systems development culture is established and approved by the Seller Program Manager, then the Seller Management, in concert with key stakeholders, evolves a vision of the culture. This vision is expressed in terms of engineering process features that include the following: planning, risk assessment, risk reduction, documentation, accountability,

Software Organization's Vision of Culture

Engineering Process Features	Existing Process Features	Envisioned Process Features
Planning	Happens after work starts	Happens before work starts
Risk Assessment	Rarely done	Consistently done
Risk Reduction	Rarely done	Provided by Product Assurance
Documentation	Sparse	Up-to-date
Accountability	Diffused	Obtained at CCB Meetings
Customer/ Seller Interaction	Informal	Customer Project Manager to Seller Project Manager
Business Method	Unstructured	**Systems Engineering Environment (SEE)**

FIGURE 7–5 The vision of the software systems development culture helps to set the organization's strategic focus for process improvement.

customer/seller interaction, and business method. For example, as shown in Figure 7–5, the vision can be expressed by the organization's existing engineering process features and the organization's envisioned process features.

To change existing engineering process features, the organization needs to (1) articulate what features are important to the organization, (2) acknowledge the current status of the features, (3) define what the future status of the features should be, and (4) make a commitment to change the engineering process features. Commitment to change is critical for successful implementation of the vision of the culture. Without organizational commitment—top to bottom, bottom to top, or some combination— it is difficult, if not impossible, to implement the vision. In general, the less the commitment, the longer the time frame for implementing the vision.

As shown in Figure 7–5, the SEE is where the organization's business methods are housed. The organization's vision of its software development environment can be represented by the SEE. The SEE is an environment where coordinated and consistent development of software systems can be accomplished. The Seller PEG Manager is the person who is responsible for the evolution of the SEE.

Seller Process Engineering Group (PEG) Manager—Plans, Evolves, and Improves Systems Engineering Environment (SEE)

Given that an organization commits to implementing a vision of its engineering culture, then the Seller PEG Manager sets out to plan, evolve, and improve the SEE. This phase will be discussed in detail, but for now, it is important to understand that people at all levels in the organization need to participate in evolving the SEE. With this multilevel participation, approved ADPE elements (i.e., policies, guidelines, procedures, and standards) can be promulgated for use. In some situations it is also desirable to have the customer participate in evolving the ADPE elements.

Seller Management and Staff—Evolve Toward Vision of the Culture

During the fourth cultural evolution process phase, the seller management and staff use the approved ADPE elements, evolve toward the vision of the culture, and provide suggested ADPE improvements to the Seller Program Manager. Feedback to the top of the organization from the bottom and middle of the organization helps to demonstrate clearly to senior management that people in the organization are committed to evolving the culture.

We want to make one last point before we present our plan for the rest of this chapter. Basic strategies for change include the following:

- **Provide information and education.** This strategy enables you to let the people know how change is going to affect them. People need to learn the skills and acquire the knowledge necessary to perform their roles and responsibilities in the new culture.

- **Exercise power.** This strategy is both positive and negative. Positive control includes the use of resources to implement change. For example, senior management can commit money for training. Negative control, however, pushes people and demands that people behave in a certain manner. Although negative control gets people's attention for the short term, it can lead to resistance and lack of commitment over time.

- **Effect organizational norms and values.** This strategy is aimed at impacting what people believe is the way to do everyday business. For example, an organization's normative behavior might be reflected by people putting forth minimum effort to get a job done. As a result, the organization may decide to change this normative behavior. The organization wants everyone to go the extra mile to get the job done. Organizational norms and values are what holds an organization together. Effecting change in norms and values provides a lasting change—a new way of doing business that is accepted as the way to do things.

These three strategies for change can be used like spices—individually, or be blended together. We offer the following short examples:

- Education can reduce anxiety about a person's role in the new way of business. "The PEG has established a training program that includes workshops and seminars to learn the new ways of doing business. In addition, support groups have been established to provide everyone with a forum for discussing lessons learned while implementing the new ways of doing business."

- A positive use of power by a manager can affect a person's schedule. "There will be a meeting tomorrow to discuss our new organizational software systems development process."

- Power blended with information and education can help to ease a person's fear about change. "Sally will present a one-hour briefing to explain your role in our new process."

- A lasting organizational change is achieved, in part, through shared ownership of the new ways of doing business. "With the use of input from the staff, the new organizational software systems development process empowers the development teams to *apply prescriptively* the development process to their particular projects."

People want to understand the purpose of the cultural change (Why?); the overall picture (What is the future going to look like?); the plan to effect the change (How are we going to get there?); and the part each person is to play in the change (What is my role?). When explaining the cultural change, you need to account for different personalities. You have to adapt your discussions appropriately and blend your strategies carefully.

With respect to the rest of the chapter, our approach is to examine cultural change issues associated with ADPE implementation from a number of organizational perspectives (including those of people like Jan Talent). The plan for this chapter is the following:

- In **Section 7.2—Cultural Change Nuggets**, we present the nuggets that you can expect to extract from this chapter.

- In **Section 7.3—Process Engineering Group (PEG)**, we address ADPE implementation from the perspective of the organization responsible for writing the ADPE elements and seeing to it that they are implemented and continually improved. Because of the PEG's central role in effecting cultural change within both the seller and the customer organizations, this section is the most extensive in this chapter.

- In **Section 7.4—Seller Project Participants and Project Managers**, we address the challenges to ADPE implementation from the perspective of the seller project-level individuals who will have to adapt to the policies, guidelines, procedures, and standards that will govern their work.

- In **Section 7.5—Buyer/User Project Management**, we discuss the challenges to ADPE implementation from the perspective of those individuals who give technical direction to seller project managers for accomplishing project work.

- In **Section 7.6—Buyer/User Senior Management**, we address the impact on buyer/user senior management that ADPE implementation brings about. Here, buyer/user senior management encompasses (1) the customer management that is paying the seller to set up an ADPE, (2) the customer management that is providing technical direction to the PEG manager, and (3) levels of customer management that sit over (1) and (2).

- In **Section 7.7—Seller Senior Management**, we discuss the key role that seller senior management plays in effecting software systems development cultural change through ADPE implementation.

- In **Section 7.8—Cultural Change Summary**, we summarize the key points developed in the chapter. We include a table of implementation guidance associated with each of the perspectives considered.

7.2 CULTURAL CHANGE NUGGETS

Figure 7–6 lists the nuggets that you can extract from this chapter. We briefly explain these nuggets. Their full intent will become apparent as you go through this chapter.

1. **ADPE implementation is cultural change.** To view implementation otherwise is a recipe for failure. Sellers must take steps to ensure that seller management and staff are on board with the ADPE way of doing business. Senior seller management must recognize that adopting ADPE practices involves growing pains. Similarly, buyer/user senior management must recognize that changing the way its organization does business with a seller is not going to happen overnight—and cultural change can be painful.

2. **ADPE implementation requires management buy-in at all levels in an organization.** In particular, managers of the Jan Talents of the world need to impress upon them that ADPE implementation is a requirement—not an option.

3. **If you are a seller, seriously consider putting into each manager's salary review the extent to which the manager has bought into ADPE implementation.** At review time, each manager should be prepared to present to his or her boss objective evidence of ADPE compliance (e.g., a folder of CCB minutes). It takes more than asserting that the customer says everything is fine.

4. **If you are a buyer/user, you should support training of your managers in the "new" way of business that ADPE implementation defines.** At a minimum, this training should consist of attendance at seller briefings of ADPE element content. Buyer/user managers should attend such briefings.

5. **ADPE practices must be sufficiently specific so that they convey something that actually can be applied to develop software products, but they cannot be so specific that they tie the hands of various people within an organization and actually impede product development.** ADPE elements should not be written in a cookie-cutter manner.

6. **To overcome resistance, build upon those in the organization who embrace implementing new ways of doing business.** Have these people pilot proposed ideas for ADPE elements. Nothing succeeds like success. Trial-use ideas that gain the acceptance of working-level troops will gravitate quickly throughout an organization, thus hastening cultural change. For example, if some in your organization have experience

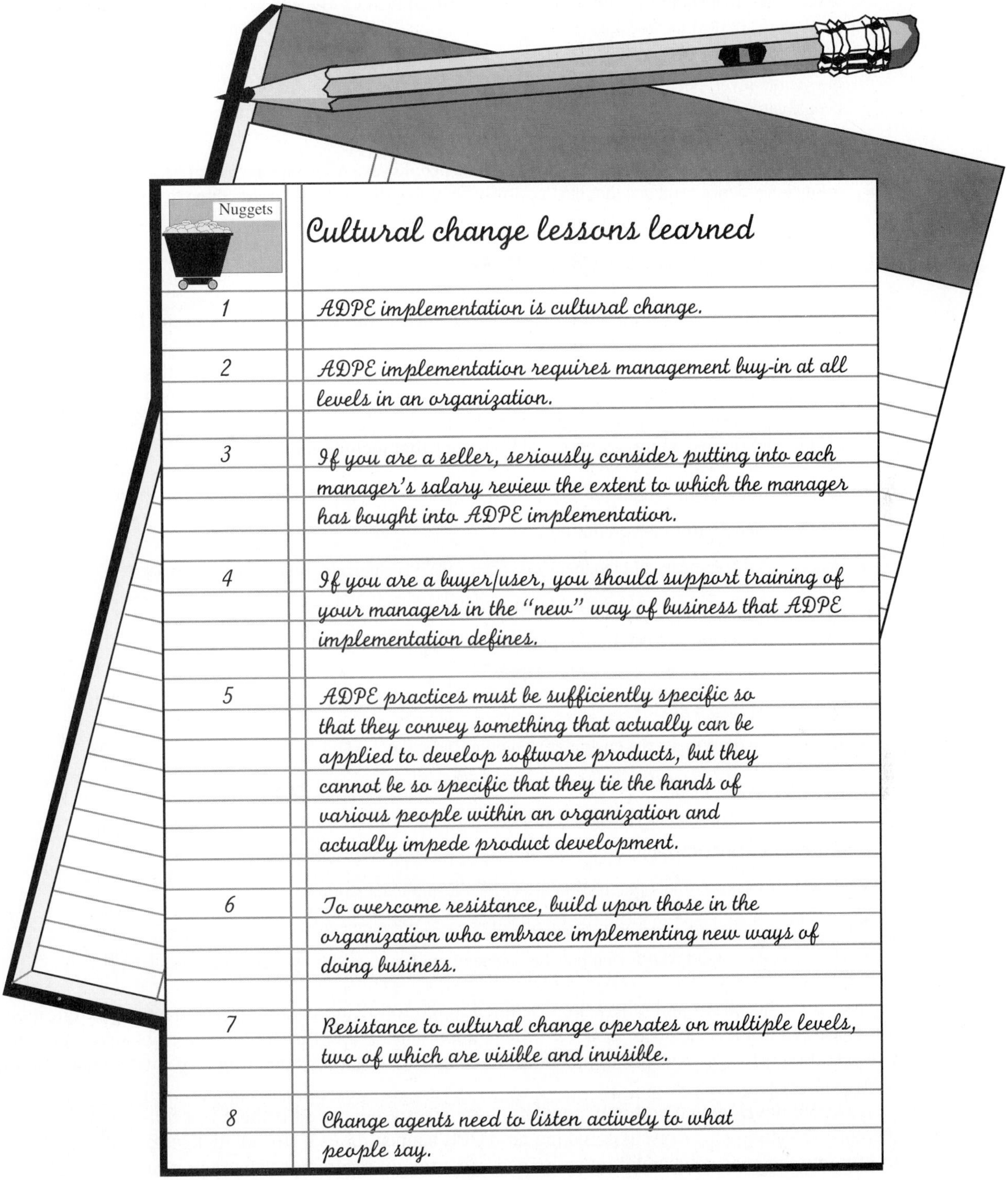

Nuggets	Cultural change lessons learned
1	ADPE implementation is cultural change.
2	ADPE implementation requires management buy-in at all levels in an organization.
3	If you are a seller, seriously consider putting into each manager's salary review the extent to which the manager has bought into ADPE implementation.
4	If you are a buyer/user, you should support training of your managers in the "new" way of business that ADPE implementation defines.
5	ADPE practices must be sufficiently specific so that they convey something that actually can be applied to develop software products, but they cannot be so specific that they tie the hands of various people within an organization and actually impede product development.
6	To overcome resistance, build upon those in the organization who embrace implementing new ways of doing business.
7	Resistance to cultural change operates on multiple levels, two of which are visible and invisible.
8	Change agents need to listen actively to what people say.

FIGURE 7–6 ADPE implementation strikes at the core of organizational and personal practice. Altering these practices is thus tantamount to effecting cultural change at the organizational and personal level. Here are key cultural change concepts explained in this chapter. These nuggets are your guide to bringing about cultural change within your organization through ADPE implementation.

with CCBs, invite others in your organization to attend their CCB meetings to experience firsthand how the CCB works in the real world.

7. **Resistance to cultural change operates on multiple levels, two of which are visible and invisible.** At the visible level, people resist *change*; at the invisible level people resist *loss*. At the visible level, other people can observe the *resistance*; at the invisible level, other people cannot observe the *losses*, *doubts*, and *fears* (real or imagined) that reside in each individual.

8. **Change agents need to listen actively to what people say.** A change agent can become frustrated when trying to convince someone that the "new way" of doing things is the "right" thing to do.

7.3 PROCESS ENGINEERING GROUP (PEG)

This section addresses cultural change in terms of ADPE implementation from the PEG perspective. The PEG is responsible for establishing, maintaining, and updating the SEE. In this chapter, we focus on the PEG's responsibilities in the *process* domain—i.e., its ADPE responsibilities. We note that in the software industry, a typical label given to the organization responsible for software process matters is the "software engineering process group (SEPG)."

In this section, we address a series of questions that include the following:

- What are some qualifications for people who work in the PEG?
- How do you establish PEG credibility?
- What type of comments and feedback on specific ADPE elements should the PEG expect?
- How should the PEG be incorporated into an organization?
- What are some of the impediments to successful ADPE implementation?
- What can you do to set up a flexible ADPE?
- How do you fund a PEG?
- What can be done to get the customer to support the seller's ADPE?
- How can the PEG address seller and customer cultural-change challenges?
- What are some of the individual responsibilities for implementing an ADPE?
- What is "prescriptive application," and how does it factor into ADPE elements?
- How does the size of an organization affect ADPE implementation?
- How long should the PEG wait before updating an ADPE element?
- How specific should ADPE elements be—general guidance or step-by-step procedures?

Each of these questions and others are discussed in the following paragraphs. Some of these questions are discussed in more detail in Chapter 8. It is important to note that there is no right set of answers. Our intention is to sensitize you to potential challenges for your consideration as you take your cultural change journey.

ADPE development and implementation are greatly facilitated if there is a full-time PEG. Even then, as we subsequently discuss, making an ADPE happen poses a stiff challenge. But, if you choose to buy into the concepts heretofore examined, we strongly recommend that you establish a PEG as a standing organizational element. Sellers should encourage buyers to pay for such an organization. Otherwise, sellers should bite the bullet and fund such an organization.

Staffing a PEG can be a challenge. In any organization, good people are at a premium—and your PEG must be staffed with good people. The following are some general qualifications for good PEG people:

- Fifteen or more years experience in the software industry, with some personal experience in each of the disciplines of management, development, and product assurance. Particularly important is experience working with customers to help define software requirements.

- Experience defining software systems development processes.

- Experience as a software systems development customer. This experience can include interfacing with vendors of off-the shelf software products trying to work out problems with the products.

- Software engineering teaching experience (including publication of papers and books), preferably at professional conferences as opposed to the classroom.

Regarding the teaching experience, it is interesting to note that the "credentials" of publications can work against a PEG member if not handled carefully. A PEG staffed with full-time people can be perceived as an ivory tower organization that has no sense of what it takes to get the job done. If PEG members have written textbooks, they run the risk of having their ADPE work being labeled "academic," with little or no connection to the real world of doing software systems development. Once this label is affixed, the people working on projects tend to ignore the ADPE work turned out by such individuals. One way to avoid this scenario is for PEG staff to work closely with project teams to show them—on the job—how the guidance in ADPE elements can play itself out in the real world—to the benefit of all involved. For example, we believe that a key element of the software systems development process is independent product assurance review. A PEG staff member should review a document to show others (a) the way that it is done and (b) the value it adds to project work (by, e.g., giving visibility to potential problems before they adversely impact project progress). Nothing can raise the credibility of the PEG staff in the eyes of others than demonstrating the process on real work.

Another comment is in order regarding the software engineering teaching experience. People, particularly project managers, who do not want to participate in the ADPE way may use the PEG textbook and publication credential for disinformation purposes. That is, such managers will convey to their staffs that the ADPE way is academic because it comes from a textbook. They will then assert that the ADPE way has little or no applicability to their work. If senior management directs subordinate management and staff to follow the ADPE way, this disinformation attack can be contained if not thwarted. This senior management direction can take many forms. For example, a senior manager can simply deny a subordinate manager's requests for going around the ADPE way. Or, a senior manager can tie a subordinate manager's salary review to ADPE compliance. Of course, if a senior manager gets inundated with requests for relief from the ADPE way from a majority of subordinate managers, then it might be that the ADPE is out of sync with business reality. However, sometimes there is a fine line between organizational insurrection and simple resistance to cultural change. As we discuss in a subsequent section, it is part of the job of seller senior management to sort out where the organization is on this resistance spectrum.

One way to establish PEG credibility in the eyes of others that we have found practical is to have at least one PEG member also concurrently serve as a technical manager. Such an individual can serve, say, half time on the PEG staff and half time as a front-line technical manager responsible for one or more software systems development projects. This arrangement provides a "down-in-the-trenches" feedback mechanism that can give the PEG good insight into what makes sense to institute and what will not work. Furthermore, this arrangement can help deflect criticism that the PEG resides in an ivory tower and has no firsthand feel for what is involved with getting the job done. This arrangement can be particularly effective if the technical manager supervises project managers. In this circumstance, the technical manager can get good insight into which ADPE practices make sense to standardize by observing actual results on multiple projects. This circumstance also offers the PEG the opportunity to enrich ADPE element content by offering examples of different ways that certain principles laid out in ADPE elements can be implemented. For instance, regarding an ADPE element defining CCB practices, a technical manager of project managers has an opportunity to see different ways in which CCB meeting information requirements are satisfied in meeting minutes. One project may choose to record verbatim CCB discussions and associated decisions, while another project may simply choose to condense such information into a sentence or two per discussion/decision. This spectrum of practice will help the PEG refine the guidance in a CCB ADPE element regarding what makes sense to record at a CCB meeting.

PEG credibility is absolutely essential if that organization is to be successful in fulfilling its primary mission—transitioning the software systems development process from ill-defined to well-defined development practices via ADPE implementation. Why? Boiled down to its essence, the ADPE is a prescription for acceptable engineering social behavior. As Figure 7–7 implies, the practices set forth in the ADPE define the "right engineering thing to do." These practices establish norms of software systems development behavior *throughout an organization* that help the system developer and the customer interact harmoniously. Over time, these norms become institutionalized, thereby precipitating software systems development cultural change within both the seller and the customer orga-

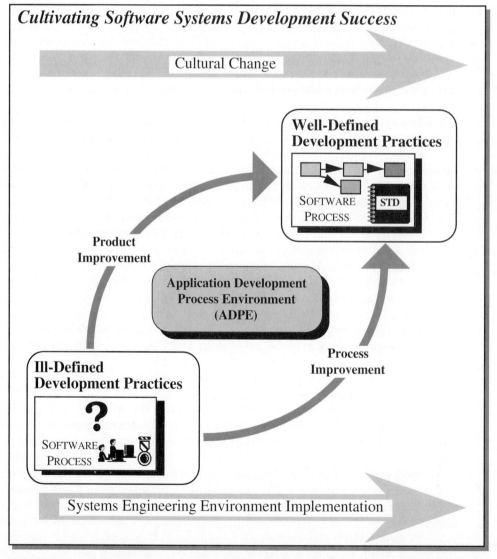

FIGURE 7–7 Cultivating software systems development success involves cultural change that, in part, is tied to ADPE implementation. The ADPE can be viewed as a code of software systems development practices defining the "right engineering thing to do."

nizations. In the absence of such norms, software systems development within an organization will invariably degenerate into process anarchy—with little likelihood of consistent, successful process repeatability.

However, it is basic human nature that people resist doing things in other people's ways. One reason for this resistance is that breaking habits (good, bad, or otherwise) is generally painful. A corollary to this fact of life is that resistance tends to magnify the more experienced the individual is. Thus, for example, as shown in Figure 7–8, people such as Sam, Pam, and Ham within a seller organization may have become accustomed to doing things their own way. Their experience has taught them what is needed to get the job done. They are naturally reluctant to cast aside what has worked for them in favor of some other process simply because it is for the greater organizational good. Thus, a critical element of PEG practice is to ensure that project staff is given an opportunity at least to comment on proposed ADPE elements as they are being developed.

Furthermore, the PEG must make it evident to project staff that all comments are indeed considered during element development or updating. The PEG must also make it evident that not everybody's comments can be incorporated. The larger the organization, the more diverse the background of its members. This diversity will, in general, give rise to a diverse set of comments and attitudes that the PEG will have to struggle to accommodate.[7]

To provide insight into the challenge facing the PEG regarding its response to comments on ADPE elements, it is useful to illustrate the types of diversity that can arise from the community that a PEG serves. The following examples relate to the ADPE elements discussed in previous chapters:

- Regarding an ADPE element governing project planning (Chapter 2), we suggested that the element should use risk assessment as the basis for planning allocation of resources to the management, development, and product assurance disciplines. With respect to resource allocation strategies, comments can range from "show me where in the industry it has been established that 20 percent of project resources should be allocated to product assurance for a high-risk project" to "your product assurance resource percentages are too conservative for all risk categories."

- Regarding an ADPE element governing the software system development process (Chapter 3), we suggested that the process should identify the key activities involved with developing and delivering a product to the customer (e.g., peer review, technical editing, product assurance review). With respect to these key activities, comments can range from "tell me the order that I have to follow in performing these activities" to "give me the freedom to pick which of these activities I need to apply to each of my products."

- Regarding an ADPE element governing CCB practice (Chapter 4), we suggested that the element should offer guidance regarding CCB minutes. With respect to this practice area, comments can range from "just tell me that I need to take minutes" to "give me a detailed CCB minutes outline."

- Regarding an ADPE element governing independent product assurance (Chapter 5), we suggested that the element should offer guidance regarding product assurance participation in CCB meetings. With respect to this practice, comments can range from "it is a waste of time for product assurance to participate in CCB meetings" to "I want product assurance to take the minutes at every CCB meeting."

The following two final comments are in order regarding the ADPE implementation suggested in Figure 7–8:

- "Organizational Software Systems Development Process" could apply to any level within an enterprise. In general, an enterprise consists of an organizational hierarchy. At each level in the hierarchy, there may be certain policies, directives, and other enterprise legislative publications that define acceptable enterprise practice. For example, an enterprise devoted to software systems development may have an *enterprisewide*

---

[7]To offer you ideas for managing this struggle, we present a figure later in this chapter showing the process for ADPE element development (i.e, Figure 7–11). We also provide an annotated outline for an ADPE element (i.e., Figure 7–13) whose purpose is to detail the process of creating, coordinating, promulgating, and updating ADPE elements.

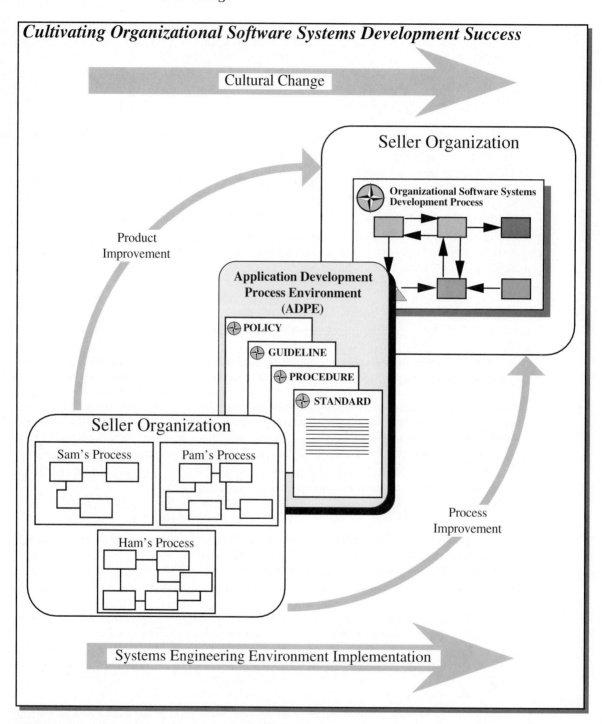

FIGURE 7–8 Individuals within the seller organization (e.g., Sam, Pam, and Ham) should be given an opportunity to contribute to the practices defined in the ADPE.

set of practices that all subordinate units have to tailor the enterprisewide practices to their specific projects. However, there may be instances in which a customer does not want the enterprisewide practices implemented for their particular project(s). In this case, the seller may have to create and implement another set of practices. As can be seen, one PEG challenge is to achieve a proper balance between (1) what may already exist that is applicable to the PEG's home organization and (2) what may need to be newly developed (and that may need to depart from what already exists).

■ "Sam's or Pam's or Ham's Process" could apply to the entire software systems development process (as described in Chapter 3) or to any element of that process (e.g., CCB operation as described in Chapter 4). The point here is that process anarchy can manifest itself across a broad range. A constant PEG challenge is to strike a balance between (1) giving Sam/Pam/Ham leeway in doing their jobs and (2) setting up an organizationwide consistent way of doing business. That is, the "organization's process" should provide a "consistent" approach that allows "diverse" implementations based on specific project characteristics. However, the process should prescribe a "minimum" set of required activities.

How should the PEG be incorporated into an organization?[8] It is not possible here to go into all the permutations for plugging a PEG into an organization. Figure 7–9 shows some of these permutations or alternative organizational arrangements. Using Figure 7–9, we offer the following general seller organizational considerations:

■ If your enterprise has a major program that will run for at least several years, you may wish to establish a PEG within the program organization. The first permutation in the figure illustrates this organizational setup. The setup shown is for a program headed by a program manager, with several project group managers (two are shown), who are responsible for managing two or more project managers. Each project manager is responsible for managing one or more software systems development projects within the program. A large project may have a project manager dedicated full time; several small projects may be managed by a single project manager. The PEG is positioned at the same level within the organization as the project group managers and a product assurance manager, who provides independent product assurance support to each project. If ADPE implementation is to take hold, the PEG should have the same organizational clout as the project group managers and the product assurance manager. As we previously emphasized, the PEG, through the ADPE, establishes the ground rules by which the managers and staff of the program are to operate. If it is organizationally subordinate to some of these managers, then PEG products (such as ADPE elements) will simply be ignored when managers higher in the organization feel more comfortable with their former way of doing business—particularly if their customers are pressuring them to revert to a former way of doing business.

We stress that, even if the PEG stands at the same level in the organization as other managers who report directly to the program manager, successful ADPE implementation is far from a foregone conclusion. If the program manager does not fully support the ADPE implementation role of the PEG, the first organizational setup shown in the figure can produce divisive infighting between the project group managers and the PEG. For example, if project group managers perceive that they can simply go around processes detailed in ADPE elements by going to the program manager to ask for relief, organizational practice will degenerate into disparate software development processes—namely, a melange of Sam's, Pam's, and Ham's processes.

One way to avoid such an impediment to successful ADPE implementation is to put into each manager's salary review the extent to which that manager has bought into ADPE implementation.[9] This approach is itself not without peril, however, for reasons such as the following:

■ The program manager has to set the example by fully supporting ADPE implementation. Simply stated, the program manager must "walk the talk." If ADPE element X says that the program manager is responsible for A, B, C, etc., then the program manager should manifestly carry out those responsibilities. Sometimes, dogmatic adherence to business rules can work against an organization. A program manager sometimes can get caught between a rock and a hard place in trying to set the example for subordinates

---

[8]This issue is discussed in more detail in Chapter 8 from the perspective of who should develop the ADPE.
[9]This issue is discussed in more detail in Chapter 8.

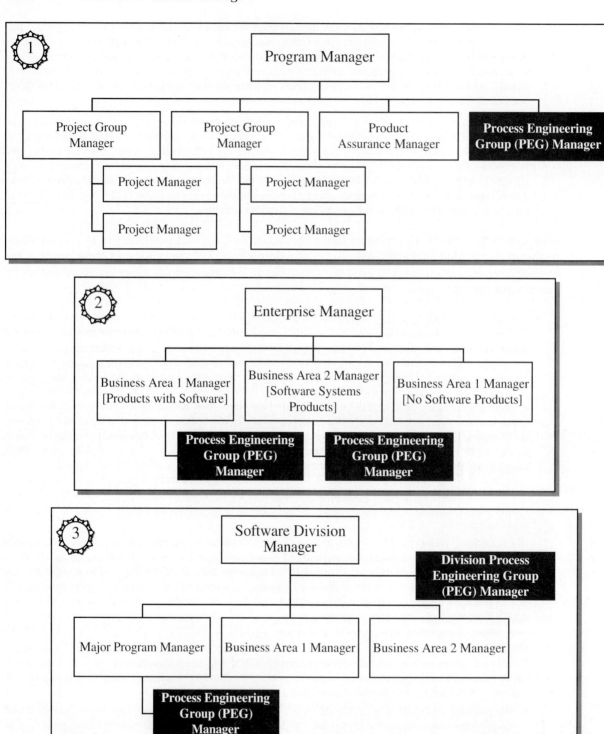

FIGURE 7–9 This figure presents several different organizational arrangements involving the process engineering group (PEG). Your organization may fit into one of these arrangements or some combination of them. Some ADPE cultural change issues are independent of the organizational arrangement—and some are not.

(particularly if his or her salary reviews depend on ADPE adherence). The program manager must keep the customer happy because that is how the program manager is often evaluated by superiors ("customer happiness" here means "continued business with the customer"). Sometimes, the program manager may have to sacrifice short-term customer happiness to achieve longer-term gains with the customer, particularly in those instances in which ADPE implementation involves significant departure from the way that customer did business with sellers in the past. On the other hand, sometimes the program manager may have to deviate from ADPE-stipulated practice because to do otherwise would irreparably damage relations with the customer.

■ Establishing a reward system based, in part, on ADPE compliance can be counterproductive. If project group managers and project managers do not really buy into the ADPE culture, they will seek ways to circumvent the culture while giving the appearance of buying in. When this situation develops, ADPE implementation becomes a sham, workers in the trenches become disillusioned, and the PEG becomes a waste of program resources. The impact on the overall program is that the program organization degenerates into individual competing fiefdoms. Such organizational factiousness does not go unnoticed by the customer—and can lead to loss of follow-on business.

The PEG must be particularly sensitive to setting up an ADPE that allows for some management flexibility to do the following:

(1) *Accommodate dilemmas such as those just posed (not only at the program manager level, but also at the project group manager level and the project manager level).*—The challenge to the PEG is allowing sufficient flexibility in ADPE ground rules while still prescribing a way of doing business that is not one step away from anarchy. One useful way to deal with this issue is to establish the following principle regarding application of ADPE business rules:

> The processes in ADPE element *X* are to be applied *prescriptively*—that is, they are to be applied in a manner that is consistent with project resources and schedule.

> It should be noted that a corollary of this principle is that processes defined in ADPE elements should rarely be "by the numbers." That is, ADPE elements should rarely include procedures that prescribe a single order for accomplishing process activities. There is generally no one way to lay out the individual steps making up a process.

(2) *Avoid the emergence of project group manager countercultures as just described.*—The challenge to the PEG is to afford managers at all levels the opportunity to comment on ADPE elements.

One additional observation is in order regarding the first PEG organizational permutation shown in Figure 7–9. You may wish to go this organizational route even if your enterprise already has an enterprisewide process improvement program. Even if your enterprise has established enterprisewide processes, the customer for your major program may have special ADPE requirements that make adaptation of the enterprisewide processes awkward or infeasible. In particular, if the customer is paying for a PEG and if that customer is relatively new to disciplined software systems development, trying to impose a highly disciplined enterprise software systems development culture on such a customer is not likely to succeed. Under such circumstances, it is preferable to develop an ADPE specific to the customer needs and to borrow small pieces from the enterprise culture that would appear to be sellable to the customer. For example, an enterprise culture may have its own software systems development terminology that is foreign to or, worse, anathema to a customer. For example, we have found that a culture with a strong Department of Defense (DoD) flavor simply does not sit well with some non-DoD organizations. While it may be true that cultural differences may be more tied to words rather than concepts (e.g., one culture's "Critical Design Review" is another culture's "Detailed Design Review"), still terminology is part and parcel of a culture and is generally difficult to change without major disruption. It is better to use terminology that a customer is comfortable with. When you are trying to sell a key process concept such as independent product assurance, it is better to iterate with a customer on product assurance terminology than to try blindly to impose terminology from an enterprise culture that may turn off a customer.

■ If your enterprise consists of several different business areas, not all of which deal with software, then you may wish to set up a PEG within each business area that deals with software. The second permutation in Figure 7–9 illustrates this organizational setup for an enterprise consisting of three business areas, two of which deal with software. The issues and approaches for their resolutions discussed previously for the first permutation apply to each PEG within this second permutation.

It is difficult to establish general principles regarding the value of trying to establish the same ADPE practices within each business area. On the surface, it would appear that, if two software business areas are part of the same enterprise, then the ADPE practices in one business area should at least considerably overlap those in the other business area. However, as we saw in discussing permutation 1, a lot of factors can influence successful ADPE implementation—within the *same* organization. It should not be surprising that when there are *two* (or more) organizations (even ones that are part of the same enterprise culture), trying successfully to institute a common ADPE culture across these organizations may prove insurmountable. For example, one business area may have a clientele that demands disciplined software systems development, while a second business area may have a clientele who has little appreciation of even the rudiments of disciplined software systems development. In such a circumstance, it would generally be counterproductive to try to institute the same ADPE implementation approach in both business areas. In particular, for the clientele for which disciplined software systems development is not an issue, independent product assurance would presumably not be an issue. Thus, ADPE element content in this environment would not have to dwell on engineering rationale for product assurance and the value its application adds to projects. On the other hand, for clientele having little appreciation for even the rudiments of disciplined software systems development, ADPE element content would have to focus considerable attention on fundamentals such as risk reduction through product assurance and other checking and balancing mechanisms. Even then, as we discussed in connection with permutation 1, it is not evident that such clientele could be persuaded to buy into such concepts.

Another potential impediment to establishing a common ADPE approach across business areas is the differences in management styles between the business areas. In discussing permutation 1, we stressed the key role that the program manager plays in bringing about successful ADPE implementation. In permutation 2, there is, in effect, a "program manager" for each business area. Given the potential impediments to successful ADPE implementation emanating from the program manager we cited in discussing permutation 1, it should not be surprising that successful ADPE implementation is strongly tied to the management style of each business area manager in permutation 2. Trying to align these management styles may not be in the best interests of each business unit—and thus not in the best interests of the enterprise. However, as each business unit establishes and refines its ADPE practices, it may, in fact, be possible to discern which of these practices can be elevated to cross-business-area practices. In this way, separate ADPE cultures can be melded over time. It may ultimately be possible to consolidate the individual business area PEGs into a single PEG having a mandate for establishing and maintaining ADPE practices across business areas.

■ If your enterprise is in the software systems development business (or primarily so) and if your business consists of a multitude of projects and programs of various sizes involving different customers, then you may wish to establish an enterprise-level PEG. This organization would be responsible for establishing ADPE elements for enterprisewide use. It may be necessary to assign some members of this organization to one or more programs or projects (here, we are using the term "program" as we did in permutation 1— namely, to denote a collection of projects) so that they can either develop program/project-specific ADPE elements or tailor the enterprise-level ADPE elements to the program/projects. Alternatively, it may be desirable to assign some members full time to, say, a major program to act as a PEG for that program. The third permutation in Figure 7–9 illustrates this organizational setup for a software division (i.e., primarily devoted to software) consisting of a major program and two business areas. The division has a PEG, and the major program has a PEG. Depending on factors such as those discussed in connection with permutation 1 (e.g., a customer unschooled in the rudiments of disciplined software systems development), it may be necessary for this program-level PEG to develop an ADPE specific to the program, borrowing wherever feasible from the division-level ADPE elements.

■ An important variation on the permutation 3 organizational setup is when the major program involves subcontractors. In this case, it is *essential* to establish a PEG within the program organization. Simply farming out representatives from the enterprise PEG to implant the enterprise ADPE culture on the program will generally not work because the subcontractor cultures have to be integrated with the culture of the prime contractor. In the real world, the way this "integration" happens is that the subcontractor cultures are subordinated to the prime contractor's culture. This subordination is far from straightforward. On the one hand, the prime contractor is responsible for satisfying the customer; the customer does not, in general, see subcontractors—to the customer, there is just a seller. So, the prime contractor and subcontractors have to appear to the customer as a single culture. On the other hand, some of the subcontractors may be the prime contractor's competitors on other jobs. Thus, the prime contractor needs to consider carefully how to train subcontractors in the ways of the prime contractor's culture. Regarding PEG staffing, one way to handle this situation is to staff it entirely with people from the prime contractor's company only—so that the ADPE concepts are clearly the prime contractor's. Alternatively, the prime contractor can staff the PEG with subcontractors as well as prime contractor people. This approach offers the opportunity to take the best from all the corporate cultures; it also facilitates subcontractor buy-in.

- Sometimes, your company may be a subcontractor. If the project or program you are working on has its own PEG, you may wish to try to become part of this organization for reasons already alluded to. If the project or program you are working on is to follow an ADPE that is part of the prime contractor's enterprise culture, then you should strive to get trained in the ways of your prime. You may even wish, if it does not compromise your competitive edge, to offer some of your company's best practices for consideration for incorporation into the prime's ADPE.

Allied to organizational considerations are PEG funding considerations. There are three straightforward funding arrangements—(1) seller organization, (2) buyer/user organization, and (3) some combination of (1) and (2). These funding arrangements depend in some instances on organizational arrangements. We will not discuss the myriad of combinations. Instead, we offer you the following suggestions to help you decide what type of funding arrangement makes sense for your environment:

- Ideally, PEG funding should come from the buyer/user. This arrangement establishes firm customer commitment to software process improvement and the attendant cultural change.

- A buyer/user may want to hire only a seller with an ADPE already developed. To ensure that the seller molds this ADPE to the customer's needs or existing environment, the buyer/user may wish to call for this molding in an RFP seeking prospective sellers. Furthermore, the buyer/user may wish to stipulate that ADPE maintenance will be on the seller's nickel after contract award. With an arrangement of this type, the buyer/user should be willing to allow the seller a larger fee than would be the case where the buyer/user pays for ADPE maintenance. The rationale for this business arrangement is that the seller is paying for business practices designed to "do things right the first time." Thus, the buyer/user should expect to reward the seller for consistently giving the buyer/user working products on time and within budget.

- In some types of contracts, particularly when the buyer/user is a government organization, it may not be possible for PEG funding to be provided by both the buyer/user and the seller. For example, for completion type contracts tendered by the U.S. federal government, the government purchases products and management from the seller. Included in "management" is the "PEG and its products—such as ADPE elements." In this case, the seller is barred by law from contributing to ADPE element development. However, the seller may be able to contribute to ADPE implementation support activities such as seller staff training in engineering principles underlying ADPE elements.

- In some circumstances, it may be desirable for the buyer/user and seller jointly to fund the PEG—even to the extent of jointly staffing the organization. This partnership arrangement may be particularly appropriate where both the buyer/user and seller have roughly equal experience in software systems development process improvement. In those cases in which both the buyer/user and seller are process improvement neophytes, it may be desirable to bring in an outside expert to act as a catalyst to direct the efforts of both sides. We stress that the partnership arrangement is perhaps the one most likely to bring about cultural change—because both sides have literally bought into process improvement.

Another key consideration to achieving buyer/user buy-in to seller PEG activity is illustrated in Figure 7–10. In this figure, we show a cover page for an arbitrary ADPE element (such as a CCB guideline as discussed in Chapter 4 or a software systems development process policy as discussed in Chapter 3). This cover page indicates that the ADPE element is part of an SEE that is governing a collection of software systems development projects (represented by the balloons) being managed under the umbrella of an effort called Program Z. The seller who prepared the element is the ABC Company. The

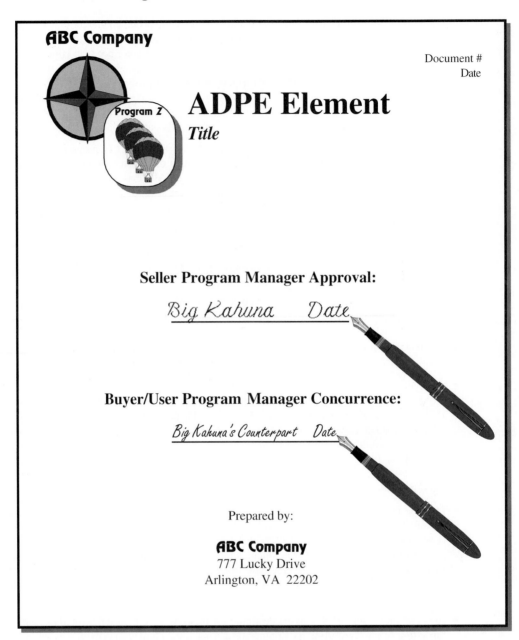

FIGURE 7–10 Although ADPE elements define *seller* software systems development business practices, buyer/user buy-in is recommended for successful ADPE implementation. Part of this buy-in should include ADPE element sign-off by a buyer/user representative who is the organizational counterpart to the seller manager who has ADPE element sign-off authority. This bipartisan sign-off formalizes the commitment of both parties to conform to the culture embodied in the element.

signature of the seller program manager, Big Kahuna, appears on the cover together with the signature of the buyer/user program manager, Big Kahuna's Counterpart. These signatures are not just a formality to give an official look to a document. The seller program manager's signature testifies to the fact that the ABC Company is committed on Program Z to the business practices set forth in the ADPE element. The buyer/user program manager's signature testifies to the fact that the customer concurs with these business practices and is committed to supporting them.

What does "the customer is committed to supporting these business practices" mean? We have stressed in preceding chapters that the business of software systems development involves continual interaction between the buyer/user and the seller. This continual interaction means that the buyer/user's behavior is an integral part of the seller's business practices. Thus, for example, we stressed in Chapter 5 that the CCB role in the acceptance testing process is critical for ensuring that the computer code to be delivered contains the capabilities that the customer asked for. We stressed that the customer must participate in the acceptance testing CCBs if the customer is to reduce misunderstandings regarding the capabilities to be included in the delivered computer code. Thus, when the buyer/user program manager signs the cover of an ADPE element governing the acceptance testing process, that manager is committing the buyer/user organization to buyer/user test CCB participation as set forth in the element.

We explained earlier in this chapter that institutionalizing the business practices in ADPE elements within the seller organization is a major PEG challenge. But, as the preceding discussion suggests, that challenge is only half the battle. If the buyer/user does not commit to these business practices too, then ADPE implementation will come up short. Having the buyer/user program manager sign off ADPE elements in a manner like that shown in Figure 7–10 is a start. This sign-off gives the buyer/user a club of sorts to effect cultural change within the buyer/user organization. However, the PEG has to work the problem from within the seller organization, too. Here, we mean that the PEG has to work with seller management and staff to convince them that ADPE business practices are really in the best interests of the customer. Too often, frontline seller managers are caught between a rock and a hard place when it comes to convincing their customers that ADPE practices are to be preferred to the "old way of doing business." On the one hand, these managers, particularly more experienced ones, may not be totally convinced that the ADPE way is the better way (as opposed to what they may have been accustomed to doing in the past). On the other hand, even if they believe in the ADPE way, the customer may not feel comfortable with the ADPE way and prefer "the customer's old way." Since frontline managers rightfully feel that they must keep their customers happy, these managers often revert to the customer's old way.

How can the PEG address these cultural change challenges within both the seller organization and the buyer/user organization? The answer to this question is not simple. The following guidance helps you deal with this question:

- The PEG must involve seller management and staff in ADPE element development. This involvement helps achieve management and staff buy-in to the practices that the PEG is responsible for setting up. We subsequently define a top-level process for bringing about this involvement. This process also offers some insight into what is involved with constructing ADPE elements that will in fact establish the seller software systems development culture.

- The PEG should submit draft ADPE elements for buyer/user review and comment. This step is mandatory if the ADPE buyer/user concurrence shown in Figure 7–10 is to happen.

- Special considerations govern ADPE content when the seller organization consists of a broad band of experience (i.e., from staff right out of school to grizzled veterans of software wars) and/or a mixture of software systems development cultures (as would be the case in which the seller organization is made up of a prime contractor and a number of subcontractors). In these situations, it is imperative to include some tutorial material in ADPE elements. The purpose of this tutorial material is to (1) define engineering terms in the vernacular so that people can communicate unambiguously with one another and (2) provide engineering rationale for the practices set forth in the ADPE elements. Thus, for example, an ADPE element on the CCB should offer rationale for why the CCB should be constituted with representatives from the management, development, and product assurance disciplines (the discussion in Chapters 1 and 2 on the CCB can be a useful starting point for this rationale). To ensure that such tutorial material does not "get in the way" of the business practices that should be the focus of ADPE elements, we suggest putting it in appendices. Even veterans of software wars can benefit from such tutorial material (even if they won't admit it). Often, such veterans have learned their trade through trial and error without understanding the engineering principles that underlie their successful experiences. This tutorial material also helps seller management and staff field challenging questions from questioning customers regarding the value of doing things the ADPE way. For example, customers often question the value that product assurance adds to a software systems development effort. To help seller management and staff respond to such customer concerns, the PEG should include in ADPE elements dealing with product assurance ideas such as the following:

> Through the application of the four processes of QA, V&V, T&E, and CM, product assurance raises the visibility of the software systems development process. This visibility provides both the customer and seller insight into the state of software products so that management can intelligently decide what to do next regarding these products. In this manner, the likelihood of product rework is reduced thereby increasing the likelihood that products will be delivered on time and within budget.

- Regarding the use of tutorial material in ADPE elements, one additional comment is in order. The PEG should take pains to know its audience. Nothing will turn off this audience more than ADPE elements that come across as preachy and condescending. ADPE elements cannot simply say do this or do that (even though some software veterans would argue that they would prefer such an approach). We have argued that ADPE elements should be set up so that they can be prescriptively applied. The PEG should use tutorial material to bring to the fore engineering principles to guide management and staff in performing this prescriptive application. For example, Chapter 4 explains that the CCB concept in its most effective form extends far beyond the traditional CM role assigned to this body. One extension to this traditional role that we have stressed is that this body can be used to do product development. To drive home this point in an ADPE element on the CCB, an appendix in this element should give an example of how the CCB can be used in this role.

- A key component of the ADPE element development process should be PEG briefings to management and staff on ADPE element content. Such briefings should occur while the elements are under development and after the elements are promulgated for use. The purpose of the briefings during development is to obtain early feedback from the seller organization on ADPE element content. This feedback also contributes to seller management and staff buy-in. The purpose of the briefings after the elements are promulgated, where the audience should be both the seller and the buyer/user, is to ensure that the practices set forth in the element are understood. In situations where there is a large seller organization (i.e., hundreds or more people) and there is a large buyer/user community, briefings should be given periodically to ensure that all involved parties are reached. Such briefings are best given to small numbers of people (tens of people at most) to allow for interchange between the attendees and the presenters. The PEG should use the briefings to convey to attendees the experiences of others within the buyer/user and seller organizations using the ADPE element being briefed. Such comments serve to enhance the credibility of the element. It also sends a message to attendees who attend later presentations that the practices in the element are, in fact, being institutionalized so that it is in the attendees' best interests to get on board with everybody else.

- In conjunction with briefings and less formal interactions between the PEG and seller/customer staff, a technique that we found useful for planting cultural change seeds is what we call "foam-board displays." These are displays of key extracts from ADPE elements or related briefing material created by mounting these extracts or material on large pieces of foam board, poster board, wood, and so forth. Here, "large" means tens of inches by tens of inches (e.g., 30" × 40"). For example, to highlight the features of the project planning risk assessment activity, it may be helpful to mount on a foam board the risk assessment criteria and the associated resource allocation percentages (e.g., in the form of pie charts as discussed in Chapter 2). Such a foam-board display can be used during a briefing on the project plan development process and/or in a one-on-one discussion of risk assessment between a PEG member and a seller or customer staff member. Its size also makes it ideal for wall mounting in prominent places. This approach to transmitting ADPE concepts brings in subliminal forces to help bring about cultural change. If you pass by a pie chart of resource allocation percentages every day in and out of your office, that pie, over time, simply becomes inseparable from other things you associate with your work environment—even if you disagree with the percentages in the chart!

We now present and walk through in detail a top-level process that a PEG can use to construct and improve upon ADPE elements. This process, shown in Figure 7–11, factors in the ideas just addressed in

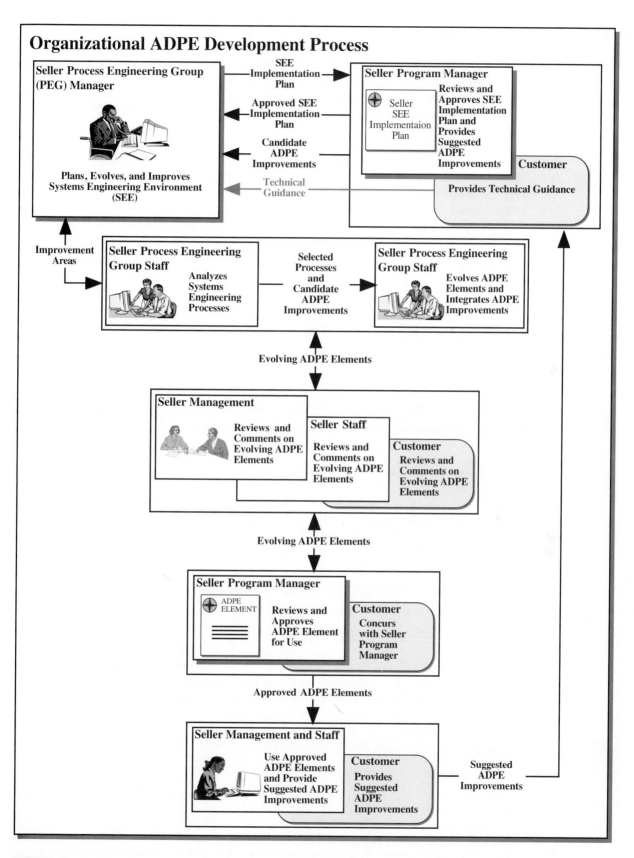

FIGURE 7-11 The development and improvement of ADPE elements involves customer personnel, seller management, and seller staff. The figure depicts a top-level ADPE element development and improvement process involving these participants.

the bulleted items. It is based on the organizational setup discussed in connection with Figure 7–9 (permutation 1)—namely, a program, managed by a program manager, consisting of a number software systems development projects, where the seller program manager interfaces with a buyer/user program manager. As we walk you through the figure, we point out variations to the process in the figure that derive from different organizational setups.

Please note that Figure 7–11 offers you a *starting point* for laying out a more detailed process that reflects your particular work environment and customer/seller contractual relationship. We suggest that one element of your ADPE should be an element that defines what your ADPE element types are (recall that in this book our ADPE element types are policy, guideline, procedure, and standard). This element should also define the process for developing and improving ADPE elements. You may wish to incorporate a figure like Figure 7–11 in such an ADPE element, together with a more detailed figure that lays out the individual steps for ADPE development and improvement. Figure 7–11 has the following eight rectangles that represent the responsible seller agents and associated process activities:

- Seller Program Manager—Reviews and Approves SEE Implementation Plan and Provides Candidate ADPE Improvements.

- Seller Process Engineering Group (PEG) Manager—Plans, Evolves, and Improves System Engineering Environment (SEE).

- Seller Process Engineering Group Staff—Analyzes Systems Engineering Processes.

- Seller Process Engineering Group Staff—Evolves ADPE Elements and Integrates ADPE Improvements.

- Seller Management—Reviews and Comments on Evolving ADPE Elements.

- Seller Staff—Reviews and Comments on Evolving ADPE Elements.

- Seller Program Manager—Reviews and Approves ADPE Elements for Use.

- Seller Management and Staff—Use Approved ADPE Elements and Provide Suggested ADPE Improvements.

Figure 7–11 also has the following shaded rounded-edge rectangles that represent the customer's responsibilities and associated process activities:[10]

- Customer—Provides Technical Guidance.

- Customer—Reviews and Comments on Evolving ADPE Elements.

- Customer—Concurs with Seller Program Manager.

- Customer—Provides Suggested ADPE Improvements.

These process activities are linked together by the major communication paths and associated information. As shown in Figure 7–11, along each communication path information is transferred from one process activity to another. The information transferred consists of the following items:

- SEE Implementation Plan.

- Approved SEE Implementation Plan.

- Candidate ADPE Improvements.

- Technical Guidance (lighter print type indicates that customer may not participate in seller ADPE development process).

---

[10]The customer responsibilities and associated process activities are shaded to denote that many times the customer is not involved with a seller's ADPE development process. We recommend that the customer participate, but we recognize that customer participation may not happen or even be practical.

- Improvement Areas.

- Selected Processes and Candidate ADPE Improvements.

- Evolving ADPE Elements.

- Approved ADPE Elements.

- Suggested ADPE Improvements.

These seller/customer activities and communication paths are described (primarily from the PEG's perspective) as follows:

- The PEG manager is responsible for planning, evolving, and improving a SEE. The PEG defines the ground rules for SEE implementation in an SEE implementation plan[11] that is provided to the seller program manager for review and approval. If the customer is paying for SEE development, someone within the customer organization with the organizational stature of the seller program manager should also review and approve the implementation plan and provide technical guidance to the seller PEG manager. The PEG manager is responsible for identifying improvement areas for investigation by PEG staff.

- The PEG staff is responsible for investigating and evaluating systems engineering processes, improvement areas, and candidate ADPE improvements. To ensure customer and seller management/staff buy-in, these investigations and evaluations should be done in concert with customer personnel, seller management (from the program manager downward, including the product assurance manager), and seller staff. For example, the PEG staff may investigate and evaluate a new way for distributing CCB minutes using a groupware software product. As part of the evaluation process, the PEG may ask one of the projects to test out the new concept. The project's input helps to achieve management/staff buy-in because the concept has been road tested by frontline project staff. The PEG investigations and evaluations, with some help from others, result in the identification of selected processes or candidate ADPE improvements for incorporation into ADPE policies, guidelines, procedures, and standards.

- The PEG staff is responsible for evolving ADPE elements and integrating ADPE improvements. Of all the activities shown in Figure 7–11, this activity is the most time-consuming. It consists of putting words and graphics on paper to create draft elements and briefing seller and customer staff along the way to ensure that ADPE content is addressing seller/customer needs.

  Putting words and graphics on paper to create the contents of an ADPE element is perhaps the most difficult part of the process shown in Figure 7–11. Ironically, even with expert writers, it is difficult to get something down on paper that the seller and customer communities can relate to. Following are some suggestions for PEG staff to consider when taking on the task of writing ADPE elements.

  - Gauge your audience carefully so that you can determine how much tutorial material to include. Put the principles and elements essentials up front. Relegate tutorial and amplifying material to appendices.

  - Use figures to document processes and clarify principles. Use tables to bring to the fore ADPE element essentials. For example, when writing an element for the CCB, consider putting in a figure such as the triangle diagram that we have used throughout this book to clarify the communications principles underlying the CCB concept. As another example, when writing an ADPE policy element, consider putting into a table the essential points of the policy. Such a table provides a handy reference for the reader to grasp quickly the policy essence. Remember, depending on the amount of tutorial material you deem is necessary to include, even ADPE policy elements can consist of tens of pages.

  - No matter how sophisticated your audience engineeringwise, define terms. Despite valiant efforts by many professional organizations such as IEEE, no standard set of software engineering terminology exists. For example, what some engineers call "quality assurance" others call "product assurance." Part of establishing an engineering culture consists of establishing a common language. The more dialects there are, the greater is the likelihood of miscommunication.

---

[11]Chapter 8 addresses in detail the SEE implementation planning activity.

- Ideally, each ADPE element should be put together by two people with complementary outlooks on what the ADPE is supposed to be. One of the ADPE authors should be a conceptual thinker who has the big picture of how all the elements are to fit together. The other ADPE author should be a detail person who can turn concepts into organizationally specific statements. As we stated earlier, it is good to have an ADPE author who spends part time as a senior manager responsible for seeing to it that ADPE practices are implemented by subordinate managers and staff. Another advantage to having a two-person team write an ADPE element is that such an arrangement serves to avoid idea burnout. Through the constant interaction between the two writers, ideas are constantly coming to the fore (and one idea generally spawns others), examined to see how they hold up under scrutiny, and refined to the mutual satisfaction of the two writers. Furthermore, since two writers necessarily have different experiences, the constant interaction between the two serves to enrich the material that each would turn out if they worked in isolation from one another.

- Above all, be receptive to comments and criticisms—and practice what your elements preach. Nothing undermines PEG credibility more than the appearance that community comments are not being addressed and that the PEG is above following the ADPE practices.

We cannot stress enough the importance of soliciting seller/customer feedback through briefings *while ADPE element drafts are being written*. Even if the PEG staff members who are writing an element are expert in the subject matter, not even experts can anticipate the myriad of issues and concerns that seller management/staff and the customer may have. Nothing can give the impression of a PEG imprisoned in an ivory tower more than a PEG that works in isolation from the community it is to serve.

If your environment consists of a seller organization made up of a prime contractor and several subcontractors and/or a customer made up of a number of organizations that have worked with different contractors in the past, *briefings on evolving ADPE content are mandatory*. This situation is the most challenging for the PEG because different seller cultures and different customer cultures have to be blended into a single way of doing business. Such cultural blending can take a long time. For example, if the seller and customer organizations are each of the order of hundreds of people, this cultural blending can take years. The PEG should keep this cultural change time scale in mind when planning ADPE implementation. We do not know the specifics of how this time scale changes with the size of the seller organization and the size of the customer organization. We can say that, when the customer organization is culturally inhomogeneous and the seller organization is a confederation of subcontractors, the time scale for homogenizing the various cultural differences will be protracted—and will become increasingly protracted the larger the seller organization is and/or the larger the customer organization. Conversely, the more culturally homogeneous the seller organization is and/or the more culturally homogeneous the customer organization is, the time scale for effecting cultural change will be correspondingly shorter. Regarding these time scales, the PEG should also keep in mind the following overriding consideration:

> The time scale for effecting cultural change can be dramatically reduced the more pliable are the involved communities. On the other hand, if seller senior managers are set in their ways and/or customers insist on doing business the "old way," effecting cultural change can take a long time (i.e., months to years)—even if the communities involved are of the order of tens of people. The PEG must therefore constantly keep in mind the fact of software systems development life that ADPE implementation is first and foremost an exercise in selling (1) seller management on the connectivity between ADPE business practices and what practices have worked in the past, and (2) customers on the connectivity between ADPE business practices and increased likelihood that the seller will deliver products with integrity.

- Figure 7–11 indicates that, linked to the PEG staff responsibility of evolving ADPE elements, are the customer responsibility and seller management and staff responsibilities of reviewing and commenting on evolving ADPE elements. This linkage is critical to effecting cultural change through ADPE implementation. Through this linkage, the customer and the seller organization are afforded the opportunity to contribute and buy into the ADPE business practices. These parties must take the time to go over this material and clarify issues for the PEG. They should be specific. For example, it is not constructive for a seller manager to offer a comment on an independent product assurance ADPE element that says in essence "I cannot live with this element because the customer thinks that product assurance is a waste of money." On the other hand, it is constructive for a seller manager in the context of this example to offer a comment such as

"I think I can sell my customer on product assurance if the element addresses how product assurance adds value to product development." When commenting on ADPE elements, the reviewers need to keep the following points in mind:

- The PEG staff is responsible for coordinating and integrating comments. There will generally be a broad spectrum of comments that the PEG receives. Some of these comments will be contradictory. For example, one comment on an ADPE element having to do with the CCB secretary might be "the project manager should take meeting minutes," while a comment from someone else might be "someone from the product assurance organization should take meeting minutes." Thus, it is generally not possible to integrate all comments into a given element. The PEG must be proactive in ensuring that the commenting communities are informed that each comment received is reviewed—even though it may not be incorporated. If the PEG is not proactive in this regard, (1) the commenting communities will soon stop commenting, (2) resistance to adopting the ADPE practices will increase, (3) turmoil between the PEG and other organizational elements will intensify, and (4) cultural change will be retarded.

- If the customer and seller management and staff abdicate their ADPE review responsibilities, they cannot subsequently say that they were unaware of the ADPE practices and did not follow them for that reason. For the process in Figure 7–11 to work, all parties involved need to approach it with the attitude that successful software systems development is a business and thus must be conducted in a businesslike manner. To treat software systems development otherwise is inviting engineering anarchy and project upheaval.

- The PEG's perspective is organizationwide. A given manager's perspective and that of staff members are generally more truncated. What may make sense in a given manager's domain simply may not make sense throughout the entire organization. Often misunderstood is the notion that "consistent business practice" is *not* equivalent to "one size fits all." This notion is a prime source of contention between the PEG and the rest of the seller organization when it comes to evolving ADPE elements. More specifically, this source of contention can be stated as follows:

> In constructing ADPE elements, the PEG must define a set of practices that can be applied uniformly across an organization. On the one hand, the practices must be sufficiently specific so that they convey something that actually can be applied to develop software products (i.e., the practices offer a *way* of doing things). For example, as we discussed in Chapter 4, an ADPE element on the CCB should specify (1) that meetings should be documented in minutes and (2) what the information *requirements* are for these minutes. On the other hand, the ADPE practices cannot be so specific that they tie the hands of various elements within an organization and actually impede product development (i.e., one size does not fit all). For example, as we discussed in Chapter 4, an ADPE element on the CCB should not dictate the amount of detail to include in the CCB minutes; rather, the element should offer guidance that ties meeting minutes detail to customer and seller management project visibility needs.
>
> We need to make an additional point about ADPE element specificity that we elaborate on in Chapter 8. In general, the more detailed an element, the more often it may have to be changed because of the dynamics of the seller and/or customer environment. For example, in Chapter 3 we indicated that, in general, an ADPE element describing a seller's software systems development process should provide guidance on a cover letter that the project or program manager is to use in releasing a product to the customer. At one extreme, this ADPE element can be a fill-in-the-blanks template where the only thing to be filled in is the product name and the date on the letter. Such an approach certainly facilitates product release, particularly in an environment where tens or hundreds of products may be released in a month. However, if the addressee on the letter (e.g., a government contracting officer or a vice president of a business enterprise) changes, then that part of the ADPE element containing the addressee's name needs to be updated to reflect this change. At the other extreme, the software systems development process ADPE element can simply say that any product the seller releases to the customer needs to be accompanied by a cover letter that the project manager prepares according to a format acceptable to the customer. In this case, the ADPE element does not need to be changed when the product addressees change. In Chapter 8 we discuss how to achieve a balance between ADPE element update frequency and business practice institutionalization. The key issue here is effecting business process improvement without disrupting cultural change.

This PEG challenge is the primary reason that we have stressed throughout this book the notion of "prescriptive application" when it comes to setting up ADPE elements. We have emphasized that management and staff should be empowered to figure out the extent to which business practices in the ADPE elements makes sense to apply on their particular projects (again, because "one size does not fit all"). This PEG challenge is also the primary reason that we have stressed throughout this book that, with the possible exception of homogeneous organizations where projects do not span a broad spectrum, specifying the order in which steps in an ADPE procedure are to be accomplished is generally not a practical idea. Rather, we have emphasized that management and staff should be empowered to figure out which order makes sense on their particular projects (again, because "one size does not fit all").

■ As Figure 7–11 shows, once the seller PEG evolves ADPE elements and integrates any ADPE improvements into the elements, the seller program manager is responsible for the review and approval of the evolving ADPE elements. Linked to this responsibility is the responsibility of the customer (i.e., buyer/user) program manager for concurring with the business practices set forth in the ADPE elements. Customer concurrence and seller program manager approval can be made a matter of record by having these managers sign and date the ADPE element cover sheet.

How does this management commitment manifest itself in an organizational setup that differs from the one in which the seller program manager approves and the customer concurs (see Figure 7–10)? The following are some organizational variations (tied in part back to Figure 7–9) and some associated suggestions for registering this management commitment:

■ The third organizational arrangement in Figure 7–9 shows, among other things, a PEG responsible for setting up an ADPE throughout an entire software division consisting of a number of business areas (two are shown) and a number of major programs (one is shown). The PEG may publish a divisionwide set of ADPE elements. To show commitment to these ADPE practices, each business area manager can sign the elements or the cover page of the entire document. Similarly, each major program manager may do likewise, unless, as shown in the figure, the major program has its own PEG responsible for setting up an ADPE for that program. This case reduces to the Figure 7–10 case with the possible additional proviso that this program-specific ADPE will use, where feasible, elements of the divisionwide ADPE. This proviso can be made explicit by referencing the divisionwide ADPE in the program-specific ADPE (if the customer served by the program manager does not object). Alternatively, the program manager can sign the divisionwide ADPE document with the understanding that the program's ADPE overrides the divisionwide ADPE in cases of conflict. To avoid bureaucracy, the divisionwide ADPE should contain a caveat to this effect. Again, the reason why many parts of a divisionwide ADPE may not be applicable to a major program is because "one size does not fit all." Implicit in the third organizational arrangement in Figure 7–9 is that the divisionwide ADPE embodies, by definition, the software systems development culture of the seller division. If the customer of the major program shown in Figure 7–9 is not another part of the seller's enterprise (i.e., the customer is another enterprise with its own separate culture), then it is unlikely that this customer will readily buy into the division's software systems development culture—unless, of course, the customer contracted with the seller for those business practices to be applied to the customer's program.

■ What makes sense to do for small projects (i.e., where the number of seller participants may be, say, five or less, including the project manager and product assurance)? Because a small project can be implanted in a wide variety of organizational environments, there is a spectrum of responses to this question. The following is a sampling from this spectrum:

■ The project may be one of several in a small software company that is running several projects of similar size. In this case, the entire company can be viewed like a major program shown in either the first or third organizational arrangement in Figure 7–9. The PEG may be a one-person organization, and may be staffed only part time. The president of the company or a senior executive may be the PEG. Here, the president of the company can sign the cover sheet of each ADPE element to demonstrate to the customer the company's commitment to the customer. If the project is pivotal to the company, the president can also urge the customer to sign on the cover sheet so that both parties formalize their commitments to following the ADPE business practices. This arrangement is particularly desirable if the customer wants the seller to tailor the company's existing ADPE elements to the specific needs of the project. Furthermore, if the customer is willing to pay for this tailoring, then the customer's signature should be mandatory.

- The project may be part of a company whose main line of business is not software but that does have a software organization. In the extreme, such an organization may not even have a PEG and may be relying on externally produced software practice documents such as IEEE standards, the SEI Capability Maturity Model for Software, ISO 9000 practices, textbooks, or some combination of these entities. In this case, the head of the software organization can direct the project manager to commit to using the externally produced "ADPE elements" in the project plan. If the software organization does have a PEG, then, following the logic in the preceding small-company case, the head of the software organization can sign the ADPE element cover sheets. If the elements are being produced specifically for the project (as may be the case if the first part of the project is to set up an ADPE before actual product development is to begin), the head of the software organization can direct the project manager to sign each ADPE element cover sheet. In addition, to solidify customer commitment to the ADPE business practices, the project manager may wish to have the customer sign each ADPE element cover sheet.

- The project may be part of a *systems* development effort in which the project is to develop software to drive one or more system components. Such "embedded software" as it is typically referred to can be critical to the overall operation of the system. It is not unusual for the development of such embedded software to be hidden from the view of managers responsible for the development of other system components—particularly if the system under development contains a myriad of subsystems (e.g., an automobile or an airplane). Often, the development of embedded software is subject to the strictures of the system-level analogues to ADPE elements. Even under such circumstances, it is important for the managers responsible for the embedded software to give visibility to their business practices and give visibility to their commitment to follow these practices. The customer in these instances is typically another engineering organization. To ensure that the software business practices meld with these other engineering practices, the head of the software organization (which, in the simplest of situations may be the software project manager) should sign each ADPE element cover sheet. So, too, should the engineering managers who are the customers for these software products sign these cover sheets. We stress that all these suggestions regarding embedded software developed on small software projects as we have here defined "small" apply to embedded software in general. In fact, the larger the size of the project responsible for producing embedded software, the more important it is to apply the suggestions discussed here. We close this discussion of embedded software and the need for formal management commitment to ADPE practices, with the following observation borne out by much software industry experience:

  > If all this signature business sounds like a lot of bureaucracy, keep in mind that faulty embedded software can make its presence painfully obvious when an automobile stops running, an airplane stops flying, or a medical device kills or injures a patient.

- Next in the process in Figure 7–11 is the "rubber-meets-the-road step." Here, seller management and staff perform assigned work on seller projects using the approved ADPE elements. As discussed in preceding chapters, this work is performed through interaction with the customer. Both the customer and the seller get a firsthand feel for those ADPE business practices that make sense—and those that seem to stand in the way of getting work done. Because these practices represent in varying degrees a different way of doing business for the parties involved, determining what makes sense and what seems to be standing in the way of getting work done is far from straightforward.

As with anything new, there is a settling-in period. The PEG must be prepared during this period to hear a lot of complaining. In the extreme, this complaining can border on rebellion. Strong senior management support is necessary to help weather the initial storm of protest due to the transition. Gaining this support in itself may be a challenge because some of the complaining may come from some senior managers.

It is important for senior management to stay the course during the period immediately following ADPE element promulgation. Depending on seller organization size, the settling-in period can span weeks to months—in general, the larger the organization, the longer the period. After the settling-in period, real issues and difficulties with the ADPE elements will begin to surface. To lessen turmoil during the settling-in period, we suggest that ADPE elements that are formally promulgated be derived from the most successful practices that may already have been in place prior to formal ADPE element promulgation. In this way, the practices appearing in the elements are simply a codified version of many of the things that people have already been doing. In many ways, the approved ADPE elements embody many lessons learned while developing software systems. One way that we have found useful for laying the groundwork for practices that will eventually be folded into ADPE elements is to incorporate some trial-balloon ADPE elements into the SEE implementation plan, try them for a while, and then start the process of evolving the trial elements.

We also need to emphasize that incorporating existing practices into ADPE elements can be a two-edged sword. On the one hand, it can lessen the turmoil during the settling-in period as we have noted. On the other hand, it can leave the impression with seller management and staff that they do not have to read the elements—because they already know what the elements contain. People will not read them—even those within the seller organization who fully support the ADPE practices. One way for the PEG to address this problem is to stress during ADPE element briefings (both prepromulgation and postpromulgation) that the elements need to be read from cover to cover—even though the elements contain some "old" or "familiar" material.

The fact that people may be reluctant to read the ADPE elements poses another challenge for the PEG. Seller management and staff are focused on getting the work done for their customers. In many organizations, there is not a lot of slack time (if there is, both seller and customer senior management may start asking questions like "What the hell are people doing with their time?"). So, reading ADPE elements is usually not high on people's list of priorities. On the one hand, if an element is too long, people will balk at even picking it up. On the other hand, if the element is so short that it does not help people do their jobs, it will not be worth reading. Chapter 8 addresses the issues associated with the number and size of ADPE elements needed to establish an ADPE.

■ The "final" step in the Figure 7–11 process consists of the customer and seller management and staff providing feedback to the seller program manager regarding suggested ADPE improvements. With the feedback coming from the middle and bottom of the organization to the top of the organization, support for the engineering norms gets blended into the ADPE elements. Complementing this "bottom-up" feedback is "top-down" support from the seller program manager. The seller program manager can make a strong statement of support for changing the culture by participating in the change. This combination of feedback and support helps to implement the ADPE elements.

Once the program manager reviews the feedback, candidate ADPE improvements are passed on to the PEG manager. The program manager may pass the suggested ADPE improvements straight to the PEG manager for review and comment. This "bottom-up" feedback precipitates revisits to one more preceding steps in the process. As seller management and staff perform work for the customer by presumably following the ADPE practices, improvements to these practices will generally become apparent. With the caveats noted earlier about the settling-in period, the PEG needs to review these suggestions and/or candidate ADPE improvements (depending upon how the program manager wants to set up the review cycle).

We suggest that the PEG get out into the workplace and experience firsthand what is working and what is not. For example, the PEG can coordinate with a project manager to attend a project CCB meeting to see how practices set forth in a CCB ADPE element are playing out on a real project. The ADPE element that contains your version of Figure 7–11 should spell out a mechanism for receiving comments on ADPE elements from the customer and from the seller management and staff. One way that we have found useful is to indicate that "suggestions should be in a memorandum and can be submitted to the program manager or PEG manager at any time."

Chapter 8 discusses ADPE element update frequency. For the present, we note that there are times when it may become necessary to distribute an interim update to an element. By *interim,* we mean a "change to a relatively small portion of an element because something is proving to be unworkable or some conditions have changed since the element was promulgated that invalidate something stated in the element." For example, suppose an ADPE element on the CCB is promulgated after the promulgation of an ADPE element on the product development process. Suppose further that this latter element included the CCB as part of the process and called it "configuration control board." Finally, suppose that while the CCB ADPE element was being developed that it was decided by the customer and/or seller management that "change control board" more accurately reflected the concept called out in the product development process ADPE element and being elaborated on in the CCB ADPE element. In this example, then, it would be necessary to issue an interim update to the product development process ADPE element to reflect this terminology change. A simple way to handle this interim update would be to make it a part of a memorandum that might be used to promulgate the CCB ADPE element.

We have completed our walkthrough of Figure 7–11. To conclude this section, we return to the following key points regarding the construction and application of ADPE elements cited during this walkthrough:

- **One size does not fit all.** In constructing ADPE elements, the PEG must define a set of practices that can be applied uniformly across an organization. On the one hand, the practices must be sufficiently specific so that they convey something that can actually be applied to develop software products (i.e., the practices offer a *way* of doing things). On the other hand, the ADPE practices cannot be so specific that they tie the hands of various components within an organization and actually impede product development.

- **Prescriptively apply ADPE elements.** The one-size-does-not-fit-all challenge is the primary reason that we stress throughout this book the notion of "prescriptive application" when it comes to setting up ADPE elements. We emphasize that management and staff should be empowered to figure out the extent to which business practices in the ADPE elements makes sense to apply on their particular projects. Specifying the order in which steps in an ADPE procedure are to be accomplished is generally not a practical idea. Rather, management and staff should be empowered to figure out which order makes sense on their particular projects. A possible exception to this empowerment principle is a homogeneous organization where projects do not span a broad spectrum. In this circumstance, it may make good business sense to specify an order for the steps specified in an ADPE element—or, at least specify a preferred order.

To appreciate fully the implications of these statements, it is worthwhile to probe what "prescriptive" fundamentally means. Since we have repeatedly stated that the ADPE is a framework within which consistent software systems development can be successfully carried out, it is also worthwhile to consider what "framework" fundamentally means.

We turn to the dictionary. It turns out that "prescriptive" and "framework" each has a broad range of definitions, depending on which dictionary is consulted. We have taken definitions from the 2000-page *The Random House Dictionary of the English Language* (the unabridged 1967 edition) because they reflect the spirit of what we are trying to convey in engineering terms.

- Prescriptive—giving directions
- Framework—a skeletal structure designed to support or enclose something

To understand the way that we are using the term "prescriptive application" of an ADPE element, we first need to explain how the qualifier "prescriptive" applies to ADPE element **content.** ADPE elements are the most useful and require infrequent change when they "give directions." By *giving directions* we mean "giving guidance—*not* detailed, step-by-step instructions." We recognize that some people use the phrase "giving directions" to mean "giving precise instructions." Others use this phrase to mean something in between our use and this precise-instruction use.

Thus, ADPE content should give directions to the extent that they provide management and staff the starting point for tailoring to the specific needs of their project work. In earlier chapters, we describe this tailoring by saying that "management and staff apply the ADPE practices consistent with the schedule and resource constraints of their projects." People, particularly those with experience, have to be given leeway to apply their experience. This leeway we have expressed as "prescriptive application of the ADPE practices." And it is this leeway that opens the door for people to adapt to the ADPE culture.

We are thus using the phrase "prescriptive application" in the same sense that "prescriptive" is used to qualify the word "grammar." The same dictionary defines *prescriptive grammar* as "grammar that is considered in terms of what is correct, and therefore good usage." Similarly, *prescriptive application of ADPE practices* means "application that is good usage of available time and resources."

To understand the way that we are using the term "framework" as it applies to the ADPE, we combine the notions of "leeway" and "prescriptive application." When an ADPE is a framework in the sense of "a skeletal structure designed to support a way of doing things by bordering it with acceptable practices" (borrowing from the dictionary definition), it cultivates cultural change. *Skeletal* here means what we just said above, that is

> ADPE practices must be sufficiently specific so that they convey something that actually can be applied to develop software products, but they cannot be so specific that they tie the hands of various elements within an organization and actually impede product development (i.e., one size does not fit all). That is, an ADPE that fosters cultural change is one that (1) is prescriptive in content and (2) can be prescriptively applied.

These words are the bottom line regarding the PEG's approach to bringing about ADPE-based cultural change. The principal corollary to this bottom line then is that the PEG should stay away from producing ADPE elements that are recipelike practices. We believe that software systems development cannot be reduced to a recipe of single instructions. People and their ability to apply themselves cognitively to software systems development are the most important ingredients (no pun intended) for achieving software systems development success.

Figure 7–12 depicts this bottom line and its relationship to the notions of the "ADPE as a business practice framework" and "prescriptive application of these practices."

In cultivating cultural change, the PEG must keep in mind the underlying currents of people's own experiences. Remember, Sam, Pam, and Ham—like most people in the software industry—are naturally going to resist doing things the organization's way if they do not have room to maneuver. Sometimes, maneuvering can degenerate into subterfuge. The PEG must recognize that, within any organization, interpretations of what "playing by the ADPE rules" means will generally span a broad spectrum. Some people will try to carry things out meticulously according to what is written (e.g., if a CCB is to meet at least monthly, they will tend to meet more frequently; if a suggested format for CCB minutes is included in an element, they will pattern their minutes after that format and then some). Others will follow the spirit of the ADPE rules but will be somewhat less fastidious in their application (e.g., if an ADPE element calls for product assurance participation in CCB meetings, they may have product assurance attend some meetings, but always copy them on CCB minutes). And still others will draw a line in the sand and say that they will simply not follow some ADPE practices (e.g., if an ADPE element calls for customer participation in the acceptance testing process to decide TIR resolutions, they will adopt the attitude that they know what the customer wants so that the customer does not need to be involved in the acceptance testing process).

To aid in ADPE implementation, we suggest that the PEG should focus its attention on the people in the middle of the spectrum. Once these individuals become more like the people who follow the ADPE rules meticulously, the resistors will face increasing pressure to get on board. The PEG must also recognize that some people are never going to change—and that it is simply not cost-effective to keep beating on those people to change. Remember, the captain who went down with the *Titanic* was informed—so history tells—that his ship was in iceberg-infested waters. Like this captain, there are some in the software industry who simply believe that software disaster cannot happen to them—because their way of doing things is tried and true. If the PEG has done a good job in following a process of getting organizational inputs to mold an organizational practice framework in the manner suggested in Figure 7–12, then such some outliers will either self-destruct or eventually come on board.

The PEG must carefully listen to its constituency. If outliers constitute a large minority or a majority, then something is breaking down. The PEG must be prepared to work with the organization to get a better handle on what is working and change what is not. One word of caution is in order regarding responding to cries for change. The PEG must be prepared to ride out this storm. The PEG needs to distinguish between the turmoil resulting from (1) the organization's adapting to a new way of doing

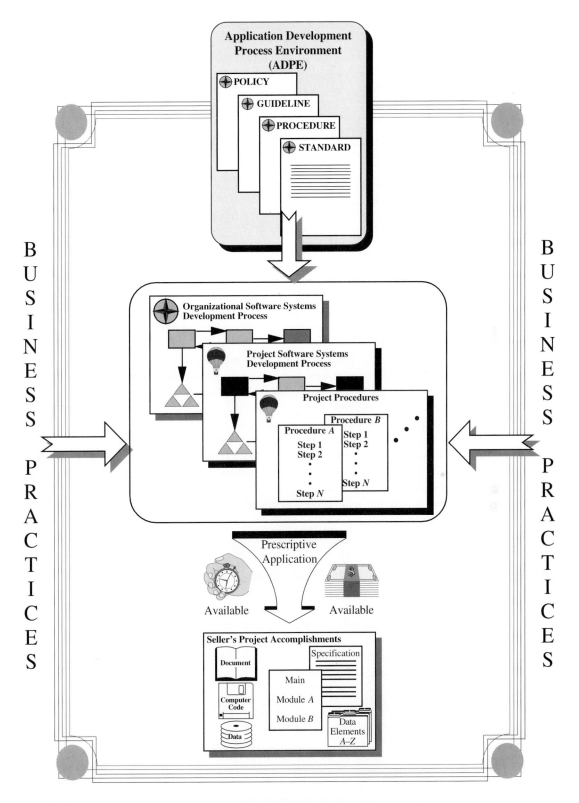

FIGURE 7–12 An ADPE that cultivates cultural change is one that establishes a business practice framework. The framework should stay away from recipelike practices and allow for prescriptive application.

things and (2) awkward or unworkable business practices. It is undesirable, at least in organizations consisting of a hundred or more people, to change an ADPE element more frequently than twelve to eighteen months. The guidance here is that the PEG should plan for ADPE element change by allowing for a settling-in period and *then* responding to organizational outcries for change.

One final comment is in order regarding Figure 7–12 and achieving cultural change through ADPE implementation. Software industry experience shows that an effective way to induce cultural change is to *set up* an organization with a specific process improvement goal. In this circumstance, everybody who comes into the organization is committed to this goal. By definition, then, everybody is on board. It typically takes several years to elevate the process maturity of an organization *one* SEI level.[12]

Figure 7–13 contains an annotated outline for helping you get started in building an ADPE element around a process like that shown in Figure 7–11—that is, an element that details the process of creating, coordinating, promulgating, and updating ADPE elements.

Our discussion of the PEG's perspective in bringing about cultural change through ADPE implementation has touched upon the perspectives of others within the seller and buyer/user organization. We now turn to these other perspectives to highlight the other forces that play a key role in shaping ADPE element content. Our discussion of these other perspectives must be more general than the discussion of the PEG perspective in this section. It is simply not feasible to consider in detail the myriad of organizational variations that exist in the software industry. Furthermore, because we discussed at length the PEG perspective and because the PEG should be the focus of organizational process definition and improvement activity, many of the details of the other perspectives have their roots in the PEG perspective already considered. For example, we discussed in connection with Figure 7–11 the roles that seller senior management and buyer/user senior management play in the ADPE element promulgation process. In particular, we explained the significance of having a senior seller manager such as a program manager and this manager's buyer/user counterpart each sign the cover sheet of an ADPE element. We pointed out that these signatures are not just a formality to give an official look to a document. The seller program manager's signature testifies to the fact that the seller's company is committed to the business practices set forth in the ADPE element. The buyer/user program manager's signature testifies to the fact that the customer concurs with these business practices and is committed to supporting them.

We begin with the seller project-level perspective, namely, that of the project participants and the project manager.

7.4 SELLER PROJECT PARTICIPANTS AND PROJECT MANAGERS

This section addresses ADPE implementation from the perspective of the seller project-level individuals—i.e., members of the product development organization, the managers who direct their efforts, and members of the product assurance organization—who will have to adapt to the policies, guidelines, procedures, and standards that will govern their work.

We address a series of questions that include the following:

- What do seller project participants and project managers feel when faced with trying to conform to ADPE business practices?

- How do some seller project participants and project managers show their resistance to or acceptance of the ADPE business practices?

---

[12]In the early 1990s, Motorola set up an organization in India in this manner. This organization elevated its software process to a very mature level (some reports indicated that the organization achieved SEI Level 5, the most mature level in the SEI scheme) in the space of several years.

[Your Organization's Name and Logo]

Document #
Date

[Your Org.'s Name] [Element Type]
ADPE Elements

Document #
Date

1.0 PURPOSE

This section states the purpose of the element. This purpose is to define the types of elements that make up your organization's ADPE (e.g., policy, guideline, procedure, and standard). This section should also indicate that this element describes the ADPE implementation and improvement process. Furthermore, this section should indicate that this element identifies the organizations responsible for (1) developing, (2) reviewing and commenting on, (3) approving, and (4) promulgating ADPE elements.

2.0 BACKGROUND

This section gives an overview of the organization, project, and/or program to which the ADPE elements are to be applied. This section should also define the concepts of SEE, ADPE, and ADTE or their counterparts in your organization.

3.0 RESPONSIBILITIES

This section delineates the organizational responsibilities regarding the development, review, approval, promulgation, and improvement of ADPE elements.

4.0 ADPE IMPLEMENTATION PROCESS

This section defines and walks through the process for establishing and maintaining the ADPE. This section should contain your version of an organizational ADPE development process. Our experience shows that, if you want to have a detailed breakout of the individual steps underlying your version of the ADPE development process, this breakout should be placed in an appendix to avoid overwhelming readers, particularly management, with detail.

5.0 ADPE ELEMENT DEFINITIONS AND FORMAT CONVENTIONS

This section defines the elements that make up your ADPE. It is helpful to put these definitions in a table together with an example extract to illustrate the orientation of each element.

APPENDIX

It is useful to have at least one appendix containing and explaining your step-by-step version of your organizational ADPE development process.

FIGURE 7–13 An annotated outline for getting you started defining a process to govern ADPE element development and improvement.

- How can the PEG try to reduce resistance or increase acceptance?

- What are the special issues that arise when the seller organization is made up of several different corporations, each with different software systems development cultures?

Each of these questions and others are discussed below. As stated before, there is no right set of answers. We offer the following discussion as food for thought about cultural change.

ADPE development and implementation depends, in part, on such factors as the age of the organization, organizational work experiences, how long the employees have been with the organization, employee work experiences, and management commitment. Regardless of these factors or other factors, when a person is faced with change, there are questions that surface. For example, a project participant that is going to attend a briefing about a new organizational product development process may ask questions or raise concerns that include the following:

> What is this process improvement stuff about? I've been doing fine without it. Now I have to go to a briefing on some organizational product development process. What does this process mean to me? What is my role? Hey, maybe this new process will let me make a contribution. After all, I do a pretty good job.

There will be a full spectrum of reactions, and adapting to the ADPE way of doing things generally means that people will have to modify their engineering behavior to some degree. This behavior modification generally causes pain because people may perceive they are giving up something. In fact, they may be giving something up, but at the same time, they may be gaining something. For ADPE implementation to take hold, each individual must believe that the net gain in individual and organizational effectiveness more than compensates for the loss associated with modifying personal behavior. As shown in Figure 7–14, if the organization's process is based on prescriptive application of the ADPE way, the perceived individual loss of "freedom to adapt" is countered by the freedom to adapt to the organization's process. Also, if the individual has a say in framing the organization's process, the individual's perceptions of loss of familiarity with doing things and the ability to innovate are countered by incorporating into the organization's process, where feasible, the individual's suggestions.

In mature organizations, the individual replaces personal loss with personal gain and organizational gain. For example, if a project participant has been working on essentially the same aging software system or systems for a number of years, (e.g., three to seven years), the participant feels comfortable with the day-to-day tasks. Life is fairly routine. However, one day the customer decides to replace the aging system and articulates something like the following:

> I want to replace our old system. I want to migrate from our current database technology to an object-oriented database. The new software language will be C^{++}. I want to use a combination of CASE technology and . . . I need the system yesterday. . . and I want the system to be independent of specific individuals. . . . I don't want to be held hostage . . . people are getting too expensive. . . .

This story all sounds familiar. Maybe the technologies have changed, but technologies always change. It is the last part of the customer's comments that are relatively new— ". . . independent of specific individuals . . . I don't want to be held hostage." Of course the customer's words could be different, but the point is that project participants need to stay current and mobile. A person who can work on several different types of projects has more flexibility and stability than someone who has too narrow a set of capabilities. We are suggesting that, for the long haul, it is important, if not necessary, for an individual to adapt, to some extent, to the organization's way of doing business. This adaption helps the individual maintain professional mobility.

What does this cultural change via an ADPE mean for the project manager? First, the project manager will probably have some of the same reactions as the project participants. After all, project managers are humans too! Second, project managers typically take on an additional leadership role.

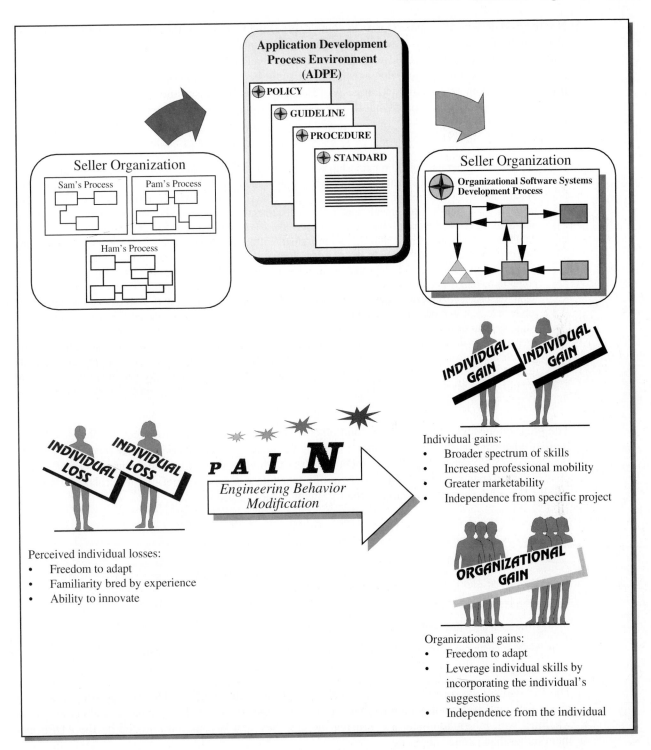

FIGURE 7–14 Individuals must perceive individual and/or organizational gains for ADPE implementation to take hold.

Not only do they need to understand (to some degree) the technology that they are implementing, but also they need to understand how to complement project participants' skill sets with each other and to match participants with specific technical tasks that need to be performed. Project management is tricky business, and the project manager's skills cannot be reduced to cookie-cutter steps. We suggest that project managers carefully examine ADPE engineering processes and determine how, in specific terms, the processes will impact what they do on a day-to-day basis. Consider the simple story that follows.

A project manager has a good relationship with the customer. The customer has been used to calling up the manager or project participants and specifying system requirements over the phone. Sometimes the customer talks about such requirements in face-to-face conversations. However, rarely do these requirements make their way into a requirements specification document that is approved by the customer. After all, Bob and Sally have been working on the project for years, and they know what the customer wants. A new ADPE element is introduced into the organization, and the new product development process states that "all customer requirements should be (1) put in writing, (2) reviewed for testability, and (3) approved, in writing, by the customer." The project manager's reaction might be something like "my customer is not going to be happy about this . . . this process is going to slow down development activities." On the other hand, the project manager's reaction might be "good . . . this is really going to help us to think through the job better . . . it will take some convincing, but I'll be able to better manage the customer's expectations of what needs to be done, what resources are really required. . . ." In this case, it may be that the project manager increases the control of the project, increases personal productivity, increases the chance for potential growth, etc. However, the project manager, the participants, and the organization need to recognize that the desired changes regarding customer requirements take time. Time is one reason why it is important for all organizational levels, and if possible, the customer, to be involved with the cultural change journey.

The program manager, PEG manager, and others should also be working to effect the changes. In particular, what can the PEG do to support effecting the change? As discussed earlier (see Figure 7–11), the PEG can set up an ADPE development process that involves seller management, seller staff, and if possible, customer personnel. The PEG should schedule a series of briefings to explain ADPE elements. These briefings should answer the following basic questions:

- What is the purpose of the ADPE element?
- What does the ADPE element look like?
- How is the ADPE element to be implemented?
- Who is responsible for what?
- How soon does this ADPE element take effect?
- What support can be expected from the management, the PEG, and the customer?

The PEG should be careful not to overwhelm people with the briefing. The briefing should address these questions and paint a picture that the audience can relate to. If audience members are overwhelmed with information and a confusing picture, they will become intimidated by the ADPE element rather than excited about it.

If the organization can afford it or the customer is willing to pay for it, the briefings should be scheduled during the regular working day, and the people's time should be paid for by the organization. However, because of increased competition, decreased resources, etc., it is often necessary to hold such briefings during lunch hour or after the normal business day. Attendance under such circumstances should not go unnoticed by management. People who are willing to help implement and evolve the culture should not go unrewarded. Each organization has its own way of showing its appreciation. Some organizations give more formal training, tuition reimbursement, and allowances for seminars for those who go the extra mile.

Another ADPE training approach is to set up annual refresher training on all the ADPE elements. In such a setting, a series of briefings, examples, and short training exercises are presented over a two- or three-day period. At the end of the training, the program manager presents certificates of accomplishment. Again, the training should not be overwhelming, but at the same time, the training cannot be a waste of everyone's time. People at all levels in the organization should participate in setting up the curriculum. The training should be viewed as valuable. If it is possible, the customer should participate. Joint customer/seller training is an effective ingredient for implementing cultural change.

We also suggest that the briefings can be given by people who are not members of the PEG. The briefers need to be respected in the organization. Ideally, the briefers have participated in the ADPE element development process. Many times, the first set of briefers are the organization's early adapters who embrace new ideas and technology.

Are there special issues when the seller organization is made up of several corporations? In general, the prime contractor should treat the subcontractor personnel as if they are employees of the prime. If the subcontractors are part of an integrated team, then they should be afforded the same training as the prime. Nondisclosure agreements can be signed to protect prime contractor proprietary information.

Who pays for the subcontractor personnel's training time? The answer to this question depends, in part, on what time of the day the training takes place. If the training occurs during "off hours," then the prime contractor could provide the training materials (in addition to providing the instructor) as a way of recognizing the subcontractor's going the extra mile. Of course, costs can be shared. The point is that the contractor team needs to come together with a mutually agreeable solution so that there is a consistent engineering approach across company lines.

Another subcontractor issue that needs to be addressed is the level of authority that subcontractor personnel can assume. Generally, the prime contractor is held responsible for all contracted technical work. Often the prime's personnel hold the management positions one layer below the program manager, the PEG manager position, and the independent product assurance manager position. Most other positions are open to the subcontractors. If the organization is deep enough, management positions can be open to the subcontractors. If the subcontractors can offer only project participants, their people have limited growth opportunities. The prime wants the subcontractor's best personnel. However, by limiting the subcontractor's participation, the prime could actually foster personnel turnover.

How are subcontractor personnel selected for open positions? This issue, along with the others just discussed, is part of the larger issue of what the image (and hopefully reality) the contractor team presents to the customer. The answer depends, in part, on the way in which the seller development organization wants to present itself to the customer. We are not going to discuss all the possible situations. However, if it is possible, an integrated team approach can be effective. In this case, the prime selects personnel who are the most capable to do the work, regardless of company affiliation. This is a win-win situation for the customer, prime, and subcontractor.

Up to this point in the book, we have primarily presented ADPE implementation from the seller's viewpoint. However, it is important to recognize that the customer community may have its own ADPE implementation program. Customer organizations, like seller organizations, can have a broad spectrum of success implementing an ADPE. This spectrum can be defined by the following three categories:

- **No ADPE Program.** In this category, the organization does not have any documented practices in place. Many times, such organizations are successful through the individual heroics of Sam, Pam, and Ham. We are not saying that such organizations produce "poor" quality products. However, we are saying that, in such organizations, consistent software systems development success may be chancy.

■ **Immature ADPE Program.** In this category, the organization has some documented practices in place and some of the people use them. Such an organization has a PEG in place, as well as an ADPE implementation plan. Success in such organizations is due to a combination of following their documented practices and from the individual heroics of Sam, Pam, and Ham. An ADPE training program is usually in place to help with the ADPE implementation.

■ **Mature ADPE Program.** In this category, the organization has documented practices in place, and most people use them. Such an organization has a PEG in place, an ADPE implementation plan, an ADPE training program, as well as mentoring and/or coaching programs in which people consistently help one another. In such organizations, the watchword is "teamwork." People think in terms of organizational success, as well as personal success. People actively contribute to the refinement and implementation of ADPE practices. The well-honed ADPE helps to stabilize the organization by providing consistent and well-understood practices for successful software systems development. At the same time, people increase their professional mobility because they are not captive to a narrow range of job options.

At one end of the spectrum, customers with no ADPE programs may want to hire seller organizations that also have no ADPE programs. However, such customers may also be willing to do business with seller organizations with immature or mature ADPE programs. Customers may be looking for help in implementing their programs, and so they may contract only with sellers who have experience dealing with cultural change issues while implementing a mature ADPE culture. At the other end of the spectrum, customers with mature ADPE programs may refuse to do business with seller organizations with no ADPE programs.

There are a number of customer/seller ADPE combinations. In the following two sections, we consider some of these combinations. In particular, the following two sections highlight some of the ADPE implementation issues from the viewpoints of the buyer/user project management (Section 7.5) and buyer/user senior management (Section 7.6).

7.5 BUYER/USER PROJECT MANAGEMENT

This section discusses ADPE implementation from the perspective of the buyer/user project management. Here, "buyer/user project management" is used to label those individuals on the customer side who give technical direction to seller project managers for accomplishing project work.

Figure 7–15 shows a customer organization's ADPE implementation status versus a seller organization's ADPE implementation status. Implementation status values are "No ADPE," "Immature ADPE," and "Mature ADPE." As shown in the figure, at some of the intersections of a seller organization ADPE implementation status and a customer status, we have entered a possible customer reaction to the seller's status. For example, for the case in which the seller organization implementation status is "No ADPE" and the customer's status is "No ADPE," the customer reaction may be as follows: "Customer project management supervises seller's staff." This value may indicate that the customer perceives the seller's staff (i.e., seller project participants) as an extension of the customer's staff. The customer provides day-to-day supervision of and direction to the seller's staff. From the customer's point of view, this arrangement may be seen as an effective way to develop software. In fact, this arrangement may be the case. Potential issues to consider are the following:

■ Who is in charge? Seller management or customer management?

■ Who is responsible if a software product does not work?

■ Whom do the seller staff report to?

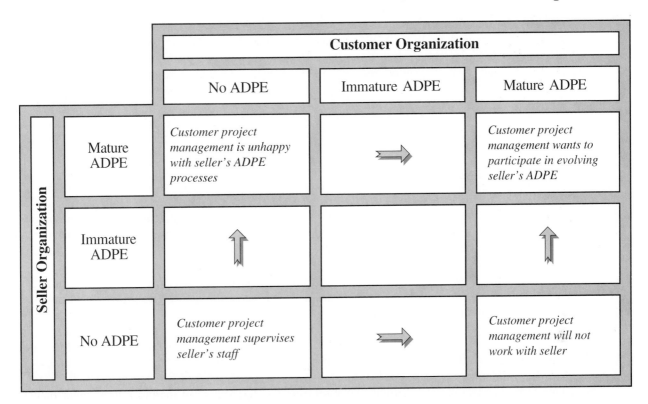

FIGURE 7–15 ADPE implementation issues depend, in part, on how far along the customer and seller organizations are in their respective ADPE implementations. This figure indicates a few potential **customer project manager** reactions to seller ADPE implementation.

- Are such staff augmentation contracts legal? If not, why not? What is allowable?
- What restrictions do government employees have concerning the supervision of private contractors?
- What is the customer's organizational policy concerning the supervision of private contractors?

For the case in which the seller organization implementation status is "No ADPE" and the customer's status is "Mature ADPE," the customer's reaction may be as follows: "Customer project management will not work with the seller." In this case, the customer may not want to spend time working with a seller organization that does not have in place a documented way of doing business. The customer recognizes that seller personnel come and go. The customer may not want to get into a situation where the project is tied to one or more key seller individuals. Of course, people are key. However, if the seller has some documented processes in place, the customer management may view the potential down time due to seller personnel turnover as reduced.

For the case in which the seller organization implementation status is "Mature ADPE" and the customer's status is "No ADPE," the customer reaction may be as follows: "Customer project management is unhappy with seller's ADPE processes." In this case, the customer project management may view the seller's ADPE processes as a burden. If the customer project management is used to supervising the seller's staff, the customer management may experience some of the real and perceived losses that people experience during a transition to a new or different way of doing things. This situation may be a frustrating experience for both the seller and the customer.

For the case in which the seller organization implementation status is "Mature ADPE" and the customer's status is "Mature ADPE," the customer reaction may be as follows: "Customer project management wants to participate in evolving seller's ADPE." In this case, the customer project management may view the seller's ADPE processes as a major plus. Given that both organizations have their own ADPE implementation programs, the customer project management may want to share lessons learned with the seller and get involved with fine-tuning seller (and maybe customer) processes. Collaboration may be a good idea, but remember to keep the customer/seller interaction on a businesslike basis.

What can happen when the seller organization implementation status is "Immature ADPE" or the customer's status is "Immature ADPE"? Things may get a little more complicated. In this case, some of the seller and customer staff are on board with the program, and some are not. This situation can cause lots of confusion and can contribute to inconsistent software systems development efforts. For example, suppose Sally on the seller's side is on board, and so is her customer counterpart. Suppose further that over time, Sally moves on to another project where the customer is not on board. Now Sally is faced with the situation in which the customer project management is going to be unhappy with Sally's use of the seller's ADPE processes. Both Sally and the customer may be unhappy. This case could be a lose-lose situation. Conversely, consider what may happen if Sally is not on board and moves to a project where the customer is on board. This case may result with Sally's getting on board or the customer's asking Sally to be removed from the project.

Now let's take a look at the same types of situations at the next higher levels in the seller and customer organizations.

7.6 BUYER/USER SENIOR MANAGEMENT

This section addresses ADPE implementation from the perspective of the buyer/user senior management. Here, "buyer/user senior management" is used to label those individuals on the customer side who (1) manage the buyer/user project management, (2) are paying the seller to set up an ADPE, and (3) manage the managers in (1) and (2).

In general, these customer senior managers, coming as they do from different parts of an organization, have different agendas. This situation is particularly so if the customer is a large government organization or a large corporation. Consequently, aspects of ADPE implementation that may please one of these senior management organizations may antagonize another. For example, one customer senior manager may be pleased with the visibility that manager may have into the seller's way of doing business brought about by ADPE implementation. On the other hand, another customer manager may be against anything the seller does simply because that manager was forced to take the business to that seller because of a more senior customer manager or because of contractual agreements.

Figure 7–16 shows a customer organization's ADPE implementation status versus a seller organization's ADPE implementation status. We use the same layout for Figure 7–16 as we used in Figure 7–15. Implementation status values are "No ADPE," "Immature ADPE," and "Mature ADPE." As shown in the figure, at some of the intersections of a seller organization ADPE implementation status and a customer status we have entered a possible customer reaction to the seller's status.

For example, for the case in which the seller organization implementation status is "No ADPE" and the customer's status is "No ADPE," the customer reaction may be as follows: "Customer senior management just wants the products." In this case, the customer senior management just wants the seller to deliver the products. The customer may not be really interested in how the seller develops products. The customer just wants the products.

For the case in which the seller organization implementation status is "No ADPE" and the customer's status is "Mature ADPE," the customer's reaction may be as follows: "Customer senior management will not contract with seller." In this case, the customer senior management may not want to spend any resources with a seller organization that is perceived as not having a mature ADPE implementation program in place. Perhaps the seller organization is perceived as not keeping pace with evolving software development practices. With competition as tough as it is, many customer organiza-

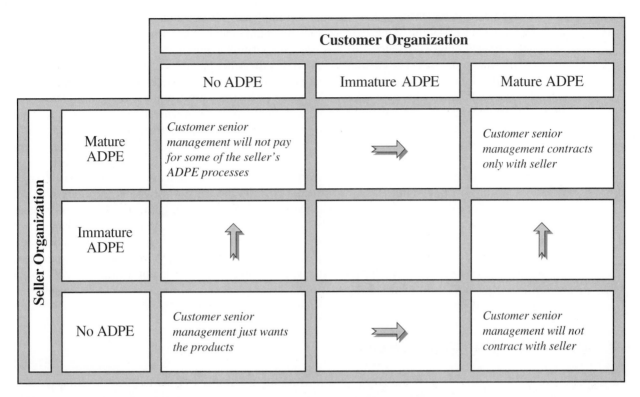

FIGURE 7–16   This figure indicates a few potential **customer senior management** reactions to seller ADPE implementation.

tions use such criteria as "No ADPE" to filter out seller organizations. Again, the issue is not that key individuals do not do a great job and produce a great product. Many times key individuals do make the difference between a failure and a success. However, customer organizations may want sellers to embody those "key individuals'" contributions in processes so that successes can be *consistently* repeated, even if key individuals leave the seller organization.

For the case in which the seller organization implementation status is "Mature ADPE" and the customer's status is "No ADPE," the customer reaction may be as follows: "Customer senior management will not pay for some of the seller's ADPE processes." In this case, the stakes may go up. Customer senior management may be accustomed to more successes than failures, and that's one of the reasons the manager has risen in the ranks. However, one visible failure may end a career. If this situation is the case, then things can get stressful in a hurry if schedules start to slip. Schedule slippage may be due to the seller's inability to come to closure with the customer on requirements. For example, the seller follows a product development process that requires the customer to sign off on requirements. If the customer is used to dealing with "No ADPE" sellers, then enough time may not have been planned for coming to closure. The customer may not have planned for such time in the past and may not have known to adjust his or her thinking. The seller was chosen because of a reputation for excellent work, but the customer did not fully understand how things were going to work. Perhaps, in haste to get the work, the seller did not fully communicate how business was to be conducted. On the other hand, maybe the seller did communicate what was required, but the customer did not fully appreciate the seller's proposed schedule. In the past, the customer said do it, and somehow it got done. Regardless, the project falls unacceptably behind schedule, and the customer senior management pays the price. The seller may also pay the price, but either way, it looks like another possible lose-lose situation.

For the case in which the seller organization implementation status is "Mature ADPE" and the customer's status is "Mature ADPE," the customer reaction may be as follows: "Customer senior management contracts only with seller." In this case, the customer senior management may have put in place ADPE-like processes. The customer expects that the seller has similar processes. In this case, the customer expects the seller to speak the same kind of ADPE language. Without such ADPE processes, the seller need not apply. There are sellers who have or who are putting in place the requisite qualifications. Seller organizations are aware that more and more customer organizations are getting educated about ADPE-like practices. A final thought—once a seller organization has the status of "Mature ADPE," the seller must maintain and continue to improve on the processes to keep pace with (or take the lead from) the competition.

What can happen when the seller organization implementation status is "Immature ADPE" or the customer's status is "Immature ADPE"? This case is similar to the corresponding case considered in Figure 7–15 where the *customer* project management was in the same situation. Since some of the seller and customer staff are on board with the program and some are not, things may get a little more complicated. Confusion and inconsistency can become organizational watchwords. This situation can benefit from education and information about ADPE implementation. The more that is communicated, the more that there is a possibility for understanding and improvement. One of the most effective tools any organization has is communication.

Now let's take a look at the same types of situations at an equivalent level in *seller* organizations.

7.7 SELLER SENIOR MANAGEMENT

This section addresses ADPE implementation from the perspective of the seller senior management. Here, "seller senior management" is used to label those individuals on the seller side who supervise seller project managers or managers of seller project managers.

Figure 7–17 shows a customer organization's ADPE implementation status versus a seller organization's ADPE implementation status. This figure is laid out the same as Figures 7–15 and 7–16. The major difference is that Figure 7–17 is from the seller's point of view about the customer's ADPE status. Implementation status values are the same as before. However, at some of the intersections of a seller organization ADPE implementation status and a customer status we have entered a possible *seller* reaction to the *customer's* status.

For example, for the case in which the seller organization implementation status is "No ADPE" and the customer's status is "No ADPE," the seller reaction may be as follows: "Seller senior management decides to pursue No-ADPE-like work." This value may indicate that seller senior management has decided that there is a certain class of contract work (i.e., ADPE-like work) that they are not going to pursue, at least in the near term. The seller senior management may recognize the cost of "retooling" its processes and "training" its people. The business decision may be to pursue only those organizations that have "No ADPE"-like environments.

For the case in which the seller organization implementation status is "No ADPE" and the customer's status is "Mature ADPE," the seller's reaction may be as follows: "Seller senior management recognizes the need for change." This customer/seller combination can arise when the seller decides to expand the organization's horizons. In this case, the seller may want to spend the necessary resources to open up the marketplace and work for a customer organization that expects a consistent way or ADPE-like way of doing business. The seller recognizes the fact that seller personnel come and go. Seller senior management recognizes this fact and decides to commit resources to transition the organization. Seller senior management recognizes that people are key. However, the seller also realizes that in order for the organization to survive in the long haul, change must take place. Plans are made to get some documented processes in place.

For the case in which the seller organization implementation status is "Mature ADPE" and the customer's status is "No ADPE," the seller reaction may be as follows: "Seller senior management rec-

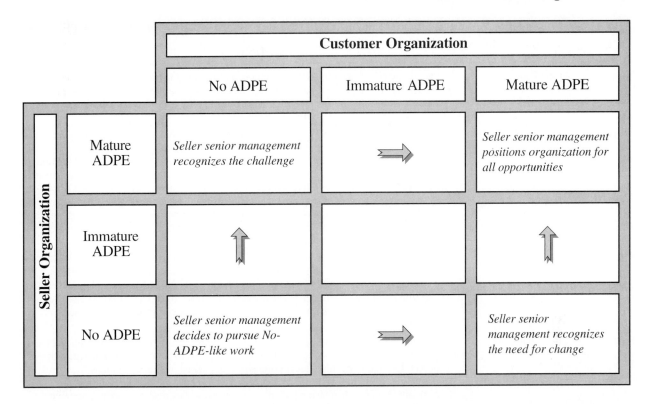

FIGURE 7–17 This figure indicates a few potential **seller senior management** reactions to customer ADPE status.

ognizes the challenge." In this case, the seller recognizes that it will take time to help the customer transition to ADPE-like processes. If the customer wants to transition to a mature ADPE program, the seller's job is made easier. Seller senior management commitment is critical. Without customer willingness and seller commitment, this case may be a frustrating experience for everyone.

For the case in which the seller organization implementation status is "Mature ADPE" and the customer's status is "Mature ADPE," the seller senior management reaction may be as follows: "Seller senior management positions organization for all opportunities." In this case, the seller senior management may view the customer's ADPE processes as a major plus. Given that both organizations have their own programs, the seller senior management may want to share lessons learned with the customer and get involved with fine-tuning customer (and maybe seller) processes. Collaboration may be a good idea, but remember to keep the seller/customer interaction on a businesslike basis.

What can happen when the seller organization implementation status is "Immature ADPE" or the customer's status is "Immature ADPE"? As we have just discussed, things may get more complicated. Confusion can abound. This situation is where the seller senior management can demonstrate its commitment to help the seller's personnel and the customer to effect a cultural change. This case then becomes a win-win situation for both the seller and the customer.

We want to make one last point before we move on to the summary section. Simply stated, implementing change for the sake of change is not useful. Changing the way an organization does business is complicated and complex. People are critical to an organization's success, as are effective and useful processes. People who have been successful have valuable lessons learned that should be carefully examined and considered for incorporation into an organizational process. At the same time, while lessons learned are valuable, so are small changes and innovations to existing processes. Small changes to proven processes and innovative approaches help to stretch the organization beyond its cur-

Perspective	Guidance
Process Engineering Group	Involve project-level staff in ADPE development by soliciting their inputs during and subsequent to ADPE element development. This approach helps to achieve buy-in from the individuals who must live with ADPE elements. The result is unforced cultural change. Avoid producing recipelike ADPE elements.
Seller Project Participants	Recognize that the PEG's job is to help you and those to whom you report to do your job and their jobs better. The more experienced you are, the more inclined you may be to resist ADPE practices that may differ from your way of doing things. Remember that the **organization** is the ADPE focus. The ADPE establishes the organization's business practices—and thus its culture. Work with the PEG to refine these practices. Remember, while everybody should be heard, it is simply not possible to establish practices that let everybody do his or her own thing—that is anarchy. Do not take personally the nonincorporation of your suggestions into ADPE elements. A true measure of experience (and professional maturity) is willingness to adapt personal practices to organizational practices.
Seller Project Manager	Set the example for your staff by promoting buy-in to the organizational practices set forth in the ADPE. Why make your already harried job more tumultuous by resisting ADPE implementation? When the PEG sends out ADPE elements for review and comment, exploit the opportunity to make your needs known. But remember, the ADPE is put there to define consistent business practices for the organization—not to accommodate your personal preferences.
Buyer/User Project Management	You are paying the seller to give you what you asked for. Recognize that both you and the seller will mutually progress in understanding what needs to be done. A competent seller sets up an ADPE to facilitate this mutual progression of understanding. It is simply counterproductive to resist getting acclimated to ADPE business practices. Remember, you have the opportunity when hiring the seller to make your business practice requirements known. Remember, too, that you have hired the seller because you were looking for someone to develop software systems for you. While the "old way of doing business" may be all right in certain circumstances, work with the seller to see what makes sense to do now.
Buyer/User Senior Management	When you hire a seller, offer incentives for setting up an ADPE. Two notable ways to provide these incentives are (1) pay for the PEG (and adequately staff it) and (2) tie the seller's fee to performance. Take care to get a balanced view of how well the ADPE is working by querying seller management as well as your own project managers. Do not undermine fee determination by attributing your project managers' shortcomings to the seller's project managers. Remember, your project managers will tend to resist the seller's ADPE practices because they will naturally be more comfortable with the old way of doing business. Actively promote the new way by, for example, encouraging your project managers to participate in seller-led training activities aimed at explaining the new way and its benefits. Remember that when the buyer/user and seller enter into a contract to do business the ADPE way, then both parties should be accountable for the way they conduct the business of software systems development. Insist that your project managers support the CCB process to bring about buyer/user and seller accountability.
Seller Senior Management	Walk the talk. Set the example for your project managers and staff by showing that you are committed to doing business the ADPE way. Among other things, this commitment means working with the customer to obtain his or her buy-in to the ADPE way. Without senior seller management commitment to the ADPE way, the organization will fracture into competing subcultures. This dissention will not be lost on the customer, who may question the seller's commitment to the buyer/user—with a loss of (follow-on) business.

rent capabilities and help it to grow. Each adaptation and innovation must be carefully weighed. There-fore, it is important that all levels in the organization participate in the cultural change journey and that they carefully select a path that makes sense for the people and the organization.

7.8 CULTURAL CHANGE SUMMARY

Table 7–1 summarizes the key points developed in the chapter. It offers cultural change guidance associated with each of the perspectives considered in the preceding sections.

We have completed our discussion of bringing about cultural change through SEE implementation. The next chapter, Chapter 8, which concludes the book, talks about SEE implementation planning. We provide guidance on how to write an SEE implementation plan to establish the framework for doing the things discussed in the preceding chapters. We have chosen to end the book by discussing what should normally be done first in bringing about software process improvement through an SEE—namely, planning. It is simply easier to discuss the planning process once you understand the key factors bearing upon SEE implementation. The final chapter leads you through a series of issues that help you pull together the concepts from the preceding chapters to help you construct an SEE implementation plan for your organization.

Process Improvement Planning

Make no little plans; they have no magic to stir men's blood and probably themselves will not be realized. Make big plans; aim high in hope and work, remembering that a noble, logical diagram once recorded will never die, but long after we are gone will be a living thing, asserting itself with ever-growing insistency. Remember that our sons and grandsons are going to do things that would stagger us. Let your watchword be order and your beacon beauty.

—Attributed to Daniel M. Burnham (1846–1912), American architect and city planner. While Burnham expressed these thoughts in a paper he read before the Town Planning Conference, London, 1910, the exact words were reconstructed by Willis Polk, Burnham's San Francisco partner. Polk used the paragraph on Christmas cards in 1912 after Burnham's death in June of that year. Henry H. Saylor, "Make No Little Plans," *Journal of the American Institute of Architects,* March 1957, pp. 95–99[1]

8.1 INTRODUCTION

The purpose of this chapter is to give you guidance for writing an SEE implementation plan. Armed with this guidance, you can establish the framework for applying to your organization the things discussed in the preceding chapters. Our approach is to present and discuss key SEE implementation issues. The aim of this discussion is to provide you with insight into how to lay out an SEE implementation approach that makes sense for your organization. For example, we discuss the rate at which ADPE elements should be developed and implemented. We describe some of the key factors bearing upon this rate (e.g., the software and system engineering experience level of your organization's management and staff). These factors should help you plan an ADPE development and implementation rate appropriate for your organization.

Before we address process improvement planning issues, we set context. Figure 8–1 reminds us that, as we repeatedly stress in the preceding chapters, consistent successful software systems development requires sustained effective communication between the software seller and the software customer. Reduced to the simplest terms, the concepts and principles examined in these chapters have their roots in this premise. We now recall some of these concepts and principles through an overview of the preceding chapters. To aid you in this recall, Figure 8–2 highlights the theme of each of these chapters.

---

[1]Suzy Platt, ed. *Respectfully Quoted: A Dictionary of Quotations from the Library of Congress* (Washington, DC: Congressional Quarterly Inc., 1992), p. 256.

THE WIZARD OF ID   by Brant parker and Johnny hart

FIGURE 8–1   At the most fundamental level, the avenue to consistent successful software systems development is sustained effective communication between the wizard (i.e., software seller) and the king (i.e., software customer). (*The Wizard of ID,* September 30, 1983. Reprinted by premission of Johnny Hart and Creators Syndicate, Inc.)

- Chapter 1 (Motivation) introduced key concepts to establish a working vocabulary for the rest of the book (e.g., software, software process, product and process "goodness," culture). We emphasized that customer/seller faulty communication underlies a majority of software systems development problems. We stressed that software process improvement is first and foremost a cultural change exercise. We introduced the requisite software systems development disciplines—management development, and product assurance. We introduced the change control board (CCB) as a mechanism for sustaining effective communication among these disciplines throughout a software systems development project. We introduced the notion of "prescriptive application" of an organization's documented software systems development process. We explained why prescriptive application is one of the keys to institutionalizing the process. We introduced the concept of "systems engineering environment." We explained that the book's approach to cultivating consistent successful software systems development has its roots in the SEE concept. The SEE also provides the means for effecting improvement to the software development process. Consistent successful software systems development and software process improvement are thus intertwined in the SEE concept.

- Chapter 2 (Project Planning Process) provided you with guidance for effectively planning software systems development work. We referred to the document containing planning information as the "project plan." We indicated that the project plan is a gauge used, in part, to think through what needs to be done, to estimate how much the effort may cost, and to determine whether software systems development work is unfolding as it was envisioned. We stressed that project planning is an ongoing negotiation between the customer (king) and the seller (wizard). We showed you how to plug the CCB apparatus into your project plan so that the wizard and king could effectively interact throughout the project. We showed you how the life cycle concept can be used to drive out specific tasks to be performed. We illustrated this fundamental point with three example life cycles—(1) six-stage classical development, (2) prototype development, and (3) (data-centered) information engineering. We showed you how to design a simple risk assessment approach for allocating resources to the three sets of requisite software systems development disciplines—management, development, and product assurance—thereby showing how you can explicitly incorporate risk reduction into your project budget. Most importantly, we showed you how to plan for change. We organized this project planning guidance into an easy-to-use package by showing you how to develop an ADPE element defining your organization's project planning process.

- Chapter 3 (Software Systems Development Process) established the focus for the remainder of the book. We defined principles for defining a software systems development process. We explained that a process constructed by applying these principles is likely to yield consistently "good" products—i.e., products that your customer wants and that are delivered on time and within budget. To help you apply these principles, we illustrated them by defining a top-level process that you can use as a starting point to formulate a process for your own organization. We again stressed the critical importance of maintaining the wizard and king dialogue by making the CCB a key element of the top-level process. We emphasized that, in general, the process cannot be reduced to a rigidly defined procedure with a definite order to the steps to be followed. Rather, we stressed that prescriptive application of the process was key to achieving consistent soft-

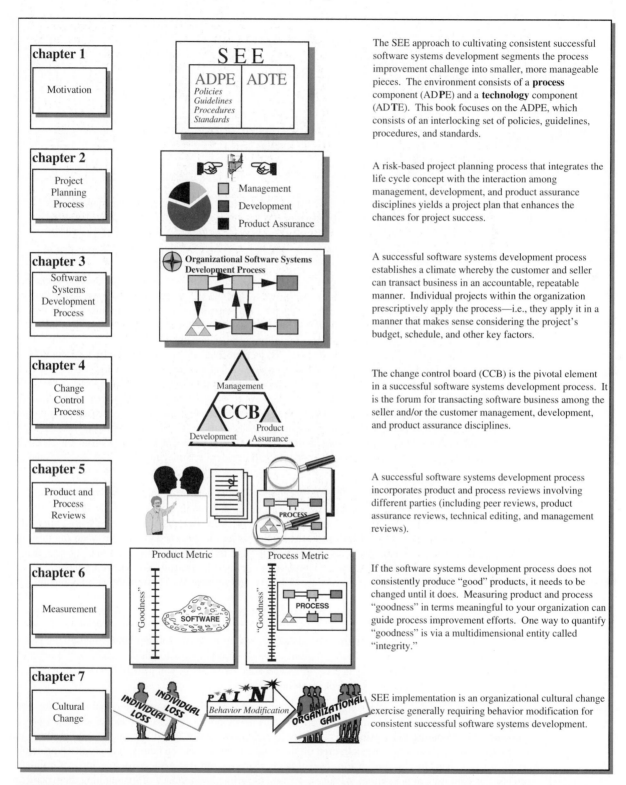

chapter 1

Motivation

The SEE approach to cultivating consistent successful software systems development segments the process improvement challenge into smaller, more manageable pieces. The environment consists of a **process** component (AD**P**E) and a **technology** component (AD**T**E). This book focuses on the ADPE, which consists of an interlocking set of policies, guidelines, procedures, and standards.

chapter 2

Project Planning Process

A risk-based project planning process that integrates the life cycle concept with the interaction among management, development, and product assurance disciplines yields a project plan that enhances the chances for project success.

chapter 3

Software Systems Development Process

A successful software systems development process establishes a climate whereby the customer and seller can transact business in an accountable, repeatable manner. Individual projects within the organization prescriptively apply the process—i.e., they apply it in a manner that makes sense considering the project's budget, schedule, and other key factors.

chapter 4

Change Control Process

The change control board (CCB) is the pivotal element in a successful software systems development process. It is the forum for transacting software business among the seller and/or the customer management, development, and product assurance disciplines.

chapter 5

Product and Process Reviews

A successful software systems development process incorporates product and process reviews involving different parties (including peer reviews, product assurance reviews, technical editing, and management reviews).

chapter 6

Measurement

If the software systems development process does not consistently produce "good" products, it needs to be changed until it does. Measuring product and process "goodness" in terms meaningful to your organization can guide process improvement efforts. One way to quantify "goodness" is via a multidimensional entity called "integrity."

chapter 7

Cultural Change

SEE implementation is an organizational cultural change exercise generally requiring behavior modification for consistent successful software systems development.

FIGURE 8–2 The preceding chapters capture the essence of things that you need to consider in planning for implementing a systems engineering environment (SEE) in your organization. SEE implementation is a structured way of institutionalizing consistent successful software systems development. This chapter integrates the ideas from the preceding chapters to guide your SEE implementation planning activity.

ware systems development. That is, the process should specify *what* is to be done; individuals should be empowered to figure out how to do the what. We showed you how to plug a specific life cycle into the top-level process to explain how a project unfolds during process application. We showed you how to design a form to help you track a product as it wends its way through your software systems development process. We explained that the process does not stop once the product goes out the seller's door. Rather, we discussed the customer and seller responsibilities after the seller has delivered the product to the customer. We folded the chapter's process definition ideas into an easy-to-use package—namely, an annotated outline for an ADPE element defining your organization's software systems development process. We explained why this element is a good place to begin setting up your ADPE.

■ Chapter 4 (Change Control Process) focused on the forum for sustaining effective communication between the wizard and king as well as among the wizard's staff—the change control board (CCB). We provided you with guidance for setting up CCBs for your software systems development process. We also provided guidance for managing unplanned, as well as planned, change. We thereby closed the loop introduced in Chapter 2 where we emphasized that you need to account for the unknown in your project plan as well as accounting for the known. Chapter 4 also closed the loop introduced in Chapter 3, which stressed that, by integrating the customer/seller CCB into your software systems development process, you make product acceptance by the customer almost a foregone conclusion. We showed you how to do this integration by stepping through change control mechanics for both planned and unplanned changes. We explained the CCB role in traversing a project life cycle. We introduced the following three scenarios, each regulated by a CCB, that we asserted govern all of change control:

  ■ Do we want something new or different?

  ■ Is something wrong?

  ■ Should we baseline the product?

We showed you what to record at CCB meetings and gave examples of CBB minutes. We offered you guidance for choosing a CCB chairperson and a CCB voting mechanism. We offered you guidance for determining when CCB hierarchies are appropriate and how to set them up. We gave you detailed guidance for constructing change control forms to support the preceding change control scenarios. We also gave example forms to help you get started in applying this guidance. We organized the CCB concepts and guidance into an easy-to-use package by showing you how to develop an ADPE element defining your organization's change control boards.

■ Chapter 5 (Product and Process Reviews) focused on the product and process reviews needed to give visibility into what is happening on a software project. To establish context for the chapter, we asserted the following:

  ■ Each software project should be approached with the candid realization that it is a voyage through iceberg-infested waters (or worse!).

  ■ If this attitude is adopted, then common sense and the natural instinct for self-preservation can lead to only one conclusion—that some way must be found to steer clear of the icebergs to the extent prudently possible.

  ■ Product and process reviews are techniques for steering clear of the icebergs.

We defined a two-dimensional review taxonomy that consists of the following product and process reviews:

■ Management Reviews

  ■ Product and Process Programmatic Tracking

  ■ Product and Process Technical Oversight

■ Development Reviews

  ■ Product and Process Peer Reviews

  ■ Technical Editing of Software and Software-Related Documents

■ Product Assurance Reviews

  ■ Product Quality Asurance, Verification and Validation, Test and Evaluation, and Self-Comparison

  ■ Process Quality Assurance at the Product Level and at the Project Level

The product reviews identified were, for the most part, those called out in Chapter 3 when we defined a top-level software systems development process. The process reviews identified were extensions to the product reviews. For example, for *management*, we called out two types of reviews—programmatic tracking and technical oversight—for both a specific product and the software systems development process.

We organized the chapter along the lines of the systems disciplines. Because we believe that application of the product assurance disciplines offers the greatest potential for reducing risk on a software project, the chapter devoted considerable attention to the product assurance product reviews. In particular, the chapter stepped through the mechanics of product assurance document reviews and acceptance testing. In this book, acceptance testing constitutes that activity in the software systems development process where the wizard formally demonstrates to the king that the software system and supporting databases do what they are supposed to do. Acceptance testing is therefore the bottom line of the process. For this reason, the chapter includes a detailed discussion of requirements testability with a worked out example.

For reviews not addressed (e.g., unit and integration attention), the chapter offered suggestions for extending the taxonomy to include such reviews. To help you apply the review guidance presented in the chapter, we showed you how to develop an ADPE element for product assurance reviews. We showed you how to integrate other product and process reviews into this element. Because peer reviews are generally recognized as adding significant value to the software systems development process, we showed you how to develop a peer review ADPE element.

- Chapter 6 (Measurement) provided you with guidance for measuring product and process "goodness." Borrowing from the mathematical discipline of vector analysis, we quantified "goodness" as the length of a vector in a space that we labelled "integrity." The dimensions in this space are the product or process attributes that we are interested in measuring. For example, for a product we might want to measure the extent to which customer requirements are satisfied and/or whether delivery was on time and/or delivery was within budget. For a process, we might want to measure, for example, whether peer reviews were conducted and/or whether product assurance reviews were performed and/or whether risk assessment was performed during project planning. We illustrated how to set up value scales for the attributes and gave you guidance for establishing value scales that make sense for your organization. We illustrated how to measure the integrity of a requirements specification, a user's manual, computer code, and a project plan. We illustrated how to measure the integrity of the process introduced in Chapter 3. To help you apply the chapter's integrity measurement approach, we reduce it to a small number of easy-to-follow steps. These steps also show you how to relate process integrity and product integrity measurements to one another to help you focus your process improvement efforts.

The product/process integrity measurement approach presented is actually a very general approach to quantifying almost any object. We thus call this approach "object measurement," or **OM**[SM]. To hint at its general applicability, we applied **OM**[SM] to the Software Engineering Institute's Capability Model for Software (CMM[SM] for Software) to show how the model's key process areas (KPAs) could be quantified.

In addition to product integrity and process integrity measurements, we showed how to establish other process-related measurements tied to one or more components of the software systems development process. The approach was based on taking simple averages involving the number of times a particular activity or set of activities was performed on various projects within an organization. For example, we defined the following measurements that might be useful for an organization to collect for the purpose of assessing process effectiveness:

- Average number of peer reviews required to produce deliverables that are accepted by the customer (i.e., the customer returns the Acceptance of Deliverable form indicating "the product is accepted as delivered").
- Percentage of deliverables delivered on time to the customer during a specific period for certain projects, where "on time" is according to delivery dates specified in project plans or CCB minutes.
- Average number of drafts required to produce a project plan resulting in a project.
- Customer perception of the seller organization.

We organized the chapter's measurement guidance into an easy-to-use package by showing you how to develop an ADPE element defining your organization's product and process metrics and your organization's approach to applying them to improve your software(-related) products and software development process.

- Chapter 7 (Cultural Change) focused on the human, as opposed to engineering, issues bearing on successful software systems development. The chapter proceeds from the following premise, which is grounded in experience:

  > Getting a process on paper is a challenge, but getting the people in the organization to commit to the change is *the* challenge. People commit to change for their own reasons, not for someone else's reasons. Therefore, when people are asked to commit to change, their first concern may be their perceived losses.

  We stressed that SEE implementation is first and foremost a cultural change exercise—an exercise in behavior modification. As we explain in the current chapter, this consideration bears heavily on developing a realistic SEE implementation plan. Successful software implementation is predominantly a people management exercise and not an engineering management exercise. Most of us do what we do (whether it is developing software systems or brushing our teeth) because we feel most comfortable doing things our way. It should therefore not be a surprise that persuading people in the software systems development world to do things someone else's way (i.e., the organization's way) can be a daunting challenge—fraught with surprises.

  We examined the role in bringing about cultural change of the organization responsible for writing the ADPE elements (i.e., the process engineering group [PEG]) and seeing to it that they are implemented and continually improved. We alerted you to considerations bearing upon PEG member qualifications (e.g., hands-on experience developing software systems).

  We discussed how to deal with ADPE implementation challenges arising from the wizard's project-level individuals who will have to adapt to practices set forth in the ADPE elements that govern their work. On the customer side, we discussed how to deal with ADPE implementation challenges arising from those kings who give technical direction to wizard project managers. In this vein, we discussed how to get the customer to be part of ADPE implementation. We also discussed the pros and cons of getting the customer to be accountable for ADPE implementation, as well as the seller.

  We examined the key role that seller senior management plays in effecting software systems development cultural change through ADPE implementation. On the other side, we examined the impact on customer senior management that ADPE implementation brings about.

  We provided you with guidance for extracting key ideas from ADPE elements and packaging them for distribution to your organization as a means for effecting cultural change (e.g., the use of prominently displayed foam boards showing key process concepts such as requirements based acceptance testing).

  We discussed the role of training in effecting cultural change. In particular, we stressed the key role that ADPE element briefings to wizard and king staff plays in getting the organization to assimilate desired engineering behavior. Allied with the role of training in bringing about cultural change, we examined the role of mentoring and coaching. We discussed how to sell ADPE implementation as a career growth opportunity.

  We looked at organizational factors bearing upon how long it takes to bring about cultural change.

  We examined why an ADPE element defining the ADPE element development and improvement process is intimately tied to organizational cultural change.

  We concluded the chapter by giving you an annotated outline for an ADPE element defining the ADPE element development and improvement process. This element provides the framework for evolving the ADPE in a self-consistent manner.

Where do you go from here? How do you put together the concepts and guidance from the preceding chapters to lay out an approach for consistent successful software systems development or to improve what you already have? As Figure 8–3 indicates, this chapter is aimed at helping you plan an SEE implementation approach.

We stress at the outset that this chapter is intended for both wizards and kings. If you are a wizard, this chapter will help you respond to a king's request for a wizard whose skill lies not in handwaving but lies in setting up and following processes that consistently yield products with integrity (ideally, you should not have to wait for a king to ask you for a repeatable way of doing business). If

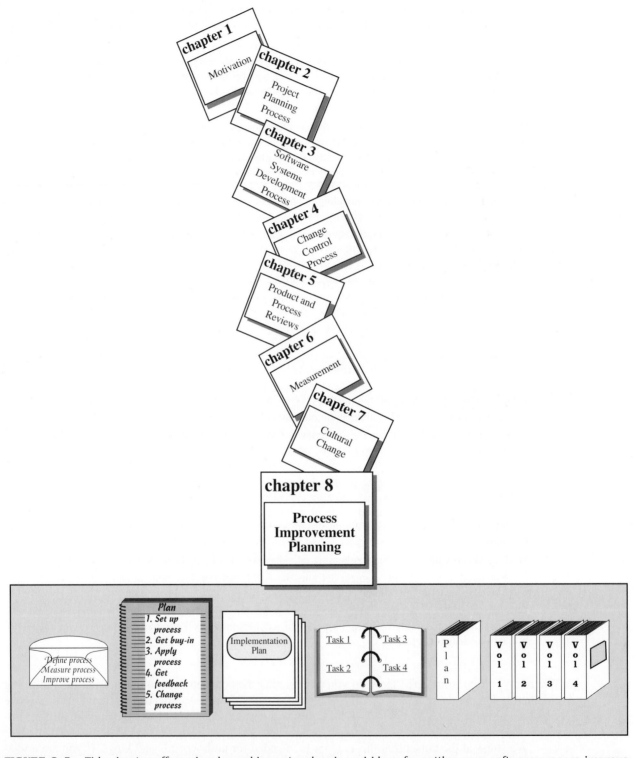

FIGURE 8–3 This chapter offers planning guidance to wizards and kings for setting up a software process improvement approach via SEE implementation. The chapter helps you select concepts from the preceding chapters to construct this approach. The concept of *implementation plan* as used in this chapter means "anything from notes scratched on the back of an envelope to a multivolume formal and highly detailed document—whatever makes sense for your organization." Reduced to simplest terms, *plan* in this chapter means "think and coordinate before doing."

you are a king, this chapter will help you (1) construct an SEE implementation approach to include in a request for proposal (RFP) that you want a wizard that you intend to hire to follow or (2) give guidance in an RFP to a wizard that you want to hire to construct an SEE implementation approach to include in the wizard's proposal or (3) give guidance to a wizard that you have already hired to construct an SEE implementation approach.

As Figure 8–3 indicates, "implementation plan" as used in this chapter spans a broad spectrum. It could be something as informal as notes scribbled on the back of an envelope highlighting the handful of things that need to be accomplished to set up and operate within an SEE. At the other end of the documentation spectrum, "implementation plan" could be a multivolume tome (for, say, a large systems development effort with major software content, or for a large organization handling fifty to several hundred or more concurrent software systems development efforts). Or "implementation plan" could be something in between these two documentation extremes. No matter where in the spectrum it lies, the purpose of the plan is to bring involved parties within an organization into the same frame of reference for setting up a consistent way of doing software systems development business.

This chapter serves as a guide to help you work your way back into previously introduced ideas to integrate them into an SEE implementation approach that makes sense for your organization. Since we do not know the details of your organization, this chapter bounds your thinking by giving you factors to consider when laying out an implementation approach. For example, we give you things to consider bearing upon how frequently ADPE elements should be updated so that you can include in your implementation plan an element update schedule.

The plan for the remainder of this chapter is the following:

- In **Section 8.2—SEE Implementation Planning Nuggets**—we present the nuggets that you can expect to extract from this chapter.

- In **Section 8.3—Key SEE Implementation Planning Issues**—we present and discuss nineteen issues that you can draw upon to decide what may be important for your organization regarding SEE implementation.

- In **Section 8.4—Cultivating Successful Software Systems Development Projects**—we offer some closing remarks about the book.

8.2 SEE IMPLEMENTATION PLANNING NUGGETS

Figure 8–4 lists the nuggets that you can expect to extract from this chapter. To introduce you to this chapter, we briefly explain these nuggets. Their full intent will become apparent as you go through the chapter.

1. **Plan your process improvement with business practices defined in ADPE elements. Your SEE implementation plan should propose an element phase-in strategy, with your first element defining your software systems development process.** As we showed in Chapter 3, this element establishes the context for most or all other ADPE elements. The software systems development process element is itself thus a plan for subsequent ADPE development. *Any* SEE should include at least this element.

2. **The primary objective of SEE implementation is to establish organizationwide business practices that do not depend on particular individuals for their successful accomplishment.** This objective should not be misunderstood. Removing dependence on particular individuals for successful software systems development does *not* mean that SEE implementation is designed to put people out of work. Good people are certainly needed to achieve successful software systems development. The intent of establishing organizationwide business practices is to plug all these people into a *consistent* way of doing things, so that on any given day good work will be done no matter who is doing the work. These business practices leverage the goodness of people across the organization and provide them with professional mobility. For example, Chapter 4 showed how to set up an ADPE element governing an organization's CCB meetings. Specifically, we explained how this element can be used to specify organizationwide practices for setting up, conducting, and documenting CCB meetings. These practices allow CCB meetings to be conducted and

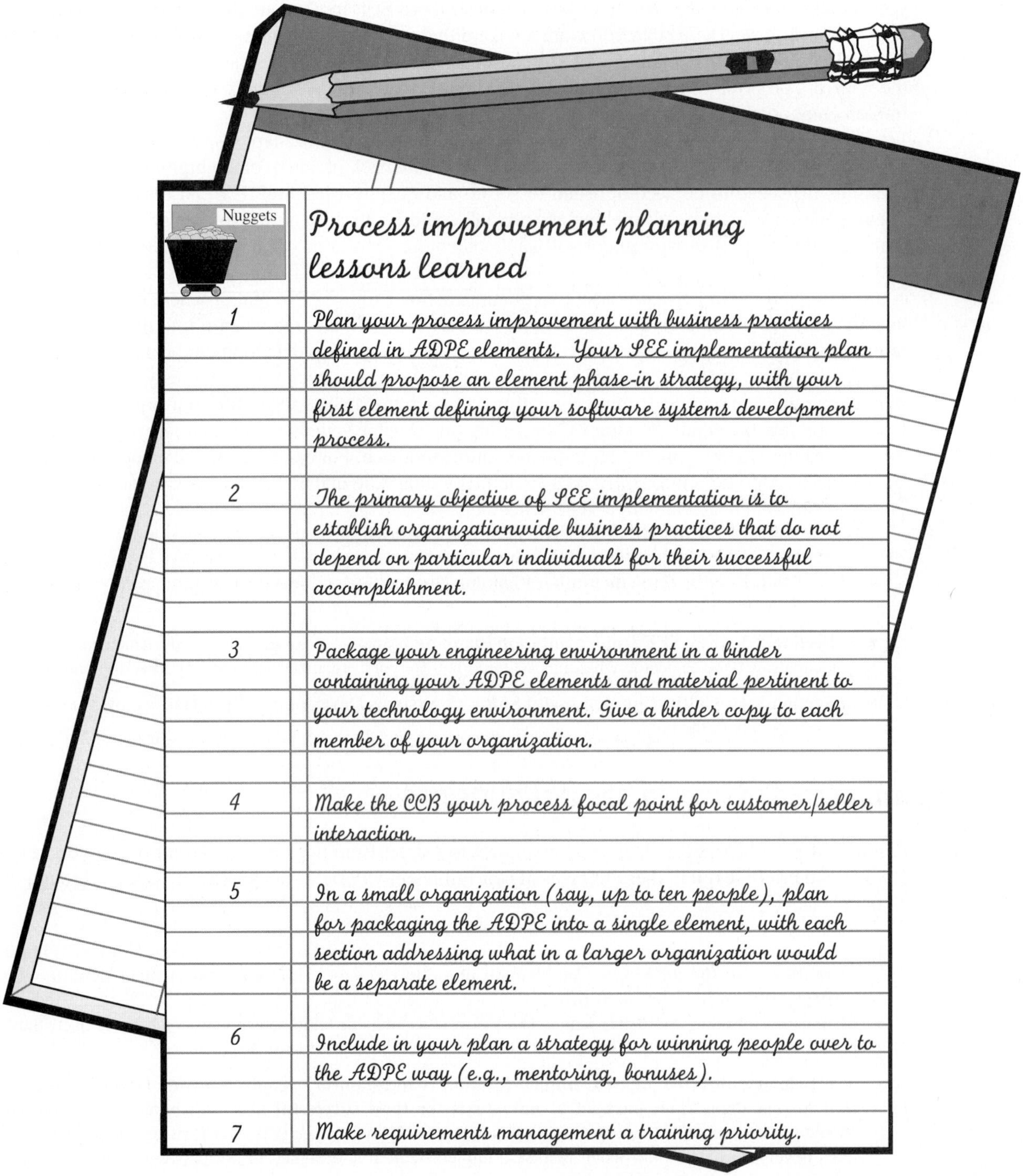

Process improvement planning lessons learned

Nuggets

1   Plan your process improvement with business practices defined in ADPE elements. Your SEE implementation plan should propose an element phase-in strategy, with your first element defining your software systems development process.

2   The primary objective of SEE implementation is to establish organizationwide business practices that do not depend on particular individuals for their successful accomplishment.

3   Package your engineering environment in a binder containing your ADPE elements and material pertinent to your technology environment. Give a binder copy to each member of your organization.

4   Make the CCB your process focal point for customer/seller interaction.

5   In a small organization (say, up to ten people), plan for packaging the ADPE into a single element, with each section addressing what in a larger organization would be a separate element.

6   Include in your plan a strategy for winning people over to the ADPE way (e.g., mentoring, bonuses).

7   Make requirements management a training priority.

FIGURE 8–4   Here are some key process improvement planning concepts explained in this chapter. These nuggets are your guide to plan SEE implementation realistically. A realistic SEE implementation plan starts you toward *consistent* successful software systems development. *To plan realistically* in this chapter means "laying out an approach that motivates people to (1) overcome their resistance change and (2) implement SEE business practices."

documented on any given day in the same way that they are conducted and documented on any other day—no matter who is conducting and documenting them. Good people are, of course, needed to make these meetings worthwhile—that is, to help carry through on software project work.

3. **Package your engineering environment in a binder containing your ADPE elements and material pertinent to your technology environment. Give a binder copy to each member of your organization.** SEE implementation cannot begin to happen unless the SEE gets into the hands of your organization's people. One standard way to promulgate ADPE elements and the associated technology environment is to place this material in a binder (hard copy or electronic) and give each member of your organization a copy when that person joins your organization. The binder should also contain an explanation of the SEE concept and the relationship of this concept to your organization's business objectives. It should also contain instructions for adapting its contents to the specific project work to be accomplished by the binder recipient. For example, each binder should have space for project-specific material such as a copy of the customer's statement of work (SOW) and the project plan governing that recipient's work. Your organization should set up a process for sending SEE updates to binder recipients.

Of course, packaging the SEE in a binder and giving binder copies to each member of your organization does not make the business practices in the binder happen. Among other things, your organization should establish a policy delineating that each individual is responsible for (1) reading its contents, (2) following the practices documented therein, and (3) promoting these practices with your organization's customers. To make this policy happen, you will need to offer training and incentives. The training should be aimed at explaining such things as the engineering principles underlying ADPE elements and the value added of following the practices; the training should also stress that following the practices offers the individual career growth opportunities because the individual is not a captive of a particular project function (e.g., with a documented configuration management process, individuals currently handling configuration management functions can move on to other things because these documented functions can be performed by other individuals). But documenting your business practices (through ADPE elements or by other means) itself will generally not make SEE implementation happen. People will need to be offered incentives to adapt themselves to these business practices (e.g., salary raises tied to the degree to which an individual can demonstrate that he or she has followed the SEE way on project work).

4. **Make the CCB your process focal point for customer/seller interaction.** At the outset of this chapter, we reiterated that the avenue to consistent successful software systems development is the sustained effective communication between the wizard (i.e., software seller) and the king (i.e., software customer). Chapter 4 detailed how the CCB is a mechanism for sustaining this communication. Chapter 3 explained how the CCB serves to focus project activity. A CCB mechanism should be put in place even before you document your organization's software systems development process. Customer/seller interaction should be formalized (via a CCB mechanism) at project outset—even without a CCB ADPE element. CCB rules can be stipulated in the project plan. Lessons learned from iterating on such rules during the early stages of setting up an SEE can be folded into such an element (to be promulgated after a software systems development process ADPE element has been promulgated).

5. **In a small organization (say, up to ten people), plan for packaging the ADPE into a single element, with each section addressing what in a larger organization would be a separate element.** A consistent way of doing software systems development business is independent of organization size. Thus, documented business practices have a place in small as well as in large organizations. Because the number of communications paths among individuals is much less in small organizations than it is in large organizations, the amount of documentation needed to specify these practices is generally much less in small organizations than it is in large organizations. This principle should be applied when planning SEE implementation for a small organization. However, as with most software engineering principles, this principle is not inviolate. In some cases, it may be necessary to have voluminous ADPE elements even in a small organization. Such would be the case if, for example, a small organization were responsible for developing software systems whose failure might result in people getting killed, suffering injury, or sustaining large financial loss. Such would also be the case if a small organization were developing software systems under a fixed-price contractual vehicle. In this case, the seller might sustain large financial loss if the way of doing business were not clearly spelled out (particularly if the seller becomes involved in litigation). A small organization might also need voluminous ADPE elements if it were responsible for developing warranted

software systems (for example, the seller would be responsible for repairing or replacing computer code, databases, and/or documentation for, say, up to one year after purchase—at no cost to the buyer).

6. **Include in your plan a strategy for winning people over to the ADPE way (e.g., mentoring, bonuses).** We detailed in Chapter 7 how ADPE implementation is a cultural change exercise. A realistic SEE implementation plan needs to include a strategy for winning people over to the ADPE way by (1) accounting for people's natural resistance to change, (2) building upon business practices that may already exist, and (3) encouraging people to contribute to the development of new business practices.

7. **Make requirements management a training priority.** This nugget is a corollary to the message in the wizard-and-king comic strip. Requirements management is the number one challenge industrywide to successful software systems development. If it does nothing else, your requirements management training should provide guidance on how to institute effective oral and written communication between the wizard and king.

8.3 KEY SEE IMPLEMENTATION PLANNING ISSUES

This section discusses the planning issues listed in Figure 8–5. This section is intended to help you overcome the blank-page syndrome as you approach the SEE implementation planning task. You should first read through the issues. Then, cull out from this reading those issues that you think are important for your organization. The discussion of these issues included in this section should help you put together your SEE implementation approach. We give you an annotated outline for an SEE implementation plan to help you organize this material. Also, you should add to the issues addressed in this section any other issues that may come to mind as you go through the issues included in this section.

Each issue listed is discussed separately. The purpose of this discussion is to give you insight into factors bearing on the issue. With this insight, you can determine (1) whether the issue is pertinent to your organization and, if so, (2) how to address the issue in your implementation plan. Even if your implementation plan is only laid out on the back of an envelope, you will need to deal with some of these issues. The issues shown may also stimulate you to formulate other issues that are important for your organization.

The focus in this chapter is on the ADPE side of the SEE. However, we do provide you some top-level guidance regarding the ADTE. Because this book focuses on process, we do not give technology-specific guidance.

To help you see the factors bearing on the issue, we include at least one figure for each issue addressed. You may want to adapt one or more of these figures to your environment and include them in your SEE implementation plan and/or your ADPE elements.

The discussion of each issue is preceded by a statement of the issue in the form of a question. To the left of the question we include the following icon that we introduced in the Preface:

The idea behind using this icon is to remind you that, by addressing the issue, you are, in effect, planting a seed. By cultivating the seed (i.e., working on the issue within your organization), you are helping to bring about software systems development success within your organization. The man is dressed in a suit and tie to remind you that he is anticipating some formality (but not too much, since he is not dressed in a tuxedo).

We now begin the discussion of each of the nineteen issues listed in Figure 8–5.

1. What are timeline considerations for SEE implementation tasks and their phasing?

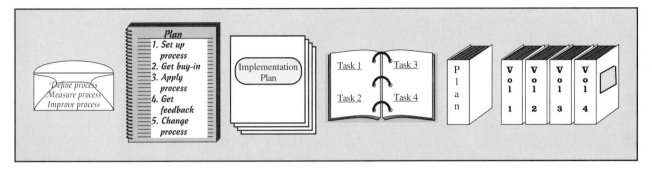

Key SEE Implementation Planning Issues

1.   What are timeline considerations for SEE implementation tasks and their phasing?
2.   How should ADPE elements be phased in?
3.   What ADPE elements should be included in your SEE?
4.   How should the ADPE be constituted—(1) from a small number of elements (i.e., approximately ten), each consisting of tens of pages or more, or (2) from a large number of elements (i.e., tens or more), each consisting of a couple of pages, or (3) some combination of (1) and (2)?
5.   How frequently should an ADPE element be updated?
6.   What amount of detail should be included in individual ADPE elements?
7.   How can you define a plan for an application development technology environment (ADTE) for your organization?
8.   How do you package ADPE elements and related items?
9.   How should ADPE implementation be handled if your organization is small? (Here, *small organization* means "an organization having only a few projects, each involving only a small number of people [say, up to ten] so that all involved parties frequently come in contact with one another.")
10. What is an austere SEE implementation approach?
11. How can mentoring and coaching be leveraged to facilitate implementation of ADPE practices?
12. What strategies can be adopted to meet the cultural change challenges posed by SEE implementation?
13. How do you deal with the business reality of the almighty dollar in bringing about ADPE implementation?
14. How do you account for the reality that people within an organization span a broad spectrum of willingness to adapt to the engineering environment?
15. Who should develop the SEE in your organization?
16. How do you frame an SEE implementation policy?
17. How do you plan ADPE implementation improvement at the project level?
18. How can process and product measurement be integrated with your organizational process?
19. How should you structure an SEE implementation plan?

FIGURE 8–5   Here are the key SEE implementation planning issues addressed in this chapter. These issues are things that you should consider when planning an SEE implementation approach for your organization.

SEE Implementation	Planned Start	Duration in Work Days (5 Days/Week)	Planned Finish	2000 Q1 Q2 Q3 Q4	2001 Q1 Q2 Q3 Q4	2002 Q1 Q2 Q3 Q4	2003 Q1 Q2 Q3 Q
Write Implementation Plan	Jan 2, 2000	60	Mar 27, 2000				
Prepare and Use Trial ADPE Elements	Feb 1, 2000	180	Oct 10, 2000				
Prepare Software Systems Development Process ADPE Element	Sep 30, 2000	64	Dec 29, 2000				
Promulgate Software Systems Development Process ADPE Element	Jan 2, 2001	0	Jan 2, 2001				
Prepare CCB ADPE Element	Jan 2, 2001	50	Mar 13, 2001				
Promulgate CCB ADPE Element	Mar 15, 2001	0	Mar 15, 2001				
Prepare ADPE Element Development Process ADPE Element	Mar 15, 2001	50	May 24, 2001				
Promulgate ADPE Element Development Process ADPE Element	May 28, 2001	0	May 28, 2001				
Measure ADPE Processes	Jan 2, 2001	554	Feb 17, 2003				
Develop and Promulgate Additional ADPE Elements	May 28, 2001	450	Feb 17, 2003				
Revise Promulgated ADPE Elements	Jan 2, 2002	450	Sep 24, 2003				

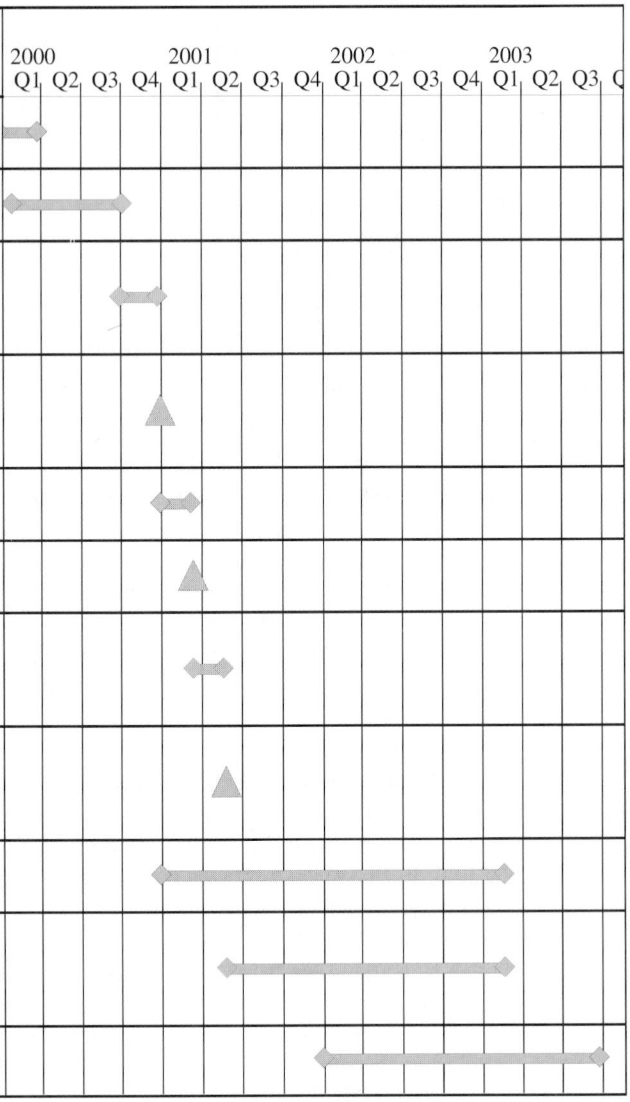

FIGURE 8–6 To help you plan SEE implementation, here is a *representative* timeline of tasks and their phasing. For completeness, we show the task for writing the SEE implementation plan itself. Time for training people on the ADPE is not shown. This training activity should be coupled to the preparation and promulgation of individual ADPE elements.

A key element of any planning activity is scheduling. To help you plan SEE implementation, we show in Figure 8–6 a *representative* timeline of tasks and their phasing. For completeness, we also include in the timeline the task for writing the SEE implementation plan itself. Before examining this figure in detail, we note that buyers may want to use this timeline as a starting point for specifying an SEE implementation approach to include in an RFP. The buyer may want candidate sellers to specify in their proposals how they would pursue such an approach.

We now consider some of the key planning factors associated with the Figure 8–6 timeline. The task durations shown in Figure 8–6 will generally vary across a broad range. They depend on factors such as the following:

- Size of your organization.

- Number of organizational elements that you want to involve in the review of ADPE elements.

- Funding cycles for your work.

- Software engineering savvy of the people in your organization.

In general, the larger your organization, the more varied may be the backgrounds of the people. Assessing the audience for the ADPE elements may be more challenging, and hence more protracted, in larger organizations. More iterations of drafts of a given element may be required before the element can be promulgated.

Another factor bearing on task duration is the number of organizational elements that you want to involve in the review of ADPE elements. In large organizations, particularly those with many layers, sending ADPE drafts up and down the chain of command can take a lot of time. It is generally a good idea to let everyone in your organization have a crack at reviewing an ADPE element draft at least once. This approach fosters buy-in to the ADPE way—but can add considerable time to the ADPE element development cycle. In addition, as we discussed in preceding chapters, we recommend that the customer be made part of the ADPE review process, an action which tends to draw out the ADPE element development cycle even more.

One way to accommodate lengthy review cycles and still move ahead with getting some business practices in place is, as Figure 8–6 indicates, to prepare and use trial ADPE elements. Some of these trial elements may be included in the SEE implementation plan. The idea is to get something in place, as rough as it may be. Experience gained from using these trial elements can be fed into the development into more polished ADPE elements.

Funding cycles for your organization can play an important role in the pace of SEE implementation. If, for example, your organization is funded on a yearly basis and funding for the next year is contingent upon doing good work in the current year, you may need to have several clearly defined milestones every twelve months to make manifest SEE implementation progress to increase the likelihood of funding for the next year. You may therefore have to turn out a number of ADPE elements in a relatively short period of time. This constraint has to be traded off with the factor just discussed regarding the number of organizational elements that you want to involve in the review of ADPE elements. Of course, if you have only one year (or less) to set up and follow ADPE practices, then the duration of the tasks shown in Figure 8–6 will be weeks or even days. The point is, no matter what your funding cycles may be, it is feasible (and we hope you now believe it is desirable) to set up a consistent way of doing software systems development via an SEE.

Another key factor bearing on the rate of ADPE element development and implementation is the software engineering savvy of the people in your organization. By *software engineering savvy* we mean "understanding that it is indeed preferable to apply engineering discipline to software systems development rather than approach it as a stream-of-consciousness exercise in artistic expression." In general, the less experienced your people are in this regard, the more time will be required to develop ADPE elements and get them to catch on. With a less experienced organization, it will generally be necessary to include more tutorial information in ADPE elements. This task is not easy. The tutorial material will need to be located where it does not obfuscate the description of the business practices the organization is to follow. One way to perform this separation is to place tutorial material in appendices. Regarding the pace of ADPE implementation, it is more difficult to generalize as to whether more experienced organizations will adopt the ADPE way more rapidly than will less experienced organizations. Sometimes, more experienced people are so set in their ways that they are highly resistant to changing their way of doing things. On the other hand, less experienced people may resist carrying out the ADPE way because they are unsure of why it may be more beneficial to follow than their former way of doing things. For example, the concept of independent product assurance can take a lot of getting used to by people whose prior experience with checking work was limited to their own checking (this attitude may be present in both software veterans and software novices). One final comment regarding "software engineering savvy" is in order:

> There may not be a direct correlation between the number of years a person has worked in the software in-dustry and the amount of software engineering savvy that person has. It is not uncommon to see people with ten or more years of experience in the software industry who hold the belief that you should "code first and ask questions later."

Figure 8–6 does suggest an order for the first couple of ADPE elements that should be promulgated—(1) Software Systems Development Process, (2) CCB, and (3) ADPE Element Development Process. In preceding chapters, we explored at length the rationale for this order. By way of a reminder, the Software Systems Development Process ADPE element sets the context for most other elements; the CCB ADPE element serves to standardize and give visibility to decision making, particularly with re-spect to customer/seller interaction; the ADPE Element Development Process element is to the ADPE what the Software Systems Development Process element is to software-(related) products. This third element thus defines a consistent way that the ADPE is developed (and improved). The experience gained developing the first two elements can be fed into the development of this third element to pro-vide insight for streamlining the ADPE element development process.

Another consideration heavily influencing the timeline in Figure 8–6 is that, once promulgated, an ADPE element should be given time to take hold before making any substantial changes to it. If, for example, your organization is involved in a multiyear process improvement program, then we suggest that no element should be changed less than twelve to eighteen months after it has been promulgated. If your program is of shorter duration, then your cycle times for promulgating and revising elements should be in terms of weeks.

Another factor bearing on the timeline in Figure 8–6 is the rate at which organizational cultural change can be expected to take place. As we stressed in Chapter 7, SEE implementation is essentially a cultural change program. Thus, SEE implementation planning must account for the resistance inherent in any cultural change activity. Later in this section we address specific issues that provide insight into how to encourage cultural change. For now, we offer the following factors that you should consider when timelining your SEE implementation approach:

- People need to see the net benefit of, in the case of SEE implementation, following the ADPE way. Your SEE implementation plan should therefore point out some of these benefits. Example benefits include the following:
  - A defined way of doing things helps people understand what is expected of them.
  - Individuals can receive rewards for contributing to and following the ADPE way.
  - Individuals are not restricted by inflexible organizational practices. The ADPE way should not be inflex-ible. We repeatedly stressed the need for setting up an ADPE based on prescriptive application of its practices. Prescriptive application is itself an incentive, since it demands of the individual to think about what makes sense in a particular situation regarding ADPE application.
- A necessary (but not sufficient) condition for encouraging cultural change is getting senior management buy-in to the ADPE way. This buy-in can be enormously difficult to achieve. Since, by definition, senior management is "in charge" at various levels within the organization, getting this buy-in is tantamount to asking them to give up some of their sovereignty. Using the argument "it is the right thing to do" will prob-ably not work. What generally works is appealing to the argument of competition. If your competitors are adopting or already have successfully adopted a consistent way of building good software systems, senior management will probably be more inclined toward supporting the ADPE way—particularly if you explain how the ADPE way can reduce software systems development risk (as, indeed, we argue throughout the preceding chapters). We stress that, if senior management does not buy into the ADPE way, the SEE imple-mentation approach you propose is doomed to failure. Your organization will likely fractionate into com-peting fiefdoms—and the ADPE way will be the subject of implicit, if not explicit, derision.

■ If senior management buy-in is not an issue, to accelerate cultural change you may want to consider making employee commitment to the ADPE way a condition of employment. That is, you may want to include in an employee's hiring agreement the stipulation that the employee agrees to follow the ADPE way as a condition of employment. To put some teeth into this approach, you may want to include in the agreement that the person will undergo a trial period of, say, ninety days during which time the person must complete mutually agreed-upon tasks demonstrating that he or she understands and practices the ADPE way. If the person falls short in this regard, then the person is not hired. To work, this approach must be supported by a ADPE training program.

The preceding discussion suggest an order for the first couple of ADPE elements that should be promulgated. We now expand upon this discussion and look at the issue of ADPE element phasing.

> 2. How should ADPE elements be phased in?

Let us now consider in more detail ADPE element linkages. This look may help you gain more insight into the factors governing ADPE element phasing. Figure 8–7 shows the following sequence of ADPE elements that might be one way to start your ADPE (we indicate in parentheses where you can find an annotated outline for the element):

1. Software Systems Development Process Policy (Chapter 3)

2. Change Control Board Guideline (Chapter 4)

3. Independent Product Assurance Policy (Chapter 5)

4. Configuration Management Guideline (Figure 8–8)

5. Acceptance Testing Cycle Procedure (Chapter 5)

Before examining Figures 8–7 and 8–8, we explain why the ADPE element governing the development of ADPE elements, which appears in Figure 8–6, does not appear in the preceding list. This element sits above all other ADPE elements and can be developed and promulgated at any time convenient for your organization. In discussing Figure 8–6, we indicated why it may be a good idea to promulgate it after the first two items listed are put in place. However, if, for example, your organization can afford to keep doing business in its old way while it is setting up an ADPE, then it may make sense to put in place the process for developing ADPE elements before any other elements are developed. Such an approach may work if your organization is not anticipating a major shift in the type of software systems development work that it will do during, say, the next six to twelve months. Under such circumstances, the heroics of individual staff members may still get your work done on time and within budget (provided you do not experience major staff turnover).

Figure 8–7 shows how each element in the sequence plugs into its predecessor. In general, a set of ADPE elements will plug into each other in more than pairwise fashion. Figure 8–7 highlights the pairwise relationships tied to the implementation chronology to suggest why the sequence shown makes sense. Of course, for your organization, other sequences (with possibly other elements) may make better sense, depending on which element features may be of importance to your organization. For example, if configuration management is a priority for your organization, it may make sense to promulgate the CM element before the CCB element. The CM element would, of course, address CCB issues in anticipation of a CCB element. Alternatively, the CCB and CM elements could be merged into a single element—depending on the prominence that you want to give to the CCB in your overall software systems development process.

We explain in the following list how the sequence in Figure 8–7 is constructed. Using similar arguments, you can construct an element sequence that makes sense for your organization. You can use

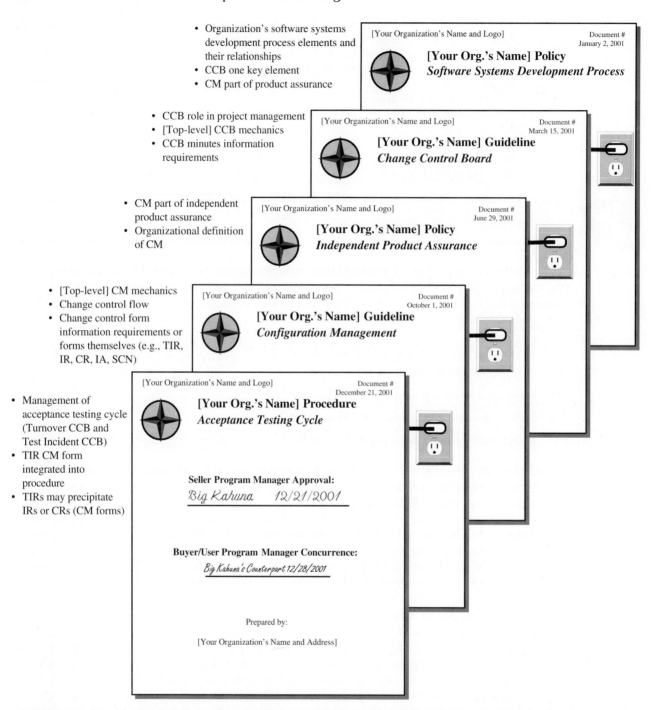

- Organization's software systems development process elements and their relationships
- CCB one key element
- CM part of product assurance

- CCB role in project management
- [Top-level] CCB mechanics
- CCB minutes information requirements

- CM part of independent product assurance
- Organizational definition of CM

- [Top-level] CM mechanics
- Change control flow
- Change control form information requirements or forms themselves (e.g., TIR, IR, CR, IA, SCN)

- Management of acceptance testing cycle (Turnover CCB and Test Incident CCB)
- TIR CM form integrated into procedure
- TIRs may precipitate IRs or CRs (CM forms)

[Your Organization's Name and Logo]   Document #
January 2, 2001
[Your Org.'s Name] Policy
Software Systems Development Process

[Your Organization's Name and Logo]   Document #
March 15, 2001
[Your Org.'s Name] Guideline
Change Control Board

[Your Organization's Name and Logo]   Document #
June 29, 2001
[Your Org.'s Name] Policy
Independent Product Assurance

[Your Organization's Name and Logo]   Document #
October 1, 2001
[Your Org.'s Name] Guideline
Configuration Management

[Your Organization's Name and Logo]   Document #
December 21, 2001
[Your Org.'s Name] Procedure
Acceptance Testing Cycle

Seller Program Manager Approval:
Big Kahuna   12/21/2001

Buyer/User Program Manager Concurrence:
Big Kahuna's Counterpart 12/28/2001

Prepared by:

[Your Organization's Name and Address]

FIGURE 8–7   A key element of SEE implementation planning is ADPE element phasing. To get you started addressing this planning issue for your organization, the figure shows some elements, their relationships, and an order for their development. Your SEE implementation plan should propose a strategy for ADPE element development. It is desirable to start with an element that defines your overall software systems development process. This element provides the context for most subsequent elements. In particular, it shows how they are to plug into one another.

[Your Organization's Name] Guideline
Configuration Management

Document #
Date

1.0 PURPOSE

This section states the purpose of the element. This purpose is the following:

- Define your organization's method for tracking, controlling, and accounting for changes to (software) product parts and changes to (software) part relationships.
- Set forth generic configuration management (CM) practices and guidance for implementing these practices on each project within your organization. [If your organization has only similar projects, then the practices can be defined in specific, "how-to-do-it" terms and be made applicable to all your projects.]
- Delineate the guideline implementation responsibilities of organizational elements and/or individuals and, if desired, your customer(s).

  If CM is an aspect of your organization's product assurance activity, then this element should explicitly link to your organization's product assurance ADPE element. Alternatively, the information in this CM guideline could be incorporated into the product assurance ADPE element (e.g., as an appendix).

2.0 BACKGROUND

This section gives an overview of your organization, your business, your customers, and the types of contractual vehicles you use to conduct business (e.g., fixed price, memorandum of understanding, time and materials). It should also explain the classes of products your organization develops (e.g., documents, computer code, databases) that will be the focus of CM activity.

3.0 ORGANIZATIONAL CONFIGURATION MANAGEMENT REQUIREMENTS

This section presents requirements for setting up CM practices on your organization's projects. Example requirements include the following:

- **Part Labeling**—establish a configuration item (CI) labeling scheme for identifying product parts to be controlled.
- **Labeling Depth**—decide on the depth of the CI hierarchy. This depth may change throughout the product lifetime. The greater the depth, the greater the visibility into product changes, and the greater the effort required to track changes.
- **Forms**—define forms for documenting and tracking (candidate) product changes.
- **Forms and CCB Support**—use forms in conjunction with a project CCB to give visibility to proposed and implemented changes.
- **Forms Library and Product Assurance**—use the product assurance organization to (1) keep forms library up-to-date, (2) make this information available at CCB meetings and other project meetings, (3) maintain the forms project archive.
- **Change Confirmation**—use the product assurance organization to confirm that approved changes have been incorporated. Confirmation should be a matter of record either at CCB meetings or other project meetings.
- **Forms Automation**—automate form data entry and archiving to the extent practical considering (1) project budget, (2) schedule, and (3) value of change control data beyond the termination of the project.

4.0 CONFIGURATION MANAGEMENT CONCEPTS

This section gives background for implementing the requirements given in the preceding section (e.g., definitions of "configuration," "baseline," "change control board [CCB]," and "CM functions"). Appendices can provide additional details that augment this background information.

FIGURE 8–8 An annotated outline for getting you started defining a (software) configuration management guideline for your organization.

[Your Organization's Name] Guideline
Configuration Management

5.0   CONFIGURATION MANAGEMENT IMPLEMENTATION RESPONSIBILITIES

This section delineates the responsibilities of each agent within your organization (e.g., project manager, manager of project managers, manager of the process engineering group, product assurance manager, product assurance analysts) for implementing the guidance set forth in the remainder of the guideline. With customer approval, it may also be desirable to delineate the responsibilities of customer agents (e.g., customer project manager) for guideline implementation (e.g., CCB participation).

APPENDICES

Appendices can contain details for carrying through the guidance set forth in the body of the guideline. For example, appendices might include such things as (1) change control scenarios and supporting forms (see Chapter 4), (2) detailed guidance for preparing a project-specific CM plan (e.g., specific suggestions for accomplishing each of the four CM functions, how to decide whether a project should use change control forms, how to set up a library for controlling products during development and subsequent to delivery) , (3) change control form information requirements, (4) example change control forms, and (5) instructions for filling out change control forms (including worked-out examples).

FIGURE 8–8   *Continued*

this sequence to construct a timeline like the one shown in Figure 8–6 to include in your SEE implementation plan.

1. For reasons stated earlier, the Software Systems Development Process Policy is constructed first. It defines the organization's way of building software(-related) products. It includes the CCB as one key element of the process. It also includes the product assurance activity which, in turn, includes configuration management.

2. The Change Control Board Guideline is constructed next. It elaborates on the CCB role in project management set forth in the Software Systems Development Process Policy. The guideline also specifies top-level CCB mechanics such as how to run a CCB meeting, who should take minutes, and who should be the chairperson. The guideline also specifies information requirements for CCB minutes and a template for packaging these information requirements.

3. The Independent Product Assurance Policy is constructed next. It stipulates that configuration management is one of the product assurance processes. It gives an organizational definition of configuration management. That is, it specifies whether the product assurance organization is to perform configuration management or to monitor those who do. The policy may also stipulate the CCB role in the product assurance T&E process.

4. The Configuration Management Guideline is constructed next. As indicated in Figure 8–8, the guideline specifies configuration management requirements for software projects (e.g., parts labeling, change control forms, change confirmation). It specifies configuration management mechanics, such as the generic change control steps (including the role of the CCB). It specifies information requirements for change control forms and, possibly, example forms. As indicated in Figure 8–8, appendices in the guideline can contain details for implementing the requirements set forth in the body of the guideline. For example, an appendix may contain detailed guidance for preparing a project-specific configuration management plan. Another appendix may contain instructions for filling out change control forms given either in the body of the guideline or in the appendix.

5. The Acceptance Test Cycle Procedure specifies the management of the acceptance testing cycle, including the roles of the Turnover CCB and Test Incident CCB as discussed in Chapter 5. The procedure explains how the change control Test Incident Report (TIR) form called out in the Configuration Management Guideline is integrated into the acceptance testing cycle. The procedure also explains how TIRs may precipitate other change control forms such as Incident Reports (IRs) or Change Requests (CR) called out in the configuration management guideline.

We note that, for small organizations, the five elements shown in Figure 8–7 may be collapsed into a single element. In this consolidated element, each chapter may address what in Figure 8–7 is a separate element. This approach might also be used in an organization where SEE implementation needs to take place over a relatively short time frame.

Other alternatives to the sequence in Figure 8–7 include the following:

- The Acceptance Testing Cycle Procedure is incorporated into the Independent Product Assurance Policy as an appendix.

- The CCB Guideline is incorporated into the Configuration Management Guideline as an appendix, with this latter guideline being produced after the Software Systems Development Process Policy.

- The Configuration Management Guideline and the Acceptance Testing Cycle Procedure are incorporated into the Independent Product Assurance Policy as appendices.

Now that we have looked at SEE timeline and ADPE element phase-in factors, we look at factors bearing on the overall make-up of the ADPE.

3. What ADPE elements should be included in your SEE?

When planning an engineering environment to define your software systems development business practices, the specific elements to include in the ADPE is a key consideration. It is difficult to provide guidance regarding the specific elements to include for reasons such as the following:

- The enterprise in which your organization is embedded may already have certain policies and directives that govern all work and/or software-specific work. In such cases, it would generally be counterproductive to create elements that duplicate existing business practices. For example, your enterprise may be a software business that has a set of life cycles that govern the different types of work that it does (e.g., a prototype development life cycle, an information engineering life cycle, a "maintenance" life cycle). These life cycles may be set forth in a document or documents that define the specific activities to be followed in developing software-(related) products. In this case, it would probably be redundant to develop an ADPE element that corresponds to the Software Systems Development Process Policy that we discussed in Chapter 3. ADPE elements may still need to be developed because enterprise policies and directives are silent with respect to needed practices. To provide connectivity with existing policies and directives, needed ADPE elements would reference these enterprise publications and/or incorporate pertinent material from them. For example, an enterprise directive or policy may call for configuration management to be instituted on all software systems development projects and may further stipulate that the projects are responsible for setting up configuration management practices. In this case, an ADPE element addressing the "how-to-do-it" of configuration management would be useful to develop. To provide context, the element would cite the enterprise configuration management directive or policy.

- A government enterprise may have hired your organization to develop software systems according to practices set forth in government standards (this situation is common on military programs). In such cases, these standards would constitute at least part of your ADPE. ADPE elements may still have to be developed to address practices only alluded to in the government-provided standards. For example, one standard may be the analog to the Software Systems Development Process Policy discussed in Chapter 3. This standard may call for peer reviews but may give no additional guidance on how peer reviews are to be conducted. In this case, it would probably be helpful to develop an ADPE element to address peer review procedures to augment the government-provided standards.

- Your organization may have been hired to do software systems development work over a relatively short period of time (say a year or less). Furthermore, the buyer who hired you expects you to have defined software business practices. In anticipation of such work, you may want to have a small number of ADPE element templates that can be (quickly) adapted to your client's specific needs—either during the first couple of weeks of the work or during your response to the client's RFP. The ADPE make-up in such circumstances will generally be much different from what it would be for circumstances in which a client has hired you for several years, and the first year, say, is to be used in part to plan and begin developing an SEE.

- Your organization may be caught up in a rapidly expanding business base. For example, because of a ballooning customer base, your organization may have to develop information management systems that must (1) operate within tightly constrained cycles (because of, for instance, customer billing cycles) and (2) be modified rapidly in response to rapidly changing requirements (for instance, to service more customers in a shorter amount of time because of competitive pressures). Such circumstances are not uncommon in the commercial business world and present special challenges regarding software systems development. On the one hand, the organization cannot stop developing its software systems to put in place or upgrade its engineering environment. On the other hand, the organization must take action to discipline its software systems development practices to head off software failures and facilitate system upgrades and replacements—otherwise, the bottom line is impacted, and the business will be crushed by its own success. The rapid pace of business growth may thus limit the ADPE elements to a small number that address only the most essential practices—leaving the remaining practices to the know-how of the individuals. For example, in the extreme, it may be feasible only to put in place an element like the Software Systems Development Process Policy discussed in Chapter 3—and nothing else. Such an element would capture in the large all the things that need to be done—the details (e.g., how to conduct peer reviews or perform independent product assurance) would be left to the know-how of the individuals to put in place on individual projects.

Given the preceding caveats, we now offer suggestions for planning what to include in your ADPE. Of course, as we stress throughout this book, plans will change. So, you should keep in mind that the following discussion is to help you overcome the blank-page syndrome when it comes to planning your ADPE makeup. You will find that as you put ADPE elements in place, your specific ADPE needs will undoubtedly evolve. In fact, as we discuss later, one of the elements to include in your ADPE is one describing the process for developing and evolving the other ADPE elements.

Figure 8–9 shows twelve candidate ADPE elements. Eight of these are addressed in previous chapters, where, among other things, we provide an annotated outline for each. An annotated outline for another element was presented earlier in this chapter (Figure 8–8). Annotated outlines for the remaining three are provided in figures after Figure 8–9. For ease of reference, we list here the twelve elements and the chapter or figure where you can find an annotated outline for each. Figure 8–9 does not imply an implementation order.

1. Software Systems Development Process Policy (Chapter 3)

2. Change Control Board Guideline (Chapter 4)

3. ADPE Elements Standard (Chapter 7)

4. Independent Product Assurance Policy (Chapter 5)

5. Document Templates Standard (Figure 8–10)

6. Project Plan Development Process Procedure (Chapter 2)

7. Measurement Guideline (Chapter 6)

8. Acceptance Testing Cycle Procedure (Chapter 5)

9. Project Tracking Guideline (Figure 8–11)

10. Configuration Management Guideline (Figure 8–8)

11. Peer Reviews Guideline (Chapter 5)

12. Software Development Life Cycle Definition Guideline (Figure 8–12).

To help you decide the breadth and depth of an ADPE for your organization, Table 8–1 summarizes the purpose and features of the twelve elements shown in Figure 8–9. This table can help you organize your ADPE planning approach. The column labelled "Purpose" reminds you of this book's approach to defining the focus of the ADPE elements included in the table. For your organization, you may want a different focus for a given element, or you may want to consolidate the focus with one or more other elements. In this case, simply redefine the purpose (and possibly rename the element). For example, the table indicates that the Project Plan Development Process element focuses on the organization's project planning process and the steps involved with producing a project plan. You may want to expand the scope of this element to encompass all forms of planning involved with software systems development. In this case, the element might be retitled, for instance, "Planning Process." This retitled element would define the various processes involved with producing different types of software-related plans (e.g., product assurance plans, test plans, configuration management plans, reliability and maintainability plans).

The column labelled "Comments" offers additional insight into the role and orientation of the elements listed. Among other things, this column offers suggestions for consolidating two or more elements (e.g., folding the Acceptance Testing Cycle element material into an appendix in the Independent Product Assurance element or the Configuration Management element).

We remind you that the elements listed in Table 8–1 are those discussed in preceding chapters or introduced and discussed in this chapter. With the possible exception of the "Software Systems Devel-

(*text continues on page 439*)

FIGURE 8–9 It is difficult to provide guidance regarding the specific ADPE elements to include in an SEE. The figure shows a set of elements to start your thinking for addressing your global SEE needs. We label the specific elements using the designation "policy," "guideline," "procedure," or "standard." As we discussed in preceding chapters, you may want to establish a different taxonomy for your elements. Even if you use our taxonomy, what we show as, e.g., a "procedure" you may want to cast as a "guideline."

[Your Organization's Name and Logo]

Document #
Date

 [Your Organization's Name] Standard
Document Templates

Rest of
ADPE

Document #
Date

1.0 PURPOSE

This section states the purpose of the element. This purpose is the following:

- Present a list of candidate document types for consideration when planning or replanning a software systems development project.
- Provide templates for these document types to serve as a starting point for constructing each document.
- Provide guidance for identifying document sets appropriate to projects of different classes within the organization.
- Allow the seller and customer to define expectations about a document.

2.0 BACKGROUND

This section gives an overview of the project and the organization within which it operates. This section should also briefly discuss the concepts of SEE, ADPE, and ADTE or their counterparts in your organization, and the relationship of this ADPE element to these counterparts.

3.0 DOCUMENT TEMPLATES DESCRIPTION AND USE

This section describes the generic format of the templates (e.g., Title, Identification Number, Description/Purpose, Relationship to Other ADPE Elements, Preparation Instructions, Format/Content Requirements). This section should also indicate whether electronic versions of the templates are available and, if so, where they can be found (e.g., in the organization's local area network). The templates themselves may be placed in an appendix for ease of reference.

4.0 DOCUMENT CATEGORIES

This section defines document categories, and groups the templates by these categories as a project planning aid (e.g., one categorization might be *Planning*, *Product Specification*, *Product Design and Development*, *Product Installation, Use, and Operation*, and *Product Evaluation and Tracking*).

5.0 DOCUMENT SELECTION AND PACKAGING GUIDANCE

This section provides a starting point for deciding which (1) document types are appropriate for a given project and (2) document types may be consolidated into a single document. The approach here is to group projects by categories and give guidance on documents by category. You may wish to categorize projects by size (e.g., "small," "medium," or "large"), contract type (e.g., fixed price, cost plus fixed fee, time and materials), risk ("high," "medium," or "low"), etc. You may wish to indicate mandatory and optional document types for each project category.

6.0 DOCUMENT REVIEW GUIDELINES

This section, which should be tied to your software systems development process ADPE element, contains document review guidance in terms of such things as review type (e.g., peer, grammar/format, management), review agent (e.g., technical editor, product developer), and review focus (e.g., for a product assurance review, *conformity* to ensure document conforms to SOW, *traceability* to ensure document content links with predecessor documents, etc.).

APPENDIX

It is useful to have at least one appendix containing the templates. The templates to include will generally change over time as your organization matures.

FIGURE 8–10 An annotated outline for getting you started defining a standard for software and software-related documents. The key point to keep in mind is that this ADPE element is not just a collection of document templates—rather, it defines a process for deciding what documents to use when and provides document review guidance. Thus, you should keep in mind that, to give this element substantive value for your organization, you should ensure that it plugs into the rest of your ADPE, particularly your software systems development process. The outline shows you a way to bring about this plug-in for your software systems development process ADPE element.

[Your Organization's Name] Guideline
Project Tracking

1.0 PURPOSE

This section states the purpose of the element. This purpose is the following:

- Define your organization's method for tracking and reviewing software systems development project accomplishments and results against documented estimates, commitments, and plans.
- Define your organization's method for adjusting planned project activities based on actual accomplishments and results.
- Delineate the guideline implementation responsibilities of organizational elements and/or individuals and, if desired, your customer(s).

2.0 BACKGROUND

This section gives an overview of your organization, your business, your customers, and the types of contractual vehicles you use to conduct business (e.g., fixed price, memorandum of understanding, time and materials). It should also explain corporate practices for project tracking that may be applicable to software systems development projects.

3.0 ORGANIZATIONAL PROJECT TRACKING REQUIREMENTS

This section presents requirements for setting up project tracking practices on your organization's projects. Example requirements include the following:

- **Schedule Tracking**—establish a means for tracking planned completion of project activities, milestones, and commitments against (1) the project plan, (2) updates to this plan, and (3) plan changes recorded in CCB minutes or other project correspondence .
- **Resource Tracking**—establish a means for tracking planned resource expenditures against (1) the project plan, (2) updates to this plan, and (3) plan changes recorded in CCB minutes or other project correspondence.
- **Risk Tracking**—establish a means for tracking risks associated with schedule, resource, and technical aspects of the project. (Risk tracking should be coupled with product assurance activity.)
- **Software Engineering Activities Tracking**—establish a means for tracking technical activities. (This tracking should be coupled with the use of the seller deliverable tracking form.)
- **Corrective Action**—establish procedures for taking corrective action in response to schedule, resource, risk, and software engineering activity tracking. These procedures should include the CCB.

4.0 PROJECT TRACKING CONCEPTS

This section gives background for implementing the requirements given in the preceding section (e.g., definitions of *risk, milestone, commitment, tracking,* and *earned value*). This section should explain, illustrate, and contrast various ways of preparing and presenting project tracking information (e.g., timelines, bar graphs, pie charts).

APPENDICES

Appendices can contain details for carrying through the guidance set forth in the body of the guideline. For example, appendices might include such things as (1) example graphs showing planned versus actual resource expenditures, (2) detailed guidance for preparing a project-specific risk management plan , (3) example spreadsheets for software engineering activity tracking , and (4) example corrective action reports.

FIGURE 8–11 An annotated outline for getting you started defining a project tracking guideline for your organization. This element should be coordinated with the Change Control Board Guideline discussed in Chapter 4, particularly with respect to the use of CCB minutes for project tracking purposes. This element should also be coordinated with the Software Systems Development Process Policy discussed in Chapter 3 with respect to the seller deliverable tracking form.

[Your Organization's Name] Guideline
Software Development Life Cycle Definition

1.0 PURPOSE

This section states the purpose of the element. This purpose is the following:

- Establish guidance for defining a life cycle or life cycles for a software systems development effort within your organization.
- Provide guidance for using life cycle stages for project planning and project accomplishment purposes.

2.0 BACKGROUND

This section gives an overview of your organization, your business, your customers, and the types of contractual vehicles you use to conduct business (e.g., fixed price, memorandum of understanding, time and materials). This section should relate your organization's business to the types of software systems development efforts that your organization typically performs (e.g., information management systems for a customer's banking activity, command and control systems for a customer's military support activity, prototype systems for a customer's research and development activity).

3.0 GUIDING PRINCIPLES

This section establishes principles for defining a life cycle for a particular software systems development effort. Example principles include the following:

- A **stage** is a set of activities whose purpose is to yield a set of software(-related) products and/or perform one or more services.
- Reduced to its simplest terms, there are four stages of software maturation: **WHAT**, **HOW**, **BUILD**, and **USE**. These generic stages enable a software systems development team to (1) specify *what* the software and supporting databases are to do, (2) specify *how* the software and supporting databases are to do the *what*, (3) *build* the computer code and supporting databases that implements the *how*, and (4) *use* the computer code and supporting databases to perform the *what*.
- For a particular software systems development effort, each generic stage unfolds into one or more stages defining the particular work to be accomplished on the effort expressed in terms the customer and seller can mutually understand. This unfolding, or *instantiation*, gives visibility to that particular effort, thereby helping the customer and seller mutually progress in their understanding of the remaining work to be accomplished.
- As shown in the figure below, the four generic stages are wrapped around an area wherein the seller's output from each stage is reviewed by product assurance activities so that management can decide what to do next. Product assurance serves as a checking and balancing mechanism on the product development activities performed in each stage. Management, in concert with product developers and product assurers, uses product assurance results to decide what life cycle stage to visit next (some stages may have to be revisited one or more times).

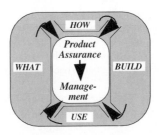

FIGURE 8–12   An annotated outline for getting you started preparing a life cycle guideline for your organization. This element should be coordinated with the Project Plan Development Process Procedure discussed in Chapter 2. This element should also be coordinated with the Software Systems Development Process Policy discussed in Chapter 3, particularly with respect to offering guidance on plugging a life cycle into the development process.

[Your Organization's Name] Guideline
Software Development Life Cycle Definition

Document #
Date

3.0 GUIDING PRINCIPLES *(Continued)*

- Software systems development proceeds iteratively through the life cycle via synergistic interaction among (1) product developers, (2) product assurers, and (3) management.
- The number and definition of the stages for a particular software systems development effort is fundamentally determined by the amount of visibility desired for the effort. At a second level, the number and definition of stages depends on the following factors:
  a. The estimated budget and schedule for accomplishing the entire project
  b. The degree of uncertainty regarding *what* is wanted
  c. The consequences of software failure (e.g., if failure would result in death or injury, the need would exist for greater visibility into the software systems development process and, thus, the need would exist for more life cycle stages)
  d. The technological challenge posed by *what* is wanted
  e. The benefits of software success (e.g., if each software development dollar invested had the potential for returning ten dollars in savings to the customer after the software system becomes operational by automating currently manual operation, then the need would exist for greater visibility into the software systems development process to realize these potential savings)
  f. The degree of "comfort" that the customer has with the software systems development team (e.g., if the customer is somewhat uncertain at project outset about the development team's understanding of the customer's requirements, then the need would exist for greater visibility into the software systems development process, and thus, the need would exist for more life cycle stages)

4.0 EXAMPLE LIFE CYCLE MODELS

This section shows how to apply the Section 3 principles to the generic four-stage life cycle to construct different life cycles based on project characteristics. For example, if the *what* on a project is uncertain (i.e., requirements are uncertain), it may be desirable to define a *Preliminary Requirements Specification Stage* and a *Detailed Requirements Specification Stage*. This approach enhances the visibility of the requirements definition process, thereby reducing the uncertainty associated with the *what*. As another example, if the *what* poses a technological challenge, it may be desirable to define a *Preliminary Design Specification Stage* and a *Detailed Design Specification Stage* as an instantiation of the HOW Stage. As a third example, if the project schedule does not allow for separate *what* and *how* activities, it may be desirable to have the WHAT Stage and the HOW Stage instantiated as a *Detailed Requirements Definition Stage,* which is then coupled to an instantiation of the BUILD Stage called *Prototyping Stage*. This latter stage would involve coding, which would be used to flesh out (iteratively) a design from the requirements developed in the *Detailed Requirements Definition Stage*. [Note: For information engineering projects, the generic four-stage life cycle is replaced with a six-stage life cycle whose stages are the following (four of the stages correspond to the generic four-stage life cycle): (1) PLANNING (to account for enterprisewide requirements), (2) ANALYSIS (WHAT), (3) DESIGN (HOW), (4) DEVELOPMENT (BUILD), (5) IMPLEMENTATION (USE), and (6) RETIREMENT (to account for phasing out of one or more systems within an enterprise).]

APPENDICES

Appendices can contain details for carrying through the guidance set forth in the body of the guideline. For example, appendices might include such things as (1) example management, development, and product assurance project tasks for one or more of the life cycles discussed in Section 4 and (2) a detailed list of candidate activities associated with each of the four generic life cycle stages (e.g., for the WHAT Stage, some candidate activities might be requirements discovery, requirements modeling, requirements verification, and requirements updating).

FIGURE 8–12 *Continued*

TABLE 8–1   Purpose and Features of Candidate ADPE Elements for Your ADPE.

Element Title	Purpose	Comments
Software Systems Devclopment Process	■ Identify the generic activities performed by your organizational elements in developing a software product (i.e., documentation, computer code, database) for delivery to your customer ■ Describe the roles of customer organizational elements and your organizational elements in performing these generic activities ■ Delineate implementation responsibilities	■ **Mandatory element** ■ Establishes the context for other elements ■ Each project adapts the generic activities to the character of the work to be performed (e.g., all projects perform peer reviews; different projects may conduct peer reviews differently)
Independent Product Assurance	■ Define your organization's statement of principles governing independent product assurance activities ■ Define product assurance processes and explain how they reduce software systems development risks ■ Delineate the implementation responsibilities of organizational elements and/or individuals and, if desired, your customer(s)	■ Independent product assurance as we define it is not the only way to set up a checking and balancing mechanism on a software project ■ One alternative is to have a so-called "Quality Assurance Organization" check the activities of all parties involved in a project (including the activities of the party that we call the "product assurance organization") ■ Decide on your checking and balancing approach and develop an ADPE element to define the activities associated with this approach
Configuration Management	■ Define your organization's method for tracking, controlling, and accounting for changes to (software) product parts and changes to (software) part relationships ■ Set forth generic configuration management (CM) practices and guidance for implementing these practices on each project within your organization [if your organization has only similar projects, then the practices can be defined in specific, "how-to-do-it" terms and be made applicable to all your projects] ■ Delineate the implementation responsibilities of organizational elements and/or individuals and, if desired, your customer(s)	■ If CM is an aspect of your organization's product assurance activity, then this element should explicitly link to your organization's product assurance ADPE element ■ Alternatively, the information in this CM element could be incorporated into the product assurance ADPE element (e.g., as an appendix) ■ Another alternative is to replace this element with one or more books or other CM publications—possibly with some instructions for adapting the material to your organization's way of doing business ■ CM scope should extend to all development products called out in the Software Systems Development Process element
Measurement	■ Identify the measurements to be performed to (1) quantify where your organization is product- and process-wise, (2) quantify differences from this baseline assessment, (3) establish quantitative process and product goals, and (4) quantify progress toward achieving these goals ■ Define the approach for incorporating process and product improvements based on the measurement activity ■ Delineate implementation responsibilities	■ Element should be put in place generally only after other elements have been in place for some time ■ Avoid measurement for measurement's sake—use measurement to answer questions your organization needs answered quantitatively
Project Tracking	■ Define your organization's method for tracking and reviewing software systems development project accomplishments and results against documented estimates, commitments, and plans ■ Define your organization's method for adjusting planned project activities based on actual accomplishments and results ■ Delineate the implementation responsibilities of organizational elements and/or individuals and, if desired, your customer(s)	■ Element may be unnecessary if your organization has standard project tracking practices ■ CCB minutes and deliverable tracking form described in Chapter 3 should be exploited for tracking purposes

TABLE 8-1 *Continued*

Element Title	Purpose	Comments
Peer Reviews	• Define your organization's approach [and, possibly, procedures] for preparing for and conducting product reviews primarily involving product developer and product assurance peers • Delineate responsibilities for preparing for and conducting peer reviews • Provide checklists and forms to facilitate and standardize peer review preparation and accomplishment • Provide instructions for completing checklists and forms provided • Delineate implementation responsibilities	• This element should stress that peer reviews (1) provide a *controlled* mechanism for refining products, (2) provide *technical* feedback to the lead developer, and (3) are *not* a measure of the lead developer's performance • This review balances the product developer's approach with the insights of others having applicable and comparable experience • Information in this element could be incorporated into the Software Systems Development Process element
Change Control Board	• Provide guidance for establishing CCBs • Define the role of CCBs in project efforts • Provide guidance for conducting CCB meetings • Delineate implementation responsibilities	• **Mandatory element** • Have trial-use element ready to use as soon as possible • CCB should be the primary vehicle for holding management accountable for their decisions
Software Development Life Cycle Definition	• Establish guidance for defining a life cycle or life cycles for a software systems development effort within your organization • Provide guidance for using life cycle stages for project planning and project accomplishment purposes • Delineate implementation responsibilities	• This element should stress that the life cycle concept is a useful way of breaking a software systems development effort into smaller, more manageable pieces • The element should stress that rarely does a project proceed sequentially from one life cycle stage to the next. Rather, one or more stages are generally revisited one or more times • The element should stress that the life cycle stages are a way of (1) organizing work to be performed on a project and (2) identifying products to be developed
Project Plan Development Process	• Delineate your organization's project planning process • Delineate implementation responsibilities	• Have trial-use element early in your SEE development program • Refine trial-use element by exploiting lessons learned from actual project planning activities • Key project planning organizational issue: Who should develop project plans—(1) one organization, or (2) each project, or (3) some combination of (1) and (2)?
Acceptance Testing Cycle	• Define the process for determining when a software system and supporting databases are ready for customer delivery • Delineate implementation responsibilities	• Scope may be expanded to encompass other forms of testing (e.g., unit and integration) • As an option, element material may be folded into Independent Product Assurance element or Configuration Management element as appendix
ADPE Elements	• Define ADPE element taxonomy (e.g., policy, guideline, procedure, and standard) • Define the process for developing and improving ADPE elements • Delineate implementation responsibilities	• Can be developed after the Software Systems Development Process element and the CCB element or at any other time • Try to involve most of the organization in reviews of ADPE element drafts • It is generally desirable to have the customer participate in the review process and to concur formally with the element content
Document Templates	• Present a list of candidate document types for consideration when planning or replanning a software systems development project • Provide templates for these document types to serve as a starting point for constructing each document • Provide guidance for identifying document sets appropriate to projects of different classes within your organization • Allow the seller and customer to define expectations about a document	• Element is more than just document templates • In support of project planning, defines process for deciding what documents to use when • Provides document review guidance • If your organization uses separately published documentation standards, then this element can simply reference these standards

opment Process" and "Change Control Board" elements, no element listed is mandatory. The number and type of elements that you choose to construct for your ADPE will probably be quite different from those listed in the table. The table is intended to start your thinking for planning your global ADPE needs.

We also remind you that the ADPE taxonomy we use in this book (i.e., "policy," "guideline," "procedure," and "standard") is just one way to categorize ADPE elements (for this reason, we have omitted these labels from the first column in Table 8–1). Furthermore, within this taxonomy, these labels may sometimes be used interchangeably for various reasons. For example, as indicated in Figure 8–9, the Software Systems Development Process element is labelled "Policy." From its statement of purpose and the definition of ADPE element "procedure" given earlier in this book, it might have made more sense to label this element "Procedure." However, because in some organizations the label "policy" carries more of an authoritative ring than does "procedure," this label may be more appropriate.

Before closing the discussion of the issue "What ADPE elements should be included in your SEE," we return briefly to Figures 8–10, 8–11, and 8–12.

Figure 8–10 (Document Templates Standard) stresses that the real value of including documentation standards in your ADPE extends beyond the document outlines. The Document Templates element should plug into the rest of the ADPE by addressing such key considerations as (1) a process for deciding what documents to use on which types of projects and (2) document review guidance (e.g., important things to look for in a document of a given type—for instance, does a software test plan contain a discussion of the system to be tested?).

Regarding Figure 8–11 (Project Tracking Guideline), project tracking techniques addressed should also incorporate items included in other ADPE elements. For example, as discussed in Chapter 4, CCB minutes should include, among other things, an action item list with due dates. These lists provide a project tracking technique that should be explicitly called out in the Project Tracking element. Also, as described in Chapter 3, the seller deliverable tracking form is used to track a product as it wends its way through the organization's software systems development process. For this reason, this form should be addressed in the Project Tracking element as a project tracking aid.

Figure 8–12 (Software Development Life Cycle Definition Guideline) provides guidance for constructing a life cycle or life cycles pertinent to a given software project. As such, this guideline is a project planning aid. For this reason, some organizations may find it helpful to fold the material in this guideline into a appendix to the Project Plan Development Process element discussed in Chapter 2, rather than placing the material in a stand-alone element. The heart of the material is the guiding principles, examples of which are shown under Section 3 in Figure 8–12. These principles are tied to the generic four-stage life cycle (i.e., WHAT, HOW, BUILD, and USE) introduced in Chapter 1, which is shown in the figure. They explain how to unfold the generic stages into stages that account for project particulars (e.g., schedule constraints, technology considerations, requirements uncertainty). Section 4 of the guideline indicates that example life cycle models should be included to illustrate the application of the guiding principles. Figure 8–12 also suggests that appendices can be used to illustrate how the life cycle constructed can be used to drive out management, development, and product assurance tasks. This process is explained and illustrated in Chapter 2.

We now discuss an SEE implementation issue pertaining to ADPE element structure. To this point, we have implicitly assumed that ADPE elements are generally documents of more than a couple of pages. Also, as suggested in Figure 8–9, we have implicitly assumed that an ADPE should be constituted with ten or so elements. The issue that we now consider examines these assumptions.

4. How should the ADPE be constituted—(1) from a small number of elements (i.e., approximately ten), each consisting of tens of pages or more, or (2) from a large number of elements (i.e., tens or more), each consisting of a couple of pages, or (3) some combination of (1) and (2)?

An important SEE implementation planning issue is how to structure the ADPE. Figure 8–13 highlights key factors bearing upon this issue. One alternative is to produce ten or so elements, with each element consisting of tens of pages or more. A second alternative is to produce tens or more elements, with each consisting of a couple of pages. A third alternative is some combination of the first and second. In the following sections we discuss SEE planning considerations regarding each alternative. For the first two alternatives, the discussion follows the bullets shown in Figure 8–13.

ADPE Constitution Alternative (1)—Tens or So Elements, Each Consisting of Tens of Pages or More

- Element development time may take months or longer. One reason for this protracted development time is deciding how much tutorial information to include, how much guidance and "how-to-do-it" to include, and how to organize these two classes of material. For example, in the CCB guideline, things such as the following may be useful to include in an element consisting of tens of pages:

  - It may be useful to incorporate tutorial information explaining, for example, a key engineering principle that management, development, and product assurance disciplines are needed to maintain effective communication between the wizard and king—and why. Through such explanatory material, people will have a better understanding of how to set up and run CCB meetings on their particular projects. Absent such information, people may struggle with, for example, getting closure at CCB meetings on things that need to be done to move a project ahead. Tutorial material is particularly important in an organization predominated by inexperienced staff (i.e., a staff with only several years' software industry experience on average).

  - It may be useful to incorporate guidance on CCB minutes. Here, there is a broad spectrum of possibilities. Some experienced members of your organization may say that all they need in the way of guidance in this regard is a simple statement such as, "Take minutes at each CCB meeting." Other members may say that they want *what* to record in minutes (i.e., CCB minutes information requirements). Still other members may say they want a specific format for CCB minutes. Because of such a broad spectrum of possibilities, it may take considerable time to strike some sort of happy medium in the CCB element regarding CCB minutes guidance detail.

  - It may be useful to incorporate examples illustrating the range of activities that can be folded into CCB operation. For instance, it may be useful to show how the CCB can be used to do software systems *development*. As a specific illustration, the CCB element may explain how to use one or more CCB meetings between the seller and customer to thrash out what "user friendly" may mean in terms of specific functions that can be tested.

- Elements consisting of tens of pages or more allow for integrating and detailing of a number of concepts. For example, in Chapter 2, we discussed how risk assessment should be a key part of the project planning process. We explained how to integrate risk assessment with other parts of project planning, such as using a life cycle to drive out specific project tasks to be accomplished. As another example, earlier in the current chapter we explained how to integrate within a Document Templates element the concepts of (1) document sets appropriate for different types of projects within an organization and (2) document review guidance.

- As mentioned earlier, elements consisting of tens of pages or more have room for both instructional (i.e., tutorial) material as well as business practices. Integrating these two types of material generally permits the material to be more easily assimilated (particularly if examples are included). In addition, by including explanations of underlying engineering principles, elements can generally be more easily adapted to different situations. For example, a principle underlying the CM function of "control" is to give visibility to candidate and approved changes. Generally, this visibility is achieved through "paperwork" (here, "paperwork" also includes electronic as well as hard copy). That is, some paperwork is needed on each project to follow product evolution—but how much? We assert that the minimum paperwork requirement is CCB minutes capturing decisions made regarding product evolution. If it is anticipated that many changes may be made to products, then more extensive paperwork will be needed. This more extensive paperwork includes change control forms (such as those discussed in Chapter 4). Carrying this paperwork example a little fur-

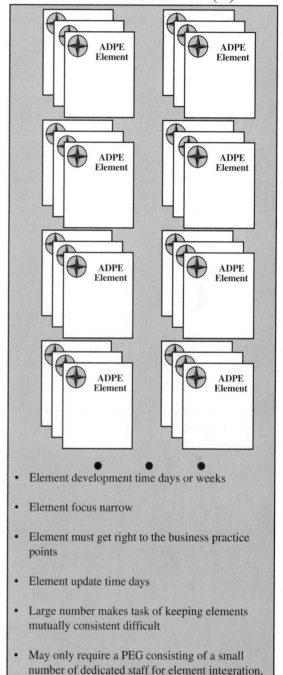

ADPE Alternative (1)

- Element development time months or longer

- Element can integrate and detail a number of concepts

- Element has room for both instructional (i.e., tutorial) material as well as business practices

- Element update time weeks or longer

- Small number facilitates task of keeping elements mutually consistent

- Dedicated PEG staff generally needed

ADPE Alternative (2)

- Element development time days or weeks

- Element focus narrow

- Element must get right to the business practice points

- Element update time days

- Large number makes task of keeping elements mutually consistent difficult

- May only require a PEG consisting of a small number of dedicated staff for element integration, training, and maintenance and a number of part-timers to write individual elements

FIGURE 8–13 An important SEE implementation planning issue is the following: How should the ADPE be constituted—(1) from a small number of elements (i.e., approximately ten), each consisting of tens of pages or more, or (2) from a large number of elements (i.e., tens or more), each consisting of a couple of pages, or (3) some combination of (1) and (2)? Here are some considerations to help you address this issue in your SEE implementation plan.

ther, it may be useful to include in your organization's CM element a rule of thumb for gauging when a project needs to augment paperwork support for change control beyond CCB minutes to include forms. The following is an example of such a rule of thumb:

> If it is anticipated that throughout the current fiscal year of the project at least one deliverable may require consideration of at least ten changes, then change control forms should be used to track product changes.

- Elements consisting of tens of pages or more may require weeks or longer to update. The update time may be particularly protracted if the element contains complex flow diagrams and extensive supporting text. Update time also depends on the process you set up for constructing, reviewing and revising ADPE elements, as discussed in Chapter 7. The greater the number of reviewers, the more protracted will be the update time.

- An ADPE consisting of a relatively small number of elements facilitates the task of keeping the elements mutually consistent. Mutual consistency is particularly important regarding definitions of terms (e.g., two different definitions of "high-risk project") and different words to refer to the same concept (e.g., "change control board" and "configuration control board").

- A process engineering group (PEG) may generally need to be *dedicated* to developing and maintaining a set of ten or so elements, each consisting of tens of pages or more. A group of dedicated staff facilitates the task of weaving a consistent approach into the ADPE. For example, it can take considerable time to hammer out the organizational software systems development process element. As we pointed out in Chapter 3, the heart of this element is the organizational process flow diagram. Generally, just a couple of dedicated people should try to get the flow down on paper—and then solicit feedback from the rest of the organization. It is generally easier for a small group of dedicated staff to establish a consistent approach to documenting ADPE elements. It is generally helpful for an ADPE to present a consistent face to the rest of the organization. Furthermore, a dedicated group is more likely to take ownership of its ADPE products—and be more forceful in campaigning for their adoption.

ADPE Constitution Alternative (2)—Tens of Elements, Each Consisting of a Couple of Pages

- For elements of this type, the development time will be days or, at the outside, weeks (depending, again, on the process you set up for constructing, reviewing, and revising ADPE elements). Such relatively rapid development time can allow for more experimentation with element orientations to accommodate perceived organization process needs. Of course, as we discuss in a subsequent issue, no matter what size the element, time is still needed for people to get acclimated before the element is changed. However, with smaller elements, the impact of element changes on staff should be easier to perceive and to adjust to.

- Because the element consists of only a couple of pages, it cannot be encyclopedic. Its focus must therefore be narrow—and, thus, generally easier to assimilate than a larger and more comprehensive element. Also, staff are more likely to read through an element with a couple of pages than one consisting of ten times that number of pages. Although reading elements does not guarantee ADPE implementation success, not reading them will almost certainly undermine successful implementation.

- Again, because of its small size, the element must get right to the business practice points. This characteristic is particularly beneficial when staff needs to locate quickly a key business process point.

- For elements each consisting of a couple of pages, the update time should generally be days. This characteristic can be particularly beneficial to relieve organizational tensions arising from existing practices that many may feel need to be changed.

- A large number of elements makes the task of keeping them mutually consistent generally more difficult than keeping a smaller set consistent. Sometimes this factor may work at cross-purposes with the preceding factor. Although, as we just argued, a couple-page element may be updatable within days, changes thus introduced may cause unanticipated inconsistencies in a number of other elements. Part of the update time for a given element must thus include the analysis of impacts on a potentially large number of other elements.

- To produce a large number of small elements may only require a PEG consisting of a small number of dedicated staff for element integration, training, and maintenance. This dedicated staff would be augmented by a number of part-timers to write individual elements. Presumably, these part-timers would be subject-matter experts who could cogently and compactly produce the element text.

Before proceeding to ADPE Constitution Alternative (3), we illustrate some of the preceding Alternative (2) factors. For this purpose, we provide the sample two-page ADPE element shown in Figure 8–14. The figure shows a CM Guideline derived from the CM Guideline outline given in Figure 8–8.

The thrust of the element is to give the essential requirements for setting up CM on a project. The element empowers the project to implement the requirements in a way that makes sense for the project. This empowerment approach should be particularly effective in an organization with solid software engineering experience (which should not be confused with "software experience," which may be markedly different from the former). Among other things, such an organization, with its know-how, should be able to apply this software engineering experience to the CM Guideline requirements to produce a CM plan and procedures consistent with project needs. If an organization is short on such know-how, the Figure 8–14 guideline can still benefit the organization if it is supplied with some references that can offer this know-how. Such references would include CM textbooks (with material such as that found in our Chapter 4), government and/or industry standards (e.g., U.S. Department of Defense, Institute for Electrical and Electronics Engineers, Electronic Industries Association, International Organization for Standards, and enterprisewide CM publications. References on automated CM tool support can also help fill a know-how gap. However, a word of caution is in order regarding CM tools in particular and automated tools in general. Tools should be viewed as just that—namely, aids for accomplishing business practices more efficiently, generally through automation. By understanding engineering principles underlying ADPE elements, it is then generally easier to decide which parts, if any, of business practices that it makes sense to accomplish with tools. The notion that defining a business practice simply in terms of some tool is adequate is generally short-sighted, if not a recipe for trouble. For example, using a tape-recorder to capture what goes on at a CCB meeting is helpful only when it is understood (1) what are the meeting events that should be captured, (2) whether a hard copy of some of this recording should be prepared, and (3) what part of this recording should be committed to hard copy.

It is important to stress that using a two-page ADPE element such as that shown in Figure 8–14 and that may be short on "how-to" is not an oxymoron for establishing *consistent* business practices. That different projects using the same guideline as that shown in Figure 8–14 may set up vastly different CM implementations, does not stand in opposition to the element's purpose of establishing an organizationwide consistent CM business practice. The view adopted here is that all such projects are implementing the same set of CM requirements in different ways—and, therefore, are practicing CM in a consistent way. For example, one project may use forms to track changes, while another project may simply use CCB minutes for this tracking purpose. However, both are tracking changes in a visible, traceable way. This argument is not meant to imply that an organization cannot set up a detailed (many-paged) CM guideline that prescribes that all projects within the organization implement CM in the same, almost carbon-copy way (e.g., same change control forms, same CCB minute format, same parts identification scheme). In some organizations, this approach may be the commonsense thing to do. **The key point here is that "consistent business practice" can span a broad range of interpretation—and the interpretation appropriate to your organization should be clearly articulated in your ADPE elements.**

ADPE Constitution Alternative (3)—Combination of Some Elements, Each Consisting of a Couple of Pages with Some Elements Each Consisting of Tens of Pages or More

This alternative aims at taking the best of the preceding two alternatives. One approach here is to make the Software Systems Development Process element tens of pages or more, with a sufficiently detailed

[Your Organization's Name and Logo]

Document #
Date

[Your Organization's Name] Guideline
Configuration Management

Document #
Date

1.0 PURPOSE

This guideline defines [*your organization's name*] configuration management (CM) requirements and responsibilities. Each project is to apply these requirements to establish a CM approach via either a CM plan and/or CM procedures.

Configuration management is defined as the integrated application of the four component functions of identification, control, auditing, and status accounting, where these functions are defined as follows:
Configuration identification entails determining the constituent parts of a product and the relationship among these parts, and labeling the parts thus determined.
Configuration control provides the mechanism for precipitating, preparing, evaluating, approving/disapproving, and implementing all changes to products throughout a project. A key element of this function is the change control board (CCB), which is discussed below.
Configuration auditing consists of two primary functions: (1) **configuration verification** and (2) **configuration validation**. Configuration verification checks that whatever is intended for each component of a product configuration as specified in one baseline is actually achieved in the succeeding baseline. Configuration validation ascertains that the product configuration is congruent with the requirements for that product, i.e., that the product requirements are fulfilled.
Configuration status accounting records the activity associated with the other three configuration management activities. It provides answers to the questions "What happened?" and "When did it happen?" thereby giving visibility into the product development process and the resultant products. Recording of CCB minutes and maintaining an archive of change control forms are examples of status accounting activities.

2.0 BACKGROUND

[*Your organization's name*] develops [*your organization's product types*] that will be the focus of CM activity.

3.0 ORGANIZATIONAL CONFIGURATION MANAGEMENT REQUIREMENTS

This section presents requirements for setting up CM practices on [*your organization's name*] projects. These requirements include the following:

• **Part Labeling**—establish a configuration item (CI) labeling scheme for identifying product parts to be controlled.
• **Labeling Depth**—decide on the depth of the CI hierarchy. This depth may change throughout the product lifetime. The greater the depth, the greater the visibility into product changes, and the greater the effort required to track changes.
• **Forms**—define forms for documenting and tracking (candidate) product changes. For small projects or projects that process only a small number of changes, forms may be replaced by entries in CCB minutes.
• **Forms and CCB Support**—use forms in conjunction with a project CCB to give visibility to proposed and implemented changes.
• **Forms Library and Product Assurance**—use the product assurance organization to (1) keep forms library up-to-date, (2) make this information available at CCB meetings and other project meetings, (3) maintain the forms project archive.
• **Change Confirmation**—use the product assurance organization to confirm that approved changes have been incorporated. Confirmation should be a matter of record either at CCB meetings or other project meetings.
• **Forms Automation**—automate form data entry and archiving to the extent practical considering (1) project budget, (2) schedule, and (3) value of change control data beyond the termination of the project.

4.0 CONFIGURATION MANAGEMENT CONCEPTS

The purpose of this section is to give background for implementing the requirements given in the preceding section. CM supports product development by providing management and product developers a "parts view" of products under development. The term "**configuration**" is used to refer to this parts view. More specifically, *configuration* is defined as "a relative arrangement of parts." Configuration management keeps track of these parts arrangements, which typically manifest themselves in two forms: (1) an exploded parts diagram showing each product part and the relationship of parts to one another and (2) a list of the parts and their identifiers. Almost any object can be described in these terms. The fundamental value of expressing an object in terms of its configuration is that this view gives insight into (1) how the object is put together, (2) how it can be taken apart, (3) how it can be fixed, and (4) how parts may be added, combined, and/or eliminated.
The fundamental CM concept, *baseline*, is defined as "a line establishing a formal base for defining subsequent change." That is, a product baseline establishes the context for defining a change to that product.
[*Here you can add other CM concepts or replace those above, depending on your organization's needs.*]

5.0 CONFIGURATION MANAGEMENT IMPLEMENTATION RESPONSIBILITIES

This section delineates the responsibilities of each agent within [*your organization's name*] for implementing the guidance set forth in the remainder of the guideline.
[*Here you list each pertinent element of your organization—e.g., project manager, manager of project managers, manager of the process engineering group, product assurance manager, product assurance analysts—and their CM responsibilities. Example organizational elements and their responsibilities are given below.*]

FIGURE 8–14 Here is an example of a two-page CM ADPE element adapted from the Figure 8–8 annotated CM ADPE element outline. The slant of this element is to empower members in the organization to develop their CM approaches from the element either via a CM plan or for, say, small projects, via CM procedures. Page 2 of the element contains a CM plan outline.

[Your Organization's Name and Logo]

Document #
Date

[Your Organization's Name] Guideline
Configuration Management

Document #
Date

5.0   CONFIGURATION MANAGEMENT IMPLEMENTATION RESPONSIBILITIES (*Continued*)

- **Project Manager**—actively supports the CM practices set forth in this guideline by (1) ensuring that its contents are assimilated by all projects within the scope of the project manager's responsibility and (2) promoting its practices with [*your organization's name*] customers. Provides required direction and guidance to the project team to support implementation of the CM practices set forth in this guideline. Interacts directly with designated product assurance analysts responsible for CM throughout the development effort as defined by the project plan and the project's product assurance plan.
- **Product Assurance (PA) Manager**—is the [*your organization's name*] person responsible for providing CM support to every [*your organization's name*] project. In accordance with the project plan and product assurance plan, the PA Manager provides support to each project by assigning PA analysts with the appropriate CM skills.
- **Product Assurance Analysts**—assist with and coordinate the development of CM requirements that are tailored to a specific project. Assistance includes developing a project-specific product assurance plan for each project. Regarding CM, this plan either (1) specifies the project CM approach or (2) calls for the development of a CM plan specifying this approach. Implement CM practices on [*your organization's name*] projects in accordance with this guideline. Coordinate the implementation of CM requirements with the project manager (and, with the project manager's knowledge, coordinate with product development personnel). Serve as the liaison to [*your organization's name*] product assurance management for project CM activities.

CM Plan Topic Outline

1.0   INTRODUCTION
This section contains a high-level description of the project and the software system(s) being developed or supported.

2.0   REFERENCES
This section lists the government, industry, and local documents, standards, specifications, plans, regulations, manuals, and other documents that apply to the development and content of the plan.

3.0   CONFIGURATION MANAGEMENT ORGANIZATION
This section specifies the project organization, the configuration management organizational setup, and the associated responsibilities.

4.0   CONFIGURATION IDENTIFICATION
This section specifies the project configuration identification approach and procedures.

5.0   CONFIGURATION CONTROL
This section specifies the project configuration control approach and procedures.

6.0   CONFIGURATION STATUS ACCOUNTING
This section specifies how the status of items will be collected, verified, stored, processed, and reported.

7.0   CONFIGURATION AUDITING
This section specifies the project configuration auditing approach and procedures.

8.0   SCHEDULE
This section specifies the date and time estimates for project events such as reviews and audits.

9.0   CONFIGURATION MANAGEMENT IMPLEMENTATION
This section specifies the methods, tools and facilities used by the project team, the product assurance organization, the CCB, and other support groups for carrying out the project configuration management activities.

10.0   CONFIGURATION MANAGEMENT INVENTORY TYPES
This section specifies the project items to be configuration managed.

APPENDICES
This optional material can contain such things as the details of the product identification scheme to be used to label product parts, change control form templates, examples of filled-out change control forms, detailed library management procedures, emergency change control procedures, and relevant terms and abbreviations.

FIGURE 8–14   *Continued*

process diagram containing all the components that should be elaborated on in other elements (e.g., project planning, peer reviews, product assurance, CCB). With the possible exception of the CCB element, these other elements can be more along the lines of the couple-of-page variety, as in Figure 8–14. So, for example, several different couple-of-page elements each on a peer review procedure for a different type of peer review (e.g., document section peer review, code walkthrough). Such elements would fill in the details of the peer review component called out in the Software Systems Development Process element.

To conclude our discussion of this issue of ADPE constitution, we offer the following approach for planning a set of ADPE elements:

1. Step through the preceding discussion of the first two alternatives and attempt to decide whether the advantages in a given alternative far outweigh the disadvantages.

2. If they do, select that alternative.

3. If not, select Alternative (3). For this alternative, develop a strategy for deciding which elements should be of the Alternative (1) flavor and which should be of the Alternative (2) flavor. In your plan, remember to allow for crossovers—that is, elements that may start out from one alternative and evolve to the other. Also, allow for the number and type of elements you will need to change (for this purpose, you may need to publish an SEE plan update).

We now turn our attention to the following SEE planning issue, which we have already touched upon:

5. How frequently should an ADPE element be updated?

Figure 8–15 shows one key factor governing this issue—organization size. Organizational process improvement means, among other things, changing ADPE business practices. The trick is to figure out when a change is truly needed versus changing practices as a knee-jerk reaction to complaints from the ranks. Initial reactions to change brought about by implementation of an ADPE element may be resistance, plaintive cries for returning to the old way, and/or outright rebellion. Thus, some settling-in time is needed to observe whether the resistance, cries, and rebellion dissipate as people get acclimated to the new way of doing business. After this settling-in period, it is then helpful to examine what is not working in the "new" way and should be changed. The question then is, how long should the settling-in period be? As Figure 8–15 indicates, the period should be months for small projects/organizations (say, tens of people or less) and a year or longer for large projects/organizations (say, hundreds of people or more). The rationale underlying this rule of thumb is simply that it generally takes longer for a larger body of people to get in step than it does for a smaller body. For anyone with marching-band or chorus-line dancing experience, this observation should be self-evident.[2]

A corollary to the preceding comments is that as an element stabilizes, the intervals between updates can generally be shorter because, presumably, the changes during each subsequent update should be more localized. As a result, the time needed for the organization to get acclimated to the changes should be correspondingly reduced.

What should be done for large organizations whose project work extends only for a year or so? Should elements be updated more frequently than a year, or should the organization just try to use the practices as they are because the work that they will be applied to is going to disappear soon anyway? One way to handle this situation is to try to limit the scope of the changes so that the changes are easy to identify and relatively easy to get acclimated to. If a major overhaul of an element or elements is

---

[2]Of course, outright errors need to be corrected immediately—for example, spelling errors on a deliverable tracking form. If the organization is slow to correct errors, people may think that the organization is not serious about the element.

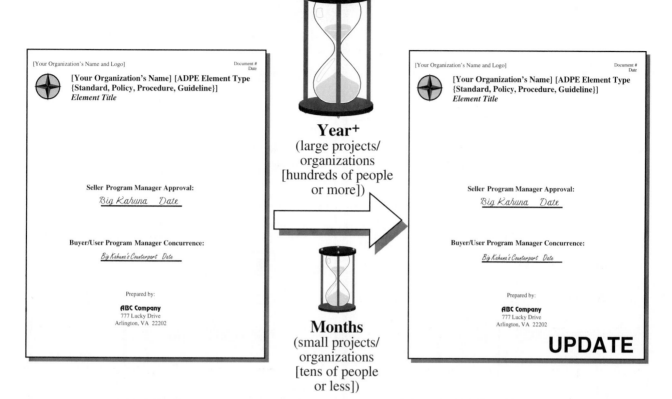

FIGURE 8–15 A key SEE implementation planning issue is the following: How frequently should an ADPE element be updated? The tradeoff here is getting people acclimated to a set of practices versus acclimating the practices to the people so that the practices (and thus the people) are useful. One factor governing ADPE element update frequency is the size of an organization. In general, the larger an organization, the longer the interval between element updates. The primary reason for this relationship is that the larger the organization, the longer it takes for a way of doing business to settle in—because it generally takes longer for a larger body of people to get in step than it does for a smaller body.

needed, then intensive training should be provided to staff in anticipation of the revised elements. This training should particularly stress the changes made to the "old" way.

In issue 4, we addressed factors bearing upon *ADPE* constitution. We now take a look at factors bearing on a related issue—namely, ADPE *element* constitution.

The issue is the following:

6. What amount of detail should be included in individual ADPE elements?

Constructing ADPE elements is generally an arduous task. Getting a feel for this "amount-of-detail" issue will help you plan ADPE element development pace.

Figure 8–16 depicts five "graphs" intended to show semiquantitative relationships among several variables bearing on ADPE element constitution. We explain each of these "graphs" in the paragraphs that follow. Each "graph" contains two "points" represented by ADPE element icons of two different

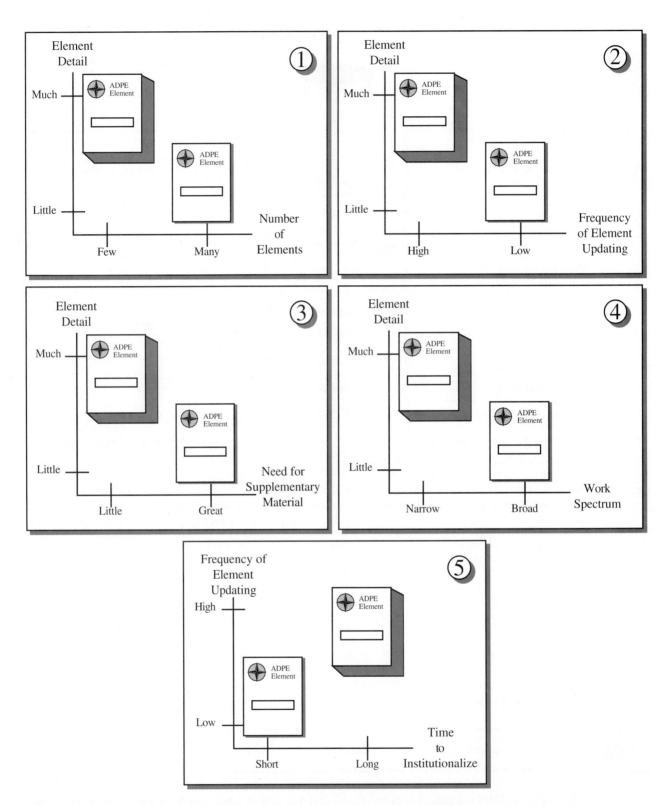

FIGURE 8–16   A key SEE implementation planning issue is the amount of detail to include in individual ADPE elements. Variables to be considered include the following: (1) number of elements, (2) frequency of element updating, (3) need for supplementary material, and (4) work spectrum. In addition, the variables generally depend upon other variables. For example, as shown in graph 5, the frequency of element updating depends upon the time to institutionalize the business practices contained in the element. For your organization, there may be other variables that you may need to consider regarding ADPE element detail.

thicknesses. Document thickness is intended to symbolize "amount of detail included in the ADPE element." This symbol should not be taken too literally. For example, by reducing the scope of a document, it is certainly possible to include a lot of detail in a small number of pages (as an extreme specific instance, you might have a single ADPE element that lists the specific steps for filling out a single change control form; such an element may consist of only a page or two). The point here is that the two document icons shown in each "graph" are intended to suggest the *range* of ADPE element size. In one organization, a five-page ADPE element on any topic may be a tome because, for example, everybody in the organization has so much software systems development experience that only the barest list of guidance statements is all that is needed to achieve consistent practice within the organization. In another organization, by contrast, five-page ADPE elements may raise more questions than they answer because, for example, the organization is new and has been put together with people from different environments who have achieved successful software systems development consistency in radically different ways.

With these above caveats, the five "graphs" shown in Figure 8–16 are intended to help you (1) visualize the tradeoffs among the variables and (2) identify other variables and associated tradeoffs that may be important for your organization. This visualization is, in turn, intended to help you figure out what may make sense for your organization regarding the amount of detail to include in your ADPE elements. We stress that the relationships depicted in the "graphs" are generalizations. For this reason, we put the word *graph* in quotes so that the relationships shown are not interpreted as rigorous mathematical dependencies. As with most generalizations, there are exceptions. The objective here is to help you with SEE implementation planning factors.

- **"Graph" 1 (Element Detail Versus Number of Elements).** The fewer the number of elements, the more detail an individual element needs. We discussed this relationship before when we addressed the issue of ADPE constitution. Here our perspective is that of the individual element. A real-world consideration regarding document thickness is that people are more likely to read a document consisting of just a few pages than one that has many more. This almost self-evident consideration should not be overlooked. A necessary (but not sufficient) condition for ADPE implementation is that the ADPE elements must be read—and, of course, understood. On the other hand, if an ADPE element consists of only a few pages but raises more questions than it answers, then subsequently produced few-page elements are likely to go unread. The name of the game here is to create elements that people will want to read because (1) the reading task is not onerous and (2) the elements will help them do their jobs.

- **"Graph" 2 (Element Detail Versus Frequency of Element Updating).** The more detail in an element, the more frequently it will have to be updated. In our discussion of issue 5, we addressed element update frequency from the point of view of organization size. Here, our focus is on element content. The dependency between element detail and element update frequency is a particular challenge when constructing ADPE elements that are procedures. Procedures are intended to provide specific instructions for accomplishing something. However, there reaches a point where the more specificity that is included, the shorter is the lifetime of the specific information included. For example, a procedure may contain a template for a cover letter to accompany a deliverable. If the template contained the specific name of the addressee and/or the name of the person signing the letter, then whenever the addressee and/or the person signing the letter changes, the element would need to be changed.

- **"Graph" 3 (Element Detail Versus Need for Supplementary Material).** The more detail in an element, the less need for supplementary material. The overall consideration here is how self-contained the ADPE should be. On the one hand, it is desirable to include in ADPE elements what the organization needs to achieve consistent software systems development success without burdening it with seeking out additional information. On the other hand, it is not practical to reproduce in the ADPE elements encyclopedic software engineering material. Balance is needed. One way to fill in details without expanding ADPE elements is to give short presentations on each ADPE element (say, one hour to a couple of hours for each element). These presentations will allow staff to relate the ADPE material to their own frame of reference, and clear up questions they may have about the material. Through such interaction, they may, for instance, annotate their ADPE elements, thereby tailoring them to their perspectives. For example, suppose your organization has an element that offers guidance on CCBs, and suppose that the element offers broad guidance on what should be documented at CCB meetings. In particular, suppose that the element contains the following CCB meeting documentation guidance:

> This documentation provides a visible trace of project activities that serves the threefold purpose of allowing (1) management intelligently to proceed with project accomplishment, (2) external auditors to verify the extent to which work was accomplished in accordance with contractual commitments, and (3) the organization to exploit lessons learned from work that has been accomplished to better perform work to be accomplished. This threefold purpose thus has a tactical component specific to project accomplishment, an after-the-fact component, and a strategic component aimed at improving overall organization operation.
>
> Documenting these meetings is simply good business practice. Experience overwhelmingly shows that memory is an unreliable source for deciding what to do next on a project and for deciding what may be applicable to another or a new project. It is particularly important to keep in mind the above stated threefold purpose of this documentation when deciding what makes sense to document. For the sake of expediency, it is often convenient to focus on the tactical component at the expense of the other two components. On the other hand, it is counterproductive to generate prodigious amounts of documentation to satisfy in particular the strategic component. It is thus necessary to strike a balance between these two extremes when deciding what to make a matter of record.

When the preceding guidance is briefed, attendees may have specific questions regarding what makes sense to document on their particular projects. For example, a particular project may involve the development of a software system whose failure may cause people to get injured or suffer large financial loss. When these project characteristics are brought up during the CCB element briefing, this guidance may be translated into the following requirement for that project (and for projects where the stakes are similar):

> The CCB minutes shall be a transcript of the entire meeting, with all conversation being made a matter of record.

Similarly, more extensive training, such as multiple-day seminars, can be used to supplement ADPE element content. For example, your organization may have an ADPE element on acceptance testing. To provide additional insight into acceptance testing mechanics and management (say, along the lines described in Chapter 5), your organization may want to offer a multiple-day seminar on these topics to ensure that the business practices in the testing element are consistently implemented. Other examples of supplementary source material include software engineering textbooks (e.g., on configuration management, peer reviews, project tracking) and industry standards (e.g., IEEE standard on software requirements specification). There are no hard-and-fast rules for deciding what to include in ADPE elements and what to point the reader to for additional insight. However, there is one overriding consideration—**if an element appears too bulky and/or the information included is not easy to assimilate, the element will likely be ignored.**

■ **"Graph" 4 (Element Detail Versus Work Spectrum).** There is an inverse correlation between the scope of an organization's work spectrum and the amount of detail incorporated into (some) ADPE elements. By "work spectrum scope" we mean the range of software systems development work that an organization performs. Examples of narrow-work-spectrum scope are the following:

  ■ Projects use information engineering (IE) in conjunction with a specific CASE tool. In this situation, ADPE elements can be IE specific and specific to the CASE tool used. For example, some CCB meetings may be labeled Joint Requirements Planning (JRP) sessions, and minutes-taking may be aided by the CASE tool. If it is desired to make the ADPE elements reasonably self-contained, then the elements can go into considerable detail regarding how IE is to be practiced within the organization. For example, a CCB element can include detailed procedures for conducting JRP sessions.

  ■ Projects use the same life cycle, and all products developed use the same suite of standards. In this situation, ADPE elements can be tied specifically to the life cycle and standards used, providing detailed guidance regarding product accomplishment during each life cycle stage. For example, suppose the life cycle contains a stage called "Requirements Definition" wherein a requirements specification is developed according to the organization's requirements specification standard. Then an ADPE element addressing software systems development practices can lay out steps for developing the requirements specification according to the standard—possibly going so far as to include (1) a complete requirements specification and (2) an explanation of how it is constructed.

- Projects develop all products according to the object-oriented paradigm. In this situation, ADPE elements can use object-oriented terminology (e.g., object, class, subclass, superclass, descendant, message, attribute, abstract data type, inheritance) and object-oriented product examples (e.g., object-oriented requirements and design specifications, where requirements and design are expressed in terms of real-world objects). Again, if it is desired to make the ADPE elements reasonably self-contained, then the elements can go into considerable detail regarding how object-oriented techniques are to be practiced within the organization (e.g., C++ coding standards).

By contrast, an example of broad-work-spectrum scope is the following:

- Projects that (1) do not necessarily include software systems development (e.g., a project that analyzes different ways to frame an information security policy), (2) use different life cycles, and (3) use different development approaches. In this situation, ADPE elements cannot detail specific life cycles. In Chapter 3, we described how to define a software systems development process into which can be plugged different life cycles. There we also described how the process could accommodate different development approaches (such as traditional software systems development and information engineering). We indicated that the process should contain activities such as peer reviews, independent product assurance, and technical editing. However, in an organization with a broad-work-spectrum scope, it may be counterproductive to, say, detail a specific procedure for conducting peer reviews. Rather, it may be necessary to include in an ADPE element several alternative peer review approaches along with some guidelines for selecting an approach to be applied to a project with certain characteristics. For example, the element might indicate that for projects with no more than, say, five people, undocumented peer reviews may be sufficient; on the other hand, the element might indicate that for projects involving the development of software-driven medical devices, all peer reviews must be documented in detail. It should be noted here that although the peer review element may not be detailed in terms of specifying the individual steps in conducting a peer review (because too many variations are possible as a result of the organization's broad work spectrum), the number of pages in the element may still be more than a few because the element has to address a number of different peer review approaches to accommodate different project needs. That is, because of the organization's broad-work-spectrum scope, ADPE elements have to replace "how-to-do-it" detail with a more broadly worded discussion of alternative applicable practices.

- **"Graph" 5 (Frequency of Element Updating Versus Time to Institutionalize).** This "graph" illustrates how the variables in the other "graphs" may themselves depend on other variables bearing on SEE implementation. "Graph" 5 has the interpretation that the lower the update frequency of an ADPE element, the shorter the time needed to institutionalize its practices. Conversely, the higher the update frequency of an ADPE element, the longer the time needed to institutionalize its practices. "Graph" 5 is intended to suggest how this correlation comes about—namely, as explained earlier, the less detailed an element, the less frequently it needs to be updated, and the shorter the time needed to institutionalize it (and conversely).

In concluding the discussion of this issue, we stress that the variables shown in Figure 8–16 may not be the only ones that you may need to consider regarding ADPE element detail. The preceding discussion is intended to illustrate in some detail (no pun intended) how to bring such variables into your SEE implementation planning picture.

We stated at the outset of this chapter that its focus is on the ADPE side of SEE implementation planning. However, we are not going to ignore totally the ADTE. We now briefly turn our attention to this SEE component. Again, as with all the issues discussed in this chapter, our purpose is to get you started planning your SEE.

7. How can you define a plan for an application development technology environment (ADTE) for your organization?

Figure 8–17 contains an annotated outline for defining a plan for establishing and evolving an ADTE. This plan could be made a part of the SEE implementation plan (e.g., as volume II, where volume I would address the ADPE).

The outline contains examples of entries that should appear in each of the five sections shown. The first three sections (Introduction, Objectives, Scope) are straightforward and are not discussed further. Regarding the remaining two sections (Policy, ADTE Components), the following comments are in order:

- The section on ADTE policy provides the plan's teeth. It establishes who within your organization and outsiders who support your organization are bound by the technology included in this plan. The policy is established to leverage employee skills within and across projects—and prevent dependency on gurus who may be part of a small community familiar with a particular technology. For example, if your organization's primary business is to develop management information systems for large corporations, the ADTE may limit the technology suite (i.e., hardware and software) to a set number of CASE tools running on a specified set of hardware platforms. As a result, your organization would have a large number of people who are trained on these tools and platforms, thereby avoiding dependence on a small community of "experts."

- The section on ADTE policy also delineates technology ground rules for the organization's customers. Of course, sellers cannot impose constraints on its customers. Technology ground rules need to be negotiated between the seller and customer. By defining such things as standard computer hardware/communications development suites, the plan limits the technology that a customer may want to bring to bear on work to be accomplished. To provide flexibility in this regard, your organization may want to include in this section a procedure for obtaining a waiver or deviation from the policy. In general, such waivers or deviations may require additional costs to be levied on the work to be performed—even if the customer provides the "nonstandard" technology. One source for these additional costs even under these circumstances is the need to train staff in the technology or to hire (higher-priced) consultants skilled in the technology.

- If there are no plan appendices, the section on ADTE components should contain itemized lists of hardware and software components (including acceptable version numbers). It should also show diagrams depicting standard hardware/communications configurations (including such things as memory sizes, mass storage capacities, and communications line transmission rates). If your organization intends to keep pace with upgrades to the technology components that make up your ADTE, you may want to relegate the technology component details to appendices (as indicated in Figure 8–17), particularly if these upgrades occur frequently. Then, when you are ready to upgrade your technology components, you may need only to update the appendices in the plan at regular intervals—for example, yearly for multiyear contracts or programs, and quarterly or semiannually for shorter arrangements.

Having discussed SEE implementation planning issues pertaining to SEE structure and substructure, we consider the following related issue before proceeding to other classes of issues:

> 8. How do you package ADPE elements and related items?

Many of us keep notebooks that contain information that we frequently need to access, such as phone numbers, addresses, and appointment dates and times. If the ADPE is to be similarly accessible, it should be packaged to facilitate access and use. We stress that, although good ADPE packaging will not guarantee ADPE element use, lack of good packaging will almost surely guarantee ADPE element nonuse.

Figure 8–18 illustrates one way to package ADPE elements and related items. It shows the contents of a three-ring binder,[3] a copy of which should be distributed to each member of your organization, with the following tabs to help organize the binder contents and facilitate information retrieval:

---

[3]Our use of the term "three-ring binder" in the subsequent discussion extends to electronic versions.

[Your Organization's Name and Logo]

Document #
Date

Plan for the [Your Organization's Name] Application Development Technology Environment (ADTE)

Document #
Date

1.0 INTRODUCTION

This section states the purpose of the plan, which is to establish a technology environment for your organization consisting of hardware (including communications components) and software development tools, and associated procedures for their use, required to develop applications. These tools include, depending on the business of your organization, such things as CASE tools, programming language compilers, local area network (LAN) application development tools, PC application development tools, database management systems, configuration management tools, and project management tools. This plan is intended for use by all your organization's staff members who are involved with developing applications.

2.0 OBJECTIVES

This section states the objectives of the plan. An example of such objectives would be the following:

- Define and describe the standard hardware, software, tools, and communications components that support application development in your organization.
- Establish standard components and identify procedures for their use where your customer does not have such standard components and procedures, and stipulate conformance to such standard components and procedures where your customer does have such standard components and procedures.

3.0 SCOPE

This section states the plan scope. An example scope statement might be the following: The components discussed in this plan include the standard hardware and software for the mainframe, minicomputer, Local Area Network (LAN), telecommunications, and personal computer (PC) environments used for development of applications within your organization.

4.0 POLICY

This section delineates the personnel associated with application development within your organization to which this plan applies (e.g., employees of your organization, contractors, subcontractors, consultants). This section should also address the policy concerning such things as customer-provided equipment and equipment acquired by a contractor that may not be part of your organization's equipment.

5.0 ADTE COMPONENTS

This section defines the hardware, software, communications components and associated procedures for their use that make up your organization's ADTE. For example, this section should specify LAN resources (e.g., file server hardware configuration, file server software configuration, network backup server, network monitoring and analysis tool, LAN printers, etc.)

APPENDICES

Appendices may be used to augment Section 5. For example, Section 5 might simply be a top-level discussion of the ADTE components. Then, appendices might contain the details. For example, if Section 5 states that the ADTE consists of a mainframe development environment and a LAN development environment, then separate appendices might detail the components of each of these environments.

FIGURE 8–17 An annotated outline for getting you started defining a plan for an application development technology environment (ADTE) for your organization.

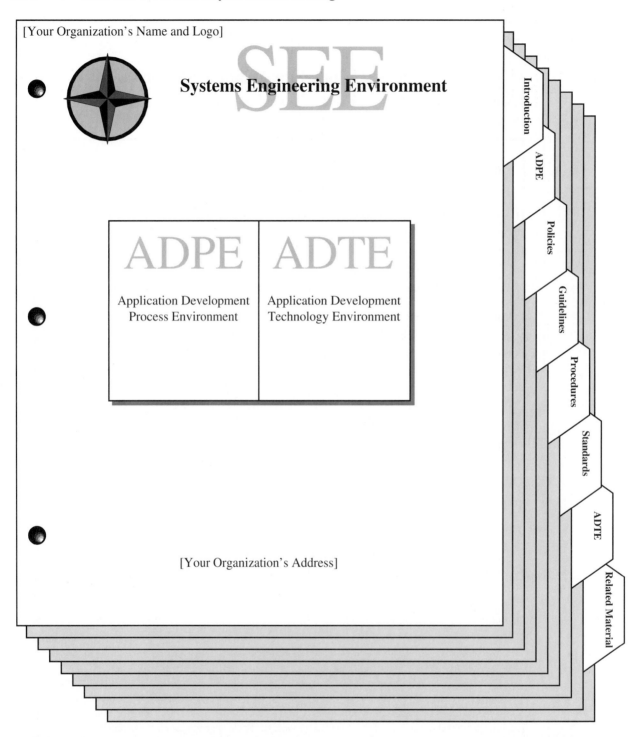

FIGURE 8–18 A good way to package your engineering environment is a binder containing your ADPE elements and material pertinent to your technology environment.

- **Introduction**. Behind this tab goes material that explains such things as your organization's mission and work spectrum, the purpose of the SEE, and the organization of the binder contents.

- **ADPE**. This tab begins the ADPE portion of the binder. The ADPE portion of the binder is organized according to the ADPE element taxonomy that you establish for your organization. In this book, we use the four-component taxonomy of "policy," "guideline," "procedure," and "standard." The ADPE tabs in Figure 8–18 reflect this taxonomy. If your organization chooses to establish a different ADPE taxonomy, then the number and names of ADPE tabs would correspondingly change.

- **Policies**. Behind this tab go your organization's ADPE policies. Other material pertaining to these policies can also be placed here, such as hard copy of briefings on ADPE policies.

- **Guidelines**. Behind this tab go your organization's ADPE guidelines. Other material pertaining to these guidelines can also be placed here, such as hard copy of briefings on ADPE guidelines.

- **Procedures**. Behind this tab go your organization's ADPE procedures. Other material pertaining to these procedures can also be placed here, such as hard copy of briefings on ADPE procedures.

- **Standards**. Behind this tab go your organization's ADPE standards. Other material pertaining to these standards can also be placed here, such as hard copy of briefings on ADPE standards.

- **ADTE**. This tab begins the ADTE portion of the binder. It can contain such things as your organization's ADTE plan, ADTE procedures that explain how to use various ADTE components such as workstations and CASE tools, and briefings on ADTE components.

- **Related Material**. This tab begins the portion of the binder that contains material that the binder recipient feels is pertinent to that person's work. Examples of such material are the SOWs and corresponding project plans that the person is working on. Other examples include articles from professional journals addressing topics bearing on the person's work (for instance, an article explaining how acceptance testing procedures can be constructed from requirements and design specifications developed using an object-oriented paradigm).

Your process engineering group (PEG) should provide every member of your organization with a copy of the binder. The PEG should be responsible for distributing updates to the binder contents. If you are a seller, you may want to provide binders to your customer.

One advantage of packaging ADPE elements and material pertinent to your technology environment in a three-ring binder is that it facilitates keeping this material current. For organizations of even modest size, where at least tens of copies of the binder need to be distributed and kept current, your SEE implementation plan should include a mechanism for distributing the binders and keeping its contents current. The plan should also include a task to cover binder preparation and the associated labor and material costs. In addition, the plan should address whether your organization wants to include your customers on the binder distribution and training list. Providing customers with the binders helps to achieve customer SEE buy-in (but does not guarantee it). In some cases, the customer may want to fund the binders. In these cases, the customer may want to place the customer organization's logo on the binder in addition to or instead of the seller organization's logo.

There are, of course, other ways to package the ADPE and related material. The packaging does not have to be hard copy. If, for example, your organization has personal computers that are networked, it may be desirable to place the material on the network for electronic access (and subsequent printing, if desired). In addition to, or instead of, providing copies of the material to each individual in your organization, you could mount the material on large poster boards or similar presentation devices and display them prominently in your organization's facilities. Whatever your packaging approach, your SEE implementation plan should address it and provide resources to make it happen.

In previous chapters, we did not say much about SEE implementation and organization size, preferring to address things that would be beneficial for organizations of any size to consider. We now turn our attention to the following SEE implementation planning issue regarding the ADPE and organization size:

> 9. How should ADPE implementation be handled if your organization is small? (Here, *small organization* means "an organization having only a few projects, each involving only a small number of people (say, ten at most) so that all involved parties frequently come into contact with one another.")

Figure 8–19 shows one compact way to address this issue. The ADPE is packaged into a single element. The figure gives an idea of how the element might be structured and what it might address. It thus gives specific suggestions for planning an SEE implementation approach built on a single ADPE element. The figure also offers a starting point for constructing such an element. The element begins with a section that states the purpose of the element and gives background on the organization's business. Each subsequent section addresses a topic that in larger organizations would be folded into a single element. The figure shows four such sections respectively addressing the following topics:

- Section 2—Project Planning

- Section 3—Software Systems Development Process

- Section 4—Change Control Board (CCB)

- Section 5—Product Development Process Measurement

These topics were selected on the basis of some of the considerations examined in previously discussed issues. For your organization, the list may need to be augmented, reduced, or otherwise modified. The figure also suggests that an appendix to the element can be used to define an approach to updating the document for purposes of improving the organization's business practices.

Figure 8–19 shows the element cast as a policy. This approach would be appropriate for a small organization whose members have strong software engineering backgrounds. In this situation, high-level statements regarding the organization's way of doing business may be sufficient. These statements would provide the basis for consistency; the staff experience would carry these statements through to the "how-to-do-it." For example, Section 4 (CCB) might simply state the following regarding the policy for CCB minutes:

> At a minimum, the following information shall be recorded:
>
> 1. Decisions (affecting project deliverables, schedule, or resources) made
>
> 2. Action items assigned
>
> 3. Issues discussed
>
> The CCB minutes format is left to the discretion of each project.

On the other hand, in a less experienced organization, it may be appropriate to cast the element as a guideline. The guideline would contain more specifics than policy-level statements such as the example given for CCB minutes. For example, in a guideline, the policy statement regarding CCB minutes might be replaced by guidance such as the following:

> All CCB meetings will be documented. Figure 2 shows the information to be recorded and the format for recording this information.

In this example, Figure 2 would be a template for CCB minutes (structured, for instance, along the lines of the CCB minutes examples given in Chapter 4).

[Your Organization's Name and Logo]

Document #
Date

[Your Organization's Name] Policy
Application Development Process Environment (ADPE)

Document #
Date

1.0 PURPOSE AND BACKGROUND

This section states the purpose of the policy. This purpose is to define the application development process environment (ADPE) for your organization. This section should give background regarding your organization's software systems development challenges, including your customers' sensitivity to the need for engineering discipline. This section should also stress how the smallness of your organization has led to the approach of packaging the ADPE into a single element.

2.0 PROJECT PLANNING

This section establishes your organization's project planning policy. Use the Chapter 2 nuggets to help you write this section. We suggest that you consider the following at a minimum: (1) the project organizational structure of management, development, and product assurance, (2) SOW risk assessment tied to this structure to allocate resources to the project, (3) a change control board (CCB) to focus project activity, and (4) a life cycle to provide the context for the work to be accomplished.

3.0 SOFTWARE SYSTEMS DEVELOPMENT PROCESS

This section establishes your organization's policy regarding software product development. Use the Chapter 3 nuggets to help you write this section. We suggest that you include at least a top-level process diagram showing the major activities in the process (e.g., peer review, independent product assurance [document audits, acceptance testing], CCB).

4.0 CHANGE CONTROL BOARD (CCB)

This section establishes your organization's policy regarding CCBs. Use the Chapter 4 nuggets to help you write this section.

5.0 PRODUCT DEVELOPMENT PROCESS MEASUREMENT

This section establishes your organization's policy regarding what is to be measured during product development. Use the Chapter 6 nuggets to help you write this section. We suggest that you focus on just a handful of quantities that will aid both seller and customer management in determining whether the development process is yielding products with integrity.

APPENDIX

You may wish to include in an appendix your organizational responsibilities regarding the development, review, approval, promulgation, and improvement of this document. For this purpose, you may want to use the general approach for developing and improving ADPE elements discussed in Chapter 7.

FIGURE 8–19 In a small organization, it may not be necessary (or practical) to detail the software systems development process via a set of ADPE elements. Under such circumstances, it may be preferable to package the ADPE into a single element. The figure offers a starting point for this approach.

Earlier we discussed ADPE element phasing. This notion can also be applied to the single-element ADPE. In this case, one section would be written and promulgated, with the other sections being shown as TBD (to be determined). For example, for the structure shown in Figure 8–19, Section 3 (Software Systems Development Process), might be promulgated first (along with Section 1 [Purpose and Background]). After a settling-in period, Section 2 (Project Planning) or Section 4 (CCB) might be promulgated next. With this promulgation order, Section 3 would have top-level information regarding the entire process (including project planning and the CCB). Project planning and CCB experience gained from the promulgated Section 3 would then be fed into the subsequently developed Section 2 (Project Planning) and Section 4 (CCB)—along with possible updates to Section 3.

The approach shown in Figure 8–19 also allows for the ADPE to grow straightforwardly as the organization grows. The single-element ADPE shown in the figure is rooted in the assumption that, in small organizations, all the organization's individuals frequently come in contact with one another. Consequently, there is less need to detail business practices in writing. These details (e.g., lessons learned) can be communicated orally through the frequent contact of the organization's individuals. As the organization grows, it will be more difficult for everybody to maintain frequent contact with one another. It will then become necessary to commit more and more of the lessons learned to writing to keep everybody in the loop. It may then become necessary to break the individual sections in Figure 8–19 into separate elements as the size of each section grows to incorporate these lessons learned. Thus, the single-element ADPE can be viewed as establishing the structure for a multiple-element ADPE.

By slightly modifying the preceding argument, a case can be made for using a single-element ADPE as a starting point for an ADPE in organizations of any size. Giving the organization a version of the "entire" ADPE early, may facilitate process institutionalization. The single-element ADPE will generally lack considerable detail when it is first promulgated. In large organizations, this lack of detail may at first lead to divergent practices. However, exposing the organization to the "entire" ADPE early may expedite getting a better fix on which lessons learned to incorporate either across the board or in separate sections. To illustrate this point, consider the following example:

> Suppose Section 3 in Figure 8–19 mandates peer reviews as part of the software systems development process, but offers no guidance on how peer reviews are to be conducted. Suppose further that the element in Figure 8–19 had a section called Peer Reviews that was marked as TBD when the element was first promulgated. Then, the organization would understand (or could be told in writing) that, initially, projects were free to conduct peer reviews however they saw fit. Then, after six months, for instance, the lessons learned from the various ways peer reviews were conducted could then be consolidated and folded into the section on peer reviews. Eventually, as lessons learned are accumulated across all the sections in the element, it may become desirable to break the sections into separate elements.

To summarize the preceding discussion, Figure 8–19 shows a way to plan for developing an ADPE for a small organization. The figure can also be viewed as phase 1 of a mutliphased plan for evolving an ADPE towards separate elements for organizations of any size.

We now turn our attention to an issue arising when an organization's resources are stretched to their limits. Specifically, what can be done when an organization (1) desires to move toward greater software systems development consistency but (2) has extremely limited resources to set up standard business practices through an SEE? To address this question, we consider the following issue:

> 10. What is an austere SEE implementation approach?

Figure 8–20 shows a combination of six candidate ADPE elements and practices for such an approach. They are arranged in the order that they should be implemented. We stress that this order is worthwhile

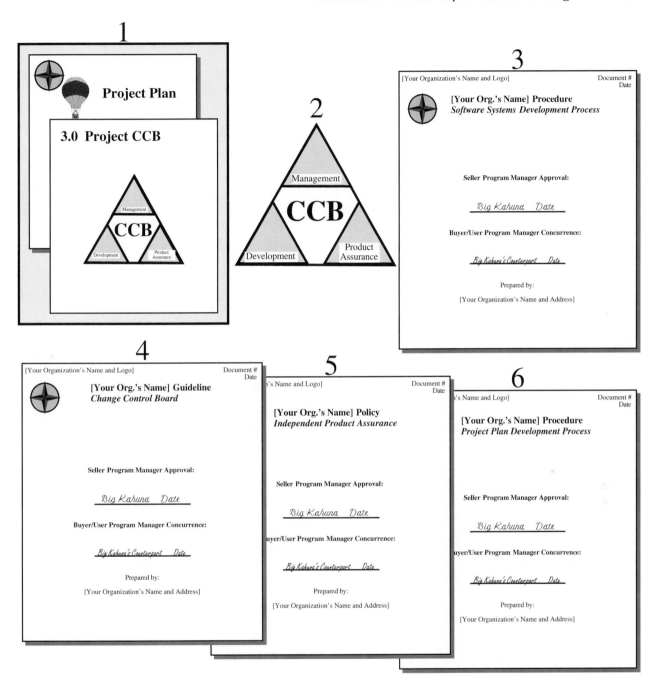

FIGURE 8–20 What is an austere SEE implementation approach? The figure shows a combination of ADPE elements and practices to consider for such an approach.

considering for *any* SEE implementation approach. We also stress that the order shown also provides a strategy for increasing austerity—namely, remove the higher numbered items first (that is, start by removing the project planning ADPE element, etc.).

1. **Project Planning Practice**. Project planning should be the first practice instituted—even before an ADPE element for this activity is formally developed. The project plan and a process for developing the plan are needed so that project members will have a documented, risk-reduced approach for starting project work. You can institute a project planning practice by using the ideas in Chapter 2. In particular, you can use the project plan outline given there as a starting point for writing project plans. You can perform risk analysis based on the ideas in that chapter to allocate resources to the management, development, and product assurance disciplines. You can plug a CCB into the project plan to focus project activity. You can transmit project planning and CCB practices to project staff via a briefing put together from ideas introduced in Chapter 2 and Chapter 4.

2. **CCB Practice**. This practice goes hand-in-hand with the first practice. The project plan can be used to define how the project CCB is to be conducted and what should be captured in CCB minutes. Figure 8–20 symbolizes these CCB practices by showing the CCB triangle icon embedded in the project plan section called "Project CCB." Experience gained from these project CCBs can be folded into the subsequently developed CCB ADPE element (shown as item 4 in Figure 8–20).

3. **Software Systems Development Process ADPE Element**. This element should be the first element developed. In Figure 8–20, the element is labelled "procedure"; in Chapter 3, we labelled the element "policy." As with other elements, the label used can have political and content overtones. "Policy" in some organizations may carry a more authoritative ring than "procedure" (or "guideline" or "standard"). In an austere SEE implementation approach, it may be desirable to label the element "procedure" and include details for each process component. By definition, an austere SEE implementation approach has only a small number of ADPE elements. It may therefore be necessary to make the few elements included more detailed than would be the case in an SEE with more elements. The earlier discussion of the issue on element detail should be revisited to help you determine how much detail to plan to include.

4. **Change Control Board (CCB) ADPE Element**. This element should be the second one developed. At a minimum, this element should spell out (1) who should attend CCB meetings, (2) what should be recorded at CCB meetings, (3) who should chair CCB meetings, and (4) what should be the CCB voting mechanism.

5. **Independent Product Assurance ADPE Element**. Throughout this book, we have explained the risk-reduction purpose and role of the independent product assurance disciplines. However, in an austere SEE implementation approach, independent product assurance may have to be limited to the role of process quality assurance (in which case, the element should be retitled to reflect this scope). In this capacity, independent product assurance would check that products are being developed in accordance with the organization's process as documented in the element shown as item 3 in Figure 8–20. Other activities that we have associated with an independent product assurance organization (i.e., product quality assurance, verification & validation, acceptance testing, and configuration management) would need to be performed by the product developers. If resources permit, it would be desirable to address in the ADPE element all product assurance activities—not just the ones performed by a group independent from the product developers. Chapter 5 provides a starting point for determining the scope of the element.

6. **Project Plan Development Process ADPE Element**. This element would commit to writing the lessons learned from carrying out the practice shown as item 1 in Figure 8–20. We recommend, as a minimum, that a project plan template be constructed to provide specific planning guidance.

To this point, we considered SEE implementation planning issues primarily bearing upon ADPE format and content. We now turn our attention to SEE implementation planning issues bearing upon applying the ADPE element business practices. The first such issue we consider deals with leveraging staff experience to bring about ADPE element institutionalization. The issue is the following:

> 11. How can mentoring and coaching be leveraged to facilitate implementation of ADPE practices?

Figure 8–21 states the purpose of "mentoring" and "coaching." These purpose statements are taken from the Software Engineering Institute's People Capability Maturity Model[SM] (P-CMM[SM]). The following discussion of this issue is adapted in part from this reference (the figure gives the complete reference—the following paragaphs give the page citations to this reference).

Before examining this issue, it is helpful to set context by stating the strategic objectives of the P-CMM, which are the following (p. xx):

- Improve the capability of software organizations by increasing the capability of their workforce.

- Ensure that software development capability is an attribute of the organization rather than of a few individuals.

- Align the motivation of individuals with that of the organization.

- Retain human assets (i.e., people with critical knowledge and skills) within the organization.

Earlier we stated that reading ADPE elements is a necessary but not sufficient condition for institutionalizing ADPE practices. How, in fact, do these practices catch on and become ingrained in the organization's way of doing business? The answers to this question are complex. However, one thing is clear from everyday experience. People mature by learning from the experience of others (sometimes negatively and sometimes positively). Mentoring and coaching are two primary means by which people learn from the experience of others. We now examine the purpose statements in Figure 8–21 to gain insight into how mentoring and coaching can be leveraged to facilitate implementation of ADPE practices. This insight is intended to help you incorporate a mentoring and coaching program into your SEE implementation plan. Since the aim here is to *leverage* mentoring and coaching, these activities should be planned—as opposed to being conducted primarily in ad hoc fashion.

One dictionary definition of *mentor* is "a trusted counselor or guide."[4] The underlying notion here is that of a personal relationship between the more experienced individual and the less experienced individual. The P-CMM extends this notion of personal relationship to groups—that is, the experienced individual can establish a personal relationship with a group. Following the words of Figure 8–21, possible outcomes of this personal relationship are skill and knowledge development, improved performance, and ability to handle difficult situations. Throughout this book, we talked about "prescriptive application" of ADPE practices—that is, applying these practices in a manner that makes sense within the context of a given project. Mentoring is a key way of passing know-how down the organizational chain to make prescriptive application happen. For example, a new project manager tasked with implementing a project plan can greatly benefit from mentoring by the manager's supervisor. The supervisor can work with the project manager to help the manager anticipate such things as schedule conflicts and resource shortfalls. For instance, the supervisor can advise the project manager to get early visibility into document development by calling first for an outline, then an annotated outline, and then a draft of the document.

How do you incorporate a mentoring program into your SEE implementation plan? Here are some ideas taken from the P-CMM to get your thinking started in this area (p. L4-1):

---

[4]*Webster's Ninth New Collegiate Dictionary* (Springfield, MA: Merriam-Webster, Inc., 1984).

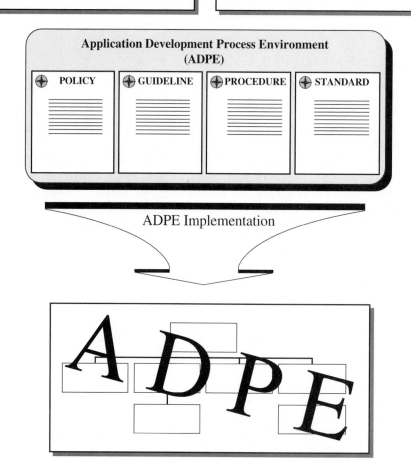

Mentoring

Purpose: Use the experience of individuals within the organization to provide *personal support and guidance* to other individuals or groups. This guidance can involve developing knowledge skills, improving performance, handling difficult situations, and making career decisions.

Experienced Individual

Coaching

Purpose: Provide *expert assistance* to enhance the performance of individuals or teams. Coaches engage in close relationships with individuals or teams to guide development of skills that improve performance.

Expert

Application Development Process Environment (ADPE)

POLICY   GUIDELINE   PROCEDURE   STANDARD

ADPE Implementation

Reference: B. Curtis, W. E. Hefley, and S. Miller, "People Capability Maturity Model^{SM}," Software Engineering Institute and Carnegie Mellon University Technical Report CMU/SEI-95-MM-02 (September 1995).

FIGURE 8–21   SEE implementation planning needs to account for mentoring and coaching. Through mentoring and coaching, how to implement ADPE practices can be transmitted from more experienced staff to less experienced staff. The key point here is that, to leverage their organizational impact, this mentoring and coaching should be planned.

Mentoring involves setting objectives for a mentoring program, designing mentoring activities to achieve these objectives, selecting and training appropriate mentors, assigning mentors to individuals or groups, establishing mentoring relationships, and evaluating the effectiveness of the program.

The organization develops one or more sets of objectives for the mentoring program. Appropriate types of mentoring relationships are designed for differing mentoring objectives within the program. Criteria are developed for selecting mentors and those chosen are trained for their assignments. Individuals or groups being mentored are provided orientation on how they can best take advantage of a mentoring relationship. Criteria are developed for assigning mentors to individuals or groups. The mentor and the individual or group being mentored establish agreements on how their relationship will be conducted. Mentors meet periodically and occasionally evaluate whether they are achieving their objectives. Advice is available to improve the effectiveness of the mentoring relationship. The mentoring program is evaluated against its objectives to identify needed improvements.

In terms of ADPE implementation and institutionalization, these ideas translate into pairing experienced individuals with other individuals and groups organizationwide to propagate the skills for carrying through on ADPE practices.

Regarding coaching, the P-CMM views it as a more focused and quantitative form of counseling than mentoring.[5] As Figure 8–21 indicates, the purpose of coaching is to provide *expert* assistance to enhance the performance of individuals or *teams*. We italicized "expert" and "teams" to stress this difference between mentoring and coaching in the P-CMM. The mentor is characterized as merely being "experienced"; the coach, on the other hand, is termed an "expert." The mentor works with individuals or groups; the coach works with individuals or teams. Here, the notion of "team," as distinct from "group," suggests that the coach is applying expertise to make the talent of the team greater than the sum of the talents of the individuals on the team. Coaches work with teams to improve their *team-based competencies* and performance. This synergy is achieved through the use of quantitative data. Just as a baseball batting coach analyzes quantitative data on pitchers who play for opposing teams to prepare the hitters to hit better against the competition, so too does the software coach analyze quantitative data on team performance to analyze skills to help the team set measurable goals for improving these skills.[6] In the P-CMM, mentoring can be thought of as a less refined form of coaching because the use of quantitative data is not mandated.

How do you incorporate a coaching program into your SEE implementation plan? Just as we did previously for mentoring, we appeal to the P-CMM for the following ideas to get your thinking started in this area (p. L5-13):

Coaching involves selecting appropriate coaches, analyzing data on personal or team performance, providing guidance on methods for improving performance, and evaluating progress towards goals for improving performance.

Coaching opportunities are pursued where coaching can provide a justifiable improvement to individual or team performance. Criteria are developed for selecting coaches. Coaches are trained in coaching skills and are assigned to an individual or team according to their expertise. Individuals or teams are provided orientation on how to best use a coach to improve performance. Coaches use data on individual or team performance to analyze skills, and they help individuals or teams set measurable goals for improving skills and performance. Coaches also track performance continuously and provide specific guidance on improving skills and performance. Individuals or teams practice the skills they are working on with the coach. Coaches provide or make inputs to appropriate rewards for improvement. Coaching activities are evaluated and improvements are made.

In terms of ADPE implementation and institutionalization, these ideas translate into pairing experts with individuals and teams organizationwide to propagate and leverage the skills for carrying though

---

[5]Some dictionaries, such as the one previously cited, list "coach" as a synonym for "mentor".

[6]Example quantitative measures are delineated in Chapter 6 in Table 6–1. For example, to improve a team's peer review skills, the coach might look at the average number of peer reviews needed by a team to produce deliverables that are accepted by the customer.

on ADPE practices. For example, a coach can work with project peer review teams to cut down on the average length of time to conduct a peer review. A coach can help realize this team performance improvement by analyzing statistics compiled on how long it takes to get through various parts of a peer review. It may turn out, for instance, that the coach uncovers through this analysis that peer review teams are spending time on trying to find solutions to discrepancies uncovered. The coach can then offer guidance to peer review teams on how to stay out of the problem-solving mode and how to stick to the classical peer review objective of giving visibility to discrepancies.

In Chapter 7, we addressed human issues bearing on bringing about organizational cultural change through SEE implementation. For purposes of planning strategies for bringing about this cultural change, we can think of SEE implementation to be like the challenges facing a mountain climber planning a way to the mountaintop. If the mountain is new to the climber, the way up will be uncertain. This uncertainty translates into potential obstacles to reaching the top. A good plan, however, can help reduce this uncertainty, thereby increasing the likelihood of reaching the top.

Figure 8–22 elaborates on this mountain-climbing analogy. The SEE implementation planning issue here is the following:

12. What strategies can be adopted to meet the cultural change challenges posed by SEE implementation?

The figure shows four such challenges and one or more strategies for meeting each challenge. The strategies shown are intended to help you build a framework for carrying through on SEE implementation. Preceding chapters offer you "how-to-do-it" guidance for constructing these strategies. The list of challenges and strategies in Figure 8–22 is not comprehensive—but these items should be considered as part of any list that you construct. To give you ideas for constructing such a list, we discuss in detail the challenges and strategies shown in the figure.

Some of these challenges may not apply to your organization, and your organization may have challenges not listed. The key point here is that your implementation plan should include such challenges and propose strategies for meeting the challenges. The perspective shown is the seller's. However, a customer organization should be prepared to support the seller in meeting these challenges so that SEE implementation becomes a win-win situation for both the seller and the customer.

Challenge: The customer does not want independent product assurance—how can this attitude be turned around?

In environments where the notion of independent product assurance is new, the customer may view this activity as an unnecessary added cost to doing business. Even in environments where the notion is not new, the customer may be reluctant because of prior negative experience (e.g., receiving a system that had been tested—at considerable cost—but that did not work in accordance with expectations).

Strategy to Meet Challenge: Show how each of the product assurance functions (QA, V&V, T&E, CM, and/or however you choose to define product assurance functions) reduces project risk, thereby adding value to the customer's product and to the product development process.

It is really not possible to *prove* the efficacy of product assurance. To do so would require doing the same software systems development project twice—once with and once without product assurance—

SEE Implementation Challenge	Strategy to Meet Challenge
The customer does not want independent product assurance—how can this attitude be turned around?	Show how each of the product assurance functions (QA, V&V, T&E, and CM) reduces project risk thereby adding value to the customer's product and to the product development process.
The seller staff and/or the customer do/does not want to follow the ADPE business way—how can this attitude be turned around?	Show how documented business practices that are followed remove dependence on the individual, thereby (1) reducing schedule risk and (2) affording the individual opportunity to grow within the organization. *[Soft Sell]* Make ADPE compliance part of each employee's performance review and reward compliance. *[Hard Sell]* Get all managers on board with the ADPE way by some combination of the preceding two strategies or by some other means, such as corporate directives and/or hiring policies. **[This strategy is mandatory.]** Give periodic briefings to the seller staff on ADPE element content before and after promulgation. After promulgation, try to make customer attendance a requirement. Establish a training program that offers the staff the opportunity to learn or augment their understanding of the engineering principles underlying the ADPE.
The seller staff will find ways to work around the ADPE way—how can this attitude be turned around or, where appropriate, be used to incorporate improvements into the ADPE way?	Show how documented business practices that are followed remove dependence on the individual, thereby affording the individual the opportunity to grow within the organization. Reward staff who follow the ADPE way and suggest improvements to it. Make the rewards part of a ceremony attended by the entire organization.
The customer will try to circumvent the seller management chain to "expedite" the incorporation of product changes—how can this attitude be turned around?	Make the CCB the focal point for customer/seller interaction. Train seller staff in the need to document interactions with the customer bearing on project work and to inform seller management of such interactions.

FIGURE 8–22   We can think of SEE implementation to be like the challenges facing a mountain climber planning a way to the mountaintop. The figure lists some of these challenges and suggests a strategy or strategies to meet each challenge.

in such a way that the only difference between the two projects is the application of product assurance. However, one way to argue is to show the value added of applying product assurance to products.

How do you show value added? One way is to measure cost savings by estimating the cost of **not** doing rework of a product after it is delivered. This estimate can be based on estimating the cost of doing postdelivery rework of a product as defined by discrepancies that product assurance discovers prior to delivery. It is generally acknowledged that it is less costly to fix discrepancies while a product is under development than it is after delivery. An applicable analogy here that it is easier, and thus less costly, to fix problems in a house while it is under construction than after it has been built. Admittedly, it may take longer to finish the house under such circumstances. However, the inconvenience to the homeowner and the added cost of fixing the problems after the homeowner has moved in are generally worthwhile avoiding.

A powerful argument that can be constructed to show the value added of product assurance is to compile statistics on the percentage of products that are accepted as delivered (i.e., that do not require rework). If most delivered products fall into this category and if product assurance is part of your product development process, then product assurance must add value (as well as the other activities in the process).

Of all the product assurance functions discussed in this book, acceptance testing is perhaps the easiest to show value added. As we explained in previous chapters, the value added of applying this function begins long before the acceptance test procedures themselves are executed. Value is added beginning with requirements analysis as part of requirements specification development. During this analysis activity, product assurance adds value by raising questions regarding the testability of requirements. If a requirement is not testable, then it is not a requirement because its presence or absence in the system being developed cannot be demonstrated.

Considerable value can be added during design specification development. During this development activity, it is desirable for product assurance to be developing test procedures. As we explained in Chapter 5, the heart of test procedure development is the nailing down of expected results—that is, being able to specify in a test procedure what a tester should see as a result of performing a specific action. This information should come from design and requirements specifications. If, while constructing test procedures, product assurance is unable to find such information, by raising questions regarding this information *while the design specifications are under development*, product assurance adds value. The value added, as we just argued, is that it is easier, and thus less costly, to incorporate such missing information into the design specification while it is under development than it would be after the specification is delivered. Furthermore, uncovering such information during design specification development, rather than after coding begins, can add considerable value by heading off costly recoding activity.

The interaction between the product development organization and the product assurance organization during requirements and design specification development just described is often not visible to software customers. We characterize this interaction (as well as the analogous interactions during coding and during other product development activities) by saying that product assurance acts as a forcing function on the software systems development process. This synergism, when applied consistently, can be of inestimable value.

Regarding this synergism, we need to stress another point. The product assurance organization cannot be constituted as an afterthought. It must be staffed with good people (that is, people well versed in the art of questioning and adept at applying this art with a benevolent attitude). Otherwise, the product assurance activity will not add value—and, in fact, may be counterproductive.

To summarize the preceding arguments, we stress that the application of product assurance does indeed cost time and money. First, it takes product assurance time to review a product, and it costs money for product assurance to perform this review. Second, addressing discrepancies that product assurance uncovers during product development adds time to the product development cycle, and it adds cost—namely, the labor to fix the discrepancies. And, indeed, addressing these discrepancies is product rework. However—and this "however" lies at the heart of the challenge under discussion—the time and money spent doing this rework while the product is under development is generally less than the time and money that would have to be spent at some later point in the project. *And that differential is the value added.*

Challenge: The seller staff and/or the customer do/does not want to follow the ADPE business way—how can this attitude be turned around?

Adopting the ADPE business practices compels almost everybody in the organization to change the way they do their jobs. Many people naturally resist change. It is therefore almost a certainty that you will encounter some resistance when you move ahead with SEE implementation. Your SEE implementation plan must include strategies for softening this resistance and creating win-win situations. We will discuss five strategies for softening resistance and creating win-win situations. These strategies are intended to spark your thinking for devising strategies appropriate to your organization. However, we do stipulate that one strategy is mandatory. There is no significance to the order of the strategies.

Strategy 1 to Meet Challenge: Show how documented business practices that are followed remove dependence on the individual, thereby (1) reducing schedule risk and (2) affording the individual opportunity to grow within the organization. *(Soft Sell)*

Let us first consider how documented business practices that are followed remove dependence on the individual, thereby reducing schedule risk. If indeed documented business practices remove dependence on the individual, then if an individual does not happen to be in the office for one or more days (for whatever reasons), others in the organization can generally pick up the slack. The net result is that the schedule should not be impacted. Of course, we are not arguing here that the individual who is out is not needed. Clearly, that individual cannot be out indefinitely because it is unreasonable to expect that other individuals can continue to do their jobs as well as somebody else's job.

What we are saying is that tasks do not need to be put on hold—thereby possibly impacting other tasks—because a particular individual is not in the office. In fact, if it is not feasible to have multiple coverage for highly specialized activities, truly robust business practices will have workarounds or alternative paths so that delays in highly specialized activities occasioned by the temporary absence of one or more individuals do not impact accomplishment of other activities. For example, if a code walkthrough has to be put on hold for a day or two because the coder is not in and if the code needs to be integrated with other code modules that are already completed, it may be possible still to integrate the incomplete code module with the other modules.

Suppose the organizational software systems development process calls for unit development folders, with each folder containing information on the development status of a particular module. This information may make it possible for others in the organization to proceed with integration testing because they would have insight into how the incomplete module might behave when integrated with the other modules. In the extreme, this information could be used to replace the incomplete module with a stub that simply acts as a pass-through for testing purposes. The key point here is that the organizational process affords others in the organization visibility into the missing individual's work, so that project work can proceed to some extent.

We now examine item (2) in the strategy statement—i.e., "documented business practices that are followed remove dependence on the individual, thereby affording the individual opportunity to grow within the organization." This strategy involves some subtle arguments that we now explore. For this purpose, we consider Figure 8–23.

The figure stresses that SEE implementation seeks to establish organizationwide *documented* business practices that, *when followed*, do not hold individuals captive to particular positions. Success-

3 **Perception—A stable organization provides me professional mobility.**

Unless an organization has *documented* practices *and uses them* (i.e., a mature organizational process), the way the organization does business will depend on the specific know-how of individuals. When those individuals are not in the office, doing business often becomes an exercise in improvisation. When those individuals permanently leave the organization, the replacement individuals will generally have difficulty getting acclimated to the idiosyncrasies of their coworkers. A key to successful SEE implementation of people-independent practices is to demonstrate that such practices foster professional mobility.

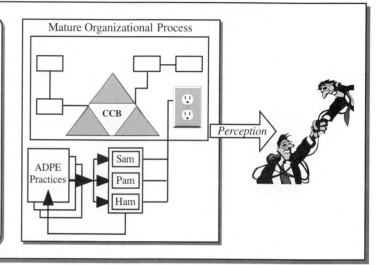

2 **Perception—A restrictive organization manipulates me.**

Some people view an organization's attempts to establish a documented process as a means to manipulate them and make them less valuable to the organization.

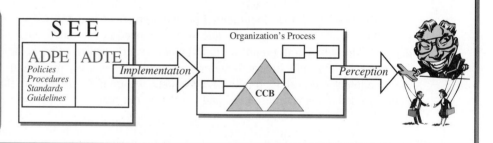

1 **Perception—A cowboy organization provides me job security.**

The reality is that in many organizations people follow some (generally undocumented) process that they and their associates have become accustomed to as they work together.

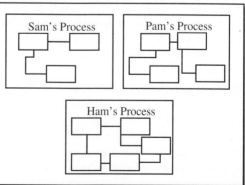

FIGURE 8–23 A key objective of SEE implementation is to establish organizationwide business practices that do not strongly depend on particular individuals for their successful accomplishment. Good people are certainly needed to achieve successful software systems development. Initially, people may have concerns and apprehensions about implementing refined or new business practices. Part of SEE implementation involves evolving an individual's perception of what this implementation means. The figure shows how an individual's perception may evolve as an organization matures.

ful software systems development requires good people—but without documented business practices that are followed, successful software systems development becomes problematic, even with good people. That is, *consistent* success is uncertain even with good people. Furthermore, these documented business practices provide an environment that encourages career growth.

We now step through the three parts of Figure 8–23 to see how career growth is a natural outcome of these documented business practices. Each part represents how an individual *perceives* an organization's impact upon his or her job. Remember, perception and reality may be two totally different things. For example, an individual may *perceive* that the organization's way of doing business reduces his or her flexibility of performing day-to-day activities. The *reality* may be that the organization's way of doing business fosters flexibility by empowering the individual to apply prescriptively the organization's business practices.

The following discussion is also intended to bring to the fore some of the concerns and apprehensions that people may have when faced with SEE implementation—so that you can plan to diminish these concerns and apprehensions.

1. Perception: A cowboy organization (i.e., where everybody does his or her own thing) provides me job security.

   People follow some (generally undocumented) process that they and their associates have become accustomed to as they work together. Sam, Pam, and Ham each has his or her own way of doing things. Amalgamated processes emerge as these and other individuals become acclimated to one another. That is, Sam and Ham develop a way of working together, Sam and Pam develop a way of working together (which, for the same type of work, may differ from the way Sam and Ham work together), etc. The processes emerge as a result of many factors including the following:

   - The prior experience of the individuals working in that corporate environment or in some other corporate environment (e.g., people who come from a corporate environment where engineering discipline was not even an afterthought will interact differently from people who come from a corporate environment where testing that used documented test procedures was necessary before a system could be released to a customer)

   - The personalities of the individuals (e.g., competitive individuals will interact differently from passive individuals)

   - The reward system (e.g., a corporate environment that rewards on-time product delivery over everything else will generally give rise to a process different from one that is used in a corporate environment that rewards error-free computer code over everything else).

   Factors such as these may foster an individual's perception that he or she has job security because he or she is the only one who knows how to perform certain tasks. This perception generally gives rise to resistance to implementing another way of doing business—such as the ADPE business way.

2. Perception: A restrictive organization (i.e., where the organization tells me how to do my job) manipulates me.

   Resistance to the ADPE business way arises for another reason. Some people view an organization's attempt to establish a documented process that all must conform to as a means to (1) manipulate them and (2) make them less valuable to the organization. This view apparently has its roots in the perception that if the organization specifies how individuals are to do their jobs, then the individual is easily replaced. It is natural for people to want to distinguish themselves from others. What is often misunderstood is that being a distinguishable member of an organization is not incompatible with following the organization's business way. The compatibility arises from the fact that each individual is responsible for applying the business way in a manner that makes sense for the situation at hand. In previous chapters, we labeled this mode of application as "prescriptive application." Applying the ADPE way is *not* a rote exercise of moving down a list of steps to be performed.

3. Perception: A stable organization (i.e., where the organization does not hold me captive to my job) provides me professional mobility.

The bottom line of the preceding arguments is that, unless an organization has *documented* practices *and uses them*, the way that the organization does business will depend on the specific know-how of individuals. As we intimated, when those individuals are not in the office, doing business becomes an improvisation exercise. Furthermore, when those individuals permanently leave the organization, the replacement individuals will generally have difficulty getting acclimated to the idiosyncracies of their coworkers (i.e., Sam's, Pam's, and Ham's way). The name of the game, then, is to have Sam, Pam, Ham, and others contribute to and adapt to the ADPE practices. That is, they help to create and plug themselves into the organization's way of doing business. If this is done with an open mind, people will find that they will have a better understanding of what to expect from one another. These clarified expectations lead to the perception that people want to work together, thereby synergizing the efforts of individuals. Over time, people shed "me-first" attitudes and replace them with teamwork attitudes. The net result is that individuals become empowered to do more (because a common purpose dominates teamwork thinking), thereby escaping the threat of being held captive to a particular position. Consequently, people increase their professional mobility, while contributing to the long-term stability of the organization.

We now consider the second strategy listed in Figure 8–22 for meeting the second challenge listed in that figure.

Strategy 2 to Meet Challenge: Make ADPE compliance part of each employee's performance review and reward compliance. *(Hard Sell)*

In many enterprises, an employee's performance is assessed periodically (e.g., quarterly, semiannually, yearly) for purposes such as setting goals, adjusting salary, and assessing promotion opportunities. Figure 8–24 shows a partial outline of a form that might be used as part of an employee's performance review. Included on the form is a section (labelled "*N*.0") containing questions and information requests aimed at assessing the employee's ADPE compliance. Such questions and information requests can be used to motivate people to acclimate to the ADPE way, particularly if they are rewarded for doing so. It should be noted that one question (i.e., How have you improved the way the organization develops products using the ADPE way?) invites suggestions for improving the ADPE way. This type of question is a concrete way of offering each employee the opportunity to participate in molding the organization's business practices. In fact, manifestly incorporating such suggestions into the ADPE way greatly increases the likelihood of employee buy-in to the ADPE way.

In more mature organizations, this strategy should be acceptable to most employees, since, by definition, disciplined engineering practices are part of the culture. However, using this strategy is not without risk. For example, employees not rewarded for what they feel is a demonstrated track record of ADPE compliance may become highly resistant to the ADPE business practices—and encourage others to do the same. The lesson here is that a modicum of consistency is needed in rewarding ADPE compliance. The questions and information requests in Figure 8–24 are aimed at pulling out evidence of ADPE compliance so that this modicum of consistency can be realized. For instance, one request is for at least five artifacts demonstrating how the employee has supported the ADPE. Example artifacts might be the following:

- One or more sets of CCB minutes signed by the customer

- A memorandum documenting a peer review

- Test incident reports (TIRs) written during an acceptance testing activity[7]

---

[7] TIRs might be appropriate for a member of a product assurance organization or for a project manager. In the case of the project manager, the TIRs can be particularly convincing evidence if they bear the project manager's signature, showing explicitly the project manager's involvement in the acceptance testing process.

Employee Performance Review and Planning Form

EMPLOYEE NAME   EMPLOYEE NO.   DATE OF HIRE

EMPLOYEE POSITION TITLE   EMPLOYEE DIVISION

-
-
-

1.0 CURRENT ASSIGNMENT

-
-
-

***N*.0 ADPE COMPLIANCE**

Have you read each promulgated ADPE element?

Have you reviewed and commented on drafts of ADPE elements submitted to you?

Have you attended the presentations explaining the content of each promulgated ADPE element?

How have you encouraged customer buy-in to the ADPE way?

How have you improved the way the organization develops products using the ADPE way?

List at least three suggestions for changing the ADPE way to make it better.

Provide at least five artifacts that demonstrate how you have supported the ADPE way.

-
-
-

FIGURE 8–24 An aggressive strategy for pursuing SEE implementation is to make ADPE compliance part of each employee's performance review. In more mature organizations, this approach should be acceptable to most employees since, by definition, disciplined engineering practices are part of the culture. The figure offers performance review ideas for addressing ADPE compliance.

Of course, some criteria may need to be established regarding such things as (1) "do all artifacts count equally?" and (2) what counts as the minimum set of responses to the questions and the information requests before the employee is entitled to an ADPE-compliance bonus.

The strategy can be reinforced by incorporating ADPE compliance into the ADPE elements themselves as part of each employee's responsibilities. Figure 8–25 shows one way to embed employee responsibility for ADPE compliance into an ADPE element. The figure shows a section of an element—labelled "*N*.0," with subsections (two are shown, "*N*.2" and "*N*.4")—dealing with ADPE element implementation responsibilities. Part of these responsibilities includes words on ADPE compliance similar to those shown in Figure 8–24.

An alternative to the reinforcing approach shown in Figure 8–25 is to remove the words appearing in Section *N* and instead place something like them in a memorandum that promulgates the ADPE element. This approach gives greater visibility to the responsibility for ADPE compliance. Figure 8–26 provides you with a starting point for a memorandum promulgating an ADPE element. The memorandum includes (in bold) the following ADPE-compliance words:

> You are expected to implement the practices set forth in this element. Your performance review will be based in part on your demonstrated application of these practices in your project work.

It should be noted that the wording in the memorandum in Figure 8–26 regarding the ADPE is based on the four-component ADPE taxonomy used in this book—namely, policy, guideline, procedure, and standard. If your organization uses some other taxonomy, the wording in your adaptation of the Figure 8–26 memorandum should reflect this taxonomy.

We now turn our attention to a third strategy, which may be linked to the preceding two strategies, for overcoming opposition to the ADPE way.

Strategy 3 to Meet Challenge: **Get all managers on board with the ADPE way by some combination of the preceding two strategies or by some other means, such as corporate directives and/or hiring policies. (This strategy is mandatory.)**

There are few instances in this book in which we say that something *must* be done. Invoking this strategy is one of those instances. If managers are not on board with the ADPE way, the people who work for them will not be on board.

Earlier we examined how mentoring and coaching can facilitate implementation of ADPE practices. Within most organizations, a prime source for this mentoring and coaching is management. Thus, if management is not on board with the ADPE way, not only will implementation of ADPE practices be blunted or curtailed, but also countercultures will emerge in the organization. Individual managers will set up their own fiefdoms with a set of practices peculiar to the fiefdom. That is, the Sam/Pam/Ham scenario discussed previously will be replicated at various levels within the organization. In the extreme, the organization can be torn apart as the fiefdoms increasingly work at cross-purposes. Furthermore, the organization will present a bewildering picture to its client community. Products developed will take on the character of the producing fiefdom. For example, one client may receive a user's manual with a delivered system, while another client may not. If customers communicate with one another, such inconsistency can drive customers away from the organization.

There are a number of ways to get managers on board with the ADPE way, including some combination of the following strategies:

- The process engineering group (PEG) should work with managers to provide them with suggestions for coaching/mentoring subordinates on how documented business practices that are followed afford individuals the opportunity to grow within the organization. For example, the PEG can help managers formulate employee career growth programs by showing how documented business practices offer employees a start-

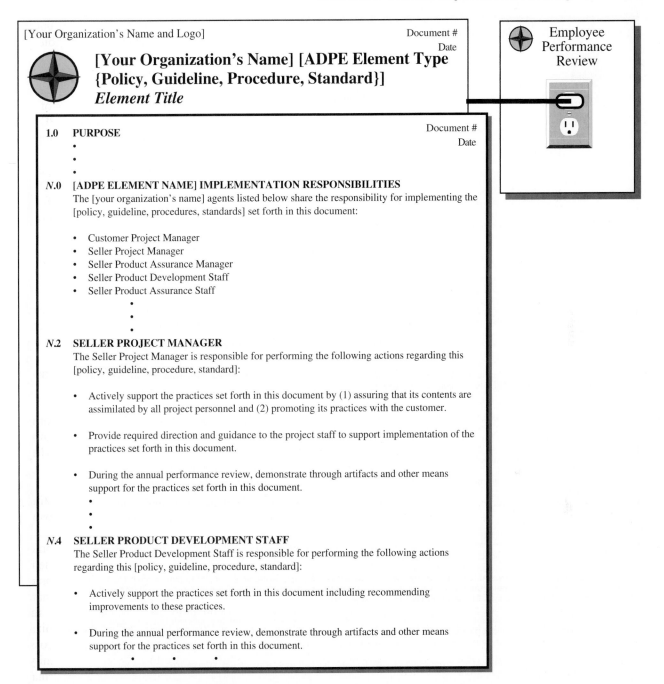

FIGURE 8–25 Here is a way to reinforce the strategy of making ADPE compliance part of each employee's performance review. The figure illustrates how to address ADPE compliance in the responsibilities section of an ADPE element.

[Your Organization's Name and Logo]   Memo ID: [*Put ID here.*]

Memorandum

To: [*Put your organization's name here.*] Management and Staff

From: [*Put your organization's name here.*] Program Manager

Date: [*Enter the memorandum's date here.*]

Subject: Promulgation of [*Put your organization's name here.*] [*Select one of the following: Policy, Guideline, Procedure, Standard.*] on [*Put topic or title of ADPE element here.*]

Reference: (a) [*Enter the name of your organization's SEE implementation plan here.*]
               [*List other references bearing on the ADPE element here—for example, corporate directives.*]

Per reference (a), [*Put your organization's name here.*] provides a development environment—the Systems Engineering Environment—where coordinated and consistent development of software systems can be accomplished. The SEE consists of two complementary components—an Application Development Process Environment (ADPE) and an Application Development Technology Environment (ADTE). The ADPE is the set of those policies, guidelines, procedures, and standards defining the engineering *processes* for developing software systems within [*Put your organization's name here.*]. The ADPE is a framework for consistent software product evolution and software systems development process accomplishment. The ADTE consists of the *technology* as embodied in hardware and software development tools, and associated procedures for their use, required to develop applications.

[*Place additional background information here, such as a list of previously promulgated ADPE elements, when they were promulgated, and their relationship to the element being promulgated.*]

Enclosed is an ADPE element entitled "[*Place the element title here.*]" This element defines [*Place the overall purpose of the element here.*] The specific purposes of this element are the following:

[*List the specific purposes of the element here. For example, if the element being promulgated is a guideline on the CCB, specific purposes might be items such as the following:*

• To define the CCB concept for {*Put your organization's name here.*} .

• To define the CCB participants.

• To present a generalized concept of change control that defines the scope of [*Put your organization's name here.*] CCB activities.

• To define methods for documenting CCB meetings and [*Put your organization's name here.*] project meetings impacting CCB meetings.

• To present guidance for developing a CCB charter defining the way that the CCB functions.

• To present guidance for conducting CCB meetings.]

As of today, the enclosed element is to be used by you to guide your work on existing projects and to plan work for your new projects. You are expected to implement the practices set forth in this element. Your performance review will be based in part on your demonstrated application of these practices to your project work.

Additional ADPE elements further defining [*Put your organization's name here.*] way of doing business will be promulgated. If you have questions concerning this element, please contact [*Place organization points of contact here, preferably those individuals who wrote the element or those who managed the individuals who wrote the element.*].

Enclosure: "[*Place the title of the ADPE element here.*]," dated [*Place the date appearing on the element here.*]

cc: [*List here the individuals who are not part of your organization's management and staff who are to receive this memorandum and the enclosed ADPE element.*]

FIGURE 8–26   Here is a starting point for a memorandum promulgating an ADPE element to your organization. The correspondence should explicitly encourage ADPE compliance. The bolded paragraph illustrates how to stipulate this encouragement.

ing point for learning new things. The PEG should also work with managers to show how documented business practices that are followed can reduce schedule risk.

■ Making ADPE compliance part of each manager's performance review is, as discussed earlier, an aggressive way to get managers (and the rest of the organization) on board with the ADPE way. This strategy has a natural leveraging effect on the organization. For managers to be rewarded for ADPE compliance, they must get subordinates to comply with ADPE business practices.

■ A strategy even more aggressive than the preceding one is to require ADPE compliance as a condition for employment. That is, ADPE compliance is made part of the manager's employment contract. An example of an ADPE-compliance contractual stipulation might be the following:

> If the manager is unable to demonstrate that those working for the manager are complying with ADPE business practices, the manager is subject to termination.

Another approach to this strategy is to require the prospective manager to go through an ADPE training program and a trial period prior to being hired. During this trial period (of, say, several months), the prospective manager would be expected to motivate subordinates to assimilate and carry through ADPE practices. Hiring of the prospective manager would be contingent upon demonstrating the ability to provide such motivation and demonstrate other management qualities that the organization deems important. Of course, once hired, the manager would be expected to continue promoting the ADPE way (e.g., by presenting ADPE briefings).

The preceding strategies are some key ways that management buy-in to the ADPE way can be achieved. They have also been presented to start your thinking for developing strategies that might be particularly suited to your organization.

The bottom line of the preceding discussion is the following:

> Management buy-in to the ADPE way must be achieved, or SEE implementation will fail. Your SEE implementation plan must therefore explicitly address how this buy-in is to be achieved.

Strategy 4 to Meet Challenge: Give periodic briefings to the seller staff on ADPE element content before and after promulgation. After promulgation, try to make customer attendance a requirement.

Earlier we stressed that promulgated ADPE elements should be required reading. However, reading alone will not result in ADPE implementation. The plain fact is that, particularly in an organization where people may be on the verge of being overwhelmed with work, reading ADPE elements will not be near the top of each staff member's list of things to do—even if the employee is interested in following the ADPE practices. To encourage reading of the ADPE elements and eventual adoption of ADPE practices, periodic briefings to the seller staff on ADPE content should be given—before and after ADPE element promulgation. Attendance at these briefings should be made mandatory—particularly in organizations where management buy-in to the ADPE may be uncertain.

Giving such briefings before element promulgation encourages buy-in to the ADPE way. Such briefings should encourage suggestions from the staff. If these suggestions are folded into the element, staff will be more inclined toward adopting the practices. Of course, it will generally not be possible to incorporate all suggestions. Some will conflict with one another, particularly in the area regarding the amount of detail to include.

After ADPE element promulgation, it is strongly suggested that customer attendance at such briefings be made a requirement—at least for the element that lays out the organization's way of doing business (i.e., the element constructed from the principles presented in Chapter 3). Since, as we discussed in Chapter 3, the customer should be made part of the organization's software systems development process, the customer needs to be made aware of what this process is if the process is to work. These briefings are part of the same thinking that encourages the customer and seller to sign each

ADPE element. The briefings and signatures are important steps toward achieving ADPE buy-in. The briefings also allow the customer to raise questions specific to that customer's work with the seller to clarify how the ADPE practices apply to that work. Such questions can also help the seller improve ADPE element content. For example, during a briefing of the seller's CCB element, the customer may question why product assurance may need to attend CCB meetings. If the element simply asserts that product assurance is required to attend, the customer's question on this issue may lead to an update to the CCB element that explains the value added of product assurance attendance at CCB meetings. For instance, product assurance can raise questions about the testability of requirements being discussed at a CCB meeting; if such questions are raised before design and/or coding activities are underway, considerable time and money can be saved by heading off costly redesign and/or recoding activities. As a specific example, suppose a response time "requirement" is articulated as follows:

> The system response time to a user query shall be three seconds.

Regarding this statement, product assurance can raise testability-related questions such as the following:

- How is the interval defining system response time to be measured? That is, what is the starting point for the interval, and what is the ending point?
- What types of queries are included? All, including such things as end-to-end database searches? Or, are only certain types of queries included because other queries would take much longer for the system to respond? For these other queries, what value is to be assigned to the response time interval?

Strategy 5 to Meet Challenge: Establish a training program that offers the staff the opportunity to learn or augment their understanding of the engineering principles underlying the ADPE.

Earlier we discussed in connection with Figure 8–16 tradeoffs associated with how much detail to include in ADPE elements. We indicated that it is neither practical nor useful to turn the set of ADPE elements into a software engineering treatise. It is often a challenge to get people to read ADPE elements, even if they consist of only a few pages. Yet, it is generally necessary to convey engineering principles to the staff if the ADPE business practices are to be applied prescriptively. More to the point of the discussion of this strategy, an often unspoken source of resistance to ADPE practices is the unwillingness of staff to make known that they may not be well versed in engineering principles. It is human nature for people not to be forthcoming regarding things they may not know.

Engineering principles provide the context for the business practice guidance, policy, and/or "how-to-do-it" that should be the heart of each ADPE element. In fact, the general structure of most of the chapters in this book is first to introduce engineering principles and then to illustrate the application of these principles to develop practical guidance for setting up practices whose application aim at consistently producing good software systems. For example, Chapter 2 of this book introduces engineering principles such as the following:

- It is necessary to plan for as yet unknown change.
- Independent product assurance serves to reduce project risk. Consequently, the amount of independent product assurance to be applied to a project should be correlated with the assessed risk of the project.

We applied the first principle listed to make the CCB the centerpiece of project change control. In Chapter 4, we detailed how to bring about this change control. Regarding the CCB concept as set forth in this book, we should stress that not everybody agrees with our views on this subject. For example, many would argue that classical project status meetings involving project management and selected members of development managers and staff can accomplish much of what we put under the CCB umbrella in this book.

Regarding the preceding independent product assurance principle, many would argue that independent product assurance as we espouse it in this book can be replaced by putting the testing function under the development organization and having an independent quality assurance (QA) organization check that all parts of the process are being accomplished (including testing). Such a QA organization may also perform document reviews, or these document reviews may be performed by members of the development staff who did not develop the document in question—so that an independent product assurance organization that performs such reviews is not needed. Furthermore, configuration management, which we place under independent product assurance, others place under the development organization. The point here is that such redistribution of functions that we put under the product assurance umbrella represents an alternative way to reduce project risk by applying the following more general engineering principle:

> To reduce software systems development project risk, it is necessary to set up checks and balances during the product development cycle. The heart of these checks and balances is to schedule and perform product reviews, using people who were not involved with the development of the product undergoing review.

As we have stated many times throughout this book, there is no one way to achieve consistent successful software systems development. We just presented arguments that attack some of the basic premises of our book to illustrate this point. Of course, we did not go through these arguments to send you the message that you wasted your time getting this far in the book. Rather, we want to drive home the point that an organization should incorporate into its ADPE implementation approach the commitment to convey to staff the engineering principles underlying ADPE elements.

So how can such principles be conveyed—given that adding to the bulk of ADPE elements by including material on engineering principles may further turn off staff to reading the elements? One approach is to establish a training program that offers staff the opportunity to learn or augment their understanding of the engineering principles underlying the ADPE. The discussion of Strategy 4 (periodic briefings on ADPE element content) offers one aspect of such a training program. These briefings could expand upon any material on engineering principles that may appear in the element. Another aspect of such a training program could be multiple-day seminars on certain topics pertaining to the ADPE—for example, requirements management, peer reviews, and acceptance testing. Such seminars could be built from widely accepted texts on the topics, and such texts could be included as part of seminar handouts. You could also construct seminars from the principles and examples set forth in this book, particularly in those areas where the book goes into considerable detail. For example, Chapter 5 sets forth engineering principles regarding various types of product and process reviews. The chapter goes into considerable detail regarding some of these reviews—in particular, product assurance document reviews and acceptance testing. We do not, however, go into the same level of detail regarding peer reviews because of the plethora of literature on this subject.

If your training budget is tightly constrained so that you can only offer staff a very limited number of classes, there is one engineering area that we would put at the top of any training list—requirements management. At the beginning of this chapter, we replayed in Figure 8–1 the wizard-and-king comic strip that we introduced in Chapter 4. The Figure 8–1 caption reads as follows:

> At the most fundamental level, the avenue to consistent successful software systems development is sustained effective communication between the wizard (i.e., software seller) and the king (i.e., software customer).

For years, we have run a three-day seminar on requirements management based on the wizard-and-king comic strip. The seminar attendees have consistently told us that this seminar is particularly effective when the attendees include both software sellers and software customers. Throughout the seminar, there is considerable interaction between the sellers and customers, primarily through exercises that the attendees work in class and then subsequently discuss. What typically emerges from these discussions is that sellers and customers each have their own way of communicating things. Thus, to achieve sustained effective communication between sellers and customers, principles of effective communication must be presented and illustrated. Probably the most important principle examined in the seminar is that of requirements testability. In fact, the section on testability appearing in Chapter 5 is used in the seminar. The capstone of the seminar is when all attendees are called upon to write test procedures from requirements and design specifications introduced in the seminar. In fact, the material used in Chapter 5 to illustrate how to write test procedures is the material used in the seminar. This classroom exercise drives home to all attendees the role of requirements in providing the basis for the seller to demonstrate formally to the customer that what the customer asked for is indeed being delivered in the software system. Sellers become sensitized to customer concerns (such as having a system that produces error diagnostics in plain English), and customers become sensitized to (1) how labor-intensive test procedure development can be and (2) how important it is to express requirements in terms that both the customer and seller understand.

We have found that this requirements management seminar effectively addresses a number of concepts examined in this book, including the following: (1) CCB, (2) acceptance testing, and (3) requirements testability. In addition, the seminar explores at length requirements topics not addressed in this book, including the following: (1) requirements "goodness," (2) requirements modeling (where different modeling techniques are introduced, such as decision tables and state transition diagrams), and (3) requirements psychology (where such issues as how the differing perspectives of management, development, and product assurance serve to individually and collectively shape requirements).

We have also found that the requirements management seminar has a good carry-over effect into the work environment. After attending the seminar, sellers pay more attention to requirements testability issues and take greater pains to develop tests based on requirements; customers pay more attention to how they express their requirements and become more tolerant of the labor needed to develop acceptance test procedures.

Part of your SEE implementation plan should include a section on training as a means for encouraging seller staff and the customer to implement the ADPE way. The starting point for this section can be the discussion in the preceding paragraphs of this fifth strategy.

Your organization will undoubtedly have its own set of training priorities. Your SEE implementation plan should address these priorities. For example, software industry experience shows that peer reviews offer a significant return on the investment in such reviews (e.g., fewer requirements discrepancies in delivered computer code). Your SEE implementation plan training section may therefore want to stress training in the mechanics of peer reviews. To build your case for emphasizing peer review training, you may want to cite industry publications touting the value added of peer reviews to the software systems development process.

We have concluded our discussion of the second SEE implementation challenge listed in Figure 8–22. This discussion focused on strategies to head off outright resistance to the ADPE way. However, outright resistance is only one form of resistance that must be dealt with if SEE implementation is to be successful. Subtler forms of resistance can present themselves. These subtler forms are the focus of the third SEE implementation challenge listed in Figure 8–22. This challenge is the following:

Challenge: The seller staff will find ways to work around the ADPE way—how can this attitude be turned around or, where appropriate, be used to incorporate improvements into the ADPE way?

We repeatedly stress that SEE implementation is a cultural change exercise. People naturally resist the loss associated with change or the transition associated with change. One form of resistance is to find ways to work around the ADPE way. This form of resistance can arise for one of the two following reasons:

- The ADPE way is awkward or just does not make good business sense
- People have not bought into the ADPE way even though it makes good business sense

The first reason can be the source of ADPE improvements, and your SEE implementation plan should address this potential process improvement source. For example, an ADPE element may specify that only the most senior manager in the organization can sign out deliverables. If the volume of deliverables is such that this senior manager proves to be a bottleneck that causes deliverables to be late, subordinate managers may choose to sign out deliverables and be prepared to defend their position to the senior manager should the senior manager call them on the matter. Ultimately, it may be decided to revise the ADPE element that specifies the deliverable sign-out procedure. The revision may be the inclusion in each project plan a table that indicates, for each deliverable, the manager who has sign-out authority. Approval by the senior manager of the project plan containing such a table is tantamount to delegating deliverable release authority to subordinate managers.

The second reason just cited—people have not bought into the ADPE way even though it makes good business sense—is another matter and is the focus of the next strategy.

Strategy to Meet Challenge: **Show how documented business practices that are followed remove dependence on the individual, thereby affording the individual opportunity to grow within the organization. Reward staff who follow the ADPE way and suggest improvements to it. Make the rewards part of a ceremony attended by the entire organization.**

The first part of this strategy we examined when we discussed the preceding challenge. The arguments presented in conjunction with Figure 8–23 apply to the challenge currently under discussion. The bottom line of those arguments was the following:

> Unless an organization has *documented* practices *and uses them*, the way that the organization does business will depend on the specific know-how of individuals. As we stated, when those individuals are not in the office, doing business becomes an improvisation exercise. Furthermore, when those individuals permanently leave the organization, the replacement individuals will generally have difficulty getting acclimated to the idiosyncrasies of their coworkers (i.e., Sam's, Pam's, and Ham's way). The name of the game, then, is to have Sam, Pam, Ham, and others blend their ways with the ADPE practices. That is, they contribute and plug themselves into the organization's way of doing business. If this is done with an open mind, people will find that they will have a better understanding of what to expect from one another. These clarified expectations lead to the perception that people want to work together, thereby synergizing the efforts of individuals. Over time, people shed "me-first" attitudes and replace them with teamwork attitudes. The net result is that individuals become empowered to do more (because a common purpose dominates teamwork thinking), thereby escaping the threat of being held captive to a particular position.

These arguments appeal to reason. Sometimes, however, such appeals fall on deaf ears. Some creative people, in particular, consider any set of practices a challenge to their inventive nature. This challenge manifests itself as ways to game the system of practices, sometimes at the expense of compromising the organization's good name. For example, people who do not believe in the value that independent product assurance can add to a product may choose to release a software system to a customer without first conducting acceptance testing. As we have previously discussed, without such testing, the risk of software failure increases.

It is therefore generally a good idea to augment appeals to reason with something more tangible. Figure 8–27 shows a number of inducements that can be offered to complement appeals to reason. These inducements include such things as the following:

- **Cash bonuses.** Monetary rewards, particularly if they are presented at a ceremony attended by the organization, serve to take some of the pain out of the changes that people are asked to make in acclimating themselves to the ADPE way.

- **Articles of clothing such as hats and T-shirts.** These items can be tagged with identifiers and/or slogans that promote the idea of SEE buy-in (e.g., "I'm plugged into the SEE").

- **Food-related articles such as coffee mugs and food.** Food-related articles can be tagged with identifiers such as "SEE" that serve as reminders of the business cultural shift associated with SEE implementation. Food can be provided at lunch-time briefings on ADPE elements.

One word of caution is in order regarding using inducements to bring about ADPE buy-in. The inducements must be offered consistently—particularly cash bonuses. It is therefore a good idea to establish criteria that clarify what an individual or group needs to do regarding ADPE implementation to be rewarded. The inducement strategy can be undermined if staff perceives inequities in the way people are rewarded. For example, it can be counterproductive to give one staff member a $500 bonus solely for making sure that project CCB minutes are signed by the customer while giving another staff member a $50 bonus for building a traceability matrix showing the explicit linkages between requirements and design specifications and test procedures.

We now turn our attention to the final SEE implementation challenge shown in Figure 8–22, which is the following:

Challenge: The customer will try to circumvent the seller management chain to "expedite" the incorporation of product changes—how can this attitude be turned around?

SEE implementation can be a cultural change for customers as well as sellers. This situation will generally exist even in those instances in which a customer asks the seller (e.g., via an RFP) to set up an SEE. It should therefore come as no surprise that, in general, a customer, like the seller staff, may resist adopting the ADPE way—and continue interacting with the seller via the pre-ADPE way. One particular manifestation of the pre-ADPE way occurs when the customer goes around the seller management chain to interact directly with product developers to "expedite" the incorporation of product changes. For example, the customer may pick up the phone and call a computer programmer (whose name for the purposes of this discussion is Guru) on the seller product development staff and make a request such as the following:

> "Say, Guru, when you get the time in the next day or so, please produce a new report that takes all the population data in the database and arranges the data by age and distance from Topeka, Kansas. Display the arrangement as a series of bar graphs, where a given bar graph shows the number of people within an age range of ten years, starting with 0 and ending with 100, living within a distance range of 50 miles from Topeka, starting with 0 and ending with 500. Thus, for example, one bar graph will show the number of people in the age range 0–10 years, 11–20 years, . . ., 91–100 years living between 51 miles and 100 miles from the courthouse building on Main Street in Topeka. Please generate a sample bar graph for me by the end of the week. Thank you for your support!"

From the customer's perspective, such interaction cuts through an organization's bureaucracy—and, on the surface, appears to be an expeditious way to transact business. From the seller project manager's perspective, however, such interaction undermines, for instance, the manager's ability to man-

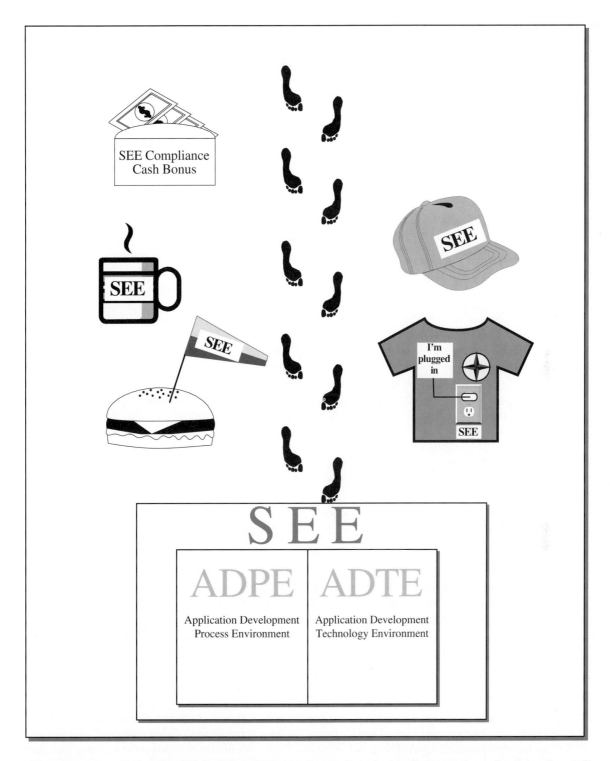

FIGURE 8–27 An ongoing SEE implementation challenge is to head off the tendency for the seller staff to find ways to work around the ADPE way. One strategy for meeting this challenge is the offering of inducements such as those shown—cash bonuses, coffee mugs, food, and articles of clothing (hats, T-shirts). Senior management and/or the organization's PEG can help achieve employee buy-in and build esprit de corps through such inducements. Inducements help reduce organizational resistance to the cultural change that SEE implementation brings. In the extreme, this resistance can manifest itself in battle cries proclaiming outright opposition such as, "I'm not going to do it!" or, "I'm going to do what I have to do (to get a product out the door)!"

age the project's cost and schedule. In this case, Guru should take the customer request to his supervisor so that the supervisor can decide what needs to be done.

The following strategy is one way to turn this customer attitude away from such practices and toward the ADPE way:

Strategy to Meet Challenge: **Make the CCB the focal point for customer/seller interaction. Train seller staff in the need to document interactions with the customer bearing on project work and to inform seller management of such interactions.**

We stress throughout this book that the ADPE practices are a way to elevate software systems development to a businesslike proposition. Through the CCB, seller and customer decisions are made a matter of record. In this way, the seller and customer become accountable for their actions.

It is simply good business to run software systems development like a business, with written records and products developed in accordance with a mutually agreed-to plan. Relying solely on the spoken word is a recipe for trouble. In particular, seller staff who take verbal direction from a customer put a project at risk. Seller staff therefore need to be trained to document interactions with the customer bearing on project work and to inform seller management of such interactions.

We want to emphasize that we are not advocating reducing software systems development to a coldly formal, paper-pushing bureaucracy. Certainly, the customer can interact with seller staff, but the customer needs to keep in mind that the customer has hired the seller to (1) *build* software(-related) products and (2) *manage* the development of these products. The customer's primary role is to give direction to seller *management* so that this management can appropriately focus the efforts of the seller staff.

Your SEE implementation plan should therefore stress that the ADPE will be set up such that the CCB is the focal point for customer/seller interaction. Each project plan should reflect this notion by including a statement such as the following:

Project decision making will be accomplished and documented at the CCB throughout the project. Decisions made outside of the CCB will be documented and appended to the minutes of the next-occurring CCB meeting.

We also want to stress that our preceding remarks about how customer/seller relationships may eventually sour are not intended to imply that both the customer and seller should enter into a contract mistrusting each other. Rather these remarks are intended to remind both parties that they should be accountable for their decisions—from the beginning of a project until its conclusion.

We have finished our examination of the four SEE implementation challenges and associated strategies for meeting the challenges shown in Figure 8–22. We have stressed in this examination that, because SEE implementation is a cultural change exercise, it will be met with resistance. The strategies discussed proceed from the proposition that if the ADPE way can be shown to be a win-win situation for both the individual and the organization, resistance to the ADPE way will subside.

We recommend that your SEE implementation plan address the challenges to SEE implementation facing your organization. The preceding extensive discussion of the challenges and the strategies for meeting the challenges shown in Figure 8–22 offers you a starting point for defining the challenges facing your organization and laying out strategies for meeting the challenges.

In the business world, the profit motive is a factor that cannot be ignored in setting up an SEE. Even not-for-profit organizations have budgets limiting what they can do. In the discussion that follows, we use the label "almighty dollar" to capture the ideas of the profit motive and budget limitations. The following SEE implementation planning issue that we now consider focuses on the business reality of the almighty dollar setting organizational priorities:

> 13. How do you deal with the business reality of the almighty dollar in bringing about ADPE implementation?

Figure 8–28 indicates some of the key factors bearing upon this issue. To help you fold these factors into your SEE implementation planning approach, we elaborate on this figure. The almighty dollar generally creates the following two pushes within a seller organization:

- **Setting organizational priorities**. As shown in the figure, the top two organizational priorities are generally (1) make a profit and (2) get and keep good people. A vicious cycle is set up whereby meeting the near-term objective of constantly getting working products out the door (to maintain the organization's profitability) locks the organization into never having time to put in place a software systems development process that does not depend on particular individuals. This cycle is difficult to break because personnel turnover forces the organization into a catch-up mode as the new personnel attempt to figure out how they fit into the way the veterans do their jobs. In short, the constant drive to maintain an organization's profitability makes the SEE implementation exercise a tough job. Even if the organization is firmly committed to putting in place documented business practices, and even if the client community it serves is pressing for such business practices (which sometimes is not the case), the day-to-day pressure of "getting the job done" often forces such commitments to be put on hold. The organization thus mortgages its future because people generally want to move on and do not want to be held captive to an organization.

- **Establishing organizational business practices**. The absence of documented business practices forces people to do whatever it takes to get a product out the door. This notion is symbolized in the figure by the worker in military garb firing away with brute-force determination to carry out the commander's (project manager's) order to take the next hill (to produce a product with integrity—that is, a product that does what the customer wants and is delivered on time and within budget).

We would not argue that, even with documented business practices, there are times when individuals within the organization must perform heroically. Things like power outages, floods, sickness, and mail that gets lost will happen and force people to take shortcuts. However, when heroic action becomes the normal mode of operation for an organization, that organization will generally decline over the long haul. Figure 8–28 sheds light as to why this decline must ultimately happen. As the figure shows, one of the top organizational priorities is "get and keep good and smart people." But good and smart people soon tire of being asked to work another weekend or through another night. Furthermore, good people soon recognize that their heroics force them into highly specialized roles, thus limiting career growth. Often, they will look elsewhere for a job.

So, how can an organization avoid the road to decline just described? The strategies shown in Figure 8–22 and discussed at length in the preceding pages offer some specific ideas for avoiding such decline. If you are a new organization, you have the opportunity to get off on the right foot by incorporating such strategies into an SEE implementation plan and making a serious attempt at implementing the plan.

But what if your organization is already caught in the downward spiral just described? Can you put documented business practices in place to stop the downward spiral? Or what if your organization is making tons of money and expanding rapidly—and beginning to burn out its people? Can you put documented business practices in place in such a dynamic environment? In both cases, we believe you can put documented business practices in place. The following are some ideas to get you started (they are listed chronologically):

1. Get senior management to support SEE implementation efforts. Such support includes (1) getting the senior management to allocate resources to a group (or individual) to start an SEE implementation effort and (2) encouraging the group (or individual) to solicit participation from others in the organization.

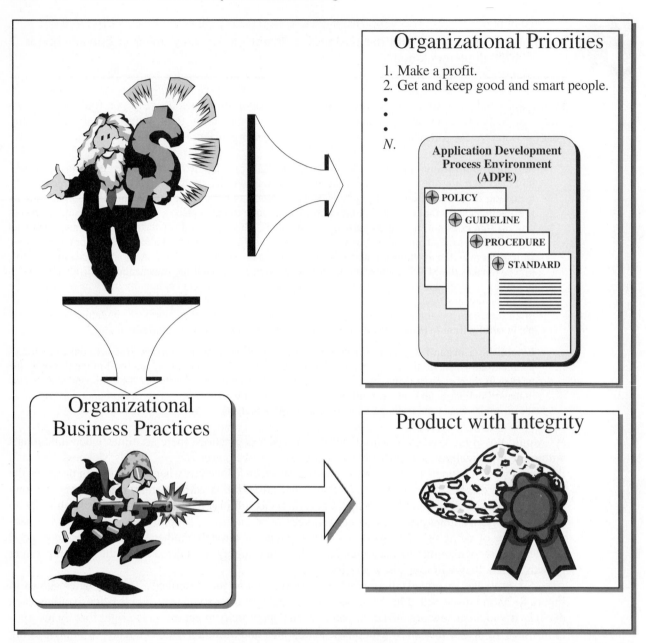

FIGURE 8–28 Business reality (the almighty dollar) often compels senior managers to walk a tightrope. They are constantly trying to balance keeping customers happy while making a profit and making sure sound engineering practices are in place and followed. In some cases, making a profit forces engineering shortcuts.

2. Have senior management inform the organization about the efforts, either via memorandum or a presentation.

3. You must still develop some kind of SEE implementation plan—at least along the lines of the back-of-the-envelope or spiral notebook variety shown at the top of Figure 8–5. Without some kind of plan, your efforts to bring some order to your organization will be hard to focus.

4. We suggest that you start with the austere SEE implementation approach discussed earlier in connection with Figure 8–20. That approach laid out priorities for setting up an SEE. You can decide how far down the

list of priorities cited there make sense for your organization. You may even want to reorder the priorities in that list. The items listed next assume the priorities cited in Figure 8–20. If you decide to reorder these priorities, you should modify the items listed below to match your reordering.

5. *While you are developing your SEE implementation plan*, start doing project planning by creating some kind of template (you can use the ideas in Chapter 2 as a starting point to create the template).

6. *While you are developing your SEE implementation plan*, start using CCBs. Use the ideas in Chapters 2, 3, and 4 to establish roles for your CCBs.

7. *While you are developing your SEE implementation plan*, start developing a process diagram for your organization using the ideas in Chapter 3. Do this development by soliciting ideas from the organization's management and staff.

8. While the foregoing activity is going on, your organization should be briefed as to what is going on in the SEE arena.

9. Publish your SEE implementation plan and brief the organization on its contents.

10. Start putting the process in your process diagram in place. Eventually, publish an ADPE element containing the process diagram.

11. Continue with the priorities shown in Figure 8–20 and/or apply other ideas given in this book.

As a final comment on this SEE implementation planning issue, we offer the following:

> If your organization is caught in the downward spiral of losing people through unrelenting demands for heroics or if your organization is drowning in its success, consider the alternative of not doing something like all or part of the eleven steps listed above.

People within an organization are not monolithic in terms of wanting to change the way that they do things. We now turn our attention to the following SEE implementation planning issue that addresses this fact of organizational life:

14. How do you account for the reality that people within an organization span a broad spectrum of willingness to adapt to the engineering environment?

One way to look at this issue is to think of a person's willingness to adapt to the ADPE way in terms of a personality spectrum in an organization. Figure 8–29 shows five typical points on such a personality spectrum. This spectrum is a continuum so that, in general, a particular individual may fall somewhere between the points indicated.

To clarify the SEE implementation planning issue associated with this spectrum, we discuss each of the five spectrum points shown in Figure 8–29.

1. **What's a process?** People at this end of the spectrum are in over their heads when it comes to understanding business processes. They may have some combination of the following backgrounds:

   a. An individual may have had no prior experience working on projects with more than several people so that the Sam/Pam/Ham process approach may have been that individual's sole exposure to an organizational way of doing things.

   b. An individual may be a recent college graduate with little or no experience working on a software project with a prescribed way of doing things.

   c. An individual may have had little or no exposure to engineering principles and concepts and their relationships (such as "life cycle," "acceptance testing," "requirements testability," "visibility," "traceabil-

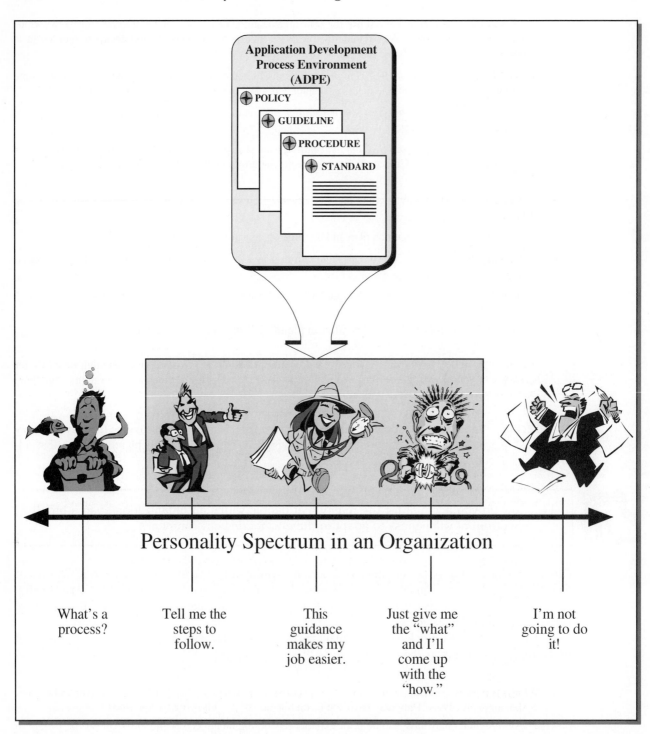

FIGURE 8–29 SEE implementation planning needs to account for the reality that people within an organization span a broad spectrum of willingness to adapt to the engineering environment. The orientation of ADPE elements should address the middle of the spectrum. All people should be given the opportunity to contribute to ADPE development.

ity"). As a result, the individual has trouble assimilating ADPE concepts and applying them to project work. Moreover, such individuals, fearing embarrassment, may be reluctant to ask questions about these concepts and how they relate to the organization's project work.

Training programs are generally needed to bring individuals at this end of the spectrum into the middle of the spectrum. This training should focus on (1) engineering principles, (2) their relationships (e.g., explanation of how test procedures give visibility to the task of demonstrating to the customer that the computer code to be delivered indeed has the functionality the customer asked for), and (3) worked out examples (e.g., of test procedures derived from requirements and design specifications).

2. **Tell me the steps to follow.** People in this region of the spectrum prefer detailed procedures, worked out examples, forms to fill out, and checklists to complete. They may have some combination of the following attitudes:

   a. An individual may have had some experience working on projects with documented processes but may be weak in understanding underlying engineering principles. Thus, the greater is the specificity of the ADPE way, the smaller is the need to try to figure out which engineering principles may need to be brought to bear to accomplish a project task. For example, an individual responsible for writing a requirements specification who is unsure of what a testable requirement is, would generally like to have detailed examples of testable requirements.

   b. An individual may be a steady performer who likes to put in a "good" eight hours and then go home to other activities.

   c. An individual may view time on the job as something to get over with. Consequently, such an individual may prefer to glide through the day without doing too much thinking.

Like the individuals at the left-hand part of the spectrum, individuals in this part of the spectrum need training programs. This training should focus on (1) explaining how, in general, there are many ways to accomplish software engineering tasks and (2) highlighting considerations that should be brought to bear to determine preferred ways to perform these tasks. Such training can give the individuals in this region of the spectrum the insight they need to apply prescriptively the ADPE way. For example, by explaining the purpose and value added of different types of process checks and balances, such individuals can determine which types of deliverables may require technical editing (e.g., a requirements specification) and which may not (e.g., a trip report that will not be distributed to anyone but the customer).

3. **This guidance makes my job easier.** People in this region of the spectrum are synchronized with the ADPE way. For them, the ADPE elements contain just the right amount of detail. They have sufficient understanding of the engineering principles underlying the ADPE so that they are able to apply prescriptively its practices. Lessons learned from applying the ADPE practices are used to apply them more effectively on subsequent work. For example, they may learn that peer review sessions should not extend beyond ninety minutes. Beyond that time, people tend to lose focus so that there is little value added.

4. **Just give me the "what" and I'll come up with the "how."** People in this region of spectrum tend to want few details. For example, they prefer to be told simply that they have to record minutes at CCB minutes. They do not want guidance on what to record or how much detail to include. They may have some combination of the following backgrounds:

   a. An individual may have a strong background in engineering principles and thus knows how to apply prescriptively the top-level guidance included in the ADPE elements.

   b. An individual may have a strong background in engineering principles and no desire to follow the ADPE way. By insisting that the ADPE be limited to broadly worded guidance, the individual can give the appearance of buying into the ADPE way while, in fact, pursuing the Sam/Pam/Ham process approach.

5. **I'm not going to do it!** People at the end of the spectrum tend to be in outright rebellion against the ADPE way. They may have some combination of the following attitudes:

   a. An individual who has been in the software industry for a long time (twenty years or more) may feel that he or she has seen it all. This attitude drives the individual to the conclusion that his or her way makes more sense than the ADPE way. That is, to an individual at this end of the spectrum, the experience folded into the ADPE way simply competes with that person's vast experience.

b. An individual may want to be in charge of the organization or in charge of the organizational element responsible for developing the ADPE.

As we discussed earlier, by making SEE buy-in a prerequisite to joining an organization, resistance to the ADPE can be sharply curtailed. In any event, an SEE implementation plan should account for the possibility of political power plays. One way to keep rebellious attitudes in check is to get SEE buy-in from the individual who heads the organization. Without this buy-in, the organization will almost assuredly fractionate into Sam, Pam, and Ham fiefdoms.

Figure 8–29 also offers planning guidance regarding the intended audience for ADPE elements—namely, the middle of the spectrum, which is shaded in the figure. In general, the elements should not try to address the vast educational needs of the people at the far left end of the spectrum, who are in over their heads processwise. Nor, in general, should the elements try to address comments submitted by people at the far right end of the spectrum. Such comments must at least be viewed with skepticism.[8] For example, if such individuals propose that the process be amended to expedite product delivery by doing away with a cover letter, this proposal must generally be viewed as a way to circumvent process checks and balances. If there is no cover letter, organizational visibility into when the product was delivered will be diminished—and eventually other shortcuts will generally creep in.

To this point, we have examined at length a number of SEE implementation planning issues having to do with (1) the form and content of the ADPE and (2) ADPE institutionalization. We now shift our focus and consider the following key SEE implementation planning issue having to do with SEE development:

15. Who should develop the SEE in your organization?

Figure 8–30 shows four alternatives and associated advantages and disadvantages. Throughout this book we use the label "process engineering group (PEG)" for the organizational entity that develops and maintains the SEE. This label can be applied to any one of the alternatives shown in Figure 8–30.

It should also be noted that, by combining two or more of the alternatives shown in Figure 8–30, additional alternatives can be constructed. Combinations can be used to exploit the advantages of the individual alternatives and soften their disadvantages. Consider, for example, the following two combinations:

1. **Alternative 1 (Full-time staff) and Alternative 2 (Part-timers)**. Here the idea is to have a small core of full-time staff and additional part-timers. This combination exploits the advantages of each alternative and softens their disadvantages as follows:

   ■ The cost of this combination would generally be less than the cost of Alternative 1 because the number of full-time staff would be less than the number of full-time staff in Alternative 1. Presumably, the labor of the part-timers in the combination would be less than the labor of the additional full-timers in Alternative 1. The part-timers would be called in by the full-timers when needed—for example, to develop a specialized ADPE element or a specialized part of an ADPE element, such as a section in a peer review guideline on object-oriented peer review checklists.

   ■ The first disadvantage of Alternative 2 (SEE implementation may be subordinated to other priorities) is softened by the small core of full-time PEG staff whose responsibility is SEE implementation. Similar arguments apply to the second and third disadvantages listed for Alternative 2—again, because the PEG also includes full-time staff.

---

[8] As stated earlier, all people in the spectrum should be allowed to contribute comments for evolving the ADPE. Even people at the far right of the spectrum (i.e., "I'm not going to do it!") should be allowed to contribute, but with one caveat—they need to use and implement ADPE elements once the organization has decided to promulgate the elements.

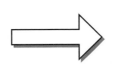

Alternative	Advantages	Disadvantages
1. Full-time staff	Dedicated to task Visible to rest of organization Visible to customer Consistent approach likely	Added cost to organization
2. Part-timers	Part of those who use SEE May be less costly than Alternative 1 Organizational buy-in more likely than in Alternative 1	SEE implementation may be subordinated to other priorities SEE may be politicized by individual's other responsibilities Consistent approach less likely than in Alternative 1
3. Outside agent (consultant)	Objective approach likely May be a true expert	Objective approach may be difficult to implement because of outsider's insensitivity to turf issues May be expensive—both to develop and update because of need to retain outsider
4. Part of each manager's job	Buy-in facilitated Little added cost	Difficult to achieve consistency across organization Documenting each manager's processes may be put on back burner Difficult to maintain Difficult for customer and outsiders to understand organization's business practices

FIGURE 8–30 Who should develop the SEE in your organization? Here are some alternatives to consider when doing SEE implementation planning. We list some associated advantages and disadvantages for each alternative.

2. **Alternative 2 (Part-timers) and Alternative 4 (Part of each manager's job)**. Here the idea is to constitute a PEG with people who have responsibilities in addition to SEE implementation. By including management in the part-timers, some of the disadvantages associated with each alternative are softened. For example, the first disadvantage of Alternative 2 (SEE implementation may be subordinated to other priorities) can be softened because management is in a position to set priorities and to work with other managers to keep SEE implementation high on the list of organizational priorities. As another example, the fourth disadvantage of Alternative 4 (difficult for customer and outsiders to understand organization's business practices) can be softened by having some part-timers who are not managers. Managers have a tendency to focus on cost and schedule considerations; business practices that give the customer and outsiders insight into the way the seller does business may be viewed by some managers as a threat to the seller's competitive advantage. PEG part-timers who are not managers but who are process experts may be able to soften some of these management views by showing how giving customers visibility into the seller's business practices serves to build trust, thereby increasing the likelihood of follow-on business. For example, having the customer participate in Test Incident CCB meetings as described in Chapter 5 and letting the customer see all TIRs generated, serves to convey to the customer that the seller has nothing to hide (of course, it also runs the risk of conveying to the customer that, if a lot of TIRs are generated, the seller's process is suspect).

The alternatives shown in Figure 8–30 are not a comprehensive list. Together with the preceding discussion of combination alternatives, Figure 8–30 is intended to get your thinking started on how to constitute a PEG for your organization. Your SEE implementation plan needs to describe your organization's approach to constituting a PEG and the rationale for the approach.

Earlier in connection with Figure 8–26 we discussed how to promulgate an ADPE element to your organization. The approach was to use a memorandum that summarized the element content and explicitly encouraged ADPE compliance. We now address the corresponding issue at the level of the SEE, namely the following:

16. How do you frame an SEE implementation policy?

Figure 8–31 shows one approach for addressing this issue. This approach is the SEE-level analogue to the ADPE-element-level approach shown in Figure 8–26.

Earlier we addressed the issue of how to package ADPE elements and related items. In Figure 8–18, we showed a tabbed three-ring binder to illustrate a way to perform this packaging. We indicated that a copy of this three-ring binder should be given to each member of the organization. The simplest way to accomplish this binder distribution is to hand a copy to each member of the organization on the day the member joins the organization. A more forceful way to handle this distribution is via a memorandum such as the one shown in Figure 8–31. The following discussion highlights key points in this memorandum:

1. In the figure, the memorandum is signed by the program manager (i.e., the manager of a number of projects or a large systems development effort). More generally, the memorandum should be signed by a senior manager who has the organizational stature to make decisions for the organization.

2. The memorandum explicitly references the organization's SEE implementation plan. To make more explicit the role that this plan has in establishing an approach to organizational consistency on software projects, the memorandum can include some remarks regarding this point (e.g., "reference [a] sets forth the organization's approach for establishing an engineering environment for achieving software systems development consistency").

3. The figure indicates that it may be appropriate to list other references in the memorandum bearing upon the policy, such as corporate directives. Such directives may address such enterprisewide policies (not neces-

[Your Organization's Name and Logo]   Memo ID: [*Put ID here.*]

Memorandum

To: [*Put your organization's name here.*] Management and Staff

From: [*Put your organization's name here.*] Program Manager

Date: [*Enter the memorandum's date here.*]

Subject: [*Put your organization's name here.*] Systems Engineering Environment (SEE) Policy

Reference: (a) [*Enter the name of your organization's SEE implementation plan here.*]
                 [*List other references bearing on the policy here—for example, corporate directives.*]

This memorandum establishes business practice policy for [*your organization's name*]. [*Your organization's name*] is in the business of [*briefly describe here the nature of your organization's work, mentioning such things as the types of products and services developed, the types of customers served, the contractual vehicle(s) governing your work*]. This policy extends to [*indicate the scope of the policy here—e.g., all projects within your organization, only certain types of projects, only certain customers*].

[*The paragraph below is an example of how you can plug the SEE concept into the policy. The wording can be used as a starting point for describing the relationship between the SEE and the business practices in your organization.*]

At [*your organization's name*], product development is coordinated and standardized via a Systems Engineering Environment (SEE). The SEE consists of two complementary components—an Application Development Process Environment (ADPE) and an Application Development Technology Environment (ADTE). The ADPE is the set of those policies, guidelines, procedures, and standards defining the engineering *processes* for developing products and services. The ADTE consists of the *technology* as embodied in hardware and software development tools, and associated procedures for their use, required to develop applications and other products. The context for the policy set forth in this memorandum is the SEE—in particular, the ADPE elements defining [*your organization's name*] product development practices.

Each ADPE element is signed by the [*your organization's name*] Program Manager and the [*customer's organization name*] Program Manager. Consequently, the ADPE is a joint [*your organization's name*]/customer commitment that [*your organization's name*] systems development business will be conducted in accordance with the ADPE.

[*The list of elements given below is the heart of the policy. They are examples of items that you may want to include in your organization's policy. Your organization's list will generally be different. The list contains items tied to your organization's business culture and cultural changes that management wishes to impose. For example, your organization's existing culture may have approached software systems development as an informal exercise in artistic expression; to remain competitive, your organization's senior management may now wish to impose discipline on software systems development through an ADPE; to effect this cultural change, this management may mandate through the policy that each member of your organization be able to demonstrate that he or she has followed the ADPE practices.*]

The elements of this policy are the following:

1.   The ADPE defines [*your organization's name*] way of engineering products and services.

2.   Each employee receives a binder containing the ADPE elements and material pertaining to the ADTE. Each employee is responsible for keeping this binder current per the instructions included in the binder.

3.   Each employee is responsible for reading each ADPE element so that the employee can assimilate and apply the practices set forth therein to project work.

4.   Each employee is responsible for attending briefings given periodically on the ADPE elements.

5.   Each employee is responsible for promoting with [*your organization's name*] customers the [*your organization's name*] business way as documented in the ADPE elements.

6.   Each employee's performance appraisal will be based in part on the employee's demonstrated compliance with this policy.

This policy is binding on all [*your organization's name*] work. It applies to all [*your organization's name*] employees.

cc: [*Customer Project/Program Manager*]

FIGURE 8–31   Here is a starting point for framing an SEE implementation policy. The figure shows how to tie the policy to your SEE implementation plan. The policy helps to encourage ADPE compliance, particularly in organizations where engineering discipline has been in short supply.

sarily having to do with software) as customer satisfaction, good products at competitive costs, and on-time delivery of products and services.

4. The memorandum defines the SEE concept (second paragraph). This information is particularly helpful for people just joining the organization. The information compactly introduces the binder recipient to its contents.

5. The third paragraph informs the recipient that each ADPE element is signed by both the program manager and the customer. The ADPE business practices are thus a joint seller/customer commitment that both parties will conduct software systems development the ADPE way.

6. The heart of the policy is the list of elements appearing at the end of the memorandum. This list should include the things that your organization considers important regarding engineering behavior. For example, the first policy element in Figure 8–31 stipulates that the ADPE way is to govern engineering behavior; the fifth policy element stipulates that "correct engineering behavior" includes promoting the ADPE way with customers. The sixth policy element picks up on an issue discussed earlier—namely, coupling each employee's performance appraisal to the employee's demonstrated compliance with the ADPE way. Your organization may want to stress items such as these to a greater or lesser degree, or stress other items all together. For instance, your organization may want to take a softer line regarding performance appraisals and ADPE compliance by rewarding compliance but not penalizing noncompliance.

7. The memorandum closes by indicating the SEE scope with respect to the organization's work and employees. The wording in Figure 8–31 indicates that the SEE business practices apply to all of the organization's work and all of the organization's employees. In some organizations, such as those whose work is not restricted to software systems development, the SEE scope may be limited to the software systems development work.

8. The memorandum indicates that the customer receives a copy. Copying the customer is particularly important if one of your policy elements includes something like the fifth one in Figure 8–31—namely, promoting the ADPE way your customers.

The bottom line of the preceding discussion of Figure 8–31 is that simply handing each employee an SEE binder and expecting that its contents will be institutionalized may be overly optimistic for all but the most mature organizations. In general, it may be necessary to give SEE implementation organizational prominence through a policy along the lines of Figure 8–31. Of course, as we discussed earlier in connection with Figure 8–22, unless senior management actively supports such a policy, SEE implementation will not happen. In particular, even if the most senior manager in the organization *signs* such a policy, that manager (and all other managers in the organization) must still *promote* the ADPE way. Therefore, your SEE implementation plan, if it is to have a chance at succeeding, must address the issue of an SEE implementation policy (and management support for the policy).

So far we talked about process improvement primarily at the organizational level. Furthermore, Chapter 7 presented an ADPE element that addressed the process of developing and improving ADPE elements. What can be said about process improvement at the project level? To offer some insight into this key question, we now consider the following issue:

17. How do you plan ADPE implementation improvement at the project level?

Figure 8–32 illustrates one way to address this issue. The figure shows an annotated outline for a project (Project *X*) software process improvement plan.

The purpose of the software process improvement plan is to lay out the approach that Project *X* intends to follow to elevate its process maturity. The context for this approach is the ADPE. That is, the plan is to specify how the project intends to take the policies, guidelines, procedures, and standards set forth in the ADPE and adapt them to the Project *X* work. For example, suppose the organization in

Project *X*

Software Process Improvement Plan for
Project Name X

1.0 INTRODUCTION

1.1 Purpose

This section explains why, in general terms, this plan is being written. Plans are to be between [n_1 to n_2] pages in length. The purpose is to provide the software process improvement plan for Project *X* in a manner that is consistent with the organization's processes as set forth in its ADPE elements. The project will use this plan to raise its process maturity.

1.2 Project Overview

This section explains the project purpose, the products to be developed, and the perceived willingness of the customer to want to improve the way the project does business.

2.0 PROJECT PROCESS IMPROVEMENT OBJECTIVES

2.1 Goals

This section contains a high-level description of the project's goals for process maturity. It is desirable to express goals for both the near term (e.g., next twelve months) and long term (say, next five years). Some words about commitment should be included—e.g., this plan is viewed as a contract of commitment between the project and senior management within the organization.

2.2 Overall Process Improvement Status

This section is used to (1) summarize the results of recent project evaluations aimed at assessing the project's process maturity and (2) describe the areas needing particular attention (e.g., product assurance).

3.0 TECHNICAL APPROACH

This section contains the project's approach for process improvement. Define the specific activities to be accomplished. Address staff training needs for managers, product developers, and product assurance personnel. Indicate how the project intends to prepare for assessments aimed at assessing the project's updated process improvement status.

4.0 SCHEDULE OF ACTIVITIES

This section shows a milestone chart or timeline indicating the actions to be taken to achieve the activities described in the plan (e.g., train staff in the configuration management process to be instituted; the purpose of this training is to explain the mechanics of the project's change management process and project personnel responsibilities for supporting this process). Provide a narrative that walks the reader through the chart or timeline.

5.0 COST

This section contains the anticipated costs for accomplishing the project process improvement effort. A table with supporting narrative may be useful for this purpose.

FIGURE 8–32 Here is an annotated outline for getting you started defining a plan for improving ADPE implementation on a particular project. It is a good idea to include in the SEE implementation plan the idea that each project in the organization should lay out its approach for process improvement within the organization's ADPE context.

which Project X operates has an ADPE guideline for project CCBs. Suppose further that the guideline gives general guidance for CCB minutes—namely that minutes are to be taken by someone, and the minutes must, at a minimum, record decisions made, actions assigned, and a summary of what was discussed. With this broad guidance, Project X may specify as part of its process improvement plan the following activities:

- Minutes will be published within three days of the meeting and sent to attendees to review while events are still fresh in their minds

- A record will be kept as to how often this stipulation was not met and why—a measure of process improvement in this area will be a decrease in the entries in this record as the project proceeds (for example, if the CCB meets every two weeks, if the project lasts a year, and if the measurement period is monthly, then if the first six measurements are 2, 2, 1, 2, 1, 0, this sequence would be considered process improvement because the trend for the last three months shows convergence toward getting the minutes to reviewers within three days of each meeting).

Section 2 of the process improvement plan stipulates process improvement goals. These goals can be expressed in a number of ways—some of which are illustrated in Figure 8–32. For example, if the organization's software systems development process stipulates that peer reviews are to be conducted on each product, a process improvement goal may be the following:

Ninety percent of all peer reviews are to be documented, where "documented" means that the following information was recorded:

- Attendees

- Product name and lead developer

- Summary of what was discussed

- Decisions made

- Actions assigned (including someone being responsible for reporting at the next project CCB that the peer review was held)

- Due dates for assigned actions

- Whether a follow-up peer review is needed—if so, whether it was scheduled as part of the current peer review.

Section 2 also addresses process improvement status as determined from project evaluations conducted by agents either external or internal to the organization. These evaluations serve to baseline where the project stands process maturitywise. In particular, such evaluations serve to identify areas needing process improvement attention. Of course, this part of Section 2 would be applicable only for ongoing projects—that is, projects that (1) have been under way for some time (say, at least a year) and have undergone some kind of assessment (including self-assessment) and (2) are planned to continue for some time into the future.

Section 3 addresses the approach for accomplishing the goals specified in Section 2. A key element of any such approach should be staff and management training. This training should be coupled to organizational training requirements—for example, attendance at ADPE element briefings. It should also include lectures/courses/seminars on software engineering principles and their application (e.g., how to write "good" requirements specifications), as well as courses/seminars on technologies that are to be applied on the project (e.g., how to use a particular CASE tool to be used to develop one or more products on the project).

Several comments regarding training are in order. Training often presents some catch-22 situations—from both the seller's perspective and the customer's perspective. We first consider the seller's perspective. On the one hand, it may be acknowledged by both project management and staff that training is needed in certain areas critical to the project; on the other hand, management and staff may balk at taking time away from project work to attend training sessions (because, for example, project schedules are tight). This argument is typically broached for training sessions that span several days. In these circumstances, management may turn to the training organization and pose a question such as the following:

> Can't the three-day requirements seminar be condensed to one day?

Sometimes it may be possible to respond affirmatively to such a question. In such cases, training can be worked into a project with a tight schedule. In other cases, it simply may not be possible to squeeze a longer training activity down to a shorter one because in so doing its *training* value has been emasculated and the activity is reduced to little more than an information briefing whose retention half-life is less than one day after the "training" session.

So how can this seller catch-22 training conundrum be avoided? One way is to consider training as project work and include it as a stand-alone task in the project plan. In this way, the tight-schedule issue that is typically raised regarding training is avoided because the training is factored into the project schedule.

This latter suggestion of factoring training into the project plan provides a segue to the customer catch-22 regarding seller training. By definition, a customer hires a seller because the seller presumably is skilled in software systems development activities and supporting technologies. If so, many customers argue, "Why should I have to pay for seller training?" To a point, this argument has validity. However, when it comes to process improvement in particular, it is a rare seller organization (and customer organization) that cannot benefit from training aimed at process improvement. And coupled with this training is the expense associated with evaluations aimed at assessing the seller's process maturity so that areas needing improvement can be identified. To try to avoid this situation, some customers include such evaluations in the process that customers use to select sellers. But even in these situations, the argument just presented still applies—namely, it is a rare seller organization that cannot benefit from training aimed at process improvement. Also, customers should recognize that such training, even if it is on their nickel, can return dividends many times the cost of the training. These dividends particularly manifest themselves as reduced rework—that is, increased likelihood of developing products right the first time.

There is another consideration that customers should factor into their perspective of paying for seller process improvement training. It is often difficult for sellers to find (and keep) people well schooled in engineering principles and required technologies. Thus, training in these areas is needed to bring existing staff and new-hires up to speed. Furthermore, as we stress throughout this book, there is no one way to define ADPE elements. Thus, even people who may have good familiarity with engineering principles will still need to be trained in the way these principles are applied in the ADPE elements defining the organization's business way. Otherwise, this business way will wind up on the shelf of good intentions and be replaced by the Sam/Pam/Ham business way(s).

Returning to Figure 8–32, Section 4 in the project process improvement plan addresses the specific activities that the project intends to follow in implementing the approach set forth in Section 3. It should contain a milestone chart or timeline, and supporting narrative indicating the timing of actions leading to the accomplishment of the goals stipulated in Section 2. Examples of such actions are the following:

- Conduct configuration management training.

- Measure process and product integrity for each project deliverable, and measure trends.

- Have process maturity assessment conducted by external agent to determine process improvement.

Section 5 lays out the cost for accomplishing the process improvement stipulated in the preceding sections. Cost is often an issue for management and can particularly be an issue if a customer is being asked to foot at least part of the process improvement bill—for the reasons just presented. The bottom line (no pun intended) here is that money spent on process improvement can return dividends many times the money that was spent. The dividend, as stated earlier, is the rework that is *not* done.

A final comment is in order regarding the cost associated with process improvement activities. Sometimes the dividends that accrue from process improvement activities cannot and should not be measured in terms of the cost of not doing rework. In fact, there are times when process improvement activities can be very expensive—and maintaining a certain level of process maturity can also be expensive. But if the software processes that are the focus of these activities produce software systems whose failure would kill or injure people (e.g., medical support systems), then the measures used to determine the return on investment in process improvement cannot, we contend, be expressed simply as monetary dividends.

This final comment on measurement provides a segue to the next SEE implementation planning issue that we consider, which is the following:

> 18. How can process and product measurement be integrated with your organizational process?

Figure 8–33 shows an approach for addressing this issue by coupling the seller deliverable tracking form introduced in Chapter 3 to the measurement techniques described in Chapter 6. The figure shows the deliverable tracking form augmented by placing product and process measurements on the back of the form.

In Chapter 3, we suggested that the seller deliverable tracking form be used to track each deliverable as it progresses through the organization's software systems development process. Therefore, by tying process measurements to the activities called out on the tracking form, a set of organizationwide measurements is obtained. These process integrity measurements, coupled with the product integrity measurements, can then be used to determine whether there is a correlation between the integrity of the products being produced and the integrity of the process used to develop these products. With this insight, the organization can identify potential areas needing attention.

The following points should be noted regarding the measurement approach in Figure 8–33:

- It is a way of doing measurement in near-real-time in the sense that the back of the form can be filled out as the product goes through the various process wickets identified on the front side of the form. Measurement simply involves having the individual who is indicated on the form circle the appropriate value (e.g., for process activity xt_{25} "performs technical editing," if the seller technical editor followed the organizational editing standards but did not edit the entire deliverable, the technical editor would circle the value 0.5). This near-real-time measurement approach of course has some obvious drawbacks—the most glaring one being that people who perform an activity are generally not objective in assessing the extent to which that activity may have been accomplished. An alternative to this self-evaluation approach is to have individuals not involved with the activity subsequently assess the activity. This evaluation can be accomplished through some combination of an audit of the project files and interviews with the people who performed the activities. If the files do not contain the information (e.g., for the technical editing activity, the files did not contain the draft of the deliverable showing the technical editor's markups), then the people who performed the activities would be interviewed. Of course, people's memories fade over time, and people also tend to report their work in the most optimistic light. Interviews thus contain the same element of bias as that found in the self-evaluation approach. Whatever approach you decide to use, you should clearly indicate in any measurements that you publish or otherwise present the potential sources of bias. Such caveats will allow the recipients of the measurement results to interpret them appropriately.

- After a value has been circled on each of the eight scales, the product and process integrity indexes can be calculated, and Kiviat diagrams can be generated. These calculation and graphing activities can be per-

SELLER DELIVERABLE TRACKING FORM

PROJECT FILE ESTABLISHMENT at Deliverable Support Center (DSC)

Product Title: _____

Lead Developer(s): _____

Contributor(s): _____

Product Control Number: _____   Charge Number: _____

Contract Number/Name: _____

Date & Time Product Is Due to Customer: _____

TECHNICAL REVIEW of PRODUCT

_____   _____
Peer Reviewer or Moderator   Technical Editor (documents only)

_____   _____
Product Assurance Reviewer or Manager   Project-level Technical Oversight Management

FINAL COORDINATION with DSC

_____   _____
Deliverable Support Center Manager   Lead Developer

PROJECT FILE MANAGEMENT

Hardcopy filed at _____

_____
Lead Developer   Electronic copy filed at _____

COMMENTS/ISSUES

_____
_____
_____
_____
_____

MANAGEMENT REVIEW and APPROVAL

_____ Project Manager	☐ concur	☐ nonconcur	_____ signature	_____ date
_____ Process Engineering Group Representative	☐ concur	☐ nonconcur	_____ signature	_____ date
_____ Business Manager (costing)	☐ concur	☐ nonconcur	_____ signature	_____ date
_____ Program Manager	☐ approved for release	☐ other action	_____ signature	_____ date
_____ Delivery and Distribution Representative			_____ signature	_____ date

CUSTOMER RECEIPT and APPROVAL

☐ Received Customer Receipt of Deliverable Form   ☐ Received Customer Acceptance of Deliverable Form   ☐ **Received written notification that deliverable requires additional work and notified Project Manager upon receipt**

[Form Number]   **Front**   **[Form Issue Date]**

FIGURE 8–33   Here is an example of how to augment the seller deliverable tracking form introduced in Chapter 3 to include organizational product and process measurements. The measurement information is placed on the back of the form. The process measurements focus on the process activities called out on the front of the form. The product measurements are tied to the product integrity attributes that your organization considers important. Two product integrity attributes are called out in the figure—on-time delivery and customer acceptance.

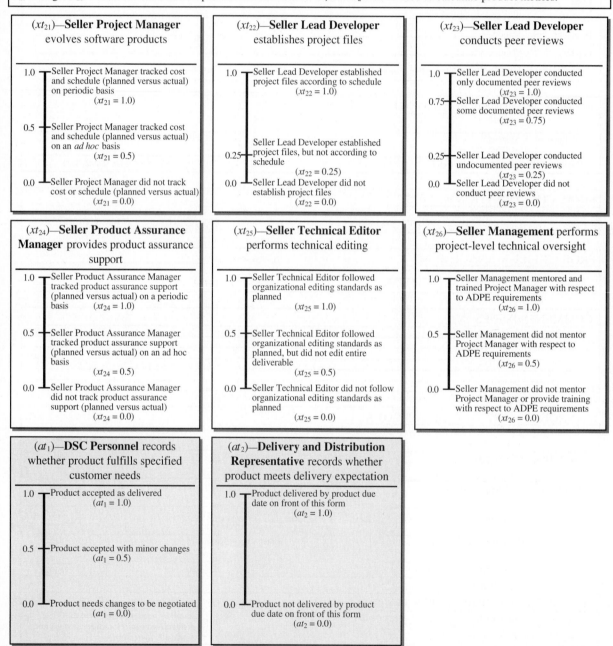

SELLER DELIVERABLE TRACKING FORM

For each box below, the responsible person (i.e., **Seller Project Manager**, **Seller Lead Developer**, **Seller Product Assurance Manager**, **Seller Technical Editor**, **Seller Management**, **DSC Personnel**, and **Delivery and Distribution Representative**) simply circles the number that indicates what action was completed. The boxes represent organizational measurements. Boxes xt_{21} through xt_{26} will be used to calculate process metrics. Boxes at_1 and at_2 will be used to calculate product metrics.

(xt_{21})—**Seller Project Manager** evolves software products

- 1.0 — Seller Project Manager tracked cost and schedule (planned versus actual) on periodic basis ($xt_{21} = 1.0$)
- 0.5 — Seller Project Manager tracked cost and schedule (planned versus actual) on an *ad hoc* basis ($xt_{21} = 0.5$)
- 0.0 — Seller Project Manager did not track cost or schedule (planned versus actual) ($xt_{21} = 0.0$)

(xt_{22})—**Seller Lead Developer** establishes project files

- 1.0 — Seller Lead Developer established project files according to schedule ($xt_{22} = 1.0$)
- 0.25 — Seller Lead Developer established project files, but not according to schedule ($xt_{22} = 0.25$)
- 0.0 — Seller Lead Developer did not establish project files ($xt_{22} = 0.0$)

(xt_{23})—**Seller Lead Developer** conducts peer reviews

- 1.0 — Seller Lead Developer conducted only documented peer reviews ($xt_{23} = 1.0$)
- 0.75 — Seller Lead Developer conducted some documented peer reviews ($xt_{23} = 0.75$)
- 0.25 — Seller Lead Developer conducted undocumented peer reviews ($xt_{23} = 0.25$)
- 0.0 — Seller Lead Developer did not conduct peer reviews ($xt_{23} = 0.0$)

(xt_{24})—**Seller Product Assurance Manager** provides product assurance support

- 1.0 — Seller Product Assurance Manager tracked product assurance support (planned versus actual) on a periodic basis ($xt_{24} = 1.0$)
- 0.5 — Seller Product Assurance Manager tracked product assurance support (planned versus actual) on an ad hoc basis ($xt_{24} = 0.5$)
- 0.0 — Seller Product Assurance Manager did not track product assurance support (planned versus actual) ($xt_{24} = 0.0$)

(xt_{25})—**Seller Technical Editor** performs technical editing

- 1.0 — Seller Technical Editor followed organizational editing standards as planned ($xt_{25} = 1.0$)
- 0.5 — Seller Technical Editor followed organizational editing standards as planned, but did not edit entire deliverable ($xt_{25} = 0.5$)
- 0.0 — Seller Technical Editor did not follow organizational editing standards as planned ($xt_{25} = 0.0$)

(xt_{26})—**Seller Management** performs project-level technical oversight

- 1.0 — Seller Management mentored and trained Project Manager with respect to ADPE requirements ($xt_{26} = 1.0$)
- 0.5 — Seller Management did not mentor Project Manager with respect to ADPE requirements ($xt_{26} = 0.5$)
- 0.0 — Seller Management did not mentor Project Manager or provide training with respect to ADPE requirements ($xt_{26} = 0.0$)

(at_1)—**DSC Personnel** records whether product fulfills specified customer needs

- 1.0 — Product accepted as delivered ($at_1 = 1.0$)
- 0.5 — Product accepted with minor changes ($at_1 = 0.5$)
- 0.0 — Product needs changes to be negotiated ($at_1 = 0.0$)

(at_2)—**Delivery and Distribution Representative** records whether product meets delivery expectation

- 1.0 — Product delivered by product due date on front of this form ($at_2 = 1.0$)
- 0.0 — Product not delivered by product due date on front of this form ($at_2 = 0.0$)

[Form Number]   Back   [Form Issue Date]

FIGURE 8–33 *Continued*

formed, for example, by somebody in the Deliverable Support Center. Spreadsheets with graphing capabilities can be used to facilitate accomplishment of these activities. The calculations can also be rolled up in various ways to get a sense of where the organization is headed. For example, the average product integrity index can be computed on, say, a monthly basis to see whether the integrity of products delivered is increasing, decreasing, staying the same, or random.

■ The approach shown in Figure 8–33 does not address all the process activities called out in Chapter 3. For example, it does not address the CCB component of the process, but there is no reason why it could not. As your organization matures over time, there may be different parts of your organizational software systems development process that you may want to measure. The approach shown here is general and allows you to adjust your organizational-level measurement activity for this purpose. Similar comments apply to the product integrity attributes shown on the form.

■ We stress that the approach shown is for organizational-level measurements because it is tied to an organizational-level tracking form. That is, the product and process attributes measured are the same for products streaming through the organizational process. By using this common set of attributes, quantitative insight into the *organization's* process can be gained—because we are comparing apples with apples across the organization. We noted in Chapter 6 that measurements at the *project* level will often involve different attributes. For example, a particular project may be using a certain technology (e.g., information engineering) and may want to measure, for instance, how many JAD (joint application design) sessions are needed to get closure on the customer's enterprisewide requirements. In this case, the project may want to set up a project-level tracking form to collect a common set of measurements. Remember—measurement for measurement's sake is a waste of time and money. As we have stressed, first decide on the questions you want answered with your measurements and then structure your measurements to get answers to these questions.

These considerations need to be factored into your SEE implementation plan if you want to include a product and process measurement program in your SEE implementation approach. However, unless your organization has some experience working with documented processes, it is not generally a good idea to embark upon a measurement program on day one. It is preferable first to document your organization's business practices—at least at the level discussed in Chapter 3—and get your people acclimated to following the practices. Then, with this process foundation in place, you can introduce a measurement program. Our observation is that people unaccustomed to working in an environment with some documented practices tend to measure things for the sake of measurement. They have trouble sorting out how to use the measurements for improving the way that they accomplish software systems development.

We now consider two questions related to the measurement issue just discussed. In addition to presenting measurement approaches tied to process and product integrity, Chapter 6 discussed other types of process-related organizational-level measurements that may be useful to collect (e.g., the average number of drafts required to produce a project plan resulting in a project). We return to this topic to address the following two measurement questions:

■ How can you make product and process measurements easy to interpret?

■ How do you sell product and process measurement as a useful activity?

Regarding the first question, it takes time for people to feel comfortable with quantifying products and processes. For example, our approach to these measurement challenges relies on the concepts of vector and vector length. These concepts are not in people's everyday vocabulary. Kiviat diagrams also take some getting used to. So, when getting started on a measurement program, you may want to try something more conventional. We illustrate this idea by using some measurement data adapted from some of our experience. This illustration will also address the second question. We show how measuring a particular process before, during, and subsequent to the documentation of the process can dramatically show the improvement of that process. This illustration should give you ideas for writing into your SEE implementation plan your approach for addressing these two measurement-related questions.

There is a tendency when compiling measurement data to perform various kinds of statistical analyses. A potential problem with such analyses is that many decision makers, in particular, have difficulty interpreting what the analysis results mean. While it is true that for statisticians and others familiar with mathematics, concepts such as "mean," "standard deviation," and "median" may be meaningful, for the general population these concepts may cause eyes to glaze over. Thus, it is important, particularly when starting a measurement program, to present results in a manner that does not assume that the intended audience speaks mathematics fluently. We now consider an example based on actual data to illustrates these points.

Figure 8–34 shows a plot of data intended to answer the following measurement question:

How effective is the organization's project planning process?

The measurement used to assess this effectiveness is whether or not the project plan was delivered on time. Each point on the plot represents a project plan (x-axis) and its *actual* delivery date in days relative to its *planned* delivery date (y-axis). More specifically, the chart shows the difference in (work) days between the actual delivery date and the planned delivery date of a series of project plans produced in an organization over a period of almost four years. If this difference is zero, the plan was delivered on time; if this difference was positive, the plan was delivered late; if this difference was negative, the plan was delivered early. The data are arranged by year. Within a year, the order of the points has no significance. That is, data point 3 in planning year 1 does not necessarily mean that the plan associated with that point was produced/delivered before the plan associated with data point 4. However, all plans in year N were delivered before all plans in year $N + 1$.

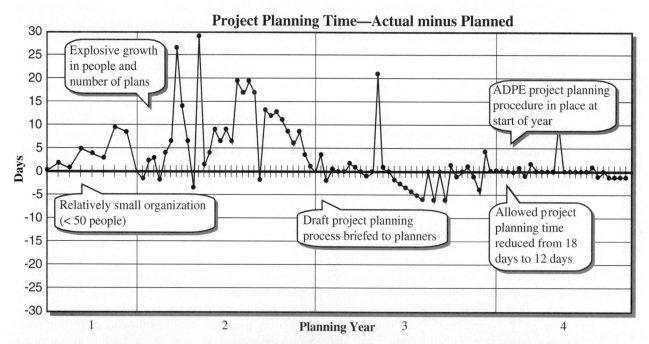

FIGURE 8–34   The figure shows a simple, yet insightful, way to show the effectiveness of part of an organization's process—in this case, project planning. The plot, adapted from actual data, shows whether or not project plans were delivered late, on time, or early over a period of several years. Each point is a project plan (x-axis) and its delivery date in days relative to its planned delivery date (y-axis). If the y-value is positive, the plan was delivered late; if this value is zero, the plan was delivered on time; if this value is negative, the plan was delivered early.

The plot is annotated to show the following significant events that took place regarding the organization:

- Initially (i.e., during year 1), the organization was of relatively small size (less than fifty people) with just a handful of projects. Project plans were written against an evolving template. There was no documented project planning process. Project plans were generally delivered late.

- During the organization's second year, the organization experienced explosive growth with the number of projects increasing tenfold. The variations in the plan delivery times resulted from the learning curve associated with new people coming on board and getting acclimated to the way that the organization did project planning through the project plan template. Most project plans were delivered late—varying from five to fifteen days for most plans, with two delivered almost a month late. A few plans were delivered early. The frenzy of planning activity consumed the organization for a number of months.

- During the organization's third year, a draft project planning process was briefed to the seller and customer organizations. This draft process was based on lessons learned during the previous year's frenzied planning cycle. As the plot shows, the process briefed served to stabilize things. With one exception, almost all plans were delivered within a few days of planned dates or were delivered early. The one exception was a plan that was delivered three weeks late. The reason for the delay was a combination of customer uncertainty on what needed to be done and seller misunderstanding of what needed to be done.

- During the organization's fourth year, an ADPE procedure documenting the organization's project planning process was put in place. The ADPE procedure folded in many of the lessons learned from the preceding years. As Figure 8–34 shows, putting this documented process in place during that year prior to the beginning of the brunt of the project planning activity served to converge the project plan delivery dates to the desired goal of "consistently on time." This convergence to consistent on-time delivery was particularly noteworthy because, at the start of that year, the time to produce a project plan was cut from approximately eighteen days to twelve days (for reasons that are not important for this discussion except to note that such things happen in the real world).

We summarize what the plot in Figure 8–34 has to say about making measurement easy to interpret and useful. In so doing, we come back to the notion of product integrity. The plot in Figure 8–34 offers the following:

- It is easy to interpret. The distribution of points and the balloons containing amplifying information tell a good process improvement story compactly.

- It shows the power of simple measurements displayed so that the numbers almost speak for themselves. The convergence to zero of the data points dramatically shows that putting a documented process in place embodying lessons learned can lead to consistency—at least for the integrity attribute of on-time delivery. Plots for other integrity attributes such as cost of producing a plan and customer satisfaction would give further insight into project planning process integrity. For example, suppose that customer satisfaction was measured in terms of what the customer indicated on the Acceptance of Deliverable form introduced in Chapter 3. Suppose further that the three choices on this form were assigned the following values:
  - Accepted as Delivered = 2.
  - Accept with Minor Changes = 1.
  - Changes to Be Negotiated = 0.

Finally, suppose that a plot of these values for all the plans given in Figure 8–34 shows in year 4, with just a couple of exceptions, a straight line that intersects the y-axis at $y = 2$ (i.e., Accepted as Delivered). Then, together with the plot in Figure 8–34, the organization could conclude the following:

> The organization's project planning process *consistently* produces project plans that are *on time* and are *accepted as delivered*. In other words, the organization consistently produced project plans with integrity.

We now conclude this section on the key SEE implementation planning issues listed in Figure 8–5 by considering the final issue listed there. This issue concerns the packaging of the SEE implementation plan and is the following:

19. How should you structure an SEE implementation plan?

Figure 8–35 is an annotated outline for helping you prepare a plan for implementing an SEE for your organization. The outline contains five sections and calls out appendices for optional material. The following comments on these sections and the appendices are from the seller's perspective, since, in general, the seller will be responsible for setting up an SEE. However, a buyer/user organization can also use the outline to specify for a seller how the buyer/user wants the seller to plan SEE implementation.

The following discussion walks through the annotated outline in Figure 8–35:

- Section 1 ("Background and Systems Development Mission") sets the stage for the SEE implementation approach set forth in Section 2. In Section 1, the seller describes the software systems development challenge facing the customer. For example, the customer may need to upgrade and integrate a number of existing systems (e.g., some systems may have no documentation, other systems may have outdated documentation, and still other systems may have outmoded hardware that needs to be replaced). To meet this challenge, the customer wants to establish a software systems development process that will guide the upgrading and integration of these systems, including bringing documentation up-to-date. The customer wants to abandon the old way of upgrading these systems because personnel turnover within the organization makes it increasingly difficult to use these systems and change them to meet evolving needs. This section should define key terms (e.g., SEE, ADPE, ADTE, independent product assurance). This section should explain that the ADPE practices serve to establish norms of software systems development behavior that help the seller and customer interact harmoniously. The section should also explain that SEE implementation is a cultural change exercise—for both the customer and the seller.

- Section 2 ("Implementation Approach") lays out the approach for establishing and maintaining an ADPE within the seller's organization. This section is the heart of the plan and can be oriented in a number of different ways, depending on where an organization is with respect to setting up a documented engineering environment. For an organization starting out in this arena, this section should be oriented along the lines of a strategy with associated milestones—as opposed to a detailed implementation plan with specific deliverables and a corresponding week-by-week or month-by-month schedule. An example milestone might be the following:

  > For an ADPE taxonomy consisting of policies, guidelines, procedures, and standards, develop and implement one element of each type within one year of the publication of this plan. One of these elements is to define the organization's software systems development process.

In subsequent years, the plan can be updated to incorporate lessons learned and to call out specific ADPE elements that are to be developed or updated and to delineate a corresponding schedule.

We note that, as with most planning documents, an SEE implementation plan can be viewed as a living document to be updated periodically. Frequent updates to a plan may, in fact, be necessary if it contains a lot of detail and if the actual implementation takes a different course. However, if process definition resources are tight or if your organization tends to downplay planning and favor just getting on with SEE implementation, then it may be preferable to write Section 2 at the strategy level with little planning detail. Orienting the section along these broad lines makes it unnecessary to update the plan. That is, the plan can be read by new employees and still reflect the general direction of the organization's evolving ADPE.

This section should describe, at least in general terms, how ADPE implementation will elevate the process maturity of the organization. For example, your organization may want to plug into certain widely recognized approaches to elevating process maturity—such as the SEI Capability Maturity Model for Software or ISO 9000. These approaches can provide guidance for identifying the kinds of ADPE elements to de-

[Your Organization's Name and Logo]

Document #
Date

Plan for Implementing a Systems Engineering Environment for [Your Organization's Name]

Document #
Date

1.0 BACKGROUND AND SYSTEMS DEVELOPMENT MISSION

This section gives insight into the software systems development challenge facing the organization. The section describes the role of the systems engineering environment (SEE) in helping the organization meet this challenge. If the document is to focus on the application development process environment (ADPE), this section addresses the rationale for this scoping. The remainder of this outline assumes this focus. This section should contain definitions of terms needed to understand the document (e.g., SEE, ADPE, life cycle, product assurance). The issue of ADPE implementation and cultural change should be addressed.

2.0 IMPLEMENTATION APPROACH

This section specifies the approach for establishing and maintaining an ADPE within your organization. It should address how ADPE implementation will elevate the maturity of the organization's software systems development process. It should discuss the factors that influence the implementation approach (e.g., the number of elements to be developed—e.g., small number of thick documents). It should describe the ADPE implementation process and offer an ADPE architecture. It should specify ADPE implementation milestones. If SEE implementation has not been stipulated by the customer as part of a procurement package, this section should address the cost of the approach.

3.0 IMPLEMENTATION ISSUES

This section presents and discusses major issues bearing on the implementation approach laid out in Section 2. The purpose of presenting these issues is to set realistic expectations regarding the implementation approach. Figure 8–5 lists issues that can be used as a starting point for issues to consider. The extensive discussion of each of the Figure 8–5 issues that we give is intended to help you (1) develop issues pertinent to your organization and (2) write this section.

4.0 ADPE IMPLEMENTATION MANAGEMENT AND STAFFING

This section delineates the responsibilities for managing the ADPE implementation approach in Section 2. The section also specifies the staffing (i.e., people) required to support the implementation approach.

5.0 REFERENCES

This section lists the references cited in the rest of the plan. It may also list references used to prepare the plan. For completeness, it may be useful to include a brief description of each reference.

APPENDICES

This optional material can contain such things as sample (draft) ADPE elements, organizational policies and/or contractual strictures constraining SEE implementation (e.g., tool suites, accreditation requirements such as ISO 9000 or SEI capability maturity, personnel educational requirements, life cycle models), customer organization, and implementation options considered but not adopted.

FIGURE 8–35 Here is an annotated outline for getting you started defining a plan for implementing a systems engineering environment (SEE) for your organization. Because our book focuses on *process*, the outline assumes that the plan focuses on the ADPE component of the SEE.

velop. As discussed in Chapter 6, the SEI approach is built upon things called key process areas (KPAs). KPAs are major building blocks in establishing an organization's process capability. One KPA is Project Planning. Thus, for an organization that wants to tie its ADPE implementation approach to the SEI's approach to elevating process maturity, this particular KPA suggests that the organization's ADPE should contain an element that addresses project planning, or have an element that contains a part that addresses project planning.

This section should describe how the ADPE is to be constituted. The discussion earlier in this chapter of Figure 8–16 regarding the amount of detail to include in an ADPE element addresses aspects of ADPE constitution. More generally, Section 2 should contain an ADPE architecture to describe ADPE constitution. The architecture sets forth the ADPE element taxonomy (e.g., in this book, the taxonomy is "policy," "guideline," "procedure," and "standard"). It should indicate a structure for the elements. For example, at the topmost level, this structure may consist of the following two categories of elements:

- Elements specific to the organization (e.g., an element defining the organization's overall process)

- Elements available from existing sources (e.g., IEEE standards, ISO 9000 standards, process-oriented textbooks such as this book)

At the second level, elements may be further categorized. For example, it may be desirable to include in the architecture the following three categories for the ADPE elements specific to the organization. These categories highlight three major aspects of *any* engineering endeavor—namely, (1) thinking before doing, (2) doing, and (3) getting organized to perform the thinking and doing. Example titles of candidate ADPE elements for each of these categories are shown to give you additional insight into our concept of ADPE architecture.

- **Planning**
  - Project Planning Procedure
  - Configuration Management Planning Guideline
  - Test Planning Guideline
  - Data Integration Planning Guideline
- **Process**
  - Software Systems Development Process Policy
  - Change Control Board Guideline
  - Document Templates Standard
  - Peer Review Procedure
- **Organization**
  - Project Manager Responsibilities Guideline
  - Process Engineering Group Policy
  - Data Administrator Guideline.

Annotated outlines for some of these items are given in this book (e.g., project planning procedure). Regarding the **Organization** category, we note that the approach in this book is to fold organizational considerations into ADPE elements that fall into the other two categories. That is, this book does not give examples of ADPE elements that are limited to organizational considerations. We show this structure to give you a starting point for handling such considerations via stand-alone elements. You could, for example, take all the sections dealing with responsibilities in the elements that we discuss in this book, remove them from these elements, and place them in stand-alone responsibilities elements. For example, you could create an element that specifies project manager responsibilities for (1) project planning, (2) managing product development within the context of the organization's software systems development process, (3) participating in CCBs, (4) giving visibility to peer reviews, etc.

Section 2 can also describe in greater detail one or more ADPE elements to give additional insight into the ADPE implementation approach. If it is desired to illustrate fully the ADPE element concept, Section 2 (or appendices) could contain sample ADPE elements. If an organization is actually doing software systems development while the SEE implementation plan is being developed, such elements may, in fact, be based on lessons learned from this development activity or draft elements prepared to support this development activity.

If SEE implementation has not been stipulated by the customer as part of a procurement package, Section 2 should address the cost of the approach. It may be necessary to present and to cost alternative approaches (e.g., low-cost approach, preferred approach, Cadillac approach). The benefits of each alternative should also be described. The pacing items for SEE implementation cost are the following:

- **PEG staff.** The number of people needed to staff the PEG is a function of what the PEG is to do. If the PEG is to write the SEE implementation plan, develop and maintain SEE elements, and prepare and give briefings on ADPE elements, then a full-time staff of three to five people can support an organization of several hundred. If PEG responsibilities extend to labor-intensive endeavors such as (1) preparing and presenting multiday seminars and (2) investigating and testing new technologies, then staffing needs can increase by a multiple of what is needed to prepare, update, and brief ADPE elements.

- **ADTE staff.** Although we have not examined ADTE issues (except for writing an ADTE plan), staffing needs can be considerable depending on the organization's needs for maintaining such technology items as networks, programming language tools, CASE tools, and database management tools. In some organizations, this staff can be incorporated into a facilities management staff. In this case, ADTE staffing needs to become part of a budget not linked to the SEE. If such is not the case, then for an organization of several hundred people, ADTE staff can be several percent of the organization's total.

- **Staff training time.** For an organization of several hundred people, this cost can quickly mount to hundreds of thousands of dollars or more per year. For example, if the organization's average loaded labor cost is $50/hour, the labor cost to train just thirty people for three days is $24 \times 30 \times \$50 = \$36,000$. This cost does not include instructor time and the labor required to prepare a three-day course. The labor required to prepare and test a several-day course can itself amount to hundreds of thousands of dollars.

- Section 3 ("Implementation Issues") discusses major issues bearing on the implementation approach set forth in Section 2. The current section in this chapter is intended to help you write this section. Your starting point is Figure 8–5. From the issues listed there and the supporting discussion you can (1) determine which issues are pertinent to your organization and/or (2) uncover other issues pertinent to your organization.

- Section 4 ("ADPE Implementation Management and Staffing") delineates the responsibilities for managing the ADPE implementation approach set forth in Section 2. These responsibilities should not be limited to the seller organization. The customer also has responsibilities in this arena. Throughout this book, we stressed that each ADPE element should be signed by a responsible customer agent as well as a responsible seller agent. This sign-off should not be just a ceremonial act. It should signify customer commitment to abiding by the ADPE practices in dealing with the seller.

  This book uses the label "process engineering group (PEG)" for the organization responsible for developing and implementing the SEE. Earlier in this section, we discussed various ways the PEG could be constituted. That discussion can be used as a starting point for addressing how ADPE implementation is to be managed and staffed.

- Section 5 ("References") should list all references cited in the plan. Particularly helpful are customer policies, directives, and plans that serve as the "biblical" basis for tasking a seller to develop and implement an SEE. For example, a customer may have a strategic plan that calls for getting more bang from the bucks invested information management systems and supporting databases. The strategic plan may further stipulate that such cost savings are to be realized through documented software systems development practices aimed at reducing rework and duplication. Such stipulations provide a natural segue for introducing the SEE concept as a consistent way to engineer software systems that do what they are supposed to do and are delivered on time and within budget.

  For completeness, it may be useful to include a brief description of each reference cited in this section. Such descriptions can give the seller early insight into the customer's commitment to following documented software systems development practices, as well as having the seller do the same.

- Appendices can be used to provide amplifying insight into the SEE implementation approach set forth in the body of the plan. This amplifying insight can be provided through such items as (1) the complete text of sample or trial ADPE elements and (2) explanation and illustration of software engineering and other engineering principles and concepts. Examples of such principles and concepts are life cycle models, checks and balances, process maturity, and requirements testability.

In closing this discussion of the annotated outline in Figure 8–35, we note that it may be useful to include an executive summary at the front of the SEE implementation plan. An executive summary is particularly helpful if (1) the plan is lengthy (say one hundred pages or more) and (2) senior management support is needed to make the plan happen. The executive summary should capture the plan's salient points

We have now completed our detailed treatment of the nineteen key SEE implementation planning issues listed in Figure 8–5. This treatment has been aimed at pulling together the ideas, concepts, and principles from the preceding seven chapters to help you organize an SEE implementation approach for your organization. By integrating the thoughts from the preceding chapters, we are helping you revisit the preceding chapters in a structured manner.

The next section offers some closing remarks about the book.

8.4 CULTIVATING SUCCESSFUL SOFTWARE DEVELOPMENT

Figure 8–36 captures the book's approach and bottom line. In one sentence, the book does the following:

> It shows how to cultivate successful software development by showing how to cultivate a systems engineering environment that helps to maintain and focus customer (king) and seller (wizard) dialogue.

Software systems development is first and foremost a communications exercise between the customer (king) and the seller (wizard). To be successful, the wizard and king must communicate effectively. Because what the wizard ultimately produces (i.e., software code) is hard to see, precise communication is particularly important.

This book describes an approach for raising the visibility of the software systems development process and resultant products as a means for aiding precise communication between the wizard and king. The approach is to establish a systems engineering environment (SEE) wherein what the wizard and king are to do is laid down (i.e., documented) and agreed to by both parties. This environment consists of two complementary components—an application development process environment (ADPE) and an application development technology environment (ADTE). The ADPE is the set of business practices that the wizard and king commit to following. The ADTE is the set of technologies that the wizard uses to develop software systems for the king. This book focused on the ADPE because, without good understanding of software systems development processes, technology has little value.

The book stresses that both the king and the wizard progress in their understanding of what needs to be done as a software project proceeds. This progression in understanding translates into changes to what needs to be done. The book spends a lot of time discussing the specifics of managing this change. Because, as we said earlier, the seller's handiwork is hard to see, managing this change is particularly challenging. The book therefore explores at length processes and techniques for raising the visibility of this handiwork and the processes used to perform this handiwork.

Overlaid on this complication that the wizard and king change their minds regarding what needs to be done as work proceeds (i.e., product change), there is another type of change going on (i.e., business process change). Business process change has to do with the way the wizard does what the king wants the wizard to do and the way that the king interacts with the wizard. This book offers suggestions for (1) overcoming resistance associated with this business process change and (2) institutionalizing the changed processes via the ADPE. Institutionalization means that the wizard and king settle into

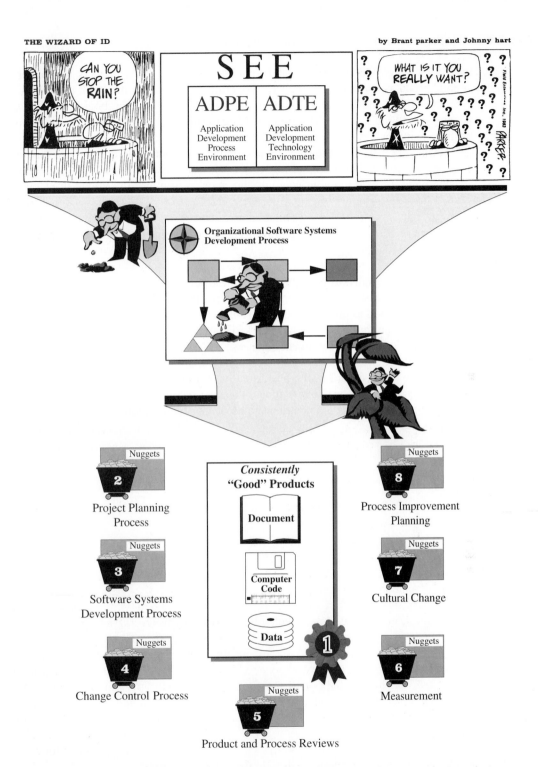

FIGURE 8–36 Reduced to simplest terms, this book shows you how to cultivate a systems engineering environment (SEE) that helps to maintain and focus dialogue between the customer (king) and seller (wizard). Maintaining this focused dialogue raises the likelihood that the customer and seller achieve common understanding of what needs to be done—without unwanted excursions. With this common understanding, the seller can develop consistently "good" products—that is, products that (1) do what the customer asked for, (2) are delivered on time, and (3) are delivered within budget. In other words, the seller can consistently deliver to the customer products with integrity. To help you to achieve this consistency, the book's essence has been reduced to a set of nuggets. (Parts of this figure were reprinted by premission of Johnny Hart and Creators Syndicate, Inc.)

the ADPE way of doing things, and thereby, hopefully, the wizard is able to produce consistently "good" products for the king. We say "hopefully" because, as the book points out, getting the ADPE practices "right" the first time is easier said than done. Thus, the book shows how to (1) control the wizard's and king's mind-changing and (2) ease the wizard and king into a consistent way of doing business with each other.

Aimed at practitioners, the book facilitates information retrieval by distilling the essence of Chapters 2 through 8 into a set of nuggets, as shown in Figure 8–36. These nuggets offer a convenient starting point for working your way into the chapters of interest to you to draw out the details that you want to apply to your organization. For example, one Chapter 2 nugget is the following:

> *Planning needs to assess risk to determine the appropriate mix of management, development, and product assurance resources.*

This nugget is intended to prompt you to go into the chapter and draw out the details presented there for doing risk assessment in support of project planning.

We have tried to provide you with some thoughts on how to cultivate successful software development. We hope that this book has sparked some ideas on how you might improve the way you conduct software systems development business.

If this book at least caused you to think about doing software systems development in a more disciplined way than you did in the past, then we communicated our message. If, in addition, this book persuaded you to try some of its ideas, then we achieved our goal—helping you reduce the ever-present software systems development risks of unsatisfied requirements, cost overruns, and schedule slippages.

Bibliography

The documents listed in this bibliography are a selected compilation of software engineering references. We also include some references from other disciplines, such as management science and organizational change engineering. The documents listed present supporting or contrasting views presented in this book. In some cases, they present detailed discussion of topics not treated in depth or only touched upon in this book (e.g., peer reviews).

Many of the documents listed contain additional references pertaining to software engineering in general and software process improvement in particular. This bibliography is thus intended to help you network your way through extant software engineering literature, with an emphasis on software process improvement.

This bibliography is not exhaustive. Most of the entries are references that the authors at least looked at during preparation of this book.

Software engineering literature is growing at a rapid rate. It is not even feasible to keep on top of the subset of software engineering publications that focus on process improvement. However, to help you in finding things that may be of interest to you in this area, we first list journals that often contain one or more articles bearing on software process improvement. We also list organizations that you can contact that will either help you get started in this area or help you expand your search on a process improvement topic of interest to you.

The IEEE Computer Society publishes the following journals that contain articles that typically appeal to a broad audience—ranging from software novices to experts. For the novice, these journals can help ease you into the world of software technology. For the expert, these journals can help update your expertise and point you to additional readings to enrich that expertise.

IEEE Software.

IEEE Computer.

The following annually published item is a good source of software engineering material:

COMPSAC XX Proceedings

Each fall since 1977, the IEEE Computer Society has held a Computer Software & Applications Conference (COMPSAC). The purpose of these conferences is to bring together software practitioners and theoreticians to exchange the latest ideas, practices, and breakthroughs in an area of software engineering covered by no other international conference—namely, applications. The papers presented at these conferences are published in the proceedings for that year. Thus, for example, the papers presented at the 1988 conference were published in the COMPSAC 88 Proceedings. The COMPSAC XX Proceedings are a good source for maintaining awareness of advances in software engineering. An interesting exercise is to note how papers in this area have evolved since 1977. These papers are also a good source of additional (and, for the most part, current) references in this area.

The IEEE also publishes software engineering standards. The following publication is perhaps the most convenient to use:

"IEEE Software Engineering Standards Collection."

This collection is published annually. IEEE standards are developed through the Technical Committees of the IEEE Societies and the Standards Coordinating Committees of the IEEE Standards Board. Members of the committees serve voluntarily and without compensation (and they may not even be IEEE members).

The collection contains a couple of dozen items, with new ones added each year as well as updates to existing standards. This publication provides a useful starting point for creating an ADPE element for document templates.

The Software Engineering Institute, based at Carnegie Mellon University in Pittsburgh, is a focal point within the United States for software process improvement technology. Founded in 1984, it is managed and partly funded by the United States Government. Its mission is to provide leadership in advancing the state of the practice of software engineering to improve the quality of systems that depend on software. The Institute's strategy for accomplishing this mission is the following:

- Improve the state of the practice of software engineering.

- Mature the profession by maturing the skills of practitioners, managers, and educators using the following approach:
  - Maturing the organizational and managerial processes through which software is acquired, developed, and maintained;
  - Maturing the technology used to develop and maintain software.

The Software Engineering Institute publishes a plethora of documents aimed at helping others mature their processes and technology bearing on their software work. Each year it conducts a symposium that affords the international software community the opportunity to keep abreast of the Institute's activities and to interact with one another to share software process improvement experiences.

For convenience, the bibliographical entries are partitioned into the following sections:

1. *Government Publications*

   The entries in this section are three Software Engineering Institute publications on the Capability Maturity Model^{SM} for Software (CMM^{SM}) and the People Capability Maturity Model^{SM}.

2. *Magazine/Journal Articles*

   The entries in this section are articles that appeared primarily in magazines or journals that deal in whole or part with software. For the most part, we selected articles published since 1990.

3. *Books*

   This section contains a list of books, most of which were published since 1990, on aspects of software engineering and other disciplines such as management science bearing on topics addressed in our book.

1. GOVERNMENT PUBLICATIONS

Curtis, B., W. E. Hefley, and S. Miller. "People Capability Maturity Model^{SM}," Software Engineering Institute and Carnegie Mellon University Technical Report CMU/SEI-95-MM-02, September 1995.

Other entries in this bibliography include another capability maturity model (CMM^{SM})—namely the Capability Maturity Model^{SM} for Software.[1] This latter model gave rise to a family of capability maturity models, one of which is the People Capability Maturity Model^{SM} (P-CMM^{SM}). This model grew out of a recognition by the SEI and others that there was more to improving software systems development than processes and technology. In fact, the executive overview of the P-CMM begins as follows:

In order to improve their performance, organizations must focus on three interrelated components—people, process, and technology. . . . With the help of the Capability Maturity Model^{SM} for Software (CMM^{SM}) [Paulk95], many software organizations have made cost-effective, lasting improvements in

---

[1]The superscript "SM" denotes "service mark." "Capability Maturity Model" and CMM are service marks of Carnegie Mellon University. These service marks began to be applied in SEI publications in the 1995 time frame, subsequent to the time that the CMM for Software first appeared. Thus, this service mark does not appear in SEI publications prior to this time.

their software processes and practices. . . . Yet many of these organizations have discovered that their continued improvement requires significant changes in the way that they manage, develop, and use their people for developing and maintaining software information systems—changes that are not fully accounted for in the CMM [for Software]. To date, improvement programs for software organizations have often emphasized process or technology, not people.

To provide guidance to organizations that want to improve the way they address these people-related issues, the SEI has developed the People Capability Maturity Model^{SM} (P-CMM^{SM}). The P-CMM is a maturity framework, patterned after the structure of the CMM [for Software], that focuses on continuously improving the management and development of the human assets of a software or information systems organization. The P-CMM provides guidance on how to continuously improve the ability of software organizations to attract, develop, motivate, organize, and retain the talent needed to steadily improve their software development capability. The strategic objectives of the P-CMM are to

- improve the capability of software organizations by increasing the capability of their workforce

- ensure that software development capability is an attribute of the organization rather than of a few individuals

- align the motivation of individuals with that of the organization

- retain human assets (i.e., people with critical knowledge and skills) within the organization (pp. xix–xx)

The discussion of mentoring and coaching in Chapter 8 is based on some ideas in the P-CMM.

Paulk, M. C., B. Curtis, M. B. Chrissis, and C. V. Weber. "Capability Maturity Model for Software, Version 1.1," Software Engineering Institute and Carnegie Mellon University Technical Report CMU/SEI-93-TR-24, February 1993.

The development of what has become known as the Capability Model for Software began in 1986. The Software Engineering Institute, with assistance from the Mitre Corporation, set about developing a software process maturity framework for the purpose of helping organizations improve their software process. The motivation for this activity stemmed from the federal government, which wanted a method for assessing the capability of its software contractors (hence, the label "capability"). In short, the federal government was looking for a way to reduce the likelihood of software disasters that had become the trademark of the industry up to that time. Version 1.0 of the CMM was released in 1991. Version 1.1 was released in early 1993. Version 2.0 is to be released later in the decade. The purpose of CMU/SEI-93-TR-24 is stated on page viii of the document as follows:

This paper provides a technical overview of the Capability Maturity Model for Software and reflects Version 1.1. Specifically, this paper describes the process maturity framework of five maturity levels, the structural components that comprise the CMM, how the CMM is used in practice, and future directions of the CMM. This paper serves as one of the best sources for understanding the CMM, and it should clear up some of the misconceptions associated with software process maturity as advocated by the SEI.

Paulk, M. C., C. V. Weber, S. M. Garcia, M. B. Chrissis, and M. Bush. "Key Practices of the Capability Maturity Model, Version 1.1," Software Engineering Institute and Carnegie Mellon University Technical Report CMU/SEI-93-TR-25, February 1993.

This document is a companion to CMU/SEI-93-TR-24 and describes the key practices for each level of the CMM. These key practices are an elaboration of what is meant by maturity at each level of the CMM. They are expressed in terms of what is expected to be the normal practices of organizations that work on large, government contracts. As the document points out on page O-3, "the CMM must be appropriately interpreted when the business environment of the organization differs significantly from that of a large contracting organization." The approach in our book is cast in a similar vein. We present software processes and offer you guidance as to how you can adapt the processes to your environment. One principle that we stress throughout our book is that of "prescriptive application of the process"—that is, application consistent with the available time and money under which a software systems development effort must operate. An echo of this idea appears on page O-3 of CMU/SEI-93-TR-25 when the document states, "the role of professional judgement in making informed use of the CMM must be recognized."

2. MAGAZINE/JOURNAL ARTICLES

Brodman, J., and D. Johnson. "Return on Investment (ROI) from Software Process Improvement as Measured by US Industry," *Software Process—Improvement and Practice*, Pilot Issue (August 1995), pp. 35–47.

Chapter 6 touched on the topic of the quantifiable benefits of software process improvement. This article reports on research that investigated published ROI claims for software process improvement programs based on the CMM for Software. The article also sought evidence of previously unpublished ROI data in organizations that had been pursuing software process improvement over several years preceding the article's publication. The United States Air Force sponsored the research. A key finding of the research was that new ROI data were found—but typically not in the classical form of the dollar amount returned for the dollar amount invested. Rather, ROI data were expressed in terms of benefits such as increased productivity, reduced schedule time, and improved quality. The article seeks to define what ROI means to government and industry. At the time of its publication, the article noted that only two Department of Defense contractors and one government organization had publicly released data documenting ROI for software process improvement. The article notes that one of the contractors had "reported as high as a 7.7 savings in program dollars for each dollar invested in process improvement" (p. 36). In the public domain, the research used two methods to gather data from industry—the questionnaire and the interview. Thirty-three companies were surveyed—some with one of the two methods and some with both. The interviews were used to define ROI and to identify the ROI data that could be collected from industry. The questionnaires were used, among other things, to identify metrics used to collect ROI data. Because ROI data per se were not abundant, the research also conducted a literature search to ferret out information on metric collection, costing software projects, and conducting inspections. This information could be used to derive ROI conclusions. The research found that there was a lack of consensus on ROI definition since, for example, "return" was defined differently in different organizations as was "investment." The research also found that the government and industry each defined and perceived ROI differently. For example, for the government, process improvement is viewed as a cost saving. "The dollars saved through reduced schedule time, higher quality, and increased productivity among its [the government's] contracting software organizations are dollars that are returned to the government, not the contractor" (p. 46). By contrast, from the contractor's perspective, ROI from process improvement in, say increased productivity, "can mean a more competitive edge in bidding for scarce government contracts and can increase the company's capacity to do work and thus perform more work within a given period of time for greater profits" (p. 46).

Mohamed, F. E., W. Tsai, and M. L. Fulghum. "Transition to Object-Oriented Software Development." *Communications of the ACM*, vol. 39, no. 2 (February 1996), pp. 108–121.

Object-oriented technology models software development based upon the way humans think. Ironically, traditional software development follows a model based upon the way that computers think. Thus, to wean people away from the traditional way toward the object-oriented way requires people to change their way of thinking. The authors stress that this weaning process is a cultural change of demanding proportions. On page 110, they assert that "it would be easier to convince people that the world is flat than to convince them to use OOSE [object-oriented software engineering]."

This article offers guidance to software development managers on how to transition to object-oriented software engineering. As such, this article provides a stepping-off point for those interested in tailoring the techniques described in our book to projects using object-oriented technology. For example, the article discusses the factors that should be considered in selecting an object-oriented technique (e.g., CASE tool support, target computer language).

Shaw, M. "Prospects for an Engineering Discipline of Software," *IEEE Software*, vol. 7, no. 6 (November 1990), pp. 15–24.

Our book is about disciplining software systems development. This article is a 1990 look at the "discipline" of software engineering. The first page of the article is emblazoned with the following sidebar that offers insight into the article's orientation:

Software engineering is not yet a true engineering discipline, but it has the potential to become one. Older engineering fields suggest the character software engineering might have (p. 15).

The article provides grassroots insight into the concept of engineering. Our book proceeds from the assumption that people participating in software systems development (buyers/users as well as sellers) need to define—in the spirit of "good engineering practice"—processes to achieve consistency in what they do. Shaw's article starts farther up the concept chain and examines notions that must be brought to bear to be able to define, among other things, workable processes (e.g., "understand the nature of proficiency," that is, what members of the development disciplines need to know to have proficiency; "encourage routine practice," that is, what are the factors bearing on, for example, routine design practice [the answer given, in part, is the engineer's command of factual knowledge and design skills, quality of available reference materials, and incentives and values associated with innovation]). This article makes useful reading for those of you interested in gaining an understanding of the fundamental "whys" underlying many of the concepts in our book. In particular, if you are a buyer/user, this article can help you determine what to look for in a seller. The article's author, a professor of computer science at Carnegie Mellon University, was chief scientist at the Software Engineering Institute during its first three years (1984–1987).

Zawrotny, S. "Demystifying the Black Art of Project Estimating," *Application Development Trends,* vol. 2, no. 7 (July 1995), pp. 36–44.

As the title intimates, this article offers practical tips for estimating the effort, duration, schedule, and costs of doing software development of information systems. As such, it is a useful supplement to the project planning concepts presented in Chapter 2. Although the article uses data and statistics tied to information systems development, many of the ideas presented can be applied to any software systems development effort. The author distinguishes between such critical estimating factors as "effort" (namely, the number of resource hours or days needed to accomplish an activity or task) and "duration" (namely, the allocation of effort across business or work days based on the rate at which effort hours will be expended). The author discusses how to account for things such as meetings, gossip, coffee breaks, and administrative tasks. The author has spent approximately thirty years in the information systems industry working for such companies as General Electric Information Services and Coca-Cola Enterprises, among others.

3. BOOKS

Adams, S. *The Dilbert™ Principle: A Cubicle's-Eye View of Bosses, Meetings, Management Fads & Other Workplace Afflictions.* New York: HarperBusiness, a Division of HarperCollins Publishers, 1996.

Scott Adams produces the widely circulated comic strip *Dilbert™*. This book is a collection of these comic strips with elaborating text to drive home points. *Dilbert™* pokes fun at the workplace, sometimes bitingly so. Many of the comic strips lampoon the software industry. The author worked for Pacific Bell for nine years where he evidently acquired the experience underlying his comic strips. The book offers some good complementary insights into much of what we say in our book regarding the disciplines of management (in particular), development, and product assurance. Some of his humor also touches on cultural change issues. For example, Chapter 24 ("Team-Building Exercises") begins with the following statement:

> If the employees in your company are a bunch of independent, antisocial psychopaths, you might need some team-building exercises (p. 280).

Through such extreme and humorous statements, Adams provokes the reader to think through organizational issues (in this case, team building), thereby coming to a better understanding of how organizations really work.

Berger, L. A., and M. J. Sikora with D. R. Berger, eds. *The Change Management Handbook: A Road Map to Corporate Transformation.* Burr Ridge, IL: Irwin Professional Publishing, 1994.

> This 489-page book is a compendium of articles written by over thirty change management experts on how to manage organizational change. Intended as a desktop resource, the book is designed to help managers anticipate and respond to change—both unexpected and foreseeable. The authors are executives, professors, and consultants. The book says almost nothing about the software industry (some companies in the software industry are mentioned, such as IBM and Microsoft). However, the book offers insight into corporate change management critical factors that help to fill in things that we only touch upon in Chapter 7 and elsewhere when we address cultural change. One section of the book (over 100 pages) is devoted to cultural change issues (e.g., critical elements of organizational culture change, cultural change and corporate strategy, and making culture change happen).

Bridges, W. *Managing Transitions: Making the Most of Change.* Reading, MA: Addison-Wesley Publishing Company, 1991 (6th printing, 1993).

> We stress throughout our book the notion that software process improvement is a cultural change exercise. The Bridges book is designed to help an organization understand change better and thereby develop improved change strategies. This book has nothing to do with software engineering but has everything to do with helping an organization bring about improved engineering practice. The book can help you better understand the ideas put forth in our Chapter 7.

Brooks, F. P., Jr. *The Mythical Man-Month: Essays on Software Engineering.* (20th) Anniversary (1995) ed. Reading, MA: Addison-Wesley Publishing Company, 1995.

> This book first appeared in 1975. The author was the project manager for the development of IBM's Operating System/360 project from 1964 to 1965. The book is a highly readable and often amusing case study of this project and includes related stories drawn from other projects. As the author indicates in the preface to the first edition, it was written to answer "Tom Watson's [IBM president] probing questions as to why programming is hard to manage" (p. viii). In the preface to the 1995 edition, the author explains the rationale for the edition as follows:
>
> > To my surprise and delight, *The Mythical Man-Month* continues to be popular after 20 years. Over 250,000 copies are in print. People often ask which of the opinions and recommendations set forth in 1975 I still hold, and which have changed, and how. Whereas I have from time to time addressed the question in lectures, I have long wanted to essay it in writing (p. vii).
>
> Accordingly, the 1995 edition contains four new chapters (16–19). The remainder of the book is a reprint of the first edition. In the September 1995 issue of *IEEE Software*, the author elaborates on why he put out a twentieth anniversary edition (pp. 57–60).
>   The book is filled with stories that highlight the idiosyncracies of software development and maintenance (as distinct from development and maintenance of nonsoftware entities). For example, in discussing software maintenance, the author describes how a software defect will often manifest itself as a local failure, when in fact it is indicative of a far more global ill. This nonlocality characteristic of many software bugs, the author points out, presents a significant maintenance challenge. Any purported fix to such a bug

must be tested not only "in the vicinity" of the code change precipitated by the bug fix, but ideally far away from this change to the outer reaches of the rest of the code. This need for global testing is one of the reasons that our book stresses the need for independent product assurance. Unlike the code developers who are generally too close to the code perhaps to sense some of these nonlocality issues, "outsiders" may be better able to give visibility to what otherwise might be hidden problems because their thinking may not be truncated.

Bryan, W., and S. Siegel. *Software Product Assurance: Techniques for Reducing Software Risk*. Englewood Cliffs, NJ: P T R Prentice Hall, 1988.

This book provides the basis for some of the items included in our book. In particular, our Chapter 4 is an update to the Bryan and Siegel Chapter 4; our Chapter 5 extends the ideas in the Bryan and Siegel Chapter 5. The seed for the product integrity index comes from Exercise 2.6 on p. 89 of this book. As noted therein, the exercise is an adaptation from an unpublished partial manuscript by E. H. Bersoff, V. D. Henderson, and S. G. Siegel.

Davis, A. M. *Software Requirements: Objects, Functions, and States*. Englewood Cliffs, NJ: PTR Prentice Hall, 1993.

We stress the importance of requirements engineering in software process improvement. This 500-page book is good for both beginners and experts wanting to know the ins and outs of how to do requirements engineering. In addition, the book contains an exhaustive annotated bibliography (more than 100 pages). It is an update to the author's book that appeared in 1990. The update was motivated by advances in requirements engineering technology, particularly in the object-oriented arena.

DeMarco, T., and T. Lister. *Peopleware: Productive Projects and Teams*. New York: Dorset House Publishing Co., Inc., 1987.

This 188-page book is an easy-to-read but content-rich collection of short essays, "each one about a particular garden path that managers are led down" (p. ix). The book is not specific to software although many of its stories have to do with software projects. The book's focus is on the people element in the [software] project game. As such, it probes in more detail some of the people issues (i.e., cultural change) that we touch upon in Chapter 1, elaborate on in Chapter 7, and briefly address in other chapters. The 26 essays that make up the book are divided into the following five parts:

> Part I: Managing the Human Resource
> Part II: The Office Environment
> Part III: The Right People
> Part IV: Growing Productive Teams
> Part V: It's Supposed to Be Fun to Work Here

Many of the essays have catchy titles and are indicative of the book's tone. The following are some examples:

> Somewhere Today, a Project Is Failing
> Make a Cheeseburger, Sell a Cheeseburger
> Quality—If Time Permits
> Brain Time Versus Body Time
> Teamicide
> Open Kimono
> Chaos and Order

Regarding the second essay in the list ("Make a Cheeseburger, Sell a CheeseBurger"), the authors provide some interesting food for thought (no pun intended) regarding why [software] systems development is inherently different from [software] production—so that managing [software] development like [software] production is not a good idea. One efficient *production* measure that the authors cite is the following (p. 7):

Standardize procedure. Do everything by the book.

This measure does not, in fact, fly in the face of the emphasis on process in our book. However, it is the reason that we spend a lot of time emphasizing the need for what we call "prescriptive application" of whatever processes are defined for a software systems development organization to follow. DeMarco and Lister essentially argue that you cannot expect to turn people in a development environment into automatons if you want them to do what they are supposed to do. In the language of our book, you need to provide the people with a way of doing business and then empower them to apply this business way in a manner that makes sense on their particular project (i.e., consistent with available time and money and the specifics of the job to be accomplished).

Down, A., M. Coleman, and P. Absolon. *Risk Management for Software Projects*. London: Mc-Graw-Hill Book Company Europe, 1994.

The preface states this book's purpose as follows: "The book focuses on the reasons for poor risk management within software development and covers a number of practical methods for resolving the problems encountered" (p. xiii). The authors' approach centers around a concept they call "optimum risk environment (ORE)." The ORE is one in which the parties involved in software systems development feel most comfortable with the perceived risks and rewards. The book explains how to (1) create the ORE, (2) manage the ORE, and (3) learn from the ORE. They call these three items the key elements in the optimum risk management process and give them respectively the names CORE, MORE, and LORE. Our Chapter 2 discusses ways to factor risk assessment into the project planning process and suggested ways for applying this assessment throughout a software project as a way of managing risk. The Down/Coleman/Absolon book examines a number of risk management issues that we only touch upon. For example, Chapter 4 ("Anticipating Risk") is a 17-page treatment of the topics of (1) identifying risks and (2) assessing risks; Chapter 5 ("Planning How to Manage the Risks"), is a 12-page treatment of the topics of (1) risk planning principles and (2) the risk management plan.

Grady, G. B. *Practical Software Metrics for Project Management and Process Improvement*. Englewood Cliffs, NJ: PTR Prentice Hall, 1992.

This 260-page book is an extension to the 1987 book by Grady and Caswell entitled *Software Metrics: Establishing a Company-Wide Program*, which described Hewlett-Packard's approach to software systems development process metrics. The book is intended for project managers. Its purpose is stated on p. 1 as follows:

This book is about practical applications of software metrics. This means that the emphasis is on proven practices and results (p. 1).

The opening words of the book define the author's concept of software metrics as follows:

Software metrics are used to measure specific attributes of a software product or software development process.

Appendix C gives a summary of definitions of most of the metrics addressed in the book (examples include "defect," "design weight," "Flesch-Kincaid readability," "hot status," "LOC [lines of code]," "patch," "stability," and "strength"). Appendix D includes a list of 396 software metrics references. Our Chapter 6 complements some of the ideas in the Grady book.

Jacobs, R. W. *Real Time Strategic Change: How to Involve an Entire Organization in Fast and Far-Reaching Change*. San Francisco, CA: Berrett-Koehler Publishers, 1994.

This 335-page book addresses the quick way to bring about organizational change. The book's thesis is that the successful organizations of the future will be those that will be able to effect fundamental, lasting, and systemwide changes—quickly. The author is a partner in a consulting firm with extensive experience working with organizations around the world to do what the book talks about. The book does not talk about the software industry. However, it addresses topics at length that we only touch upon in Chapters 7 and 8 in our discussions of ADPE implementation and organizational change. The book uses "strategic change" in the sense of uncovering new ways of doing business that push an organization forward to success now and in the future. "Real time" is used in the sense of simultaneously planning and implementing individual, group, and organizationwide changes.

Jenner, M. G. *Software Quality Management and ISO 9001: How to Make Them Work for You.* New York: John Wiley & Sons, Inc., 1995.

As the author states in his first chapter, "this book addresses the issues of managing a modern organization within the framework of the ISO 9001 requirements" (p. 3). To motivate the reader, and to inject pizzazz into a subject that, on the surface, may be hard to get excited about, the author asserts the following:

> Quality is a state of mind and can be delivered better by people who are having fun than by people who live dull, regulated lives surrounded by slogans and exhortations (p. 3).

ISO 9000 is the name that describes the International Organization for Standards' (ISO) 9000 series of management system standards. The centerpiece of the series is ISO 9001. It is titled "Quality Systems— Model for Quality Assurance in Design/Development, Production, Installation, and Servicing." Auditors outside an organization use this standard as a basis for certifying that an organization can design, develop, produce, etc. products and services (such as software) with quality. *Quality* in the context of this standard means "the totality of features and characteristics of a product or service that bear on its ability to satisfy stated or implied [customer] needs" (p. 220). The book, which is a step-by-step walkthrough (for the practitioner) of ISO 9001, deals with quality issues in a much broader context than our book in that Jenner's work is not restricted to software products. The book reinforces many of the ideas that we address, such as the critical importance of project planning (see, e.g., p. 37) and customer satisfaction (see, e.g., p. 39). Software is specifically addressed in several different places (see the book's index).

Jones, C. *Applied Software Measurement: Assuring Productivity and Quality.* New York: McGraw-Hill, Inc., 1991.

The thesis of this 493-page book is that software can be accurately measured and that the resultant measurements have practical value. The preface includes an interesting thumbnail sketch of the history of the software industry and provides insight into how software measurement got started and evolved. Included in this sketch is how the popular software metric of "lines of code" came into being. The intent of the book is to explain how to start a full corporate software measurement program encompassing productivity, quality, and human factors. The book consists of five chapters and four appendices. Chapter 2, consisting of approximately 80 pages, gives the history and evolution of functional metrics (e.g., lines of code, function points, feature points). Chapter 3 addresses the subject of United States averages for software productivity and quality. The purpose of this chapter is to set context for the mechanics of measurement dealt with in Chapter 4. Chapter 5 addresses the subject of measuring software quality and user satisfaction. This chapter offers a multiplicity of alternatives to our quantitative treatment in Chapter 6 of software quality and customer satisfaction in terms of the product integrity concept.

Kan, S. H. *Metrics and Models in Software Quality Engineering.* Reading, MA: Addison-Wesley Publishing Company, 1995.

The thesis of this book is that measurement plays a critical role in successful software systems development. To set context, the first chapter deals with the issue of what is software quality. The author argues that *quality* is best defined as "conformance to customer requirements" (p. 10). The discussion of process and product quality in this chapter offers some alternative thinking to that which we present in Chapter 6. For example, generalizing the notion of customer satisfaction to internal customers (e.g., life cycle stages), Kan suggests that process quality can be thought of in the following terms:

> If each stage of the development process meets the requirements of its intermediate user (the next stage), the end product thus developed and produced will meet the specified requirements (p. 7).

Note how this point of view is also another way of looking at the relationship between product and process quality. Chapter 2, like our Chapter 3, talks about software systems development process models. Chapter 3 provides measurement theory fundamentals, including a discussion of reliability, validity, and measurement errors. Chapter 4 is devoted to software quality metrics (e.g., function points, customer satisfaction metrics), Chapter 8 deals with the exponential distribution and reliability growth models (surprisingly without a lot of mathematics), and Chapter 11 is devoted to measuring and analyzing customer satisfaction. Section 11.4 is perhaps the most intriguing part of this latter chapter in that it addresses the issue of how much customer satisfaction is good enough.

LaMarsh, J. *Changing the Way We Change: Gaining Control of Major Operational Change.* Reading, MA: Addison-Wesley Publishing Company, 1995.

This book is one in a series aimed at engineering practitioners called the *Engineering Process Improvement Series*. The objective of the series is to provide the reader practical information for improving processes and products. The book's scope deals with engineering in general; that is, it is not limited to software engineering. The book is about how to manage change and is organized as follows (p. xiii):

■ The process of change
■ The people in the process
■ The systems that support change
■ The planning to make change happen

Our book stresses that software systems development process improvement is a cultural change exercise. Our Chapter 7 probes how to bring about that cultural change. The LaMarsh book provides additional insight into this issue from a perspective broader than software engineering. Its ideas complement and reinforce some of the notions addressed in the Bridges book cited elsewhere in this bibliography.

Möller, K. H., and D. J. Paulish. *Software Metrics: A Practitioner's Guide to Improved Product Development.* London: Chapman & Hall, 1993. (Also published by IEEE Press, USA and Canada only.)

The book's purpose and orientation are stated as follows: "This book aims to document some of the best practices of software metrics that are currently used in industry" (p. 11). Möller and Paulish define the term *metrics* to mean "quantitative methods" (p. 4). The book's approach to metrics complements our discussion in Chapter 6. Measurements that we fold into our product and process integrity indices Möller and Paulish treat as separate entities. Chapter 7 focuses on example metrics that the authors say may be useful for establishing a metrics program. Some of the metrics defined and discussed there are the following:

■ Lines of Code
■ Customer Change Requests
■ Schedule (difference between planned versus actual)
■ Requirements Specification Change Requests
■ Design Faults
■ Customer Complaint Rate ("number of customer identified faults per time period from the time of first field use of the product through its lifetime") (p. 81)

Chapter 2 provides historical perspective by summarizing the origins of software metrics (software measurement started in the 1970s).

Paulk, M. C., and others. *The Capability Maturity Model: Guidelines for Improving the Software Process*. Reading, MA: Addison-Wesley Publishing Company, 1995.

This 400-page book pulls together various concepts pertaining to the Capability Maturity Model (CMM) appearing in earlier SEI publications such as the one by Paulk and others cited elsewhere in this bibliography. It is a guide to applying the CMM for purposes of improving an organization's software systems development process. Ideas in this book complement many of the ideas in our book. Perhaps the biggest difference between the CMM approach and our approach to process improvement is our stress on the CCB as the heart of any successful software systems development process. The SEI appears to treat the role of the CCB in its classical configuration management sense. Chapter 1 gives an informative historical overview of how the CMM came to be. Chapter 6 describes the Space Shuttle Onboard Software project at IBM-Houston to illustrate what a mature organization does in producing software products with integrity. This chapter also explains how IBM-Houston evolved into a mature software systems development organization.

Pressman, R. S. *Software Engineering: A Practitioner's Approach*. 3rd ed. New York: McGraw-Hill, 1992.

The organization of this 793-page book is intended for both students and practitioners. As its title suggests, the book contains "how-to-do-it" software engineering techniques. The book is divided into five parts—(1) Software—The Process and Management, (2) System and Software Requirements Analysis, (3) The Design and Implementation of Software, (4) Ensuring, Verifying, and Maintaining Software Integrity, and (5) The Role of Automation.

Radice, R. A. *ISO 9001: Interpreted for Software Organizations*. Andover, MA: Paradoxicon Publishing, 1995.

This book is intended for the practitioner wanting to understand ISO 9001 ("Quality Systems—Model for Quality Assurance in Design, Development, Production, Installation, and Servicing") and/or who may be involved with implementing an ISO 9001 compliant program in a software organization. ISO stands for the International Organization for Standardization. The ISO mission is to provide international standardization to facilitate worldwide commerce (i.e., exchange of goods and services). ISO 9000 is a series of *generic* standards (thus they are open to broad interpretation) "for building, operating, and documenting a quality system" (p. 16). The series, originally published in 1987, consists of five major parts, one of which is ISO 9001. "ISO 9001 is a standard and model for quality assurance in design/development, production, installation, and servicing" (p. 17). In the words of the standard, a quality system is "the organizational structure, responsibilities, procedures, processes and resources for implementing quality management necessary to achieve the quality objectives stated in the quality policy." Another major ISO 9000 part is ISO 9000-3, which is a guideline for applying ISO 9001 to software.

The author analyzes each of the twenty ISO 9001 Section 4 clauses that constitute the heart of the standard (examples of the clause headings are "management responsibility," "document control," "process control," "inspection and testing," "training," and "statistical techniques"). This analysis includes the relationship of the clause to ISO 9000-3, including where 9000-3 adds interpretation beyond what is stated or implied in 9001. The analysis also includes a statement about the risks of not meeting the requirements embodied in the clause. If the risk materializes, then the risk becomes a problem.

The analysis of the twenty clauses spans pages 65 to 307 in Radice's 352-page book. Given that the standard itself is only five pages and that ISO 9000-3 is only eleven pages, the book bears testimony to the fact that 9001 is not self-evident to apply.

Using the concepts in our book, you can construct a set of ADPE elements compliant with the twenty ISO 9001 Section 4 clauses. For example, clause 13 is entitled "Review and Disposition of Nonconforming Product." This clause reads in part as follows:

The responsibility for review and authority for the disposition of nonconforming product shall be defined.

Nonconforming product shall be reviewed in accordance with documented procedures. It may be

a) reworked to meet the specified requirements,

b) accepted with or without repair by concession,

c) regraded for alternative applications, or

d) rejected or scrapped.

As we discussed in Chapters 2, 3 and 5, software product review responsibilities and disposition authority are addressed in ADPE elements for project planning, the software systems development process, and independent product assurance.

The ISO 9000 series is intended for almost any manufacturing domain (e.g., banks, legal firms, health service providers, and educational institutions).

Schulmeyer, G. G., and J. I. McManus, eds. *Handbook of Software Quality Assurance*. 2nd ed. New York: Van Nostrand Reinhold, 1992.

This 550-page book is a collection of articles by various authors on topics that in our book we put under the umbrella of product assurance. Its content is practitioner oriented. As the editors state in the book's preface, "this Handbook brings to the reader . . . a collection of experiences and expectations of some of the most notable experts in the field of software quality assurance" (p. xv).

Senge, P. *The Fifth Discipline: The Art and Practice of the Learning Organization*. New York: Doubleday, 1990.

A learning organization is one that enables individuals to work in teams. These teams learn and develop innovative ways of doing business. In this book, Senge introduces a widely accepted framework for defining and achieving a learning organization through the practice of five disciplines—personal mastery, challenging mental models, shared vision, team learning, and systems thinking. This book, which has nothing to do with software, offers some worthwhile insights into how to make organizations work more effectively. It is particularly useful for understanding some of the mechanisms underlying our discussion of cultural change in Chapter 7 and associated issues in Chapter 8. For example, Chapter 7 describes how SEE implementation is a cultural change exercise. If this exercise is viewed as evolving an organization towards a learning organization, then SEE implementation can be tied to the five learning organization disciplines. The learning organization has a strong sense of shared vision that focuses action. It enables employees to develop a high level of proficiency in their field so that they become like master craftspeople in other disciplines. It links people through teams that can work synergistically to achieve tasks that individuals cannot. The organization encourages people to question its assumptions. Such questioning can be made part of the process of developing and maintaining ADPE elements that is discussed in Chapter 7.

Sommerville, I. *Software Engineering*. 4th ed. New York: Addison-Wesley Publishing Company, 1992.

This 650-page book, first published in 1982, "is aimed at students in undergraduate and graduate courses and at software engineers in commerce and industry" (p. vii). The author is a Professor of Software Engineering at the University of Lancaster in the United Kingdom. The following extract from the book's preface perhaps explains why the book has enjoyed longstanding popularity:

This book is an introduction to software engineering which takes a broad view of the subject. As in previous editions, my intention is to introduce the reader to a spectrum of state-of-the-art software engineering techniques which can be applied in practical software projects. The book has a pragmatic bias but introduces theory when it is appropriate to do so.

Whitten, N. *Managing Software Development Projects: Formula for Success*. 2nd ed. New York: John Wiley & Sons, Inc., 1995.

The following statement from this book's preface succinctly states its thrust:

This book is a how-to, real-world, no-nonsense, practical guide to identifying and resolving the most common, major problems in software projects (p. v).

The book's intended audience is project managers, project leaders, and project members. The book consists of fourteen chapters whose titles are listed following this paragraph. As explained in the book's opening chapter, each chapter is laid out the same way—a problem encountered in software development (e.g., lack of discipline), war stories illustrating how the problem can appear within a project, and steps to follow to recognize and to avoid or recover from the problem.

Chapter 1	Defining a Software Development Process
Chapter 2	Discipline: The Glue That Holds It All Together
Chapter 3	Communicating in Harmony
Chapter 4	Project Schedule Planning: Getting in Control
Chapter 5	Project Tracking: Staying in Control
Chapter 6	Planning for Quality
Chapter 7	Managing Priorities Effectively
Chapter 8	Product Requirements: Understanding the Customer's Problem to Solve
Chapter 9	Product Objectives: Providing Direction for the Solution
Chapter 10	Product Specifications: Defining the Final Product
Chapter 11	Product Ease of Use
Chapter 12	Development Testing: Strengthening the Weak Link
Chapter 13	Vendor Relationships
Chapter 14	Postproject Review: Understanding the Past to Improve the Future

The book complements many of the ideas appearing in our book. For example, Whitten's first chapter addresses life cycle and software development process concepts, which we address in Chapters 2 and 3. He offers an eight-step approach for defining a software development process. The life cycle models he considers are the following:

Code-and-fix ["code first and ask questions later"]

Waterfall

Incremental

Iterative

He chooses these models because, as he asserts, "most models are derived, at least in part, from one or more of these basic models" (p. 19).

The book is easy to read and convenient to use.

Index